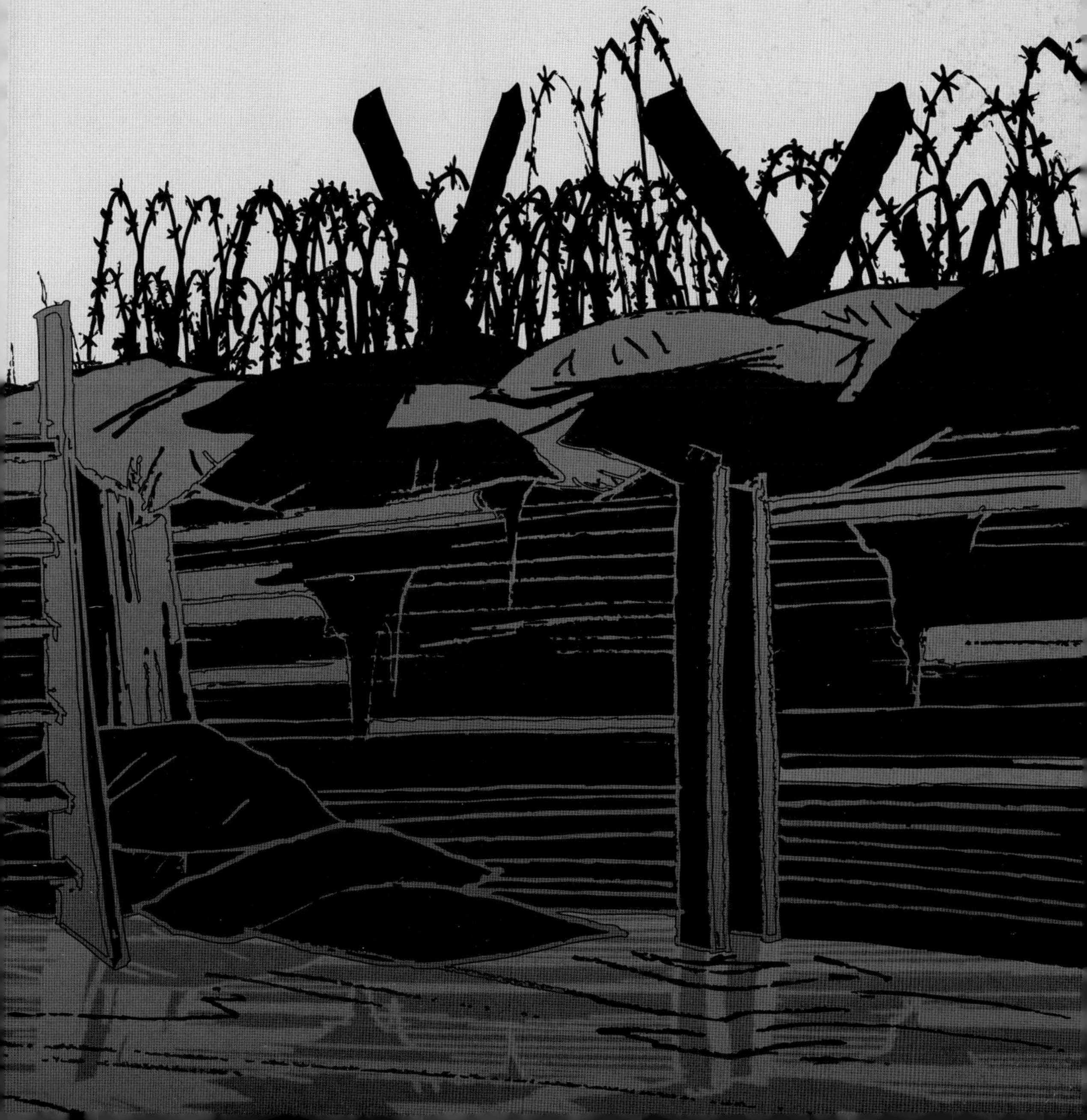

TO END ALL WARS
The Graphic Anthology of The First World War

Introduction by Pat Mills
Edited by
Jonathan Clode
John Stuart Clark

SOARING PENGUIN
PRESS

LONDON UK

To End All Wars

The Graphic Anthology of the First World War

Edited by Jonathan Clode & John Stuart Clark
Introduction by Pat Mills

Published by
Soaring Penguin Press
4 Florence Terrace
Kingston Vale
London
SW15 3RU
www.soaringpenguinpress.com

First Edition: July 2014

10 9 8 7 6 5 4 3 2 1

ISBN: 978-1-908030-13-9

Printed in Latvia

MEDECINS SANS FRONTIERES
DOCTORS WITHOUT BORDERS

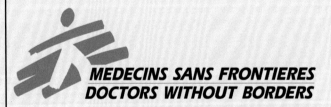

£2 of every book sold will be donated to
Médecins Sans Frontières / Doctors Without Borders.

Médecins Sans Frontières / Doctors Without Borders is an international, independent, medical humanitarian organisation that delivers emergency aid to people affected by armed conflict, epidemics, healthcare exclusion and natural disasters. MSF combines the provision of emergency medical care with a commitment to speaking out about the suffering people endure and the obstacles encountered in providing assistance. MSF offers assistance to people based only on need and irrespective of race, religion, gender or political affiliation.

MSF (UK) is a company limited by guarantee | English Charity Reg No.1026588 | English Registration No. 2853011

Table of Contents

This anthology you have in your hands is an important one because comics are one of the few media voices the establishment has yet to muzzle, doubtless because they think they don't matter. It's how a series like *Charley's War* managed to slip under the wire and spread its anti-war message to a young mass audience in the UK. Today the series is also reaching a new audience in France, where there is a huge appetite for comic interpretations of the war. In fact, inspired by the work of the great Tardi, a new generation of young artists and writers there have produced several beautiful graphic novel series on the conflict. I like to think that this anthology could be the launch pad for British creators to produce similar books. Certainly I found these stories heartfelt, passionate, clever, controversial, thought-provoking, original and often crying out for sequels. I could sense that many writers and artists were sharpening their claws for the first time and would love to see how they develop. I know, as an editor, just how difficult it is to collect and select stories and writers, and marry them up to the right artists. It is rare to achieve this successfully in Britain today, and rarer still to produce an anti-war collection with such disparate, talented but connected voices. Bravo!

This anthology is important because A Very British Lie is currently being perpetrated about World War One. In summary, the Sandhurst-trained revisionists are rewriting history in the most outrageous way to claim that 'sacrifices' like the Somme were necessary to help Field Marshal Haig win the war; even though Britain's *Daily Telegraph* itself admits, "what a terrible shame it was that Haig's progress along his learning curve had to be greased by such deep floods of blood." 'Sacrifice' seems to be the buzzword chosen by Whitehall's spin-doctors, whose mouthpieces dutifully talk about a noble sacrifice and a just war. Meanwhile the BBC's line in recent commemorative documentaries is that Britain had to fight for freedom against a Germany hell-bent on world conquest. (Britain mobilized one week *before* Germany invaded Belgium, which had long been in a secret military alliance with France and Britain.)

Apart from making people feel helpless in the face of overwhelming forces – an objective in itself – another motive in legitimizing the 'Great War' is so no one asks awkward questions about their subsequent dubious conflicts in World War Two, Korea, Iraq and Afghanistan. Equally important is the need to train the public in how they should behave in wartime: stiff upper lip and the spirit of the Blitz (the making of the British character, according to the BBC). All this is essential because beneath the flimflam lies Britain's key role, then and now, as a leading arms exporter. War is extremely profitable. Follow the money.

Here is a quick guide to some of the ways the establishment avoids dissent and *genuine* debate about the 'War To End All Wars':

*Claims *The Monocled Mutineer*, by William Allison & John Fairley, which depicts a major mutiny by British soldiers in WW1, is an unsourced work of fiction. Not true: it was authoritatively sourced and anything but fiction. The Alan Bleasdale TV adaptation caused a furor among Tory MPs and in the press, where it was branded 'a tissue of lies' grossly exaggerating 'a little disrespect to officers'.

*Ignores the shocking *new* revelation in the 2014 version of *Oh, What A Lovely War!* that Britain was trading weapons extensively with Germany *during* the war, and kept the war going for profit. Also ignores how this supposedly irrelevant musical for the Vietnam War generation still plays to packed audiences, young and old.

*Ignores a senior German diplomat who was dismayed recently to find that a key commemoration ceremony would *not* be in a spirit of reconciliation but rather in one of British jingoism, with Germany still portrayed as the aggressor. You won't find *that* reported in our supposedly free media.

*Has a media blackout on books such as *Hidden History* by Gerry Docherty and Jim Macgregor, who set out an authoritative and overwhelming case for **Britain** being responsible for World War One, *not* Germany. Their book is an absolute essential for anyone who wants to follow up on Brick's *Iron Dice* in this anthology. It is the story many of us sensed was the truth, rather than the ludicrous version they still pump out in schools. A few years ago Robert Newman's hilarious *History of Oil* (available on YouTube) came close to the truth, but *Hidden History* goes much further and fully reveals the establishment's lies, at last. Don't read it if you need to keep the ground firmly beneath your feet.

"Ignores the words of the last British Tommy, Harry Patch, who died recently and described the war as 'organized murder'. When he was asked what advice he would give young men today, he responded, "Don't join the army." His reply was *whooshed*.

As Patch calls it murder, I refer to those responsible as murderers and in the case of Haig, as an organized serial killer. Any other description is to accept the spin-doctors' highly effective and contagious cognitive dissonance that still deludes so many of us.

This startling and dramatic graphic collection of stories provides an alternative voice. The most important is Brick's war crimes tribunal story, a passionate and necessary search for justice with the Good Soldier Svejk as the inquisitor! What an excellent choice, and how gratifying to see the quintessential common man challenging his 'superiors'. It's also a valuable and cathartic image to see the leaders in the dock at The Hague. Let us hope one day it will be a reality for the recently retired world leaders who took their countries into war on the back of lies and subterfuge, but until our British war criminals – Haig, Grey, Lloyd George and more – have been publicly exposed and shamed, and their portraits turned to the wall, the psychic burden remains concealed and festering in our national psyche. We subconsciously crave for the true and still missing explanation of why this war really happened so we can have closure, which is why *The Iron Dice* story has such power.

The research on the stories looks excellent to me, particularly the impeccable work by Irish writer Steve Earles on his excellent and very moving *Bitter Harvest*. I am also very impressed by *Dead in the Water*. The artist and writer have achieved the impossible: they've made a ship story work in comics! That's a first, believe me! And it was valuable to see stories about the questionable role of the media and Bottomley, World War One's Robert Maxwell. If there is a volume two, I would love to see a story about the British spin doctor of this era, who simply made up the story of the Kaiser calling the British a 'contemptible little army', as well as those lies about the British at Mons firing as fast as machine guns. *Mud, Lice and Vice* is very brave to cover sexual disease. Another taboo subject for next time would be those 'Forced March' cocaine tablets officially but secretly given to the troops on *both* sides, leaving behind an unacknowledged post-war generation of addicts, their lives wrecked by the British Empire's greed for power.

I am also delighted to see so many stories about the African, French and German soldiers, rather than the parochial, pseudo-patriotic norm where war is a strictly British activity. We really need more stories like these to enhance the spirit of reconciliation that should be the guiding light of this centenary, especially at a time when the German war dead on the Western Front are still not accorded the same burial rights as the Allied war dead. Death is *not* the great equalizer it should be, and it is sad but not surprising therefore that Germans do not visit their war dead in the same numbers as people from other countries.

Currently, we are fed the spin-doctors' version of legalized mass murder, legitimized as 'heroic sacrifice' with challenging, embarrassing or difficult facts whitewashed from the record. I hope this collection will help to counteract their lies and commemorate the centenary as an opportunity for reconciliation and a search for the truth.

Pat Mills

March 2014

Pat Mills is the writer of *Charley's War*, a ten volume anti-war graphic novel series drawn by Joe Colquohoun, published by Titan Books. He also adapted the poem *Dead Man's Dump* with artist David Hitchcock for *Above the Dreamless Dead*, a graphic interpretation of the poetry of the conflict, published by First Second Books. He is currently writing a new WW1 graphic novel series, *Brothers in Arms*, illustrated by David Hitchcock

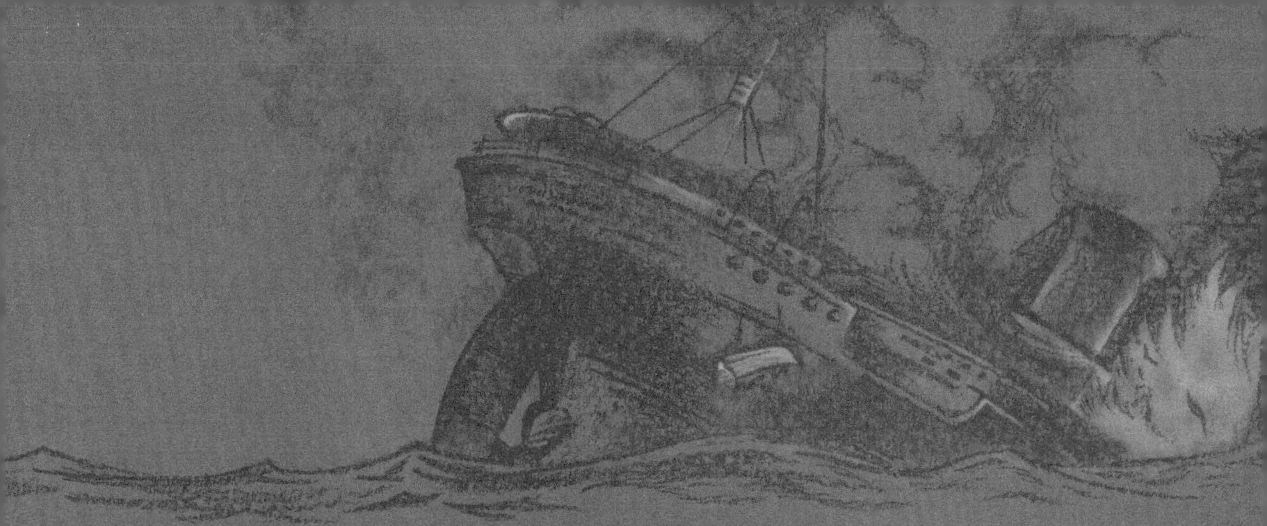

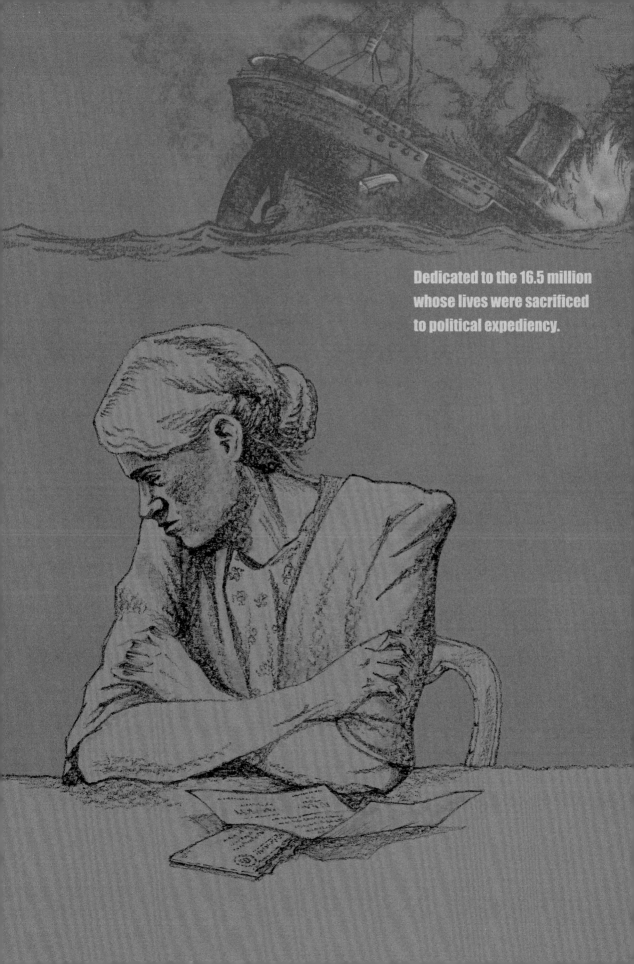

Dedicated to the 16.5 million
whose lives were sacrificed
to political expediency.

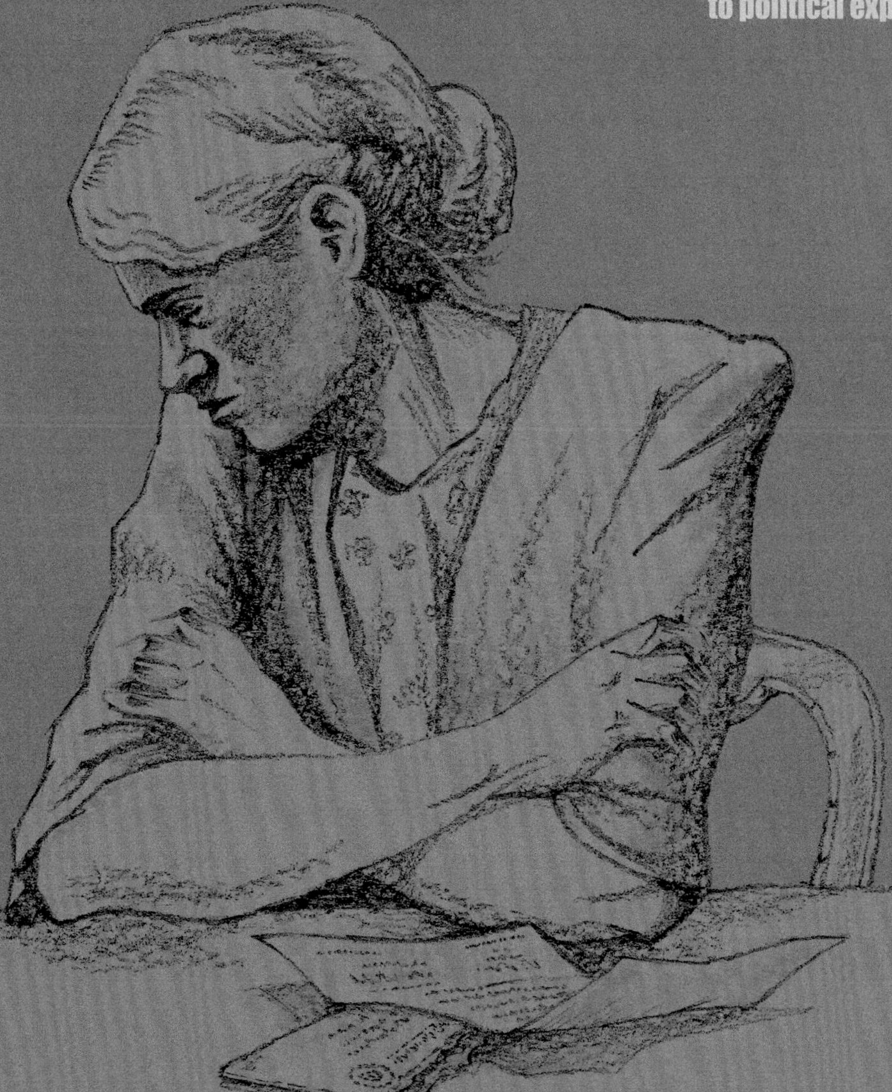

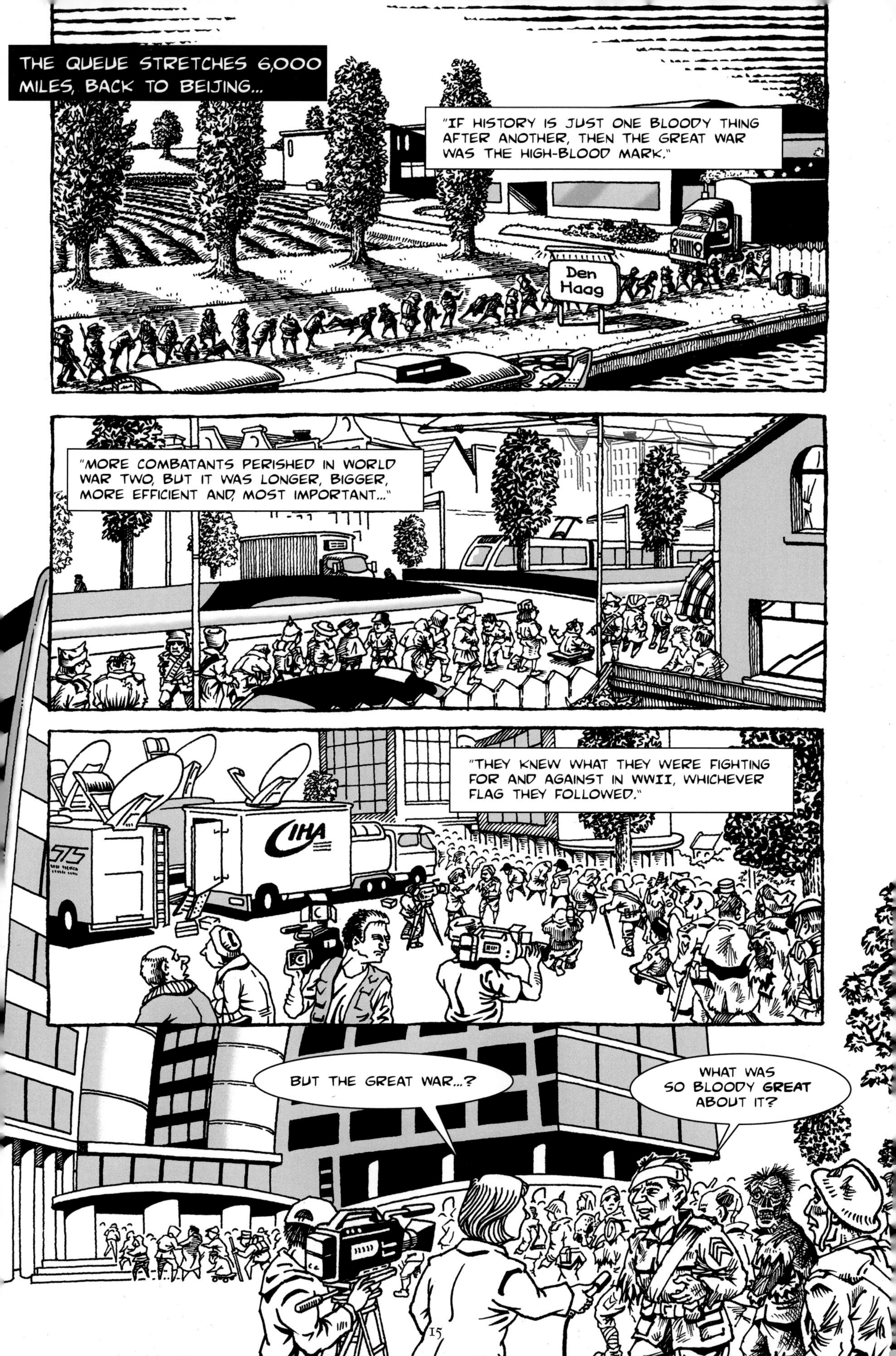
THE QUEUE STRETCHES 6,000 MILES, BACK TO BEIJING...
"IF HISTORY IS JUST ONE BLOODY THING AFTER ANOTHER, THEN THE GREAT WAR WAS THE HIGH-BLOOD MARK."
Den Haag
"MORE COMBATANTS PERISHED IN WORLD WAR TWO, BUT IT WAS LONGER, BIGGER, MORE EFFICIENT AND, MOST IMPORTANT..."
"THEY KNEW WHAT THEY WERE FIGHTING FOR AND AGAINST IN WWII, WHICHEVER FLAG THEY FOLLOWED."
CIHA
BUT THE GREAT WAR...?
WHAT WAS SO BLOODY GREAT ABOUT IT?

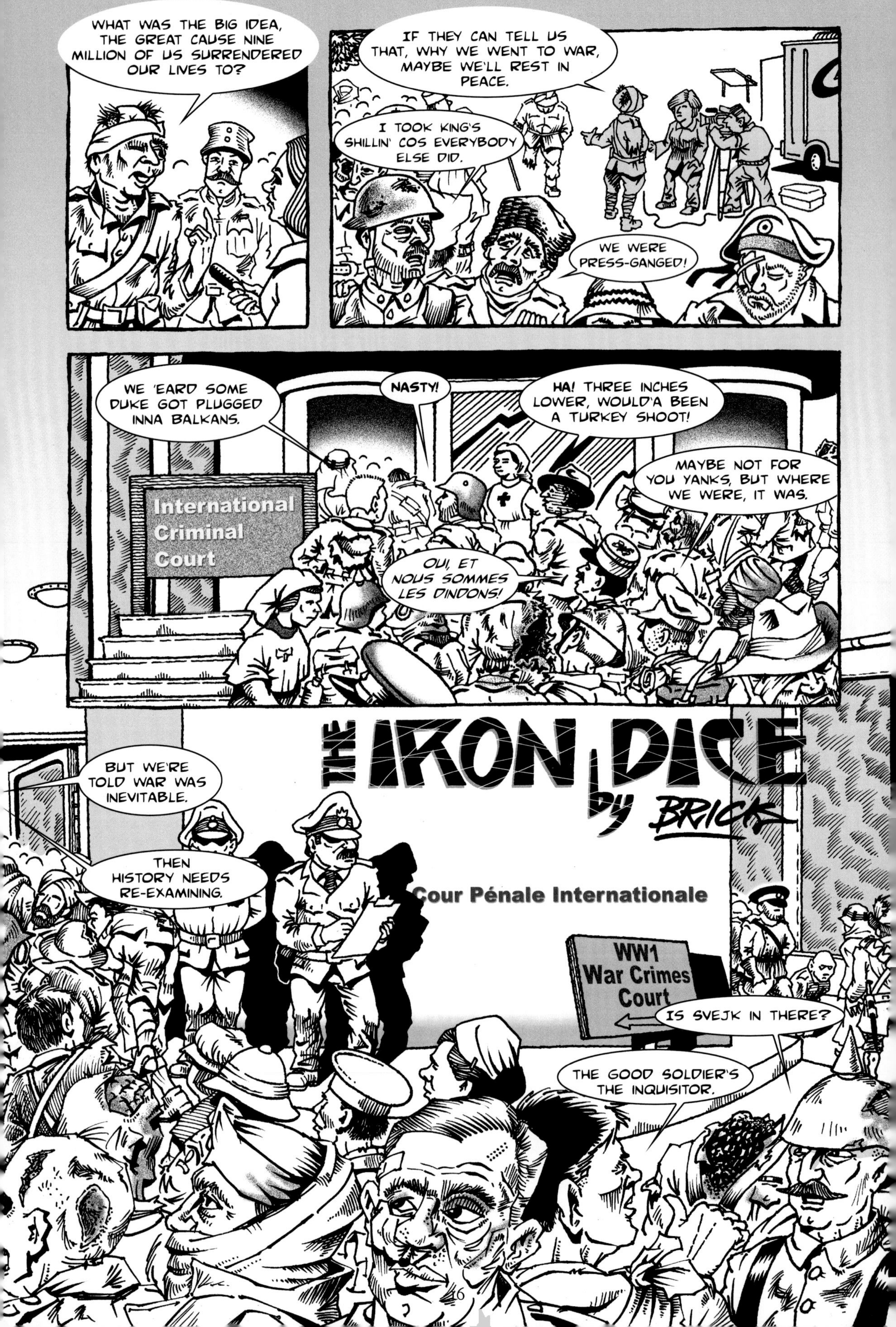
WHAT WAS THE BIG IDEA, THE GREAT CAUSE NINE MILLION OF US SURRENDERED OUR LIVES TO?
IF THEY CAN TELL US THAT, WHY WE WENT TO WAR, MAYBE WE'LL REST IN PEACE.
I TOOK KING'S SHILLIN' COS EVERYBODY ELSE DID.
WE WERE PRESS-GANGED!
WE 'EARD SOME DUKE GOT PLUGGED INNA BALKANS.
NASTY!
HA! THREE INCHES LOWER, WOULD'A BEEN A TURKEY SHOOT!
MAYBE NOT FOR YOU YANKS, BUT WHERE WE WERE, IT WAS.
OUI, ET NOUS SOMMES LES DINDONS!
International Criminal Court
THE IRON DICE
by BRICK
BUT WE'RE TOLD WAR WAS INEVITABLE.
THEN HISTORY NEEDS RE-EXAMINING.
Cour Pénale Internationale
WW1 War Crimes Court
IS SVEJK IN THERE?
THE GOOD SOLDIER'S THE INQUISITOR.

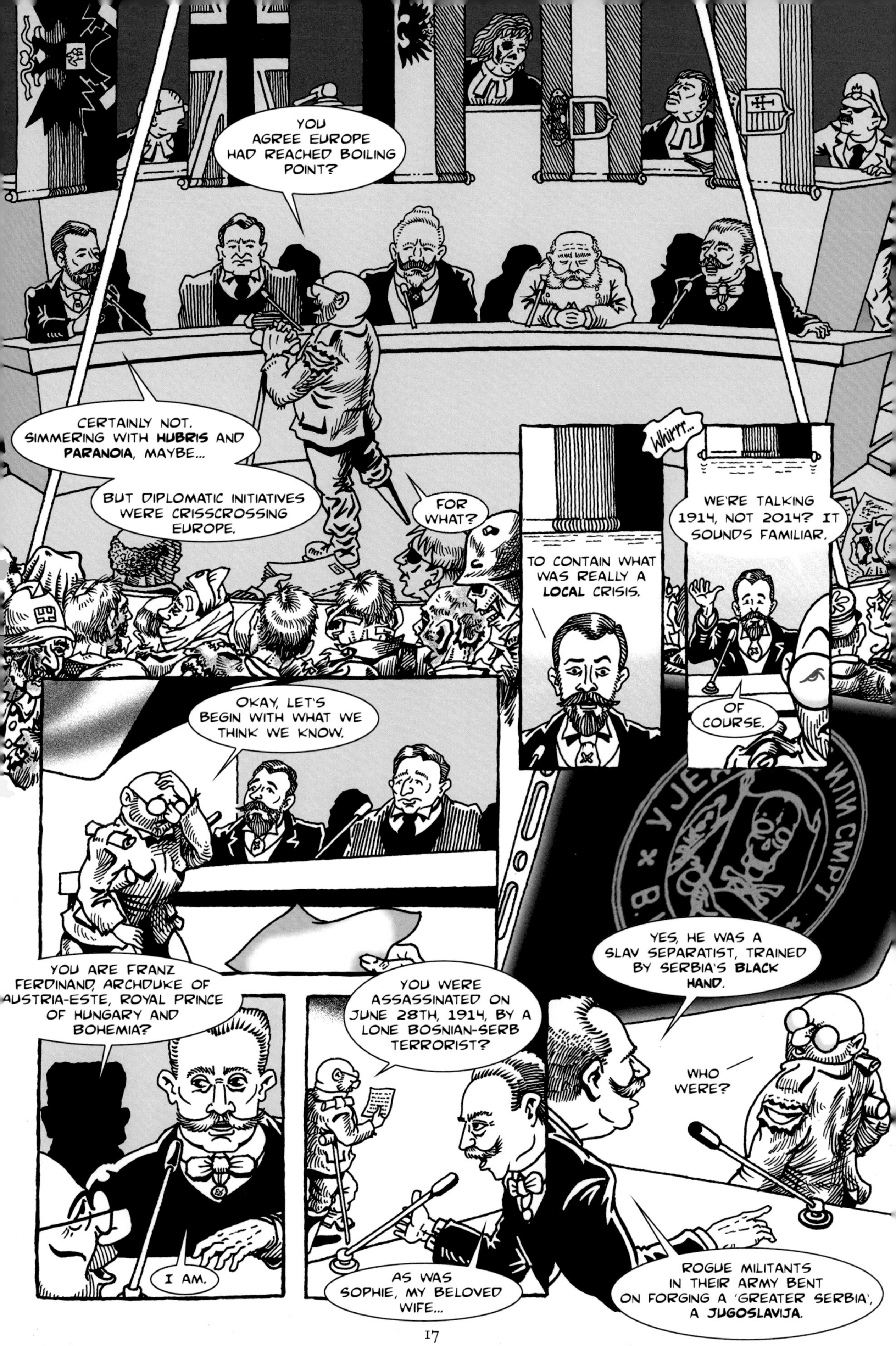
YOU AGREE EUROPE HAD REACHED BOILING POINT?
CERTAINLY NOT. SIMMERING WITH **HUBRIS** AND **PARANOIA**, MAYBE...
BUT DIPLOMATIC INITIATIVES WERE CRISSCROSSING EUROPE.
FOR WHAT?
TO CONTAIN WHAT WAS REALLY A **LOCAL** CRISIS.
Whirrr...
WE'RE TALKING 1914, NOT 2014? IT SOUNDS FAMILIAR.
OF COURSE.
OKAY, LET'S BEGIN WITH WHAT WE THINK WE KNOW.
YOU ARE FRANZ FERDINAND, ARCHDUKE OF AUSTRIA-ESTE, ROYAL PRINCE OF HUNGARY AND BOHEMIA?
I AM.
YOU WERE ASSASSINATED ON JUNE 28TH, 1914, BY A LONE BOSNIAN-SERB TERRORIST?
AS WAS SOPHIE, MY BELOVED WIFE...
YES, HE WAS A SLAV SEPARATIST, TRAINED BY SERBIA'S **BLACK HAND**.
WHO WERE?
ROGUE MILITANTS IN THEIR ARMY BENT ON FORGING A 'GREATER SERBIA', A **JUGOSLAVIJA**.

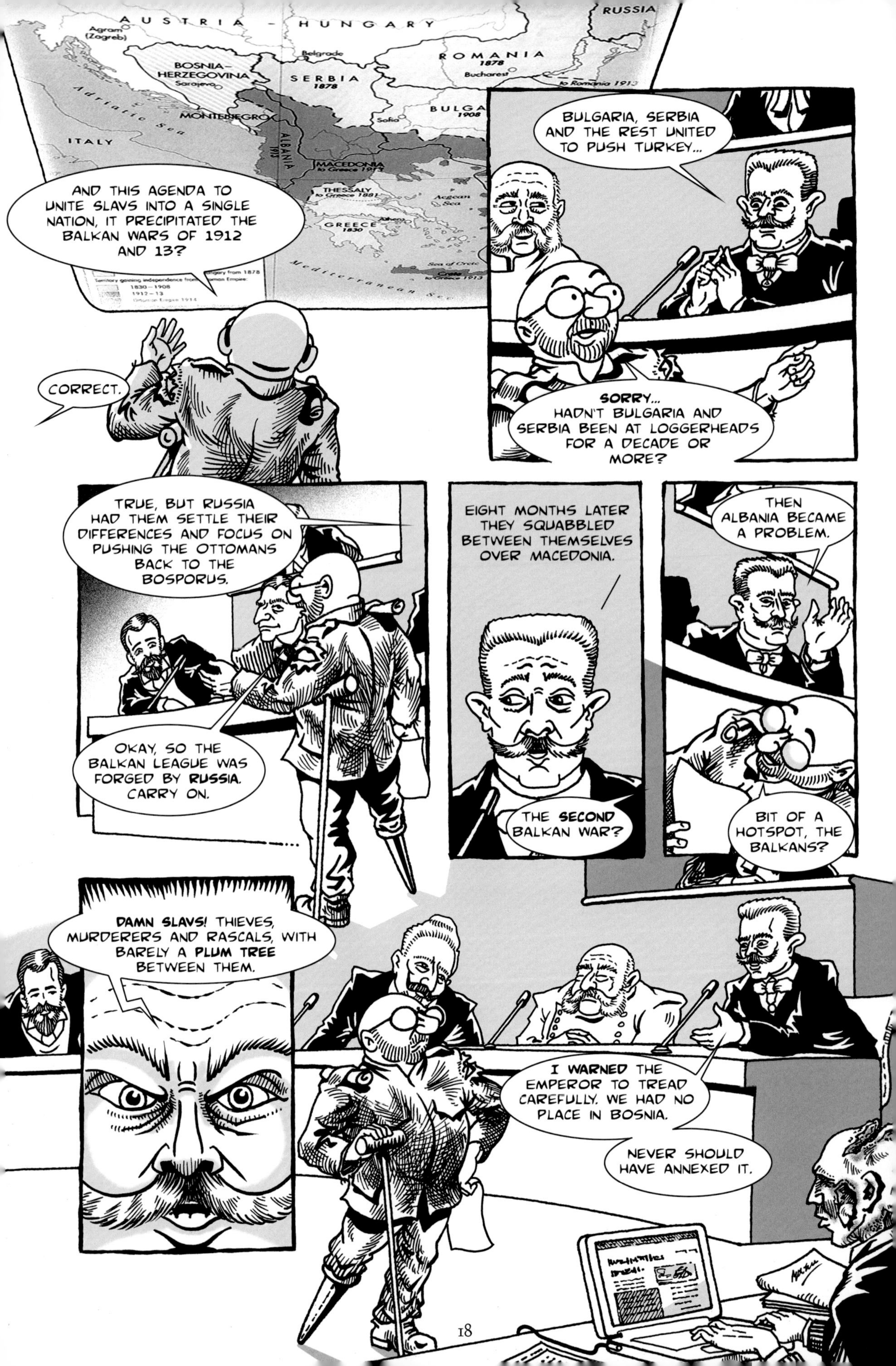

AUSTRIA - HUNGARY
RUSSIA
Agram (Zagreb)
BOSNIA-HERZEGOVINA
Sarajevo
Belgrade
SERBIA 1878
ROMANIA 1878
Bucharest
to Romania 1913
MONTENEGRO
Sofia
BULGA 1908
Adriatic Sea
ITALY
ALBANIA 1913
MACEDONIA to Greece 1913
THESSALY to Greece 1881
Aegean Sea
GREECE 1830
Athens
Sea of Crete
Crete to Greece 1913
1830–1908
1912–13
AND THIS AGENDA TO UNITE SLAVS INTO A SINGLE NATION, IT PRECIPITATED THE BALKAN WARS OF 1912 AND 13?
CORRECT.
BULGARIA, SERBIA AND THE REST UNITED TO PUSH TURKEY...
SORRY... HADN'T BULGARIA AND SERBIA BEEN AT LOGGERHEADS FOR A DECADE OR MORE?
TRUE, BUT RUSSIA HAD THEM SETTLE THEIR DIFFERENCES AND FOCUS ON PUSHING THE OTTOMANS BACK TO THE BOSPORUS.
OKAY, SO THE BALKAN LEAGUE WAS FORGED BY **RUSSIA**. CARRY ON.
EIGHT MONTHS LATER THEY SQUABBLED BETWEEN THEMSELVES OVER MACEDONIA.
THE **SECOND** BALKAN WAR?
THEN ALBANIA BECAME A PROBLEM.
BIT OF A HOTSPOT, THE BALKANS?
DAMN SLAVS! THIEVES, MURDERERS AND RASCALS, WITH BARELY A **PLUM TREE** BETWEEN THEM.
I WARNED THE EMPEROR TO TREAD CAREFULLY. WE HAD NO PLACE IN BOSNIA.
NEVER SHOULD HAVE ANNEXED IT.

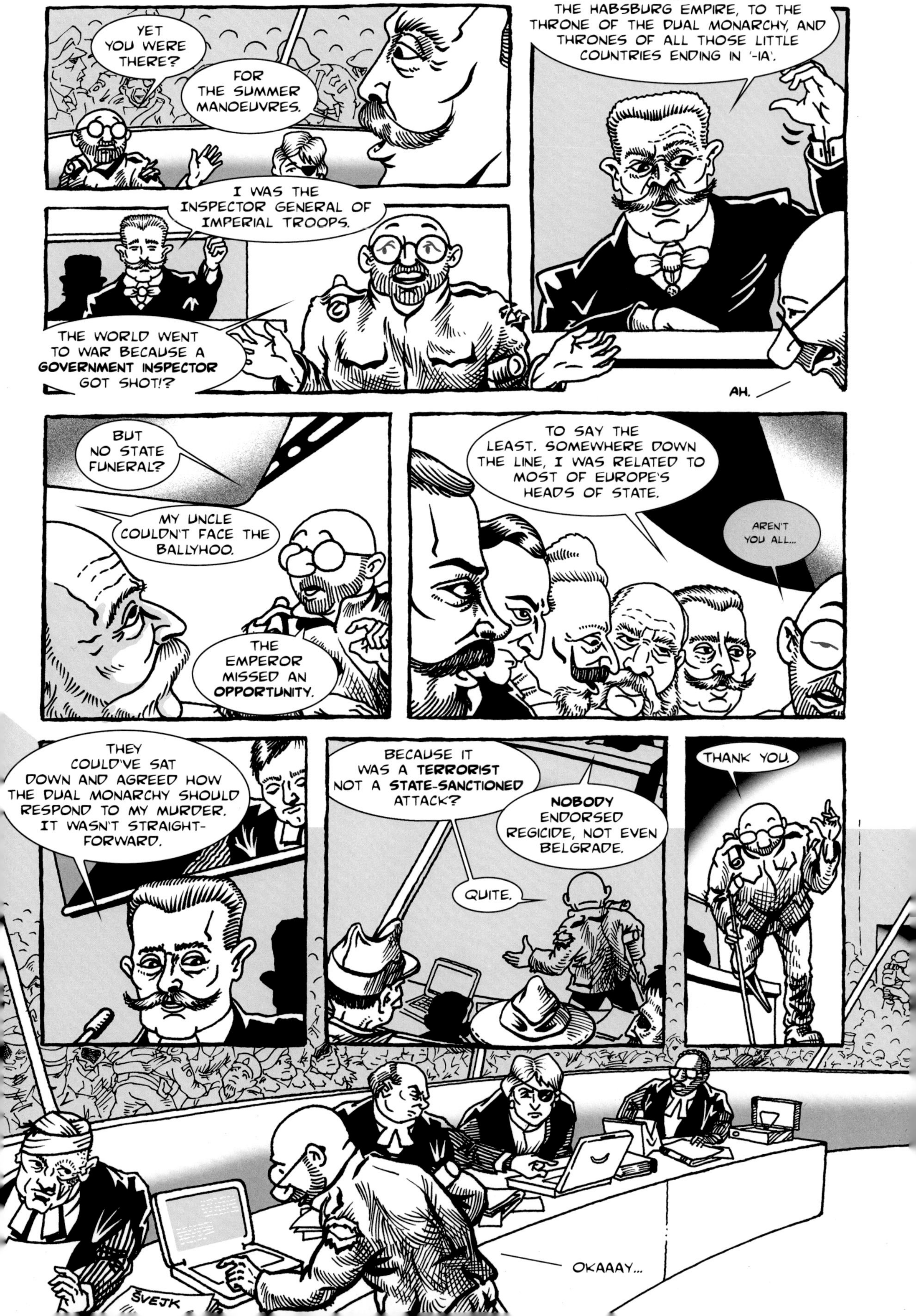
YET YOU WERE THERE?
FOR THE SUMMER MANOEUVRES.
I WAS ALSO HEIR TO THE HABSBURG EMPIRE, TO THE THRONE OF THE DUAL MONARCHY, AND THRONES OF ALL THOSE LITTLE COUNTRIES ENDING IN '-IA'.
I WAS THE INSPECTOR GENERAL OF IMPERIAL TROOPS.
THE WORLD WENT TO WAR BECAUSE A **GOVERNMENT INSPECTOR** GOT SHOT!?
AH.
BUT NO STATE FUNERAL?
MY UNCLE COULDN'T FACE THE BALLYHOO.
THE EMPEROR MISSED AN **OPPORTUNITY**.
TO SAY THE LEAST. SOMEWHERE DOWN THE LINE, I WAS RELATED TO MOST OF EUROPE'S HEADS OF STATE.
AREN'T YOU ALL...
THEY COULD'VE SAT DOWN AND AGREED HOW THE DUAL MONARCHY SHOULD RESPOND TO MY MURDER. IT WASN'T STRAIGHT-FORWARD.
BECAUSE IT WAS A **TERRORIST** NOT A **STATE-SANCTIONED** ATTACK?
NOBODY ENDORSED REGICIDE, NOT EVEN BELGRADE.
QUITE.
THANK YOU.
OKAAAY...
ŠVEJK

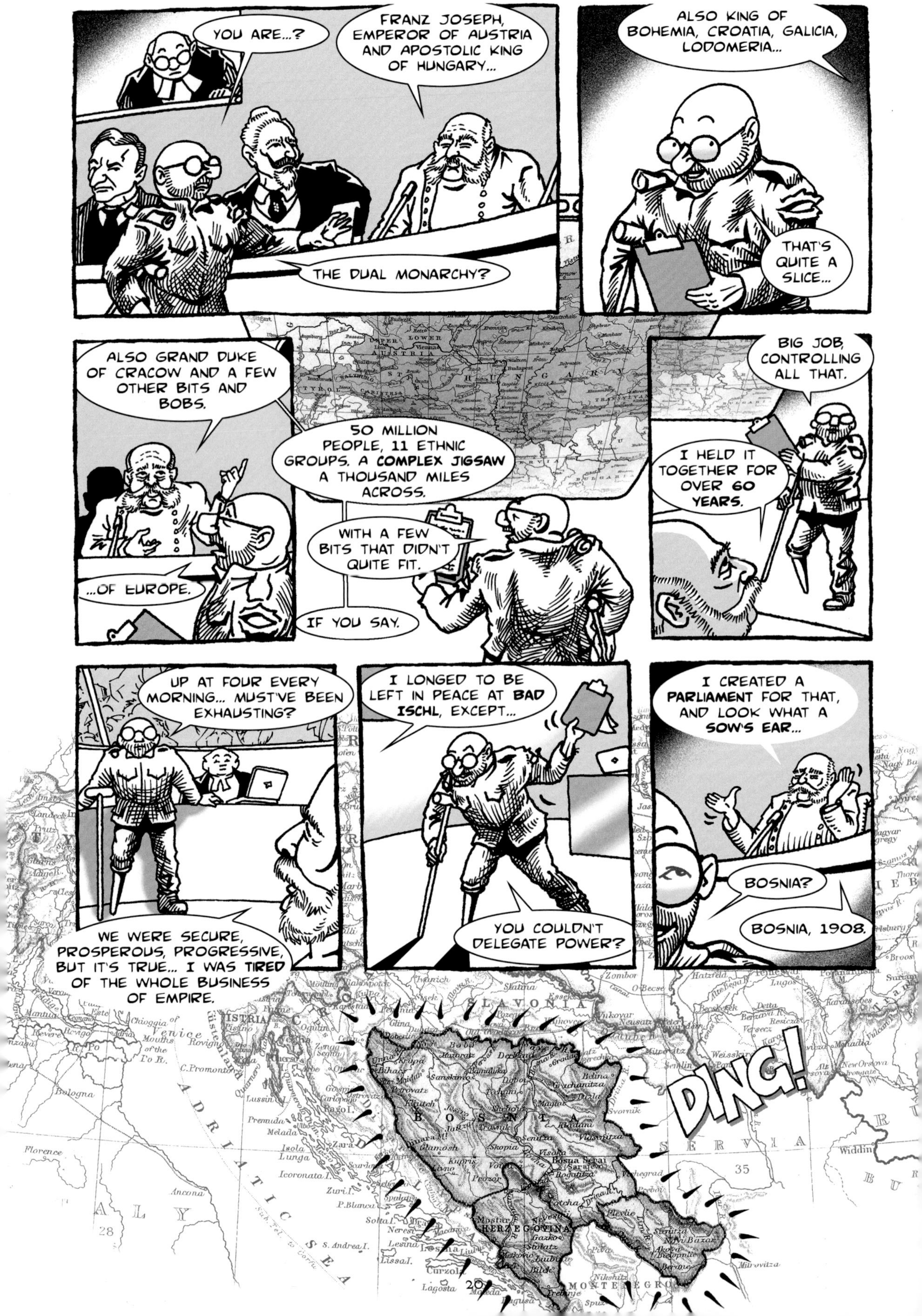
YOU ARE...?
FRANZ JOSEPH, EMPEROR OF AUSTRIA AND APOSTOLIC KING OF HUNGARY...
THE DUAL MONARCHY?
ALSO KING OF BOHEMIA, CROATIA, GALICIA, LODOMERIA...
THAT'S QUITE A SLICE...
ALSO GRAND DUKE OF CRACOW AND A FEW OTHER BITS AND BOBS.
...OF EUROPE.
50 MILLION PEOPLE, 11 ETHNIC GROUPS. A COMPLEX JIGSAW A THOUSAND MILES ACROSS.
WITH A FEW BITS THAT DIDN'T QUITE FIT.
IF YOU SAY.
BIG JOB, CONTROLLING ALL THAT.
I HELD IT TOGETHER FOR OVER 60 YEARS.
UP AT FOUR EVERY MORNING... MUST'VE BEEN EXHAUSTING?
WE WERE SECURE, PROSPEROUS, PROGRESSIVE, BUT IT'S TRUE... I WAS TIRED OF THE WHOLE BUSINESS OF EMPIRE.
I LONGED TO BE LEFT IN PEACE AT BAD ISCHL, EXCEPT...
YOU COULDN'T DELEGATE POWER?
I CREATED A PARLIAMENT FOR THAT, AND LOOK WHAT A SOW'S EAR...
BOSNIA?
BOSNIA, 1908.
DING!

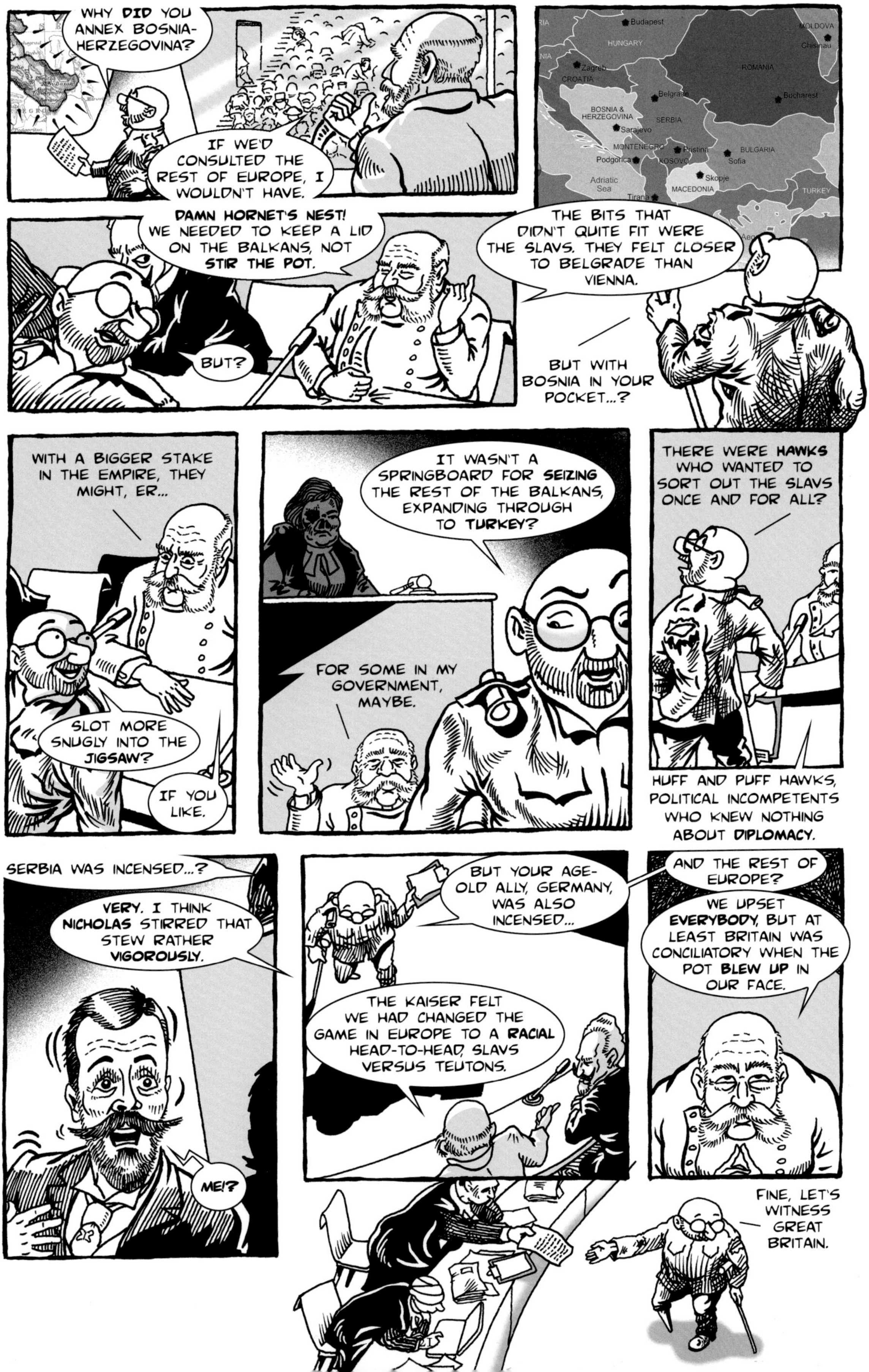
WHY DID YOU ANNEX BOSNIA-HERZEGOVINA?
IF WE'D CONSULTED THE REST OF EUROPE, I WOULDN'T HAVE.
Budapest
HUNGARY
MOLDOVA
Chisinau
Zagreb
CROATIA
ROMANIA
Belgrade
Bucharest
BOSNIA & HERZEGOVINA
SERBIA
Sarajevo
MONTENEGRO
Pristina
BULGARIA
Podgorica
KOSOVO
Sofia
Skopje
Adriatic Sea
MACEDONIA
Tirana
TURKEY
DAMN HORNET'S NEST! WE NEEDED TO KEEP A LID ON THE BALKANS, NOT STIR THE POT.
BUT?
THE BITS THAT DIDN'T QUITE FIT WERE THE SLAVS. THEY FELT CLOSER TO BELGRADE THAN VIENNA.
BUT WITH BOSNIA IN YOUR POCKET...?
WITH A BIGGER STAKE IN THE EMPIRE, THEY MIGHT, ER...
SLOT MORE SNUGLY INTO THE JIGSAW?
IF YOU LIKE.
IT WASN'T A SPRINGBOARD FOR SEIZING THE REST OF THE BALKANS, EXPANDING THROUGH TO TURKEY?
FOR SOME IN MY GOVERNMENT, MAYBE.
THERE WERE HAWKS WHO WANTED TO SORT OUT THE SLAVS ONCE AND FOR ALL?
HUFF AND PUFF HAWKS, POLITICAL INCOMPETENTS WHO KNEW NOTHING ABOUT DIPLOMACY.
SERBIA WAS INCENSED...?
VERY. I THINK NICHOLAS STIRRED THAT STEW RATHER VIGOROUSLY.
ME!?
BUT YOUR AGE-OLD ALLY, GERMANY, WAS ALSO INCENSED...
THE KAISER FELT WE HAD CHANGED THE GAME IN EUROPE TO A RACIAL HEAD-TO-HEAD, SLAVS VERSUS TEUTONS.
AND THE REST OF EUROPE?
WE UPSET EVERYBODY, BUT AT LEAST BRITAIN WAS CONCILIATORY WHEN THE POT BLEW UP IN OUR FACE.
FINE, LET'S WITNESS GREAT BRITAIN.

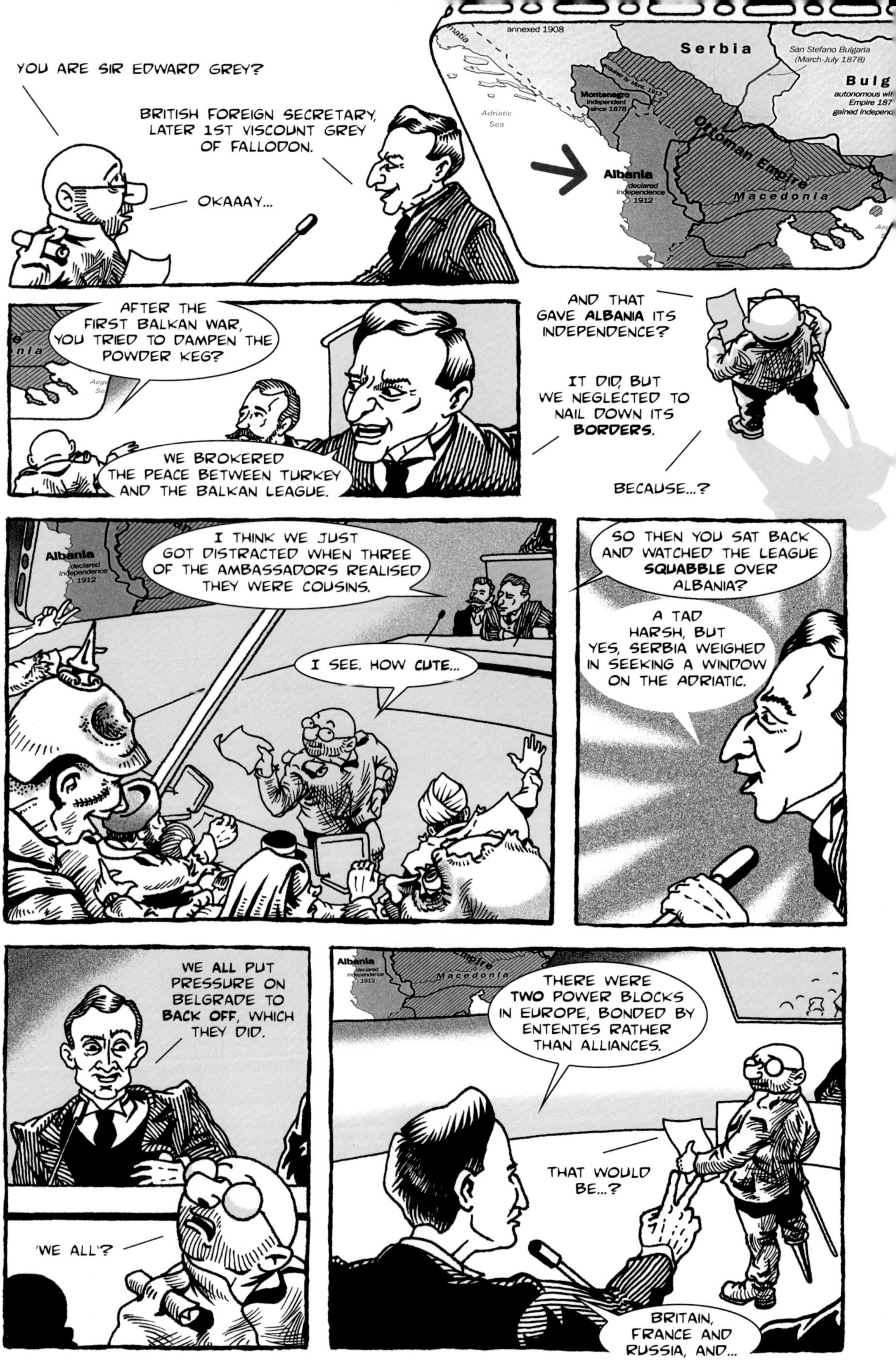
YOU ARE SIR EDWARD GREY?
BRITISH FOREIGN SECRETARY, LATER 1ST VISCOUNT GREY OF FALLODON.
OKAAAY...
annexed 1908
Serbia
San Stefano Bulgaria (March-July 1878)
Montenegro independent since 1878
Adriatic Sea
Albania declared independence 1912
Ottoman Empire
Macedonia
AFTER THE FIRST BALKAN WAR, YOU TRIED TO DAMPEN THE POWDER KEG?
WE BROKERED THE PEACE BETWEEN TURKEY AND THE BALKAN LEAGUE.
AND THAT GAVE ALBANIA ITS INDEPENDENCE?
IT DID, BUT WE NEGLECTED TO NAIL DOWN ITS BORDERS.
BECAUSE...?
I THINK WE JUST GOT DISTRACTED WHEN THREE OF THE AMBASSADORS REALISED THEY WERE COUSINS.
I SEE. HOW CUTE...
SO THEN YOU SAT BACK AND WATCHED THE LEAGUE SQUABBLE OVER ALBANIA?
A TAD HARSH, BUT YES, SERBIA WEIGHED IN SEEKING A WINDOW ON THE ADRIATIC.
WE ALL PUT PRESSURE ON BELGRADE TO BACK OFF, WHICH THEY DID.
'WE ALL'?
THERE WERE TWO POWER BLOCKS IN EUROPE, BONDED BY ENTENTES RATHER THAN ALLIANCES.
THAT WOULD BE...?
BRITAIN, FRANCE AND RUSSIA, AND...

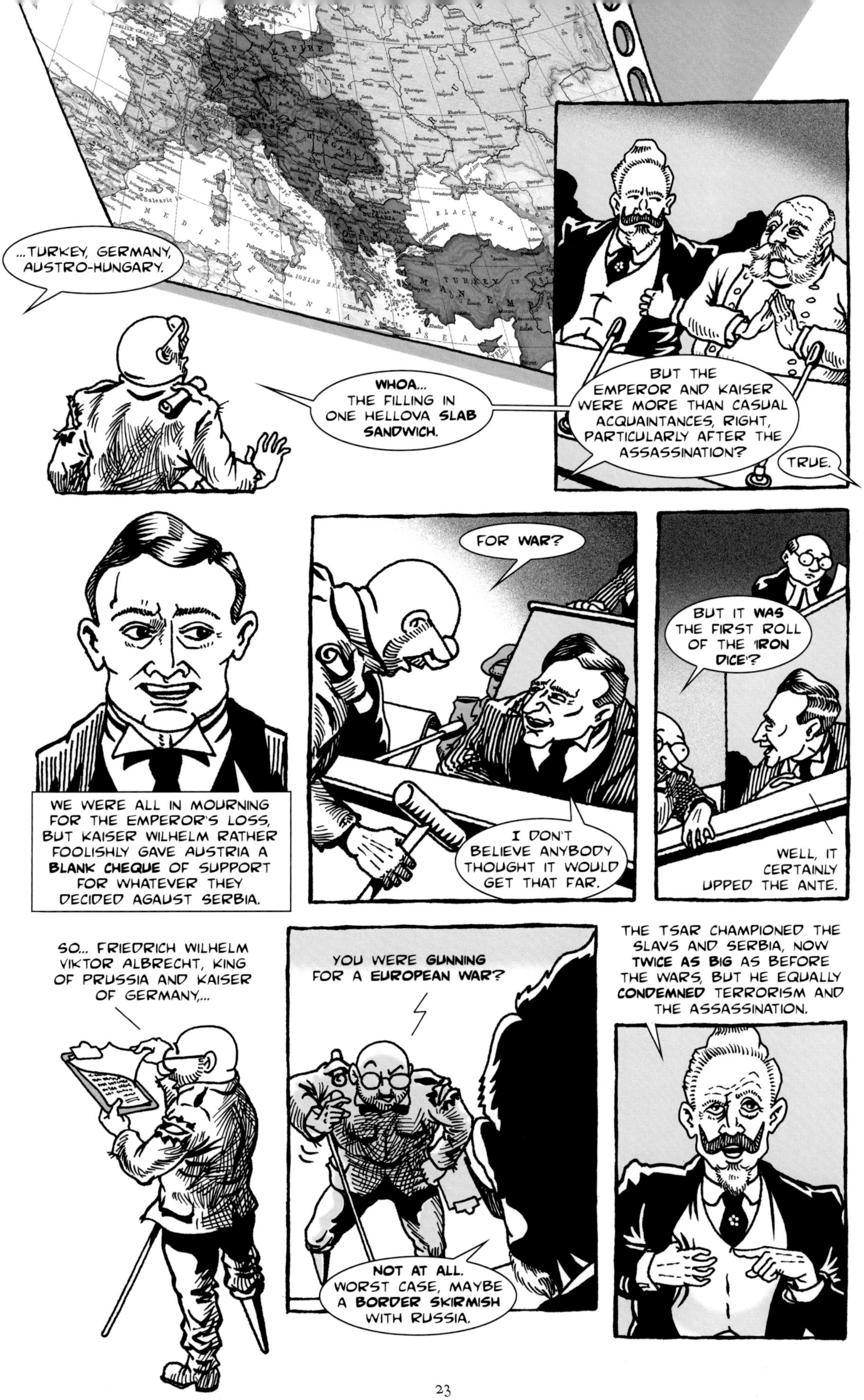

...TURKEY, GERMANY, AUSTRO-HUNGARY.
WHOA... THE FILLING IN ONE HELLOVA SLAB SANDWICH.
BUT THE EMPEROR AND KAISER WERE MORE THAN CASUAL ACQUAINTANCES, RIGHT, PARTICULARLY AFTER THE ASSASSINATION?
TRUE.
WE WERE ALL IN MOURNING FOR THE EMPEROR'S LOSS, BUT KAISER WILHELM RATHER FOOLISHLY GAVE AUSTRIA A BLANK CHEQUE OF SUPPORT FOR WHATEVER THEY DECIDED AGAUST SERBIA.
FOR WAR?
I DON'T BELIEVE ANYBODY THOUGHT IT WOULD GET THAT FAR.
BUT IT WAS THE FIRST ROLL OF THE 'IRON DICE'?
WELL, IT CERTAINLY UPPED THE ANTE.
SO... FRIEDRICH WILHELM VIKTOR ALBRECHT, KING OF PRUSSIA AND KAISER OF GERMANY,...
YOU WERE GUNNING FOR A EUROPEAN WAR?
NOT AT ALL. WORST CASE, MAYBE A BORDER SKIRMISH WITH RUSSIA.
THE TSAR CHAMPIONED THE SLAVS AND SERBIA, NOW TWICE AS BIG AS BEFORE THE WARS, BUT HE EQUALLY CONDEMNED TERRORISM AND THE ASSASSINATION.

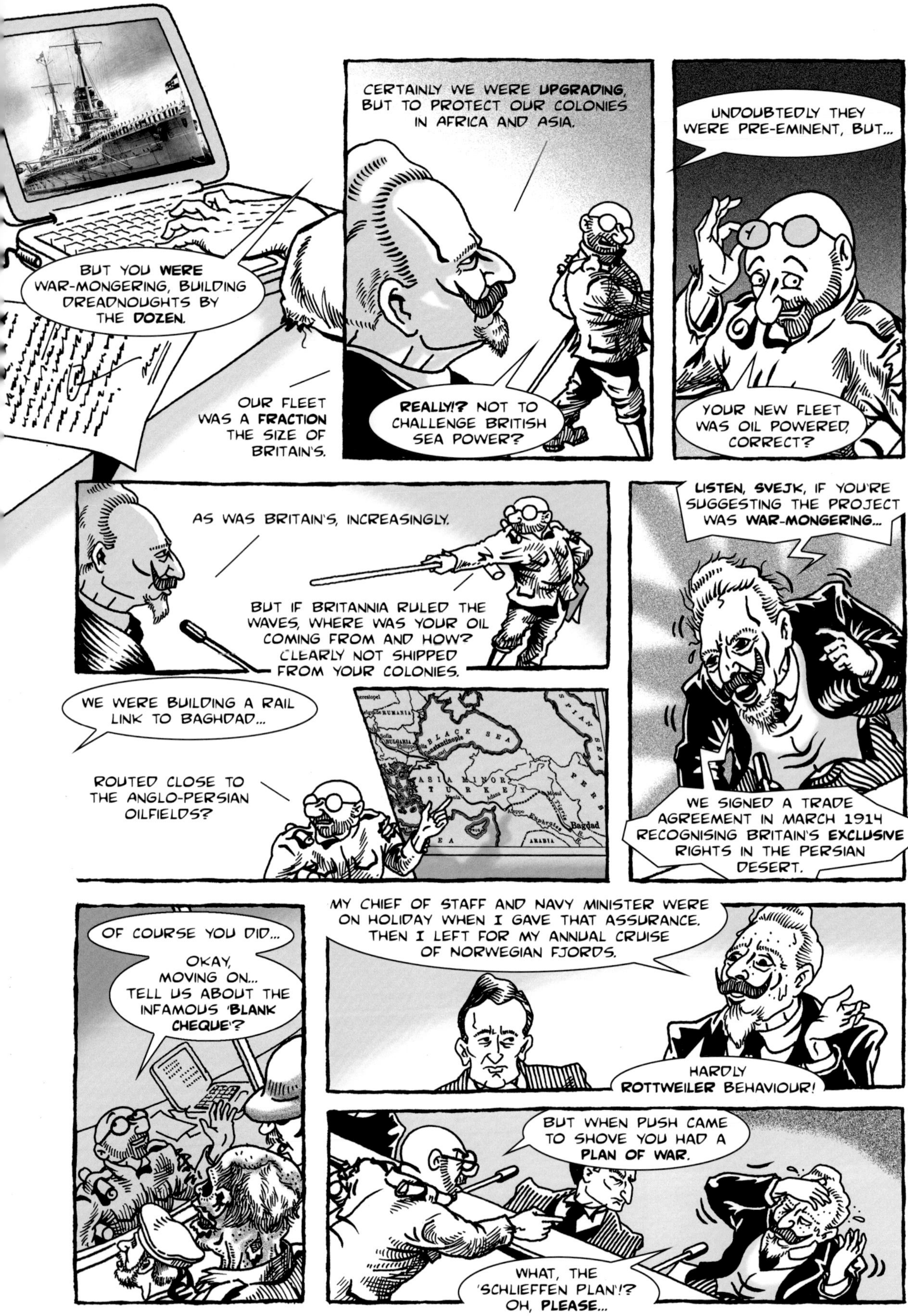
BUT YOU WERE WAR-MONGERING, BUILDING DREADNOUGHTS BY THE DOZEN.
OUR FLEET WAS A FRACTION THE SIZE OF BRITAIN'S.
CERTAINLY WE WERE UPGRADING, BUT TO PROTECT OUR COLONIES IN AFRICA AND ASIA.
REALLY!? NOT TO CHALLENGE BRITISH SEA POWER?
UNDOUBTEDLY THEY WERE PRE-EMINENT, BUT...
YOUR NEW FLEET WAS OIL POWERED, CORRECT?
AS WAS BRITAIN'S, INCREASINGLY.
BUT IF BRITANNIA RULED THE WAVES, WHERE WAS YOUR OIL COMING FROM AND HOW? CLEARLY NOT SHIPPED FROM YOUR COLONIES.
WE WERE BUILDING A RAIL LINK TO BAGHDAD...
ROUTED CLOSE TO THE ANGLO-PERSIAN OILFIELDS?
RUMANIA
BULGARIA
BLACK SEA
Constantinople
ASIA MINOR
TURKEY
Adana
Mosul
Aleppo
Bagdad
ARABIA
LISTEN, SVEJK, IF YOU'RE SUGGESTING THE PROJECT WAS WAR-MONGERING...
WE SIGNED A TRADE AGREEMENT IN MARCH 1914 RECOGNISING BRITAIN'S EXCLUSIVE RIGHTS IN THE PERSIAN DESERT.
OF COURSE YOU DID...
OKAY, MOVING ON... TELL US ABOUT THE INFAMOUS 'BLANK CHEQUE'?
MY CHIEF OF STAFF AND NAVY MINISTER WERE ON HOLIDAY WHEN I GAVE THAT ASSURANCE. THEN I LEFT FOR MY ANNUAL CRUISE OF NORWEGIAN FJORDS.
HARDLY ROTTWEILER BEHAVIOUR!
BUT WHEN PUSH CAME TO SHOVE YOU HAD A PLAN OF WAR.
WHAT, THE 'SCHLIEFFEN PLAN'!? OH, PLEASE...

I'M TELLING YOU, HUNGARY, BRITAIN, RUSSIA, OURSELVES - **EVERYBODY** URGED **PRUDENCE** IN DEALING WITH BELGRADE.

NOBODY EXPECTED AUSTRIA'S DEMANDS TO ESCALATE INTO WAR?

PULLED FROM A BOTTOM DRAW AND THICK WITH **DUST**. IT WAS OUT OF DATE, INAPPROPRIATE, AND THE **ONLY** ONE WE HAD.

EXCEPT MAYBE THAT HOTHEAD **BERCHTOLD**.

COUNT LEOPOLD, THE AUSTRIAN FOREIGN MINISTER?

ZZZZ

IDIOT BOY!

WE ALL AGREED WITH THE HUNGARIAN PRIME MINISTER, THE DEMANDS SHOULD 'NOT BE IMPOSSIBLE OF FULFILMENT'.

SO BERCHTOLD SPENDS TWO WEEKS DRAFTING DEMANDS THAT **NO** SOVEREIGN STATE COULD **POSSIBLY** AGREE TO!

WHERE WAS THE EMPEROR IN ALL THIS?

BAD ISCHL, AND **NOT** ANSWERING THE PHONE.

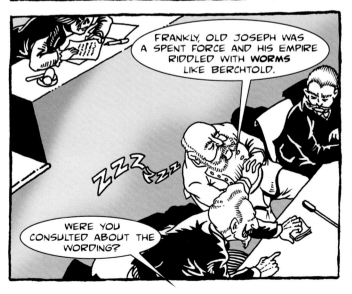

FRANKLY, OLD JOSEPH WAS A SPENT FORCE AND HIS EMPIRE RIDDLED WITH **WORMS** LIKE BERCHTOLD.

ZZZZ ZZZ

WERE YOU CONSULTED ABOUT THE WORDING?

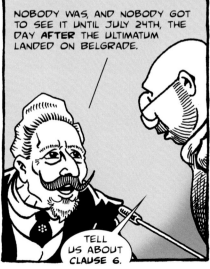

NOBODY WAS, AND NOBODY GOT TO SEE IT UNTIL JULY 24TH, THE DAY **AFTER** THE ULTIMATUM LANDED ON BELGRADE.

TELL US ABOUT CLAUSE 6.

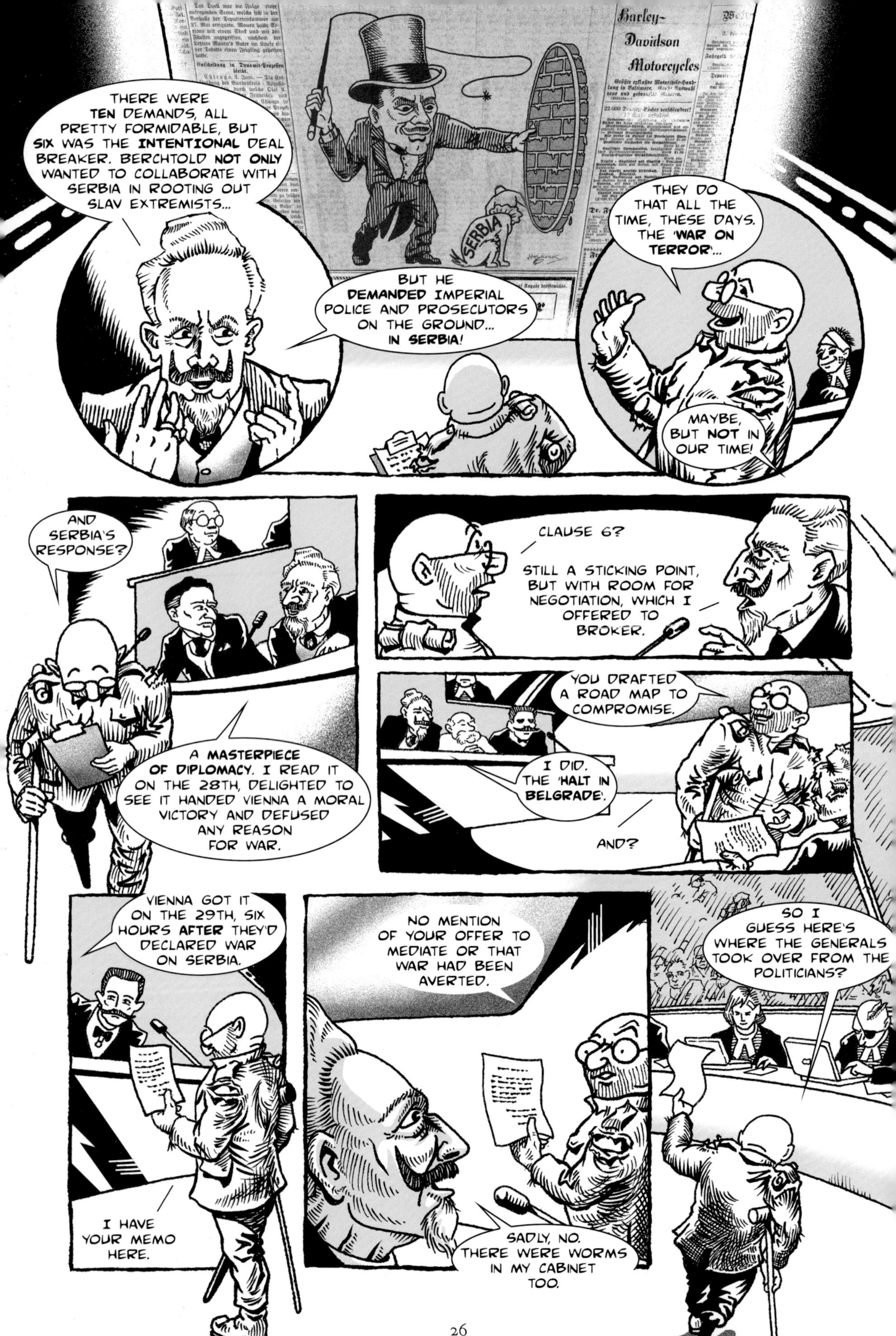
Harley-Davidson Motorcycles
SERBIA
THERE WERE TEN DEMANDS, ALL PRETTY FORMIDABLE, BUT SIX WAS THE INTENTIONAL DEAL BREAKER. BERCHTOLD NOT ONLY WANTED TO COLLABORATE WITH SERBIA IN ROOTING OUT SLAV EXTREMISTS...
BUT HE DEMANDED IMPERIAL POLICE AND PROSECUTORS ON THE GROUND... IN SERBIA!
THEY DO THAT ALL THE TIME, THESE DAYS. THE 'WAR ON TERROR'...
MAYBE, BUT NOT IN OUR TIME!
AND SERBIA'S RESPONSE?
A MASTERPIECE OF DIPLOMACY. I READ IT ON THE 28TH, DELIGHTED TO SEE IT HANDED VIENNA A MORAL VICTORY AND DEFUSED ANY REASON FOR WAR.
CLAUSE 6?
STILL A STICKING POINT, BUT WITH ROOM FOR NEGOTIATION, WHICH I OFFERED TO BROKER.
YOU DRAFTED A ROAD MAP TO COMPROMISE.
I DID. THE 'HALT IN BELGRADE'.
AND?
VIENNA GOT IT ON THE 29TH, SIX HOURS AFTER THEY'D DECLARED WAR ON SERBIA.
I HAVE YOUR MEMO HERE.
NO MENTION OF YOUR OFFER TO MEDIATE OR THAT WAR HAD BEEN AVERTED.
SADLY, NO. THERE WERE WORMS IN MY CABINET TOO.
SO I GUESS HERE'S WHERE THE GENERALS TOOK OVER FROM THE POLITICIANS?

WITH BRITAIN'S SUPPORT, I WAS STILL BOMBARDING VIENNA WITH MY PROPOSED COMPROMISE ON THE 30TH.

BUT RUSSIA MOBILISED ON THE 29TH?

THEY'D ACTUALLY HAD TROOPS IN POSITION SINCE THE 25TH, BUT YES.

THEN YOU MOBILISED, THEN THE FRENCH.

WE ONLY MOBILISED BECAUSE GREY WAS MAKING THREATS ABOUT US SUPPORTING AUSTRIA.

BRITAIN SHOULD'VE BEEN RAPPING THE TSAR'S KNUCKLES, NOT OURS.

HOWEVER...?

YOU HAVE TO UNDERSTAND THE DIFFERENCE BETWEEN MOBILISING, OR READYING THE TROOPS, AND ACTUALLY DECLARING WAR.

OKAY, SO YOU BLEW THE DUST OFF THE 'SCHLIEFFEN PLAN'?

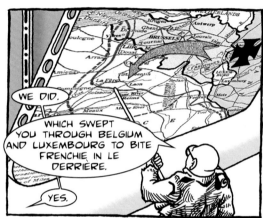

WE DID.

WHICH SWEPT YOU THROUGH BELGIUM AND LUXEMBOURG TO BITE FRENCHIE IN LE DERRIÈRE.

YES.

WHICH HAD WHAT TO DO WITH THE BALKANS?

IT WAS DEVISED DURING BISMARCK'S TIME, FOR GOD'S SAKE, TO COUNTER AN ATTACK ON TWO FRONTS.

HMM... NOT AS MUCH AS THEY DO!

BUT IT WAS THE CURVEBALL THAT SUCKED IN BRITAIN ON AUGUST 4TH?

WHICH I DEEPLY REGRET.

EXIT

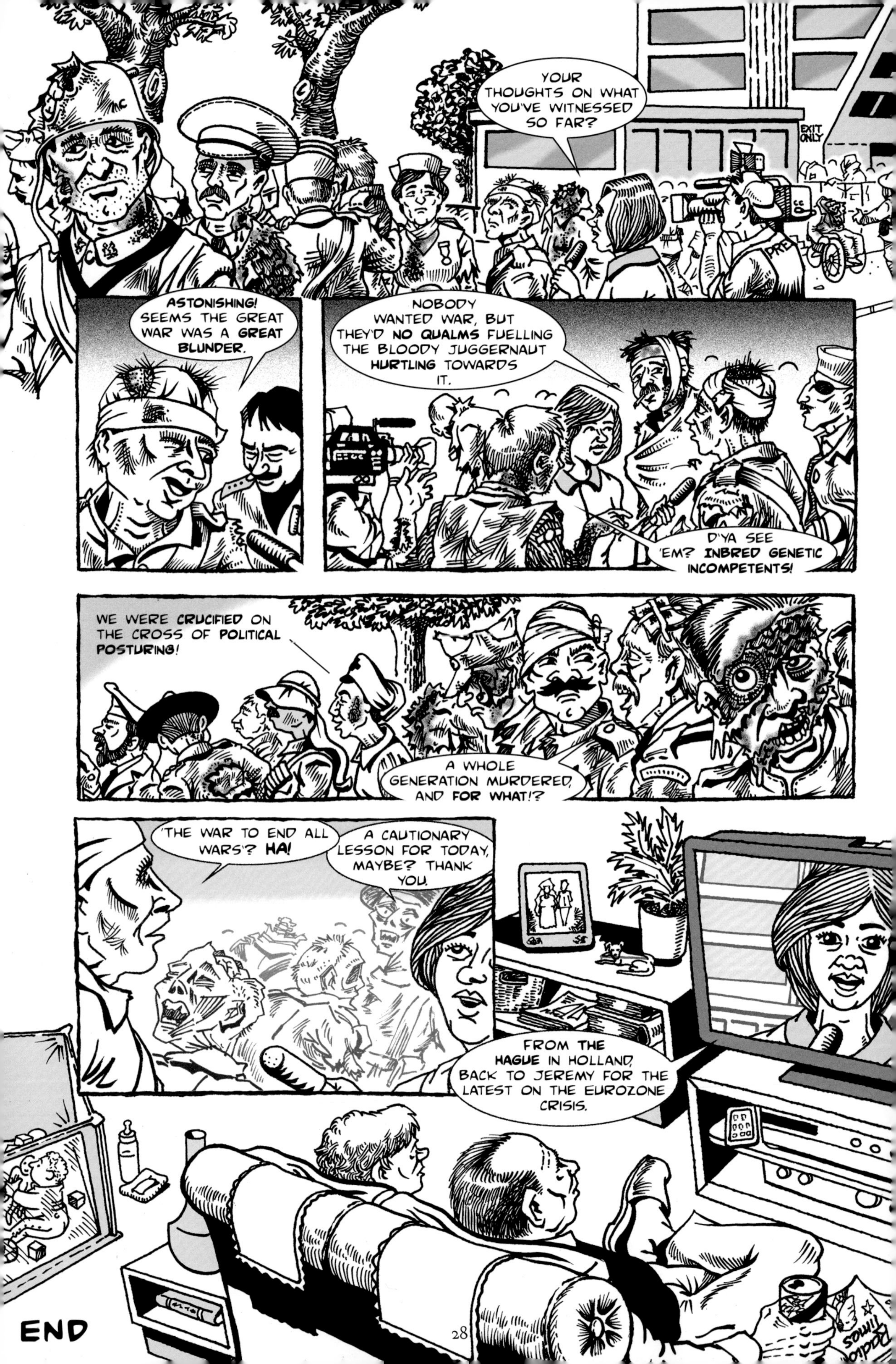
YOUR THOUGHTS ON WHAT YOU'VE WITNESSED SO FAR?
EXIT ONLY
ASTONISHING! SEEMS THE GREAT WAR WAS A GREAT BLUNDER.
NOBODY WANTED WAR, BUT THEY'D NO QUALMS FUELLING THE BLOODY JUGGERNAUT HURTLING TOWARDS IT.
D'YA SEE 'EM? INBRED GENETIC INCOMPETENTS!
WE WERE CRUCIFIED ON THE CROSS OF POLITICAL POSTURING!
A WHOLE GENERATION MURDERED, AND FOR WHAT!?
'THE WAR TO END ALL WARS'? HA!
A CAUTIONARY LESSON FOR TODAY, MAYBE? THANK YOU.
FROM THE HAGUE IN HOLLAND, BACK TO JEREMY FOR THE LATEST ON THE EUROZONE CRISIS.
END

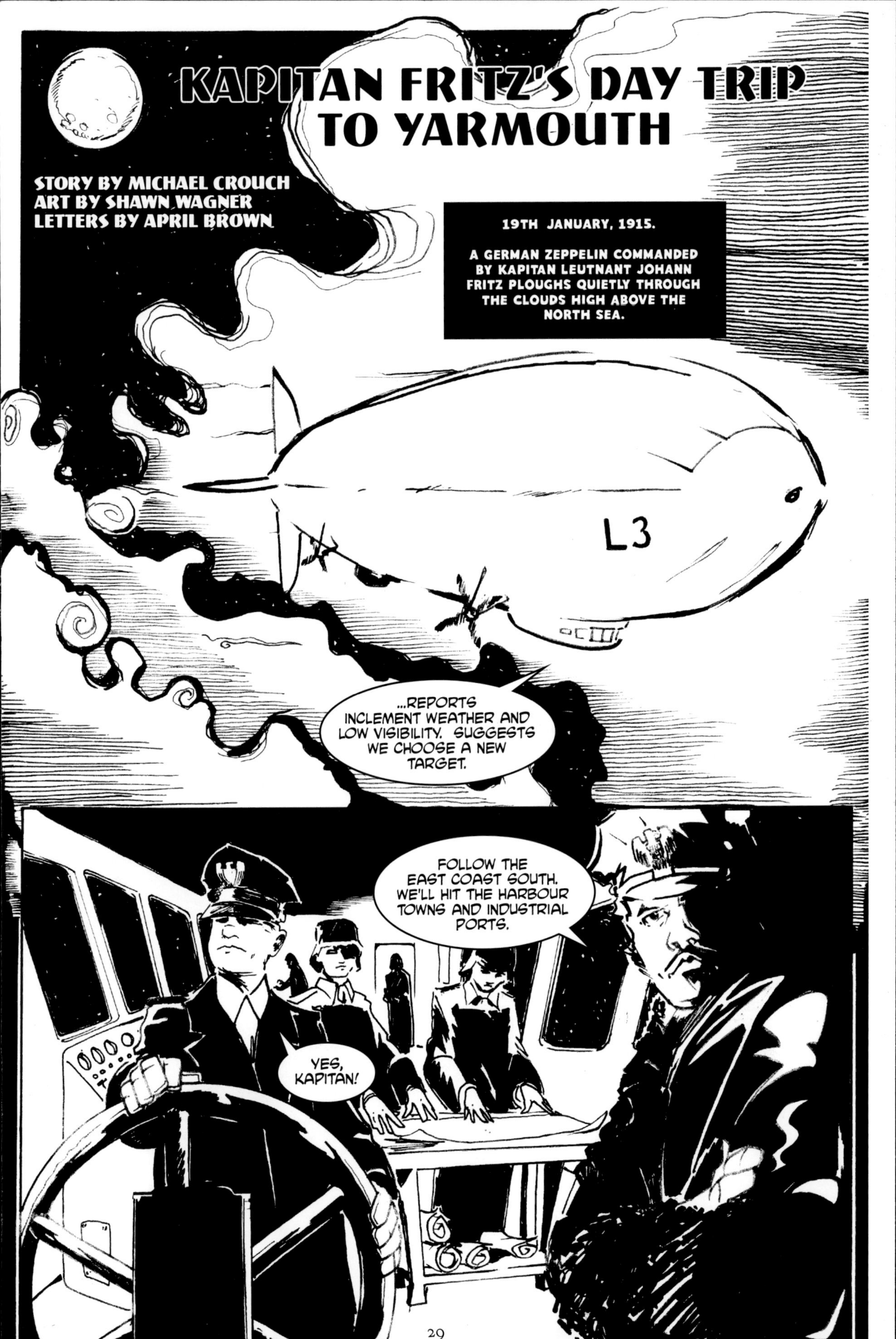

KAPITAN FRITZ'S DAY TRIP TO YARMOUTH
STORY BY MICHAEL CROUCH
ART BY SHAWN WAGNER
LETTERS BY APRIL BROWN
19TH JANUARY, 1915.
A GERMAN ZEPPELIN COMMANDED BY KAPITAN LEUTNANT JOHANN FRITZ PLOUGHS QUIETLY THROUGH THE CLOUDS HIGH ABOVE THE NORTH SEA.
L3
...REPORTS INCLEMENT WEATHER AND LOW VISIBILITY. SUGGESTS WE CHOOSE A NEW TARGET.
FOLLOW THE EAST COAST SOUTH. WE'LL HIT THE HARBOUR TOWNS AND INDUSTRIAL PORTS.
YES, KAPITAN!

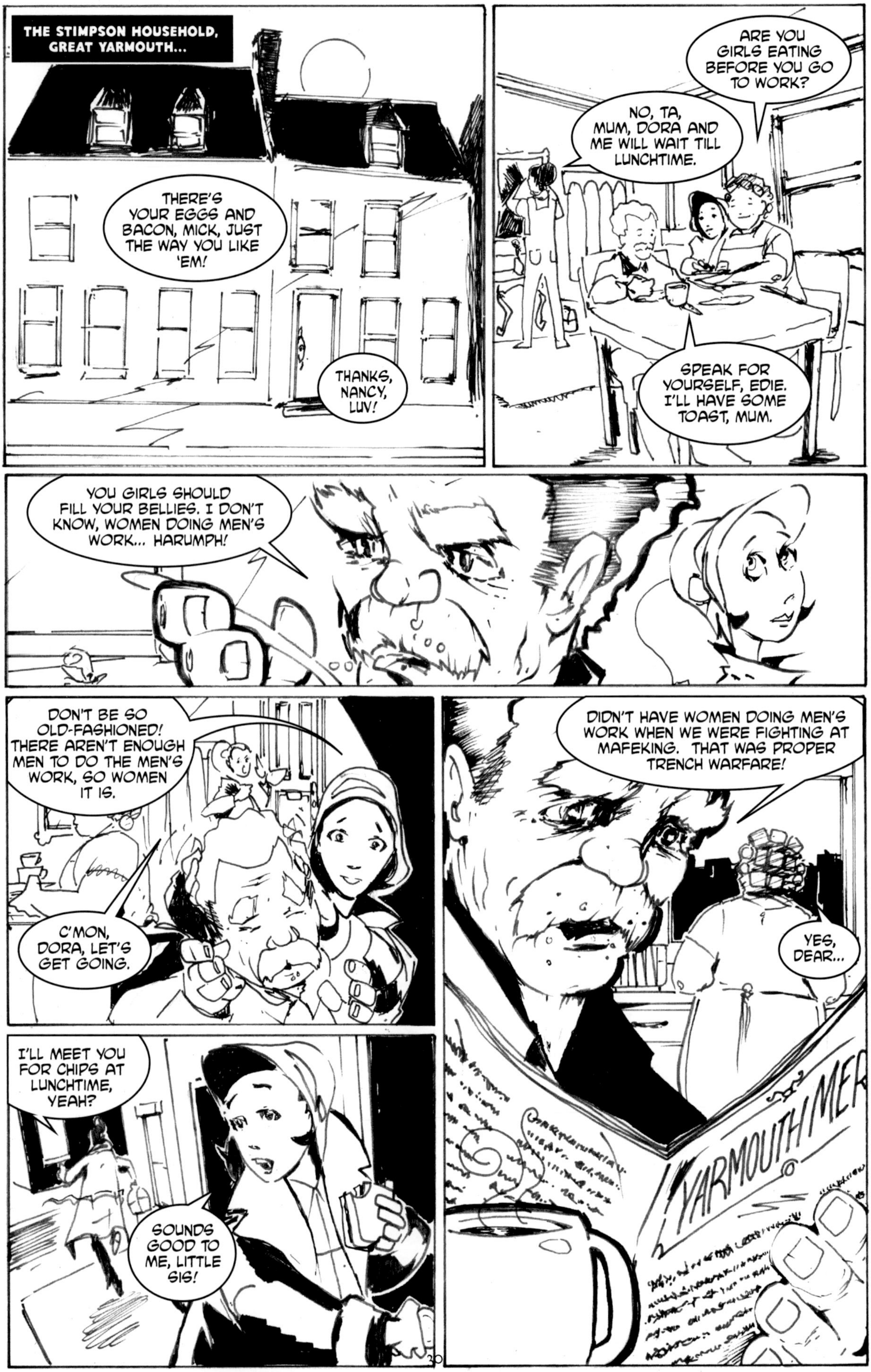
THE STIMPSON HOUSEHOLD, GREAT YARMOUTH...
THERE'S YOUR EGGS AND BACON, MICK, JUST THE WAY YOU LIKE 'EM!
THANKS, NANCY, LUV!
ARE YOU GIRLS EATING BEFORE YOU GO TO WORK?
NO, TA, MUM, DORA AND ME WILL WAIT TILL LUNCHTIME.
SPEAK FOR YOURSELF, EDIE. I'LL HAVE SOME TOAST, MUM.
YOU GIRLS SHOULD FILL YOUR BELLIES. I DON'T KNOW, WOMEN DOING MEN'S WORK... HARUMPH!
DON'T BE SO OLD-FASHIONED! THERE AREN'T ENOUGH MEN TO DO THE MEN'S WORK, SO WOMEN IT IS.
C'MON, DORA, LET'S GET GOING.
DIDN'T HAVE WOMEN DOING MEN'S WORK WHEN WE WERE FIGHTING AT MAFEKING. THAT WAS PROPER TRENCH WARFARE!
YES, DEAR...
I'LL MEET YOU FOR CHIPS AT LUNCHTIME, YEAH?
SOUNDS GOOD TO ME, LITTLE SIS!
YARMOUTH MER

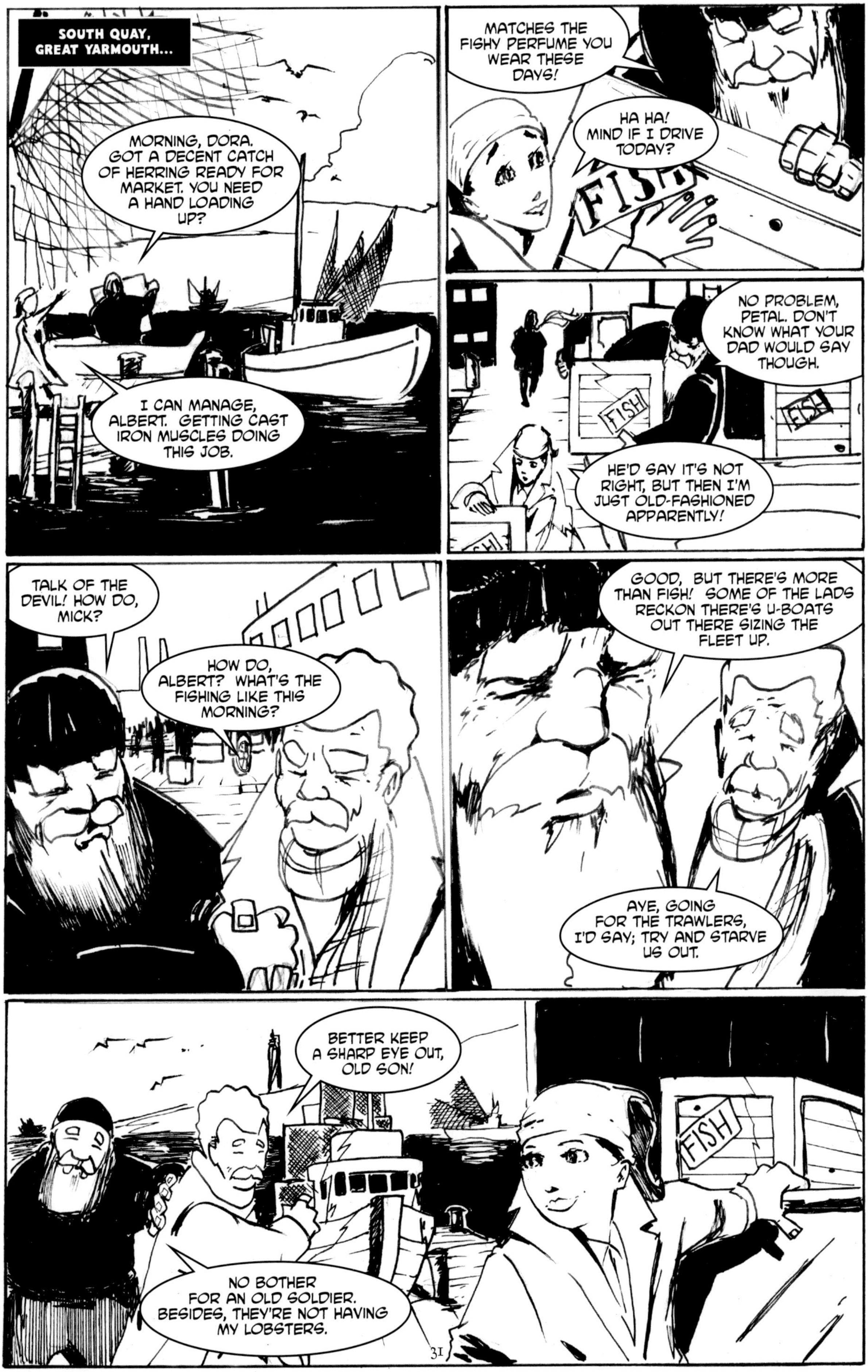
SOUTH QUAY, GREAT YARMOUTH...
MORNING, DORA. GOT A DECENT CATCH OF HERRING READY FOR MARKET. YOU NEED A HAND LOADING UP?
I CAN MANAGE, ALBERT. GETTING CAST IRON MUSCLES DOING THIS JOB.
MATCHES THE FISHY PERFUME YOU WEAR THESE DAYS!
HA HA! MIND IF I DRIVE TODAY?
FISH
NO PROBLEM, PETAL. DON'T KNOW WHAT YOUR DAD WOULD SAY THOUGH.
HE'D SAY IT'S NOT RIGHT, BUT THEN I'M JUST OLD-FASHIONED APPARENTLY!
FISH
FISH
TALK OF THE DEVIL! HOW DO, MICK?
HOW DO, ALBERT? WHAT'S THE FISHING LIKE THIS MORNING?
GOOD, BUT THERE'S MORE THAN FISH! SOME OF THE LADS RECKON THERE'S U-BOATS OUT THERE SIZING THE FLEET UP.
AYE, GOING FOR THE TRAWLERS, I'D SAY; TRY AND STARVE US OUT.
BETTER KEEP A SHARP EYE OUT, OLD SON!
NO BOTHER FOR AN OLD SOLDIER. BESIDES, THEY'RE NOT HAVING MY LOBSTERS.
FISH

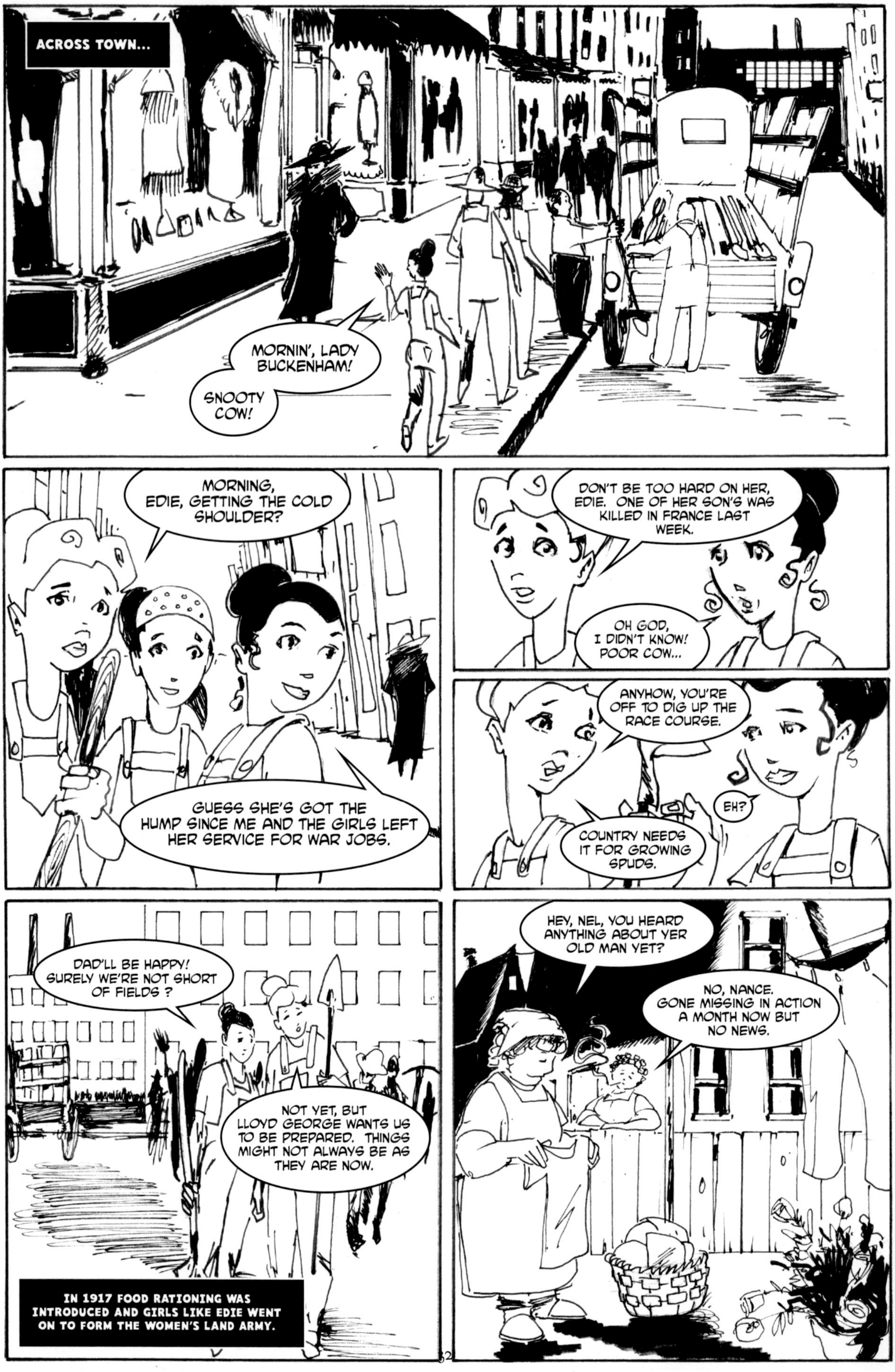
ACROSS TOWN...
MORNIN', LADY BUCKENHAM!
SNOOTY COW!
MORNING, EDIE, GETTING THE COLD SHOULDER?
GUESS SHE'S GOT THE HUMP SINCE ME AND THE GIRLS LEFT HER SERVICE FOR WAR JOBS.
DON'T BE TOO HARD ON HER, EDIE. ONE OF HER SON'S WAS KILLED IN FRANCE LAST WEEK.
OH GOD, I DIDN'T KNOW! POOR COW...
ANYHOW, YOU'RE OFF TO DIG UP THE RACE COURSE.
EH?
COUNTRY NEEDS IT FOR GROWING SPUDS.
DAD'LL BE HAPPY! SURELY WE'RE NOT SHORT OF FIELDS ?
NOT YET, BUT LLOYD GEORGE WANTS US TO BE PREPARED. THINGS MIGHT NOT ALWAYS BE AS THEY ARE NOW.
IN 1917 FOOD RATIONING WAS INTRODUCED AND GIRLS LIKE EDIE WENT ON TO FORM THE WOMEN'S LAND ARMY.
HEY, NEL, YOU HEARD ANYTHING ABOUT YER OLD MAN YET?
NO, NANCE. GONE MISSING IN ACTION A MONTH NOW BUT NO NEWS.

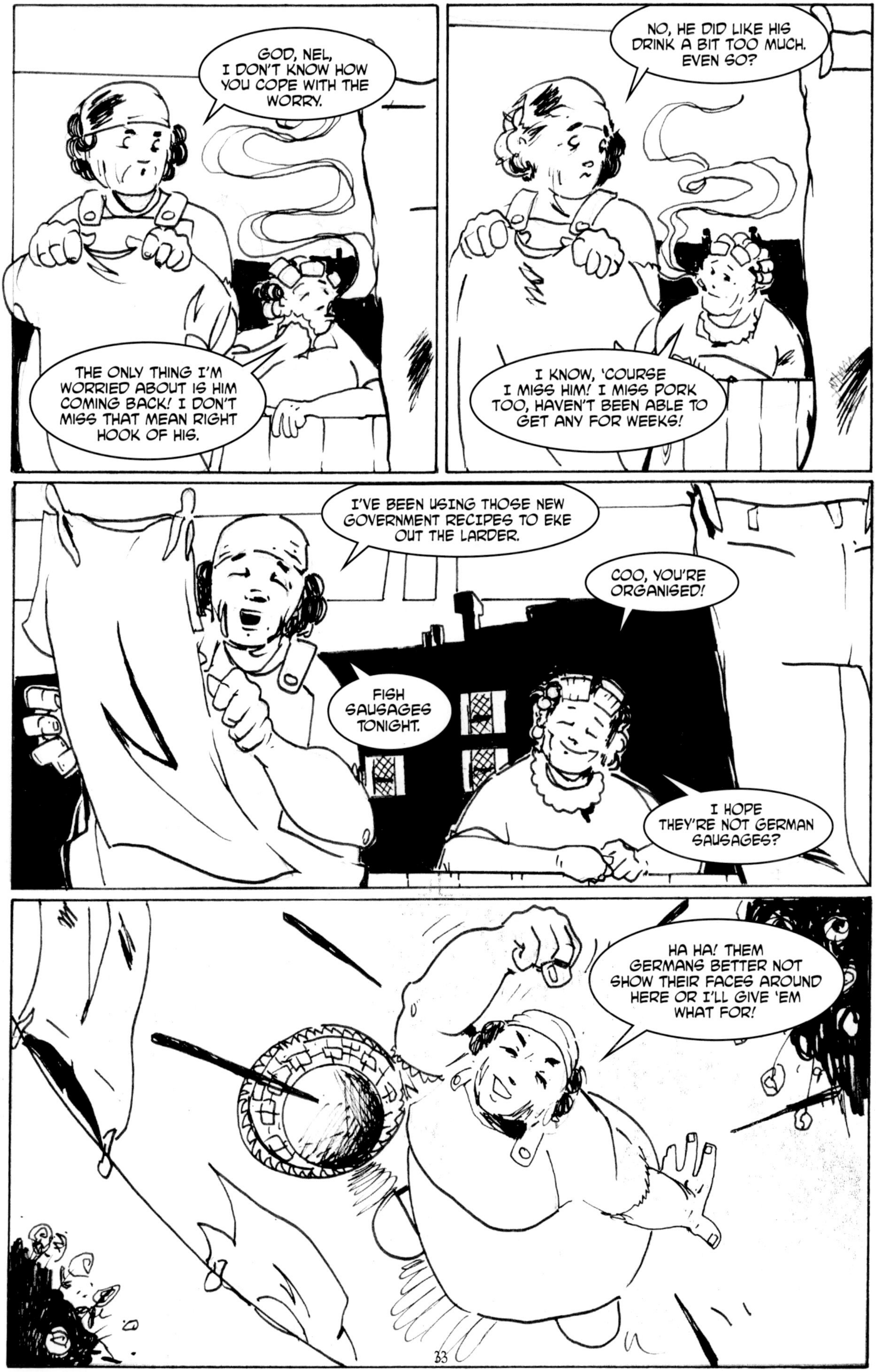
GOD, NEL, I DON'T KNOW HOW YOU COPE WITH THE WORRY.
THE ONLY THING I'M WORRIED ABOUT IS HIM COMING BACK! I DON'T MISS THAT MEAN RIGHT HOOK OF HIS.
NO, HE DID LIKE HIS DRINK A BIT TOO MUCH. EVEN SO?
I KNOW, 'COURSE I MISS HIM! I MISS PORK TOO, HAVEN'T BEEN ABLE TO GET ANY FOR WEEKS!
I'VE BEEN USING THOSE NEW GOVERNMENT RECIPES TO EKE OUT THE LARDER.
COO, YOU'RE ORGANISED!
FISH SAUSAGES TONIGHT.
I HOPE THEY'RE NOT GERMAN SAUSAGES?
HA HA! THEM GERMANS BETTER NOT SHOW THEIR FACES AROUND HERE OR I'LL GIVE 'EM WHAT FOR!

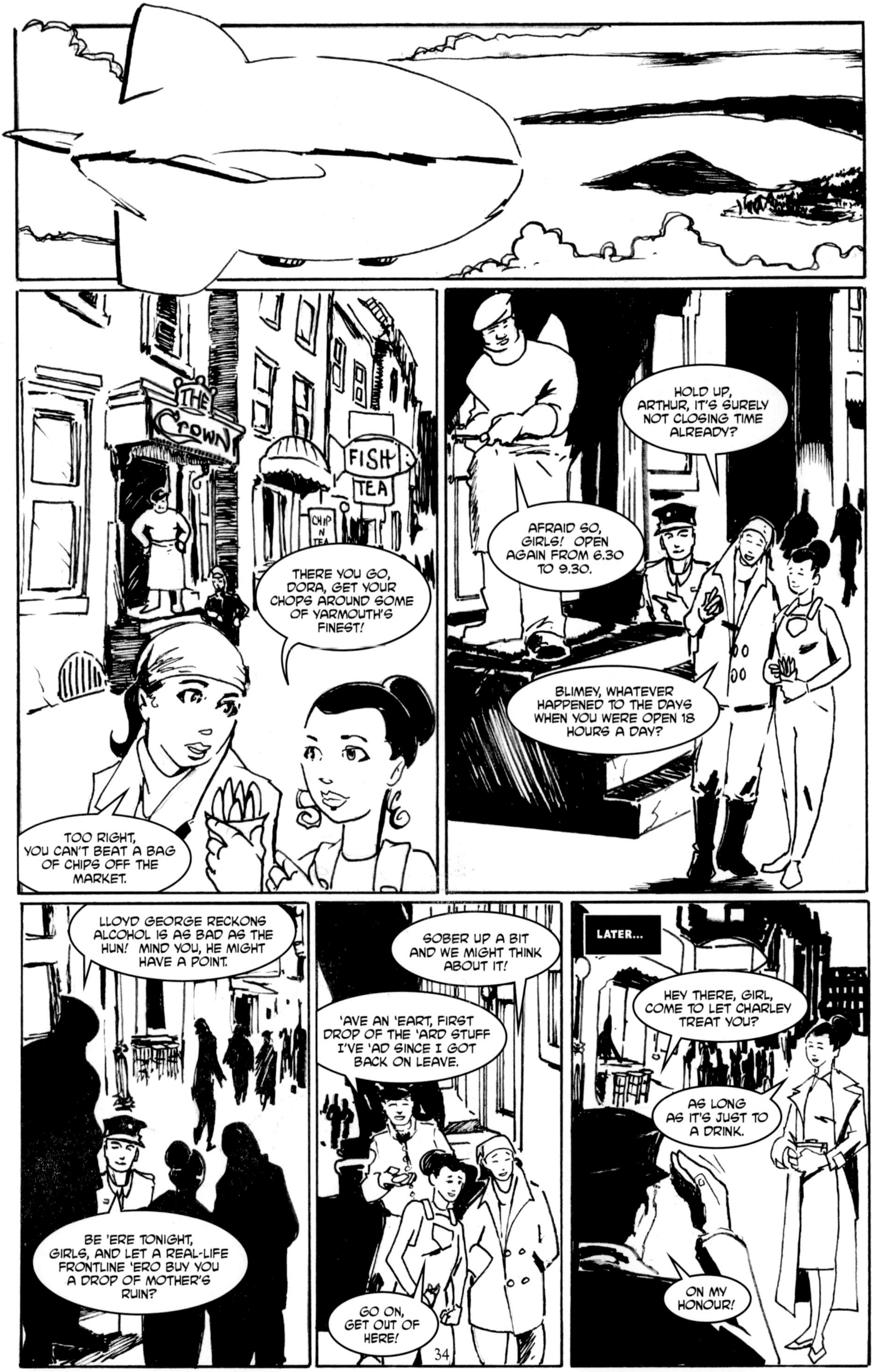
THE Crown
FISH
TEA
CHIP N TEA
THERE YOU GO, DORA, GET YOUR CHOPS AROUND SOME OF YARMOUTH'S FINEST!
TOO RIGHT, YOU CAN'T BEAT A BAG OF CHIPS OFF THE MARKET.
HOLD UP, ARTHUR, IT'S SURELY NOT CLOSING TIME ALREADY?
AFRAID SO, GIRLS! OPEN AGAIN FROM 6.30 TO 9.30.
BLIMEY, WHATEVER HAPPENED TO THE DAYS WHEN YOU WERE OPEN 18 HOURS A DAY?
LLOYD GEORGE RECKONS ALCOHOL IS AS BAD AS THE HUN! MIND YOU, HE MIGHT HAVE A POINT.
BE 'ERE TONIGHT, GIRLS, AND LET A REAL-LIFE FRONTLINE 'ERO BUY YOU A DROP OF MOTHER'S RUIN?
SOBER UP A BIT AND WE MIGHT THINK ABOUT IT!
'AVE AN 'EART, FIRST DROP OF THE 'ARD STUFF I'VE 'AD SINCE I GOT BACK ON LEAVE.
GO ON, GET OUT OF HERE!
LATER...
HEY THERE, GIRL, COME TO LET CHARLEY TREAT YOU?
AS LONG AS IT'S JUST TO A DRINK.
ON MY HONOUR!

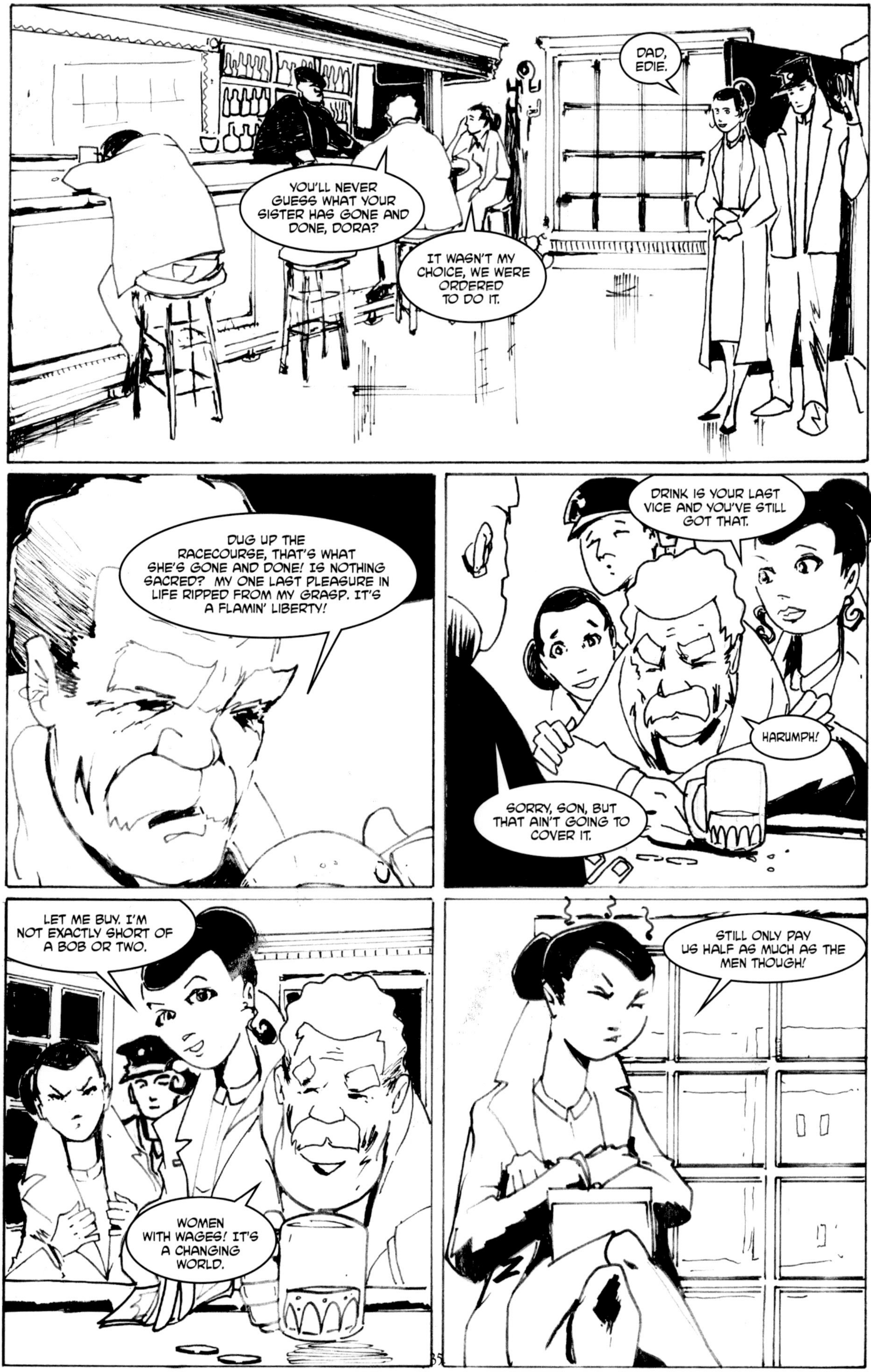
DAD, EDIE.
YOU'LL NEVER GUESS WHAT YOUR SISTER HAS GONE AND DONE, DORA?
IT WASN'T MY CHOICE, WE WERE ORDERED TO DO IT.
DUG UP THE RACECOURSE, THAT'S WHAT SHE'S GONE AND DONE! IS NOTHING SACRED? MY ONE LAST PLEASURE IN LIFE RIPPED FROM MY GRASP. IT'S A FLAMIN' LIBERTY!
DRINK IS YOUR LAST VICE AND YOU'VE STILL GOT THAT.
HARUMPH!
SORRY, SON, BUT THAT AIN'T GOING TO COVER IT.
LET ME BUY. I'M NOT EXACTLY SHORT OF A BOB OR TWO.
WOMEN WITH WAGES! IT'S A CHANGING WORLD.
STILL ONLY PAY US HALF AS MUCH AS THE MEN THOUGH!

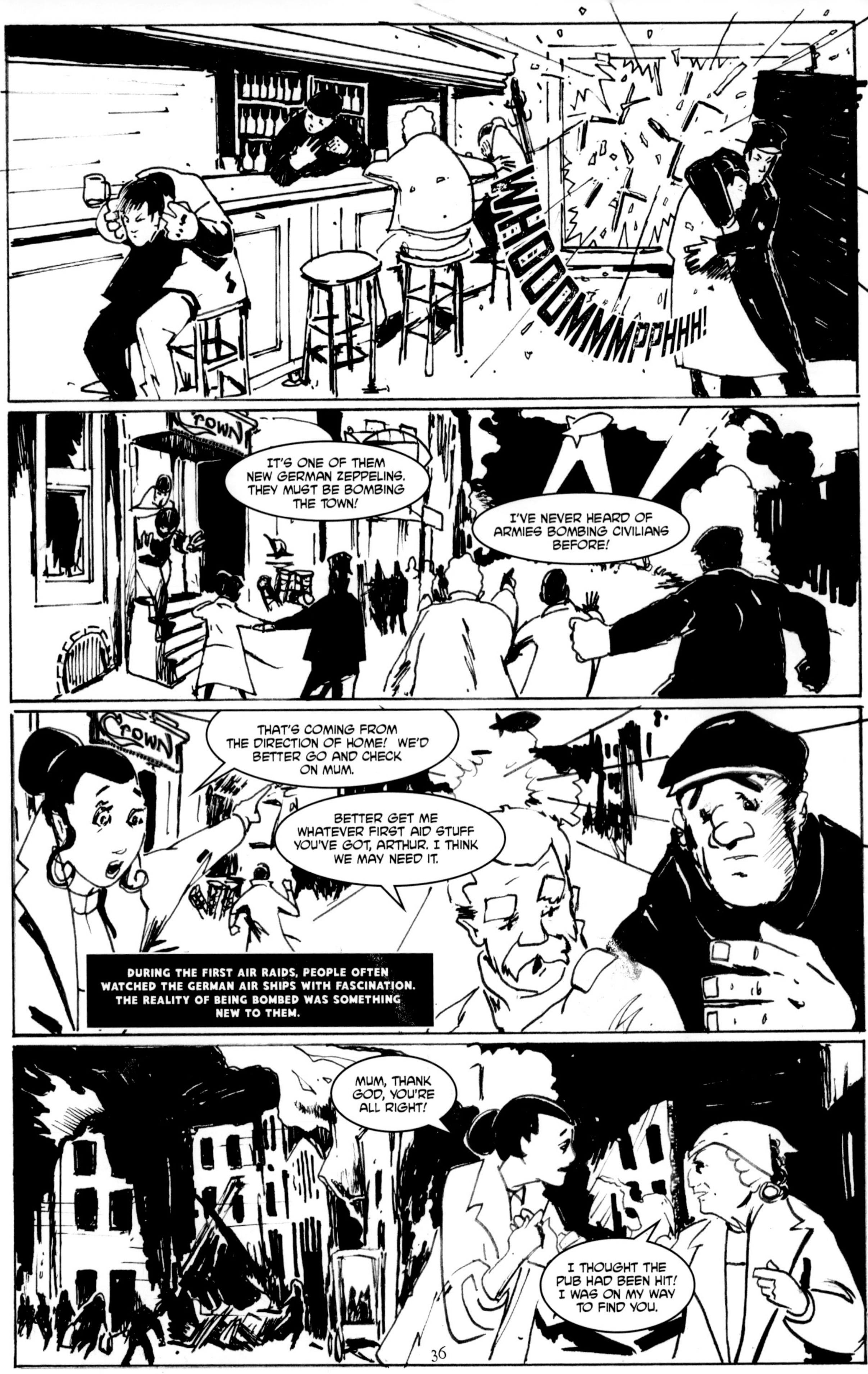
WHOOOMMMPPHHH!
TOWN
IT'S ONE OF THEM NEW GERMAN ZEPPELINS. THEY MUST BE BOMBING THE TOWN!
I'VE NEVER HEARD OF ARMIES BOMBING CIVILIANS BEFORE!
TOWN
THAT'S COMING FROM THE DIRECTION OF HOME! WE'D BETTER GO AND CHECK ON MUM.
BETTER GET ME WHATEVER FIRST AID STUFF YOU'VE GOT, ARTHUR. I THINK WE MAY NEED IT.
DURING THE FIRST AIR RAIDS, PEOPLE OFTEN WATCHED THE GERMAN AIR SHIPS WITH FASCINATION. THE REALITY OF BEING BOMBED WAS SOMETHING NEW TO THEM.
MUM, THANK GOD, YOU'RE ALL RIGHT!
I THOUGHT THE PUB HAD BEEN HIT! I WAS ON MY WAY TO FIND YOU.

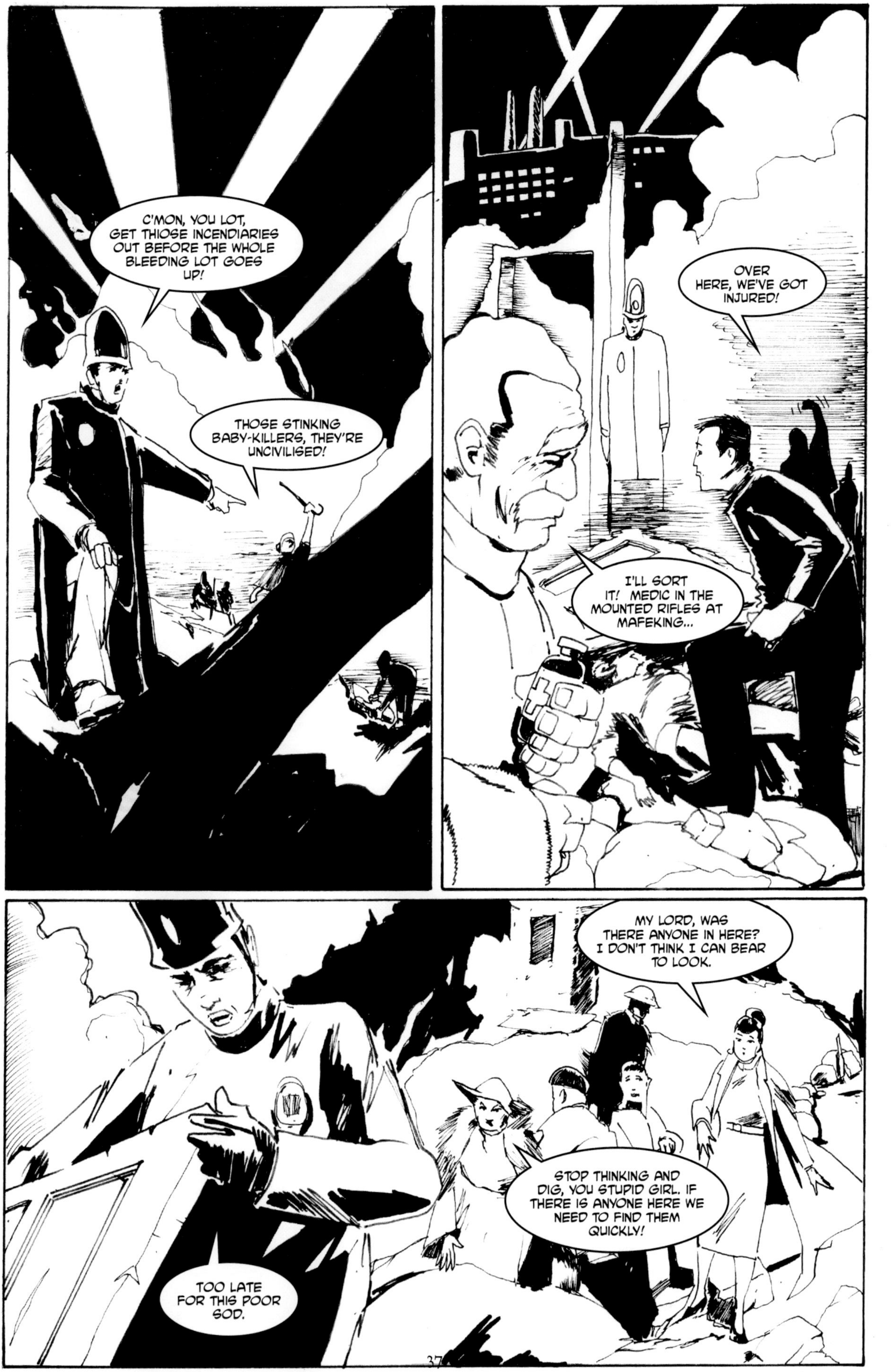
C'MON, YOU LOT, GET THIOSE INCENDIARIES OUT BEFORE THE WHOLE BLEEDING LOT GOES UP!
THOSE STINKING BABY-KILLERS, THEY'RE UNCIVILISED!
OVER HERE, WE'VE GOT INJURED!
I'LL SORT IT! MEDIC IN THE MOUNTED RIFLES AT MAFEKING...
MY LORD, WAS THERE ANYONE IN HERE? I DON'T THINK I CAN BEAR TO LOOK.
STOP THINKING AND DIG, YOU STUPID GIRL. IF THERE IS ANYONE HERE WE NEED TO FIND THEM QUICKLY!
TOO LATE FOR THIS POOR SOD.

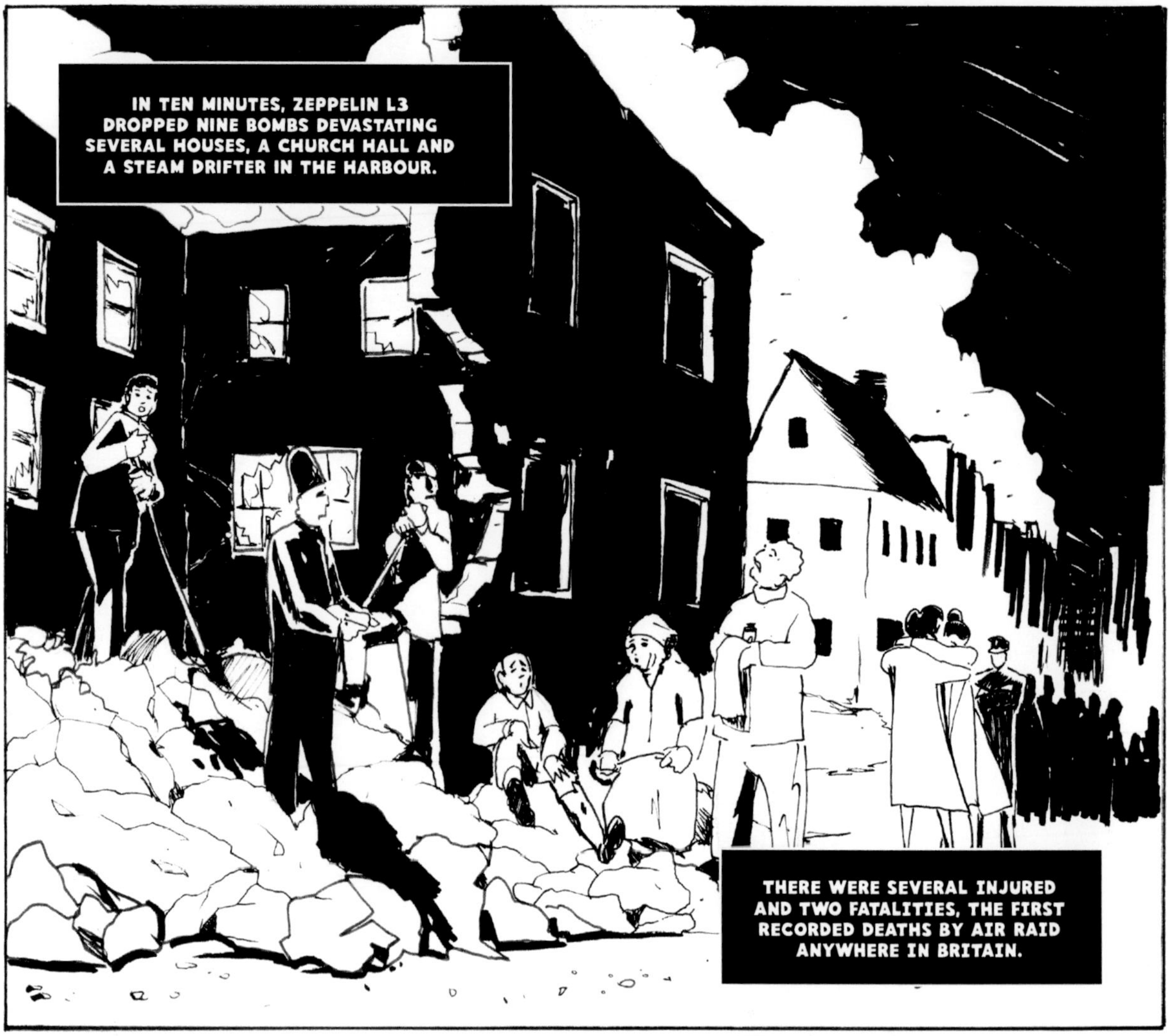
IN TEN MINUTES, ZEPPELIN L3 DROPPED NINE BOMBS DEVASTATING SEVERAL HOUSES, A CHURCH HALL AND A STEAM DRIFTER IN THE HARBOUR.
THERE WERE SEVERAL INJURED AND TWO FATALITIES, THE FIRST RECORDED DEATHS BY AIR RAID ANYWHERE IN BRITAIN.

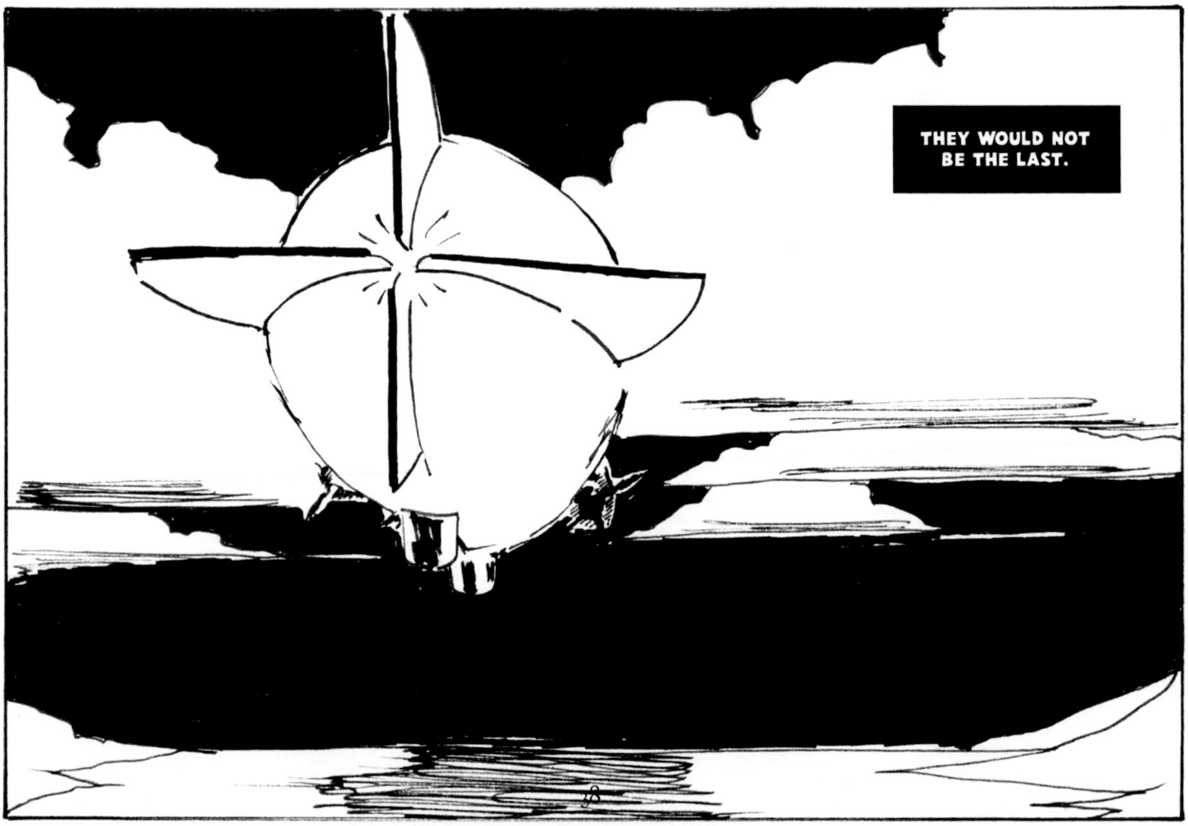
THEY WOULD NOT BE THE LAST.

8TH SEPTEMBER 1914. OUTSKIRTS OF TOURNAN-EN-BRIE.

MY NAME IS PRIVATE **THOMAS HIGHGATE**, 1st BATTALION, THE QUEEN'S OWN ROYAL WEST KENTS. LIKELY YOU KNOW ME BETTER BY MY **OTHER** NAMES...

"COWARD."

"DESERTER."

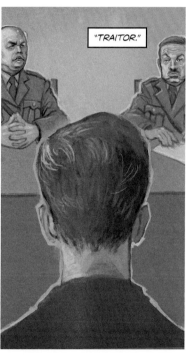

"TRAITOR."

THE COWARD'S WAR

Script: JONATHAN CLODE • Art: MATT SOFFE
Lettering: JIM CAMPBELL

"CASUALTY."

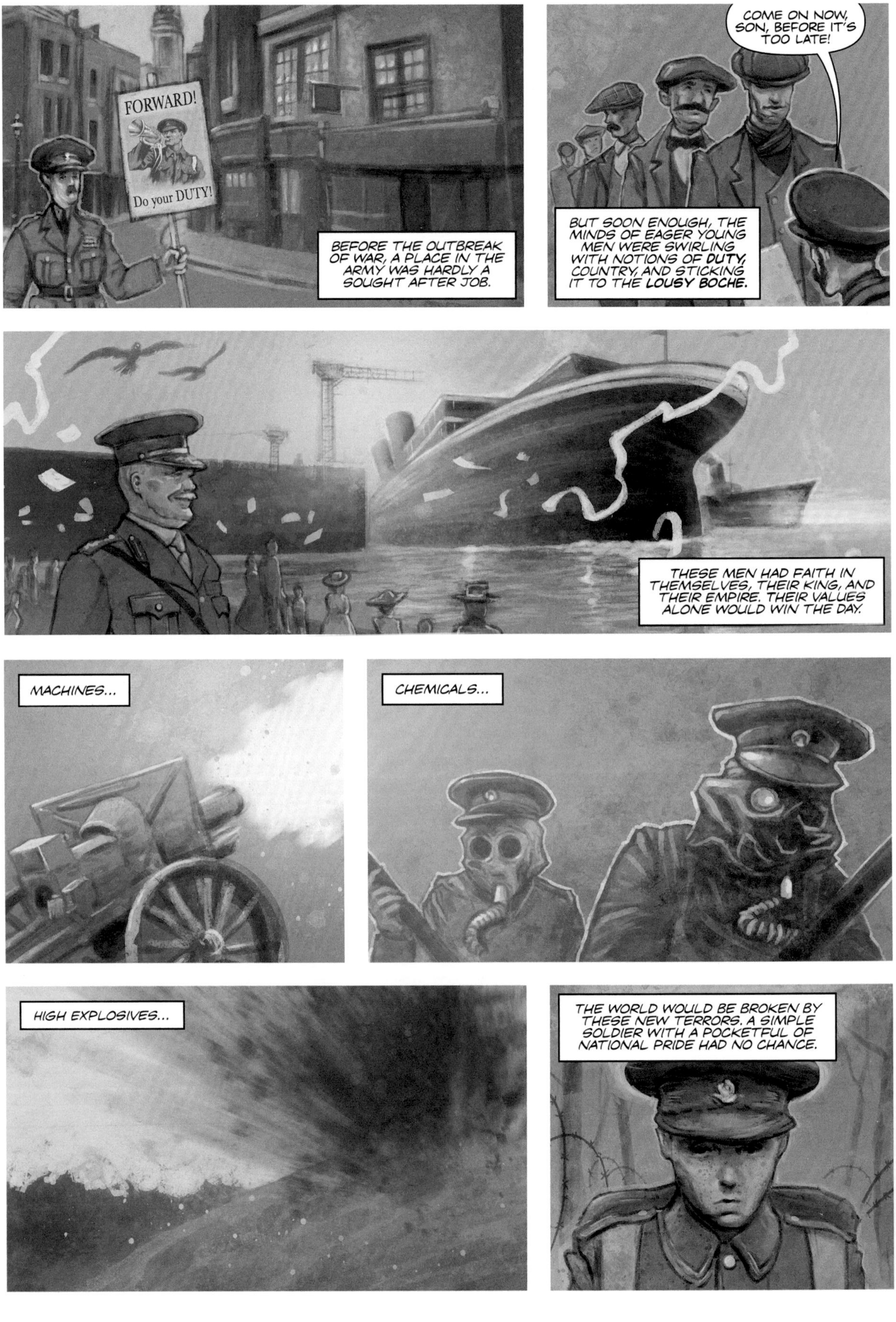
FORWARD!
Do your DUTY!
BEFORE THE OUTBREAK OF WAR, A PLACE IN THE ARMY WAS HARDLY A SOUGHT AFTER JOB.
COME ON NOW, SON, BEFORE IT'S TOO LATE!
BUT SOON ENOUGH, THE MINDS OF EAGER YOUNG MEN WERE SWIRLING WITH NOTIONS OF DUTY, COUNTRY, AND STICKING IT TO THE LOUSY BOCHE.
THESE MEN HAD FAITH IN THEMSELVES, THEIR KING, AND THEIR EMPIRE. THEIR VALUES ALONE WOULD WIN THE DAY.
MACHINES...
CHEMICALS...
HIGH EXPLOSIVES...
THE WORLD WOULD BE BROKEN BY THESE NEW TERRORS. A SIMPLE SOLDIER WITH A POCKETFUL OF NATIONAL PRIDE HAD NO CHANCE.

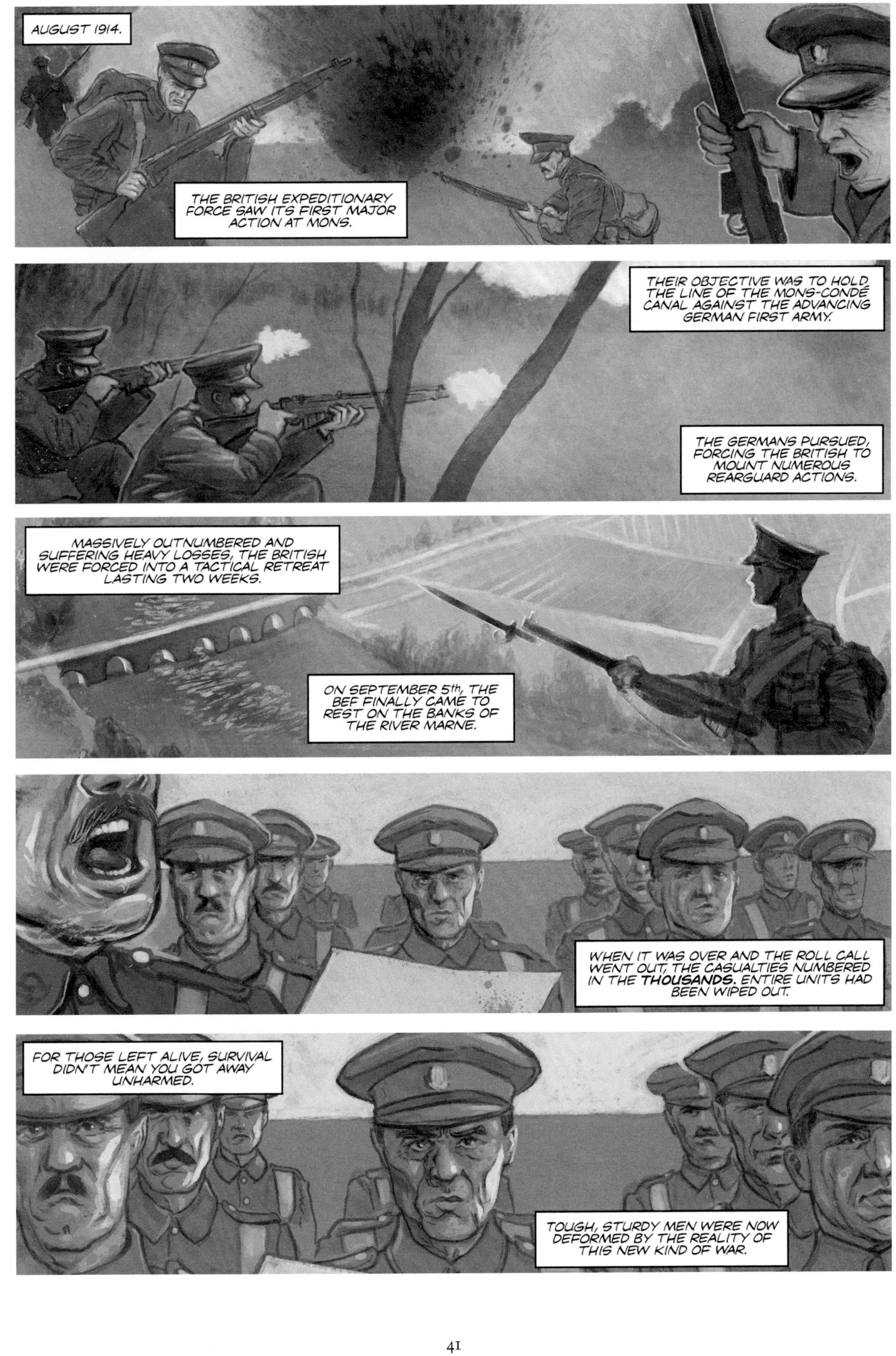
AUGUST 1914.
THE BRITISH EXPEDITIONARY FORCE SAW ITS FIRST MAJOR ACTION AT MONS.
THEIR OBJECTIVE WAS TO HOLD THE LINE OF THE MONS-CONDÉ CANAL AGAINST THE ADVANCING GERMAN FIRST ARMY.
THE GERMANS PURSUED, FORCING THE BRITISH TO MOUNT NUMEROUS REARGUARD ACTIONS.
MASSIVELY OUTNUMBERED AND SUFFERING HEAVY LOSSES, THE BRITISH WERE FORCED INTO A TACTICAL RETREAT LASTING TWO WEEKS.
ON SEPTEMBER 5th, THE BEF FINALLY CAME TO REST ON THE BANKS OF THE RIVER MARNE.
WHEN IT WAS OVER AND THE ROLL CALL WENT OUT, THE CASUALTIES NUMBERED IN THE **THOUSANDS.** ENTIRE UNITS HAD BEEN WIPED OUT.
FOR THOSE LEFT ALIVE, SURVIVAL DIDN'T MEAN YOU GOT AWAY UNHARMED.
TOUGH, STURDY MEN WERE NOW DEFORMED BY THE REALITY OF THIS NEW KIND OF WAR.

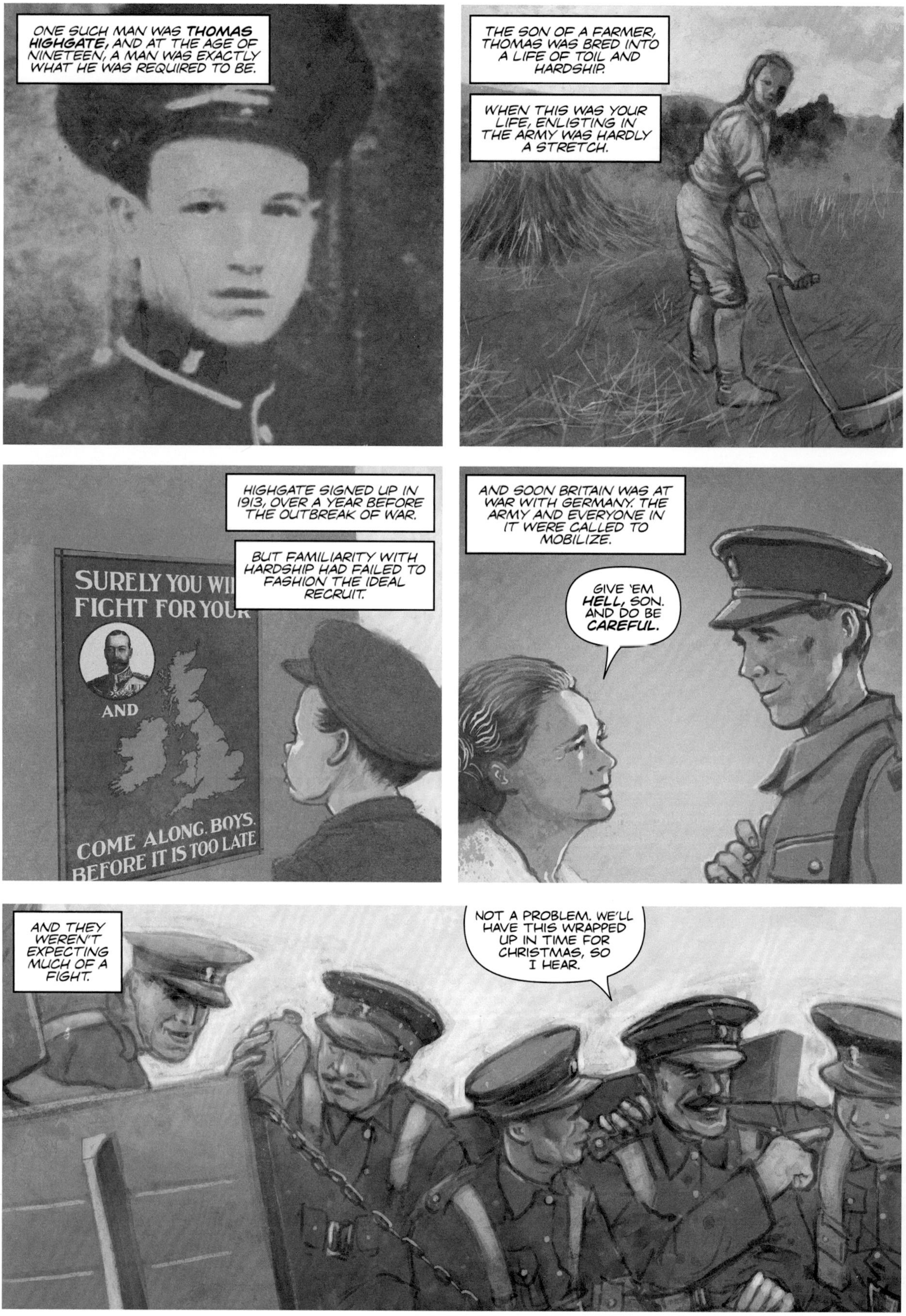
ONE SUCH MAN WAS **THOMAS HIGHGATE**, AND AT THE AGE OF NINETEEN, A MAN WAS EXACTLY WHAT HE WAS REQUIRED TO BE.
THE SON OF A FARMER, THOMAS WAS BRED INTO A LIFE OF TOIL AND HARDSHIP.
WHEN THIS WAS YOUR LIFE, ENLISTING IN THE ARMY WAS HARDLY A STRETCH.
HIGHGATE SIGNED UP IN 1913, OVER A YEAR BEFORE THE OUTBREAK OF WAR.
BUT FAMILIARITY WITH HARDSHIP HAD FAILED TO FASHION THE IDEAL RECRUIT.
SURELY YOU WI
FIGHT FOR YOUR
AND
COME ALONG. BOYS.
BEFORE IT IS TOO LATE
AND SOON BRITAIN WAS AT WAR WITH GERMANY. THE ARMY AND EVERYONE IN IT WERE CALLED TO MOBILIZE.
GIVE 'EM **HELL**, SON. AND DO BE **CAREFUL**.
AND THEY WEREN'T EXPECTING MUCH OF A FIGHT.
NOT A PROBLEM. WE'LL HAVE THIS WRAPPED UP IN TIME FOR CHRISTMAS, SO I HEAR.

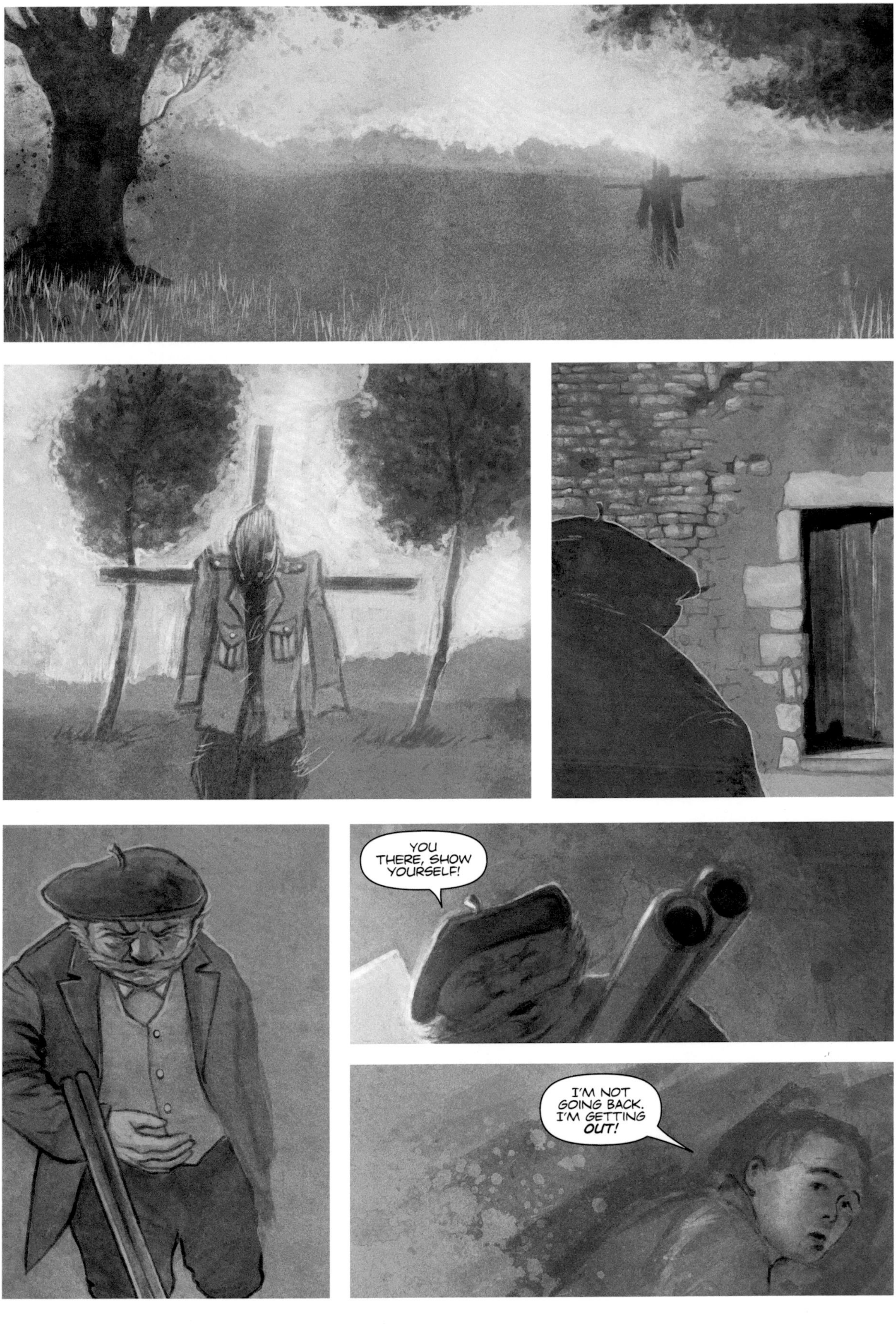
YOU THERE, SHOW YOURSELF!
I'M NOT GOING BACK. I'M GETTING OUT!

SIR, A CIVILIAN REPORTS AN ENGLISH **DESERTER** AT A FARM IN TOURNAN. HOW SHOULD WE PROCEED?

HIGHGATE'S COURT MARTIAL WAS HASTILY CONVENED. CHARGED WITH DESERTION, HE STOOD BEFORE HIS ACCUSERS UNDEFENDED.

NOT GUILTY.

MAKING A STATEMENT UNDER OATH, HE CLAIMED TO HAVE LOST HIS REGIMENT WHEN THEY SET OFF.

I FOUND MY WAY TO A FARM, AND I VAGUELY RECALL PUTTING SOME CIVILIAN CLOTHES ON.

I DON'T REMEMBER EXACTLY WHAT ELSE HAPPENED UNTIL THEY CAME DOWN TO ARREST ME...

HIS FLIMSY STORY WAS **REJECTED**.

FOR DESERTING HIS MAJESTY'S FORCES WHILE ON ACTIVE SERVICE, I SENTENCE YOU TO **DEATH** BY **FIRING SQUAD**.

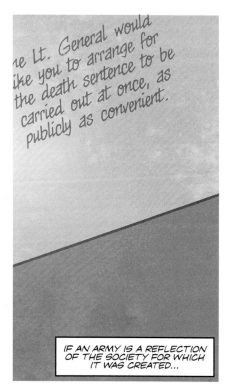

...e Lt. General would ...ike you to arrange for the death sentence to be carried out at once, as publicly as convenient.

IF AN ARMY IS A REFLECTION OF THE SOCIETY FOR WHICH IT WAS CREATED...

THOMAS HIGHGATE WAS THE FIRST **CRACK** IN ITS MIRROR.

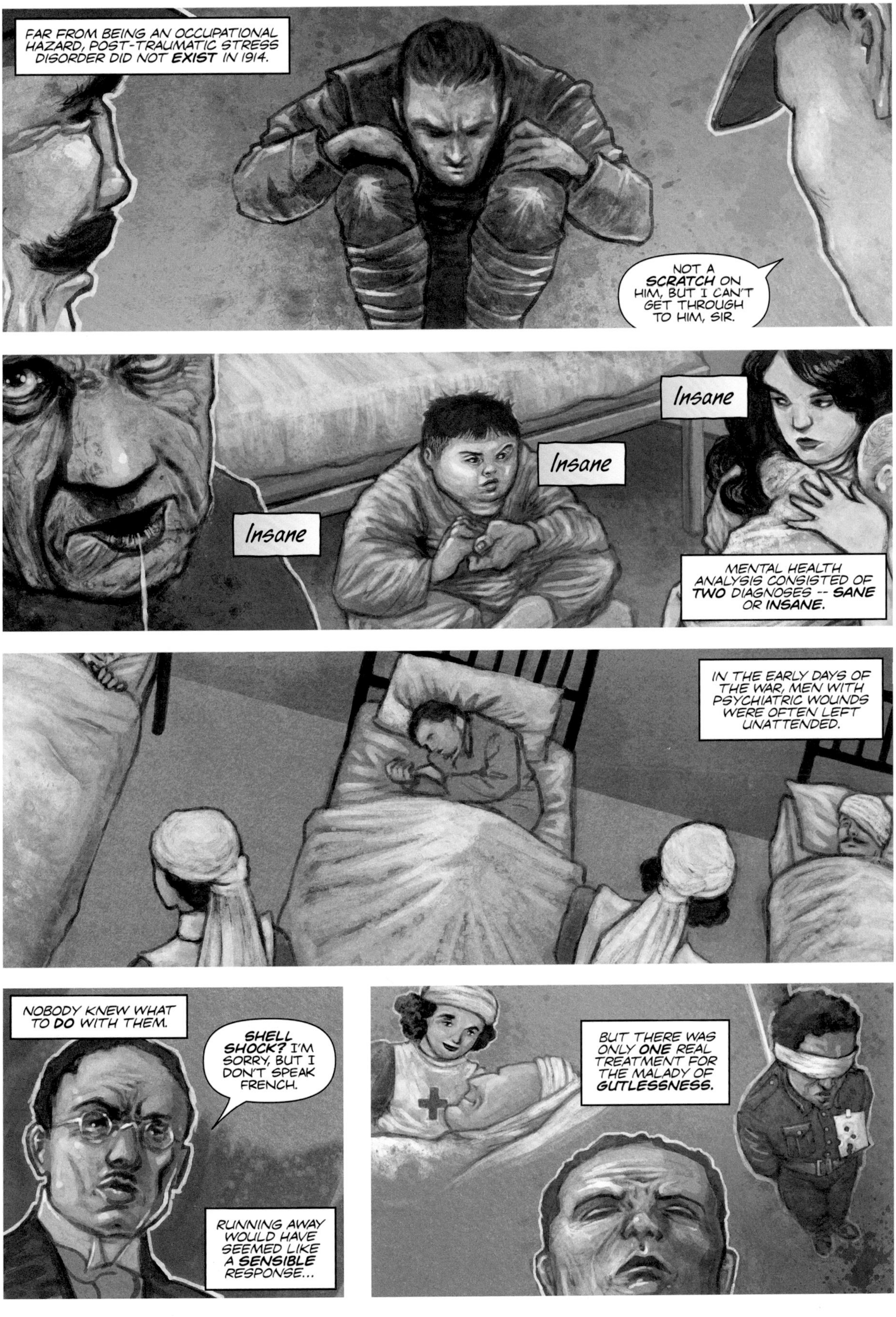
FAR FROM BEING AN OCCUPATIONAL HAZARD, POST-TRAUMATIC STRESS DISORDER DID NOT **EXIST** IN 1914.
NOT A **SCRATCH** ON HIM, BUT I CAN'T GET THROUGH TO HIM, SIR.
Insane
Insane
Insane
MENTAL HEALTH ANALYSIS CONSISTED OF **TWO** DIAGNOSES -- **SANE** OR **INSANE.**
IN THE EARLY DAYS OF THE WAR, MEN WITH PSYCHIATRIC WOUNDS WERE OFTEN LEFT UNATTENDED.
NOBODY KNEW WHAT TO **DO** WITH THEM.
SHELL SHOCK? I'M SORRY, BUT I DON'T SPEAK FRENCH.
RUNNING AWAY WOULD HAVE SEEMED LIKE A **SENSIBLE** RESPONSE...
BUT THERE WAS ONLY **ONE** REAL TREATMENT FOR THE MALADY OF **GUTLESSNESS.**

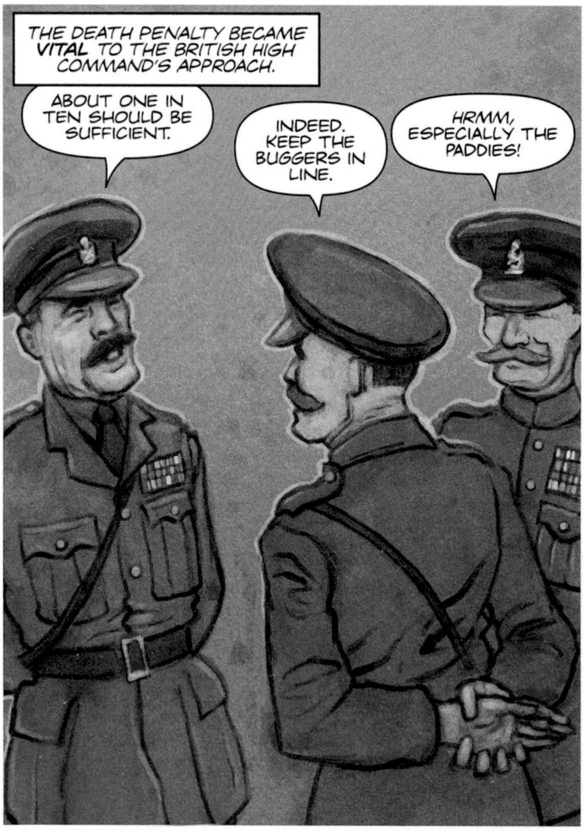
THE DEATH PENALTY BECAME **VITAL** TO THE BRITISH HIGH COMMAND'S APPROACH.
ABOUT ONE IN TEN SHOULD BE SUFFICIENT.
INDEED. KEEP THE BUGGERS IN LINE.
HRMM, ESPECIALLY THE PADDIES!

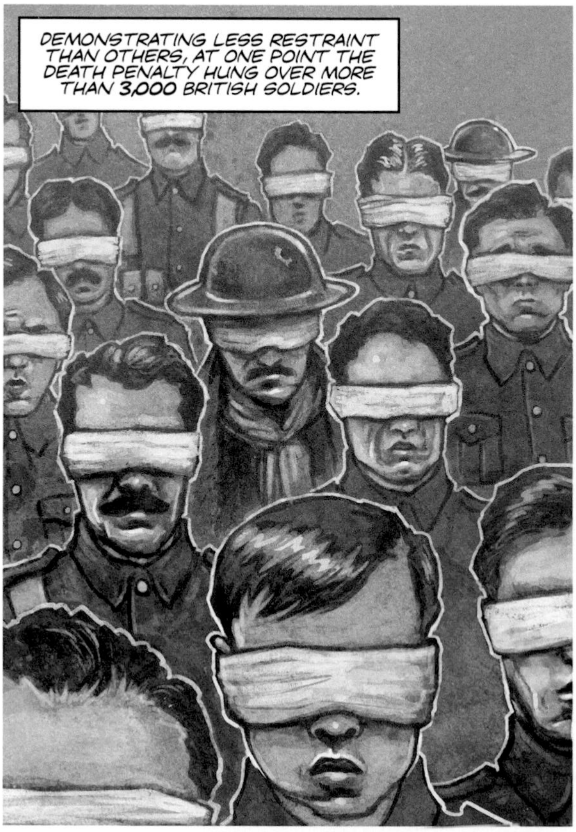
DEMONSTRATING LESS RESTRAINT THAN OTHERS, AT ONE POINT THE DEATH PENALTY HUNG OVER MORE THAN **3,000** BRITISH SOLDIERS.

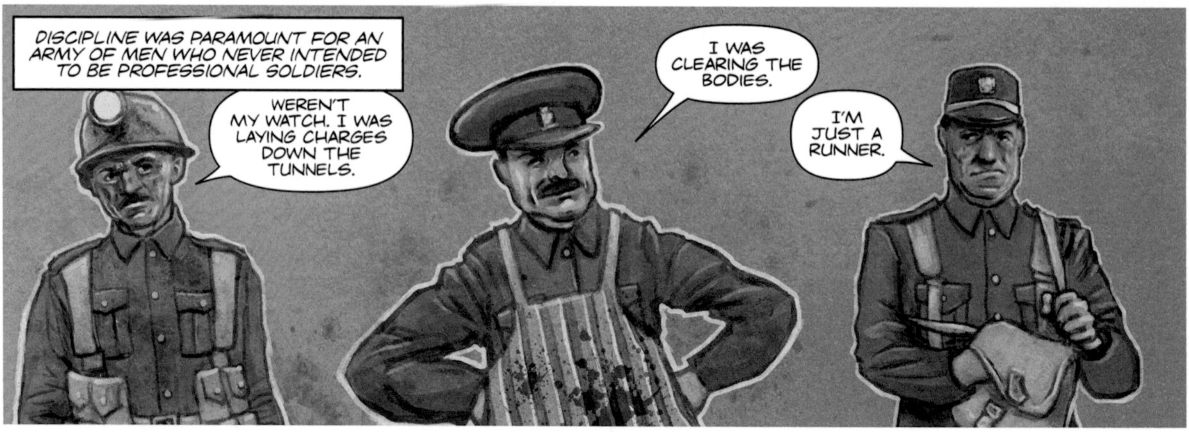
DISCIPLINE WAS PARAMOUNT FOR AN ARMY OF MEN WHO NEVER INTENDED TO BE PROFESSIONAL SOLDIERS.
WEREN'T MY WATCH. I WAS LAYING CHARGES DOWN THE TUNNELS.
I WAS CLEARING THE BODIES.
I'M JUST A RUNNER.

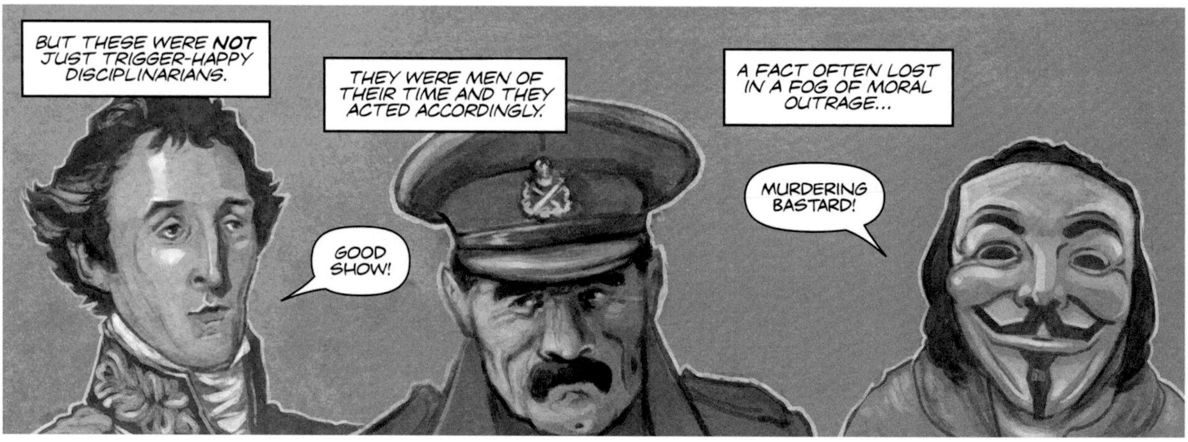
BUT THESE WERE **NOT** JUST TRIGGER-HAPPY DISCIPLINARIANS.
THEY WERE MEN OF THEIR TIME AND THEY ACTED ACCORDINGLY.
GOOD SHOW!
A FACT OFTEN LOST IN A FOG OF MORAL OUTRAGE...
MURDERING BASTARD!

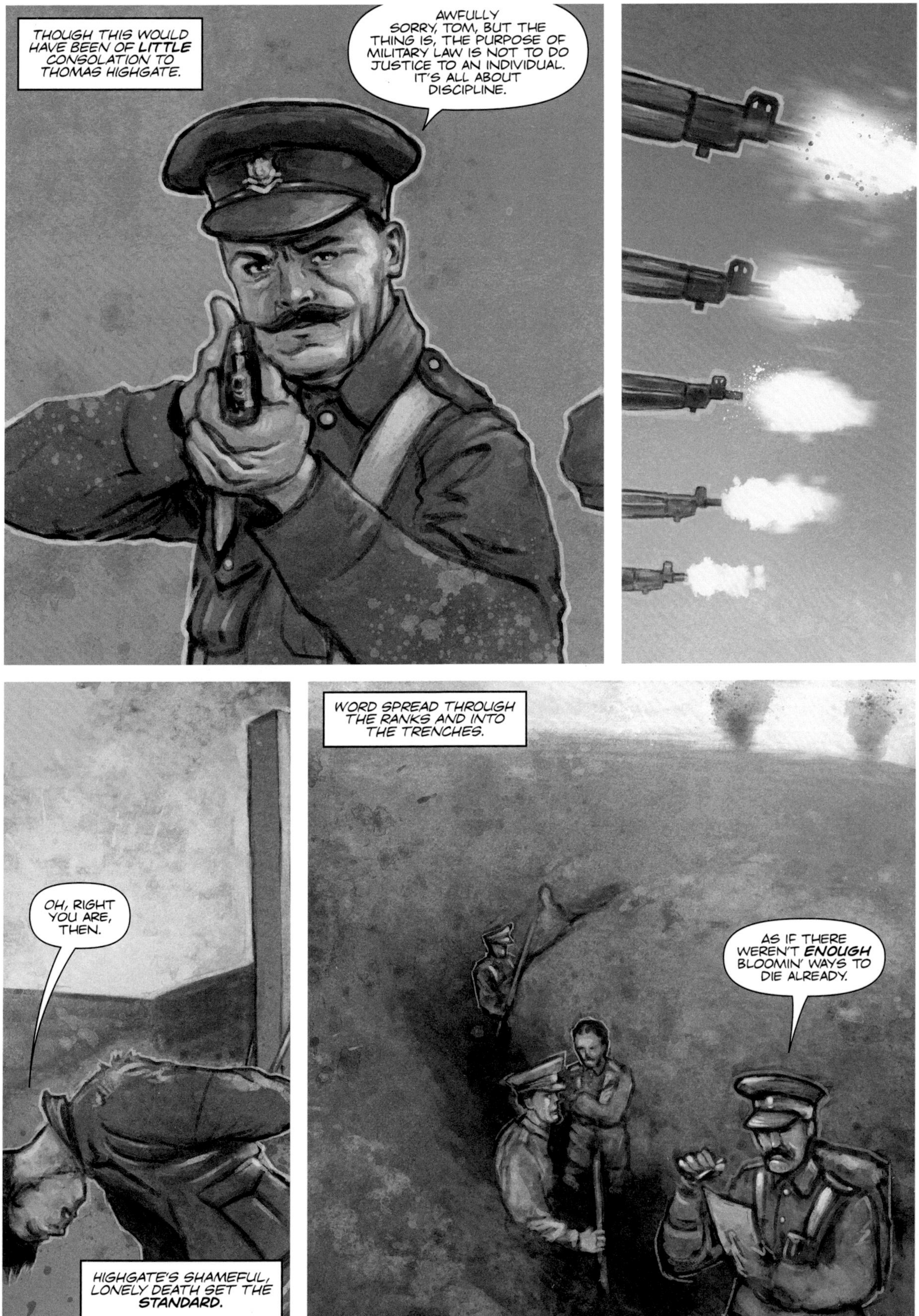
THOUGH THIS WOULD HAVE BEEN OF LITTLE CONSOLATION TO THOMAS HIGHGATE.
AWFULLY SORRY, TOM, BUT THE THING IS, THE PURPOSE OF MILITARY LAW IS NOT TO DO JUSTICE TO AN INDIVIDUAL. IT'S ALL ABOUT DISCIPLINE.
OH, RIGHT YOU ARE, THEN.
HIGHGATE'S SHAMEFUL, LONELY DEATH SET THE STANDARD.
WORD SPREAD THROUGH THE RANKS AND INTO THE TRENCHES.
AS IF THERE WEREN'T ENOUGH BLOOMIN' WAYS TO DIE ALREADY.

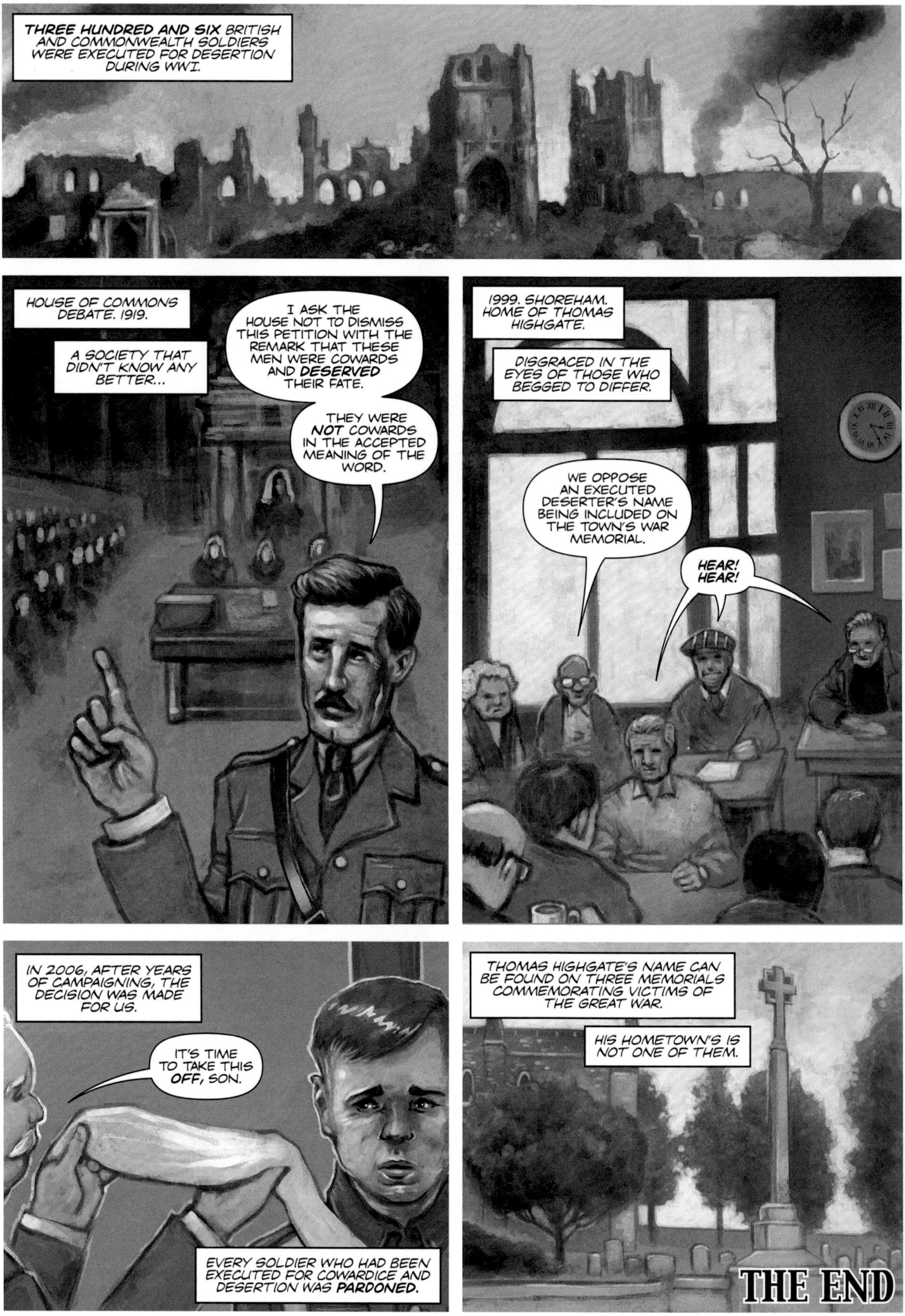
THREE HUNDRED AND SIX BRITISH AND COMMONWEALTH SOLDIERS WERE EXECUTED FOR DESERTION DURING WWI.
HOUSE OF COMMONS DEBATE. 1919.
A SOCIETY THAT DIDN'T KNOW ANY BETTER...
I ASK THE HOUSE NOT TO DISMISS THIS PETITION WITH THE REMARK THAT THESE MEN WERE COWARDS AND DESERVED THEIR FATE.
THEY WERE NOT COWARDS IN THE ACCEPTED MEANING OF THE WORD.
1999. SHOREHAM. HOME OF THOMAS HIGHGATE.
DISGRACED IN THE EYES OF THOSE WHO BEGGED TO DIFFER.
WE OPPOSE AN EXECUTED DESERTER'S NAME BEING INCLUDED ON THE TOWN'S WAR MEMORIAL.
HEAR! HEAR!
IN 2006, AFTER YEARS OF CAMPAIGNING, THE DECISION WAS MADE FOR US.
IT'S TIME TO TAKE THIS OFF, SON.
EVERY SOLDIER WHO HAD BEEN EXECUTED FOR COWARDICE AND DESERTION WAS PARDONED.
THOMAS HIGHGATE'S NAME CAN BE FOUND ON THREE MEMORIALS COMMEMORATING VICTIMS OF THE GREAT WAR.
HIS HOMETOWN'S IS NOT ONE OF THEM.
THE END

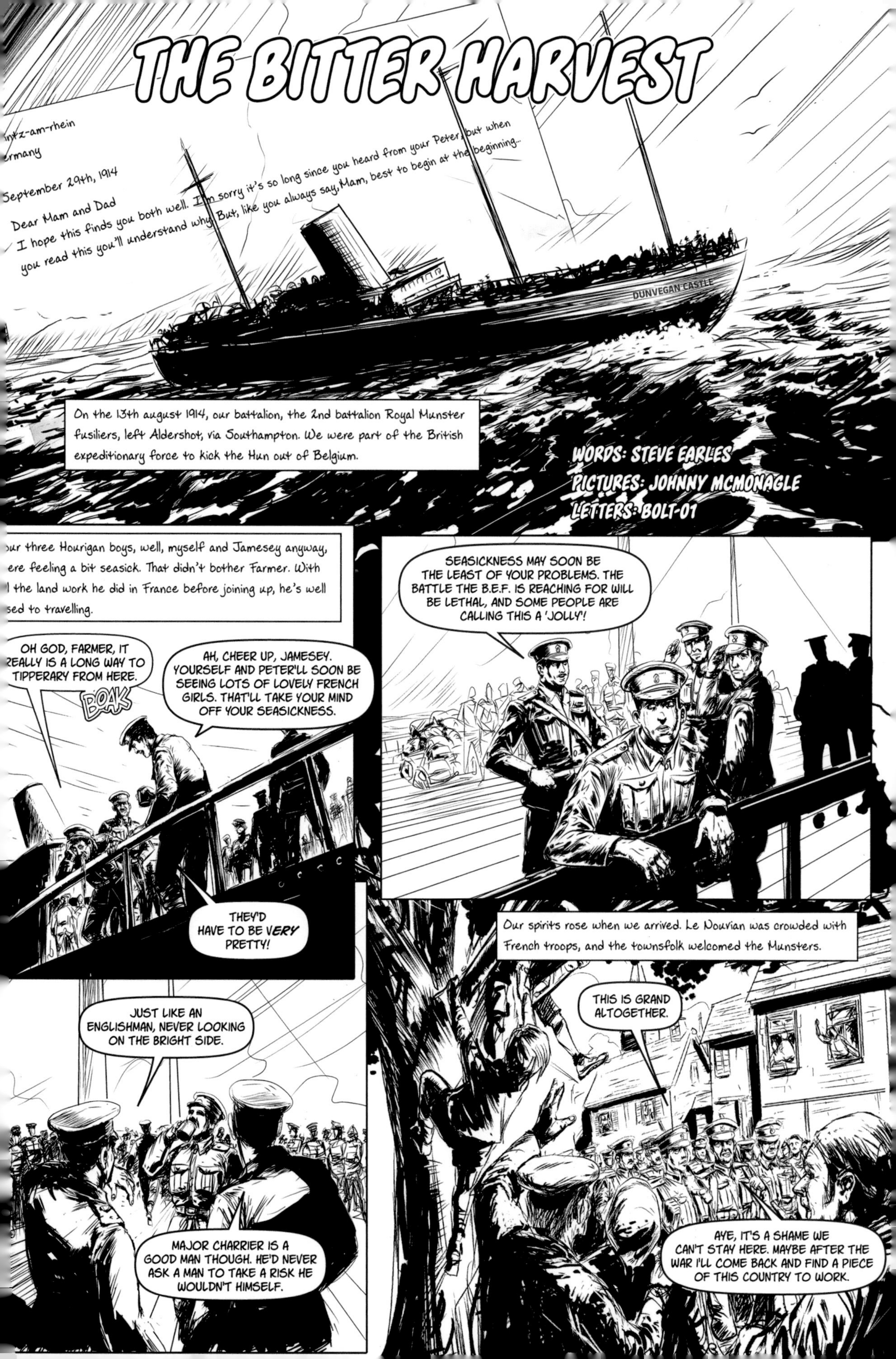
THE BITTER HARVEST
intz-am-rhein
rmany
September 29th, 1914
Dear Mam and Dad
I hope this finds you both well. I'm sorry it's so long since you heard from your Peter, but when you read this you'll understand why. But, like you always say, Mam, best to begin at the beginning...
DUNVEGAN CASTLE
On the 13th august 1914, our battalion, the 2nd battalion Royal Munster fusiliers, left Aldershot, via Southampton. We were part of the British expeditionary force to kick the Hun out of Belgium.
WORDS: STEVE EARLES
PICTURES: JOHNNY MCMONAGLE
LETTERS: BOLT-01
our three Hourigan boys, well, myself and Jamesey anyway, ere feeling a bit seasick. That didn't bother Farmer. With l the land work he did in France before joining up, he's well sed to travelling.
OH GOD, FARMER, IT REALLY IS A LONG WAY TO TIPPERARY FROM HERE.
BOAK
AH, CHEER UP, JAMESEY. YOURSELF AND PETER'LL SOON BE SEEING LOTS OF LOVELY FRENCH GIRLS. THAT'LL TAKE YOUR MIND OFF YOUR SEASICKNESS.
THEY'D HAVE TO BE VERY PRETTY!
SEASICKNESS MAY SOON BE THE LEAST OF YOUR PROBLEMS. THE BATTLE THE B.E.F. IS REACHING FOR WILL BE LETHAL, AND SOME PEOPLE ARE CALLING THIS A 'JOLLY'!
JUST LIKE AN ENGLISHMAN, NEVER LOOKING ON THE BRIGHT SIDE.
MAJOR CHARRIER IS A GOOD MAN THOUGH. HE'D NEVER ASK A MAN TO TAKE A RISK HE WOULDN'T HIMSELF.
Our spirits rose when we arrived. Le Nouvian was crowded with French troops, and the townsfolk welcomed the Munsters.
THIS IS GRAND ALTOGETHER.
AYE, IT'S A SHAME WE CAN'T STAY HERE. MAYBE AFTER THE WAR I'LL COME BACK AND FIND A PIECE OF THIS COUNTRY TO WORK.

Y'MEAN, YOU'D LEAVE THE ARMY TO FARM FULL TIME? LEAVE REGULAR WORK FOR THE LAND?

AH, SURE I ONLY JOINED TO LOOK AFTER *YOU TWO*. MAM SAID SHE'D KILL ME IF ANYTHING HAPPENED TO YOU.

SHE SAID THE SAME THING TO US!

We made our way to a place called Bouey, three miles distant to a village we would come to know all too well called Etreux.

THE KAISER KNOWS THE MUNSTERS BY THE SHAMROCK ON THEIR CAPS AND THE FAMOUS BENGAL TIGER, EVER READY FOR A SCRAP

MIGHTY LAND FOR GROWING, JUST LIKE HOME.

YOU AND YOUR PRECIOUS 'LAND', ONE MORNING YOU'LL WAKE UP AND FIND YOU'VE SPROUTED ROOTS AND LEAVES.

I COULDN'T BE FARMING, OUT IN EVERY WEATHER, NO SECURITY.

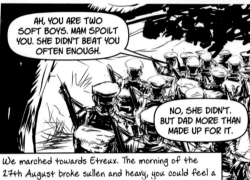

AH, YOU ARE TWO SOFT BOYS. MAM SPOILT YOU. SHE DIDN'T BEAT YOU OFTEN ENOUGH.

NO, SHE DIDN'T. BUT DAD MORE THAN MADE UP FOR IT.

We marched towards Etreux. The morning of the 27th August broke sullen and heavy, you could feel a storm coming...a terrible storm.

Major Charrier had explicit orders to hold back the Germans, unless or until he received orders to retire.

We exchanged shots with a German patrol as the rain began.

Under cover of the storm the Germans attacked en masse...

...but we gave them a bloody nose, then marched for Fesmy.

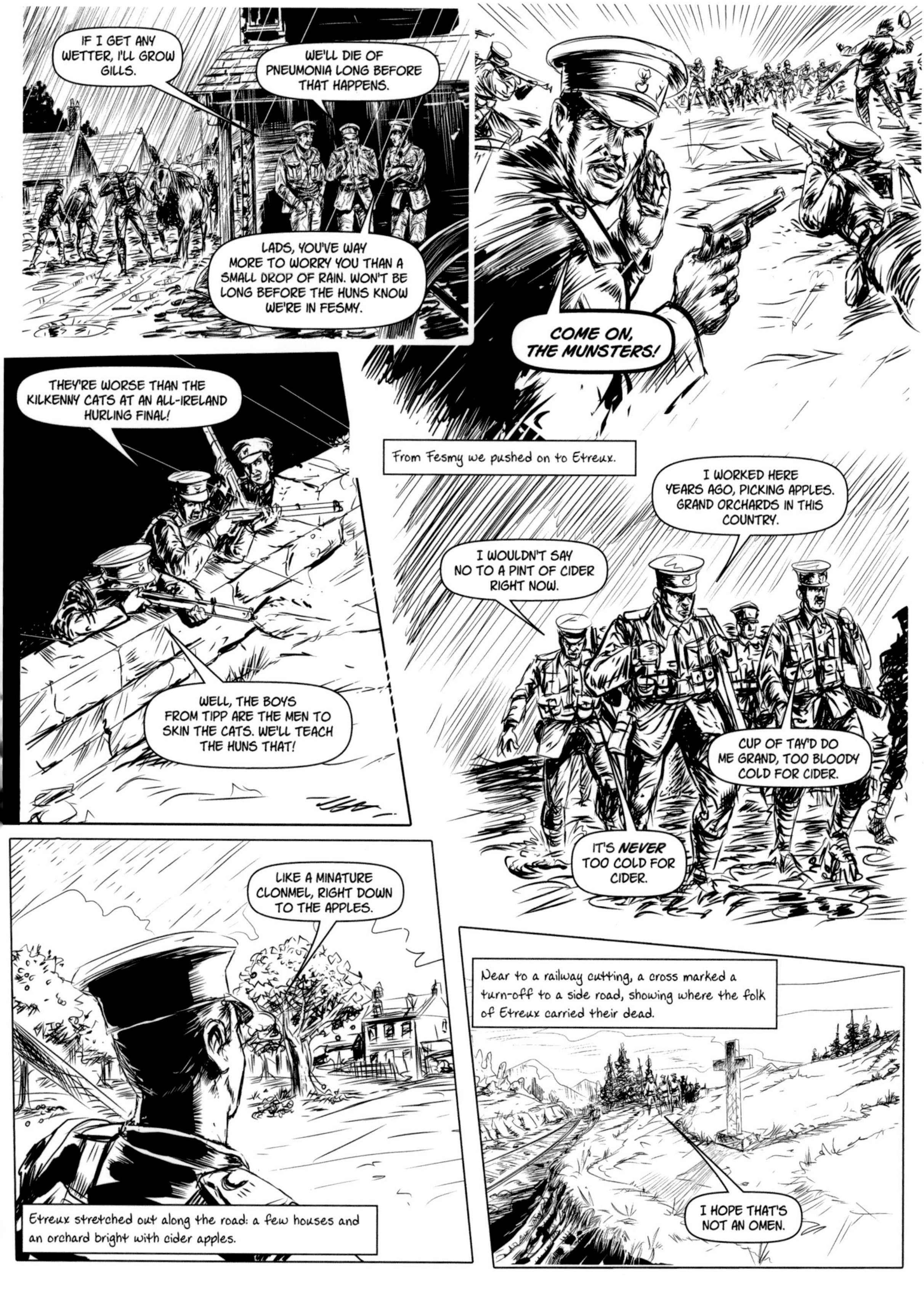
IF I GET ANY WETTER, I'LL GROW GILLS.
WE'LL DIE OF PNEUMONIA LONG BEFORE THAT HAPPENS.
LADS, YOU'VE WAY MORE TO WORRY YOU THAN A SMALL DROP OF RAIN. WON'T BE LONG BEFORE THE HUNS KNOW WE'RE IN FESMY.
COME ON, THE MUNSTERS!
THEY'RE WORSE THAN THE KILKENNY CATS AT AN ALL-IRELAND HURLING FINAL!
WELL, THE BOYS FROM TIPP ARE THE MEN TO SKIN THE CATS. WE'LL TEACH THE HUNS THAT!
From Fesmy we pushed on to Etreux.
I WORKED HERE YEARS AGO, PICKING APPLES. GRAND ORCHARDS IN THIS COUNTRY.
I WOULDN'T SAY NO TO A PINT OF CIDER RIGHT NOW.
CUP OF TAY'D DO ME GRAND, TOO BLOODY COLD FOR CIDER.
IT'S NEVER TOO COLD FOR CIDER.
LIKE A MINATURE CLONMEL, RIGHT DOWN TO THE APPLES.
Etreux stretched out along the road: a few houses and an orchard bright with cider apples.
Near to a railway cutting, a cross marked a turn-off to a side road, showing where the folk of Etreux carried their dead.
I HOPE THAT'S NOT AN OMEN.

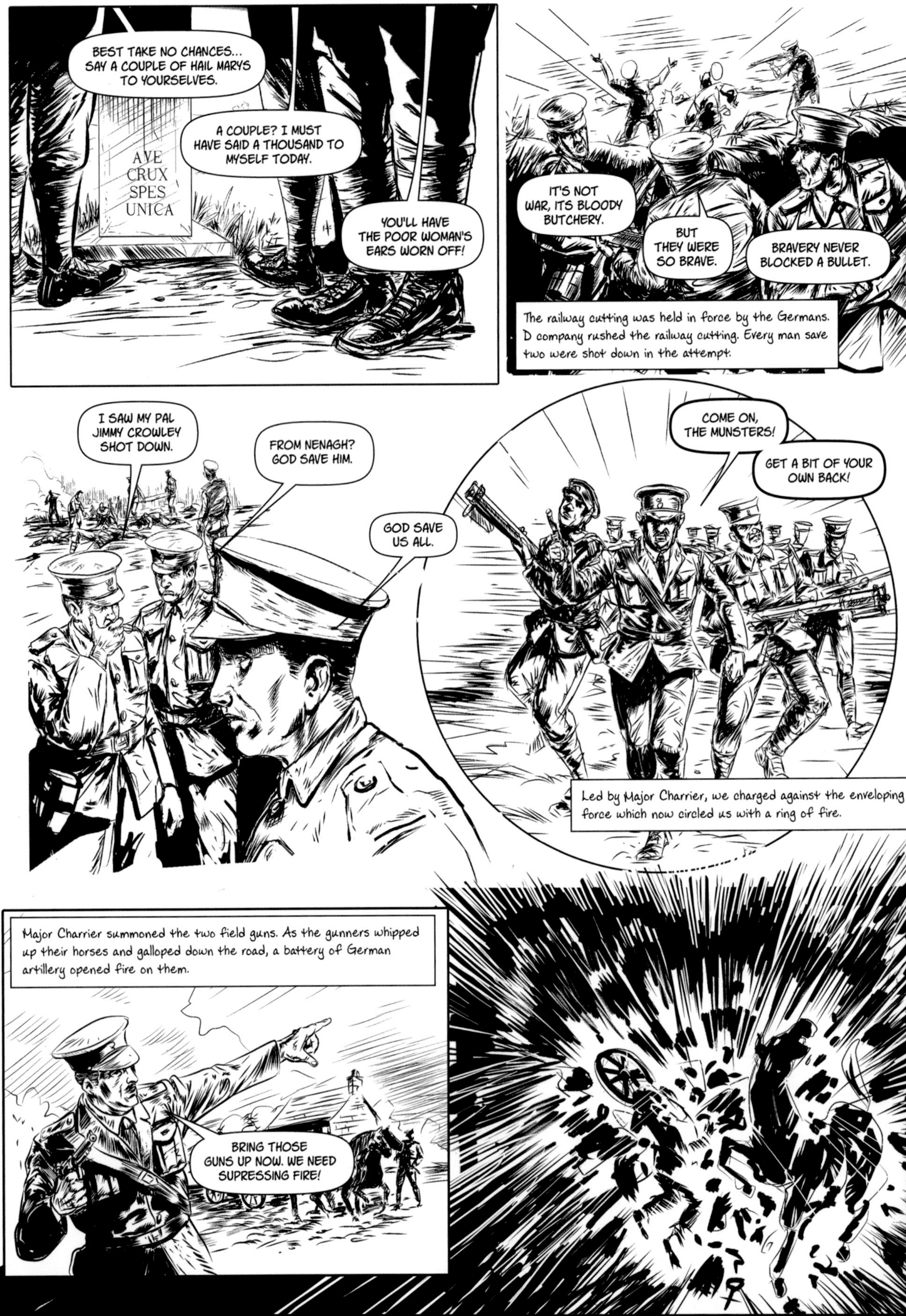
BEST TAKE NO CHANCES... SAY A COUPLE OF HAIL MARYS TO YOURSELVES.
A COUPLE? I MUST HAVE SAID A THOUSAND TO MYSELF TODAY.
AVE CRUX SPES UNICA
YOU'LL HAVE THE POOR WOMAN'S EARS WORN OFF!
IT'S NOT WAR, ITS BLOODY BUTCHERY.
BUT THEY WERE SO BRAVE.
BRAVERY NEVER BLOCKED A BULLET.
The railway cutting was held in force by the Germans. D company rushed the railway cutting. Every man save two were shot down in the attempt.
I SAW MY PAL JIMMY CROWLEY SHOT DOWN.
FROM NENAGH? GOD SAVE HIM.
GOD SAVE US ALL.
COME ON, THE MUNSTERS!
GET A BIT OF YOUR OWN BACK!
Led by Major Charrier, we charged against the enveloping force which now circled us with a ring of fire.
Major Charrier summoned the two field guns. As the gunners whipped up their horses and galloped down the road, a battery of German artillery opened fire on them.
BRING THOSE GUNS UP NOW. WE NEED SUPRESSING FIRE!

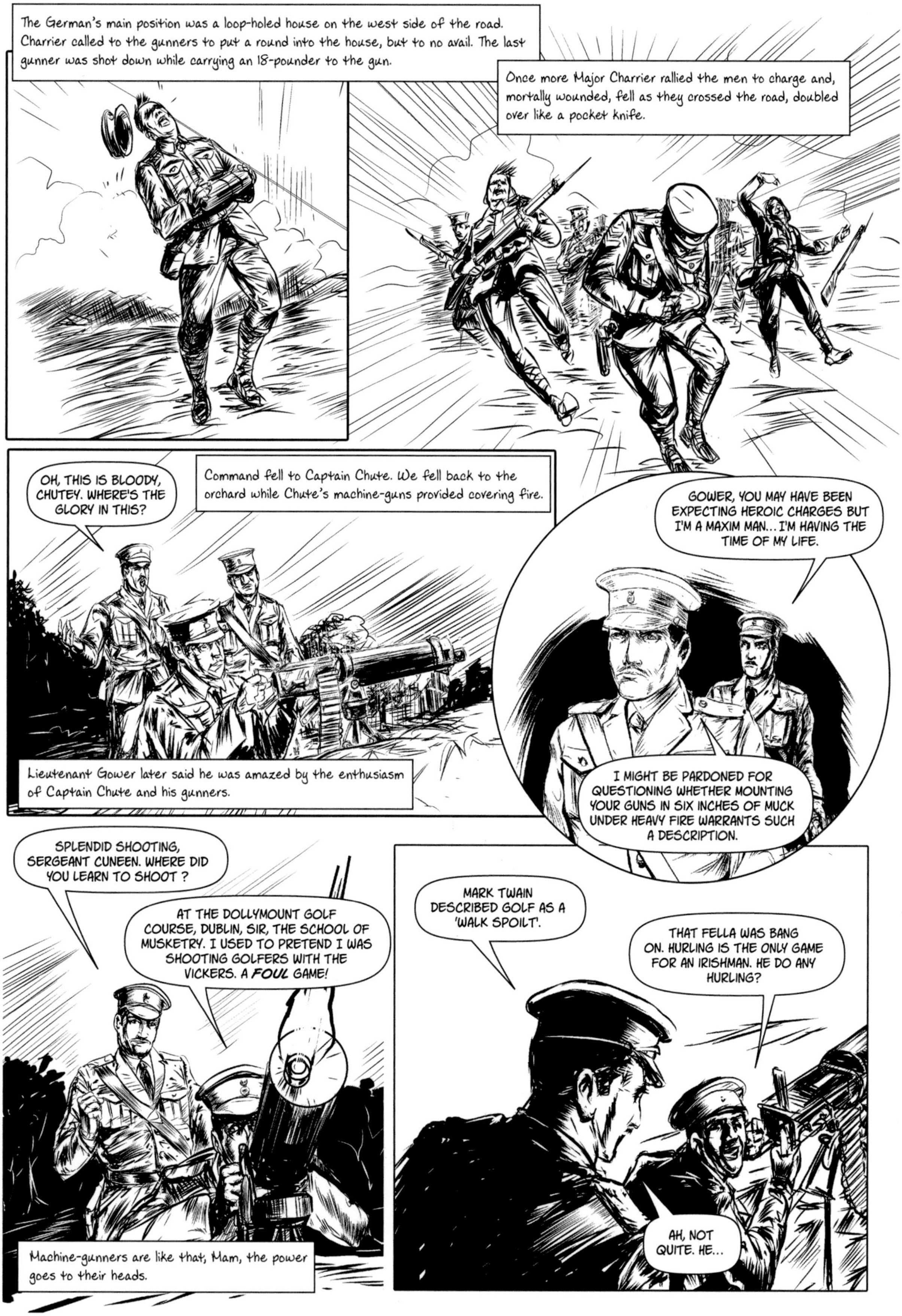
The German's main position was a loop-holed house on the west side of the road. Charrier called to the gunners to put a round into the house, but to no avail. The last gunner was shot down while carrying an 18-pounder to the gun.
Once more Major Charrier rallied the men to charge and, mortally wounded, fell as they crossed the road, doubled over like a pocket knife.
OH, THIS IS BLOODY, CHUTEY. WHERE'S THE GLORY IN THIS?
Command fell to Captain Chute. We fell back to the orchard while Chute's machine-guns provided covering fire.
Lieutenant Gower later said he was amazed by the enthusiasm of Captain Chute and his gunners.
GOWER, YOU MAY HAVE BEEN EXPECTING HEROIC CHARGES BUT I'M A MAXIM MAN... I'M HAVING THE TIME OF MY LIFE.
I MIGHT BE PARDONED FOR QUESTIONING WHETHER MOUNTING YOUR GUNS IN SIX INCHES OF MUCK UNDER HEAVY FIRE WARRANTS SUCH A DESCRIPTION.
SPLENDID SHOOTING, SERGEANT CUNEEN. WHERE DID YOU LEARN TO SHOOT ?
AT THE DOLLYMOUNT GOLF COURSE, DUBLIN, SIR, THE SCHOOL OF MUSKETRY. I USED TO PRETEND I WAS SHOOTING GOLFERS WITH THE VICKERS. A *FOUL* GAME!
Machine-gunners are like that, Mam, the power goes to their heads.
MARK TWAIN DESCRIBED GOLF AS A 'WALK SPOILT'.
THAT FELLA WAS BANG ON. HURLING IS THE ONLY GAME FOR AN IRISHMAN. HE DO ANY HURLING?
AH, NOT QUITE. HE...

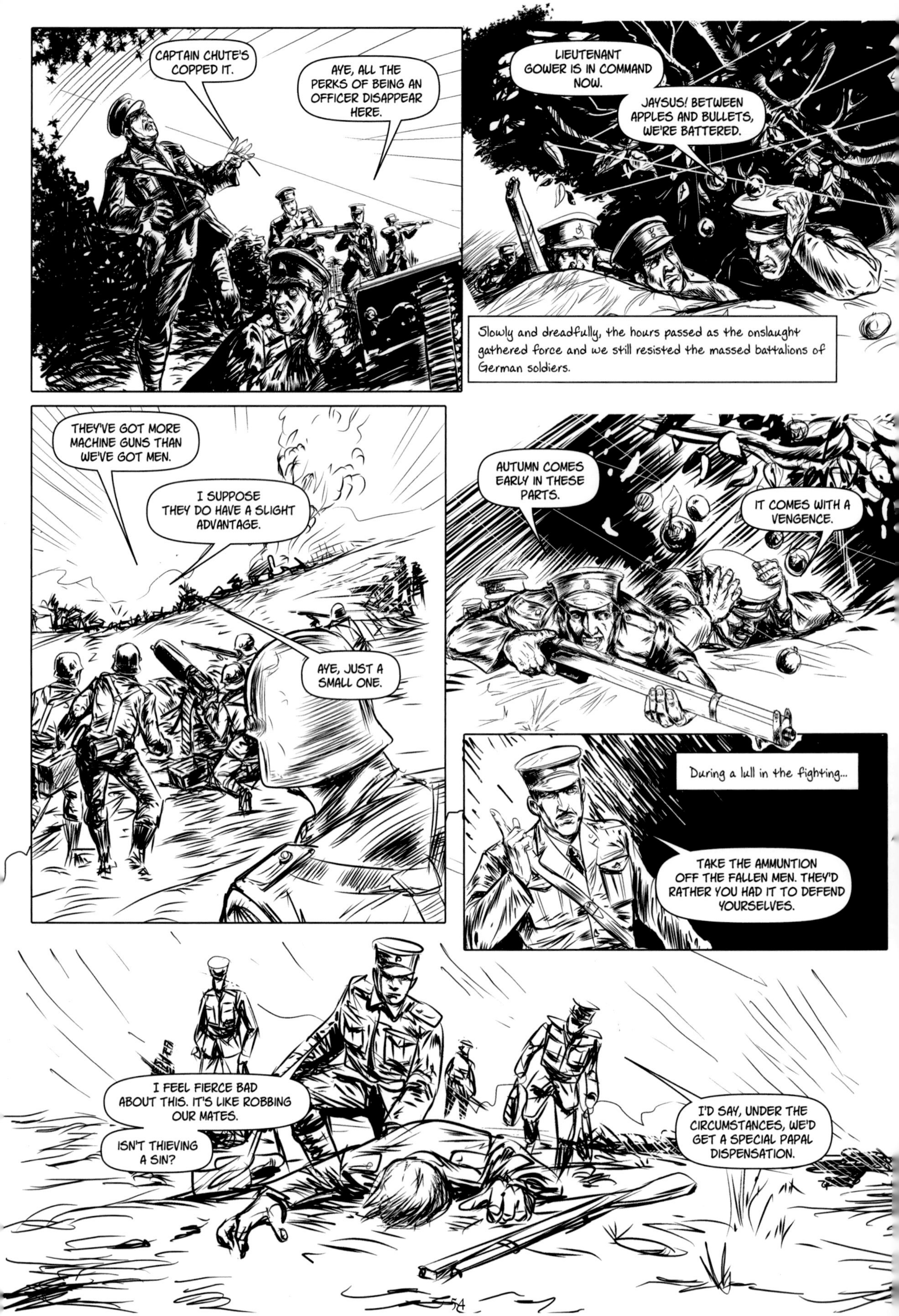

CAPTAIN CHUTE'S COPPED IT.
AYE, ALL THE PERKS OF BEING AN OFFICER DISAPPEAR HERE.
LIEUTENANT GOWER IS IN COMMAND NOW.
JAYSUS! BETWEEN APPLES AND BULLETS, WE'RE BATTERED.
Slowly and dreadfully, the hours passed as the onslaught gathered force and we still resisted the massed battalions of German soldiers.
THEY'VE GOT MORE MACHINE GUNS THAN WE'VE GOT MEN.
I SUPPOSE THEY DO HAVE A SLIGHT ADVANTAGE.
AYE, JUST A SMALL ONE.
AUTUMN COMES EARLY IN THESE PARTS.
IT COMES WITH A VENGENCE.
During a lull in the fighting...
TAKE THE AMMUNTION OFF THE FALLEN MEN. THEY'D RATHER YOU HAD IT TO DEFEND YOURSELVES.
I FEEL FIERCE BAD ABOUT THIS. IT'S LIKE ROBBING OUR MATES.
ISN'T THIEVING A SIN?
I'D SAY, UNDER THE CIRCUMSTANCES, WE'D GET A SPECIAL PAPAL DISPENSATION.

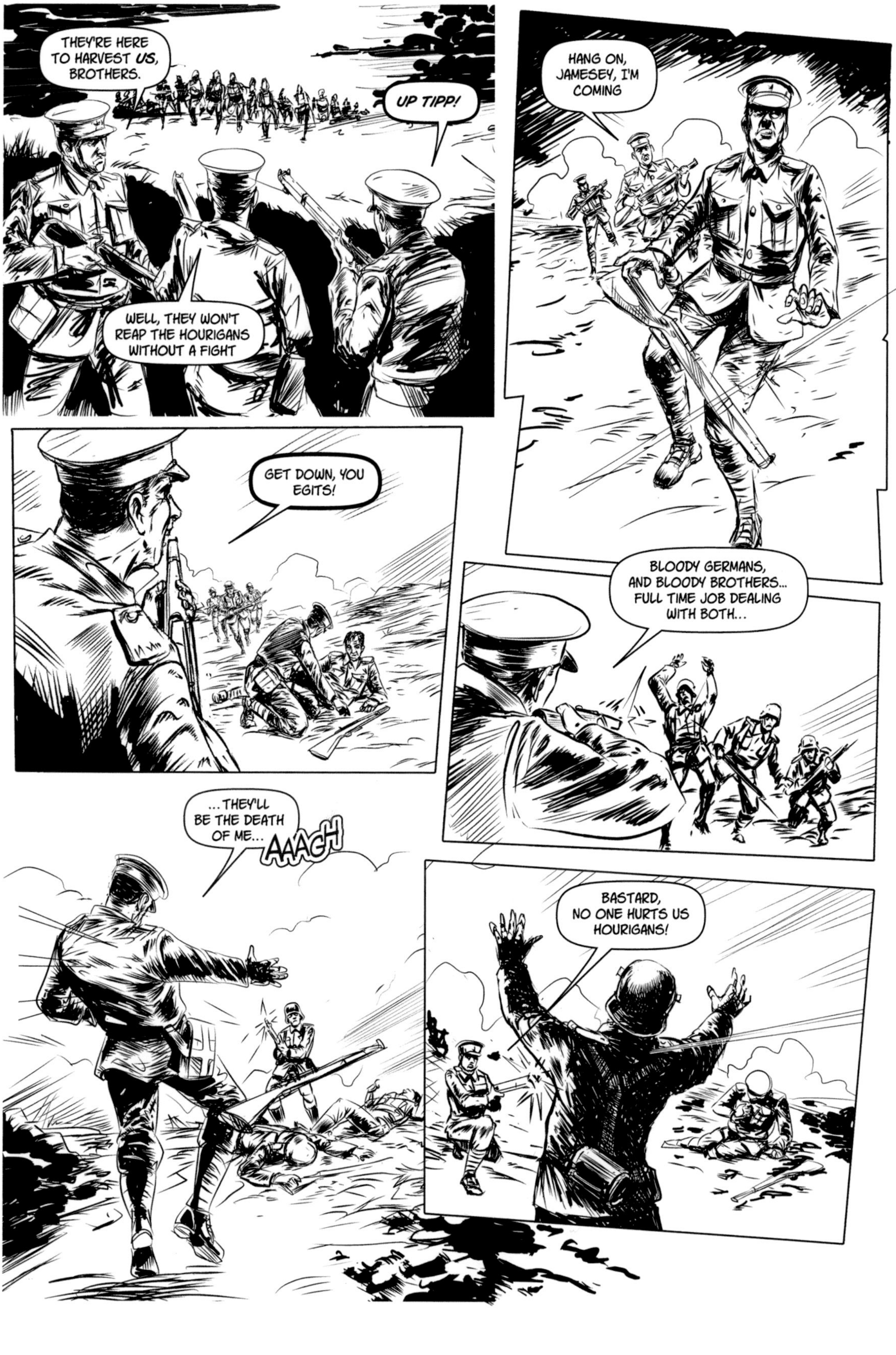
THEY'RE HERE TO HARVEST US, BROTHERS.
UP TIPP!
WELL, THEY WON'T REAP THE HOURIGANS WITHOUT A FIGHT
HANG ON, JAMESEY, I'M COMING
GET DOWN, YOU EGITS!
BLOODY GERMANS, AND BLOODY BROTHERS... FULL TIME JOB DEALING WITH BOTH...
...THEY'LL BE THE DEATH OF ME...
AAAGH
BASTARD, NO ONE HURTS US HOURIGANS!

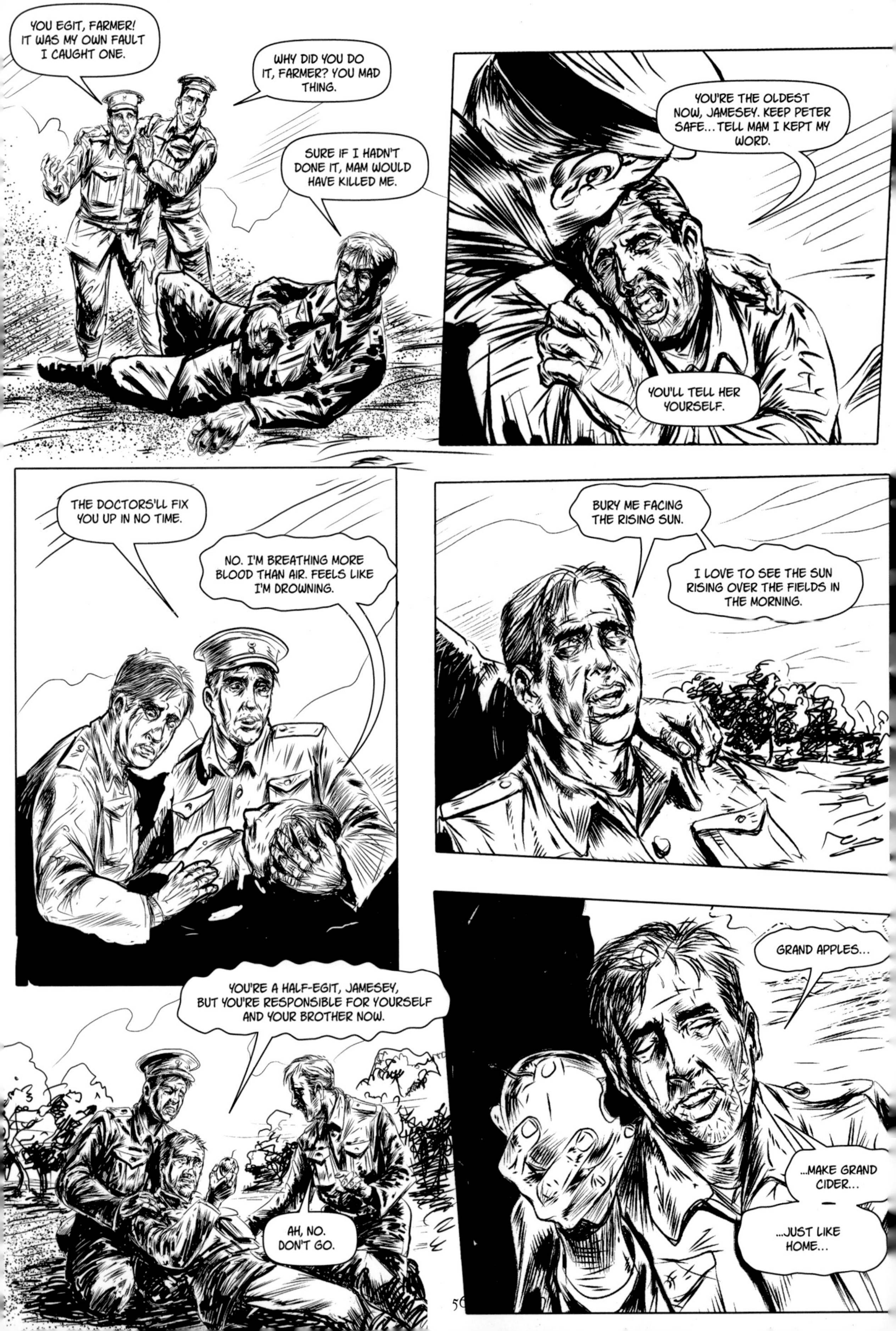
YOU EGIT, FARMER! IT WAS MY OWN FAULT I CAUGHT ONE.
WHY DID YOU DO IT, FARMER? YOU MAD THING.
SURE IF I HADN'T DONE IT, MAM WOULD HAVE KILLED ME.
YOU'RE THE OLDEST NOW, JAMESEY. KEEP PETER SAFE... TELL MAM I KEPT MY WORD.
YOU'LL TELL HER YOURSELF.
THE DOCTORS'LL FIX YOU UP IN NO TIME.
NO. I'M BREATHING MORE BLOOD THAN AIR. FEELS LIKE I'M DROWNING.
BURY ME FACING THE RISING SUN.
I LOVE TO SEE THE SUN RISING OVER THE FIELDS IN THE MORNING.
YOU'RE A HALF-EGIT, JAMESEY, BUT YOU'RE RESPONSIBLE FOR YOURSELF AND YOUR BROTHER NOW.
AH, NO. DON'T GO.
GRAND APPLES...
...MAKE GRAND CIDER...
...JUST LIKE HOME...

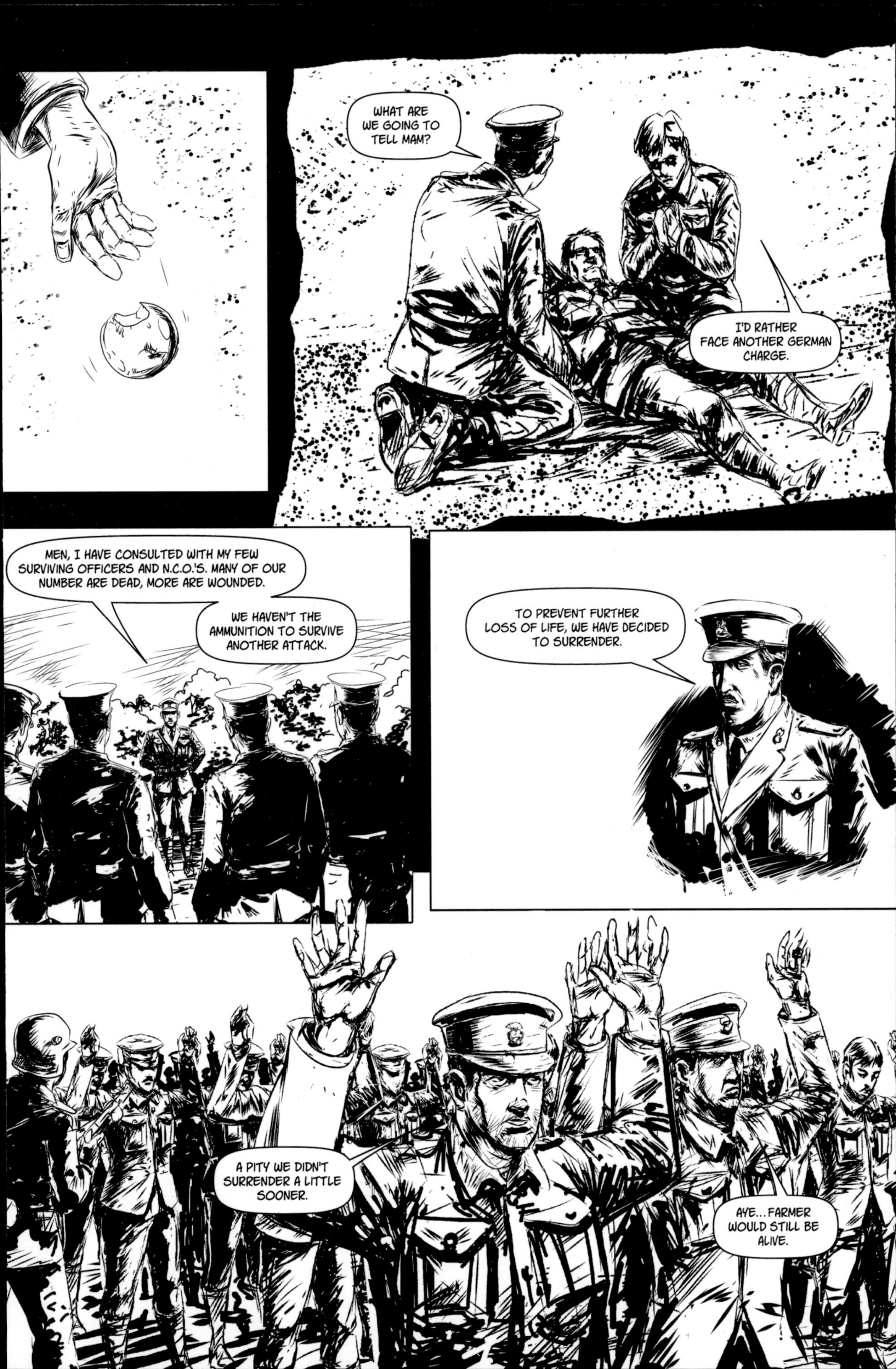
WHAT ARE WE GOING TO TELL MAM?
I'D RATHER FACE ANOTHER GERMAN CHARGE.
MEN, I HAVE CONSULTED WITH MY FEW SURVIVING OFFICERS AND N.C.O.'S. MANY OF OUR NUMBER ARE DEAD, MORE ARE WOUNDED.
WE HAVEN'T THE AMMUNITION TO SURVIVE ANOTHER ATTACK.
TO PREVENT FURTHER LOSS OF LIFE, WE HAVE DECIDED TO SURRENDER.
A PITY WE DIDN'T SURRENDER A LITTLE SOONER.
AYE... FARMER WOULD STILL BE ALIVE.

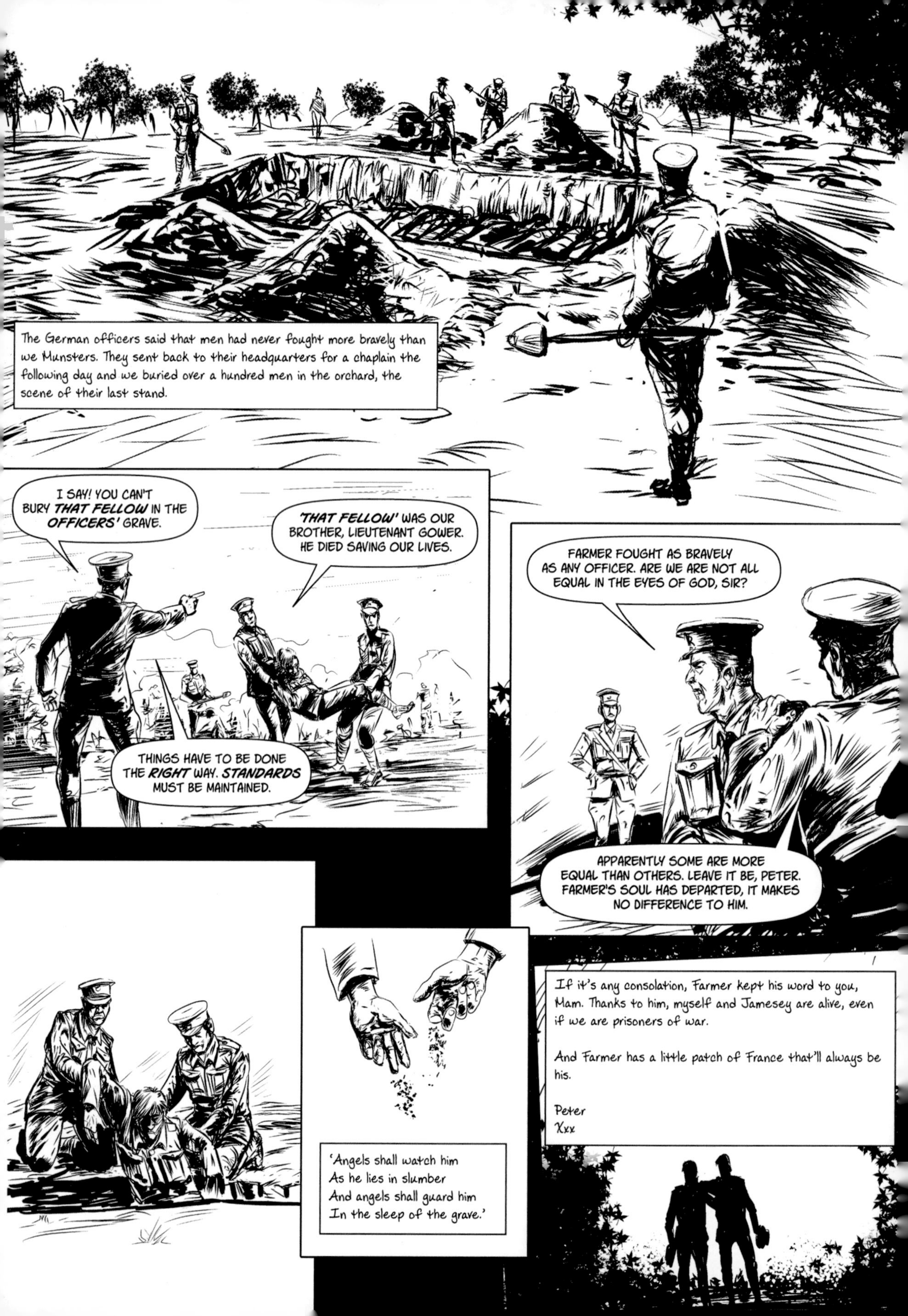

The German officers said that men had never fought more bravely than we Munsters. They sent back to their headquarters for a chaplain the following day and we buried over a hundred men in the orchard, the scene of their last stand.
I SAY! YOU CAN'T BURY THAT FELLOW IN THE OFFICERS' GRAVE.
'THAT FELLOW' WAS OUR BROTHER, LIEUTENANT GOWER. HE DIED SAVING OUR LIVES.
THINGS HAVE TO BE DONE THE RIGHT WAY. STANDARDS MUST BE MAINTAINED.
FARMER FOUGHT AS BRAVELY AS ANY OFFICER. ARE WE ARE NOT ALL EQUAL IN THE EYES OF GOD, SIR?
APPARENTLY SOME ARE MORE EQUAL THAN OTHERS. LEAVE IT BE, PETER. FARMER'S SOUL HAS DEPARTED, IT MAKES NO DIFFERENCE TO HIM.
'Angels shall watch him
As he lies in slumber
And angels shall guard him
In the sleep of the grave.'
If it's any consolation, Farmer kept his word to you, Mam. Thanks to him, myself and Jamesey are alive, even if we are prisoners of war.
And Farmer has a little patch of France that'll always be his.
Peter
Kxx

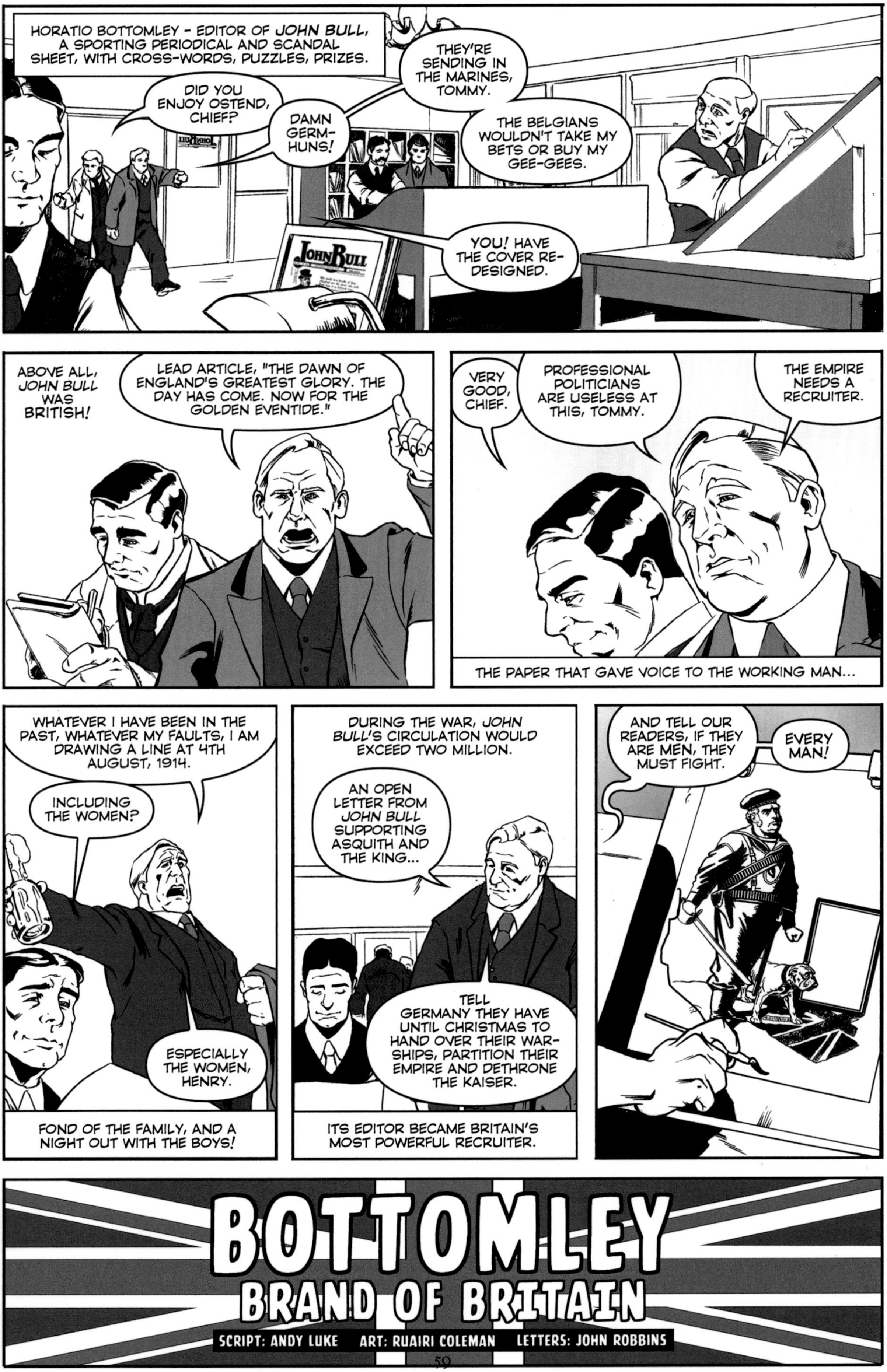
HORATIO BOTTOMLEY - EDITOR OF JOHN BULL, A SPORTING PERIODICAL AND SCANDAL SHEET, WITH CROSS-WORDS, PUZZLES, PRIZES.
DID YOU ENJOY OSTEND, CHIEF?
DAMN GERM-HUNS!
THEY'RE SENDING IN THE MARINES, TOMMY.
THE BELGIANS WOULDN'T TAKE MY BETS OR BUY MY GEE-GEES.
JOHN BULL
YOU! HAVE THE COVER RE-DESIGNED.
ABOVE ALL, JOHN BULL WAS BRITISH!
LEAD ARTICLE, "THE DAWN OF ENGLAND'S GREATEST GLORY. THE DAY HAS COME. NOW FOR THE GOLDEN EVENTIDE."
VERY GOOD, CHIEF.
PROFESSIONAL POLITICIANS ARE USELESS AT THIS, TOMMY.
THE EMPIRE NEEDS A RECRUITER.
THE PAPER THAT GAVE VOICE TO THE WORKING MAN...
WHATEVER I HAVE BEEN IN THE PAST, WHATEVER MY FAULTS, I AM DRAWING A LINE AT 4TH AUGUST, 1914.
INCLUDING THE WOMEN?
ESPECIALLY THE WOMEN, HENRY.
FOND OF THE FAMILY, AND A NIGHT OUT WITH THE BOYS!
DURING THE WAR, JOHN BULL'S CIRCULATION WOULD EXCEED TWO MILLION.
AN OPEN LETTER FROM JOHN BULL SUPPORTING ASQUITH AND THE KING...
TELL GERMANY THEY HAVE UNTIL CHRISTMAS TO HAND OVER THEIR WAR-SHIPS, PARTITION THEIR EMPIRE AND DETHRONE THE KAISER.
ITS EDITOR BECAME BRITAIN'S MOST POWERFUL RECRUITER.
AND TELL OUR READERS, IF THEY ARE MEN, THEY MUST FIGHT.
EVERY MAN!
BOTTOMLEY
BRAND OF BRITAIN
SCRIPT: ANDY LUKE ART: RUAIRI COLEMAN LETTERS: JOHN ROBBINS

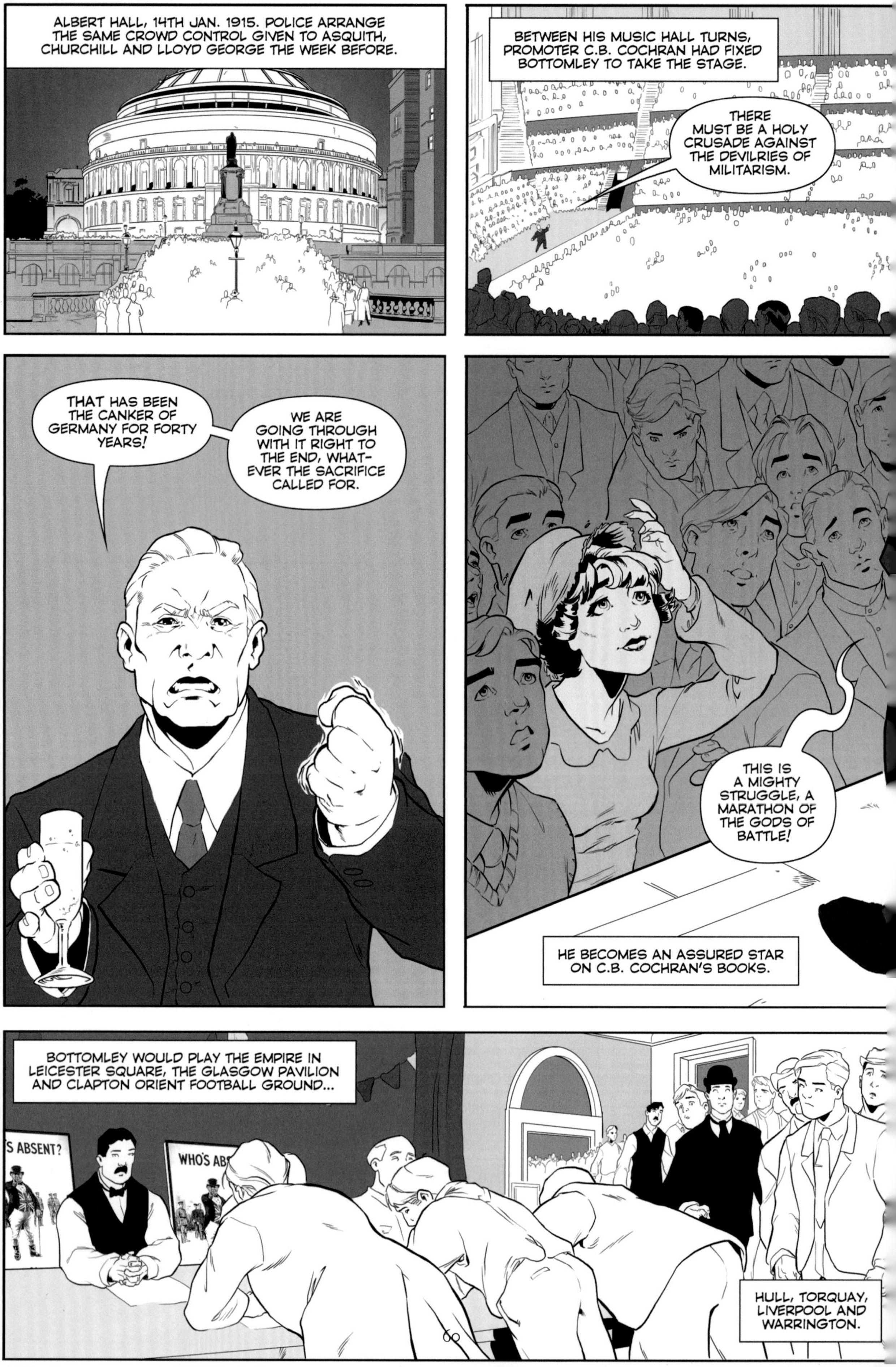
ALBERT HALL, 14TH JAN. 1915. POLICE ARRANGE THE SAME CROWD CONTROL GIVEN TO ASQUITH, CHURCHILL AND LLOYD GEORGE THE WEEK BEFORE.
BETWEEN HIS MUSIC HALL TURNS, PROMOTER C.B. COCHRAN HAD FIXED BOTTOMLEY TO TAKE THE STAGE.
THERE MUST BE A HOLY CRUSADE AGAINST THE DEVILRIES OF MILITARISM.
THAT HAS BEEN THE CANKER OF GERMANY FOR FORTY YEARS!
WE ARE GOING THROUGH WITH IT RIGHT TO THE END, WHAT-EVER THE SACRIFICE CALLED FOR.
THIS IS A MIGHTY STRUGGLE, A MARATHON OF THE GODS OF BATTLE!
HE BECOMES AN ASSURED STAR ON C.B. COCHRAN'S BOOKS.
BOTTOMLEY WOULD PLAY THE EMPIRE IN LEICESTER SQUARE, THE GLASGOW PAVILION AND CLAPTON ORIENT FOOTBALL GROUND...
'S ABSENT?
WHO'S AB
HULL, TORQUAY, LIVERPOOL AND WARRINGTON.

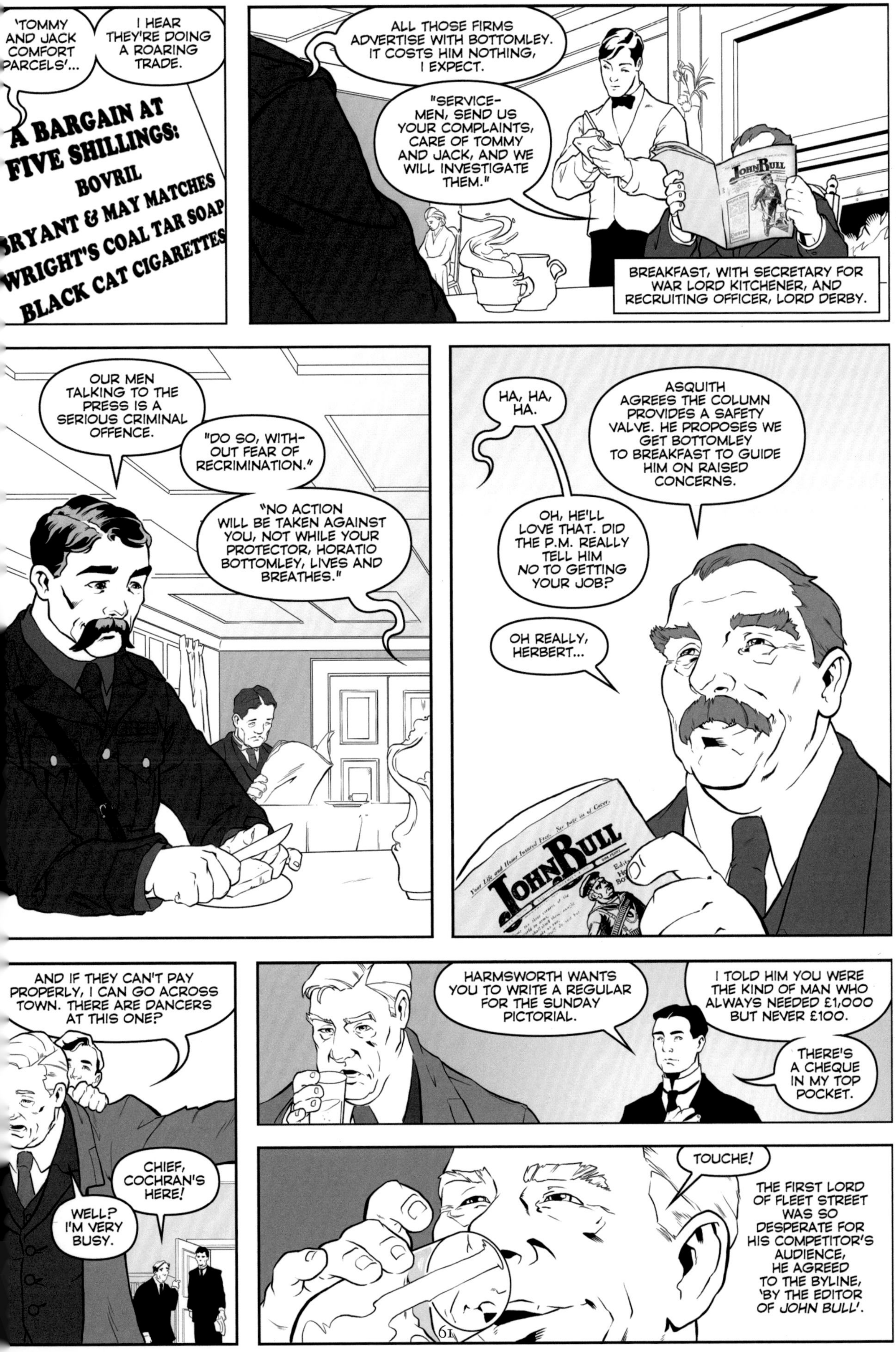
'TOMMY AND JACK COMFORT PARCELS'...
I HEAR THEY'RE DOING A ROARING TRADE.
A BARGAIN AT FIVE SHILLINGS:
BOVRIL
BRYANT & MAY MATCHES
WRIGHT'S COAL TAR SOAP
BLACK CAT CIGARETTES
ALL THOSE FIRMS ADVERTISE WITH BOTTOMLEY. IT COSTS HIM NOTHING, I EXPECT.
"SERVICE-MEN, SEND US YOUR COMPLAINTS, CARE OF TOMMY AND JACK, AND WE WILL INVESTIGATE THEM."
JOHN BULL
BREAKFAST, WITH SECRETARY FOR WAR LORD KITCHENER, AND RECRUITING OFFICER, LORD DERBY.
OUR MEN TALKING TO THE PRESS IS A SERIOUS CRIMINAL OFFENCE.
"DO SO, WITHOUT FEAR OF RECRIMINATION."
"NO ACTION WILL BE TAKEN AGAINST YOU, NOT WHILE YOUR PROTECTOR, HORATIO BOTTOMLEY, LIVES AND BREATHES."
HA, HA, HA.
ASQUITH AGREES THE COLUMN PROVIDES A SAFETY VALVE. HE PROPOSES WE GET BOTTOMLEY TO BREAKFAST TO GUIDE HIM ON RAISED CONCERNS.
OH, HE'LL LOVE THAT. DID THE P.M. REALLY TELL HIM NO TO GETTING YOUR JOB?
OH REALLY, HERBERT...
JOHN BULL
AND IF THEY CAN'T PAY PROPERLY, I CAN GO ACROSS TOWN. THERE ARE DANCERS AT THIS ONE?
CHIEF, COCHRAN'S HERE!
WELL? I'M VERY BUSY.
HARMSWORTH WANTS YOU TO WRITE A REGULAR FOR THE SUNDAY PICTORIAL.
I TOLD HIM YOU WERE THE KIND OF MAN WHO ALWAYS NEEDED £1,000 BUT NEVER £100.
THERE'S A CHEQUE IN MY TOP POCKET.
TOUCHE!
THE FIRST LORD OF FLEET STREET WAS SO DESPERATE FOR HIS COMPETITOR'S AUDIENCE, HE AGREED TO THE BYLINE, 'BY THE EDITOR OF JOHN BULL'.

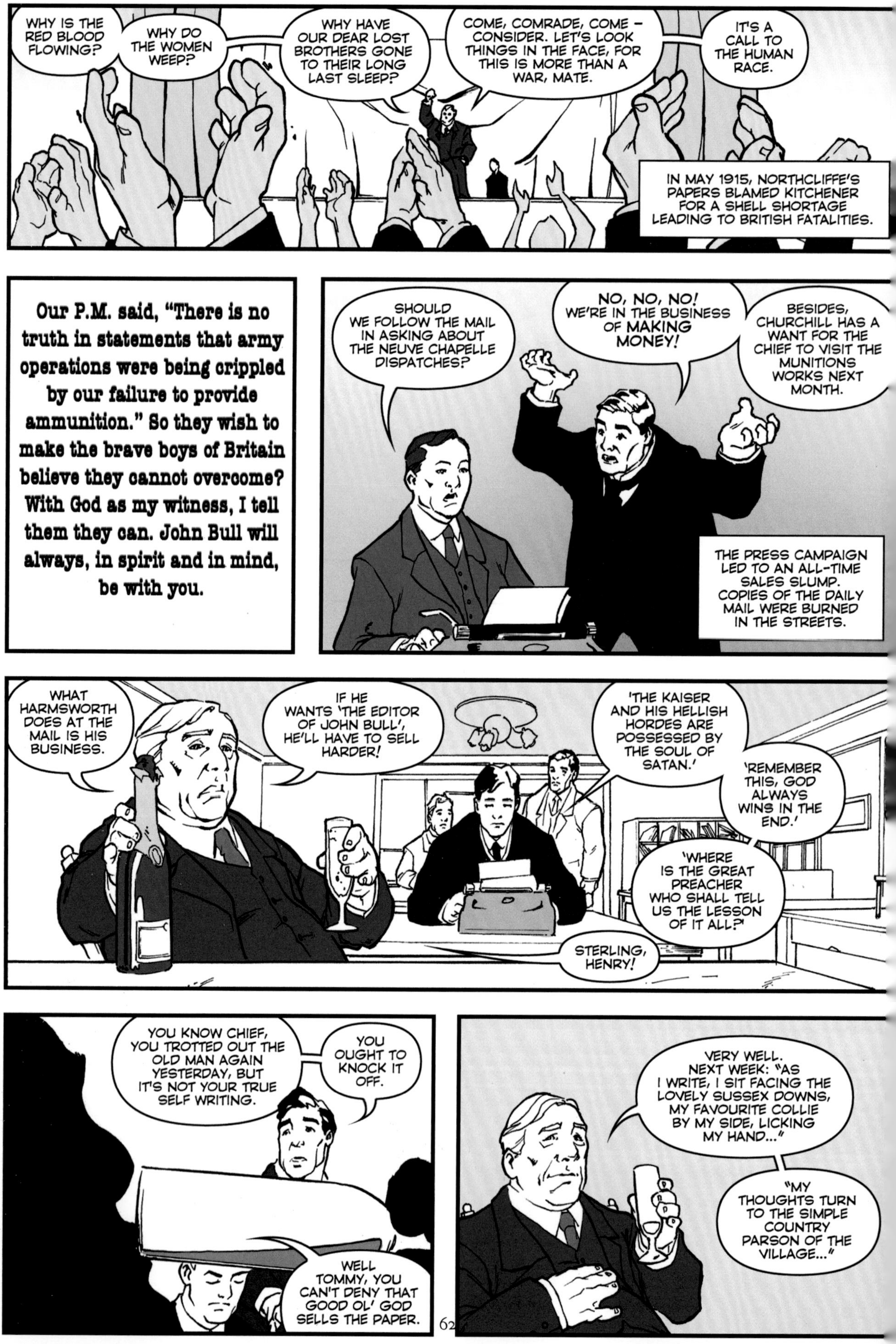
WHY IS THE RED BLOOD FLOWING?
WHY DO THE WOMEN WEEP?
WHY HAVE OUR DEAR LOST BROTHERS GONE TO THEIR LONG LAST SLEEP?
COME, COMRADE, COME – CONSIDER. LET'S LOOK THINGS IN THE FACE, FOR THIS IS MORE THAN A WAR, MATE.
IT'S A CALL TO THE HUMAN RACE.
IN MAY 1915, NORTHCLIFFE'S PAPERS BLAMED KITCHENER FOR A SHELL SHORTAGE LEADING TO BRITISH FATALITIES.
Our P.M. said, "There is no truth in statements that army operations were being crippled by our failure to provide ammunition." So they wish to make the brave boys of Britain believe they cannot overcome? With God as my witness, I tell them they can. John Bull will always, in spirit and in mind, be with you.
SHOULD WE FOLLOW THE MAIL IN ASKING ABOUT THE NEUVE CHAPELLE DISPATCHES?
NO, NO, NO! WE'RE IN THE BUSINESS OF MAKING MONEY!
BESIDES, CHURCHILL HAS A WANT FOR THE CHIEF TO VISIT THE MUNITIONS WORKS NEXT MONTH.
THE PRESS CAMPAIGN LED TO AN ALL-TIME SALES SLUMP. COPIES OF THE DAILY MAIL WERE BURNED IN THE STREETS.
WHAT HARMSWORTH DOES AT THE MAIL IS HIS BUSINESS.
IF HE WANTS 'THE EDITOR OF JOHN BULL', HE'LL HAVE TO SELL HARDER!
'THE KAISER AND HIS HELLISH HORDES ARE POSSESSED BY THE SOUL OF SATAN.'
'REMEMBER THIS, GOD ALWAYS WINS IN THE END.'
'WHERE IS THE GREAT PREACHER WHO SHALL TELL US THE LESSON OF IT ALL?'
STERLING, HENRY!
YOU KNOW CHIEF, YOU TROTTED OUT THE OLD MAN AGAIN YESTERDAY, BUT IT'S NOT YOUR TRUE SELF WRITING.
YOU OUGHT TO KNOCK IT OFF.
WELL TOMMY, YOU CAN'T DENY THAT GOOD OL' GOD SELLS THE PAPER.
VERY WELL. NEXT WEEK: "AS I WRITE, I SIT FACING THE LOVELY SUSSEX DOWNS, MY FAVOURITE COLLIE BY MY SIDE, LICKING MY HAND..."
"MY THOUGHTS TURN TO THE SIMPLE COUNTRY PARSON OF THE VILLAGE..."

WON'T THE GOVERNMENT HAVE A FIT?

THE COMMON TOMMY MUST HAVE HIS PROBLEMS ADDRESSED...

AND THAT IS THE LAW OR I'M NOT BOTTOMLEY!

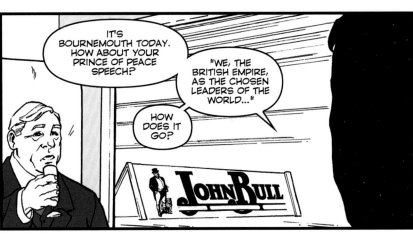

IT'S BOURNEMOUTH TODAY. HOW ABOUT YOUR PRINCE OF PEACE SPEECH?

"WE, THE BRITISH EMPIRE, AS THE CHOSEN LEADERS OF THE WORLD..."

HOW DOES IT GO?

JohnBull

HUMAN DESTINY AND PROGRESS, STAR OF BETHLEHEM, YES YES YES.

BUT FOR £200 GATE MONEY, WE'LL GIVE THE WINTER GARDENS SOMETHING SPECIAL.

HOUSTON OFTEN STOOD IN THE WINGS SHOWING THE TAKINGS ON HIS FINGERS. BOTTOMLEY WOULD THEN ADJUST HIS SPEECH ACCORDINGLY.

THIS COURT HAS REACHED THE VERDICT THAT, WITHIN SIX WEEKS OF TODAY, WE SHALL HAVE THE KRAUTS ON THE RUN.

WE SHALL DRIVE THEM OUT OF FRANCE, FLANDERS, BELGIUM, THE RHINELANDS!

BACK!

BACK!

WE SHALL GIVE THEM A TASTE OF THEIR OWN MEDICINE!

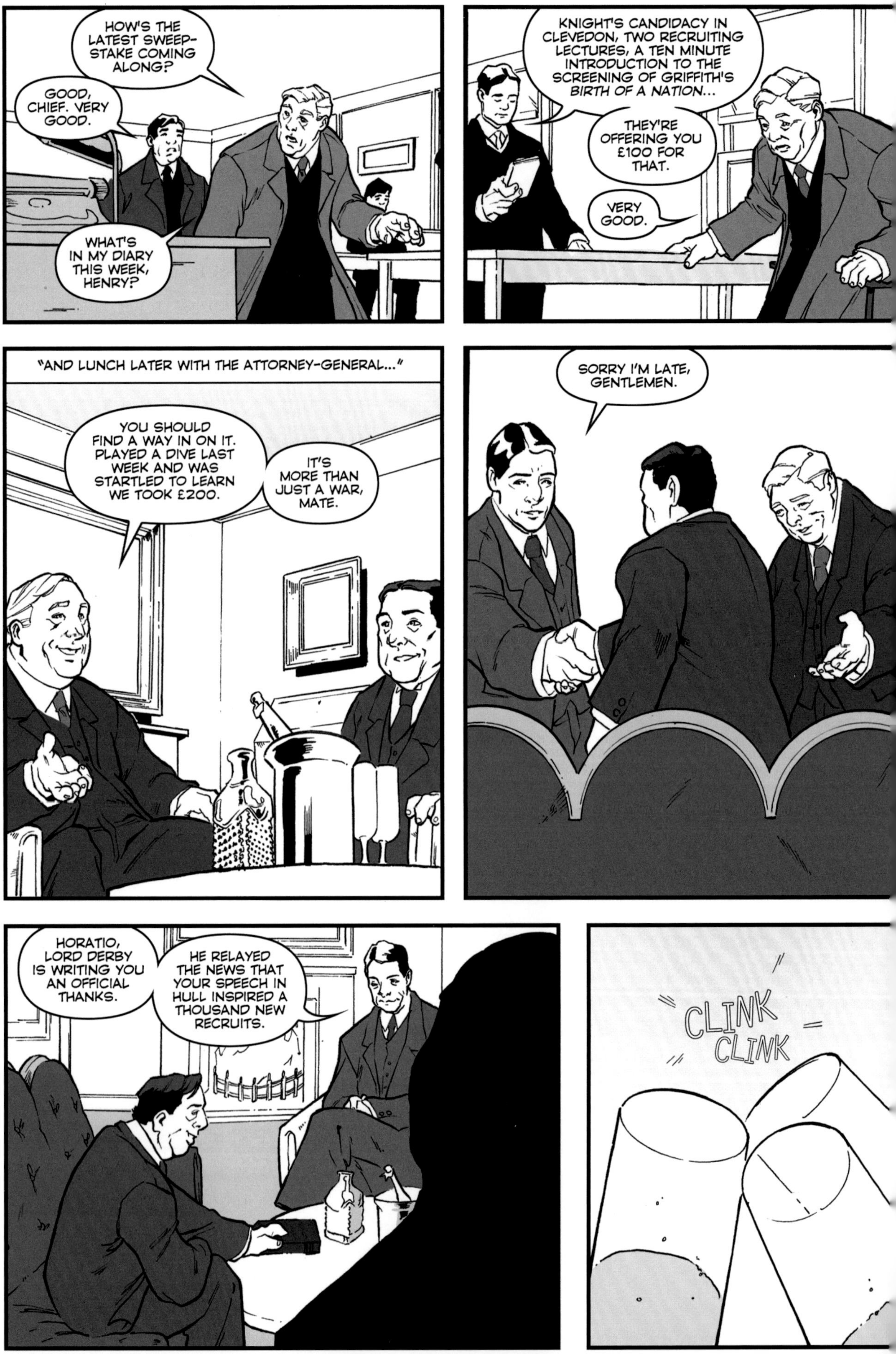
HOW'S THE LATEST SWEEP-STAKE COMING ALONG?
GOOD, CHIEF. VERY GOOD.
WHAT'S IN MY DIARY THIS WEEK, HENRY?
KNIGHT'S CANDIDACY IN CLEVEDON, TWO RECRUITING LECTURES, A TEN MINUTE INTRODUCTION TO THE SCREENING OF GRIFFITH'S *BIRTH OF A NATION*...
THEY'RE OFFERING YOU £100 FOR THAT.
VERY GOOD.
"AND LUNCH LATER WITH THE ATTORNEY-GENERAL..."
YOU SHOULD FIND A WAY IN ON IT. PLAYED A DIVE LAST WEEK AND WAS STARTLED TO LEARN WE TOOK £200.
IT'S MORE THAN JUST A WAR, MATE.
SORRY I'M LATE, GENTLEMEN.
HORATIO, LORD DERBY IS WRITING YOU AN OFFICIAL THANKS.
HE RELAYED THE NEWS THAT YOUR SPEECH IN HULL INSPIRED A THOUSAND NEW RECRUITS.
CLINK
CLINK

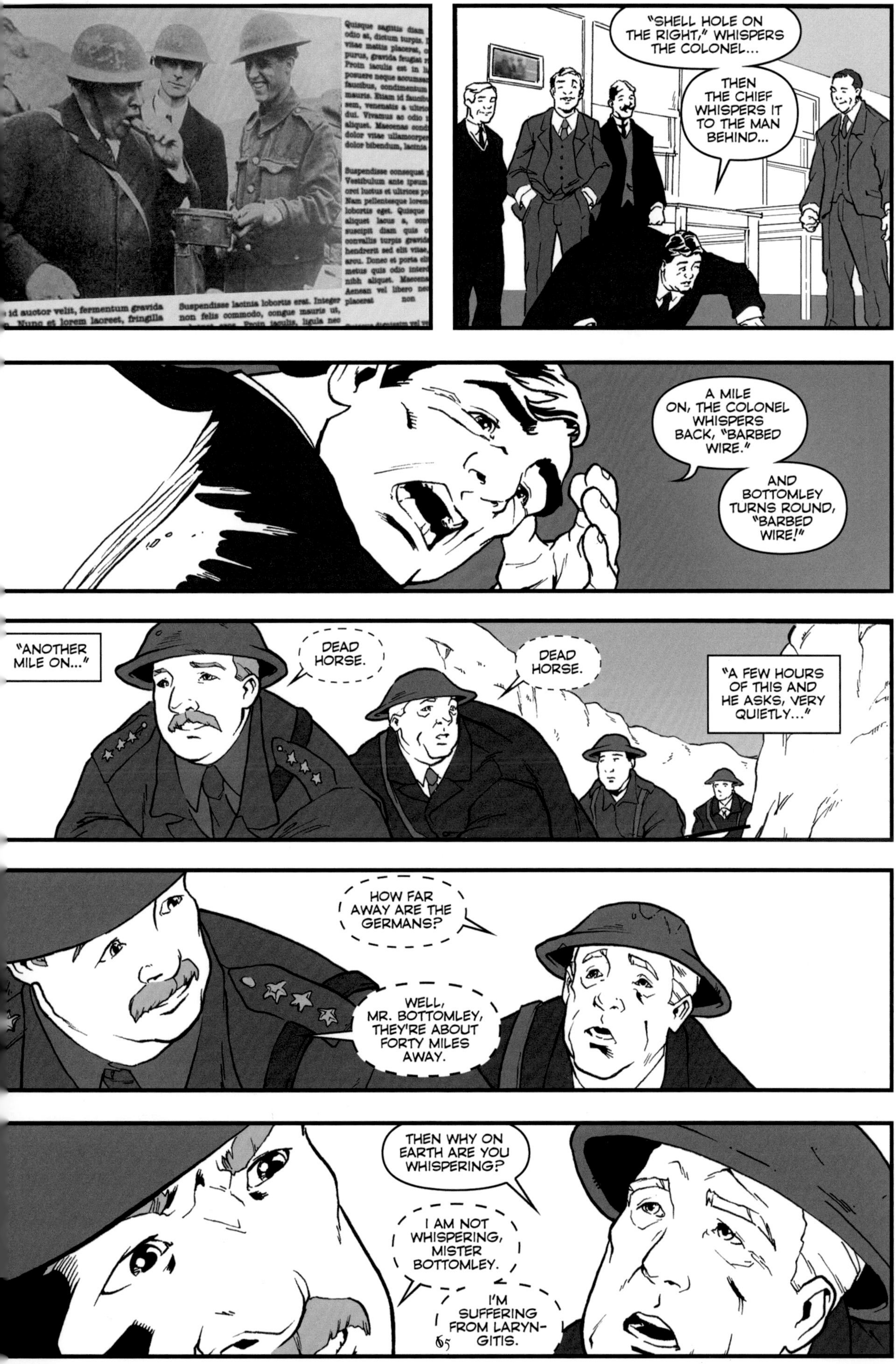

Quisque sagittis diam
odio et, dictum turpis.
vitae mattis placerat,
purus, gravida feugiat
Proin iaculis est in l
posuere neque accumsan
faucibus, condimentum
mauris. Etiam id faucib
sem, venenatis a ultric
dui. Vivamus ac odio
aliquet. Maecenas
dolor vitae ullamcorper
dolor bibendum, lacinia
Suspendisse consequat
Vestibulum ante ipsum
orci luctus et ultrices
Nam pellentesque lorem
lobortis eget. Quisque
aliquet lacus a,
suscipit diam quis
convallis turpis gravida
hendrerit sed elit vitae,
arcu. Donec et porta elit
metus quis odio interd
nibh aliquet. Maecenas
Aenean vel libero ne
placerat non
id auctor velit, fermentum gravida
Nunc et lorem laoreet, fringilla
Suspendisse lacinia lobortis erat. Integer
non felis commodo, congue mauris ut,
"SHELL HOLE ON THE RIGHT," WHISPERS THE COLONEL...
THEN THE CHIEF WHISPERS IT TO THE MAN BEHIND...
A MILE ON, THE COLONEL WHISPERS BACK, "BARBED WIRE."
AND BOTTOMLEY TURNS ROUND, "BARBED WIRE!"
"ANOTHER MILE ON..."
DEAD HORSE.
DEAD HORSE.
"A FEW HOURS OF THIS AND HE ASKS, VERY QUIETLY..."
HOW FAR AWAY ARE THE GERMANS?
WELL, MR. BOTTOMLEY, THEY'RE ABOUT FORTY MILES AWAY.
THEN WHY ON EARTH ARE YOU WHISPERING?
I AM NOT WHISPERING, MISTER BOTTOMLEY.
I'M SUFFERING FROM LARYN-GITIS.

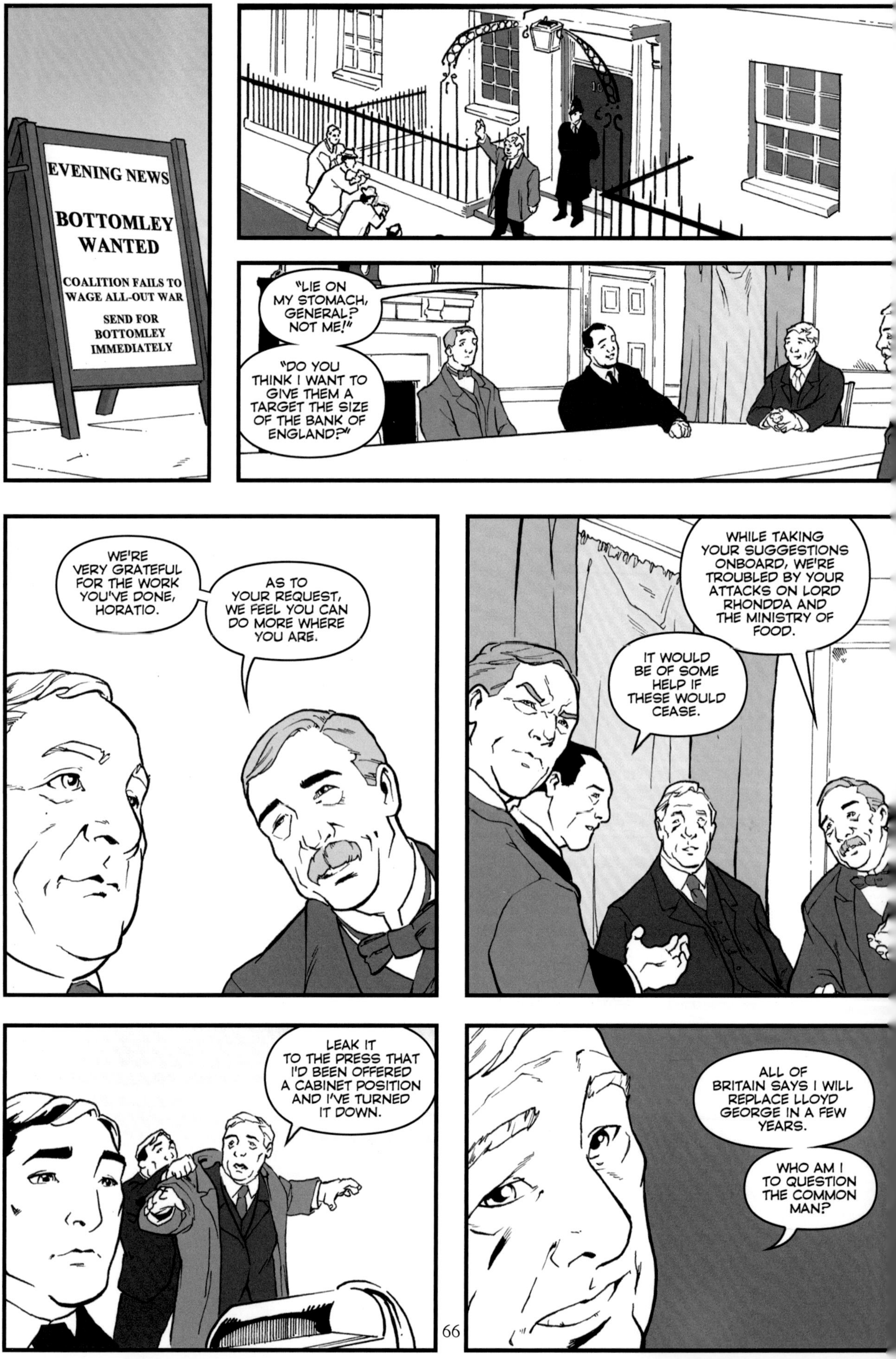
EVENING NEWS
BOTTOMLEY WANTED
COALITION FAILS TO WAGE ALL-OUT WAR
SEND FOR BOTTOMLEY IMMEDIATELY
"LIE ON MY STOMACH, GENERAL? NOT ME!"
"DO YOU THINK I WANT TO GIVE THEM A TARGET THE SIZE OF THE BANK OF ENGLAND?"
WE'RE VERY GRATEFUL FOR THE WORK YOU'VE DONE, HORATIO.
AS TO YOUR REQUEST, WE FEEL YOU CAN DO MORE WHERE YOU ARE.
WHILE TAKING YOUR SUGGESTIONS ONBOARD, WE'RE TROUBLED BY YOUR ATTACKS ON LORD RHONDDA AND THE MINISTRY OF FOOD.
IT WOULD BE OF SOME HELP IF THESE WOULD CEASE.
LEAK IT TO THE PRESS THAT I'D BEEN OFFERED A CABINET POSITION AND I'VE TURNED IT DOWN.
ALL OF BRITAIN SAYS I WILL REPLACE LLOYD GEORGE IN A FEW YEARS.
WHO AM I TO QUESTION THE COMMON MAN?

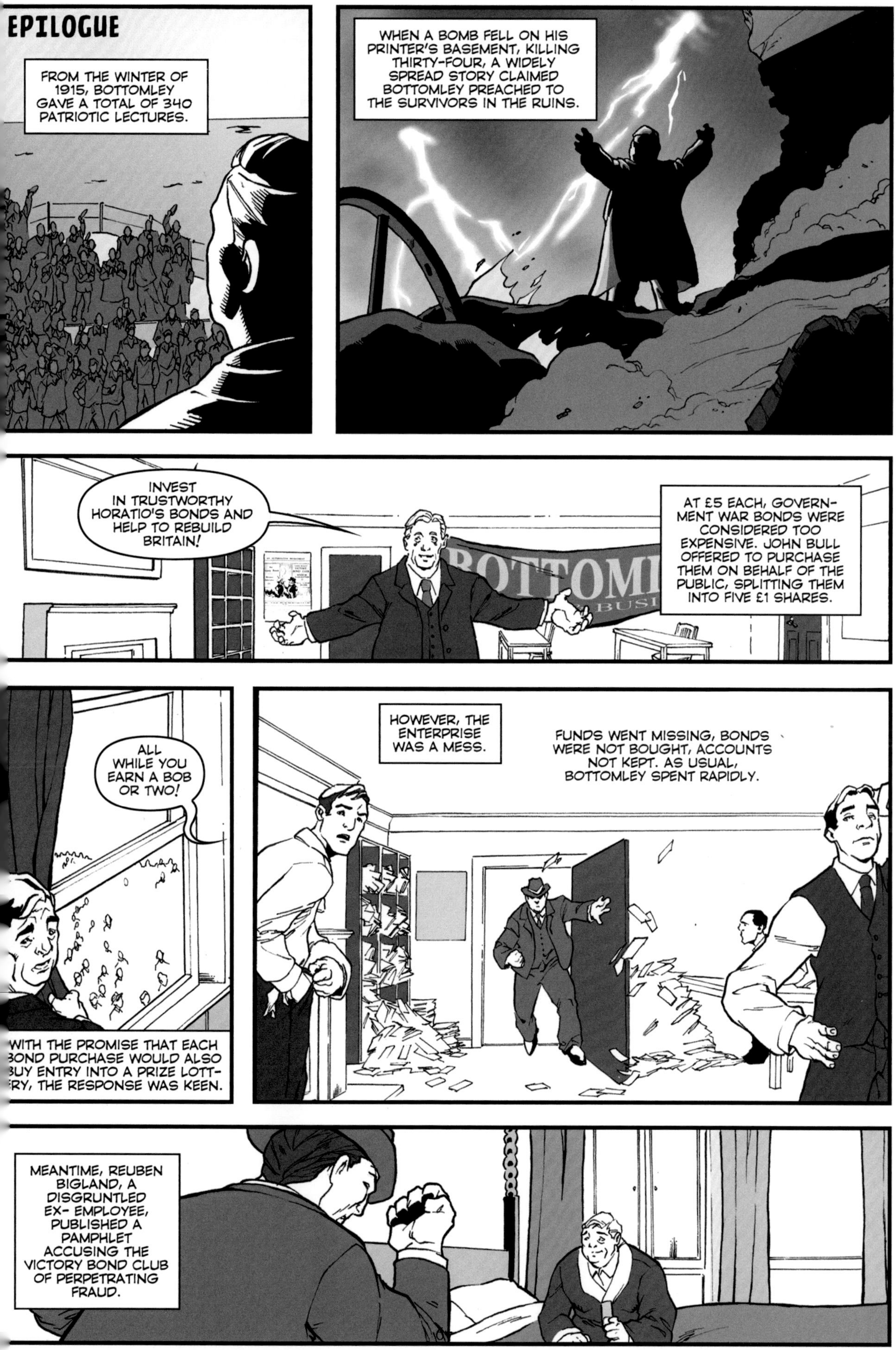
EPILOGUE
FROM THE WINTER OF 1915, BOTTOMLEY GAVE A TOTAL OF 340 PATRIOTIC LECTURES.
WHEN A BOMB FELL ON HIS PRINTER'S BASEMENT, KILLING THIRTY-FOUR, A WIDELY SPREAD STORY CLAIMED BOTTOMLEY PREACHED TO THE SURVIVORS IN THE RUINS.
INVEST IN TRUSTWORTHY HORATIO'S BONDS AND HELP TO REBUILD BRITAIN!
AT £5 EACH, GOVERNMENT WAR BONDS WERE CONSIDERED TOO EXPENSIVE. JOHN BULL OFFERED TO PURCHASE THEM ON BEHALF OF THE PUBLIC, SPLITTING THEM INTO FIVE £1 SHARES.
ALL WHILE YOU EARN A BOB OR TWO!
WITH THE PROMISE THAT EACH BOND PURCHASE WOULD ALSO BUY ENTRY INTO A PRIZE LOTTERY, THE RESPONSE WAS KEEN.
HOWEVER, THE ENTERPRISE WAS A MESS.
FUNDS WENT MISSING, BONDS WERE NOT BOUGHT, ACCOUNTS NOT KEPT. AS USUAL, BOTTOMLEY SPENT RAPIDLY.
MEANTIME, REUBEN BIGLAND, A DISGRUNTLED EX- EMPLOYEE, PUBLISHED A PAMPHLET ACCUSING THE VICTORY BOND CLUB OF PERPETRATING FRAUD.

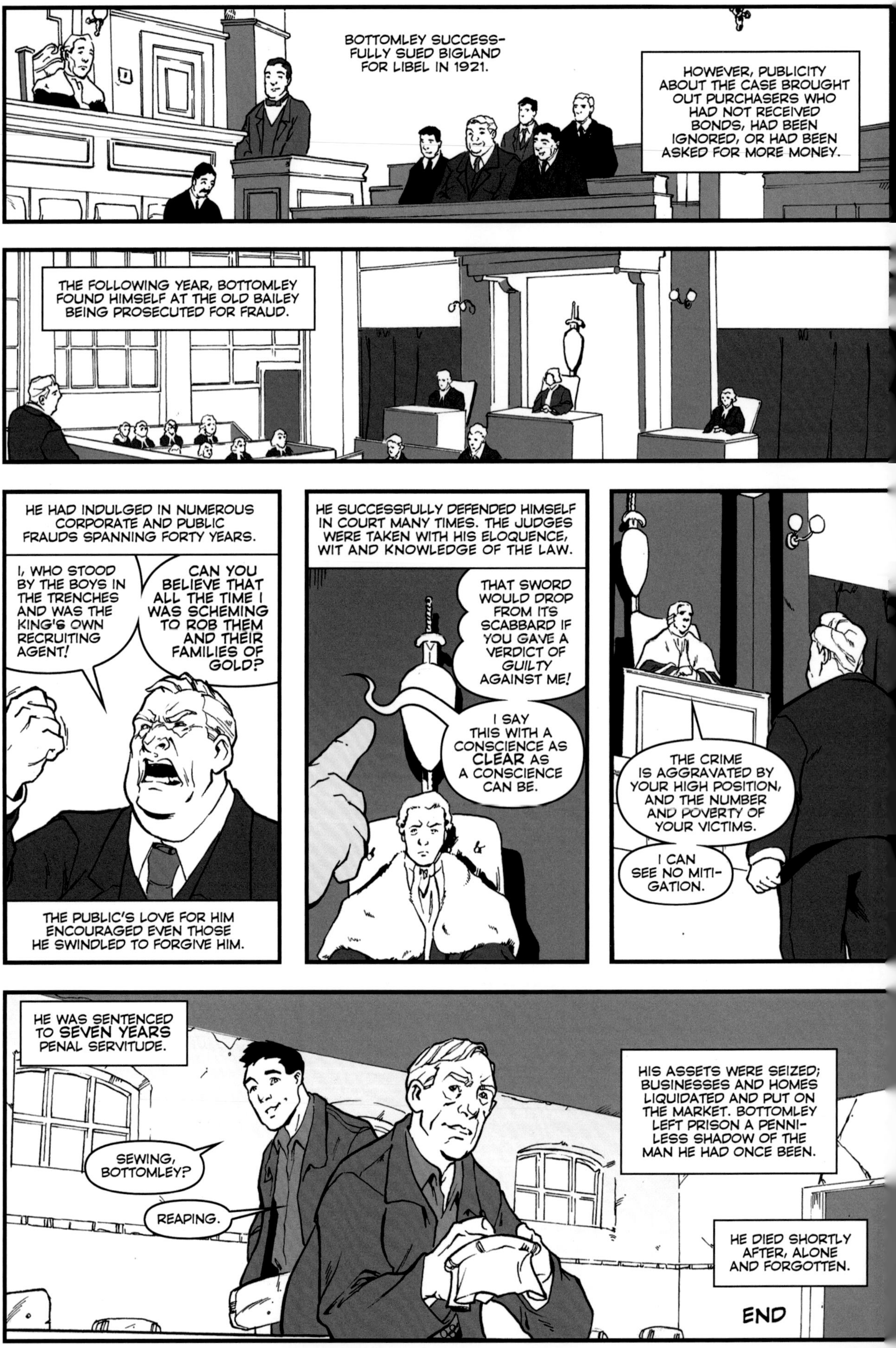
BOTTOMLEY SUCCESSFULLY SUED BIGLAND FOR LIBEL IN 1921.
HOWEVER, PUBLICITY ABOUT THE CASE BROUGHT OUT PURCHASERS WHO HAD NOT RECEIVED BONDS, HAD BEEN IGNORED, OR HAD BEEN ASKED FOR MORE MONEY.
THE FOLLOWING YEAR, BOTTOMLEY FOUND HIMSELF AT THE OLD BAILEY BEING PROSECUTED FOR FRAUD.
HE HAD INDULGED IN NUMEROUS CORPORATE AND PUBLIC FRAUDS SPANNING FORTY YEARS.
I, WHO STOOD BY THE BOYS IN THE TRENCHES AND WAS THE KING'S OWN RECRUITING AGENT!
CAN YOU BELIEVE THAT ALL THE TIME I WAS SCHEMING TO ROB THEM AND THEIR FAMILIES OF GOLD?
THE PUBLIC'S LOVE FOR HIM ENCOURAGED EVEN THOSE HE SWINDLED TO FORGIVE HIM.
HE SUCCESSFULLY DEFENDED HIMSELF IN COURT MANY TIMES. THE JUDGES WERE TAKEN WITH HIS ELOQUENCE, WIT AND KNOWLEDGE OF THE LAW.
THAT SWORD WOULD DROP FROM ITS SCABBARD IF YOU GAVE A VERDICT OF *GUILTY* AGAINST ME!
I SAY THIS WITH A CONSCIENCE AS **CLEAR** AS A CONSCIENCE CAN BE.
THE CRIME IS AGGRAVATED BY YOUR HIGH POSITION, AND THE NUMBER AND POVERTY OF YOUR VICTIMS.
I CAN SEE NO MITIGATION.
HE WAS SENTENCED TO **SEVEN YEARS** PENAL SERVITUDE.
SEWING, BOTTOMLEY?
REAPING.
HIS ASSETS WERE SEIZED; BUSINESSES AND HOMES LIQUIDATED AND PUT ON THE MARKET. BOTTOMLEY LEFT PRISON A PENNILESS SHADOW OF THE MAN HE HAD ONCE BEEN.
HE DIED SHORTLY AFTER, ALONE AND FORGOTTEN.
END

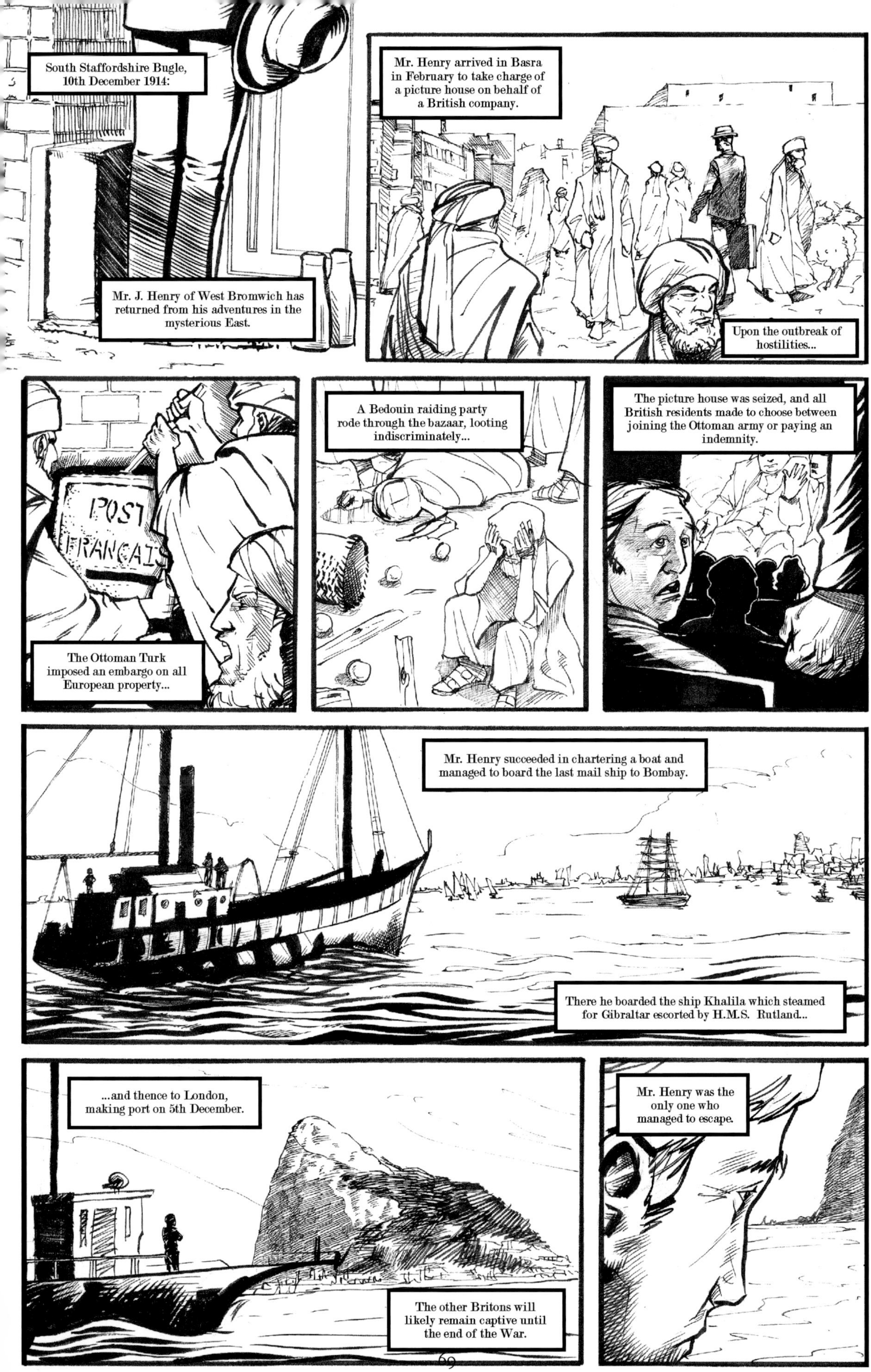
South Staffordshire Bugle, 10th December 1914:
Mr. J. Henry of West Bromwich has returned from his adventures in the mysterious East.
Mr. Henry arrived in Basra in February to take charge of a picture house on behalf of a British company.
Upon the outbreak of hostilities...
POST FRANCAIS
The Ottoman Turk imposed an embargo on all European property...
A Bedouin raiding party rode through the bazaar, looting indiscriminately...
The picture house was seized, and all British residents made to choose between joining the Ottoman army or paying an indemnity.
Mr. Henry succeeded in chartering a boat and managed to board the last mail ship to Bombay.
There he boarded the ship Khalila which steamed for Gibraltar escorted by H.M.S. Rutland...
...and thence to London, making port on 5th December.
The other Britons will likely remain captive until the end of the War.
Mr. Henry was the only one who managed to escape.

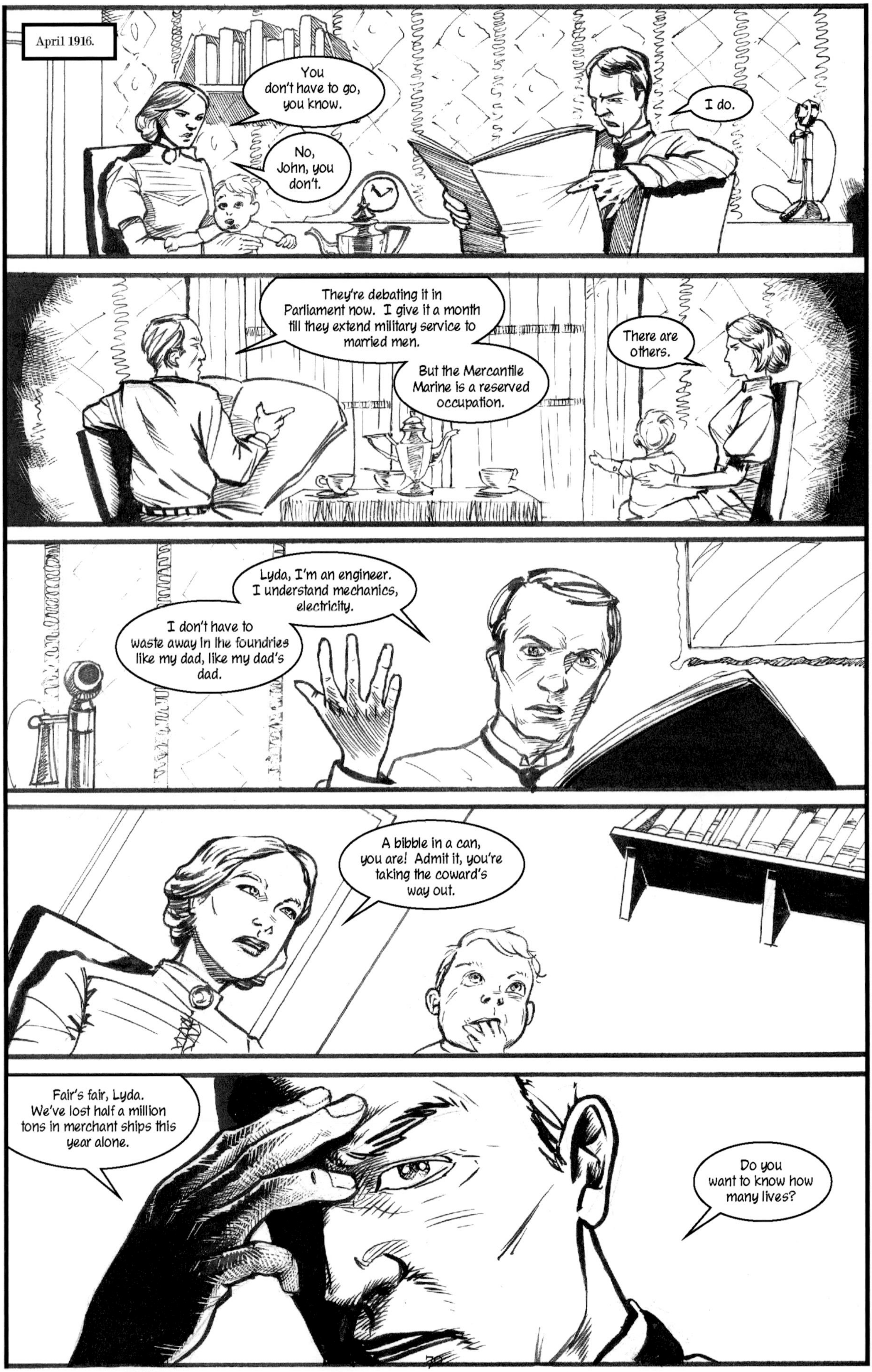
April 1916.
You don't have to go, you know.
I do.
No, John, you don't.
They're debating it in Parliament now. I give it a month till they extend military service to married men.
But the Mercantile Marine is a reserved occupation.
There are others.
Lyda, I'm an engineer. I understand mechanics, electricity.
I don't have to waste away in the foundries like my dad, like my dad's dad.
A bibble in a can, you are! Admit it, you're taking the coward's way out.
Fair's fair, Lyda. We've lost half a million tons in merchant ships this year alone.
Do you want to know how many lives?

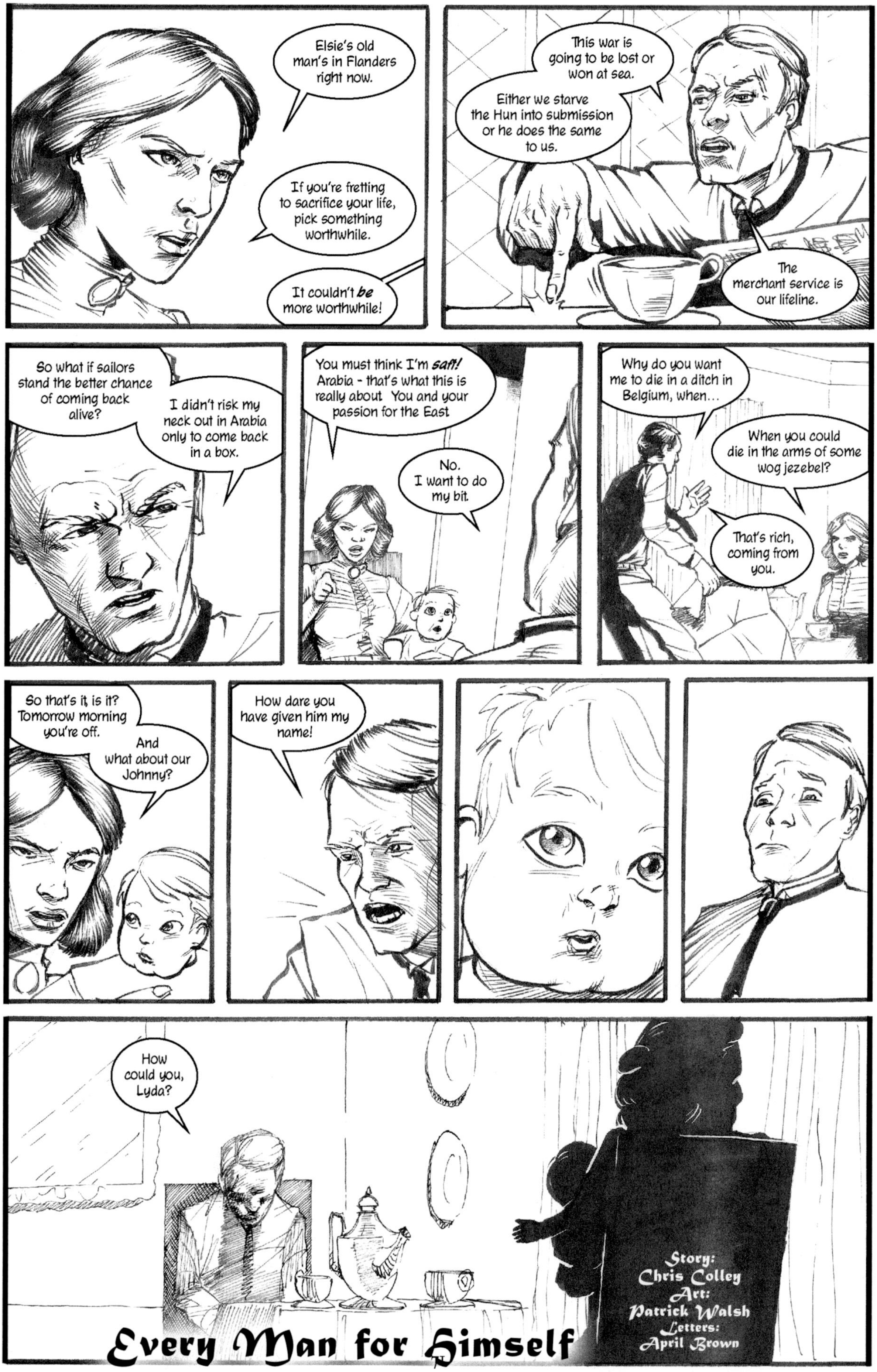

Elsie's old man's in Flanders right now.
If you're fretting to sacrifice your life, pick something worthwhile.
It couldn't *be* more worthwhile!
This war is going to be lost or won at sea.
Either we starve the Hun into submission or he does the same to us.
The merchant service is our lifeline.
So what if sailors stand the better chance of coming back alive?
I didn't risk my neck out in Arabia only to come back in a box.
You must think I'm *saft!* Arabia - that's what this is really about. You and your passion for the East
No. I want to do my bit.
Why do you want me to die in a ditch in Belgium, when...
When you could die in the arms of some wog jezebel?
That's rich, coming from you.
So that's it, is it? Tomorrow morning you're off.
And what about our Johnny?
How dare you have given him my name!
How could you, Lyda?
Every Man for Himself
Story: Chris Colley
Art: Patrick Walsh
Letters: April Brown

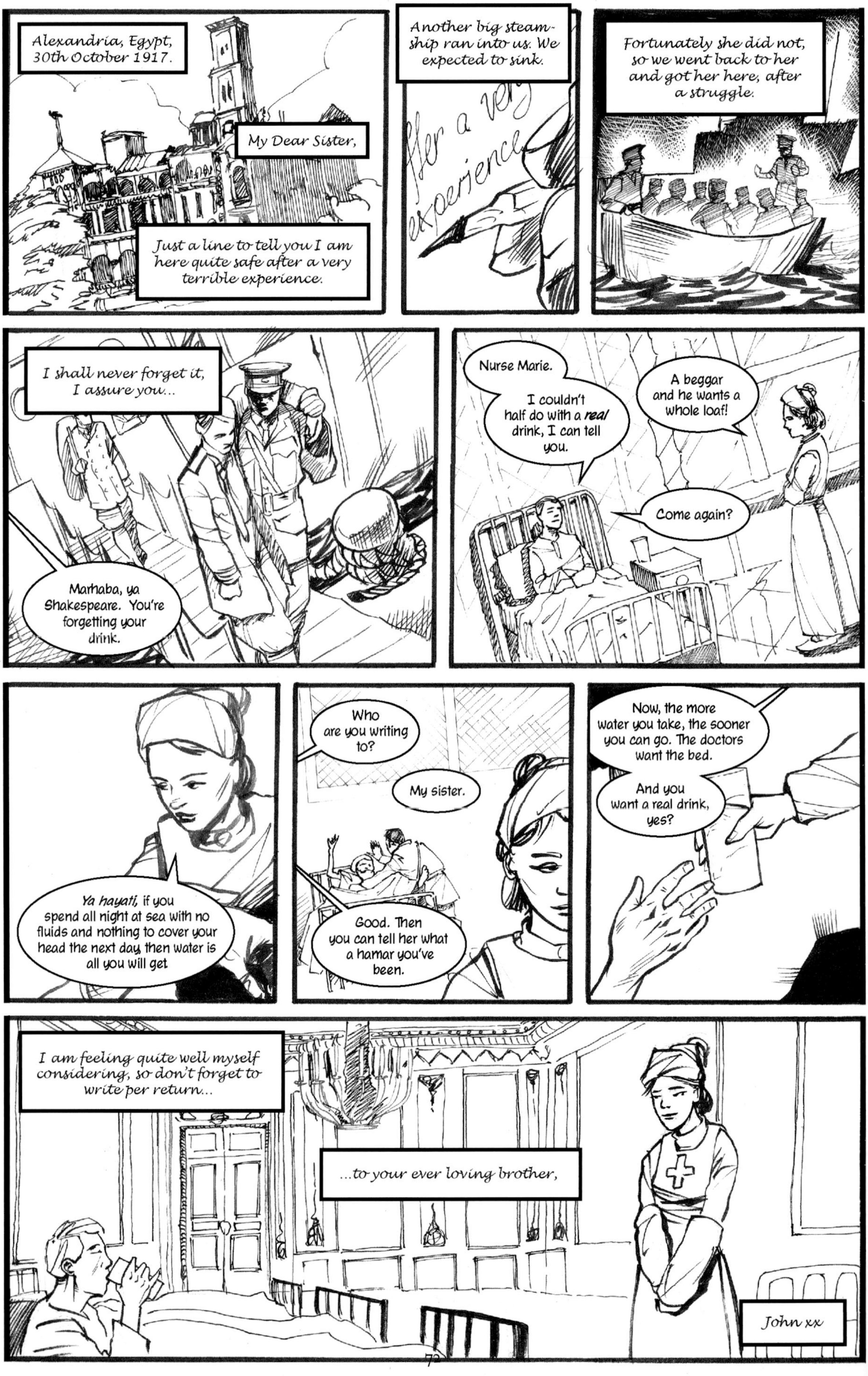
Alexandria, Egypt, 30th October 1917.
My Dear Sister,
Just a line to tell you I am here quite safe after a very terrible experience.
Another big steam-ship ran into us. We expected to sink.
Fortunately she did not, so we went back to her and got her here, after a struggle.
I shall never forget it, I assure you...
Marhaba, ya Shakespeare. You're forgetting your drink.
Nurse Marie.
I couldn't half do with a *real* drink, I can tell you.
A beggar and he wants a whole loaf!
Come again?
Ya hayati, if you spend all night at sea with no fluids and nothing to cover your head the next day, then water is all you will get.
Who are you writing to?
My sister.
Good. Then you can tell her what a hamar you've been.
Now, the more water you take, the sooner you can go. The doctors want the bed.
And you want a real drink, yes?
I am feeling quite well myself considering, so don't forget to write per return...
...to your ever loving brother,
John xx

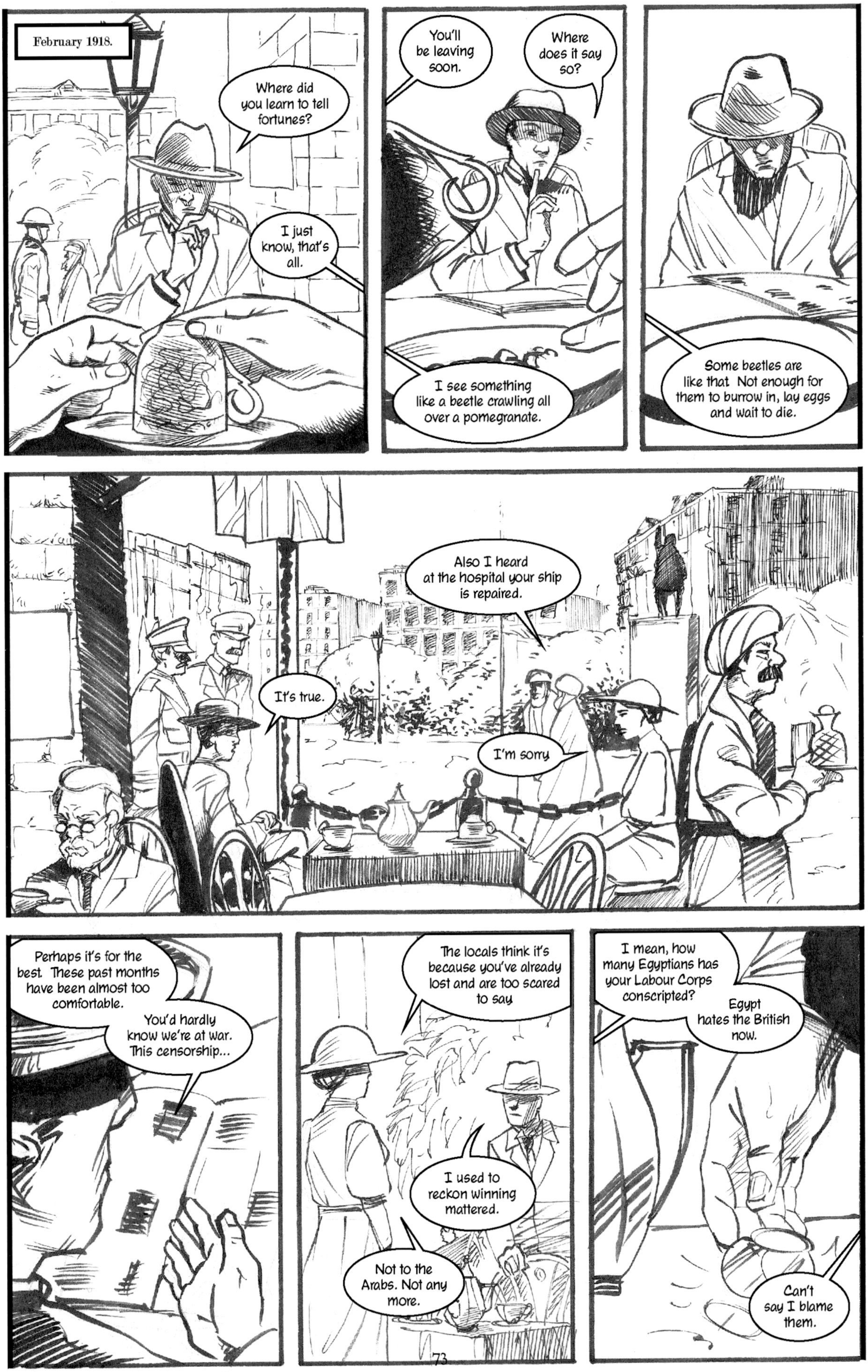
February 1918.
Where did you learn to tell fortunes?
I just know, that's all.
You'll be leaving soon.
Where does it say so?
I see something like a beetle crawling all over a pomegranate.
Some beetles are like that. Not enough for them to burrow in, lay eggs and wait to die.
Also I heard at the hospital your ship is repaired.
It's true.
I'm sorry.
Perhaps it's for the best. These past months have been almost too comfortable.
You'd hardly know we're at war. This censorship...
The locals think it's because you've already lost and are too scared to say.
I used to reckon winning mattered.
Not to the Arabs. Not any more.
I mean, how many Egyptians has your Labour Corps conscripted?
Egypt hates the British now.
Can't say I blame them.

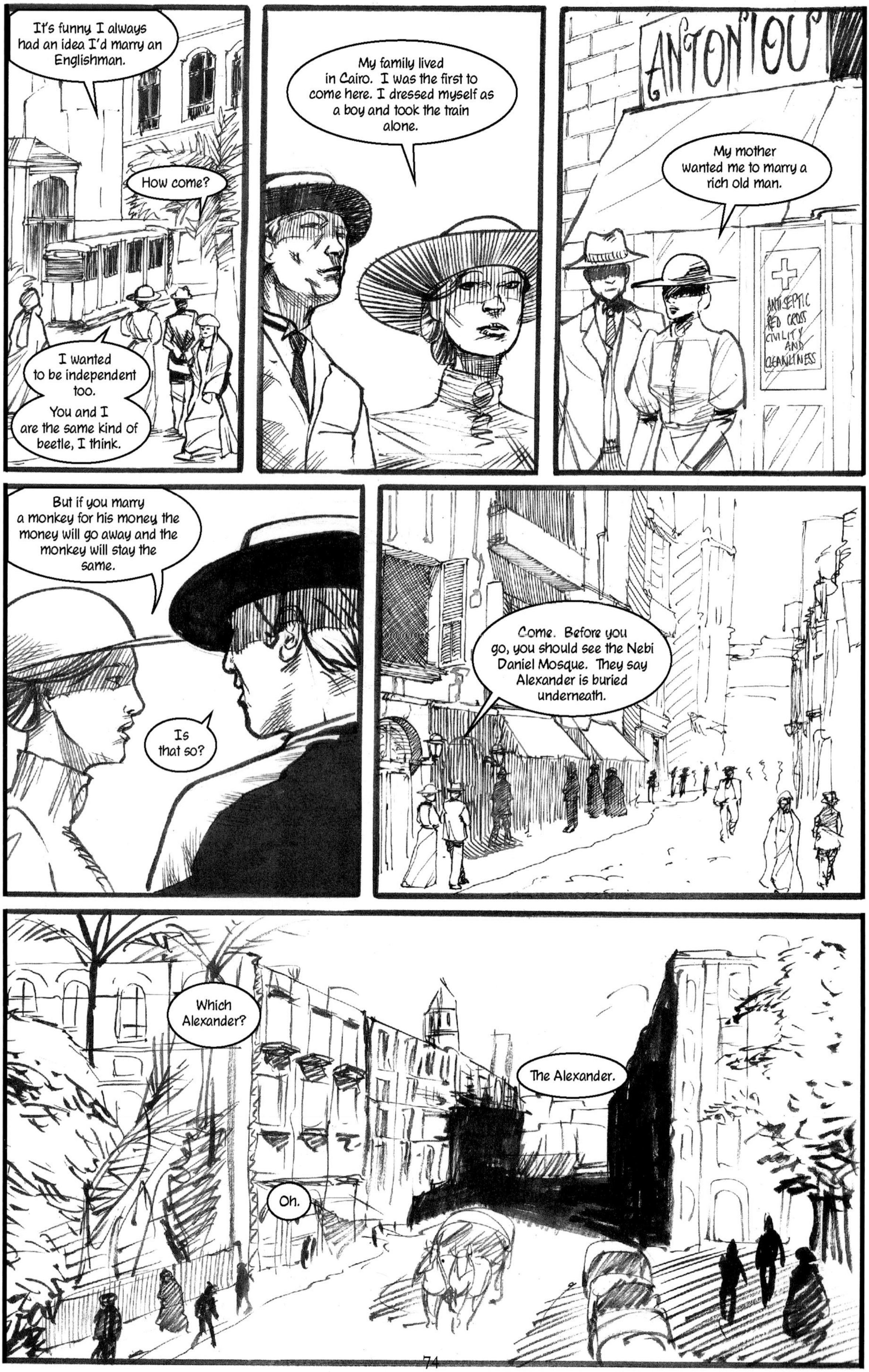
It's funny I always had an idea I'd marry an Englishman.
How come?
I wanted to be independent too.
You and I are the same kind of beetle, I think.
My family lived in Cairo. I was the first to come here. I dressed myself as a boy and took the train alone.
ANTONIOU
My mother wanted me to marry a rich old man.
ANTISEPTIC RED CROSS CIVILITY AND CLEANLINESS
But if you marry a monkey for his money the money will go away and the monkey will stay the same.
Is that so?
Come. Before you go, you should see the Nebi Daniel Mosque. They say Alexander is buried underneath.
Which Alexander?
The Alexander.
Oh.

"15th April. The ship was proceeding in convoy down The Channel, when..."

Cheer up, Jack! If I'm ever within smelling distance of Johnny Turk again, it'll be a lifetime too soon.

How's that ANZAC song go?

"Land of sand and sweating feet, Gyppo guts and camel meat, Johnny's heaven, Tommy's hell, Land of bastards - fare thee well!"

Something like that

Gabriel, you of all people...

I'm pulling your leg, you ass! Though damned if I know what you see in the place.

Well, it's got Wolverhampton licked.

Besides, Alexandria's hardly Sinai. Did you know Alexander's buried there?

Alexander who?

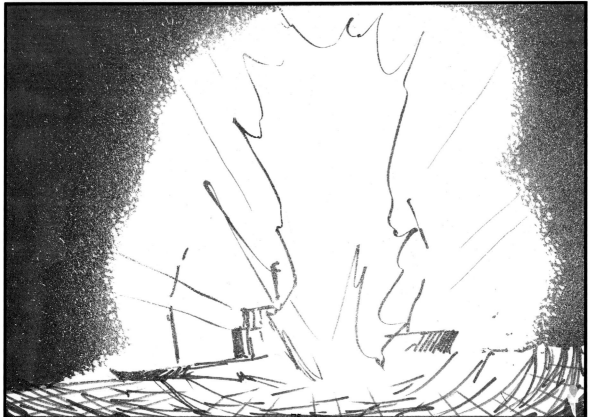

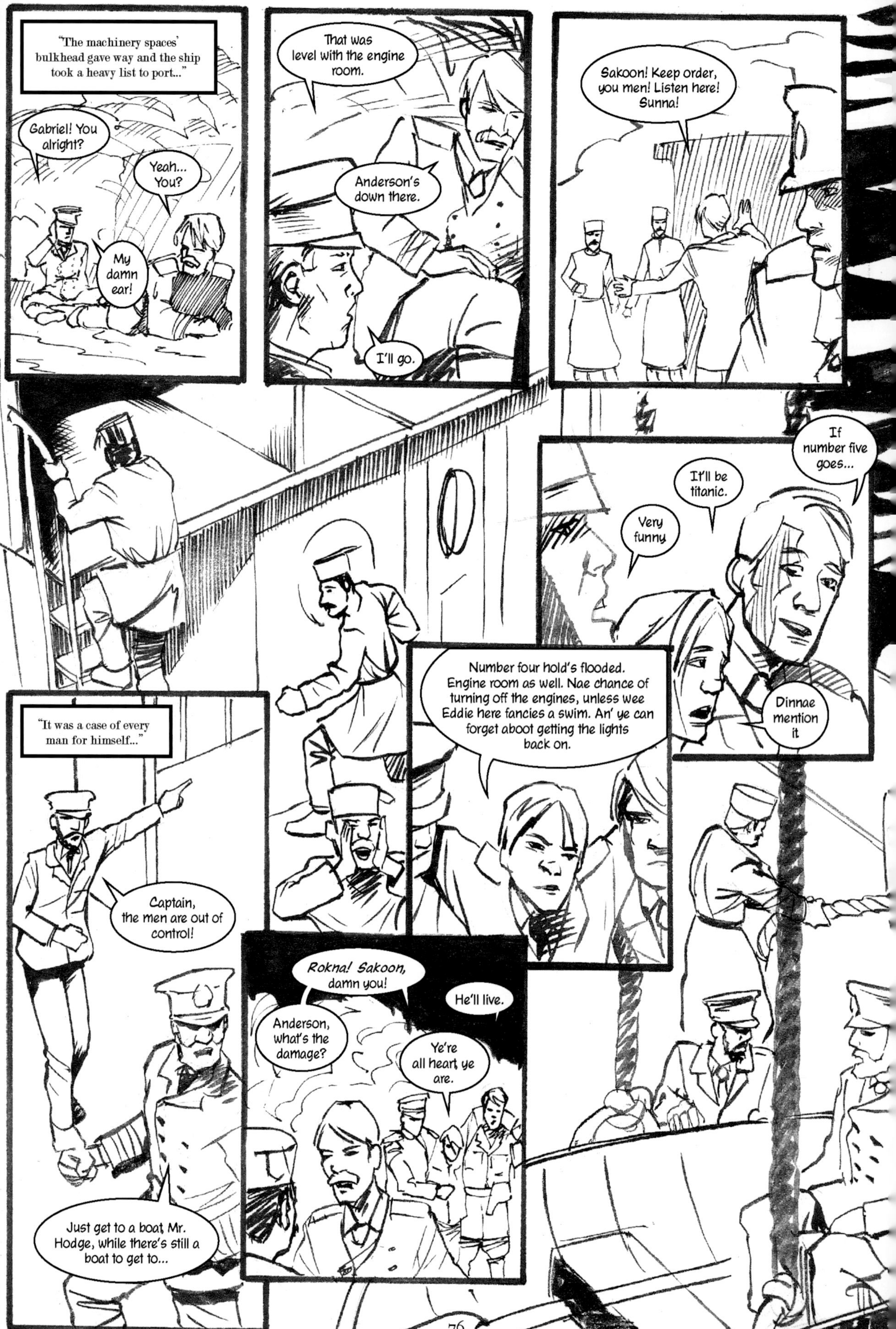

"The machinery spaces' bulkhead gave way and the ship took a heavy list to port..."
Gabriel! You alright?
Yeah... You?
My damn ear!
That was level with the engine room.
Anderson's down there.
I'll go.
Sakoon! Keep order, you men! Listen here! Sunna!
If number five goes...
It'll be titanic.
Very funny
Dinnae mention it
Number four hold's flooded. Engine room as well. Nae chance of turning off the engines, unless wee Eddie here fancies a swim. An' ye can forget aboot getting the lights back on.
"It was a case of every man for himself..."
Captain, the men are out of control!
Just get to a boat, Mr. Hodge, while there's still a boat to get to...
Rokna! Sakoon, damn you!
He'll live.
Anderson, what's the damage?
Ye're all heart, ye are.

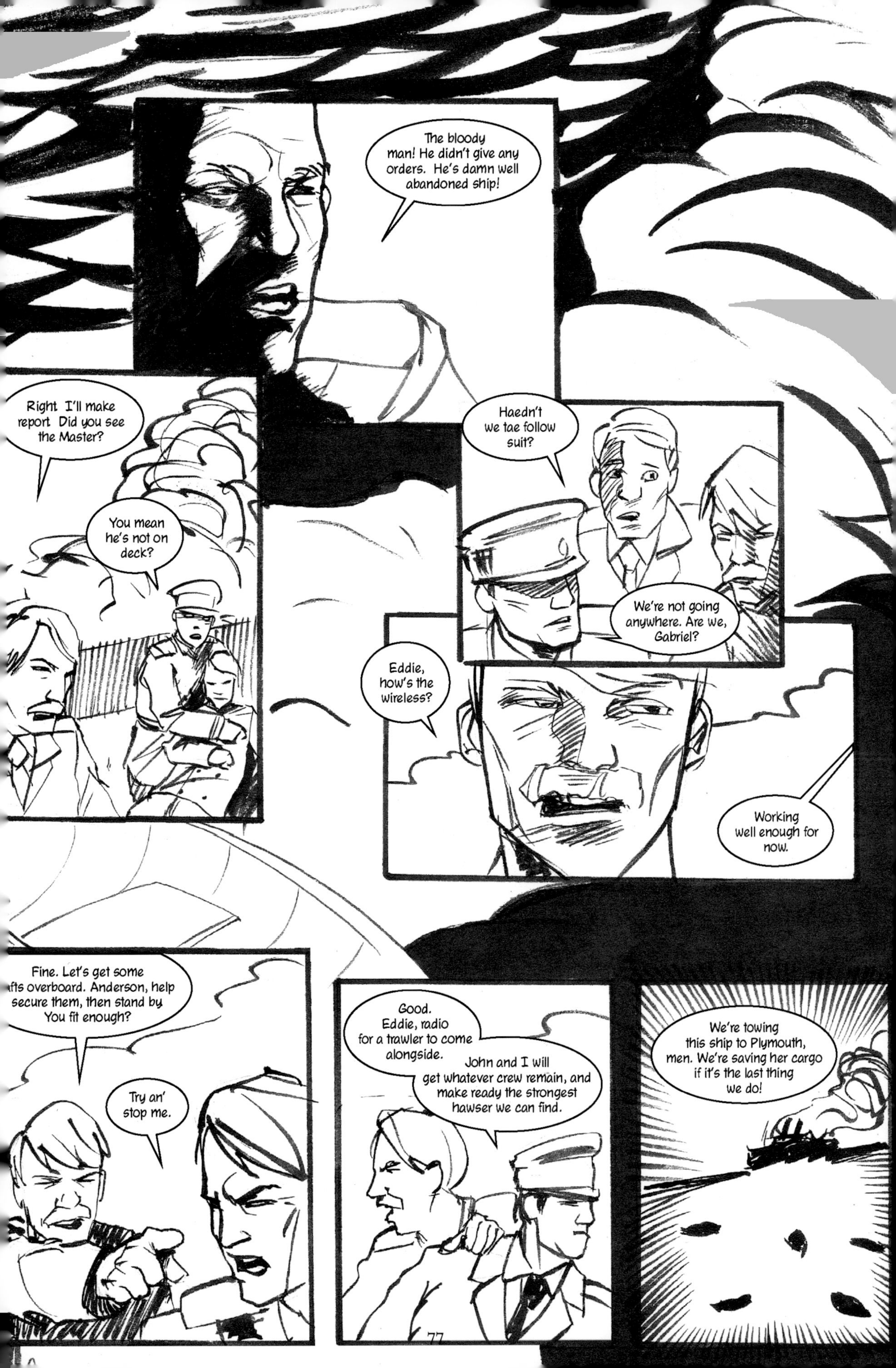
The bloody man! He didn't give any orders. He's damn well abandoned ship!
Right I'll make report Did you see the Master?
You mean he's not on deck?
Haedn't we tae follow suit?
We're not going anywhere. Are we, Gabriel?
Eddie, how's the wireless?
Working well enough for now.
Fine. Let's get some afts overboard. Anderson, help secure them, then stand by You fit enough?
Try an' stop me.
Good. Eddie, radio for a trawler to come alongside.
John and I will get whatever crew remain, and make ready the strongest hawser we can find.
We're towing this ship to Plymouth, men. We're saving her cargo if it's the last thing we do!

"Sixty survivors from S.S. Penfold were picked up from the boats."

"At 10.30pm the trawler Tom Adams came to their aid."

"With the salvage crew onboard, S.S. Penfold was brought safely into Plymouth about midnight."

"It is stated that on returning the following morning..."

"...the Officers found their cabins had been looted..."

Gabriel!

I know. Mine too.

"...locks having been broken on trunks and boxes, and personal effects removed."

Allegations of this kind are made on practically every occasion when an abandoned vessel is brought into port by the exertions of His Majesty's salvage vessels.

MERCAN MARINE S.S. PEN ALLEGATIONS OF LOOTING.

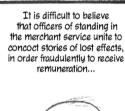

It is difficult to believe that officers of standing in the merchant service unite to concoct stories of lost effects, in order fraudulently to receive remuneration...

But there is simply no evidence on which compensation can be made.

As for the Master, the Committee consider his conduct to be highly unsatisfactory

However, in view of the fact that he has no intention of proceeding to sea again, it has been decided that no further action is necessary.

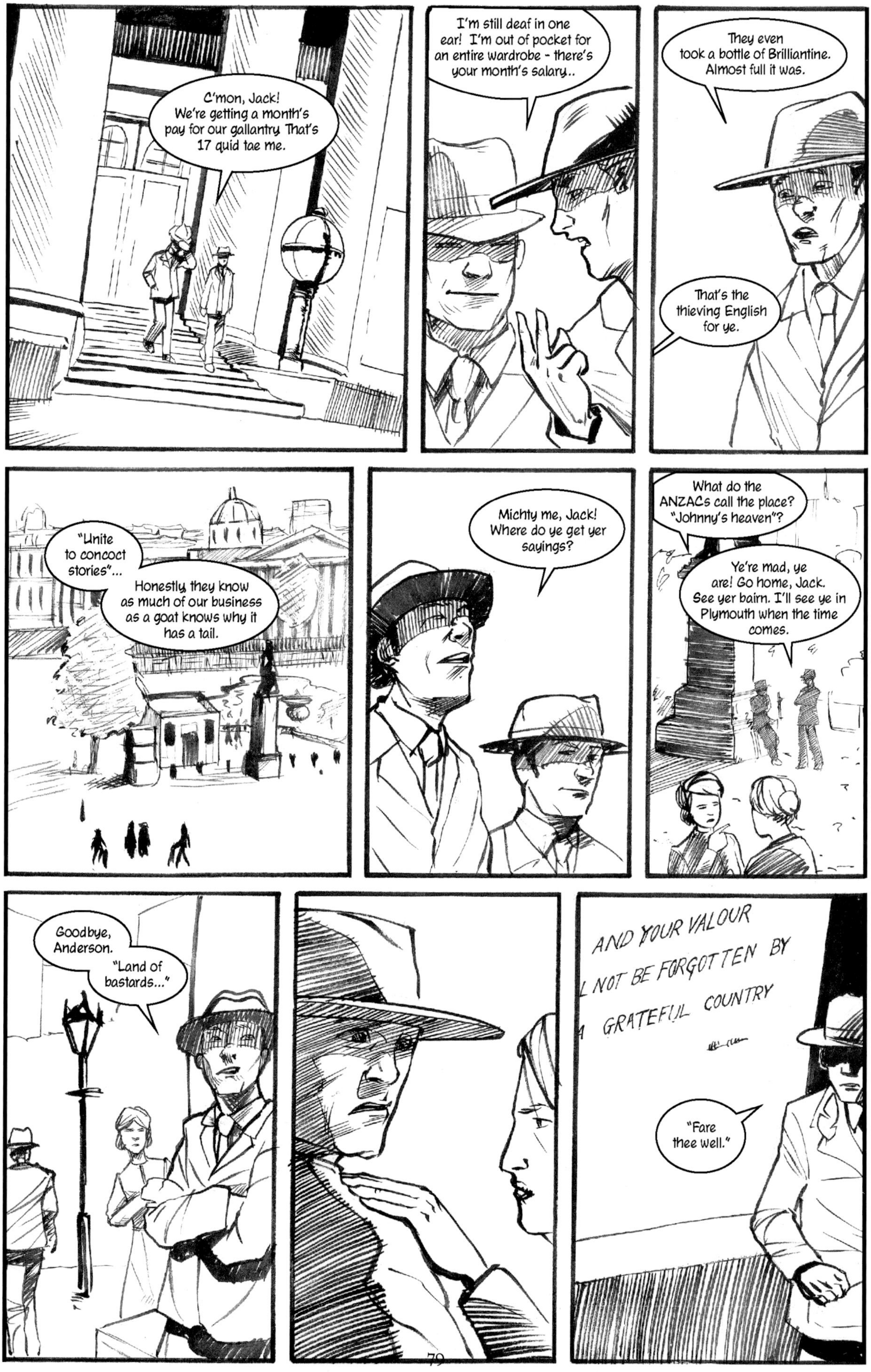
C'mon, Jack! We're getting a month's pay for our gallantry That's 17 quid tae me.
I'm still deaf in one ear! I'm out of pocket for an entire wardrobe - there's your month's salary..
They even took a bottle of Brilliantine. Almost full it was.
That's the thieving English for ye.
"Unite to concoct stories"...
Honestly they know as much of our business as a goat knows why it has a tail.
Michty me, Jack! Where do ye get yer sayings?
What do the ANZACs call the place? "Johnny's heaven"?
Ye're mad, ye are! Go home, Jack. See yer bairn. I'll see ye in Plymouth when the time comes.
Goodbye, Anderson.
"Land of bastards..."
AND YOUR VALOUR
L NOT BE FORGOTTEN BY
A GRATEFUL COUNTRY
"Fare thee well."

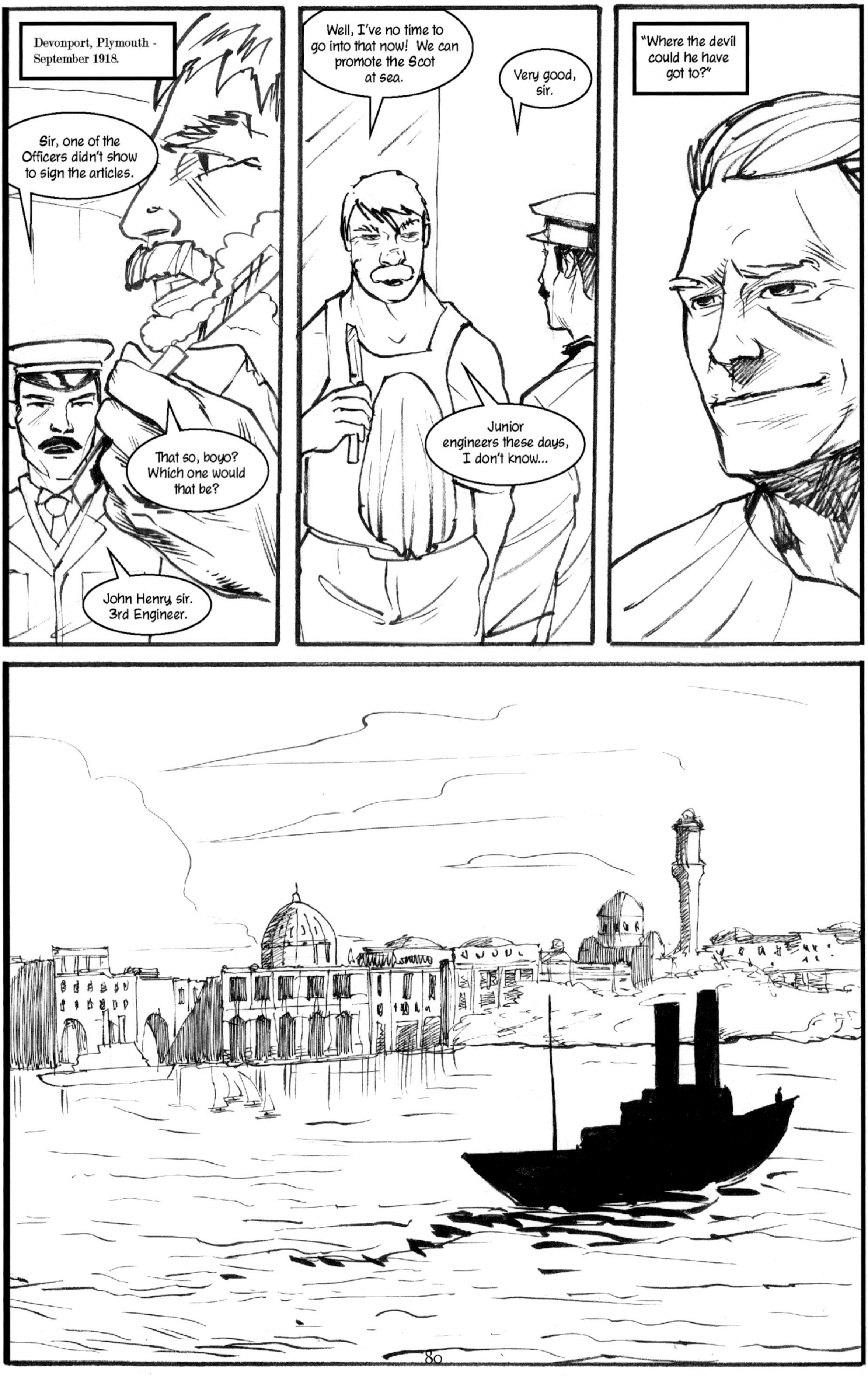
Devonport, Plymouth - September 1918.
Sir, one of the Officers didn't show to sign the articles.
That so, boyo? Which one would that be?
John Henry, sir. 3rd Engineer.
Well, I've no time to go into that now! We can promote the Scot at sea.
Very good, sir.
Junior engineers these days, I don't know...
"Where the devil could he have got to?"

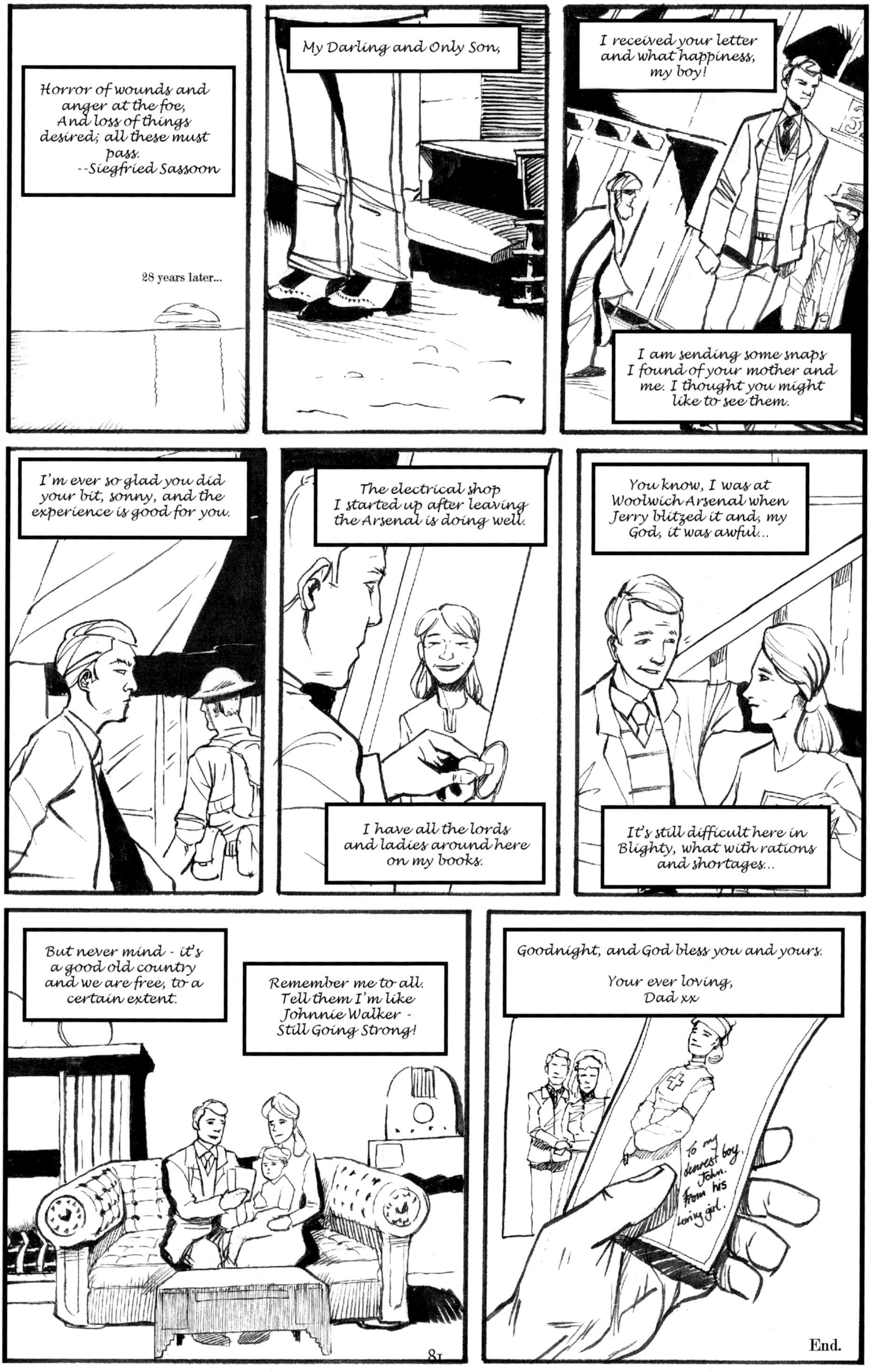
Horror of wounds and anger at the foe,
And loss of things desired; all these must pass.
--Siegfried Sassoon
28 years later...
My Darling and Only Son,
I received your letter and what happiness, my boy!
I am sending some snaps I found of your mother and me. I thought you might like to see them.
I'm ever so glad you did your bit, sonny, and the experience is good for you.
The electrical shop I started up after leaving the Arsenal is doing well.
I have all the lords and ladies around here on my books.
You know, I was at Woolwich Arsenal when Jerry blitzed it and, my God, it was awful...
It's still difficult here in Blighty, what with rations and shortages...
But never mind - it's a good old country and we are free, to a certain extent.
Remember me to all. Tell them I'm like Johnnie Walker - Still Going Strong!
Goodnight, and God bless you and yours.
Your ever loving,
Dad xx
To my dearest boy, John. From his loving girl.
End.

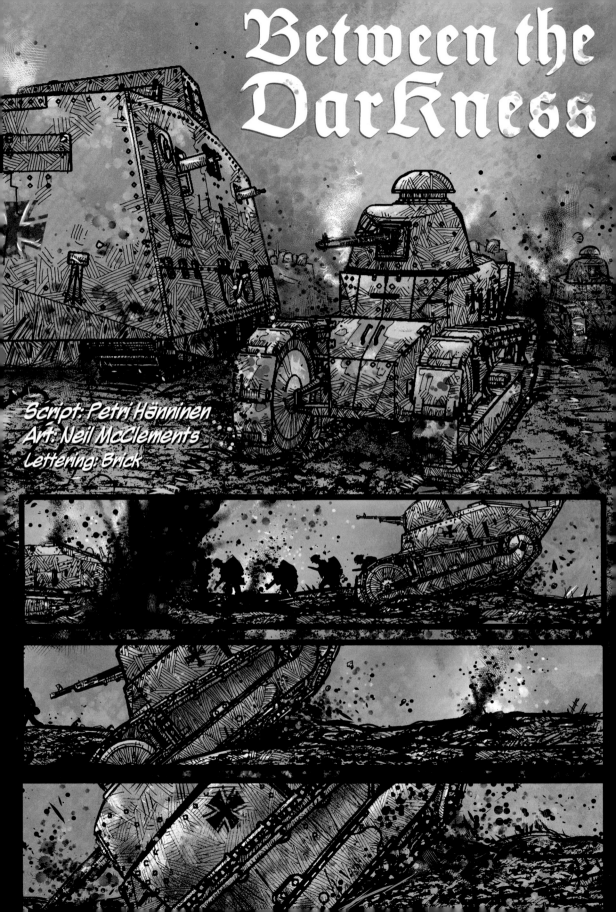

Between the Darkness

Script: Petri Hänninen
Art: Neil McClements
Lettering: Brick

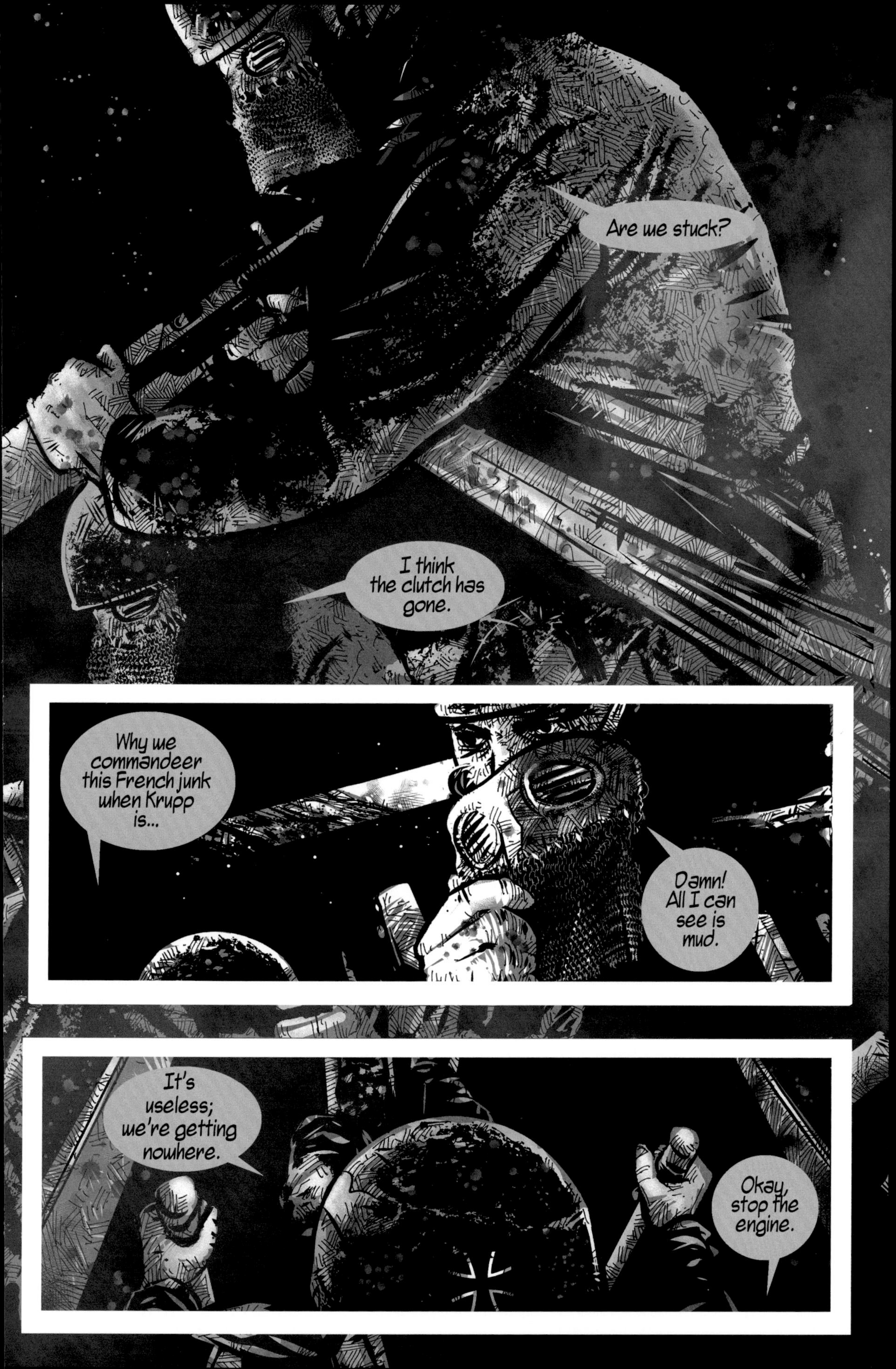
Are we stuck?
I think the clutch has gone.
Why we commandeer this French junk when Krupp is...
Damn! All I can see is mud.
It's useless; we're getting nowhere.
Okay, stop the engine.

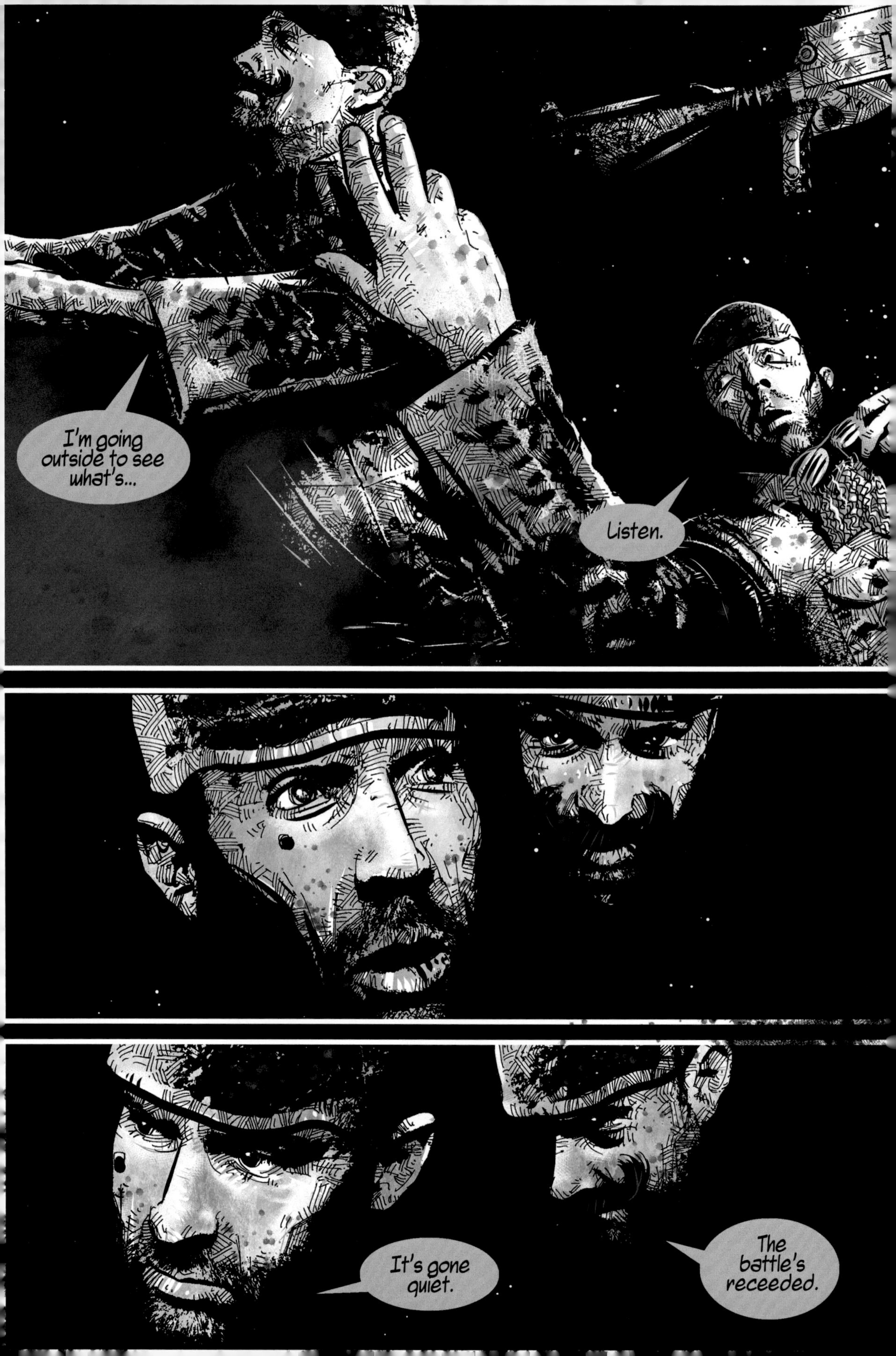
I'm going outside to see what's...
Listen.
It's gone quiet.
The battle's receeded.

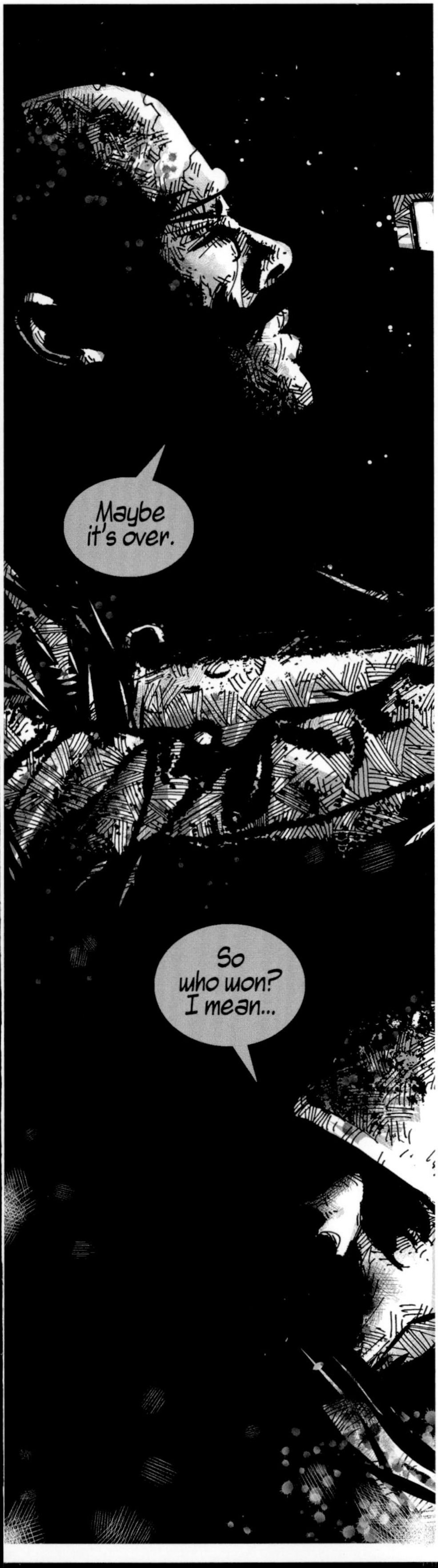
Maybe it's over.
So who won? I mean...

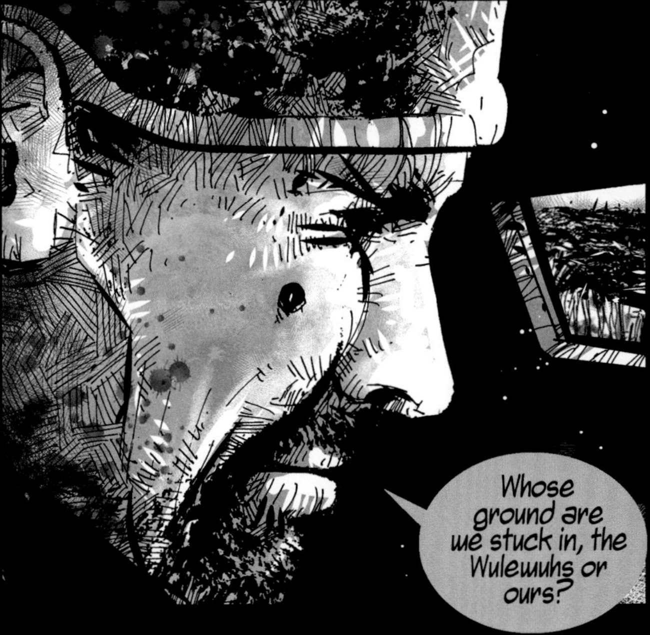
Whose ground are we stuck in, the Wulewuhs or ours?

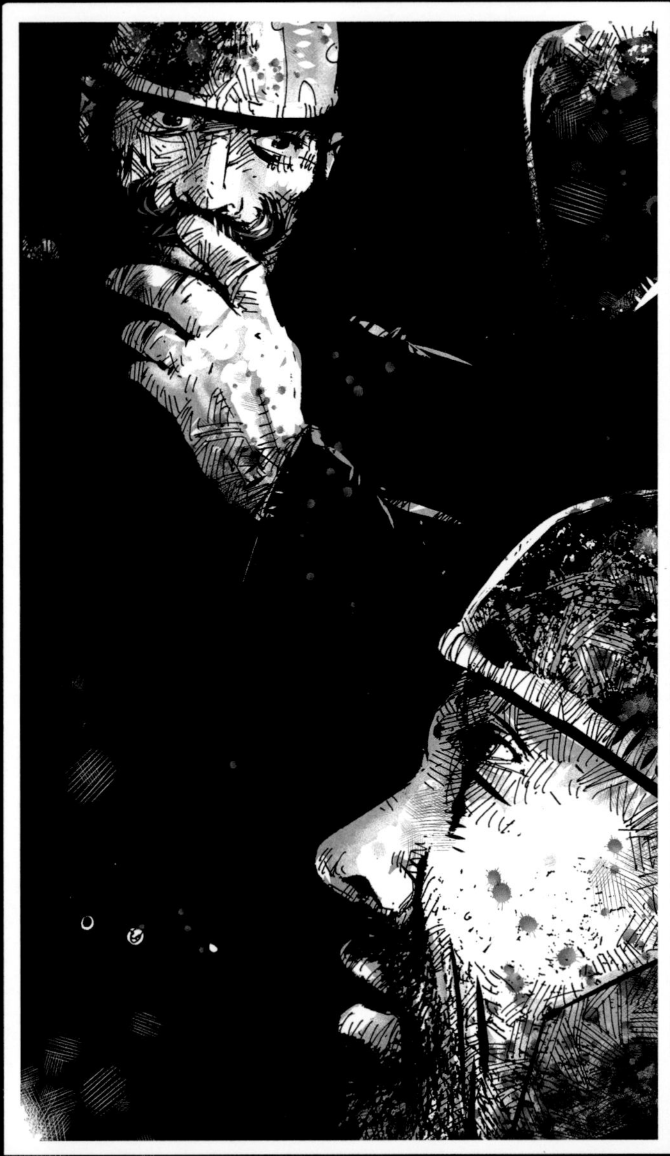

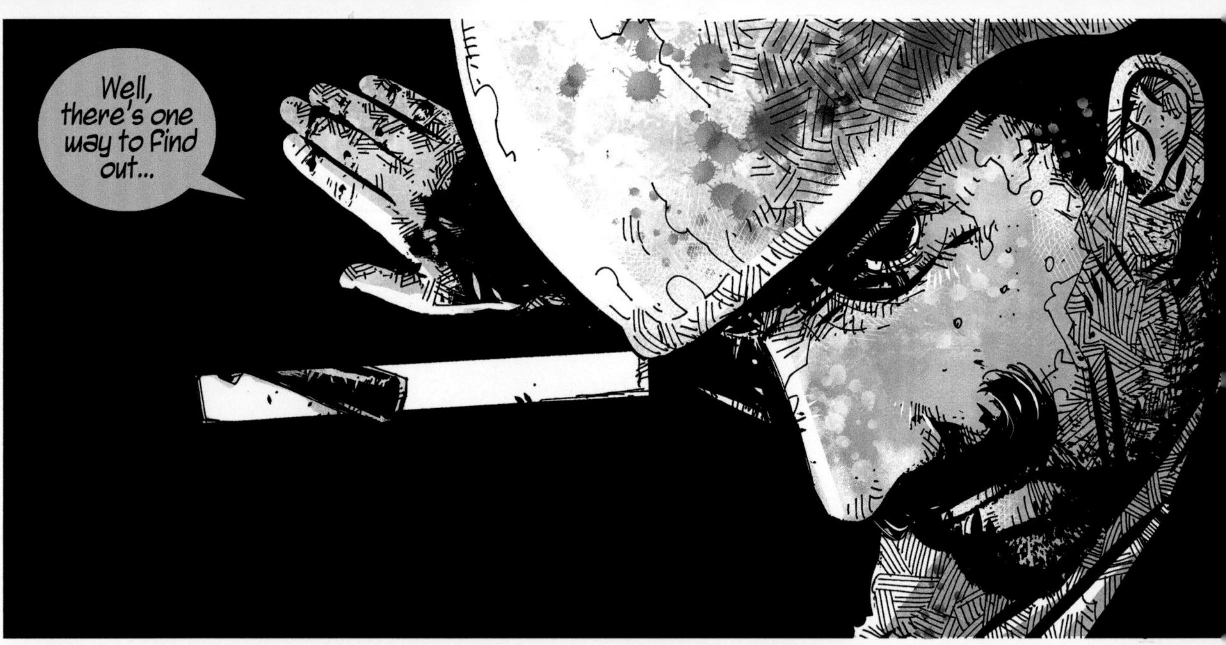
Well, there's one way to find out...

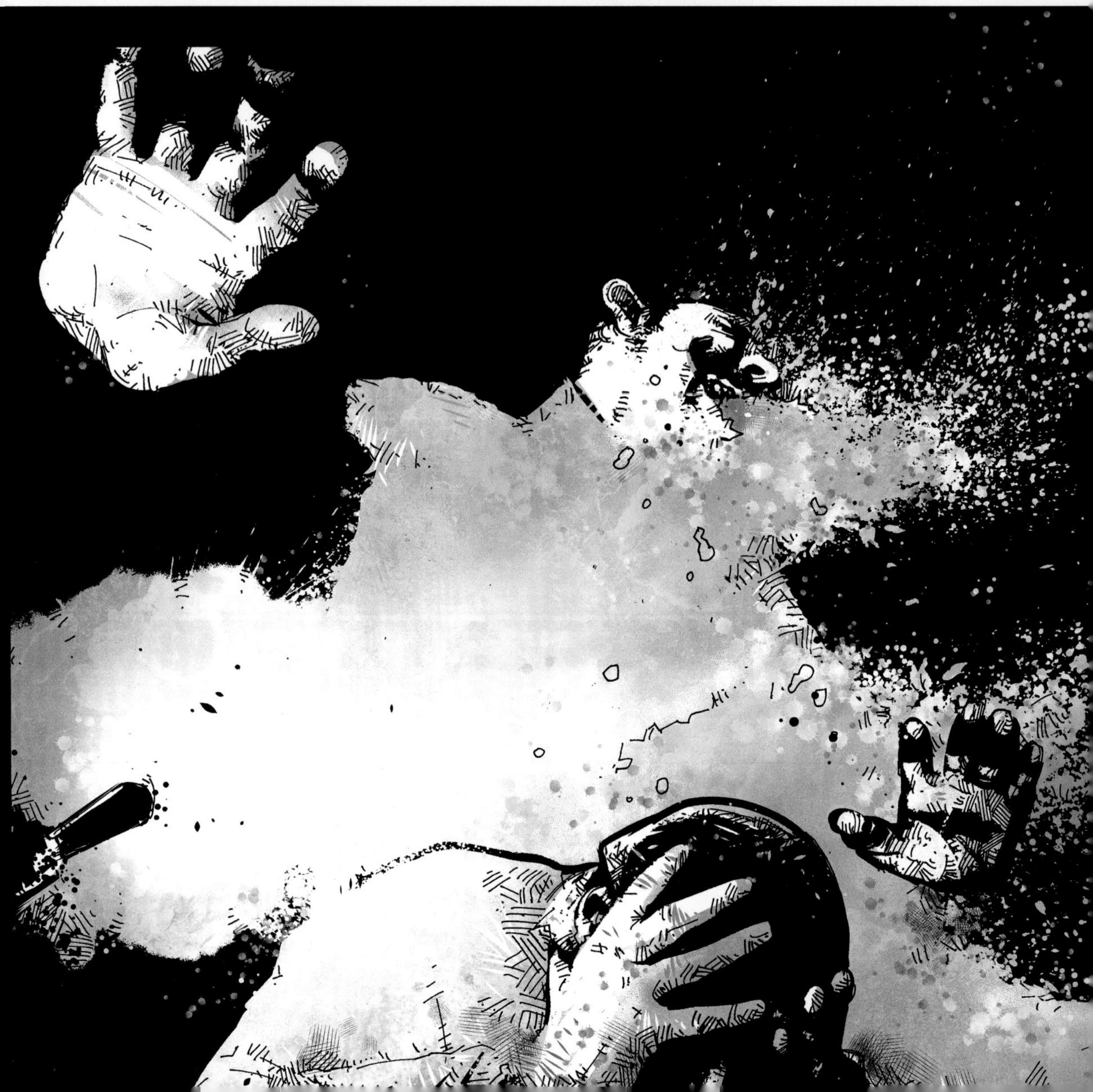

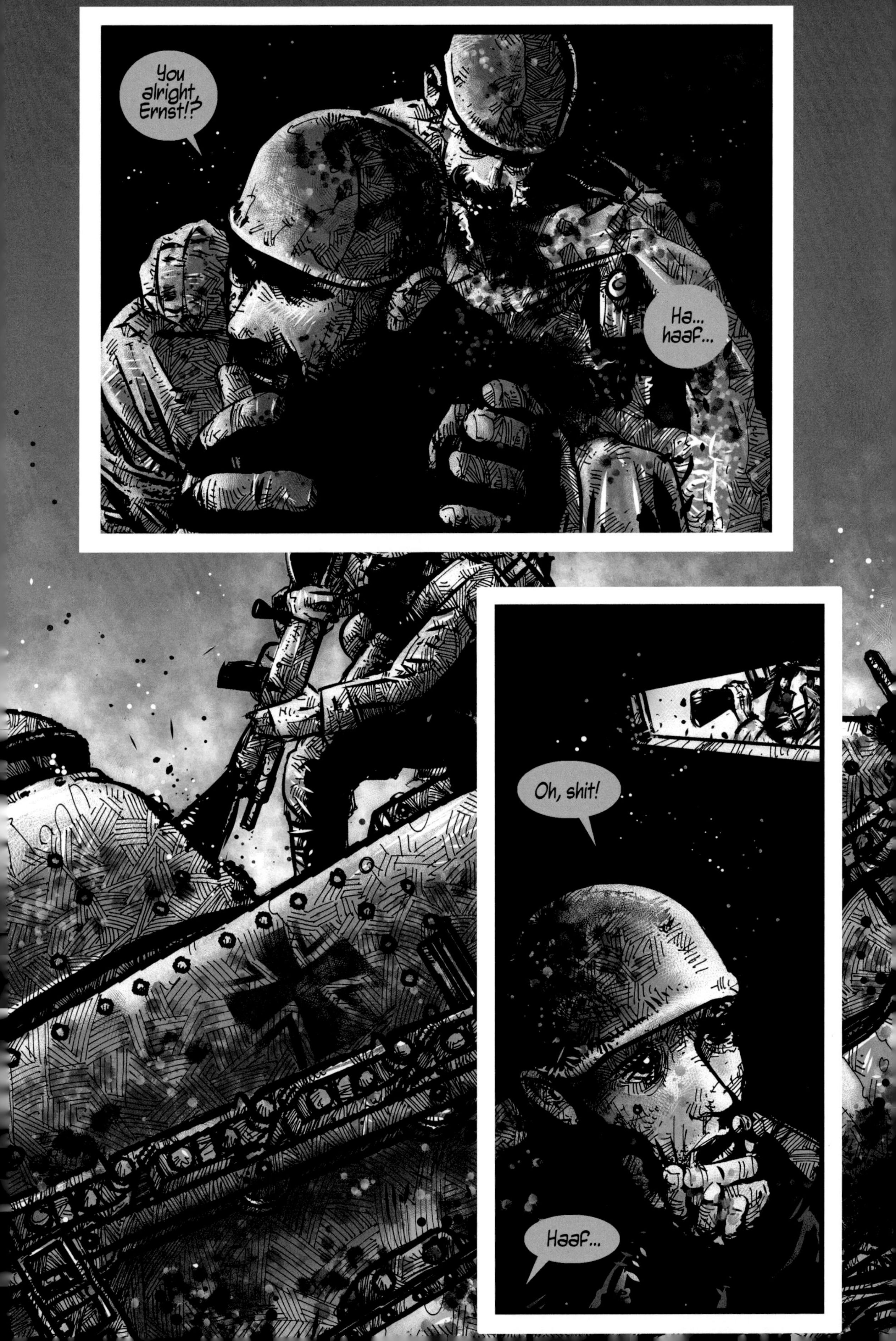

You alright, Ernst!?
Ha... haaf...
Oh, shit!
Haaf...

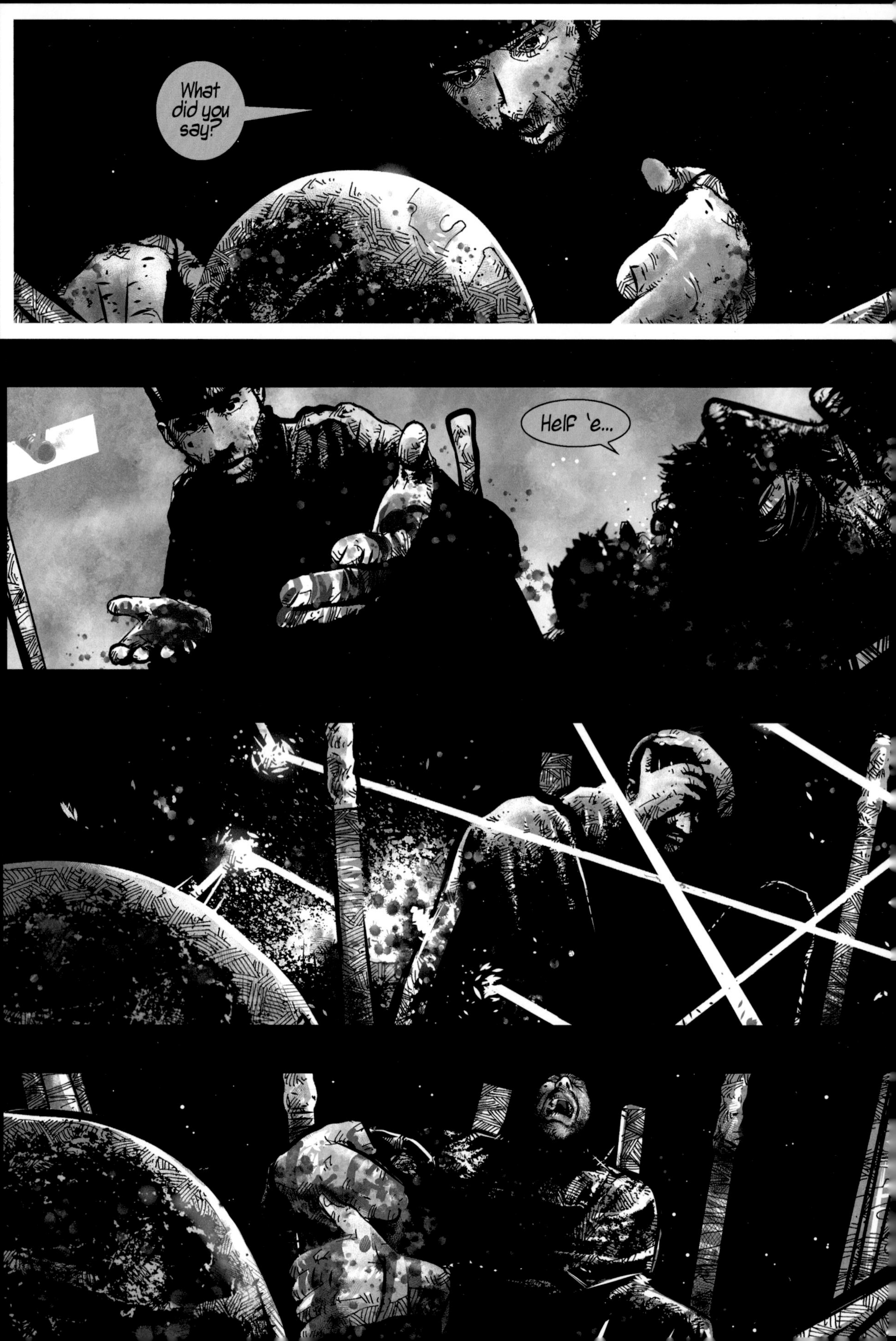
What did you say?
Helf 'e...

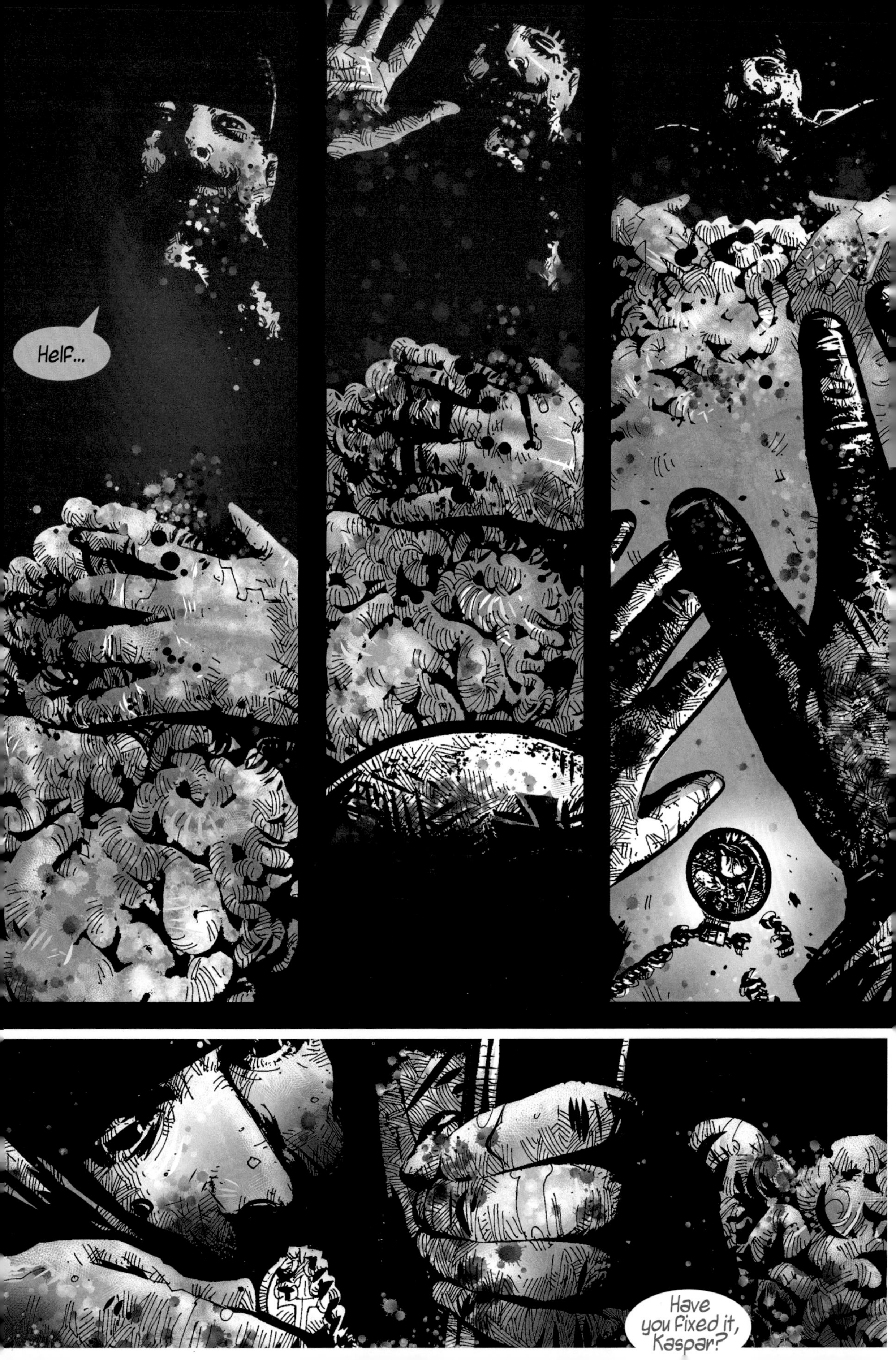
Helf...
Have you fixed it, Kaspar?

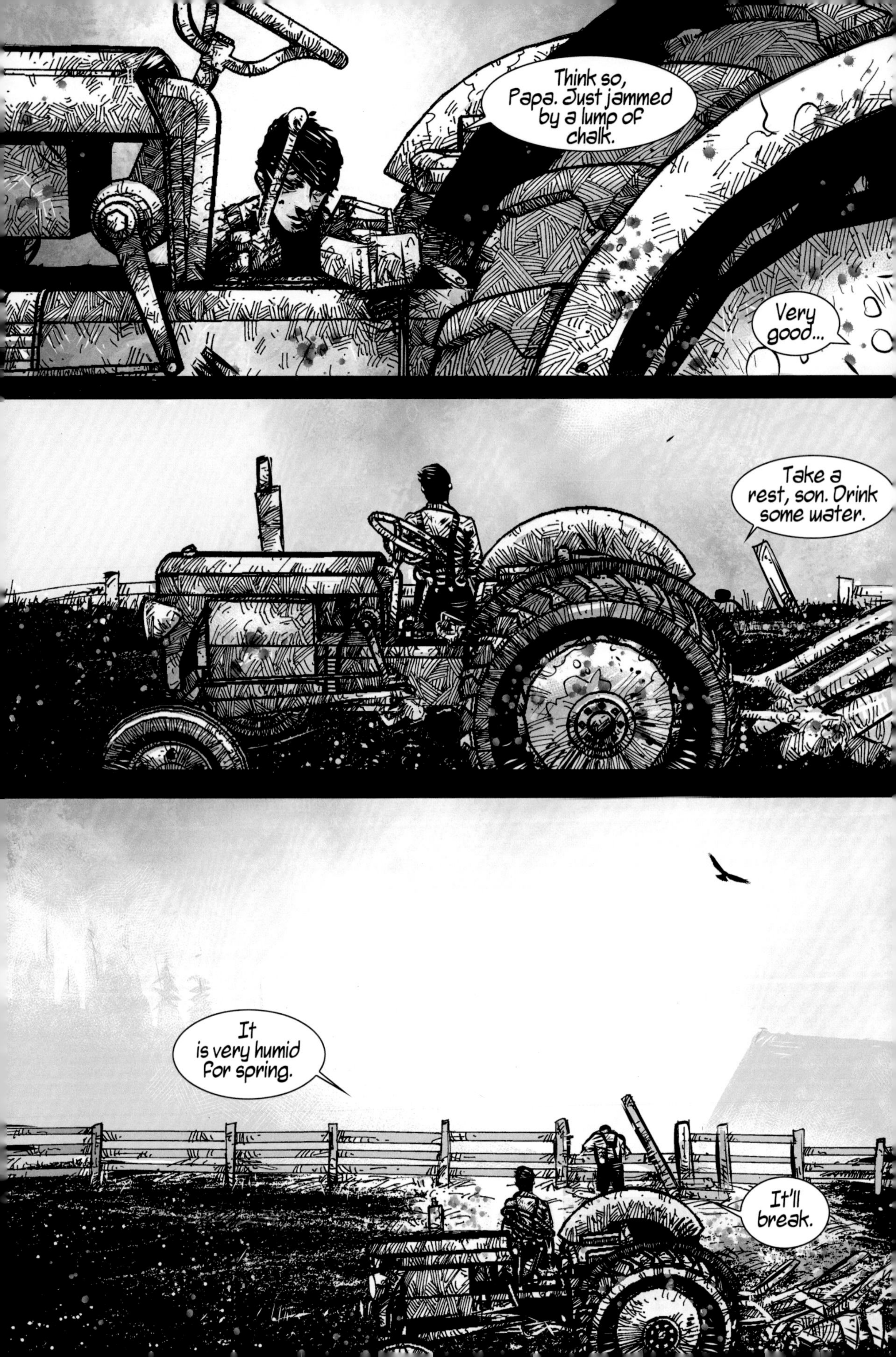
Think so, Papa. Just jammed by a lump of chalk.
Very good...
Take a rest, son. Drink some water.
It is very humid for spring.
It'll break.

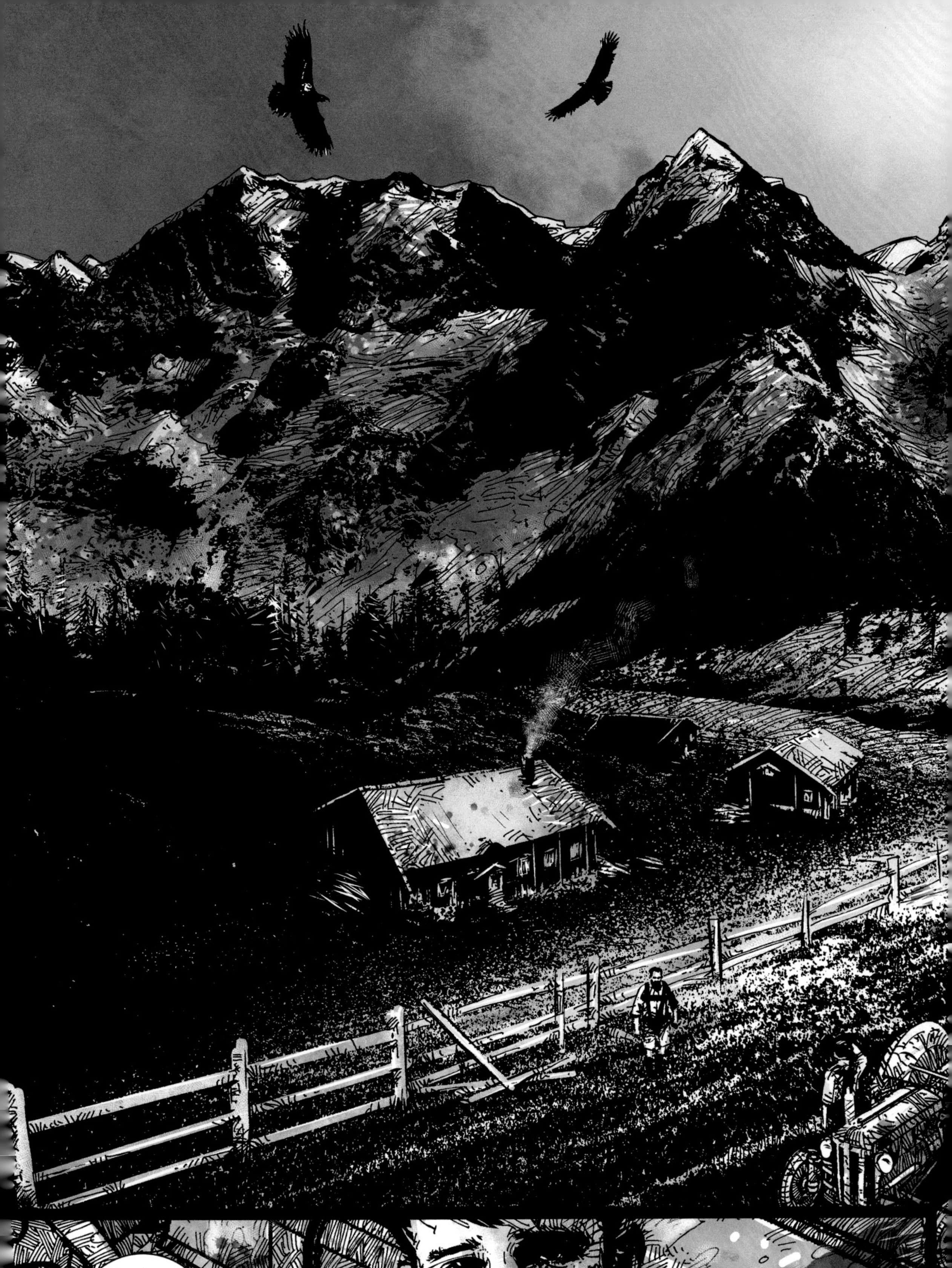

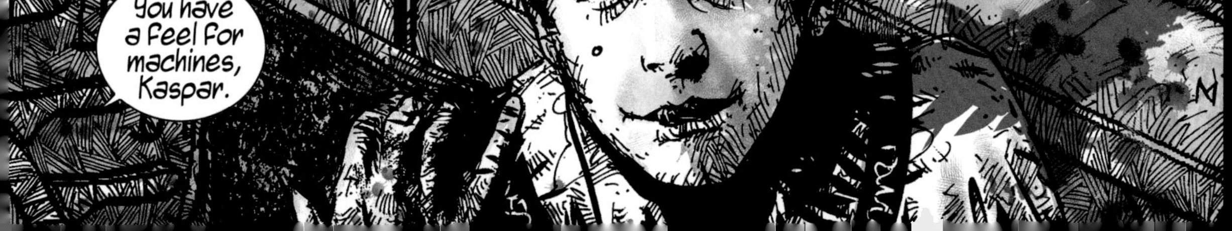
You have a feel for machines, Kaspar.

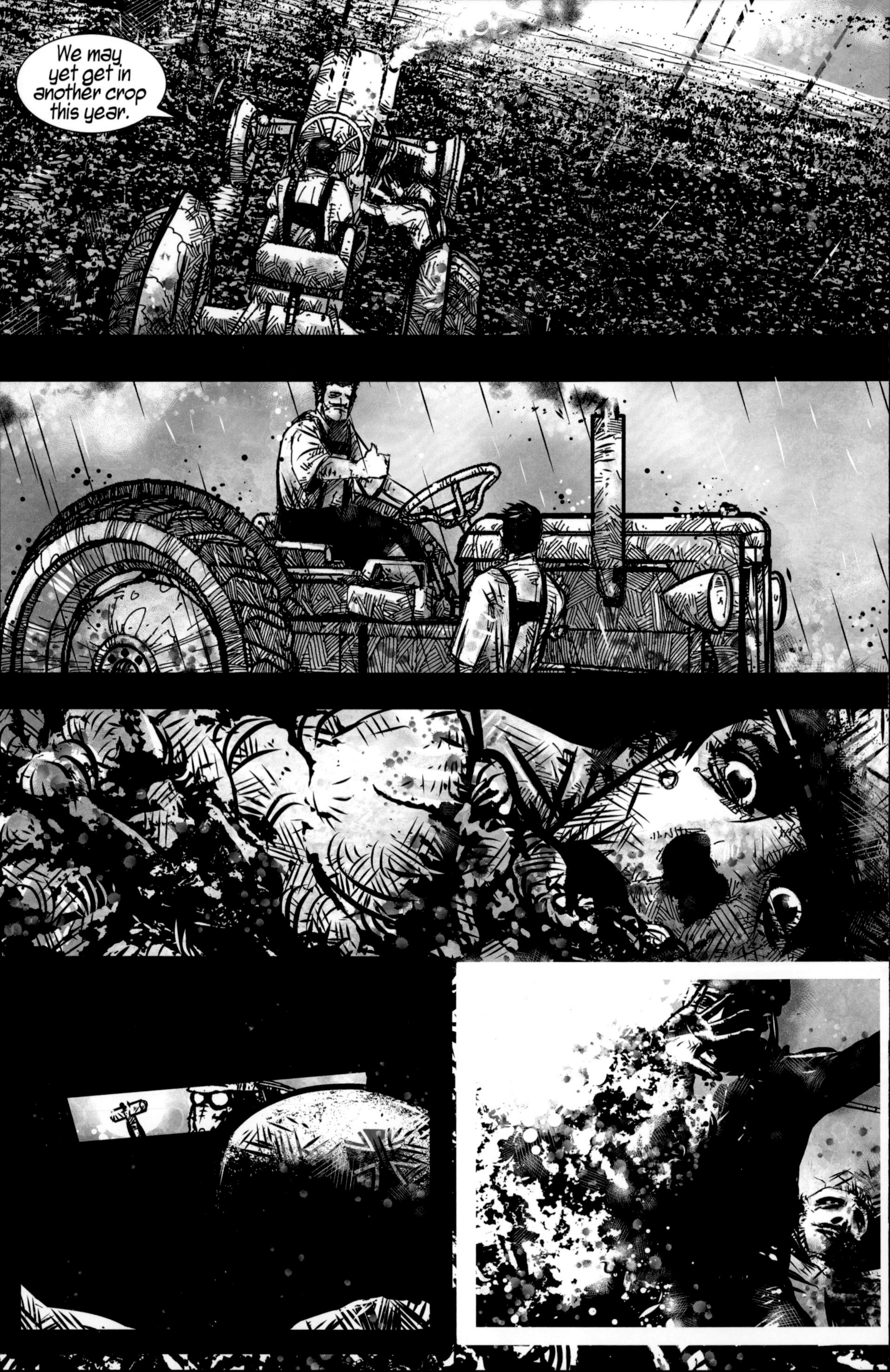
We may yet get in another crop this year.

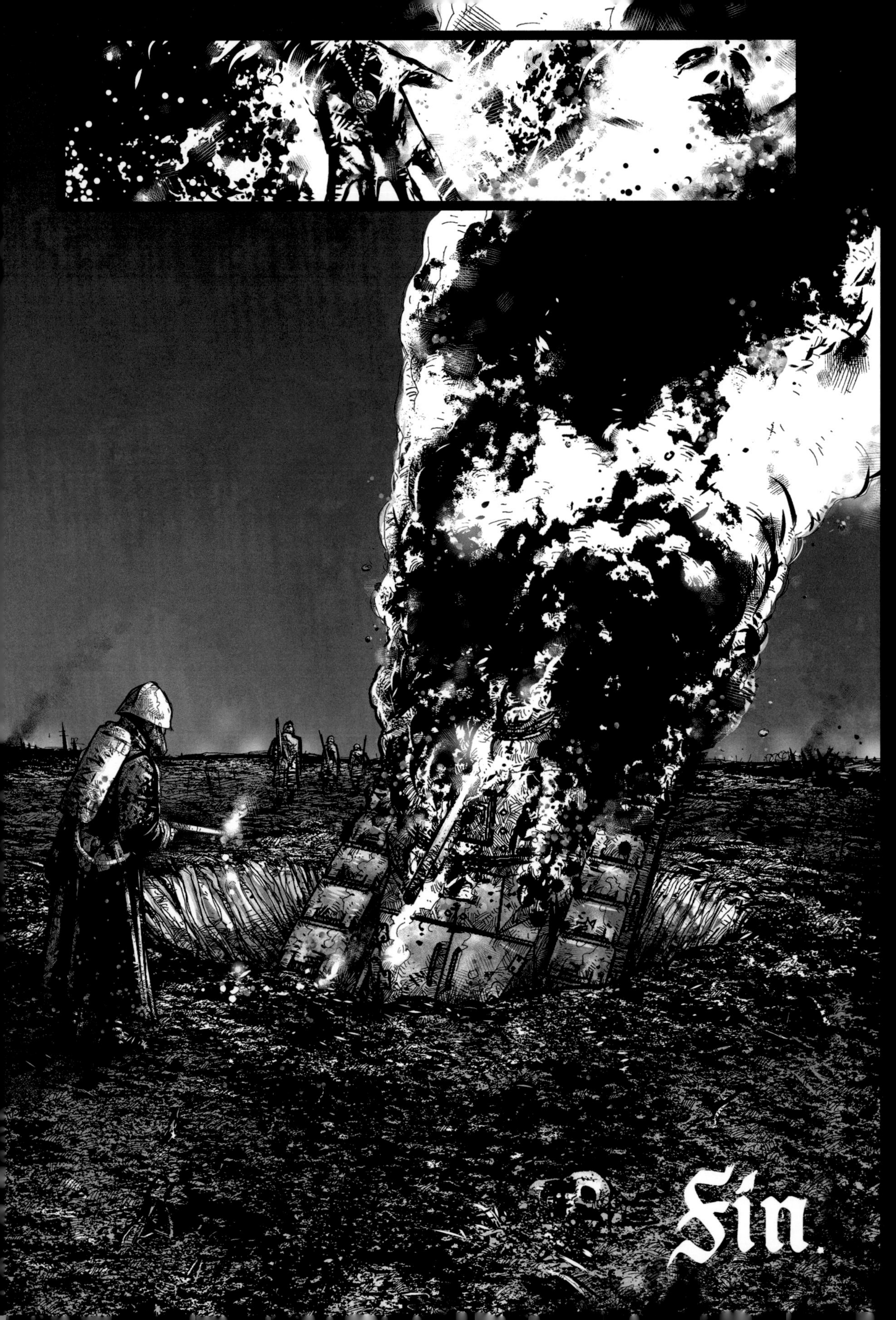
Fin.

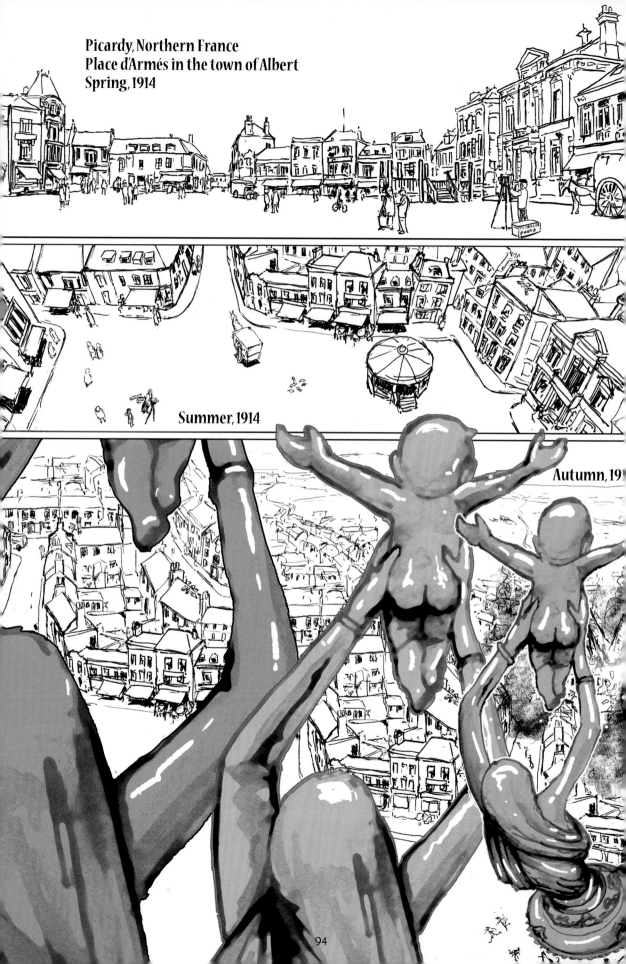

Picardy, Northern France
Place d'Armés in the town of Albert
Spring, 1914

Summer, 1914

Autumn, 19[

94

Three miles north-east of Albert

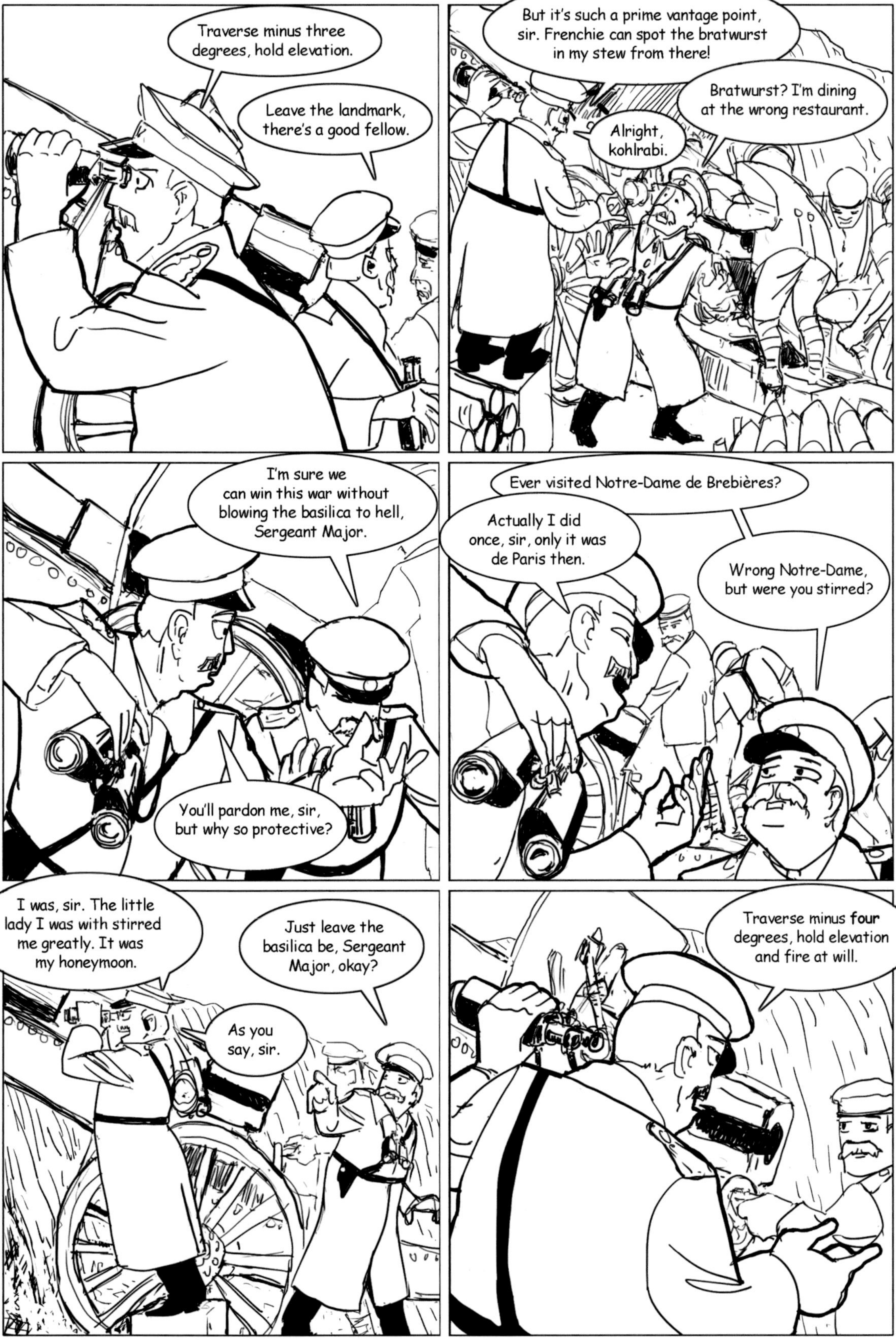
Traverse minus three degrees, hold elevation.
Leave the landmark, there's a good fellow.
But it's such a prime vantage point, sir. Frenchie can spot the bratwurst in my stew from there!
Alright, kohlrabi.
Bratwurst? I'm dining at the wrong restaurant.
I'm sure we can win this war without blowing the basilica to hell, Sergeant Major.
You'll pardon me, sir, but why so protective?
Ever visited Notre-Dame de Brebières?
Actually I did once, sir, only it was de Paris then.
Wrong Notre-Dame, but were you stirred?
I was, sir. The little lady I was with stirred me greatly. It was my honeymoon.
Just leave the basilica be, Sergeant Major, okay?
As you say, sir.
Traverse minus **four** degrees, hold elevation and fire at will.

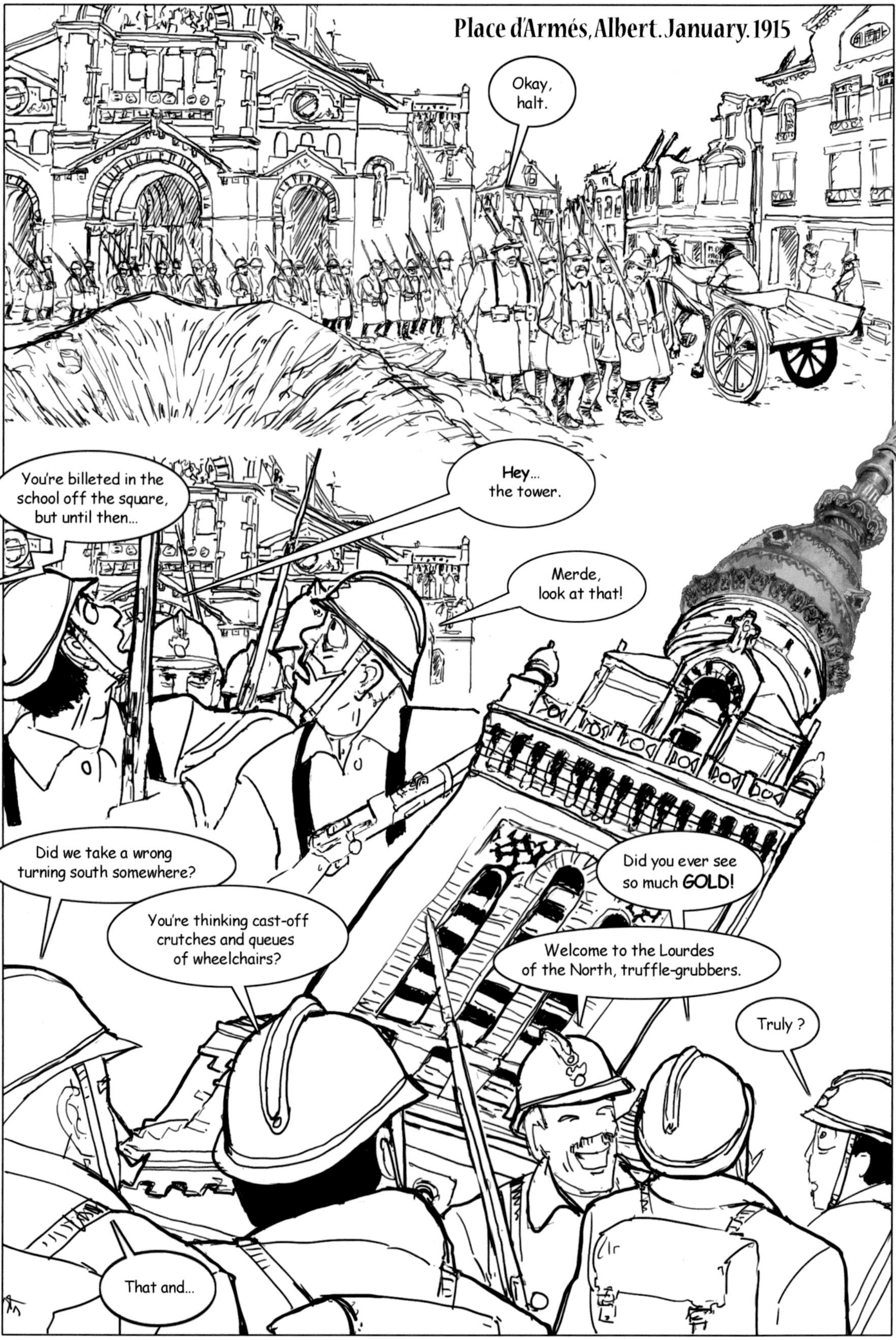
Place d'Armés, Albert. January. 1915
Okay, halt.
You're billeted in the school off the square, but until then...
Hey... the tower.
Merde, look at that!
Did we take a wrong turning south somewhere?
Did you ever see so much GOLD!
You're thinking cast-off crutches and queues of wheelchairs?
Welcome to the Lourdes of the North, truffle-grubbers.
Truly ?
That and...

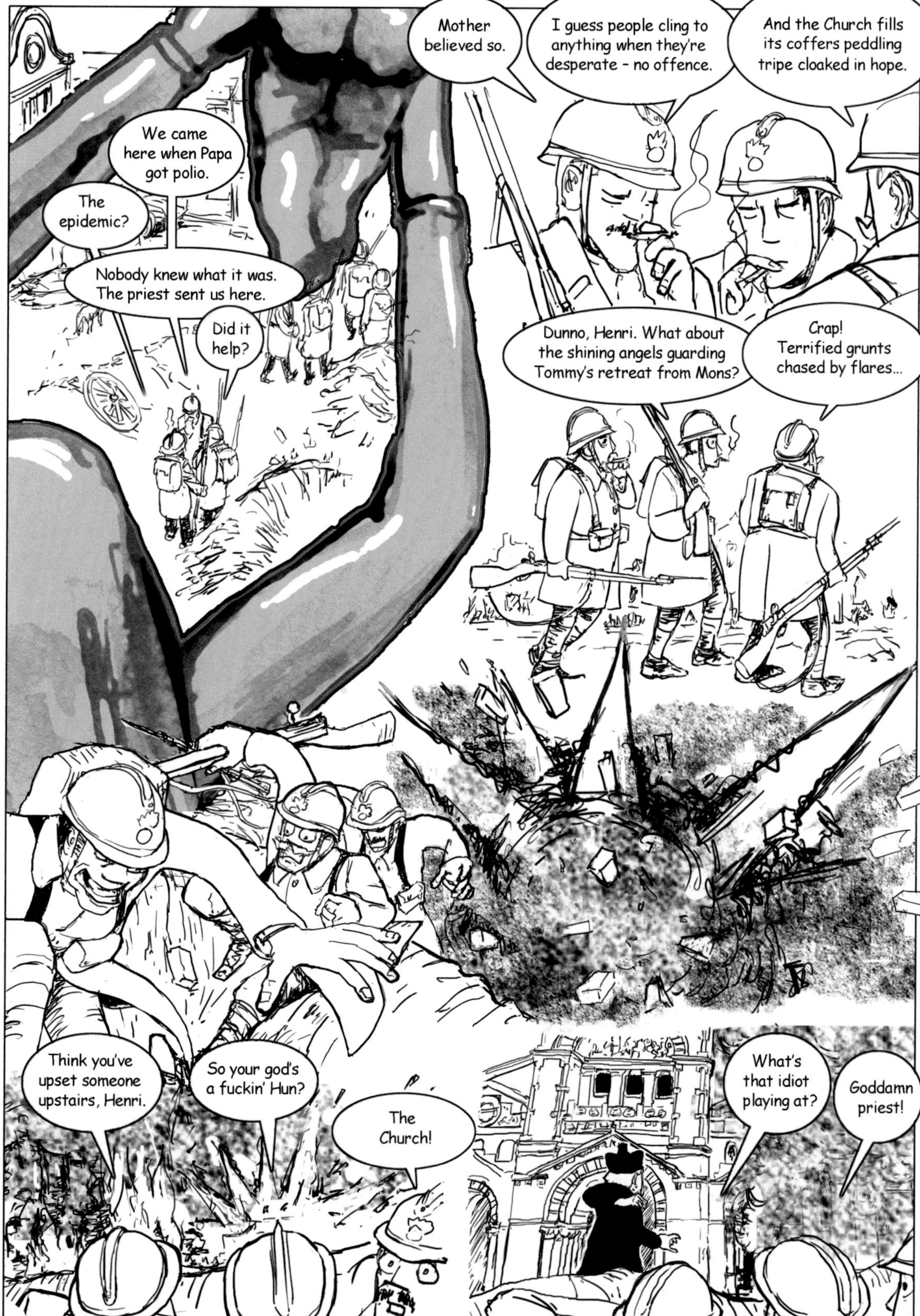

We came here when Papa got polio.
The epidemic?
Nobody knew what it was. The priest sent us here.
Did it help?
Mother believed so.
I guess people cling to anything when they're desperate – no offence.
And the Church fills its coffers peddling tripe cloaked in hope.
Dunno, Henri. What about the shining angels guarding Tommy's retreat from Mons?
Crap! Terrified grunts chased by flares...
Think you've upset someone upstairs, Henri.
So your god's a fuckin' Hun?
The Church!
What's that idiot playing at?
Goddamn priest!

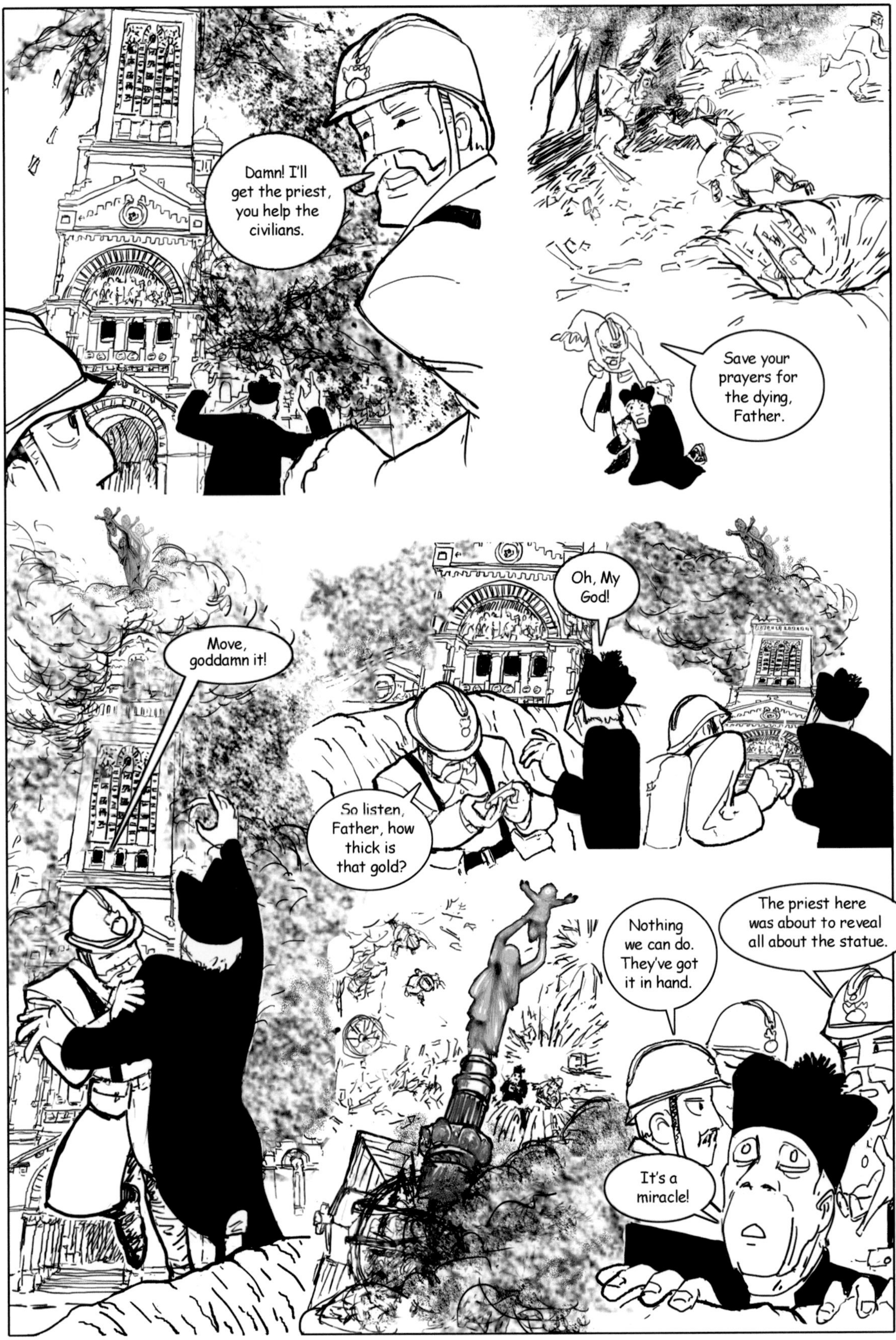
Damn! I'll get the priest, you help the civilians.
Save your prayers for the dying, Father.
Move, goddamn it!
Oh, My God!
So listen, Father, how thick is that gold?
Nothing we can do. They've got it in hand.
The priest here was about to reveal all about the statue.
It's a miracle!

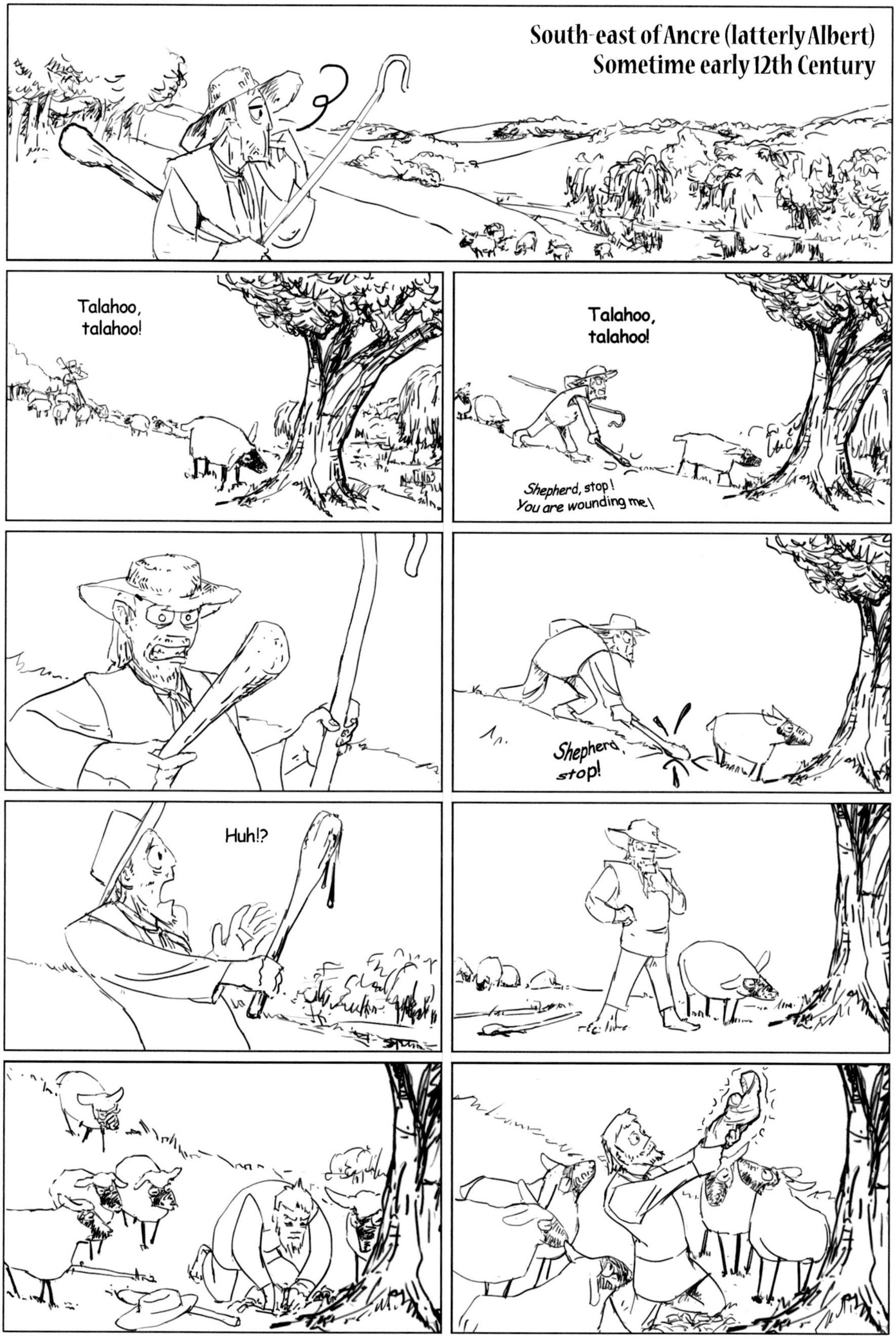
South-east of Ancre (latterly Albert)
Sometime early 12th Century
Talahoo, talahoo!
Talahoo, talahoo!
Shepherd, stop! You are wounding me!
Shepherd, stop!
Huh!?

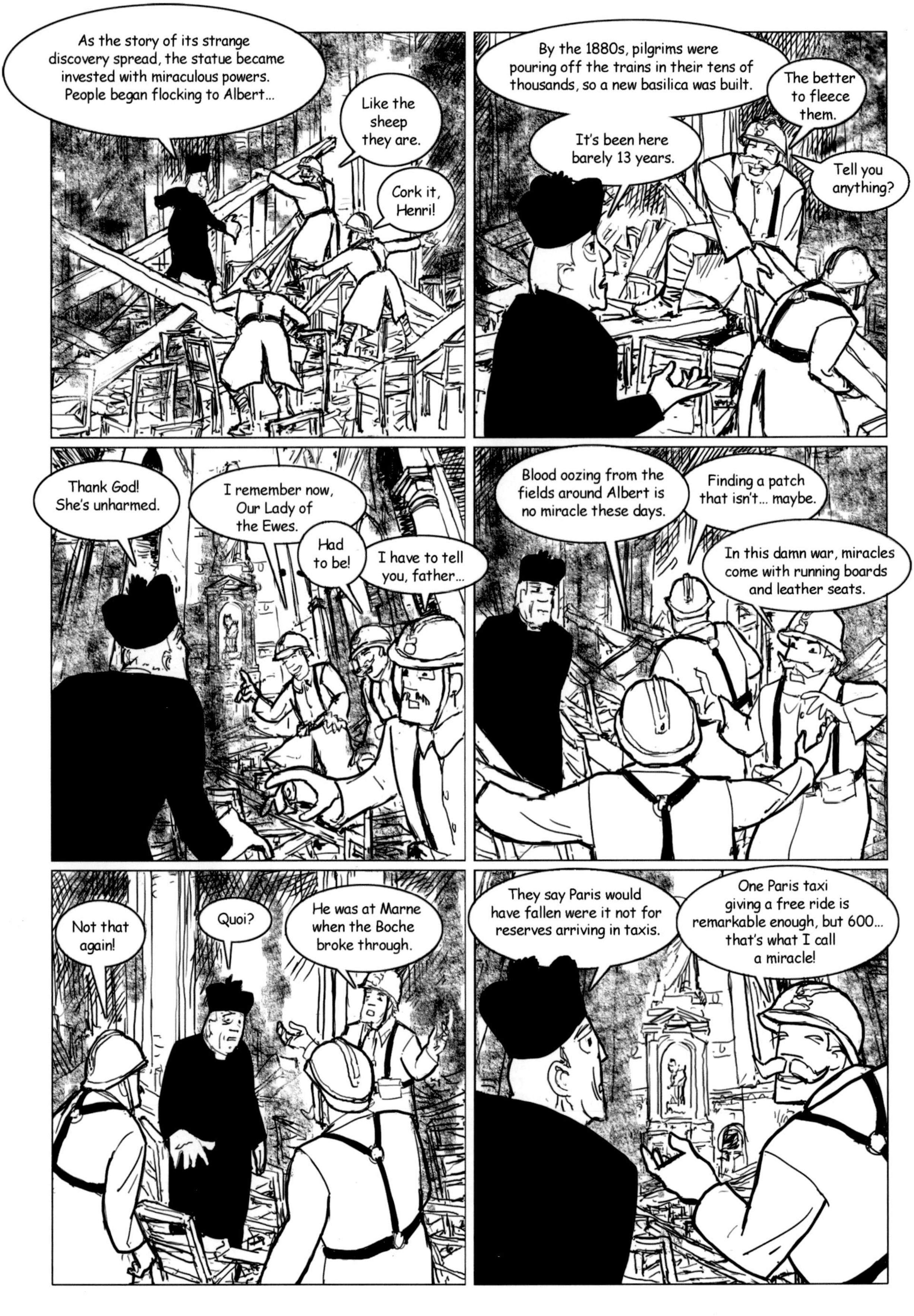
As the story of its strange discovery spread, the statue became invested with miraculous powers. People began flocking to Albert...
Like the sheep they are.
Cork it, Henri!
By the 1880s, pilgrims were pouring off the trains in their tens of thousands, so a new basilica was built.
The better to fleece them.
It's been here barely 13 years.
Tell you anything?
Thank God! She's unharmed.
I remember now, Our Lady of the Ewes.
Had to be!
I have to tell you, father...
Blood oozing from the fields around Albert is no miracle these days.
Finding a patch that isn't... maybe.
In this damn war, miracles come with running boards and leather seats.
Not that again!
Quoi?
He was at Marne when the Boche broke through.
They say Paris would have fallen were it not for reserves arriving in taxis.
One Paris taxi giving a free ride is remarkable enough, but 600... that's what I call a miracle!

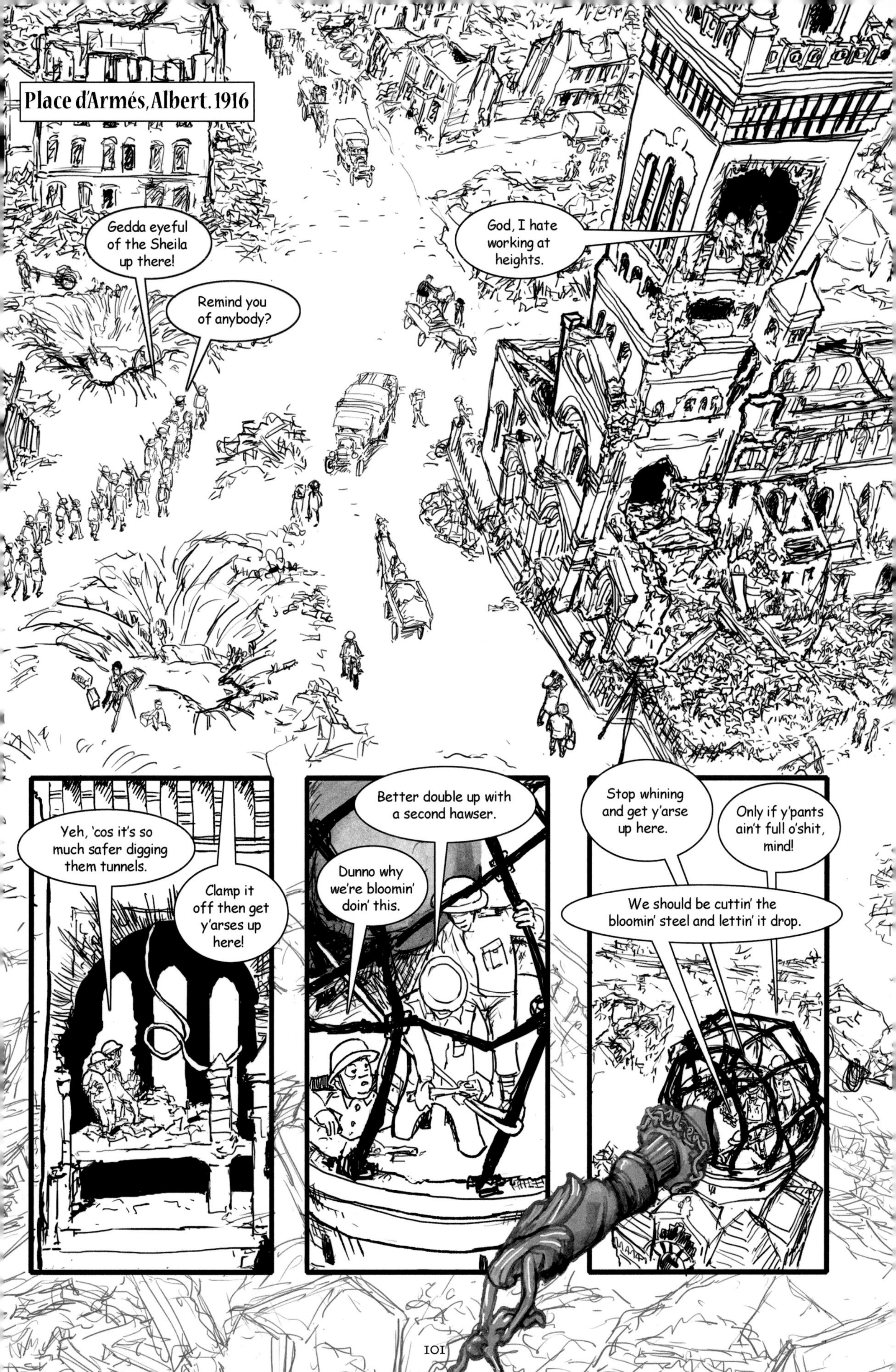
Place d'Armés, Albert. 1916
Gedda eyeful of the Sheila up there!
Remind you of anybody?
God, I hate working at heights.
Yeh, 'cos it's so much safer digging them tunnels.
Clamp it off then get y'arses up here!
Better double up with a second hawser.
Dunno why we're bloomin' doin' this.
Stop whining and get y'arse up here.
Only if y'pants ain't full o'shit, mind!
We should be cuttin' the bloomin' steel and lettin' it drop.

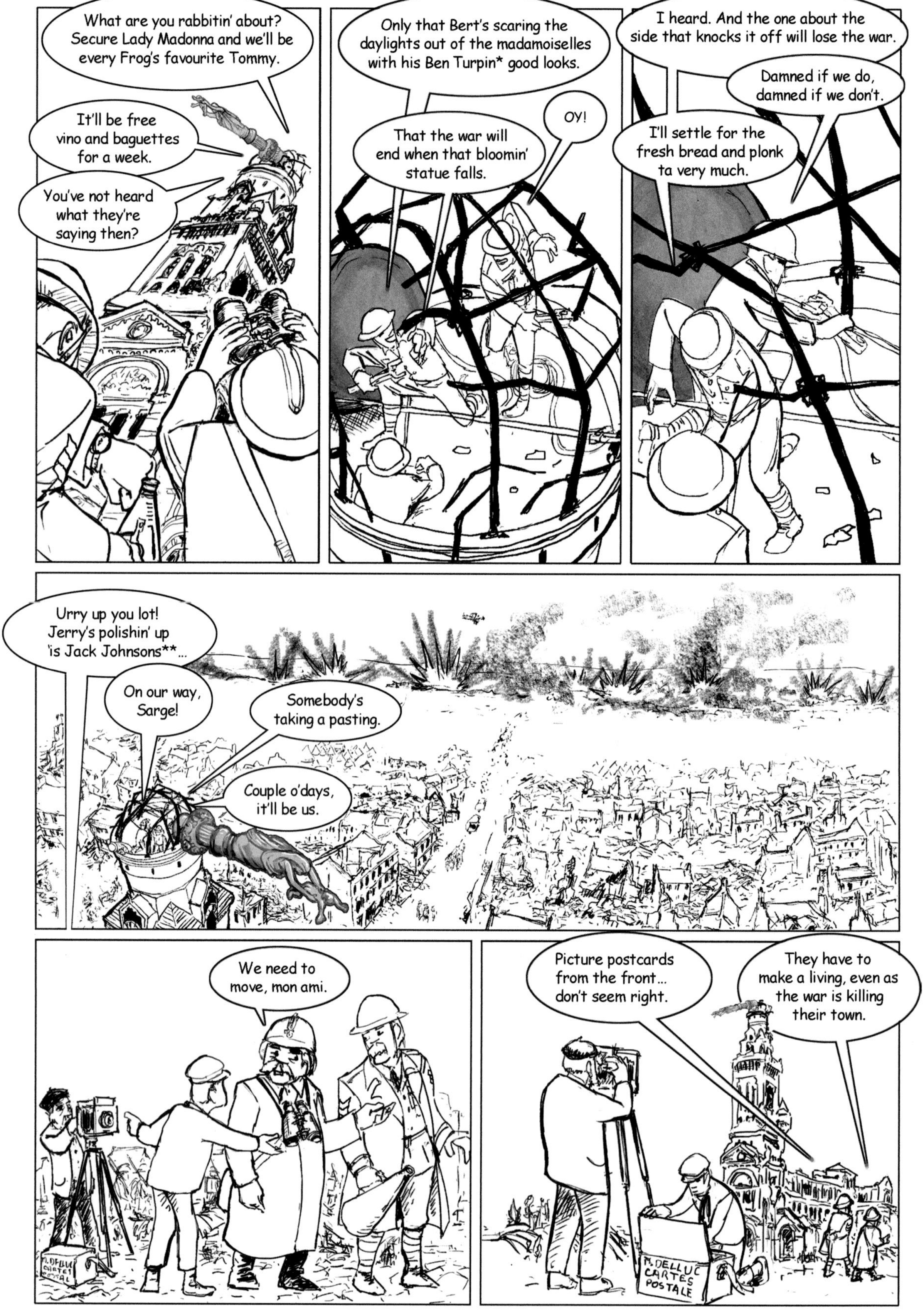
What are you rabbitin' about? Secure Lady Madonna and we'll be every Frog's favourite Tommy.
It'll be free vino and baguettes for a week.
You've not heard what they're saying then?
Only that Bert's scaring the daylights out of the madamoiselles with his Ben Turpin* good looks.
That the war will end when that bloomin' statue falls.
OY!
I heard. And the one about the side that knocks it off will lose the war.
Damned if we do, damned if we don't.
I'll settle for the fresh bread and plonk ta very much.
Urry up you lot! Jerry's polishin' up 'is Jack Johnsons**...
On our way, Sarge!
Somebody's taking a pasting.
Couple o'days, it'll be us.
We need to move, mon ami.
Picture postcards from the front... don't seem right.
They have to make a living, even as the war is killing their town.
M. DELLUC CARTES POSTALE

*Cross-eyed American silent film star ** British nickname for German 150mm artillery shells

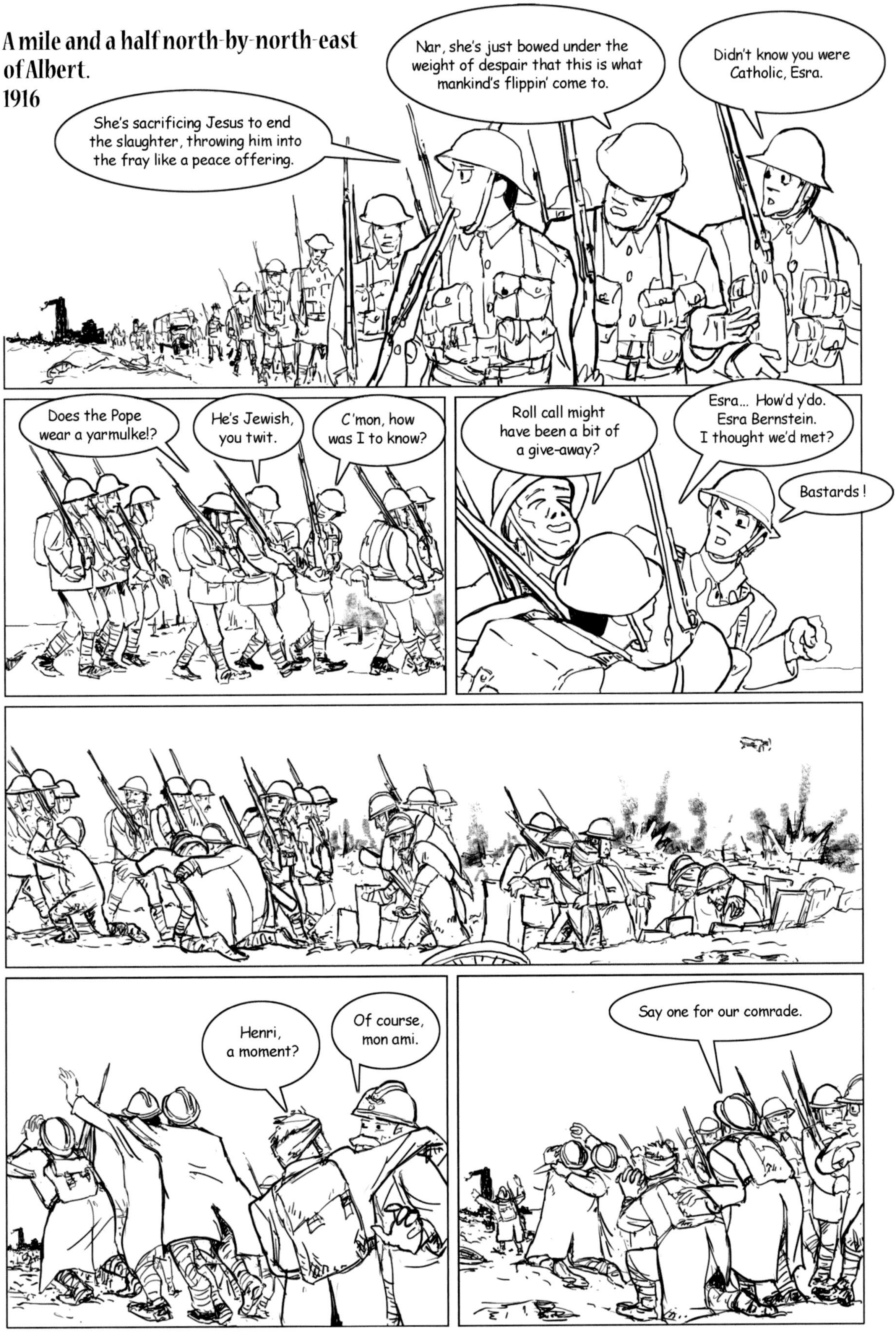
A mile and a half north-by-north-east of Albert.
1916
She's sacrificing Jesus to end the slaughter, throwing him into the fray like a peace offering.
Nar, she's just bowed under the weight of despair that this is what mankind's flippin' come to.
Didn't know you were Catholic, Esra.
Does the Pope wear a yarmulke!?
He's Jewish, you twit.
C'mon, how was I to know?
Roll call might have been a bit of a give-away?
Esra... How'd y'do. Esra Bernstein. I thought we'd met?
Bastards!
Henri, a moment?
Of course, mon ami.
Say one for our comrade.

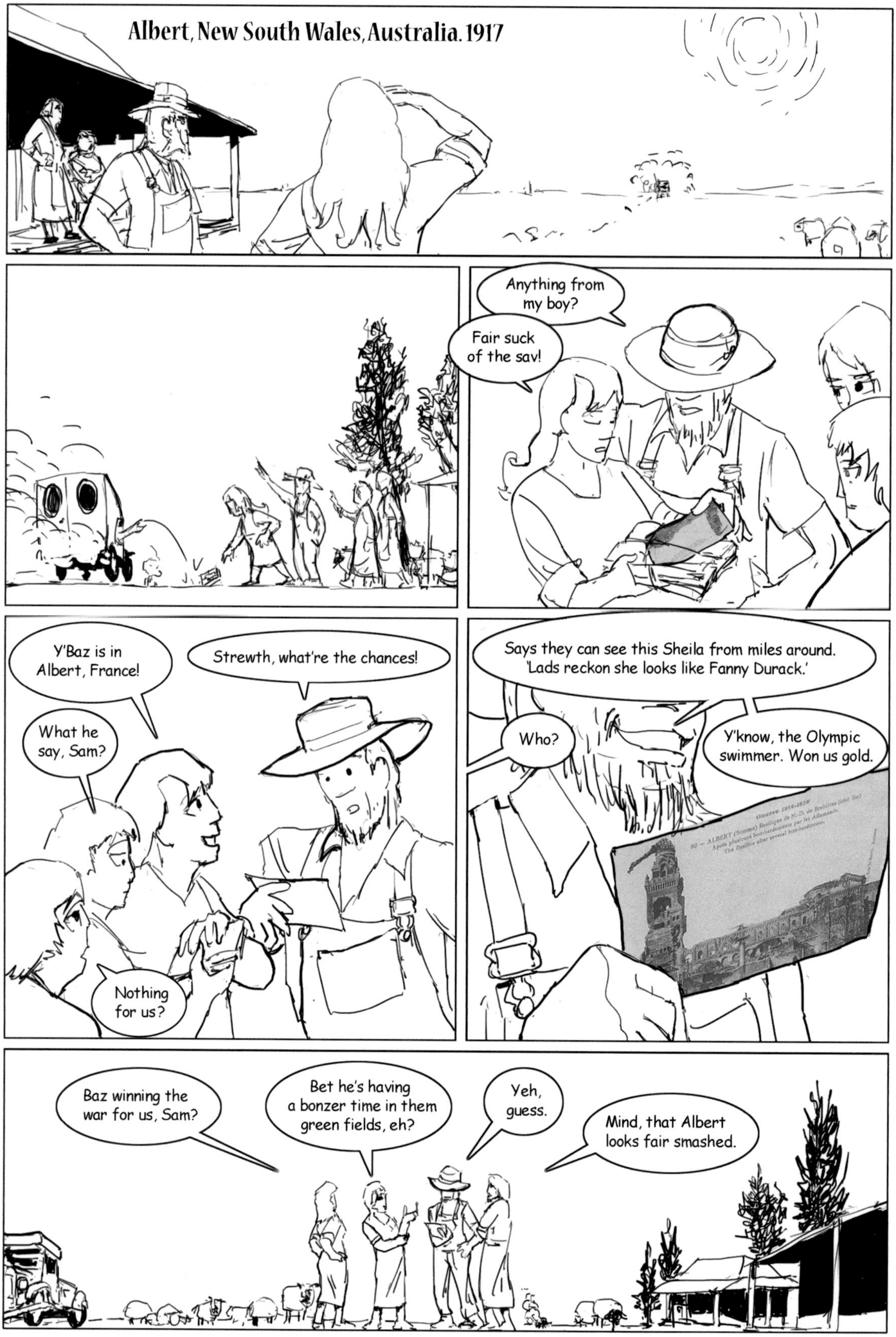
Albert, New South Wales, Australia. 1917
Anything from my boy?
Fair suck of the sav!
Y'Baz is in Albert, France!
Strewth, what're the chances!
What he say, Sam?
Nothing for us?
Says they can see this Sheila from miles around. 'Lads reckon she looks like Fanny Durack.'
Who?
Y'know, the Olympic swimmer. Won us gold.
Baz winning the war for us, Sam?
Bet he's having a bonzer time in them green fields, eh?
Yeh, guess.
Mind, that Albert looks fair smashed.

Place d'Armés, Albert. 1918

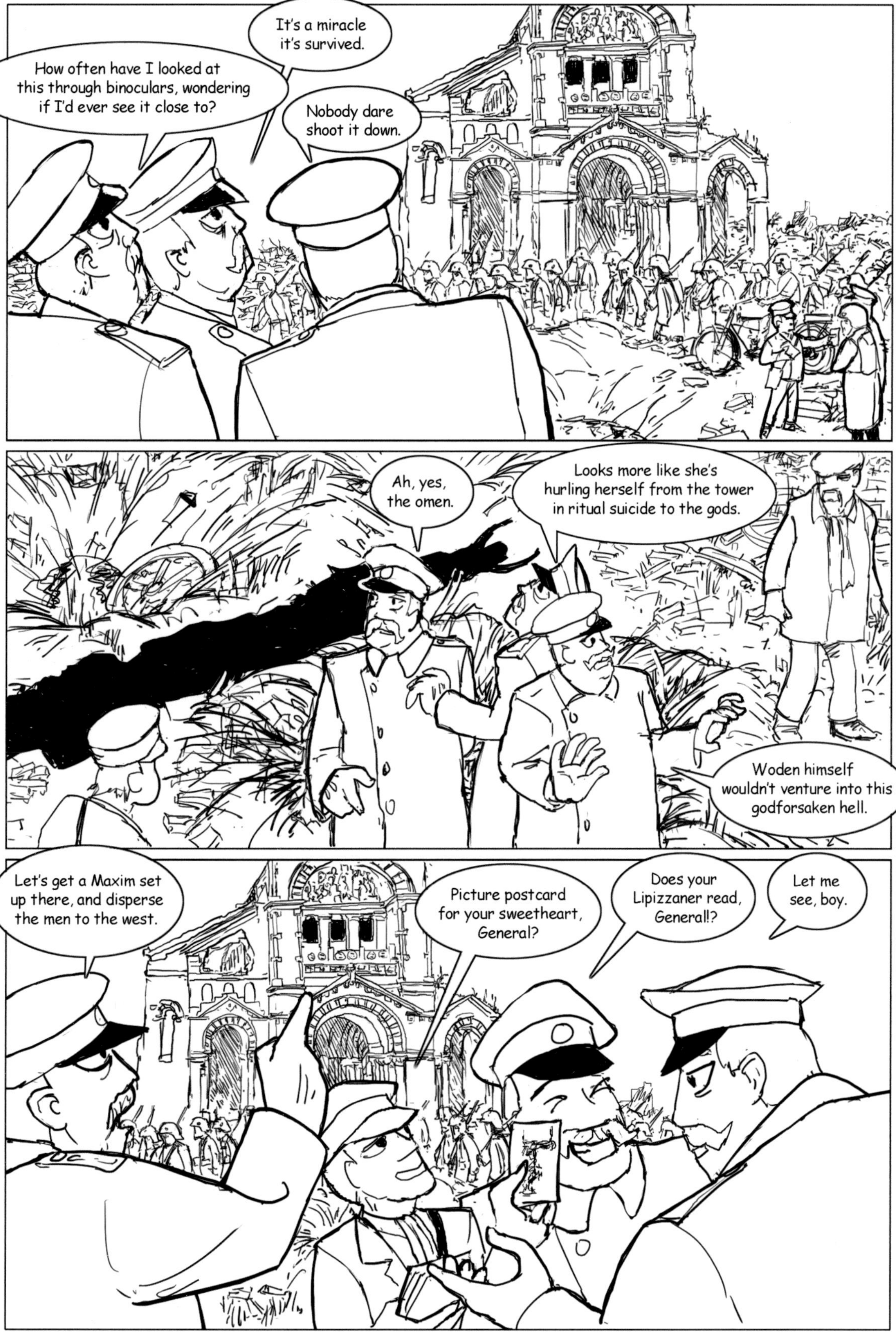
How often have I looked at this through binoculars, wondering if I'd ever see it close to?
It's a miracle it's survived.
Nobody dare shoot it down.
Ah, yes, the omen.
Looks more like she's hurling herself from the tower in ritual suicide to the gods.
Woden himself wouldn't venture into this godforsaken hell.
Let's get a Maxim set up there, and disperse the men to the west.
Picture postcard for your sweetheart, General?
Does your Lipizzaner read, General!?
Let me see, boy.

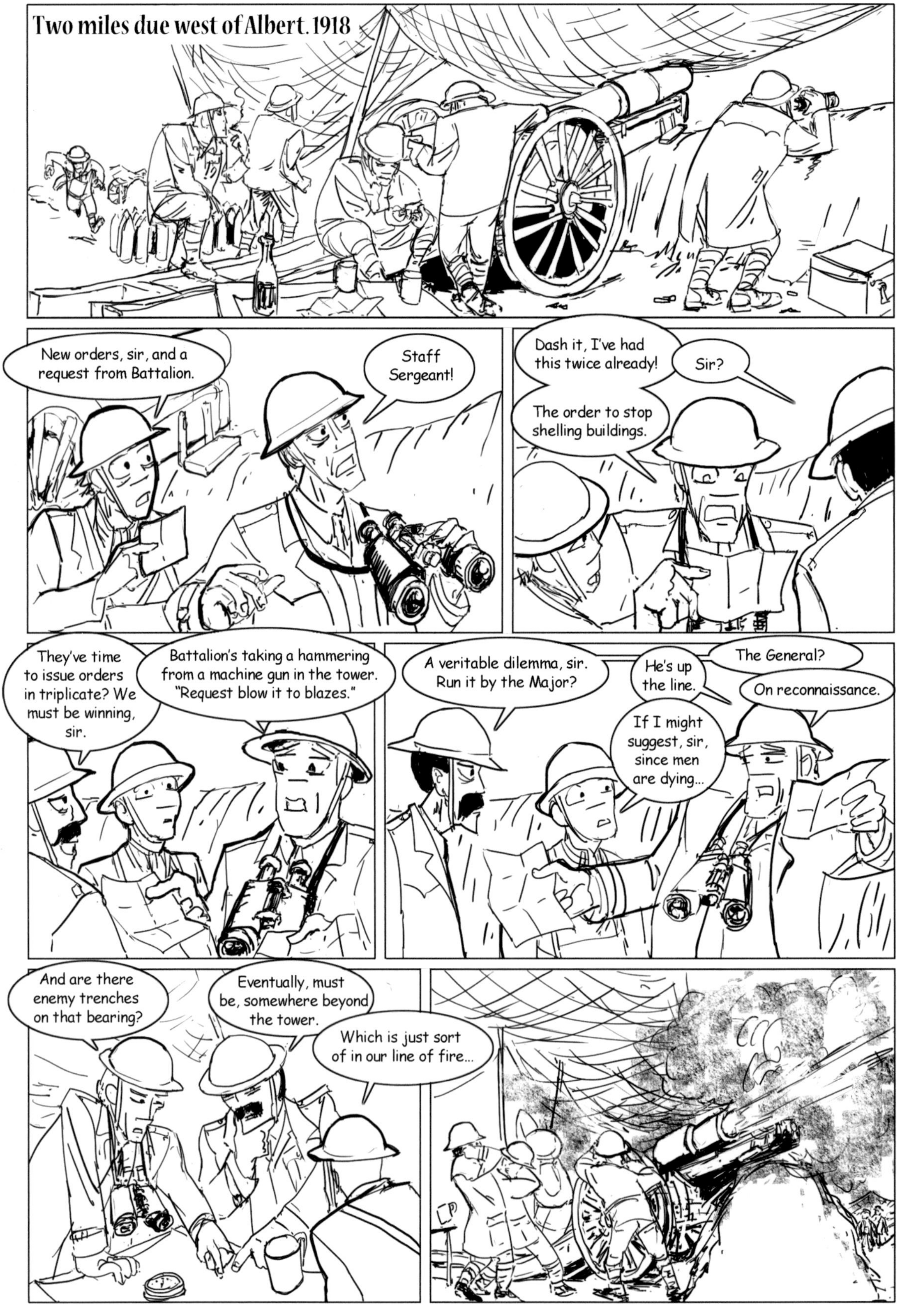
Two miles due west of Albert. 1918
New orders, sir, and a request from Battalion.
Staff Sergeant!
Dash it, I've had this twice already!
Sir?
The order to stop shelling buildings.
They've time to issue orders in triplicate? We must be winning, sir.
Battalion's taking a hammering from a machine gun in the tower. "Request blow it to blazes."
A veritable dilemma, sir. Run it by the Major?
He's up the line.
The General?
On reconnaissance.
If I might suggest, sir, since men are dying...
And are there enemy trenches on that bearing?
Eventually, must be, somewhere beyond the tower.
Which is just sort of in our line of fire...

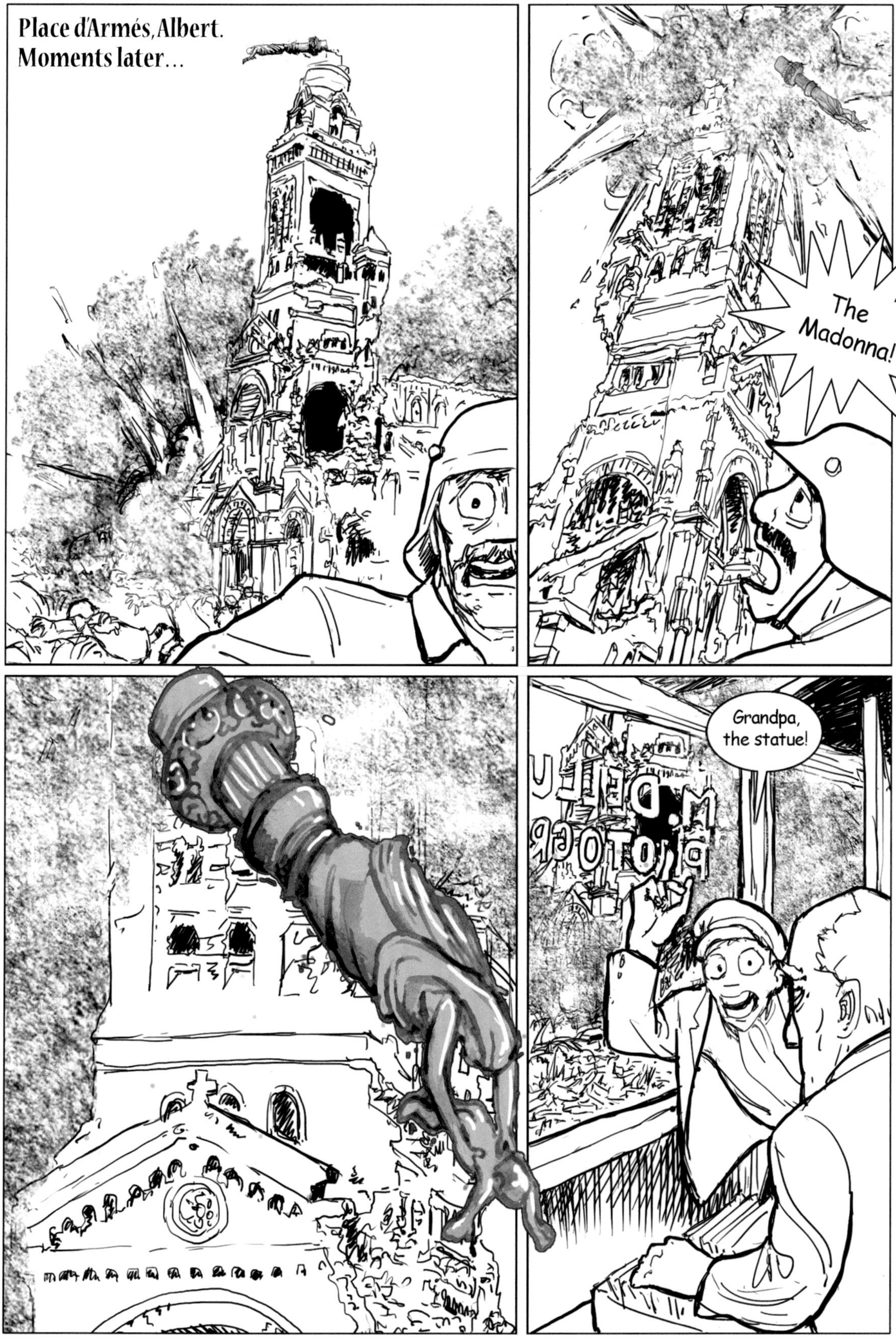
Place d'Armés, Albert.
Moments later…
The Madonna!
Grandpa, the statue!

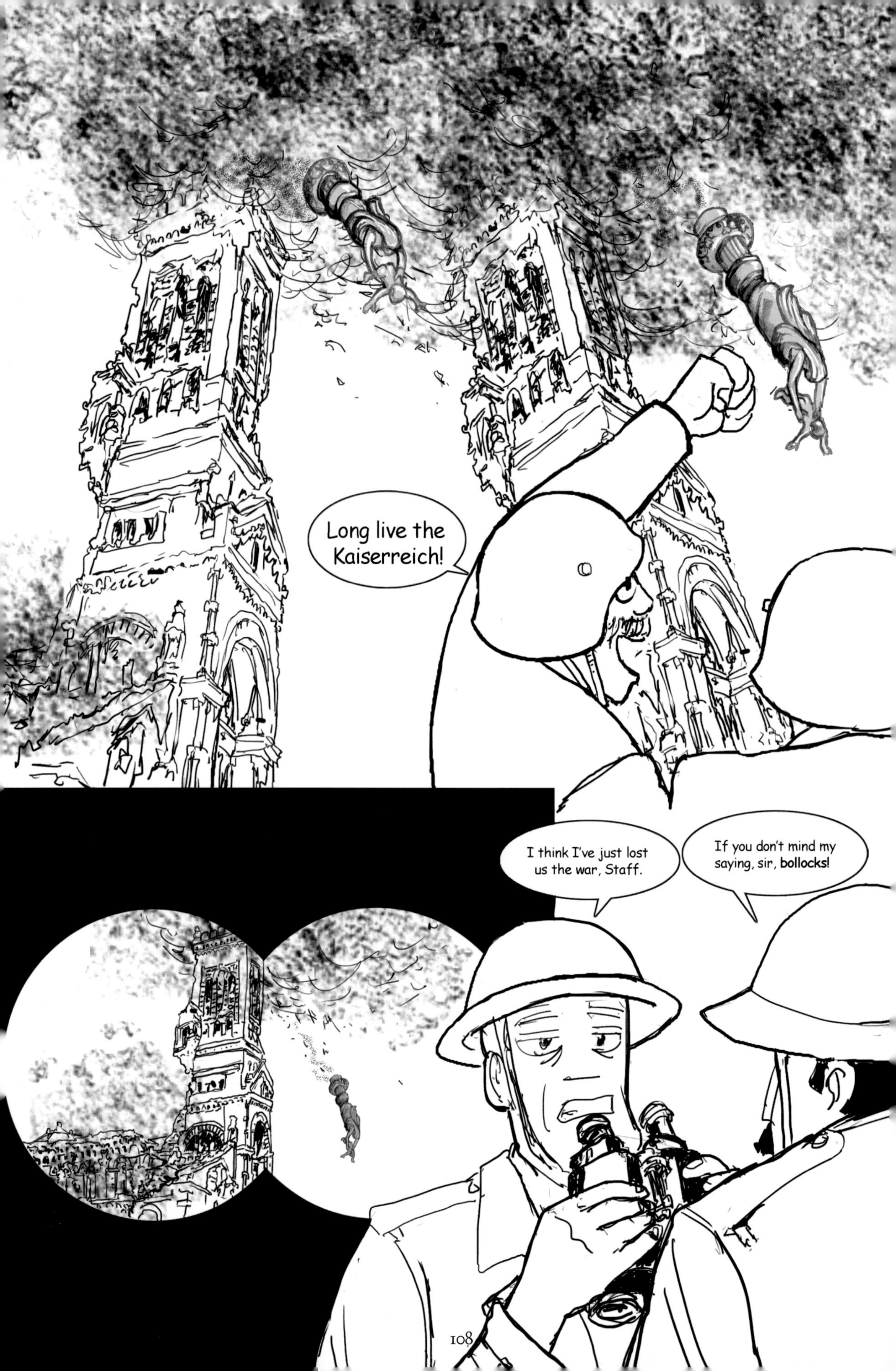
Long live the Kaiserreich!
I think I've just lost us the war, Staff.
If you don't mind my saying, sir, **bollocks!**

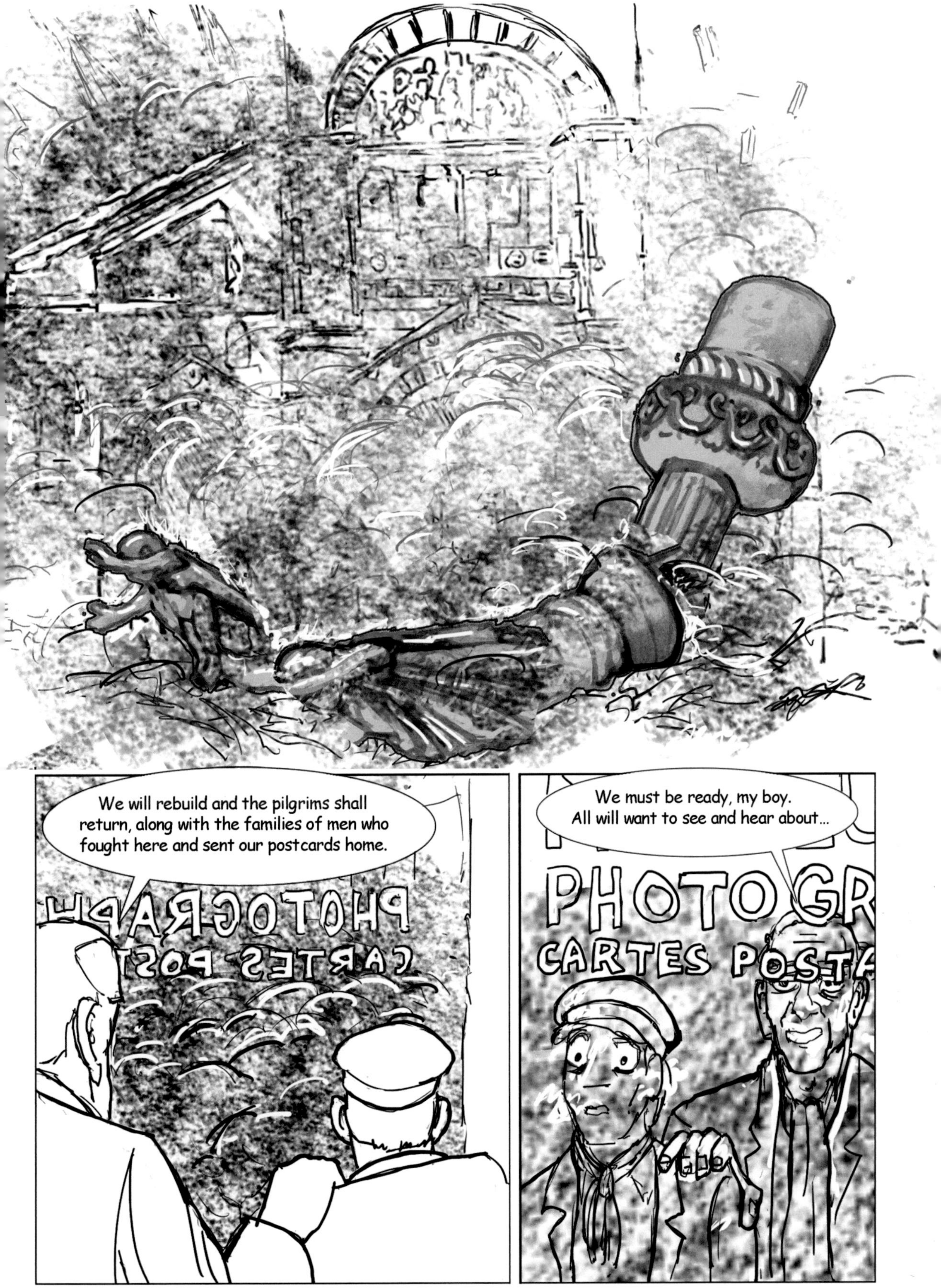
We will rebuild and the pilgrims shall return, along with the families of men who fought here and sent our postcards home.
We must be ready, my boy. All will want to see and hear about...
PHOTO GR
CARTES POSTA

The Legend of the Leaning Virgin

Story: Lotte Grünseid
Art: Jenny Linn Cole

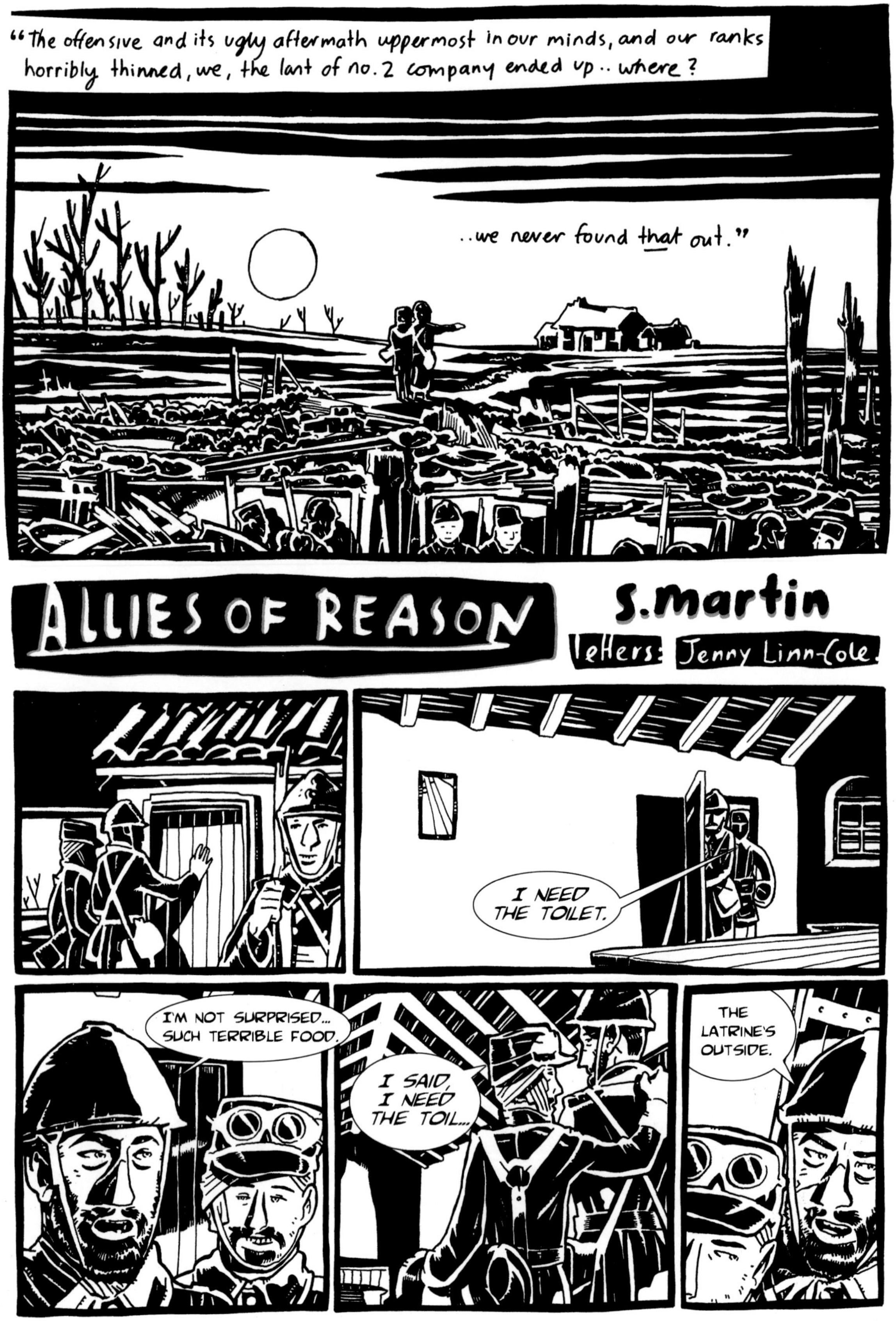
"The offensive and its ugly aftermath uppermost in our minds, and our ranks horribly thinned, we, the last of no. 2 company ended up .. where?
..we never found that out."
ALLIES OF REASON
S. martin
letters: Jenny Linn-Cole
I NEED THE TOILET.
I'M NOT SURPRISED... SUCH TERRIBLE FOOD.
I SAID, I NEED THE TOIL...
THE LATRINE'S OUTSIDE.

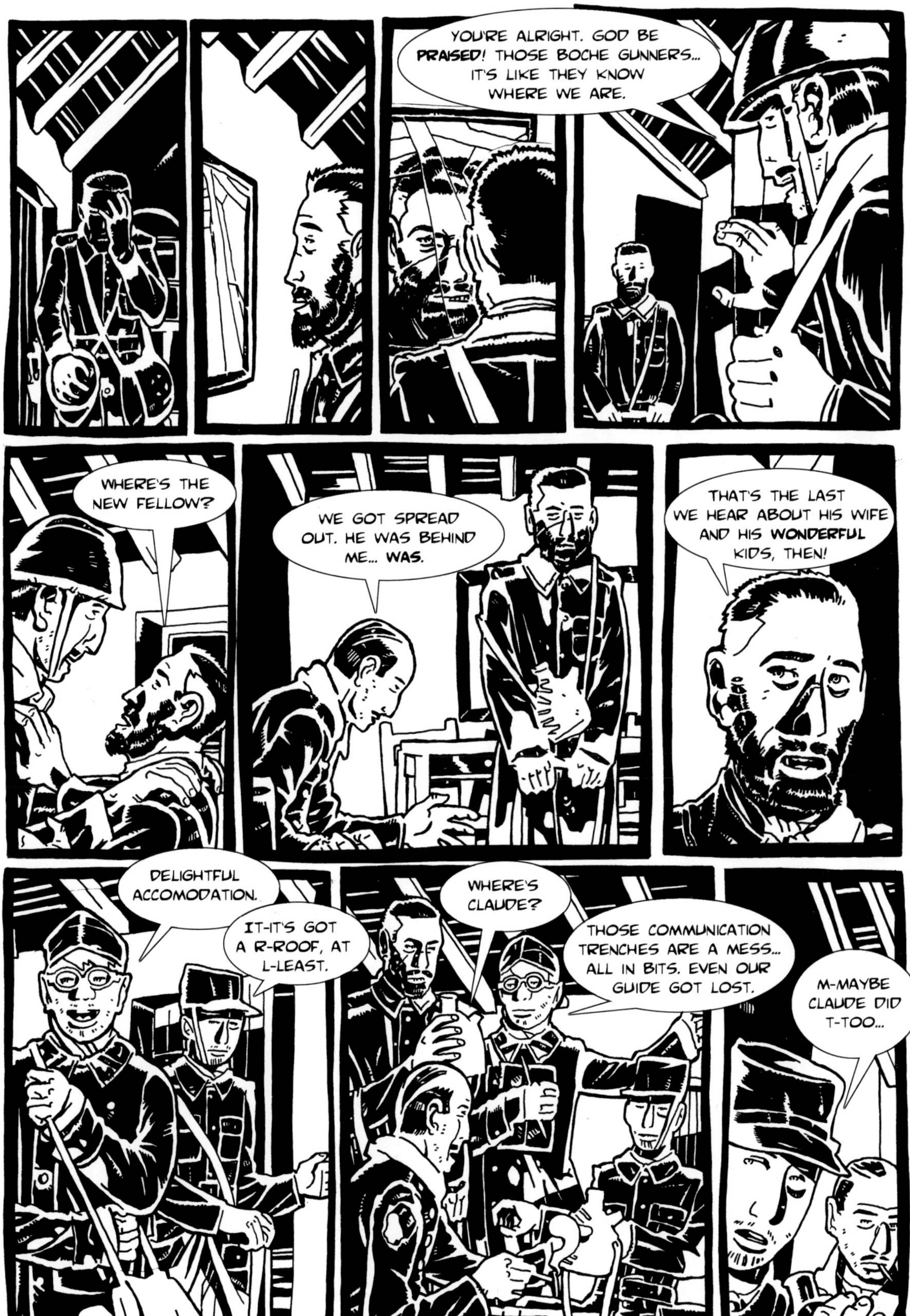
YOU'RE ALRIGHT. GOD BE PRAISED! THOSE BOCHE GUNNERS... IT'S LIKE THEY KNOW WHERE WE ARE.
WHERE'S THE NEW FELLOW?
WE GOT SPREAD OUT. HE WAS BEHIND ME... WAS.
THAT'S THE LAST WE HEAR ABOUT HIS WIFE AND HIS WONDERFUL KIDS, THEN!
DELIGHTFUL ACCOMODATION.
IT-IT'S GOT A R-ROOF, AT L-LEAST.
WHERE'S CLAUDE?
THOSE COMMUNICATION TRENCHES ARE A MESS... ALL IN BITS. EVEN OUR GUIDE GOT LOST.
M-MAYBE CLAUDE DID T-TOO...

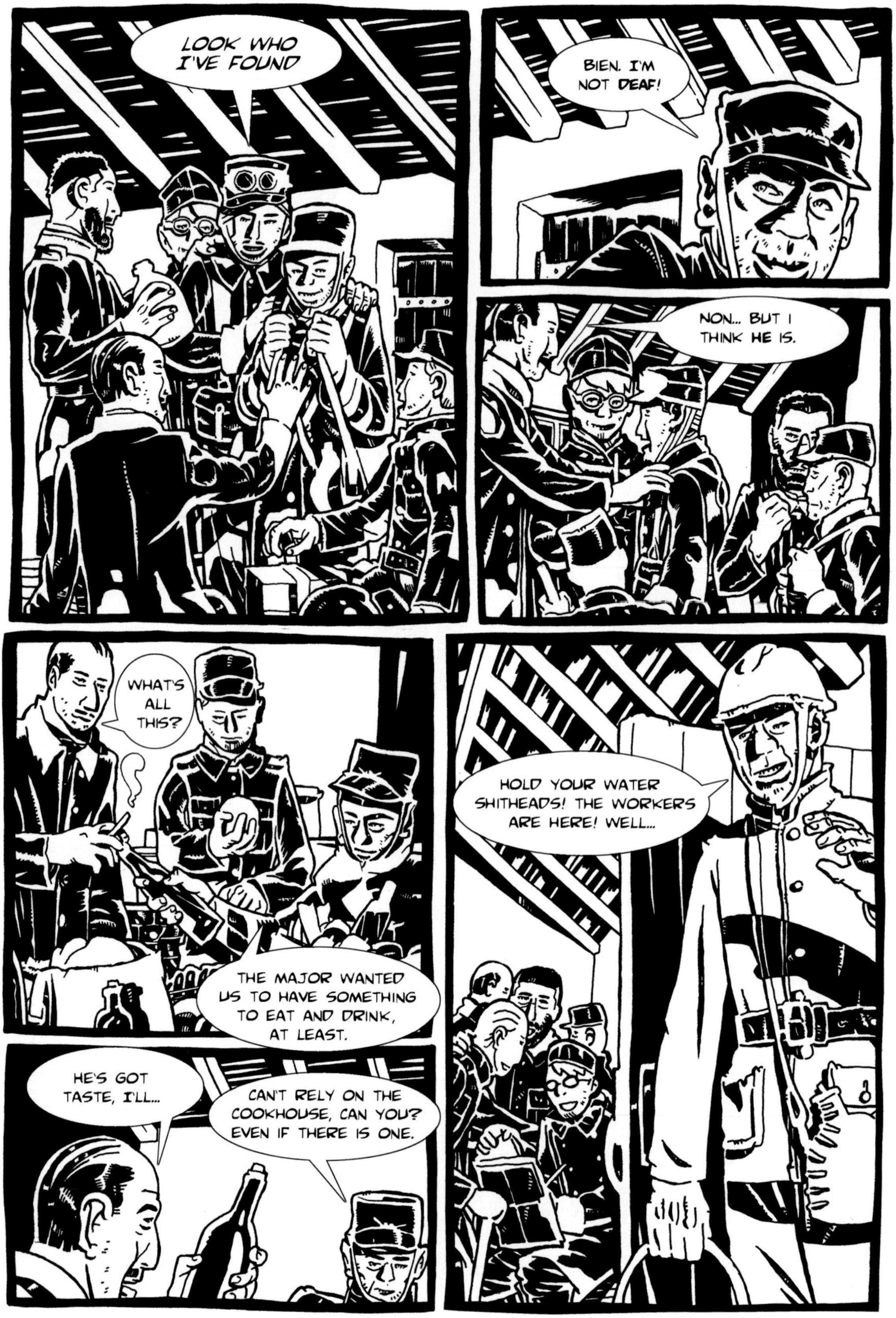
LOOK WHO I'VE FOUND
BIEN. I'M NOT DEAF!
NON... BUT I THINK HE IS.
WHAT'S ALL THIS?
THE MAJOR WANTED US TO HAVE SOMETHING TO EAT AND DRINK, AT LEAST.
HE'S GOT TASTE, I'LL...
CAN'T RELY ON THE COOKHOUSE, CAN YOU? EVEN IF THERE IS ONE.
HOLD YOUR WATER SHITHEADS! THE WORKERS ARE HERE! WELL...

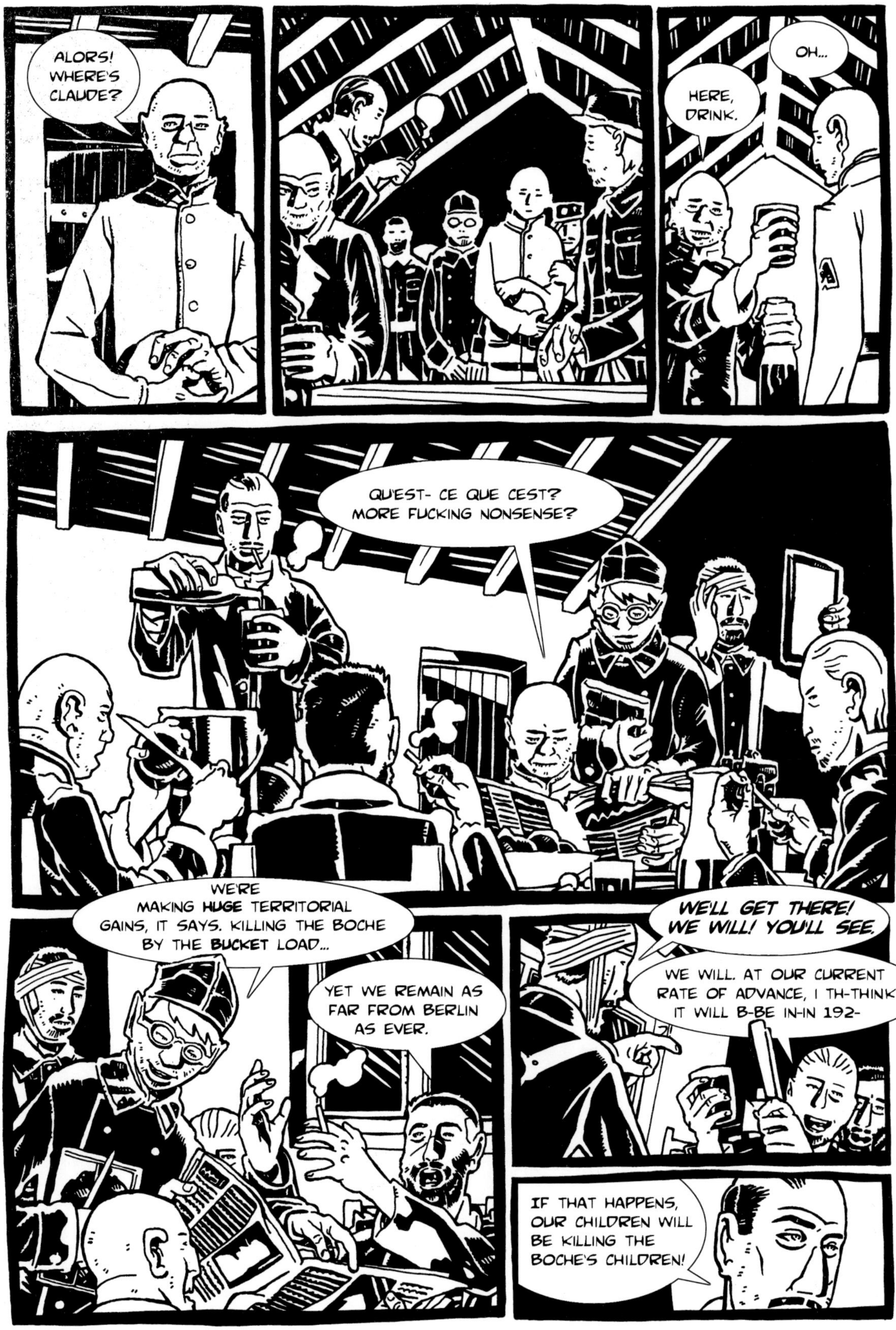
ALORS! WHERE'S CLAUDE?
OH...
HERE, DRINK.
QU'EST- CE QUE CEST? MORE FUCKING NONSENSE?
WE'RE MAKING HUGE TERRITORIAL GAINS, IT SAYS. KILLING THE BOCHE BY THE BUCKET LOAD...
YET WE REMAIN AS FAR FROM BERLIN AS EVER.
WE'LL GET THERE! WE WILL! YOU'LL SEE.
WE WILL. AT OUR CURRENT RATE OF ADVANCE, I TH-THINK IT WILL B-BE IN-IN 192-
IF THAT HAPPENS, OUR CHILDREN WILL BE KILLING THE BOCHE'S CHILDREN!

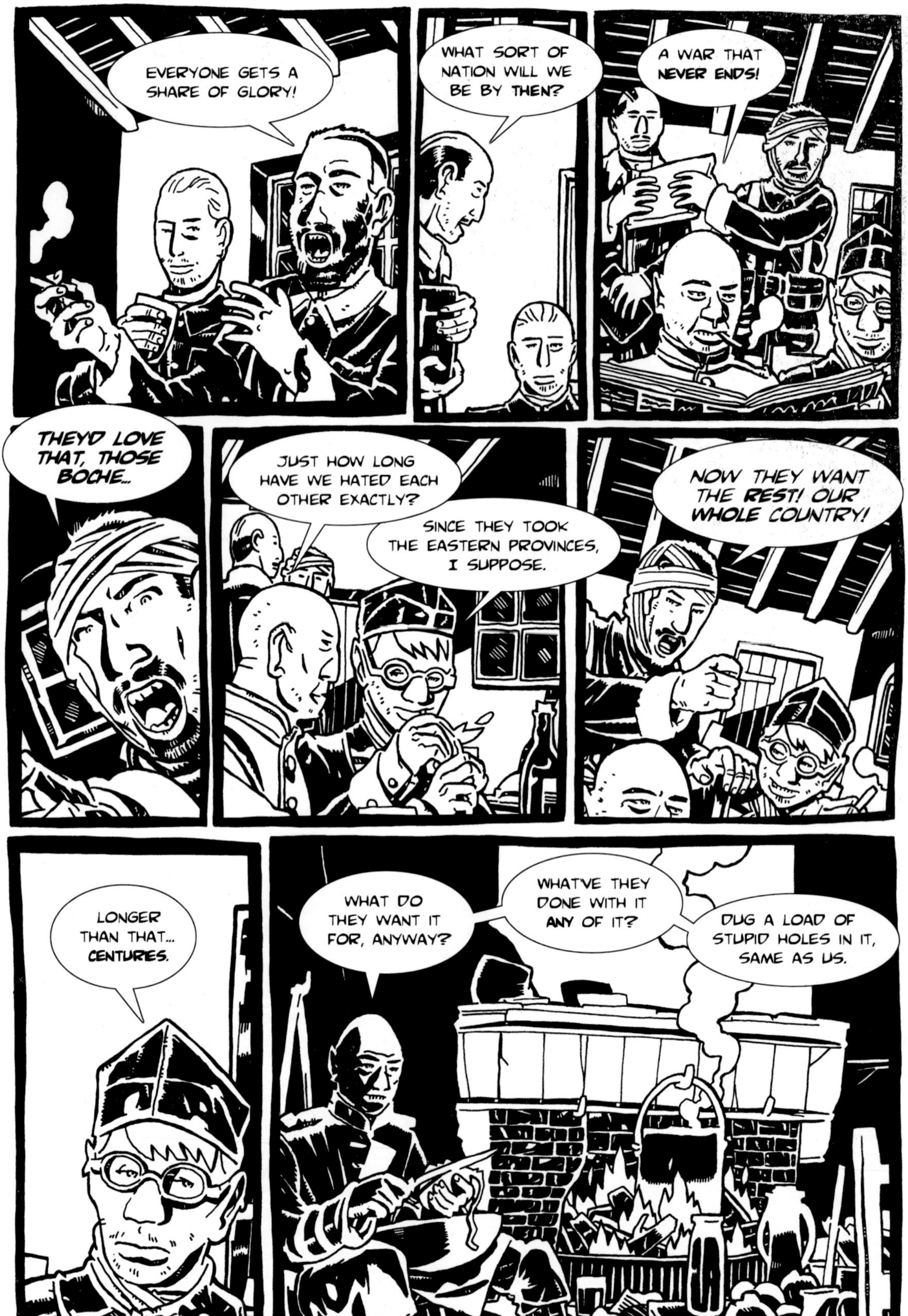
EVERYONE GETS A SHARE OF GLORY!
WHAT SORT OF NATION WILL WE BE BY THEN?
A WAR THAT NEVER ENDS!
THEY'D LOVE THAT, THOSE BOCHE...
JUST HOW LONG HAVE WE HATED EACH OTHER EXACTLY?
SINCE THEY TOOK THE EASTERN PROVINCES, I SUPPOSE.
NOW THEY WANT THE REST! OUR WHOLE COUNTRY!
LONGER THAN THAT... CENTURIES.
WHAT DO THEY WANT IT FOR, ANYWAY?
WHAT'VE THEY DONE WITH IT ANY OF IT?
DUG A LOAD OF STUPID HOLES IN IT, SAME AS US.

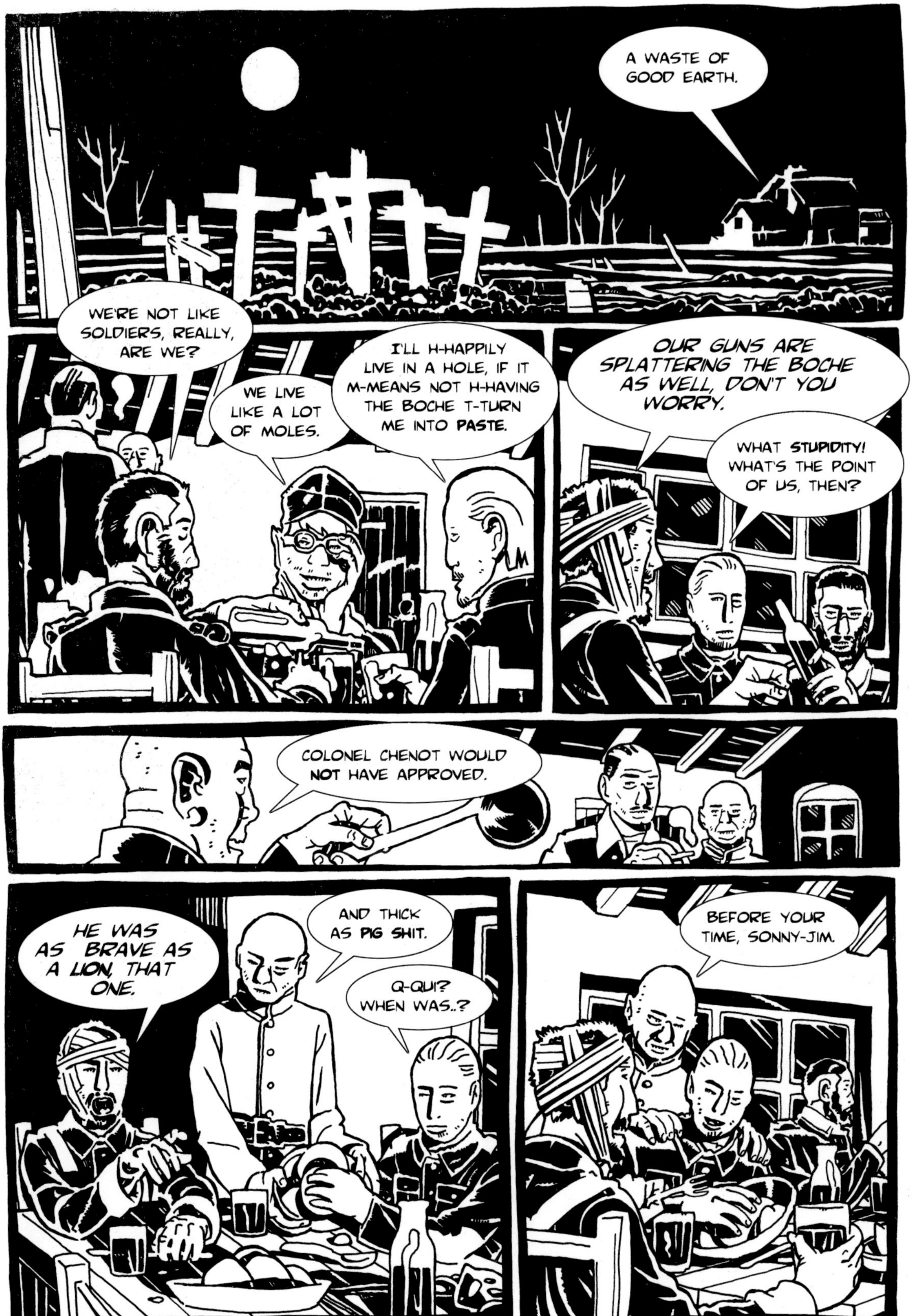
A WASTE OF GOOD EARTH.
WE'RE NOT LIKE SOLDIERS, REALLY, ARE WE?
WE LIVE LIKE A LOT OF MOLES.
I'LL H-HAPPILY LIVE IN A HOLE, IF IT M-MEANS NOT H-HAVING THE BOCHE T-TURN ME INTO **PASTE**.
OUR GUNS ARE SPLATTERING THE BOCHE AS WELL, DON'T YOU WORRY.
WHAT **STUPIDITY!** WHAT'S THE POINT OF US, THEN?
COLONEL CHENOT WOULD **NOT** HAVE APPROVED.
HE WAS AS BRAVE AS A ***LION,*** *THAT ONE.*
AND THICK AS **PIG SHIT**.
Q-QUI? WHEN WAS..?
BEFORE YOUR TIME, SONNY-JIM.

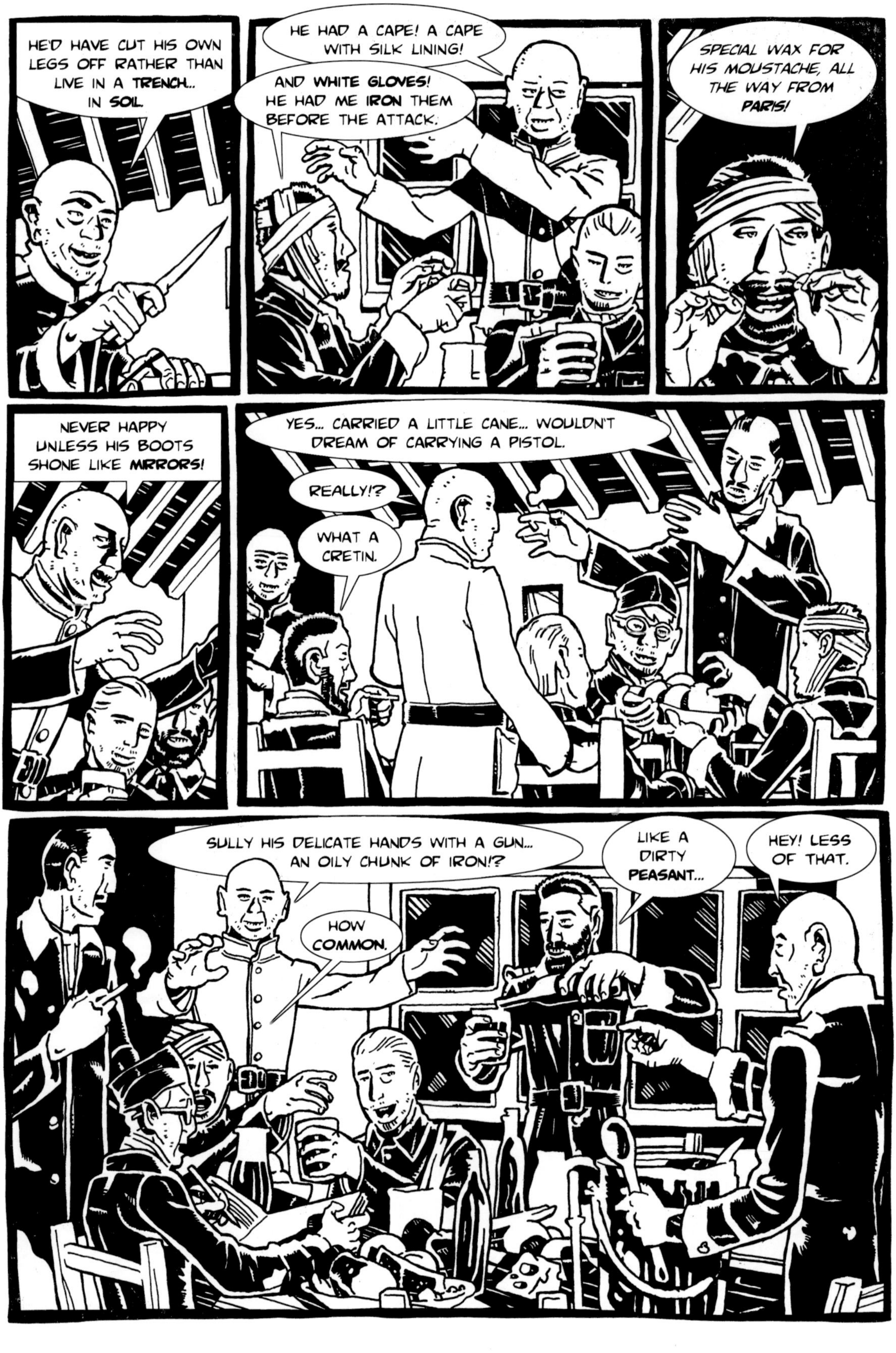
HE'D HAVE CUT HIS OWN LEGS OFF RATHER THAN LIVE IN A TRENCH... IN SOIL.
HE HAD A CAPE! A CAPE WITH SILK LINING!
AND WHITE GLOVES! HE HAD ME IRON THEM BEFORE THE ATTACK.
SPECIAL WAX FOR HIS MOUSTACHE, ALL THE WAY FROM PARIS!
NEVER HAPPY UNLESS HIS BOOTS SHONE LIKE MIRRORS!
YES... CARRIED A LITTLE CANE... WOULDN'T DREAM OF CARRYING A PISTOL.
REALLY!?
WHAT A CRETIN.
SULLY HIS DELICATE HANDS WITH A GUN... AN OILY CHUNK OF IRON!?
HOW COMMON.
LIKE A DIRTY PEASANT...
HEY! LESS OF THAT.

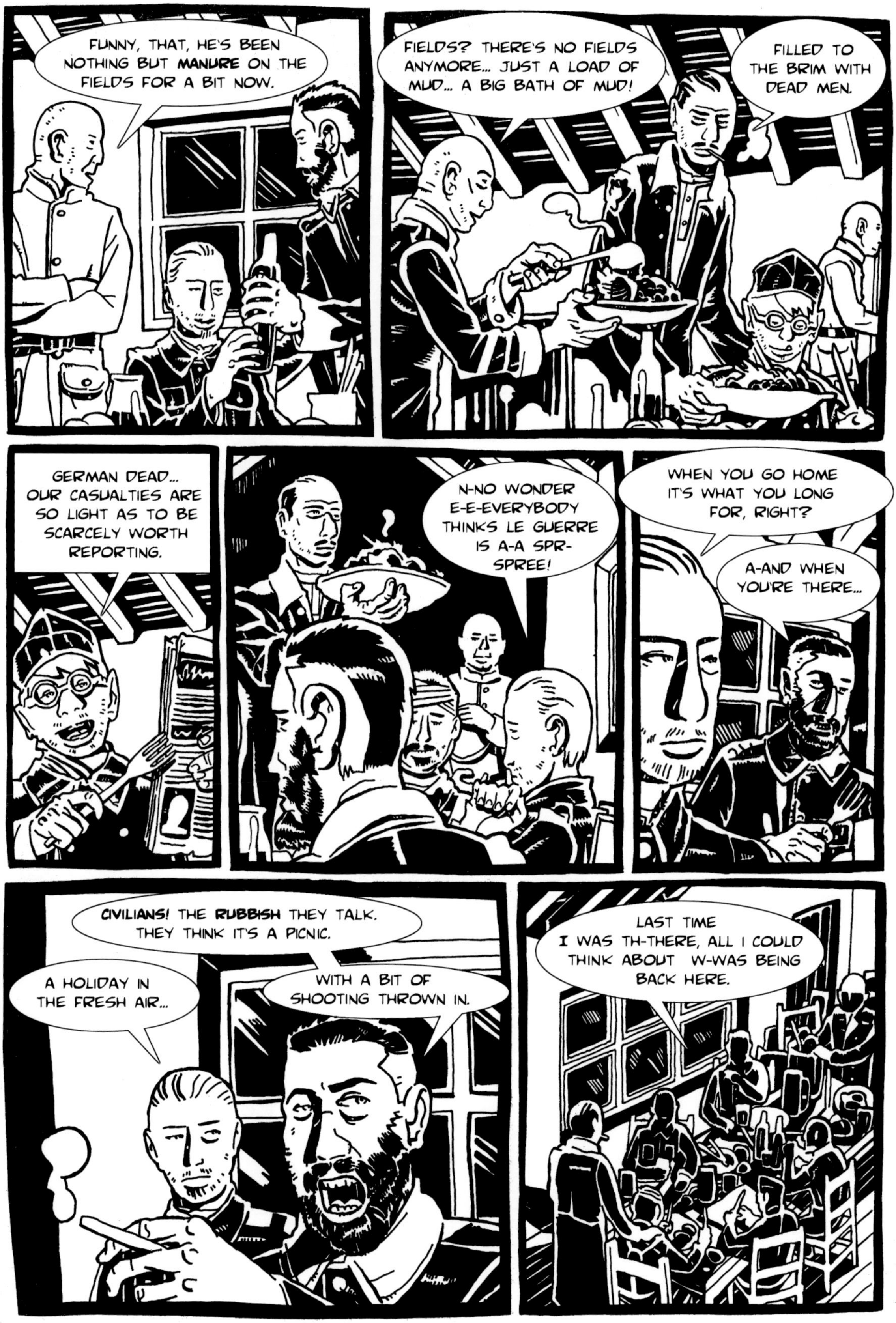
FUNNY, THAT, HE'S BEEN NOTHING BUT MANURE ON THE FIELDS FOR A BIT NOW.
FIELDS? THERE'S NO FIELDS ANYMORE... JUST A LOAD OF MUD... A BIG BATH OF MUD!
FILLED TO THE BRIM WITH DEAD MEN.
GERMAN DEAD... OUR CASUALTIES ARE SO LIGHT AS TO BE SCARCELY WORTH REPORTING.
N-NO WONDER E-E-EVERYBODY THINKS LE GUERRE IS A-A SPR-SPREE!
WHEN YOU GO HOME IT'S WHAT YOU LONG FOR, RIGHT?
A-AND WHEN YOU'RE THERE...
CIVILIANS! THE RUBBISH THEY TALK. THEY THINK IT'S A PICNIC.
A HOLIDAY IN THE FRESH AIR...
WITH A BIT OF SHOOTING THROWN IN.
LAST TIME I WAS TH-THERE, ALL I COULD THINK ABOUT W-WAS BEING BACK HERE.

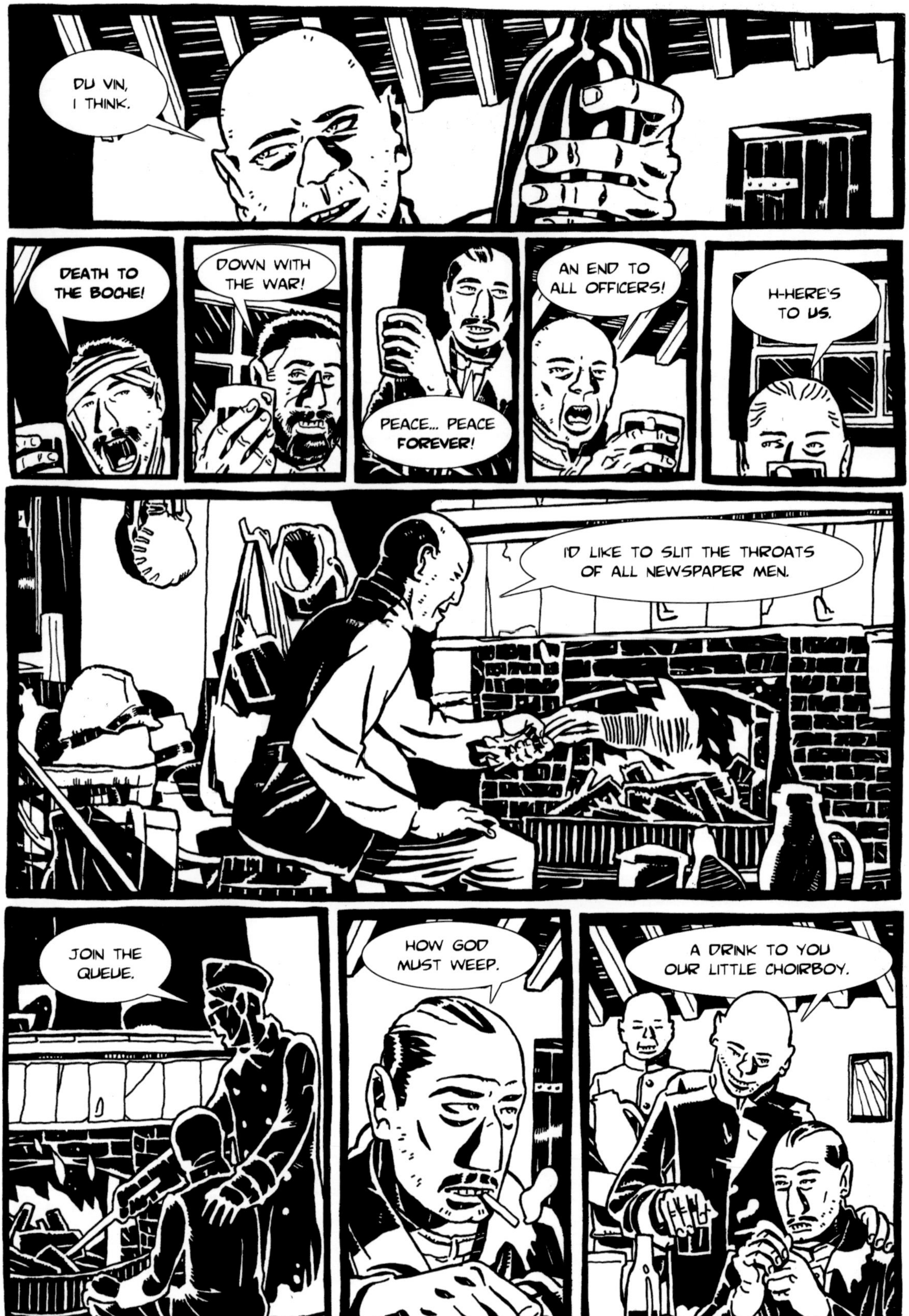
DU VIN, I THINK.
DEATH TO THE BOCHE!
DOWN WITH THE WAR!
PEACE... PEACE FOREVER!
AN END TO ALL OFFICERS!
H-HERE'S TO US.
I'D LIKE TO SLIT THE THROATS OF ALL NEWSPAPER MEN.
JOIN THE QUEUE.
HOW GOD MUST WEEP.
A DRINK TO YOU OUR LITTLE CHOIRBOY.

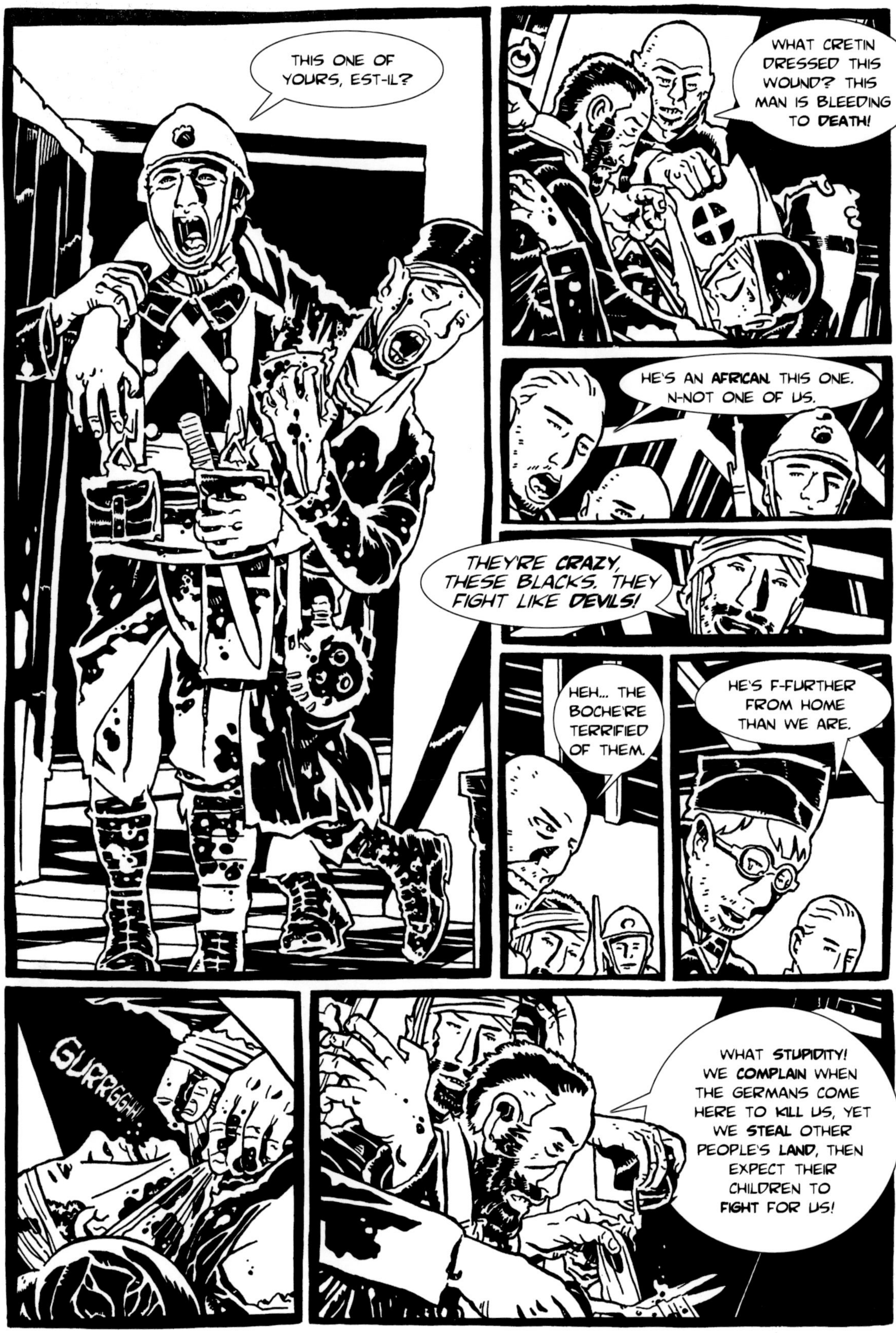
THIS ONE OF YOURS, EST-IL?
WHAT CRETIN DRESSED THIS WOUND? THIS MAN IS BLEEDING TO **DEATH!**
HE'S AN **AFRICAN**. THIS ONE. N-NOT ONE OF US.
*THEY'RE **CRAZY**, THESE BLACKS. THEY FIGHT LIKE **DEVILS!***
HEH... THE BOCHE'RE TERRIFIED OF THEM.
HE'S F-FURTHER FROM HOME THAN WE ARE.
GURRGGHH!
WHAT **STUPIDITY!** WE **COMPLAIN** WHEN THE GERMANS COME HERE TO **KILL** US, YET WE **STEAL** OTHER PEOPLE'S **LAND**, THEN EXPECT THEIR CHILDREN TO **FIGHT** FOR US!

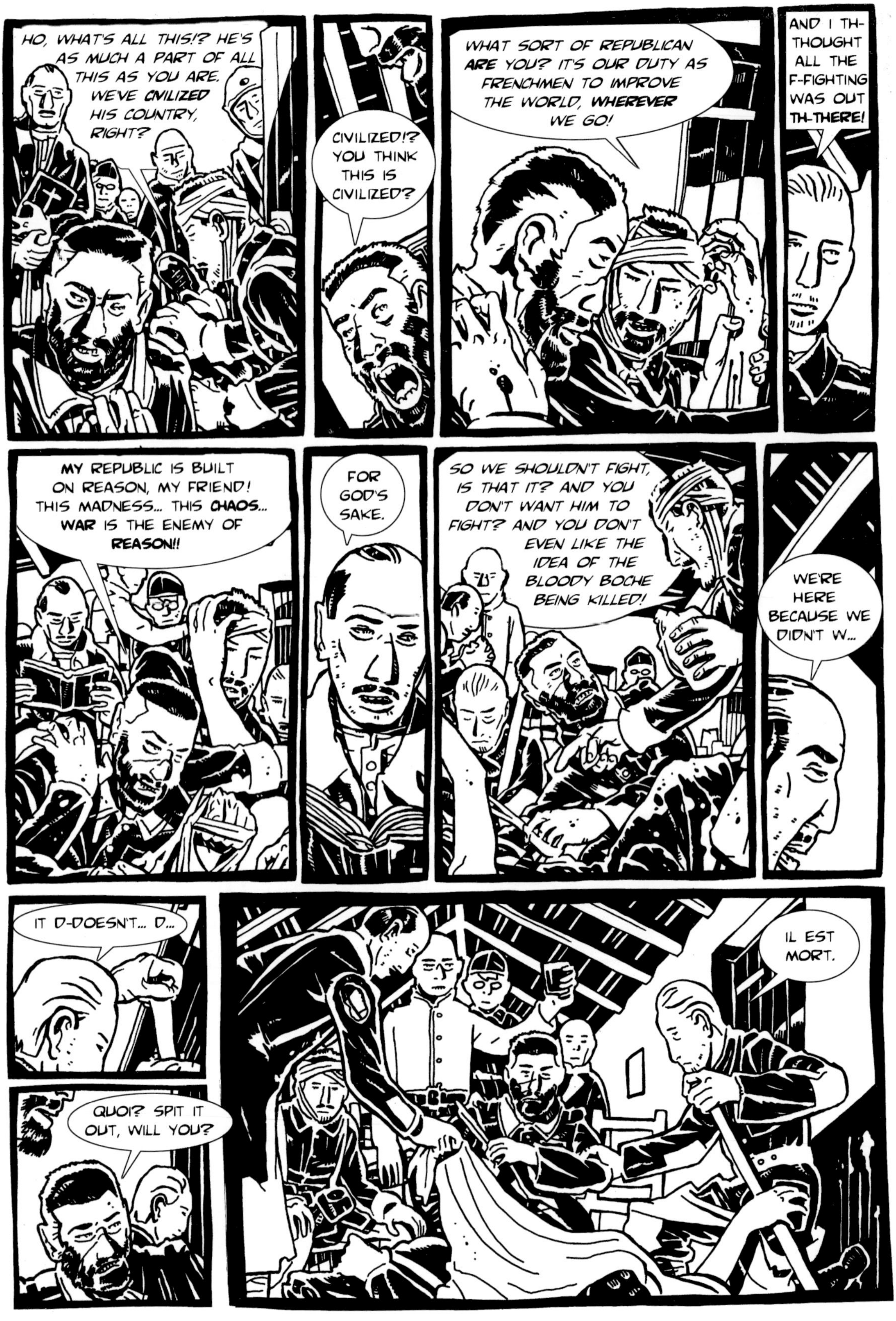
HO, WHAT'S ALL THIS!? HE'S AS MUCH A PART OF ALL THIS AS YOU ARE. WE'VE **CIVILIZED** HIS COUNTRY, RIGHT?
CIVILIZED!? YOU THINK THIS IS CIVILIZED?
WHAT SORT OF REPUBLICAN **ARE** YOU? IT'S OUR DUTY AS FRENCHMEN TO IMPROVE THE WORLD, **WHEREVER** WE GO!
AND I TH-THOUGHT ALL THE F-FIGHTING WAS OUT **TH-THERE!**
MY REPUBLIC IS BUILT ON REASON, MY FRIEND! THIS MADNESS... THIS **CHAOS**... **WAR** IS THE ENEMY OF **REASON!!**
FOR GOD'S SAKE.
SO WE SHOULDN'T FIGHT, IS THAT IT? AND YOU DON'T WANT HIM TO FIGHT? AND YOU DON'T EVEN LIKE THE IDEA OF THE BLOODY BOCHE BEING KILLED!
WE'RE HERE BECAUSE WE DIDN'T W...
IT D-DOESN'T... D...
QUOI? SPIT IT OUT, WILL YOU?
IL EST MORT.

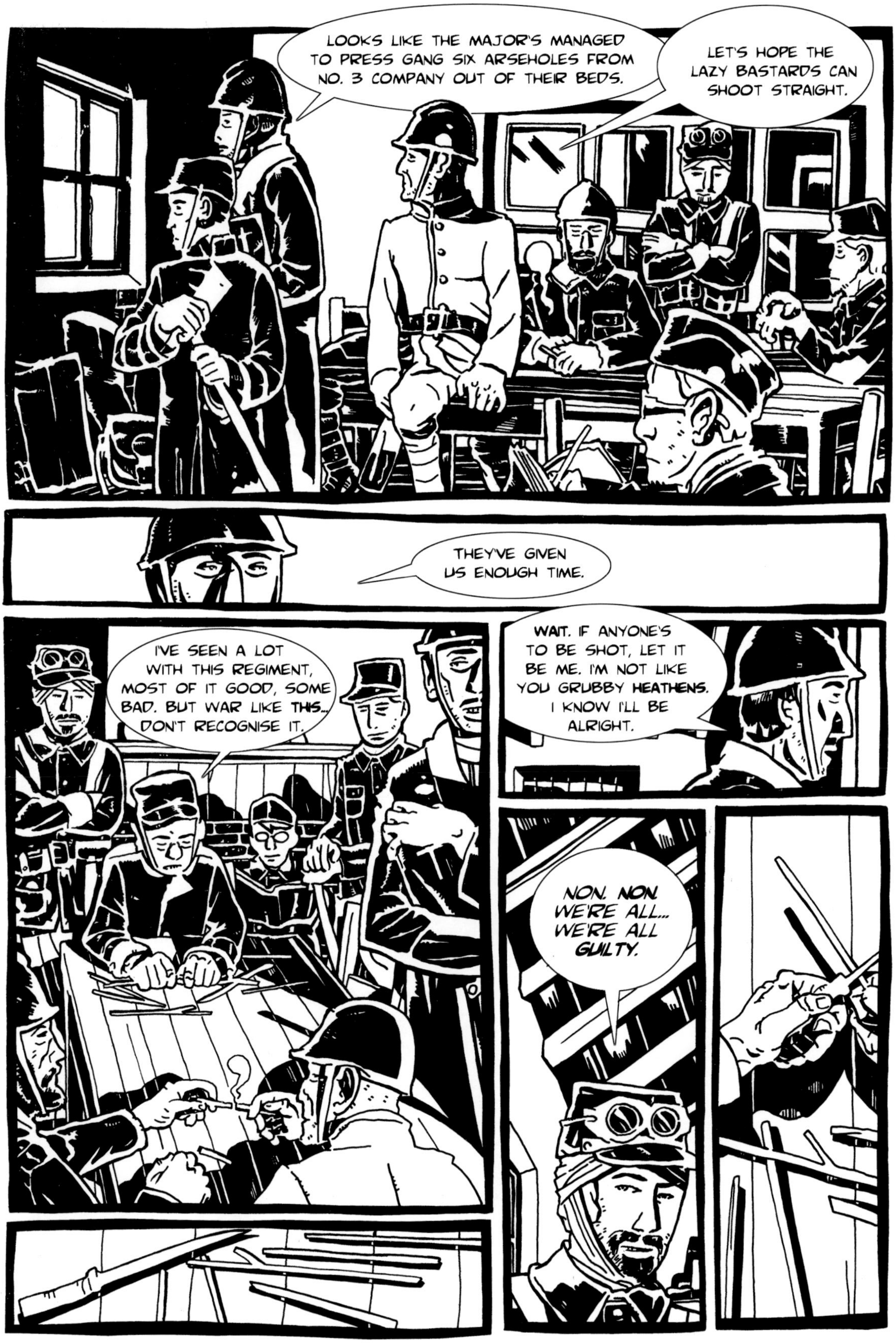
LOOKS LIKE THE MAJOR'S MANAGED TO PRESS GANG SIX ARSEHOLES FROM NO. 3 COMPANY OUT OF THEIR BEDS.
LET'S HOPE THE LAZY BASTARDS CAN SHOOT STRAIGHT.
THEY'VE GIVEN US ENOUGH TIME.
I'VE SEEN A LOT WITH THIS REGIMENT, MOST OF IT GOOD, SOME BAD. BUT WAR LIKE THIS... DON'T RECOGNISE IT.
WAIT. IF ANYONE'S TO BE SHOT, LET IT BE ME. I'M NOT LIKE YOU GRUBBY HEATHENS. I KNOW I'LL BE ALRIGHT.
NON. NON. WE'RE ALL... WE'RE ALL GUILTY.

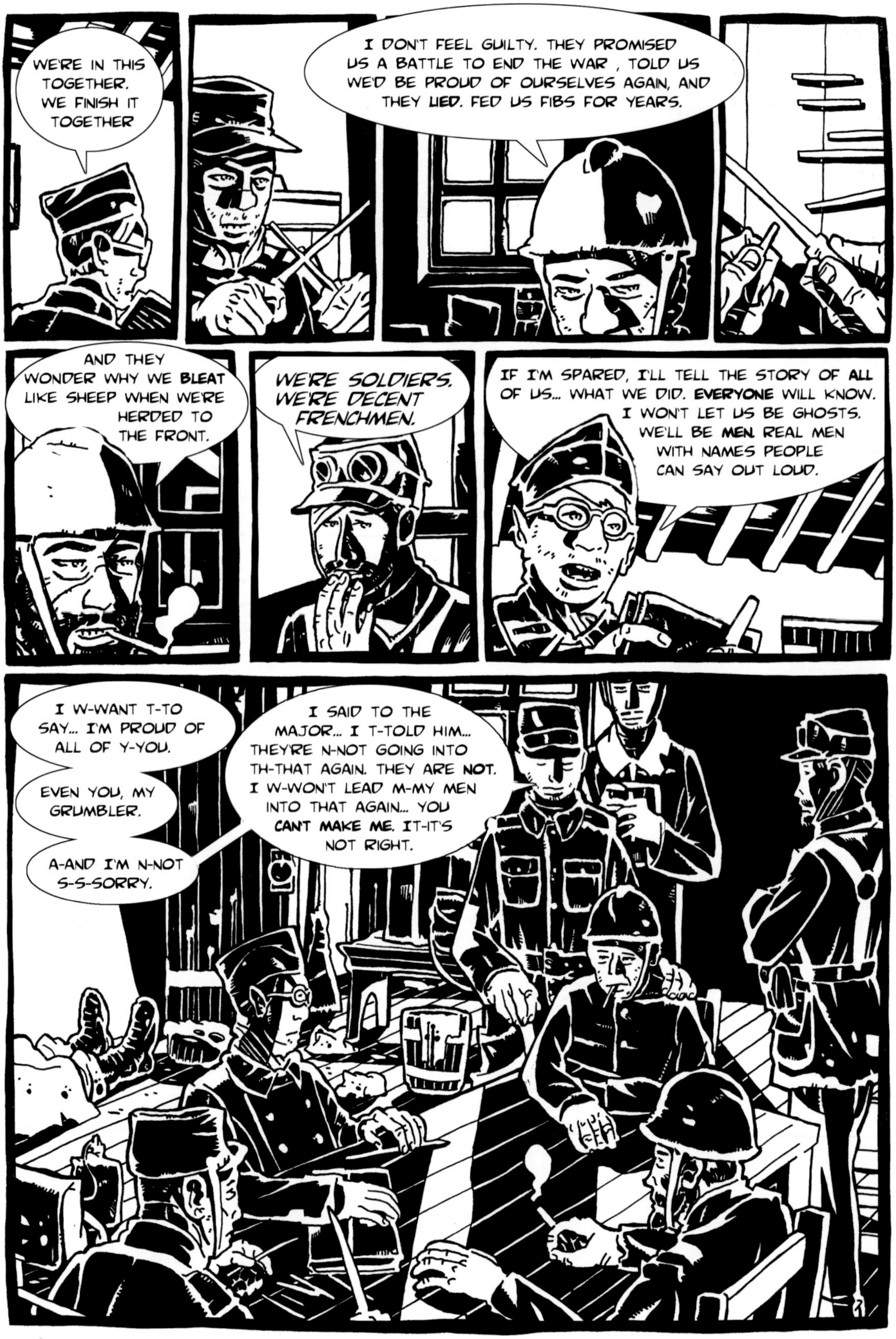
WE'RE IN THIS TOGETHER. WE FINISH IT TOGETHER
I DON'T FEEL GUILTY. THEY PROMISED US A BATTLE TO END THE WAR , TOLD US WE'D BE PROUD OF OURSELVES AGAIN, AND THEY LIED. FED US FIBS FOR YEARS.
AND THEY WONDER WHY WE BLEAT LIKE SHEEP WHEN WE'RE HERDED TO THE FRONT.
WE'RE SOLDIERS. WE'RE DECENT FRENCHMEN.
IF I'M SPARED, I'LL TELL THE STORY OF ALL OF US... WHAT WE DID. EVERYONE WILL KNOW. I WON'T LET US BE GHOSTS. WE'LL BE MEN. REAL MEN WITH NAMES PEOPLE CAN SAY OUT LOUD.
I W-WANT T-TO SAY... I'M PROUD OF ALL OF Y-YOU.
EVEN YOU, MY GRUMBLER.
A-AND I'M N-NOT S-S-SORRY.
I SAID TO THE MAJOR... I T-TOLD HIM... THEY'RE N-NOT GOING INTO TH-THAT AGAIN. THEY ARE NOT. I W-WON'T LEAD M-MY MEN INTO THAT AGAIN... YOU CAN'T MAKE ME. IT-IT'S NOT RIGHT.

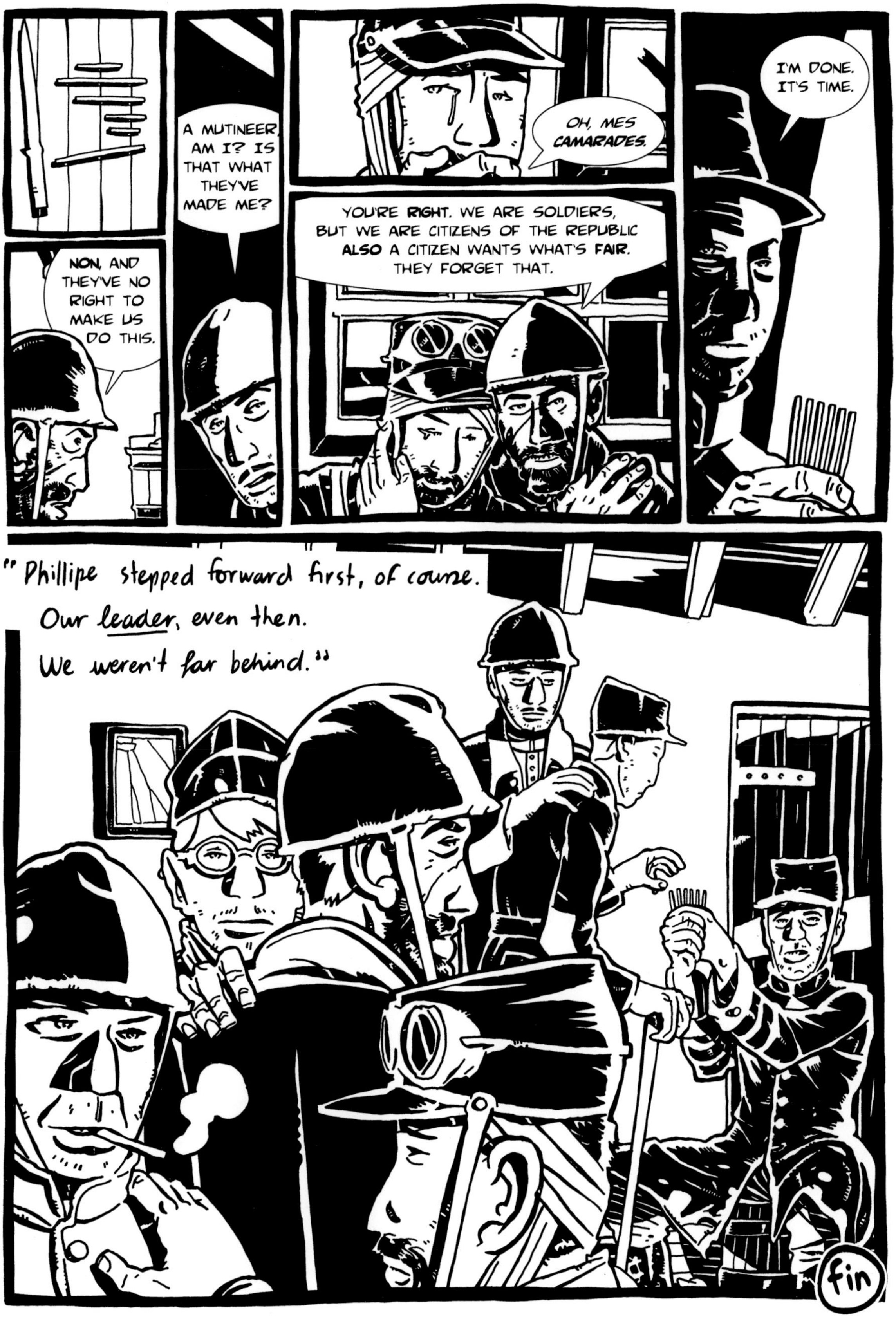
A MUTINEER AM I? IS THAT WHAT THEY'VE MADE ME?
NON, AND THEY'VE NO RIGHT TO MAKE US DO THIS.
OH, MES CAMARADES.
YOU'RE RIGHT. WE ARE SOLDIERS, BUT WE ARE CITIZENS OF THE REPUBLIC ALSO A CITIZEN WANTS WHAT'S FAIR. THEY FORGET THAT.
I'M DONE. IT'S TIME.
"Phillipe stepped forward first, of course.
Our leader, even then.
We weren't far behind."
fin

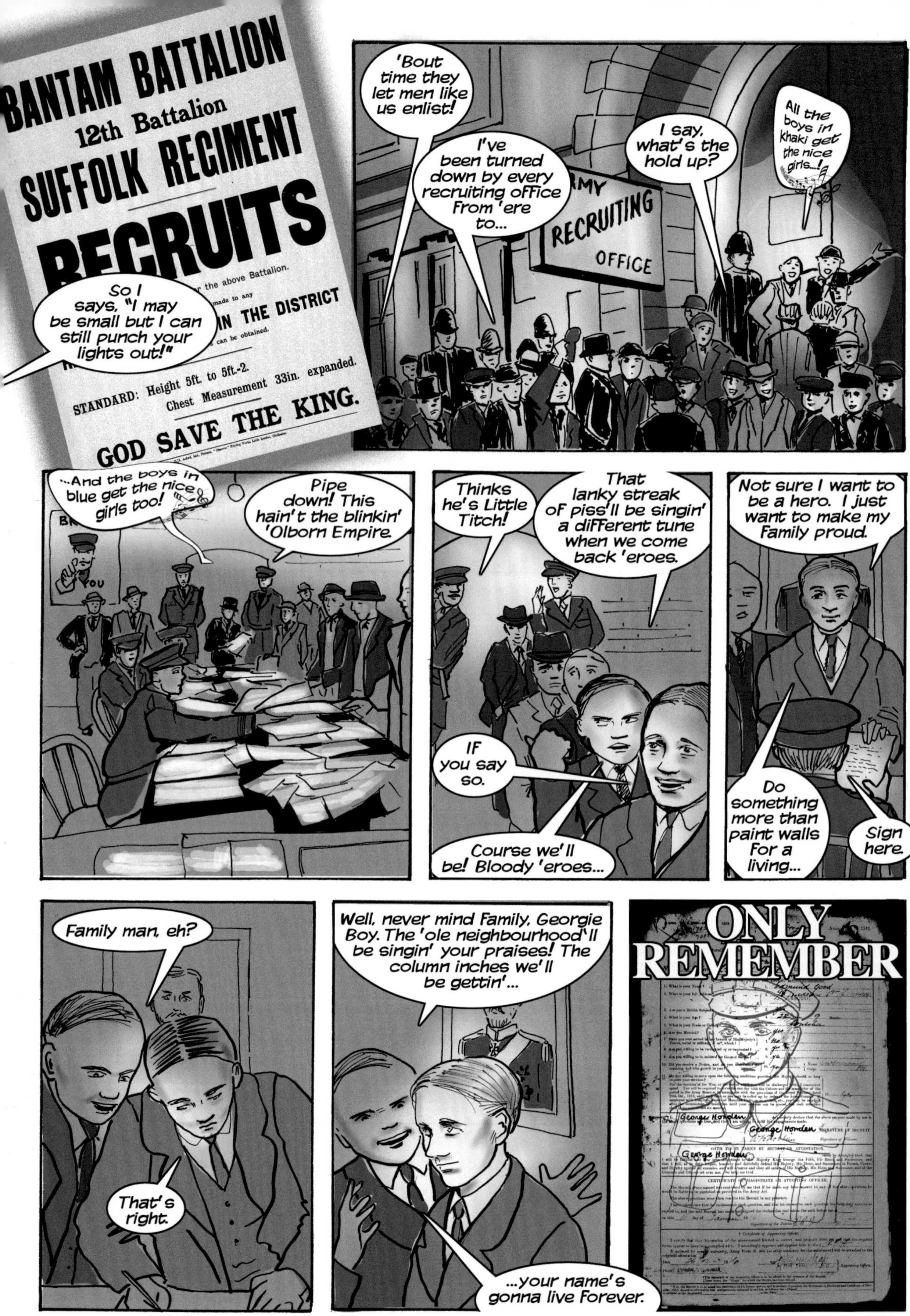

BANTAM BATTALION
12th Battalion
SUFFOLK REGIMENT
RECRUITS
r the above Battalion.
made to any
IN THE DISTRICT
s can be obtained.
STANDARD: Height 5ft. to 5ft.-2.
Chest Measurement 33in. expanded.
GOD SAVE THE KING.
So I says, "I may be small but I can still punch your lights out!"
'Bout time they let men like us enlist!
I've been turned down by every recruiting office from 'ere to...
RMY RECRUITING OFFICE
I say, what's the hold up?
All the boys in khaki get the nice girls...!
...And the boys in blue get the nice girls too!
Pipe down! This hain't the blinkin' 'Olborn Empire.
Thinks he's Little Titch!
That lanky streak of piss'll be singin' a different tune when we come back 'eroes.
If you say so.
Course we'll be! Bloody 'eroes...
Not sure I want to be a hero. I just want to make my family proud.
Do something more than paint walls for a living...
Sign here.
Family man, eh?
That's right.
Well, never mind family, Georgie Boy. The 'ole neighbourhood'll be singin' your praises! The column inches we'll be gettin'...
...your name's gonna live forever.
ONLY REMEMBER
George Horsden

Script: **Christopher & Faye Colley**
Art: **Jessica Martin & John Maybury**
Lettering: **Brick**

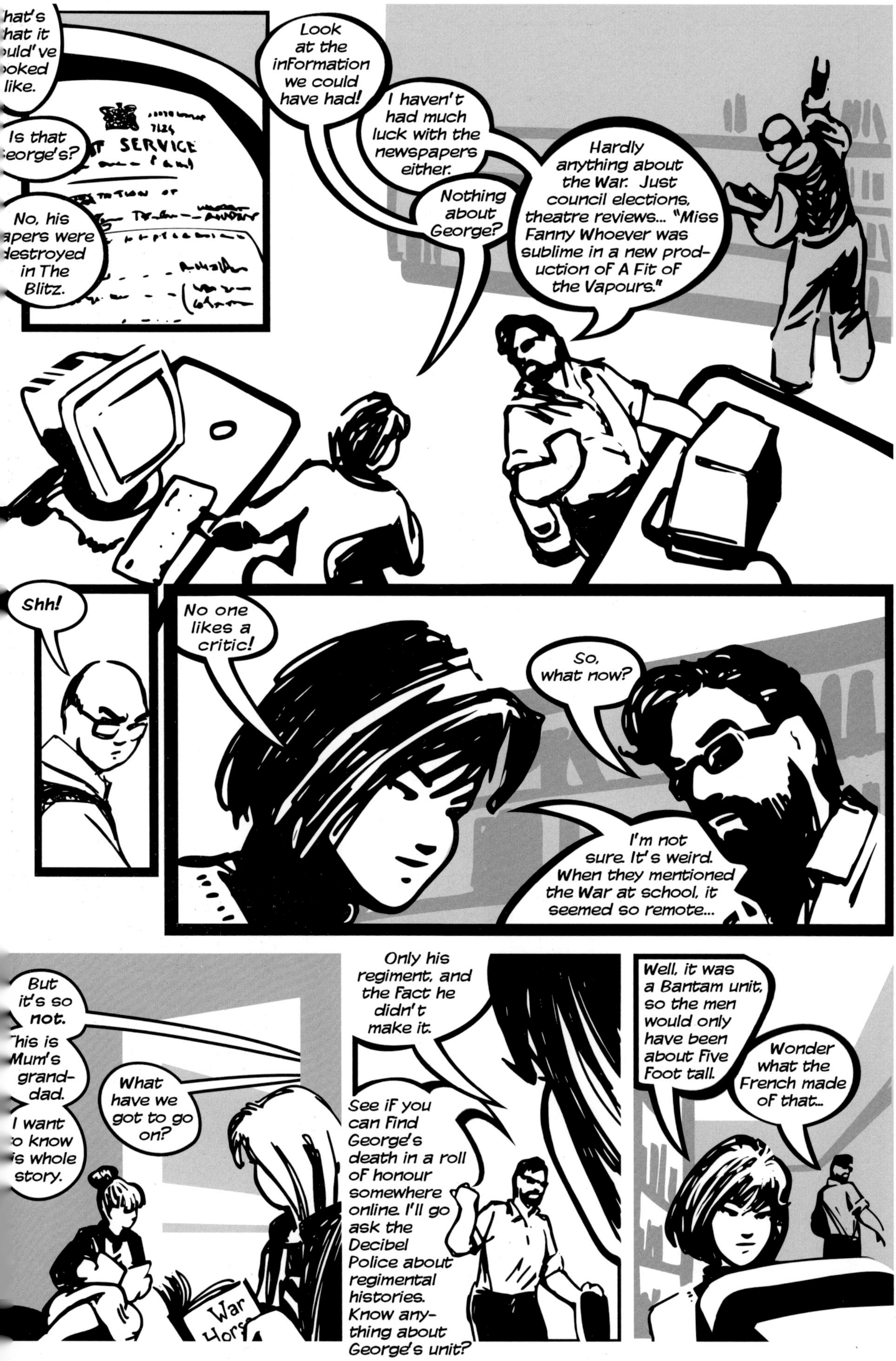

hat's
hat it
ould've
ooked
like.
Is that
eorge's?
SERVICE
No, his
apers were
destroyed
in The
Blitz.
Look at the information we could have had!
I haven't had much luck with the newspapers either.
Nothing about George?
Hardly anything about the War. Just council elections, theatre reviews... "Miss Fanny Whoever was sublime in a new production of A Fit of the Vapours."
Shh!
No one likes a critic!
So, what now?
I'm not sure. It's weird. When they mentioned the War at school, it seemed so remote...
But it's so **not**.
This is Mum's grand-dad.
I want
o know
is whole
story.
What have we got to go on?
War Hors
Only his regiment, and the fact he didn't make it.
See if you can find George's death in a roll of honour somewhere online. I'll go ask the Decibel Police about regimental histories. Know anything about George's unit?
Well, it was a Bantam unit, so the men would only have been about five foot tall.
Wonder what the French made of that...

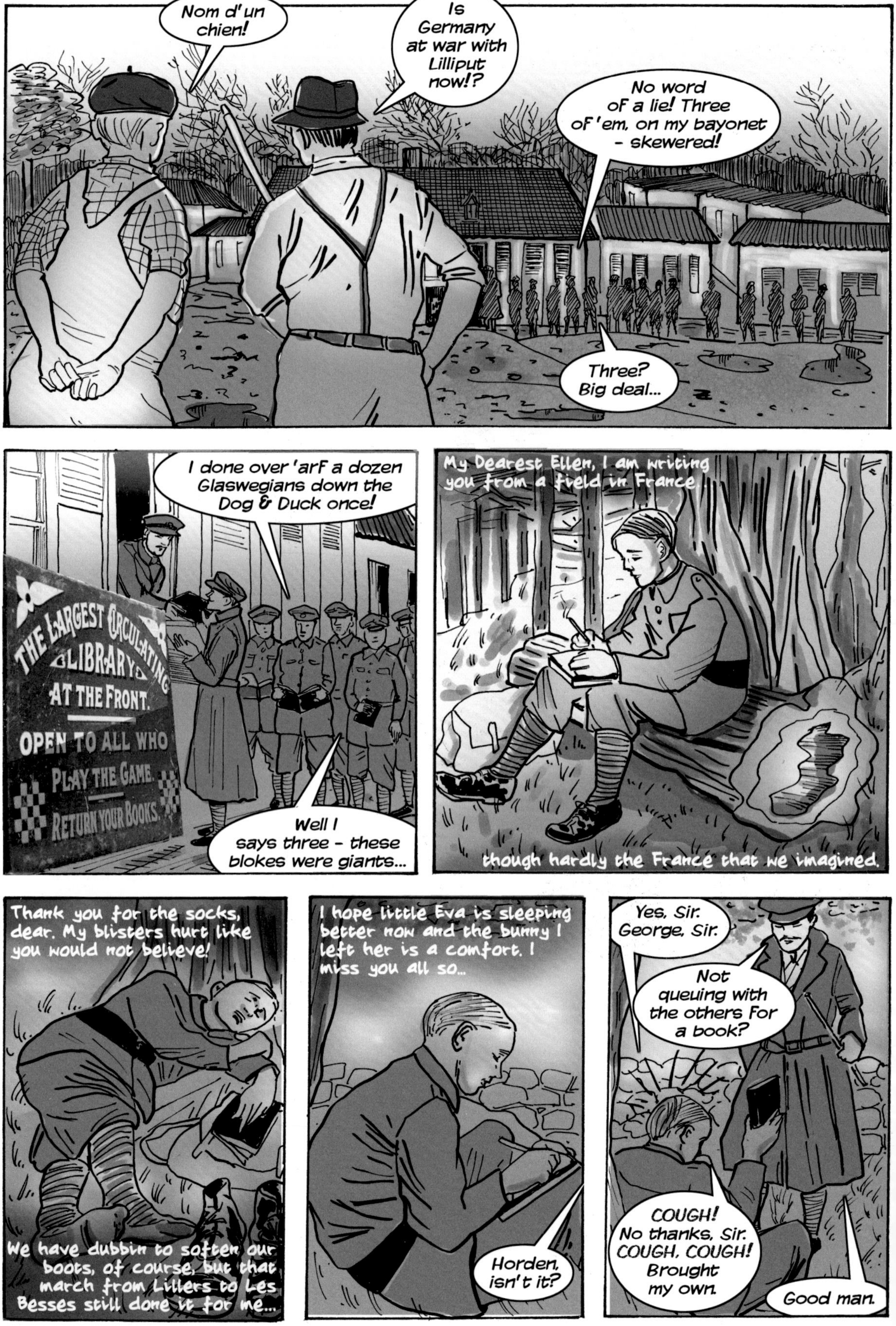
Nom d'un chien!
Is Germany at war with Lilliput now!?
No word of a lie! Three of 'em, on my bayonet - skewered!
Three? Big deal...
I done over 'arf a dozen Glaswegians down the Dog & Duck once!
THE LARGEST CIRCULATING LIBRARY AT THE FRONT. OPEN TO ALL WHO PLAY THE GAME. RETURN YOUR BOOKS.
Well I says three - these blokes were giants...
My Dearest Ellen, I am writing you from a field in France...
though hardly the France that we imagined.
Thank you for the socks, dear. My blisters hurt like you would not believe!
We have dubbin to soften our boots, of course, but that march from Lillers to Les Besses still done it for me...
I hope little Eva is sleeping better now and the bunny I left her is a comfort. I miss you all so...
Horden, isn't it?
Yes, Sir. George, Sir.
Not queuing with the others for a book?
COUGH! No thanks, Sir. COUGH, COUGH! Brought my own.
Good man.

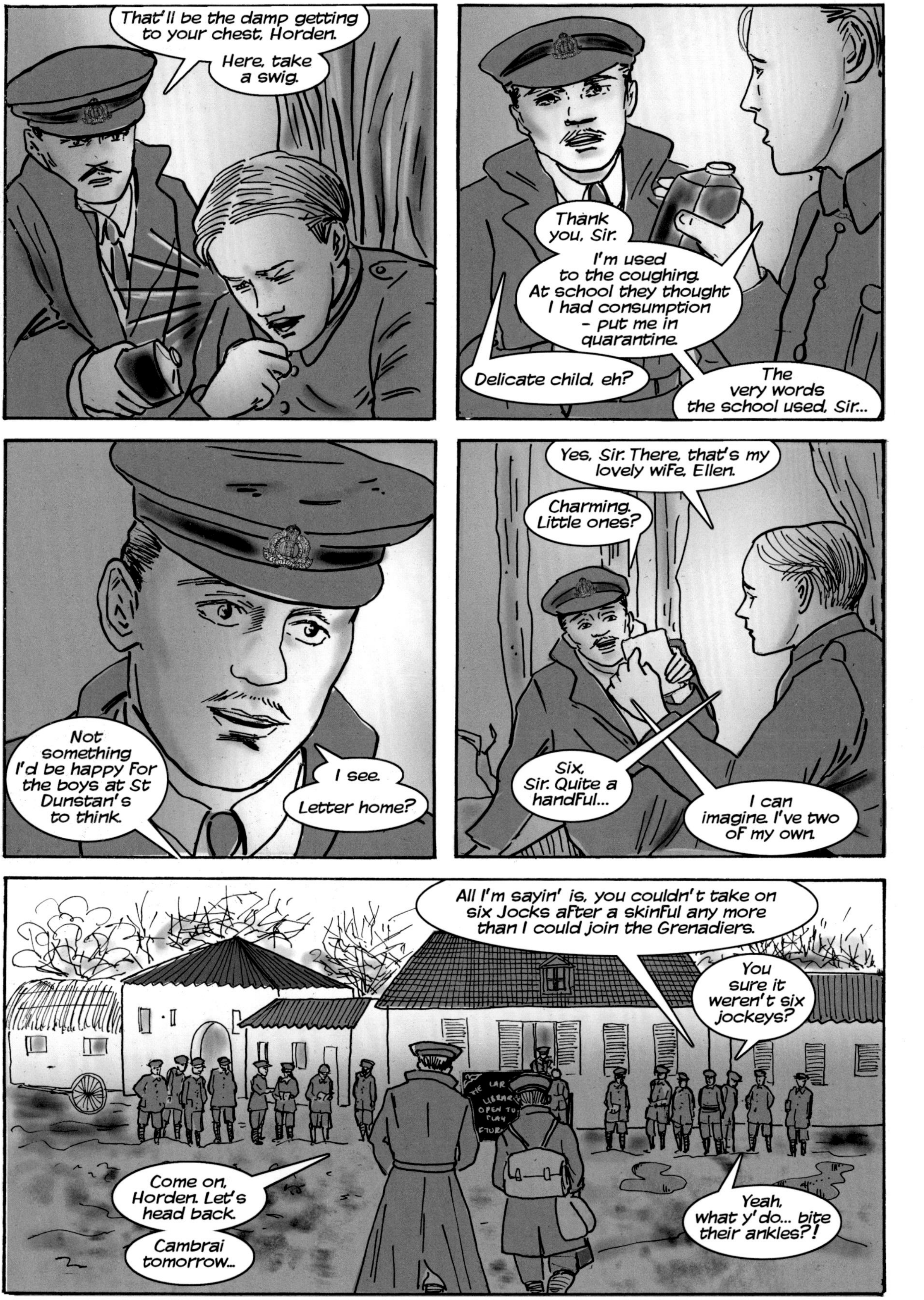
That'll be the damp getting to your chest, Horden.
Here, take a swig.
Thank you, Sir.
I'm used to the coughing. At school they thought I had consumption - put me in quarantine.
Delicate child, eh?
The very words the school used, Sir...
Not something I'd be happy for the boys at St Dunstan's to think.
I see.
Letter home?
Yes, Sir. There, that's my lovely wife, Ellen.
Charming. Little ones?
Six, Sir. Quite a handful...
I can imagine. I've two of my own.
All I'm sayin' is, you couldn't take on six Jocks after a skinful any more than I could join the Grenadiers.
You sure it weren't six jockeys?
Yeah, what y' do... bite their ankles?!
Come on, Horden. Let's head back.
Cambrai tomorrow...

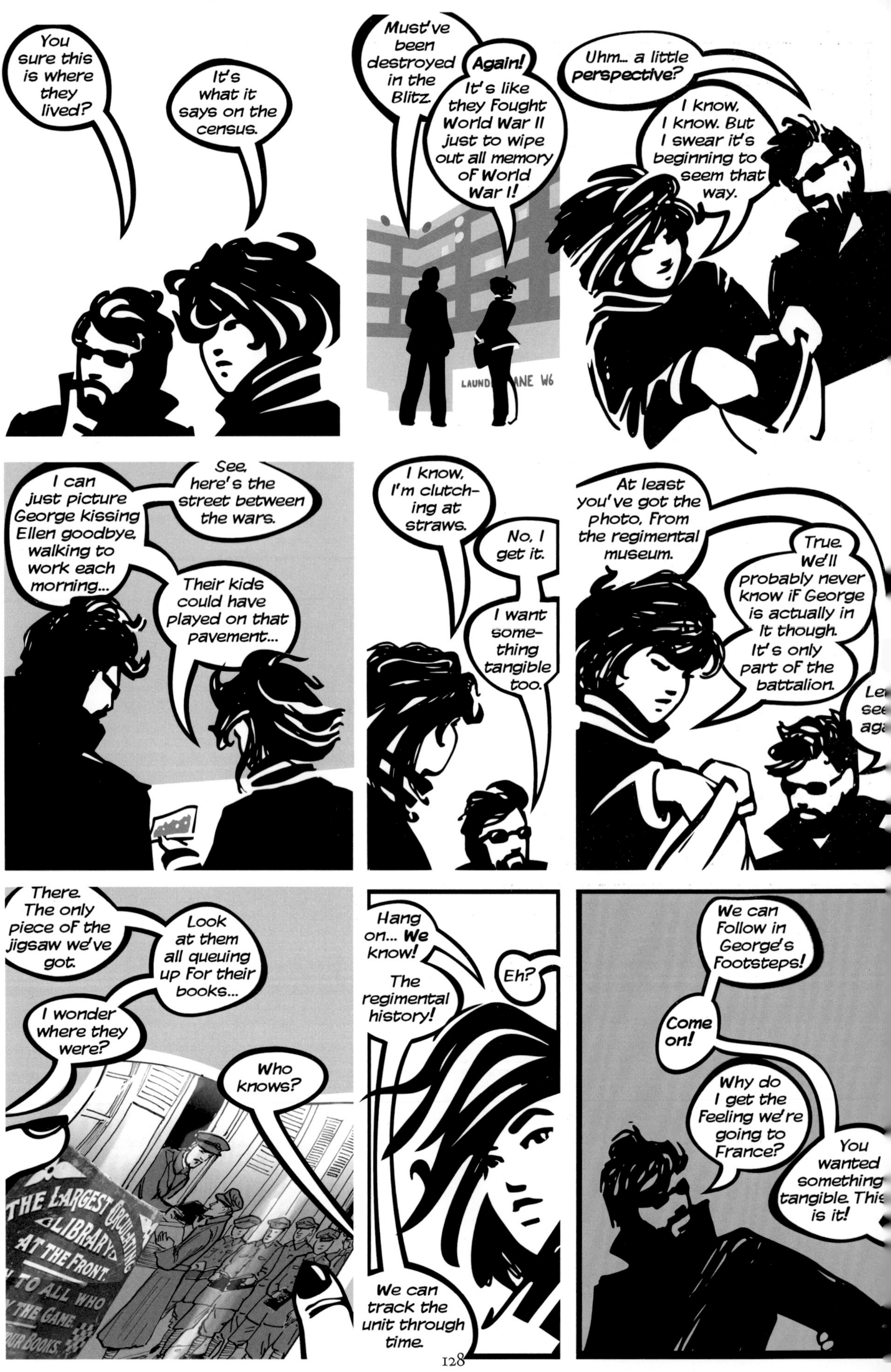
You sure this is where they lived?
It's what it says on the census.
Must've been destroyed in the Blitz.
Again! It's like they fought World War II just to wipe out all memory of World War I!
Uhm... a little perspective?
I know, I know. But I swear it's beginning to seem that way.
I can just picture George kissing Ellen goodbye, walking to work each morning...
See, here's the street between the wars.
Their kids could have played on that pavement...
I know, I'm clutching at straws.
No, I get it.
I want something tangible too.
At least you've got the photo, from the regimental museum.
True. We'll probably never know if George is actually in it though. It's only part of the battalion.
There. The only piece of the jigsaw we've got.
Look at them all queuing up for their books...
I wonder where they were?
Who knows?
THE LARGEST CIRCULATING LIBRARY AT THE FRONT.
Hang on... We know!
Eh?
The regimental history!
We can track the unit through time.
We can follow in George's footsteps!
Come on!
Why do I get the feeling we're going to France?
You wanted something tangible. This is it!

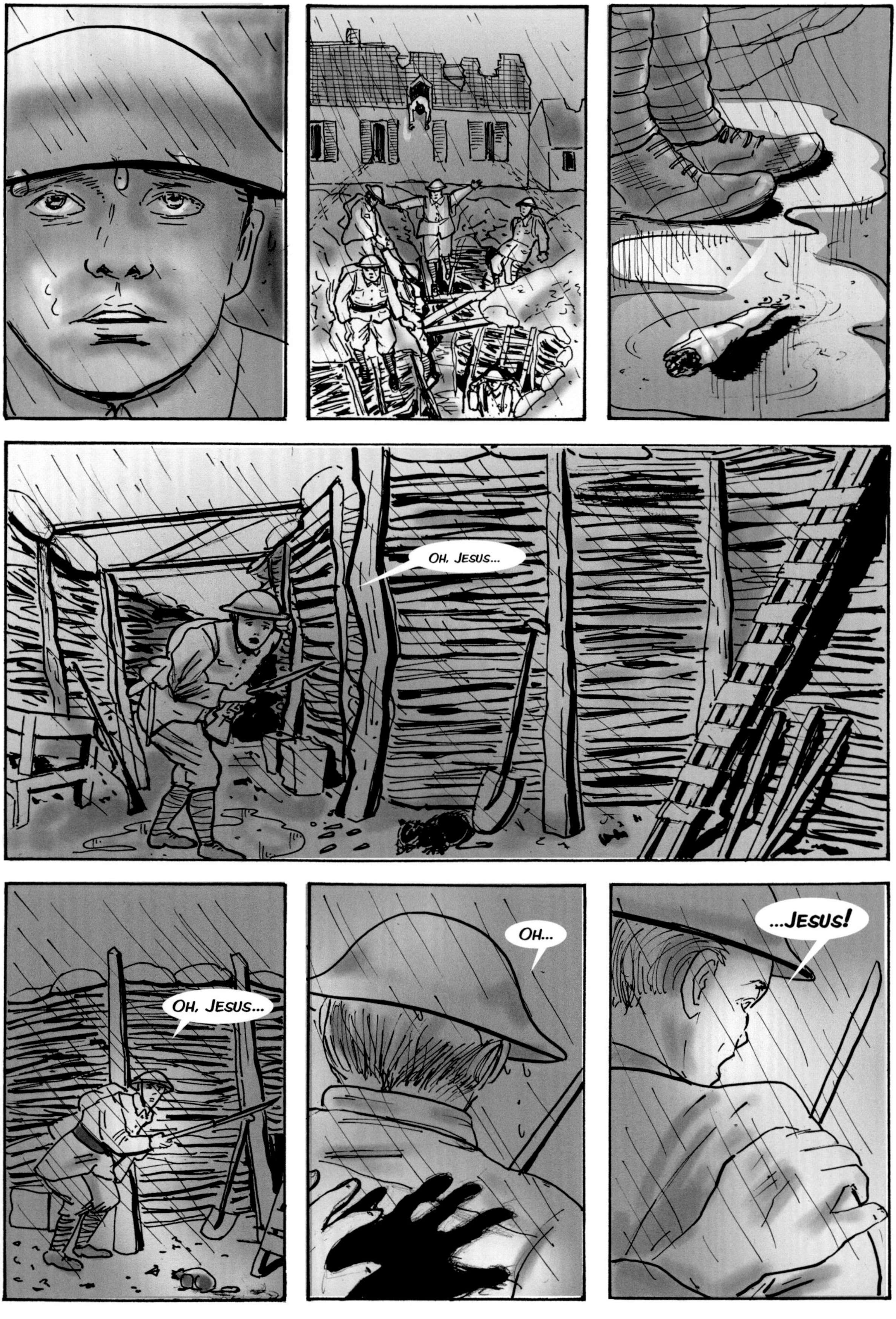
OH, JESUS...
OH, JESUS...
OH...
...JESUS!

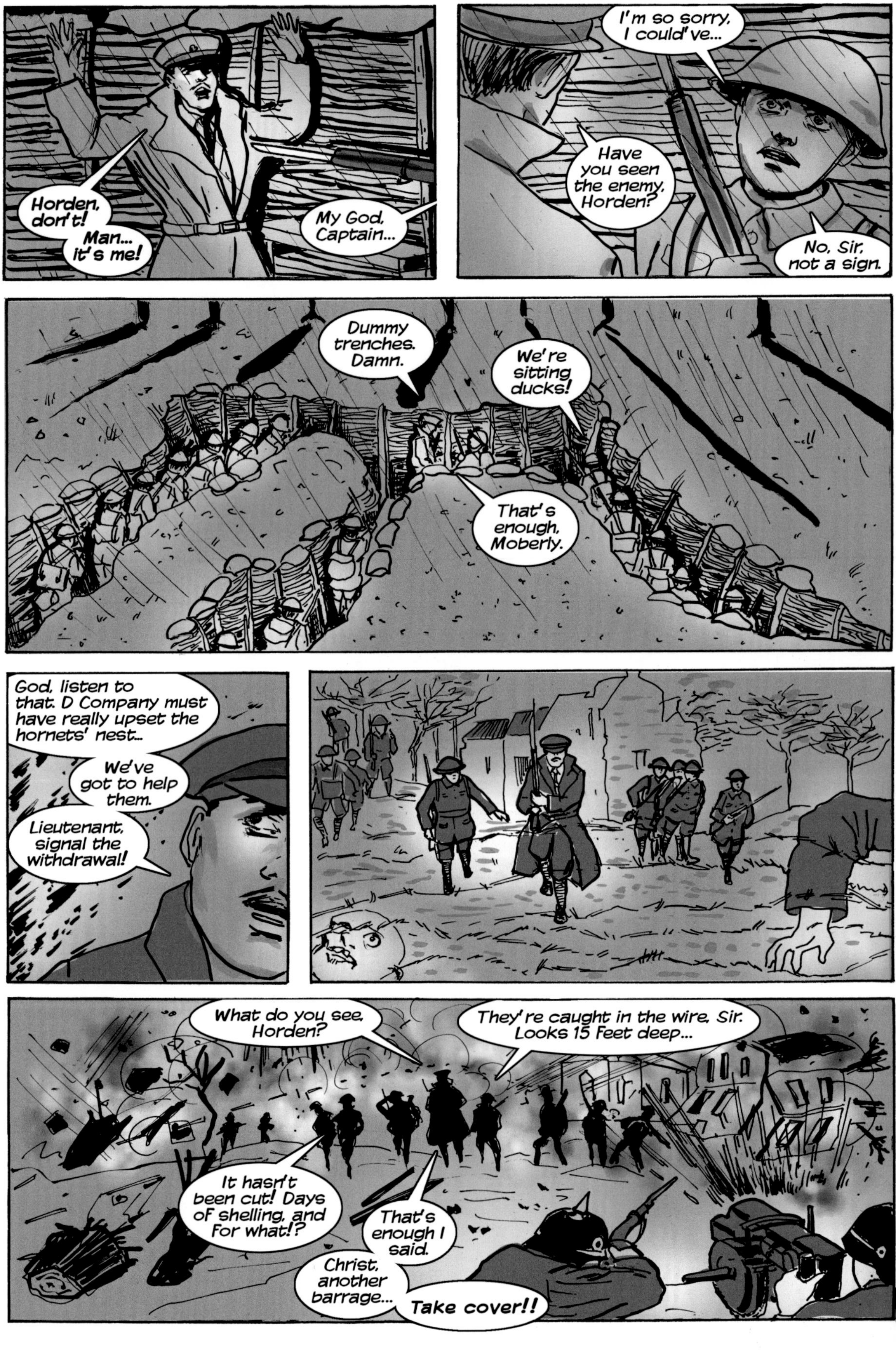
Horden, don't! Man... it's me!
My God, Captain...
I'm so sorry, I could've...
Have you seen the enemy, Horden?
No, Sir, not a sign.
Dummy trenches. Damn.
We're sitting ducks!
That's enough, Moberly.
God, listen to that. D Company must have really upset the hornets' nest...
We've got to help them.
Lieutenant, signal the withdrawal!
What do you see, Horden?
They're caught in the wire, Sir. Looks 15 feet deep...
It hasn't been cut! Days of shelling, and for what!?
That's enough I said.
Christ, another barrage...
Take cover!!

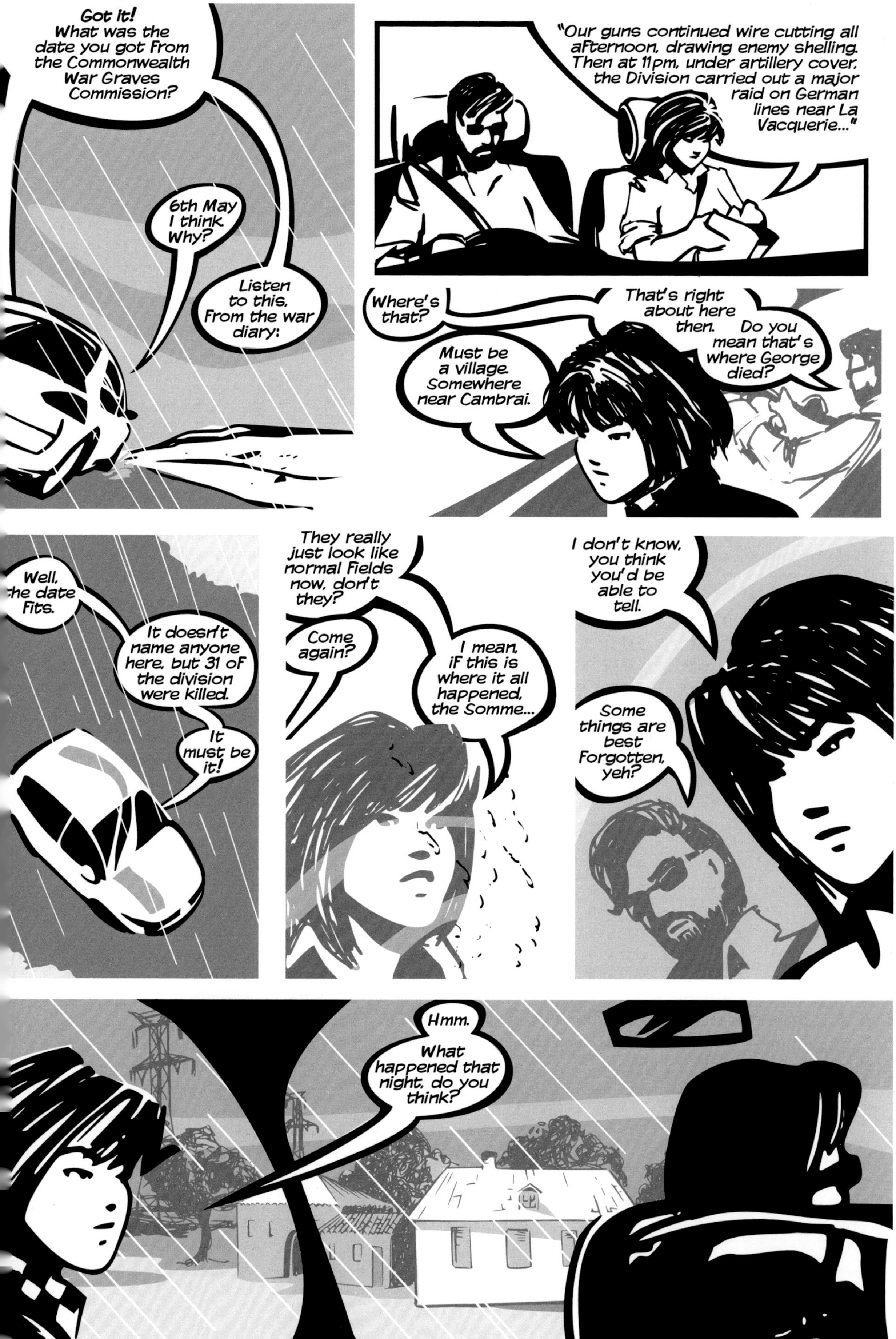
Got it! What was the date you got from the Commonwealth War Graves Commission?
6th May I think. Why?
Listen to this, from the war diary:
"Our guns continued wire cutting all afternoon, drawing enemy shelling. Then at 11pm, under artillery cover, the Division carried out a major raid on German lines near La Vacquerie..."
Where's that?
Must be a village. Somewhere near Cambrai.
That's right about here then.
Do you mean that's where George died?
Well, the date fits.
It doesn't name anyone here, but 31 of the division were killed.
It must be it!
They really just look like normal fields now, don't they?
Come again?
I mean, if this is where it all happened, the Somme...
I don't know, you think you'd be able to tell.
Some things are best forgotten, yeh?
Hmm.
What happened that night, do you think?

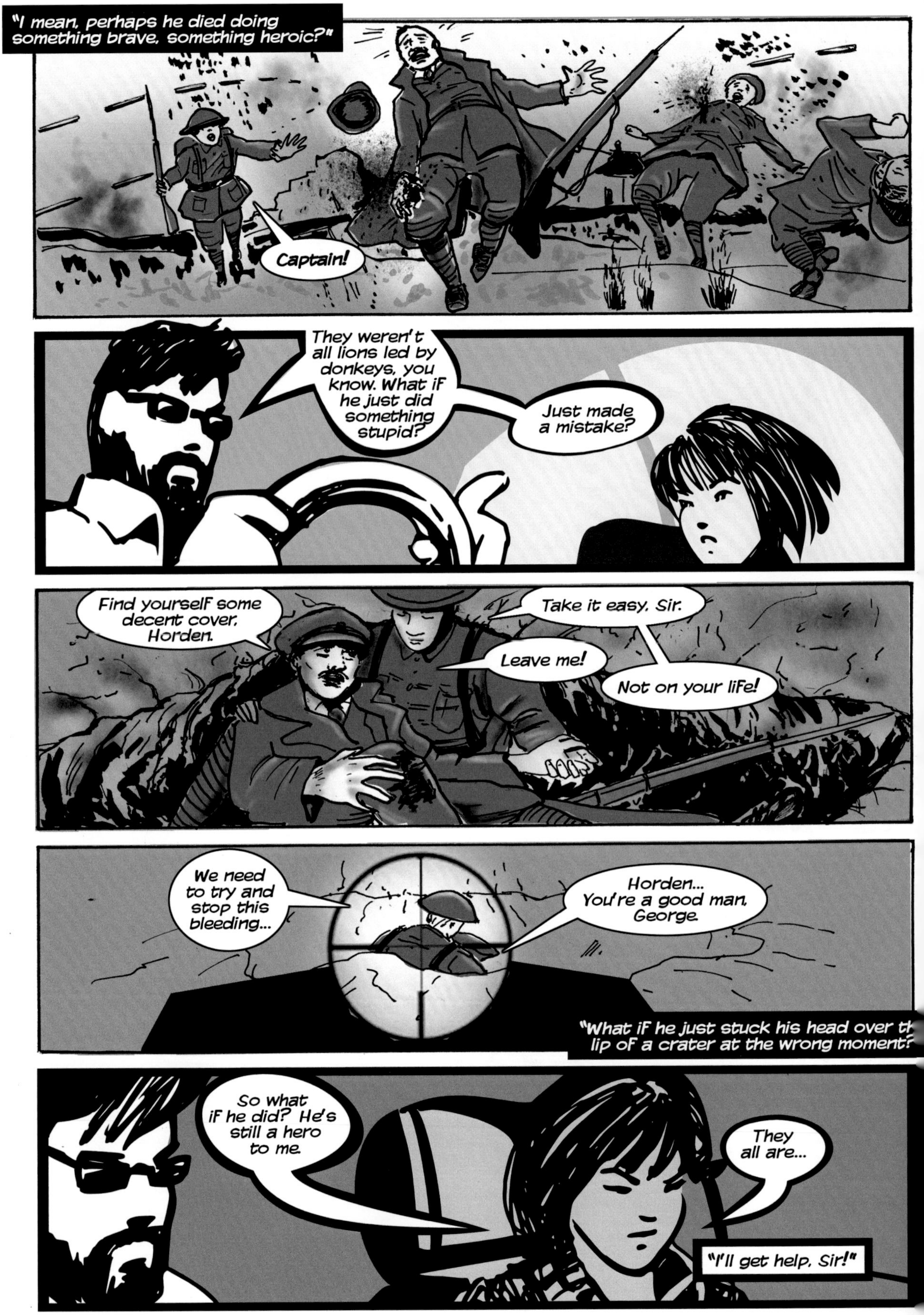
"I mean, perhaps he died doing something brave, something heroic?"
Captain!
They weren't all lions led by donkeys, you know. What if he just did something stupid?
Just made a mistake?
Find yourself some decent cover, Horden.
Take it easy, Sir.
Leave me!
Not on your life!
We need to try and stop this bleeding...
Horden... You're a good man, George.
"What if he just stuck his head over th lip of a crater at the wrong moment?
So what if he did? He's still a hero to me.
They all are...
"I'll get help, Sir!"

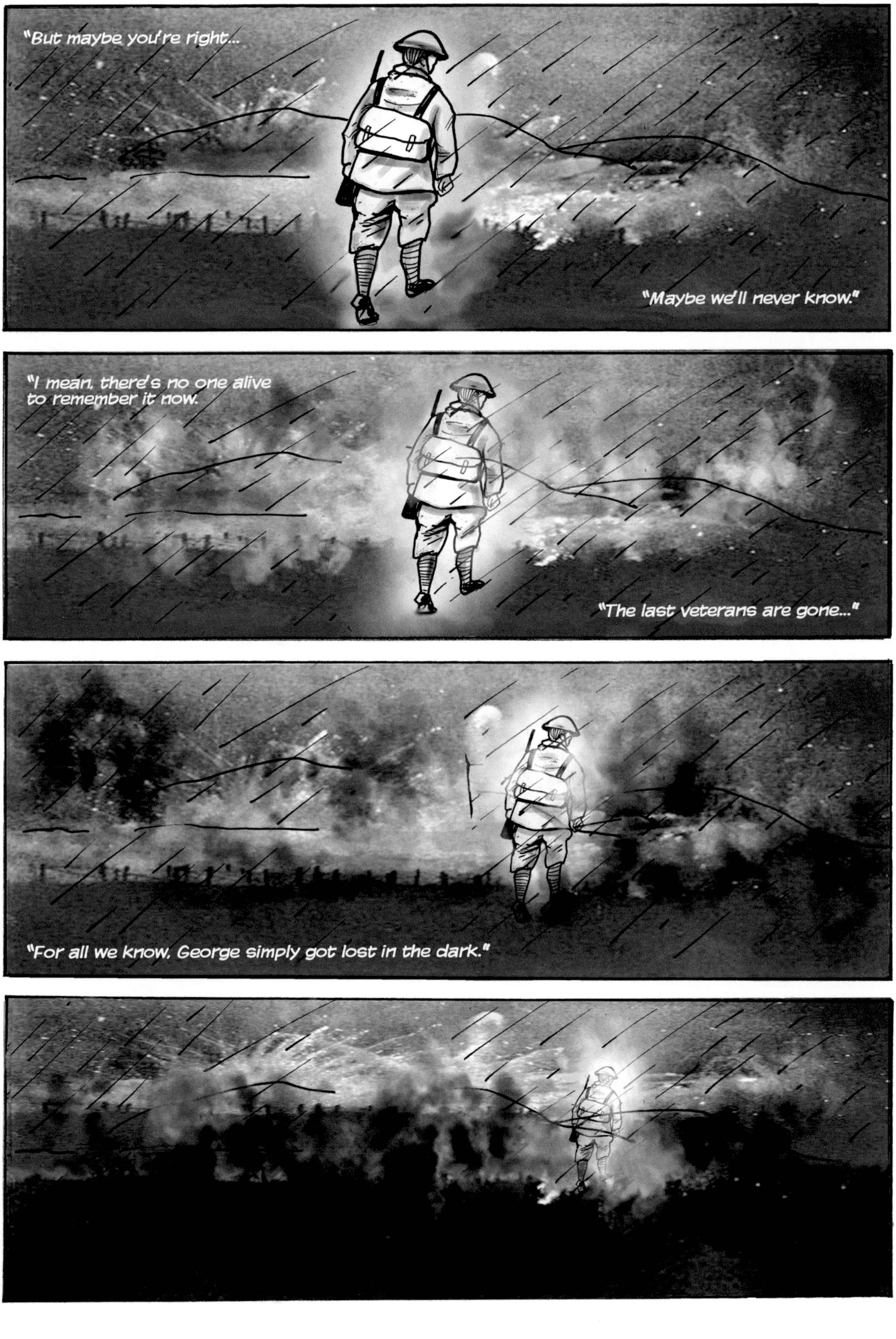
"But maybe you're right...
"Maybe we'll never know."
"I mean, there's no one alive to remember it now.
"The last veterans are gone..."
"For all we know, George simply got lost in the dark."

That was good timing. The rain's stopping.

It should be just the other side of these trees...

Well... There it is.

Whoah!

How are we supposed your find your great-granddad's amongst all these?

Look at all these names...

The War Graves people gave me the reference.

Let's see – pier 2, Face A...

It's like being lost in the trenches.

Don't joke.

Not like that. I mean, we're surrounded by them, by all the men who died on the Western Front.

No, only the ones whose bodies they **didn't** find. Just from the Somme.

THEIR NAME LIVETH FOR EVERMORE

My God.

Okay... Hopkins, Hopkinson...

Here! Here he is.

You know, we're probably the first family members who've been able to visit – to see his name.

...KINSON T. C.
...WOLD H.
...PWOOD A. F.
HO...AM T.
HORD...N G. H.
HORN...W.
HORNBY K. K.
HORNB...L.
HORN...R
HORNS...

Are you okay?

I'm sorry. It's strange.

It feels like the road has ended.

We're as close to George as we'll ever be...

But there's so much we'll never know.

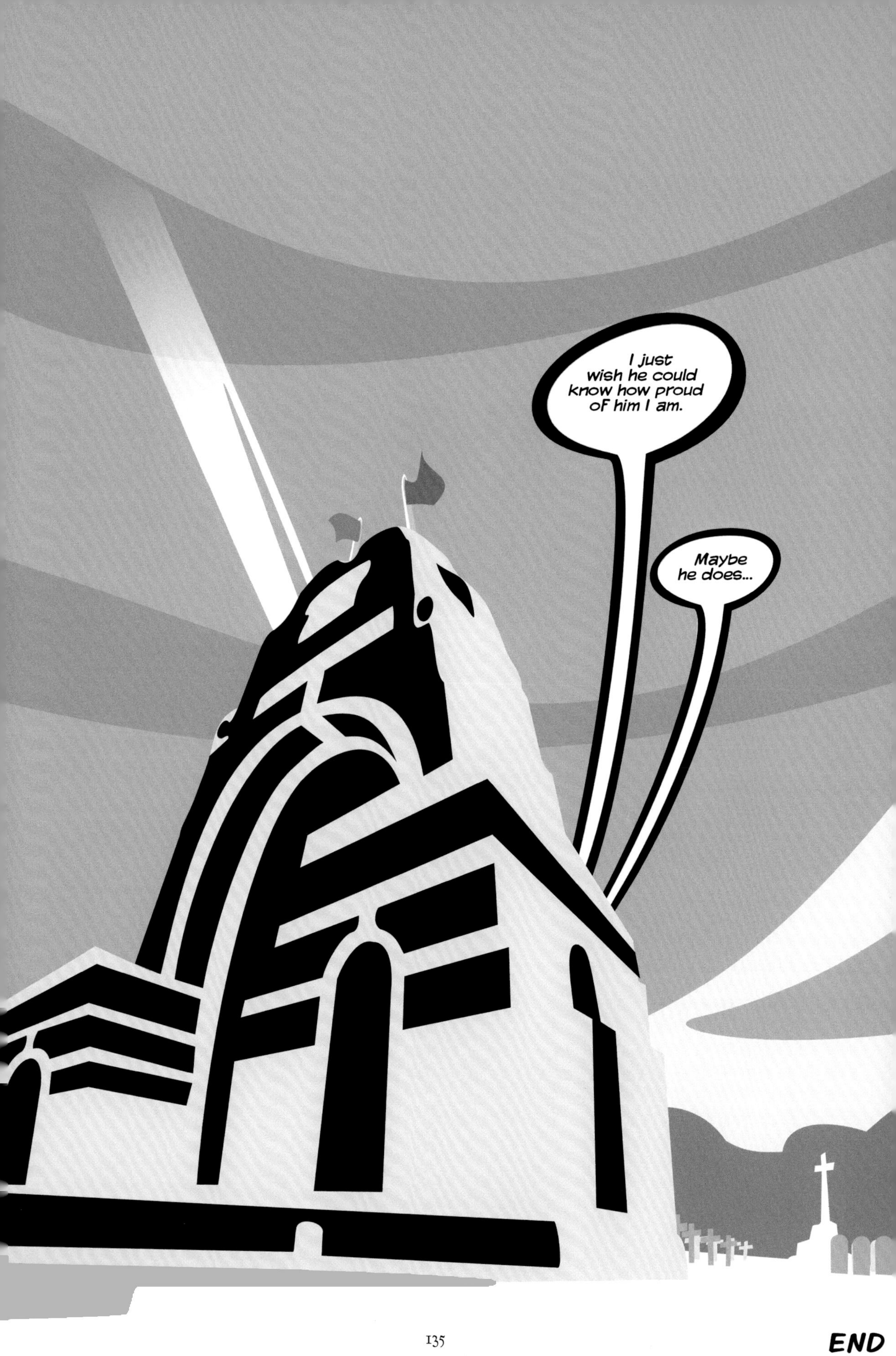
I just wish he could know how proud of him I am.
Maybe he does...

END

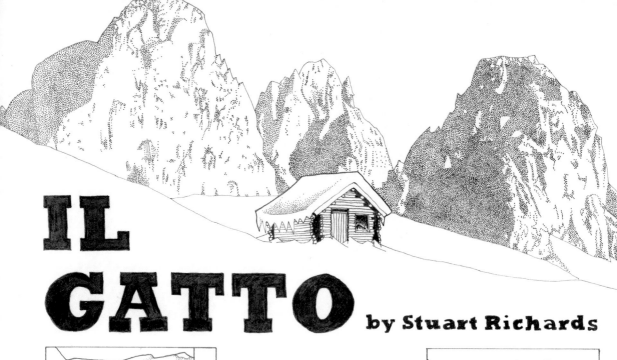

IL GATTO
by Stuart Richards

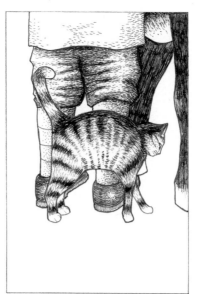
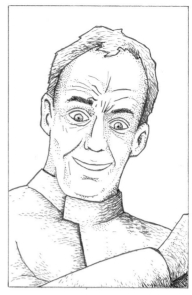

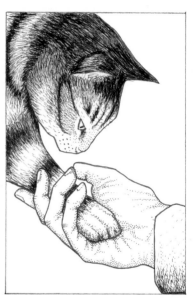

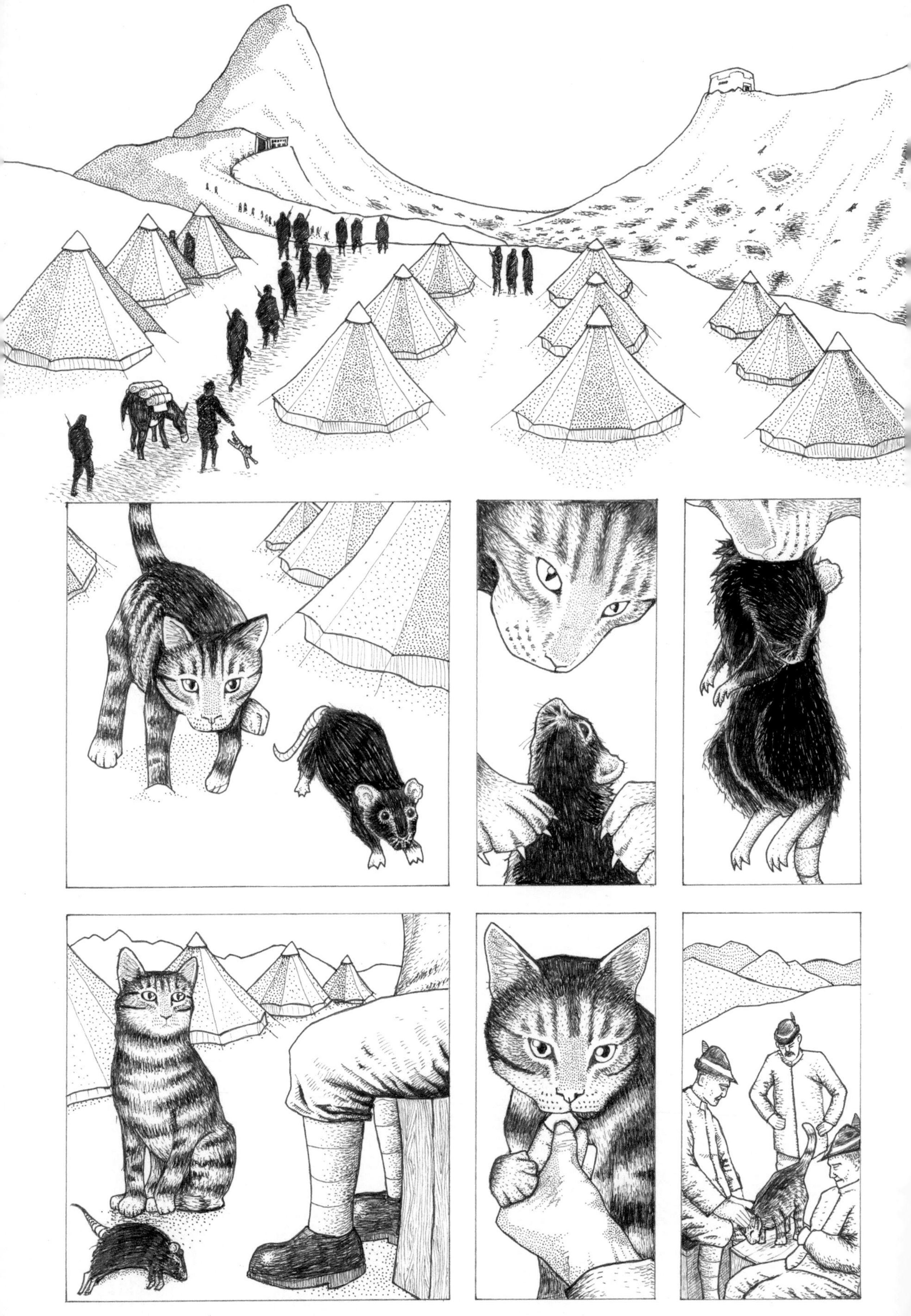

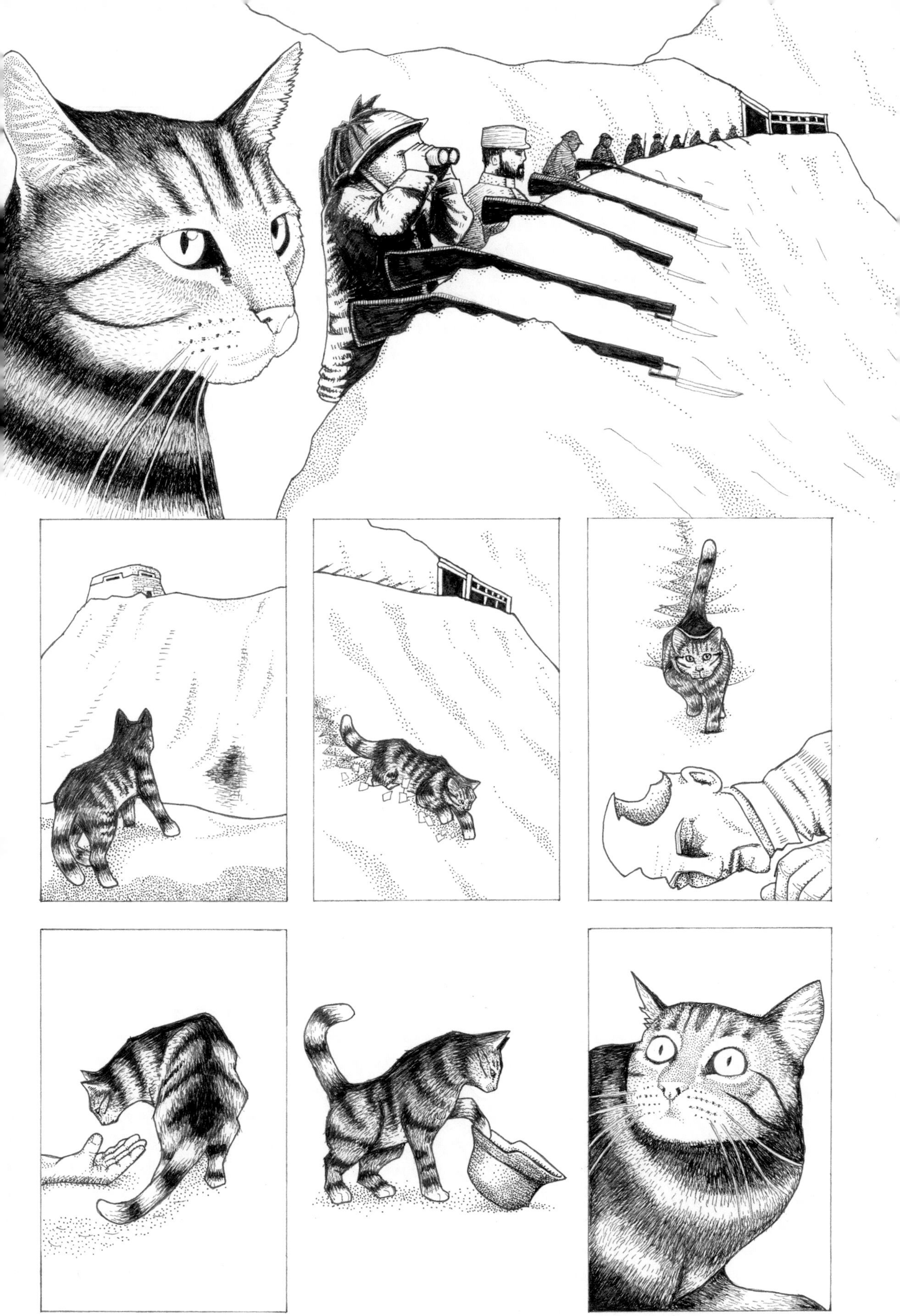

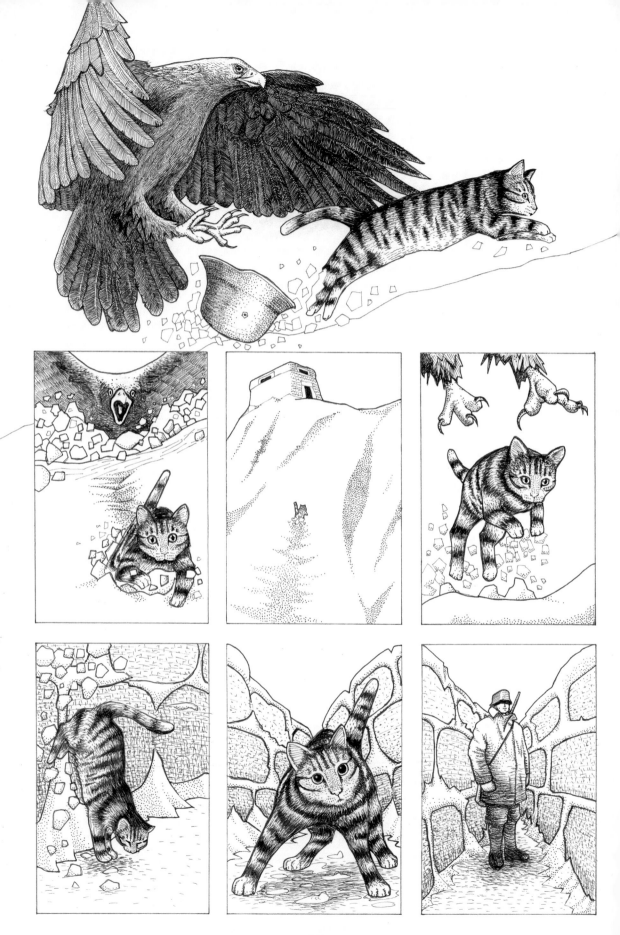

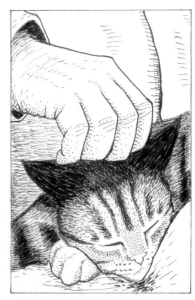

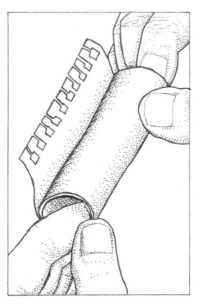

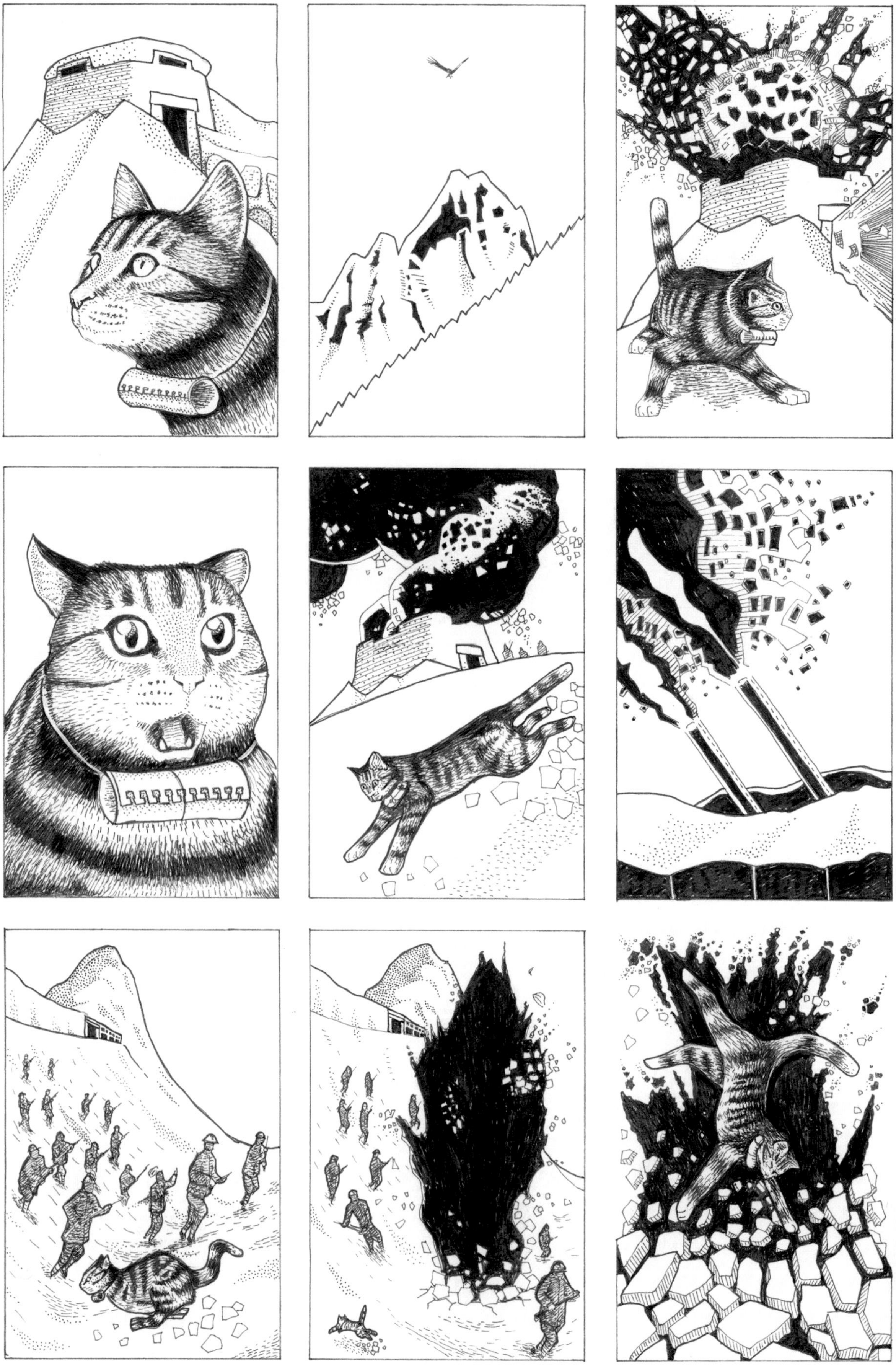

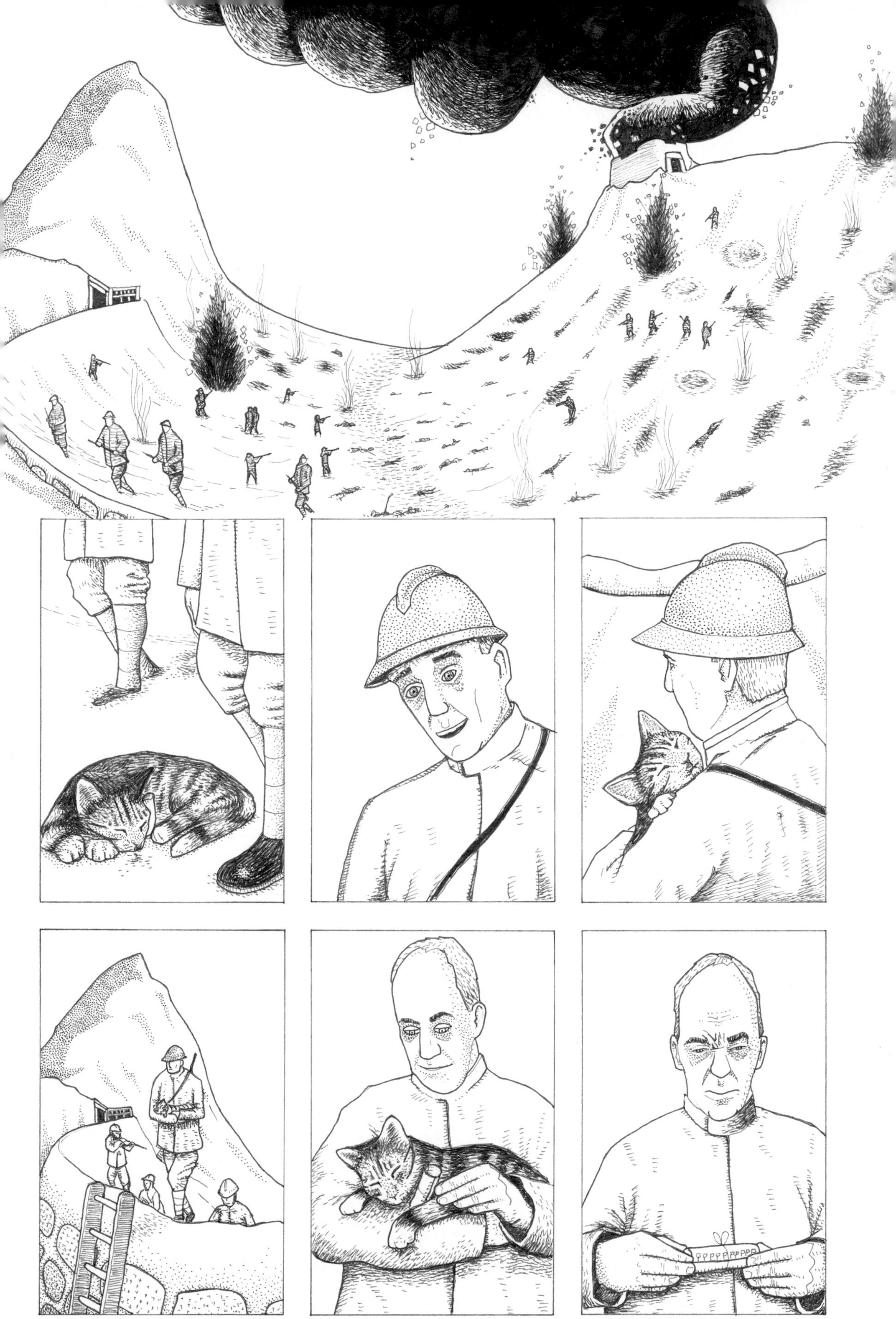

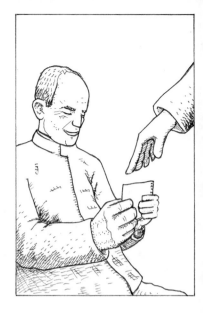
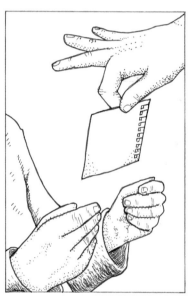

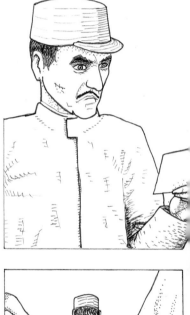
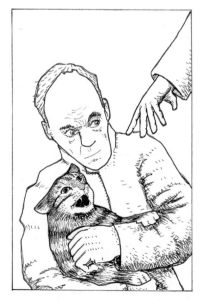

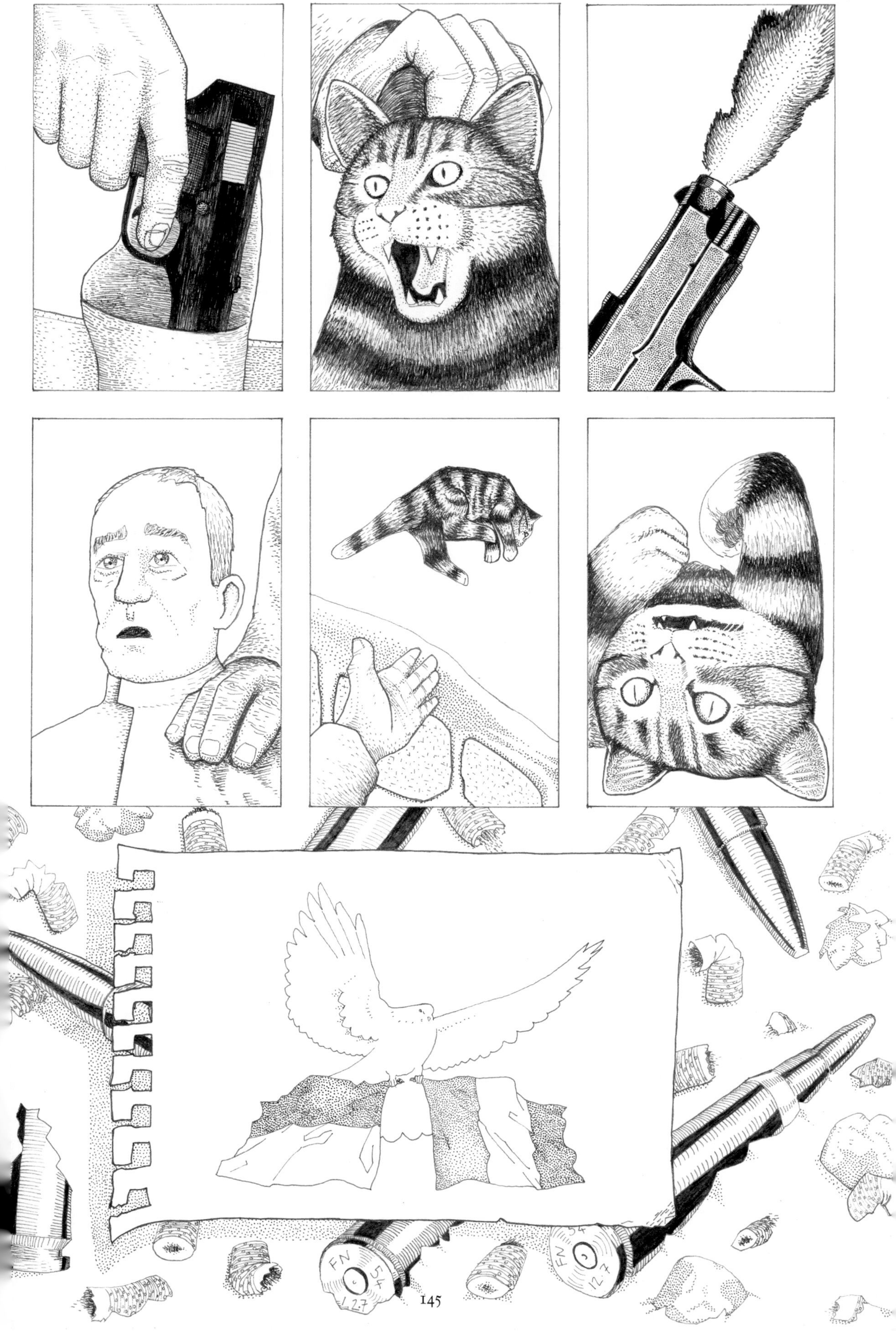
FN 54 12.7
FN 54 12.7

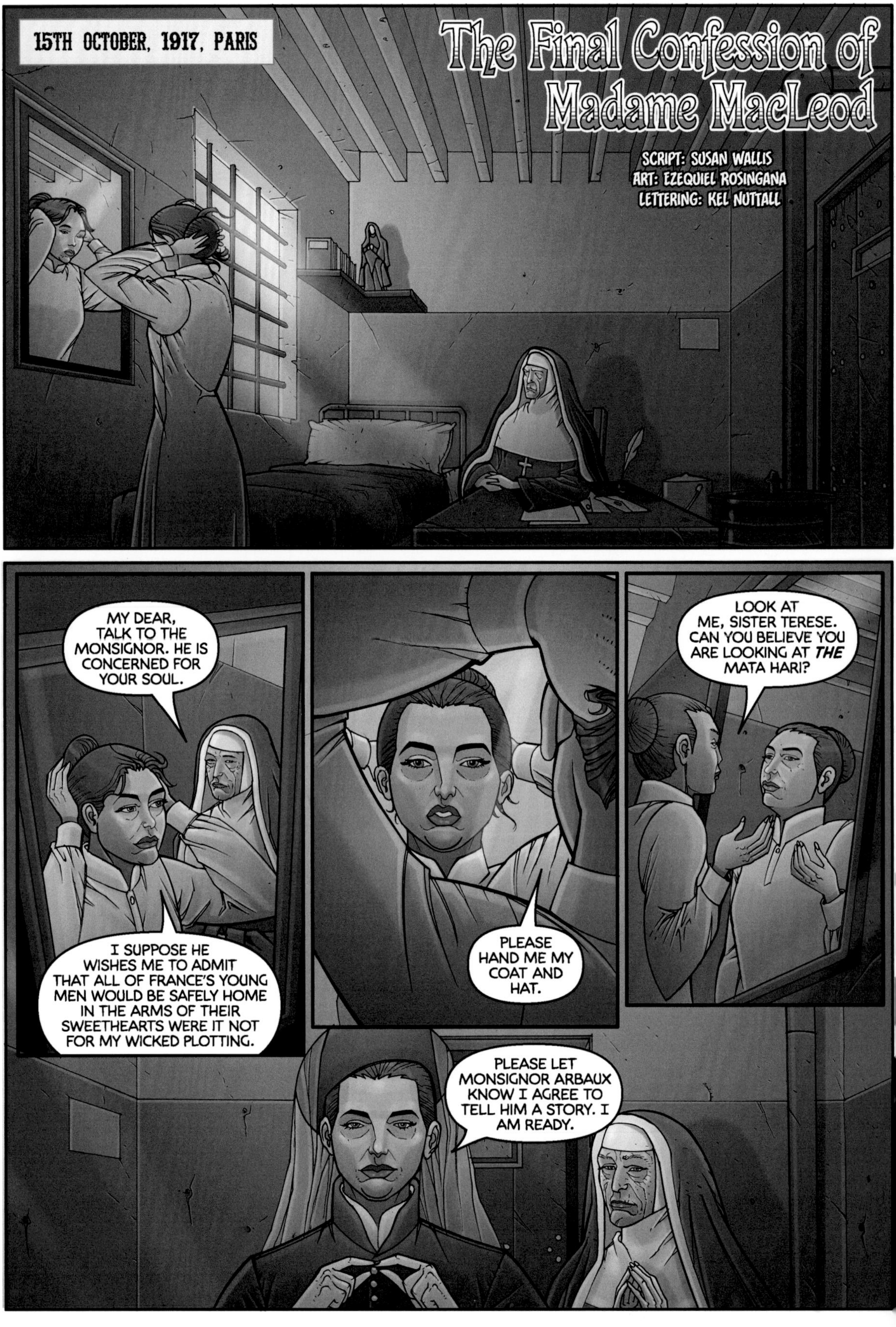
15TH OCTOBER, 1917, PARIS
The Final Confession of Madame MacLeod
SCRIPT: SUSAN WALLIS
ART: EZEQUIEL ROSINGANA
LETTERING: KEL NUTTALL
MY DEAR, TALK TO THE MONSIGNOR. HE IS CONCERNED FOR YOUR SOUL.
I SUPPOSE HE WISHES ME TO ADMIT THAT ALL OF FRANCE'S YOUNG MEN WOULD BE SAFELY HOME IN THE ARMS OF THEIR SWEETHEARTS WERE IT NOT FOR MY WICKED PLOTTING.
PLEASE HAND ME MY COAT AND HAT.
LOOK AT ME, SISTER TERESE. CAN YOU BELIEVE YOU ARE LOOKING AT *THE* MATA HARI?
PLEASE LET MONSIGNOR ARBAUX KNOW I AGREE TO TELL HIM A STORY. I AM READY.

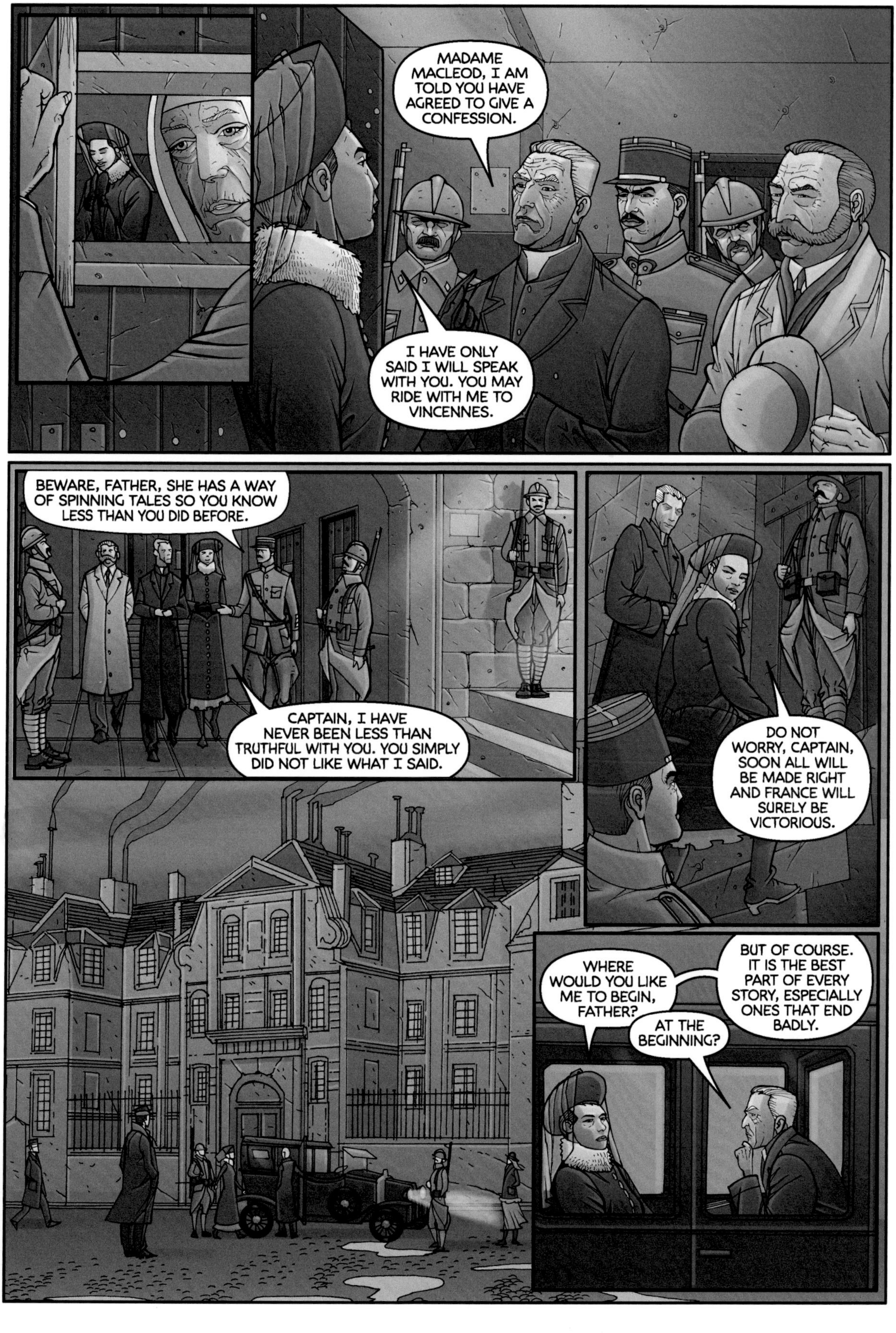
MADAME MACLEOD, I AM TOLD YOU HAVE AGREED TO GIVE A CONFESSION.
I HAVE ONLY SAID I WILL SPEAK WITH YOU. YOU MAY RIDE WITH ME TO VINCENNES.
BEWARE, FATHER, SHE HAS A WAY OF SPINNING TALES SO YOU KNOW LESS THAN YOU DID BEFORE.
CAPTAIN, I HAVE NEVER BEEN LESS THAN TRUTHFUL WITH YOU. YOU SIMPLY DID NOT LIKE WHAT I SAID.
DO NOT WORRY, CAPTAIN, SOON ALL WILL BE MADE RIGHT AND FRANCE WILL SURELY BE VICTORIOUS.
WHERE WOULD YOU LIKE ME TO BEGIN, FATHER?
AT THE BEGINNING?
BUT OF COURSE. IT IS THE BEST PART OF EVERY STORY, ESPECIALLY ONES THAT END BADLY.

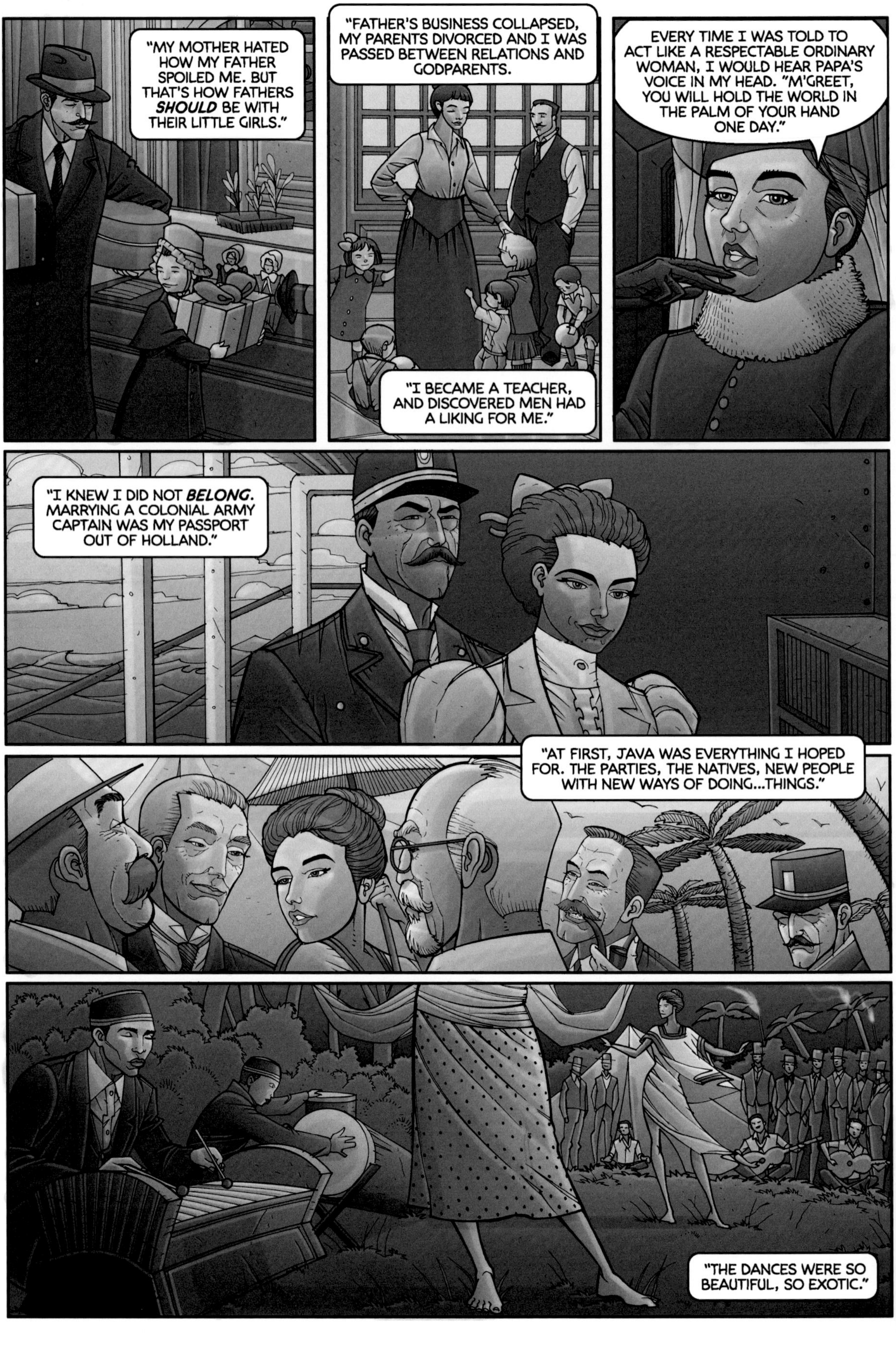
"MY MOTHER HATED HOW MY FATHER SPOILED ME. BUT THAT'S HOW FATHERS *SHOULD* BE WITH THEIR LITTLE GIRLS."
"FATHER'S BUSINESS COLLAPSED, MY PARENTS DIVORCED AND I WAS PASSED BETWEEN RELATIONS AND GODPARENTS.
"I BECAME A TEACHER, AND DISCOVERED MEN HAD A LIKING FOR ME."
EVERY TIME I WAS TOLD TO ACT LIKE A RESPECTABLE ORDINARY WOMAN, I WOULD HEAR PAPA'S VOICE IN MY HEAD. "M'GREET, YOU WILL HOLD THE WORLD IN THE PALM OF YOUR HAND ONE DAY."
"I KNEW I DID NOT *BELONG*. MARRYING A COLONIAL ARMY CAPTAIN WAS MY PASSPORT OUT OF HOLLAND."
"AT FIRST, JAVA WAS EVERYTHING I HOPED FOR. THE PARTIES, THE NATIVES, NEW PEOPLE WITH NEW WAYS OF DOING...THINGS."
"THE DANCES WERE SO BEAUTIFUL, SO EXOTIC."

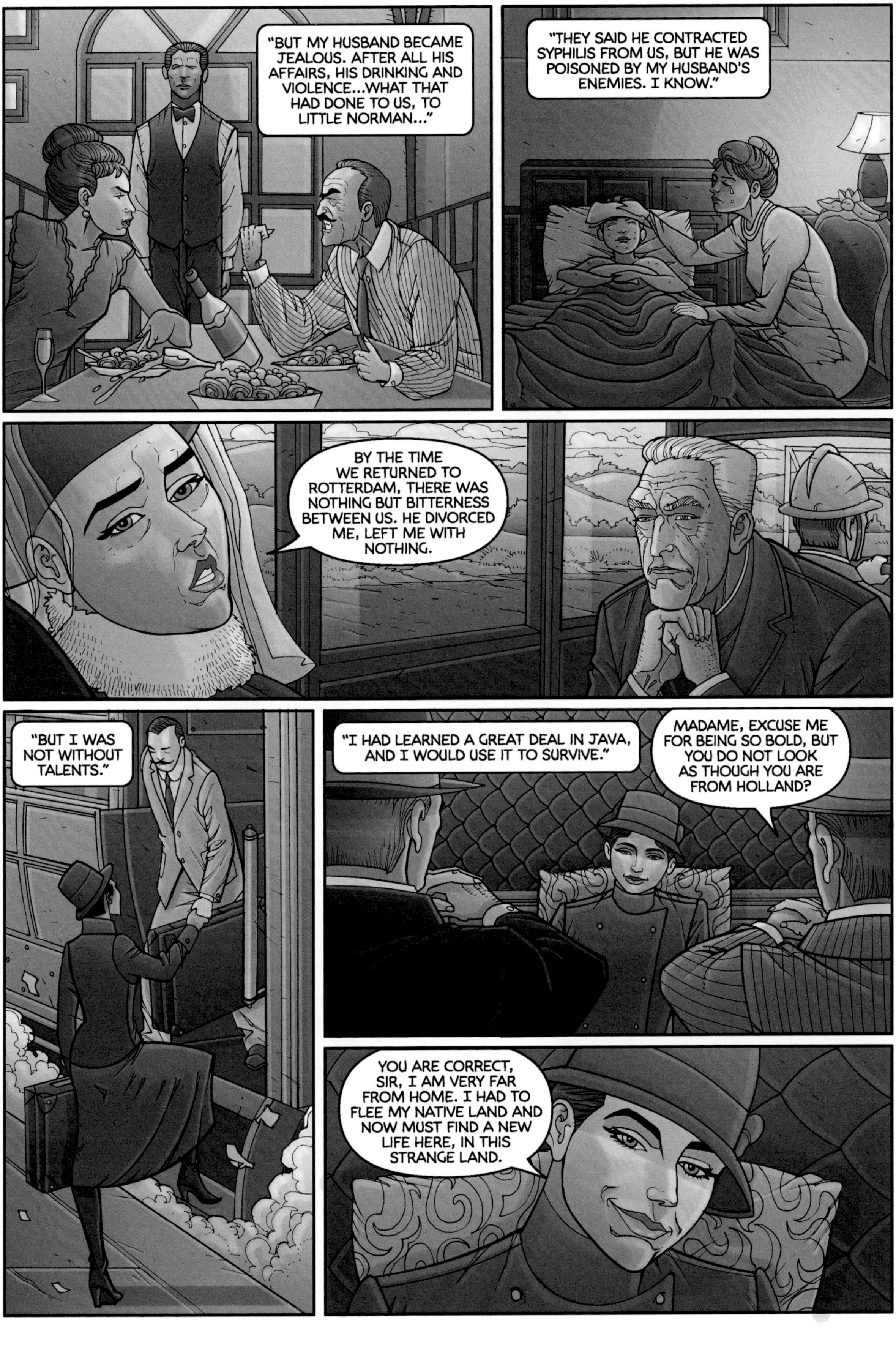
"BUT MY HUSBAND BECAME JEALOUS. AFTER ALL HIS AFFAIRS, HIS DRINKING AND VIOLENCE...WHAT THAT HAD DONE TO US, TO LITTLE NORMAN..."
"THEY SAID HE CONTRACTED SYPHILIS FROM US, BUT HE WAS POISONED BY MY HUSBAND'S ENEMIES. I KNOW."
BY THE TIME WE RETURNED TO ROTTERDAM, THERE WAS NOTHING BUT BITTERNESS BETWEEN US. HE DIVORCED ME, LEFT ME WITH NOTHING.
"BUT I WAS NOT WITHOUT TALENTS."
"I HAD LEARNED A GREAT DEAL IN JAVA, AND I WOULD USE IT TO SURVIVE."
MADAME, EXCUSE ME FOR BEING SO BOLD, BUT YOU DO NOT LOOK AS THOUGH YOU ARE FROM HOLLAND?
YOU ARE CORRECT, SIR, I AM VERY FAR FROM HOME. I HAD TO FLEE MY NATIVE LAND AND NOW MUST FIND A NEW LIFE HERE, IN THIS STRANGE LAND.

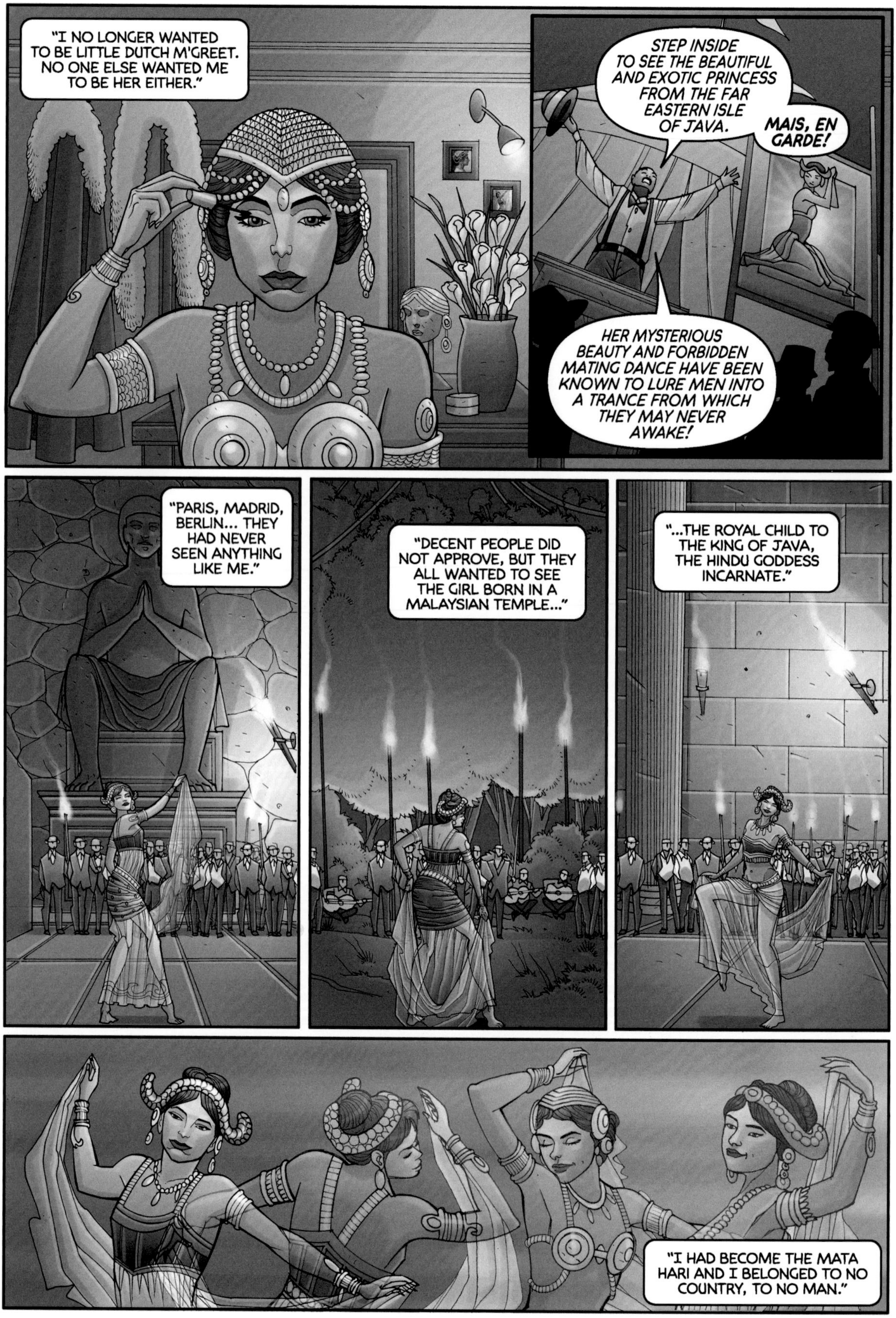
"I NO LONGER WANTED TO BE LITTLE DUTCH M'GREET. NO ONE ELSE WANTED ME TO BE HER EITHER."
STEP INSIDE TO SEE THE BEAUTIFUL AND EXOTIC PRINCESS FROM THE FAR EASTERN ISLE OF JAVA.
MAIS, EN GARDE!
HER MYSTERIOUS BEAUTY AND FORBIDDEN MATING DANCE HAVE BEEN KNOWN TO LURE MEN INTO A TRANCE FROM WHICH THEY MAY NEVER AWAKE!
"PARIS, MADRID, BERLIN... THEY HAD NEVER SEEN ANYTHING LIKE ME."
"DECENT PEOPLE DID NOT APPROVE, BUT THEY ALL WANTED TO SEE THE GIRL BORN IN A MALAYSIAN TEMPLE..."
"...THE ROYAL CHILD TO THE KING OF JAVA, THE HINDU GODDESS INCARNATE."
"I HAD BECOME THE MATA HARI AND I BELONGED TO NO COUNTRY, TO NO MAN."

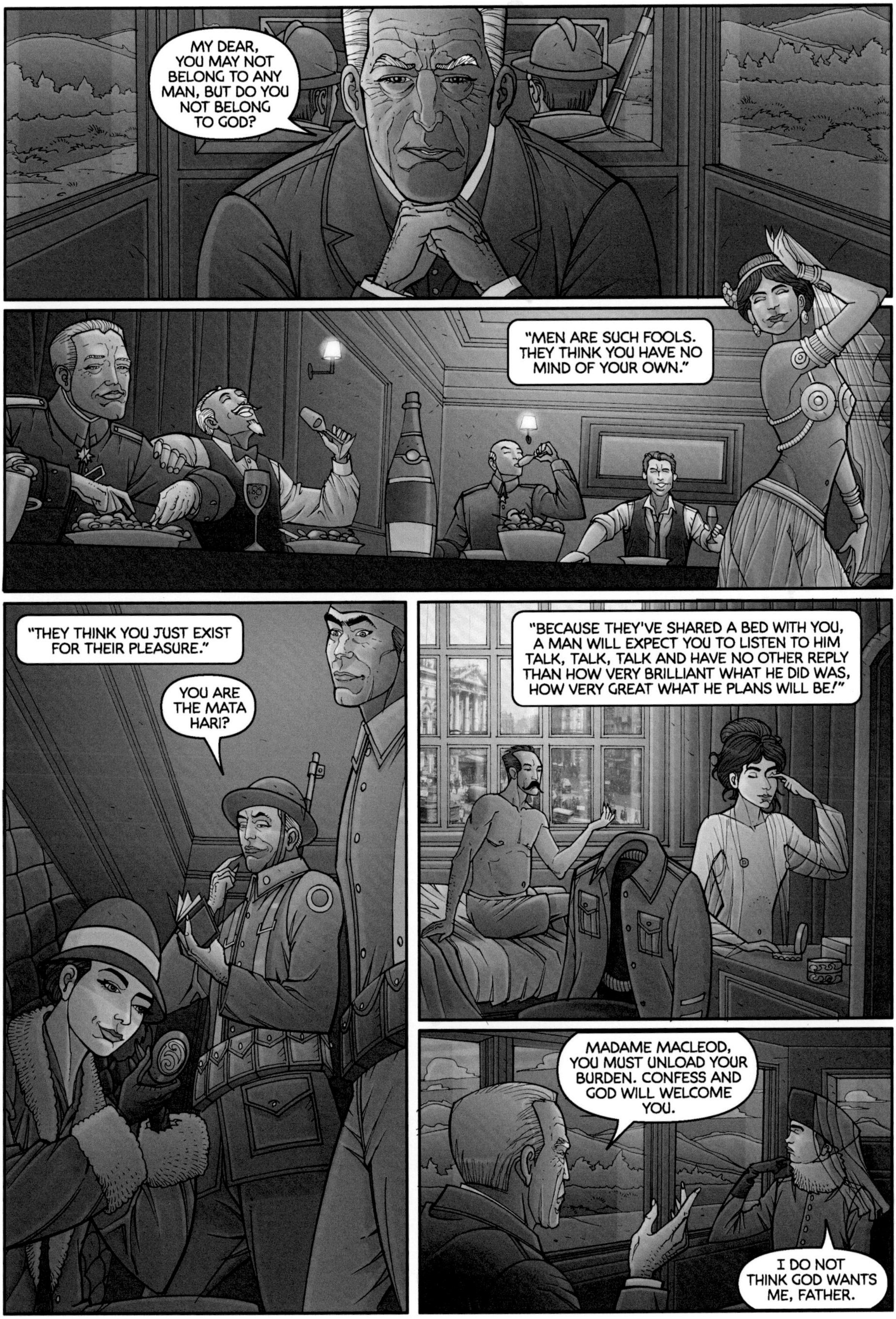
MY DEAR, YOU MAY NOT BELONG TO ANY MAN, BUT DO YOU NOT BELONG TO GOD?
"MEN ARE SUCH FOOLS. THEY THINK YOU HAVE NO MIND OF YOUR OWN."
"THEY THINK YOU JUST EXIST FOR THEIR PLEASURE."
YOU ARE THE MATA HARI?
"BECAUSE THEY'VE SHARED A BED WITH YOU, A MAN WILL EXPECT YOU TO LISTEN TO HIM TALK, TALK, TALK AND HAVE NO OTHER REPLY THAN HOW VERY BRILLIANT WHAT HE DID WAS, HOW VERY GREAT WHAT HE PLANS WILL BE!"
MADAME MACLEOD, YOU MUST UNLOAD YOUR BURDEN. CONFESS AND GOD WILL WELCOME YOU.
I DO NOT THINK GOD WANTS ME, FATHER.

THE WESTERN FRONT, 1916

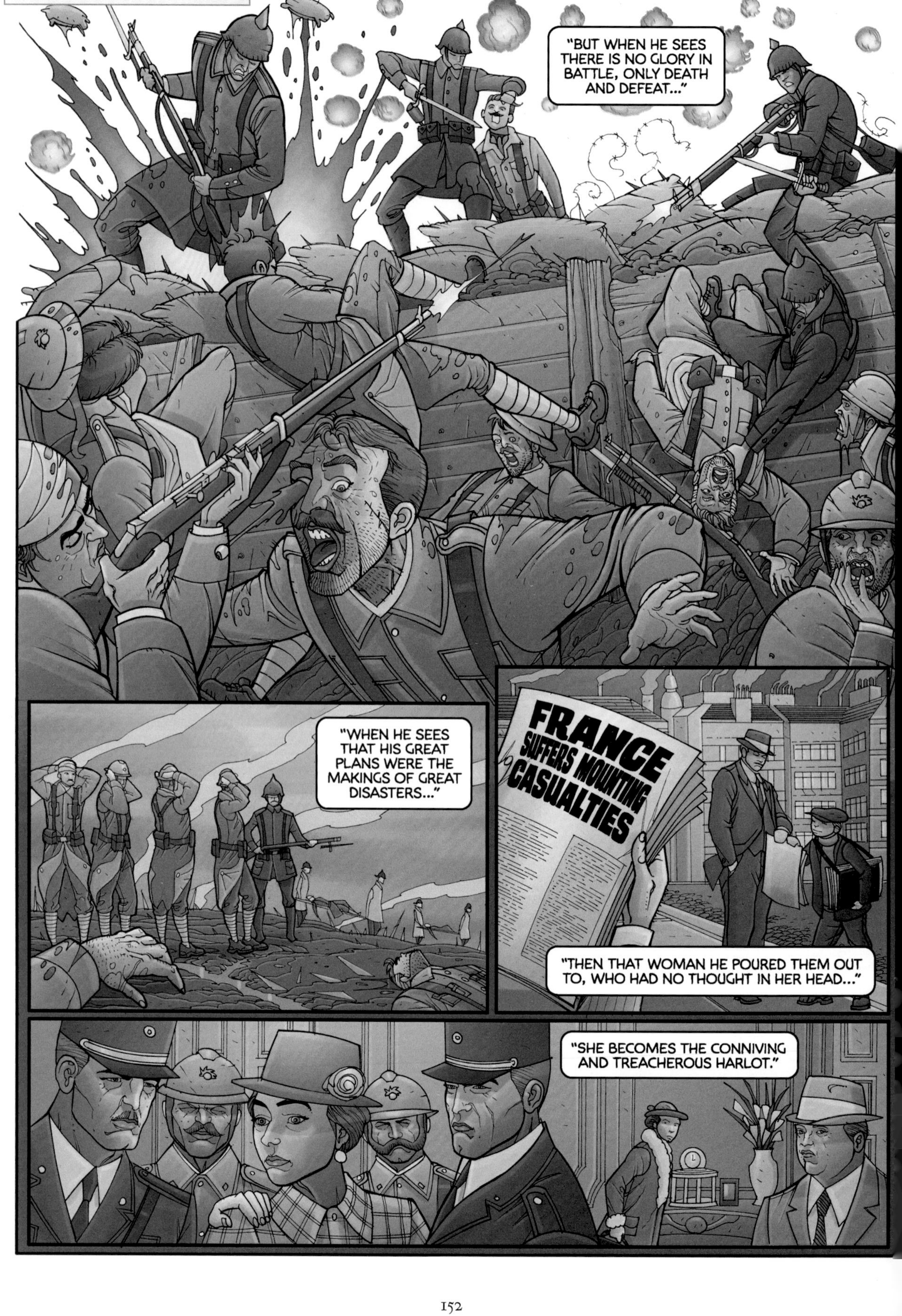
"BUT WHEN HE SEES THERE IS NO GLORY IN BATTLE, ONLY DEATH AND DEFEAT..."
"WHEN HE SEES THAT HIS GREAT PLANS WERE THE MAKINGS OF GREAT DISASTERS..."
FRANCE SUFFERS MOUNTING CASUALTIES
"THEN THAT WOMAN HE POURED THEM OUT TO, WHO HAD NO THOUGHT IN HER HEAD..."
"SHE BECOMES THE CONNIVING AND TREACHEROUS HARLOT."

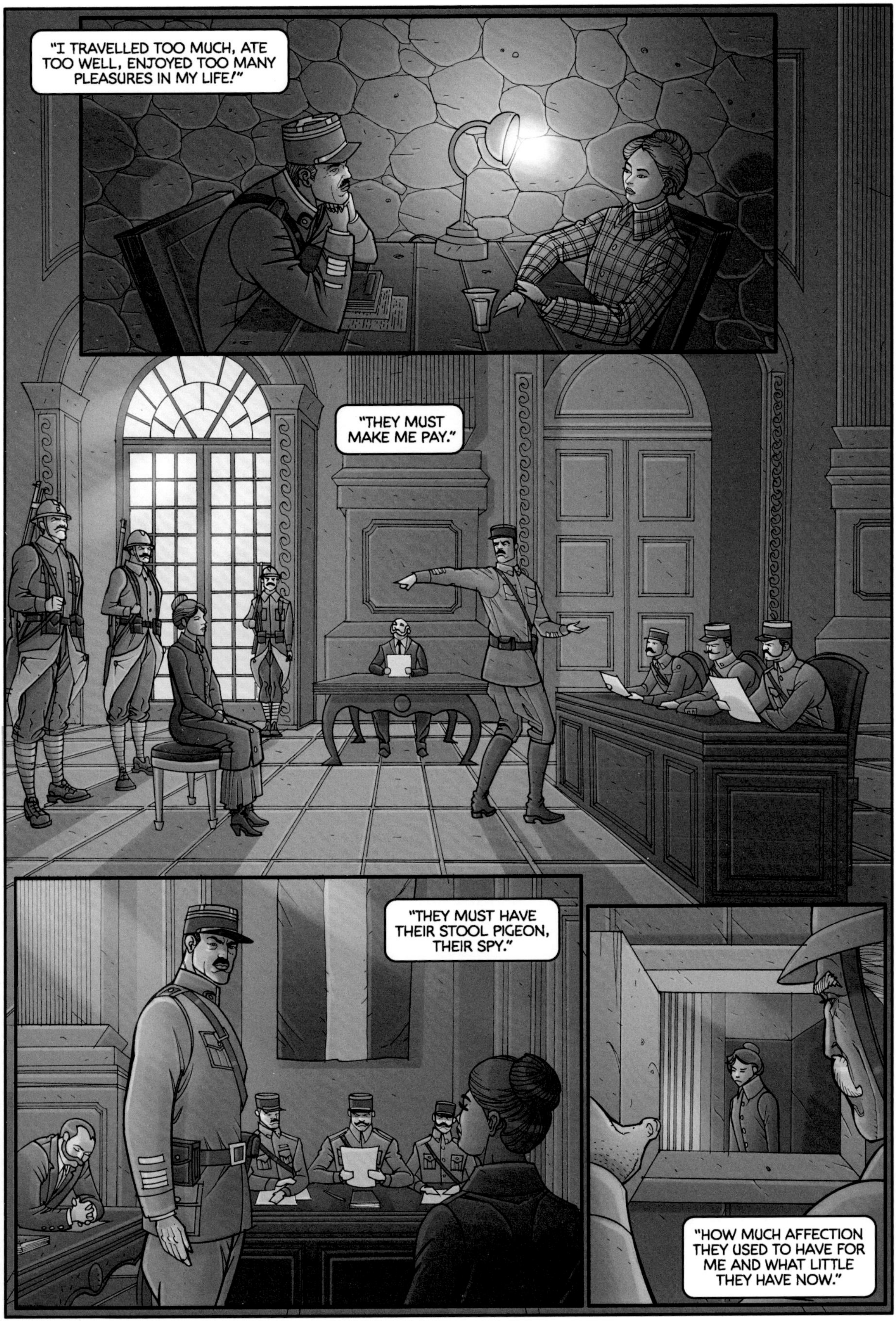
"I TRAVELLED TOO MUCH, ATE TOO WELL, ENJOYED TOO MANY PLEASURES IN MY LIFE!"
"THEY MUST MAKE ME PAY."
"THEY MUST HAVE THEIR STOOL PIGEON, THEIR SPY."
"HOW MUCH AFFECTION THEY USED TO HAVE FOR ME AND WHAT LITTLE THEY HAVE NOW."

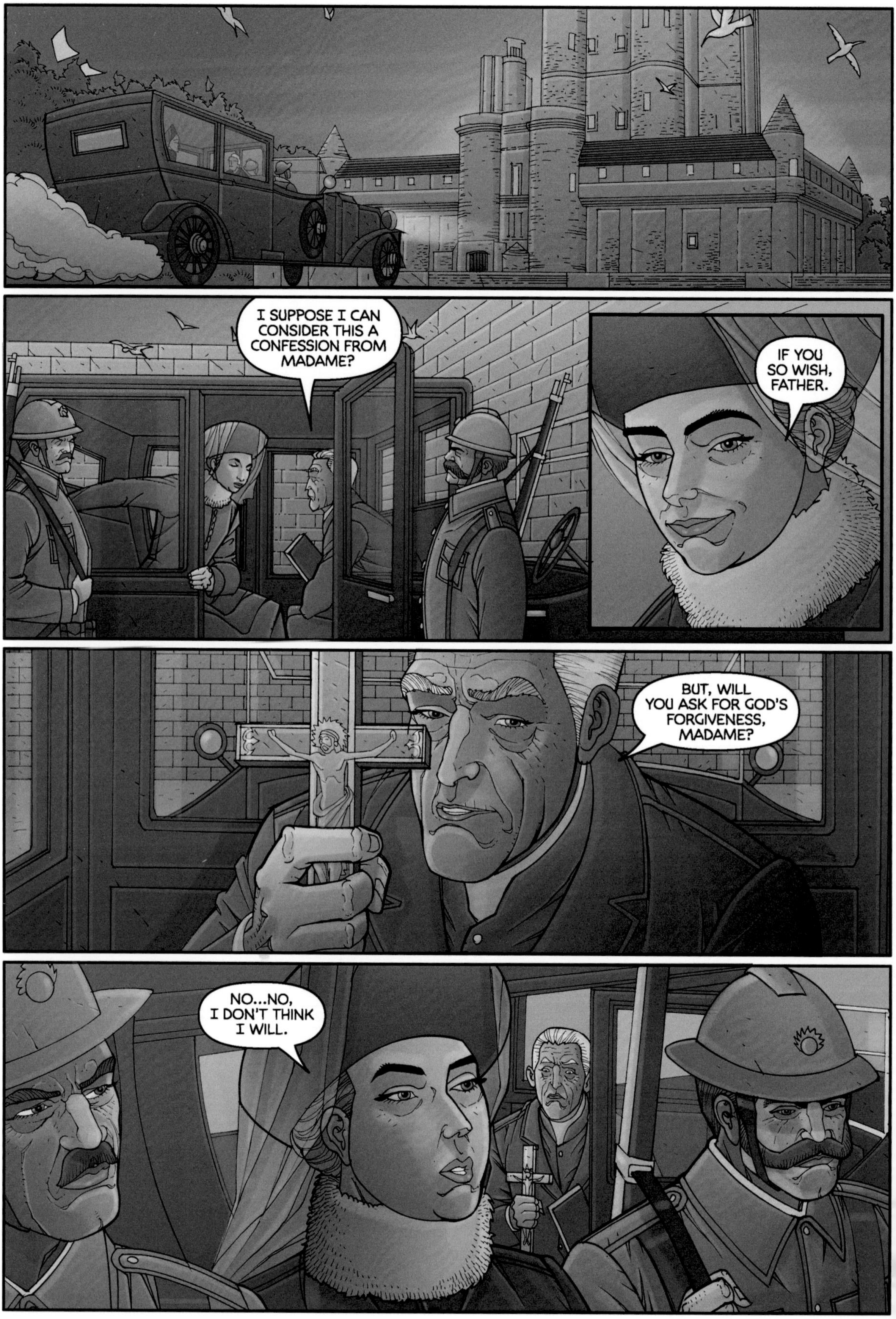
I SUPPOSE I CAN CONSIDER THIS A CONFESSION FROM MADAME?
IF YOU SO WISH, FATHER.
BUT, WILL YOU ASK FOR GOD'S FORGIVENESS, MADAME?
NO...NO, I DON'T THINK I WILL.

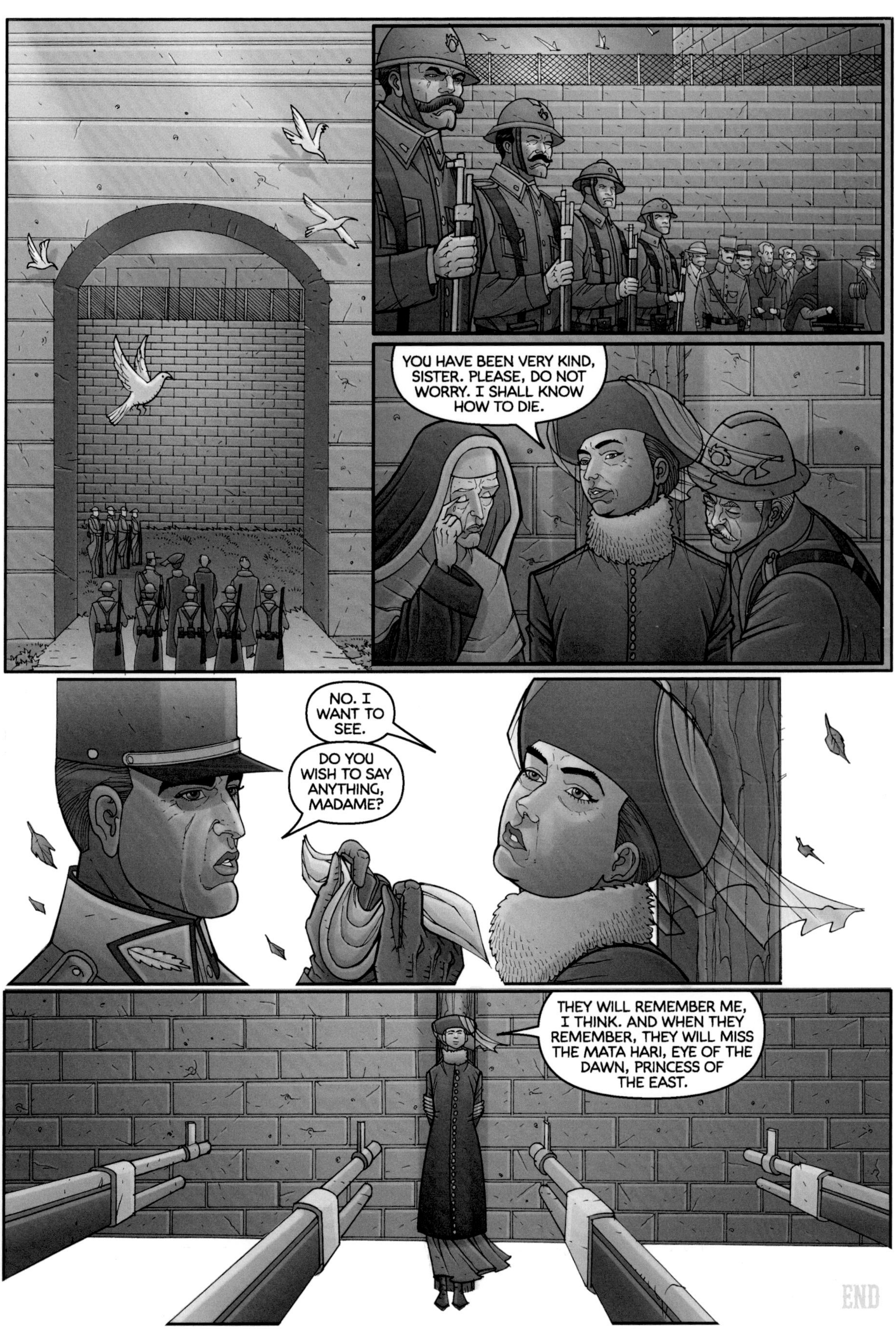
YOU HAVE BEEN VERY KIND, SISTER. PLEASE, DO NOT WORRY. I SHALL KNOW HOW TO DIE.
DO YOU WISH TO SAY ANYTHING, MADAME?
NO. I WANT TO SEE.
THEY WILL REMEMBER ME, I THINK. AND WHEN THEY REMEMBER, THEY WILL MISS THE MATA HARI, EYE OF THE DAWN, PRINCESS OF THE EAST.
END

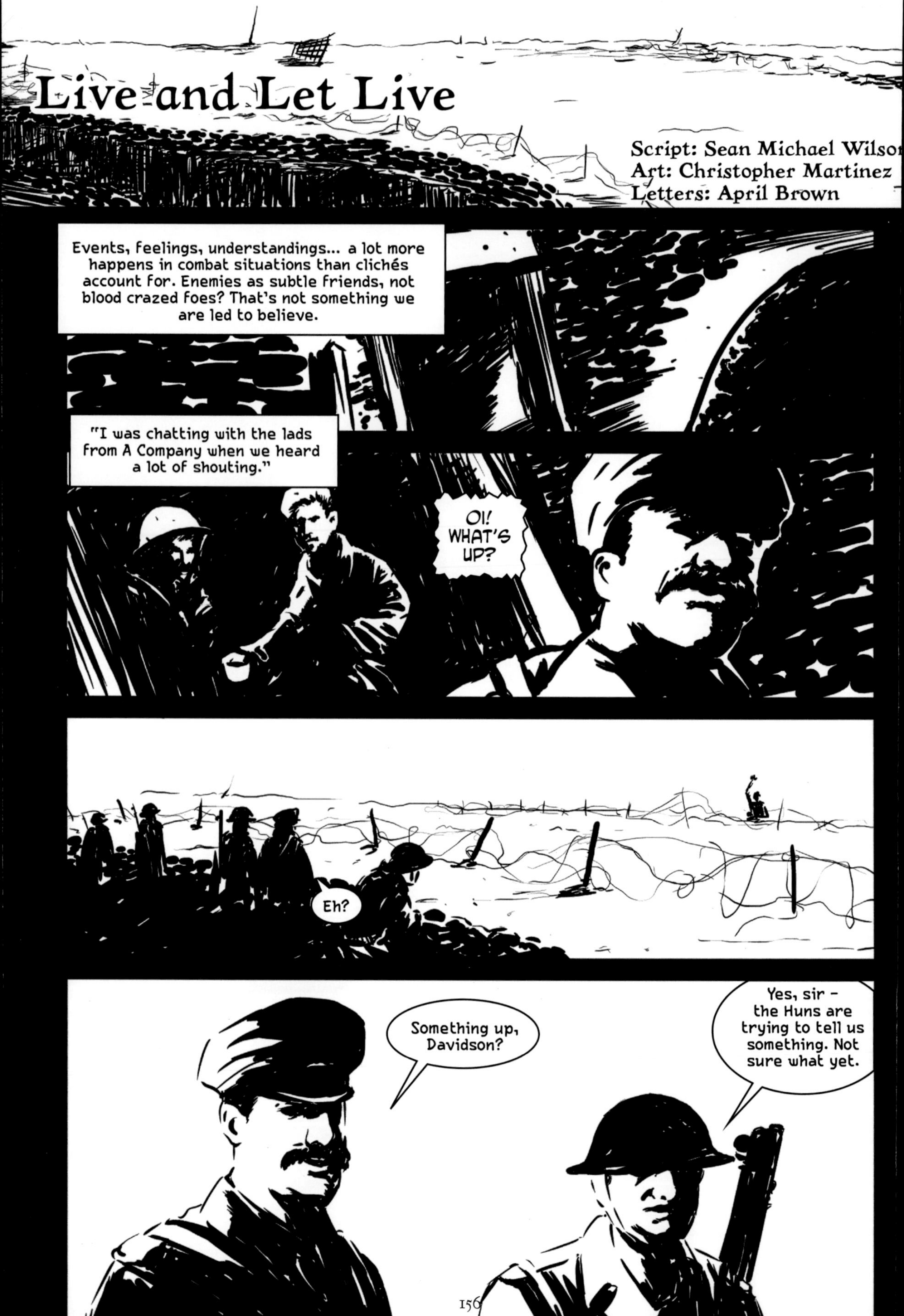

Live and Let Live
Script: Sean Michael Wilso
Art: Christopher Martinez
Letters: April Brown
Events, feelings, understandings... a lot more happens in combat situations than clichés account for. Enemies as subtle friends, not blood crazed foes? That's not something we are led to believe.
"I was chatting with the lads from A Company when we heard a lot of shouting."
OI! WHAT'S UP?
Eh?
Something up, Davidson?
Yes, sir – the Huns are trying to tell us something. Not sure what yet.

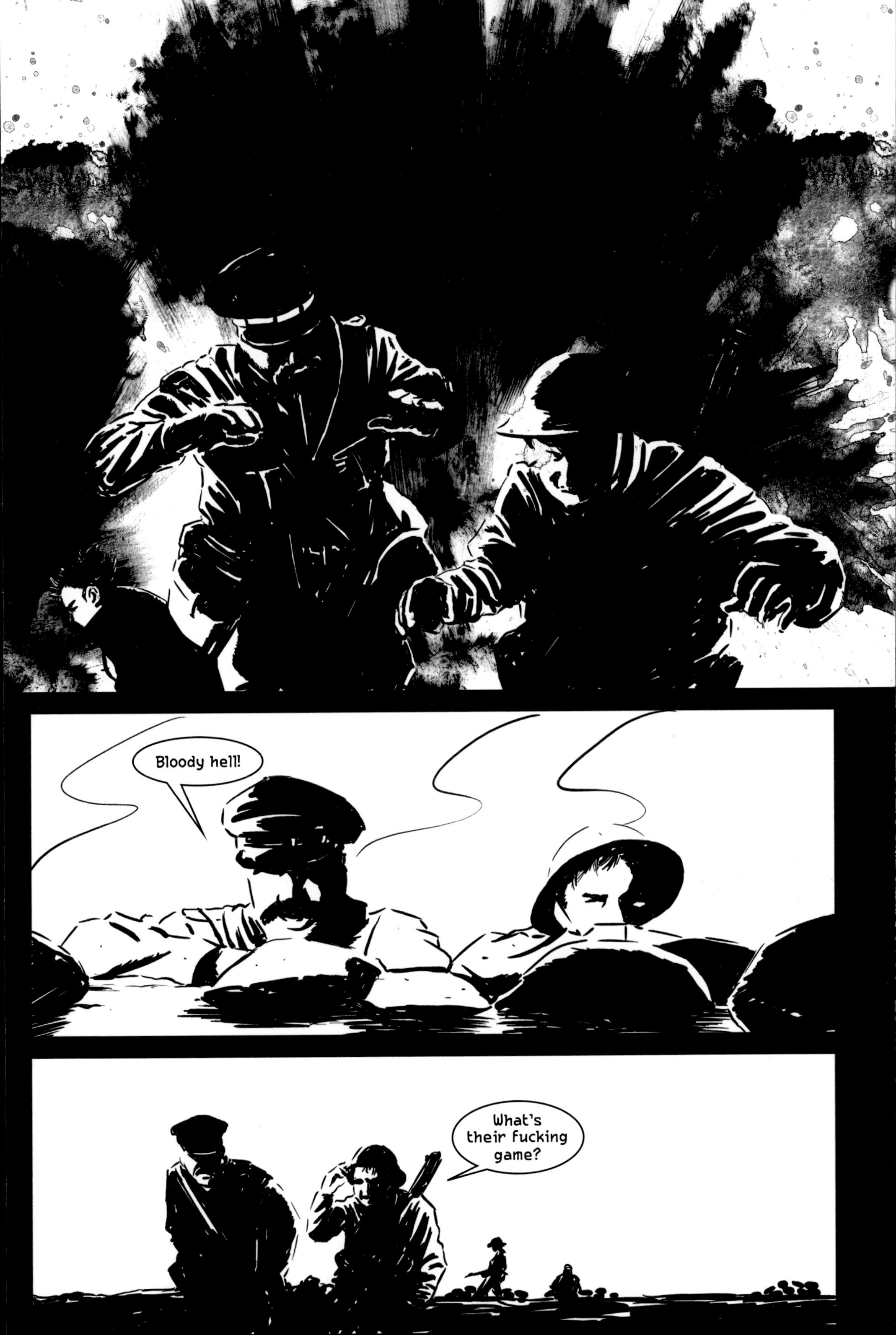
Bloody hell!
What's their fucking game?

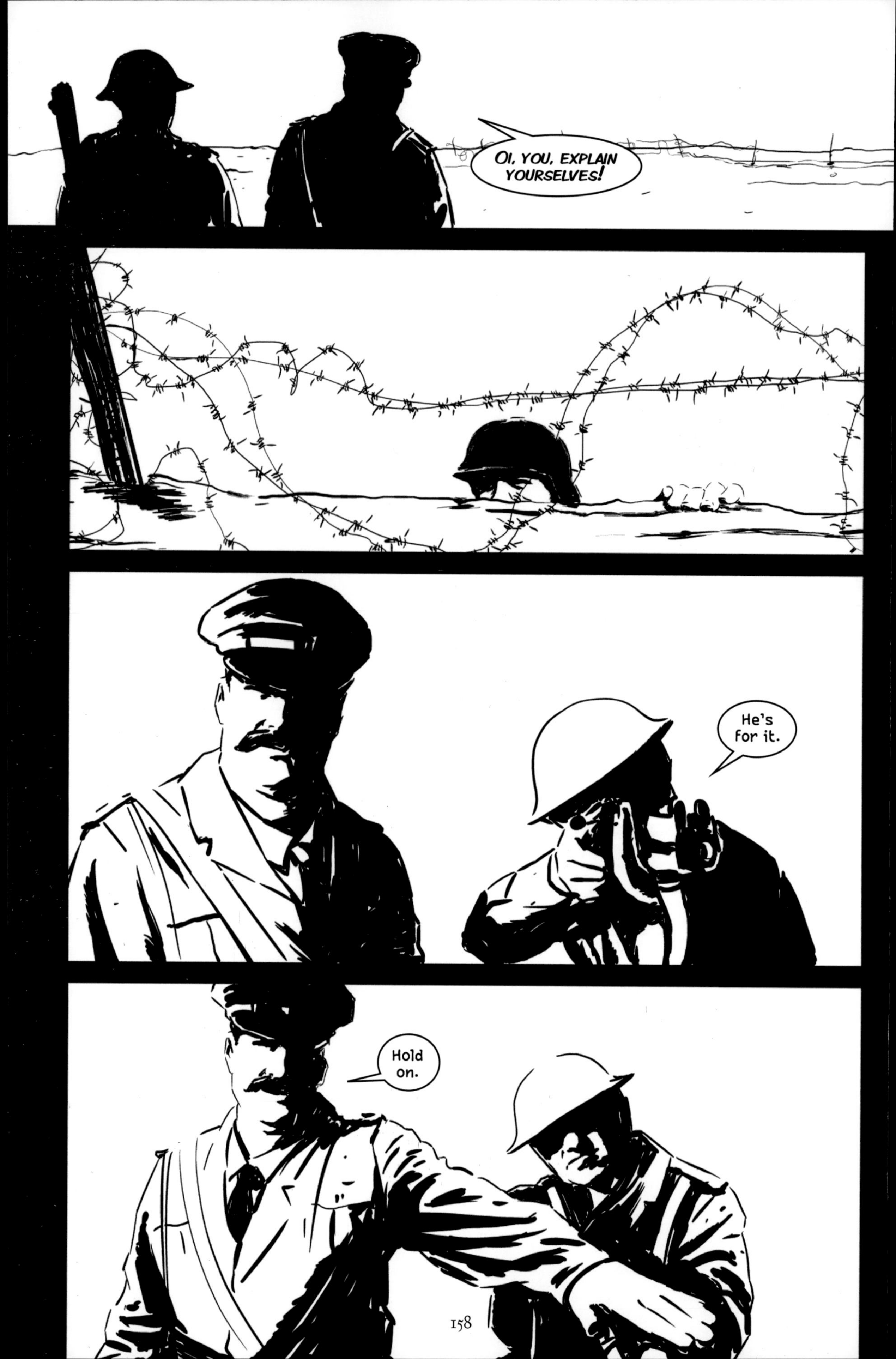
OI, YOU, EXPLAIN YOURSELVES!
He's for it.
Hold on.

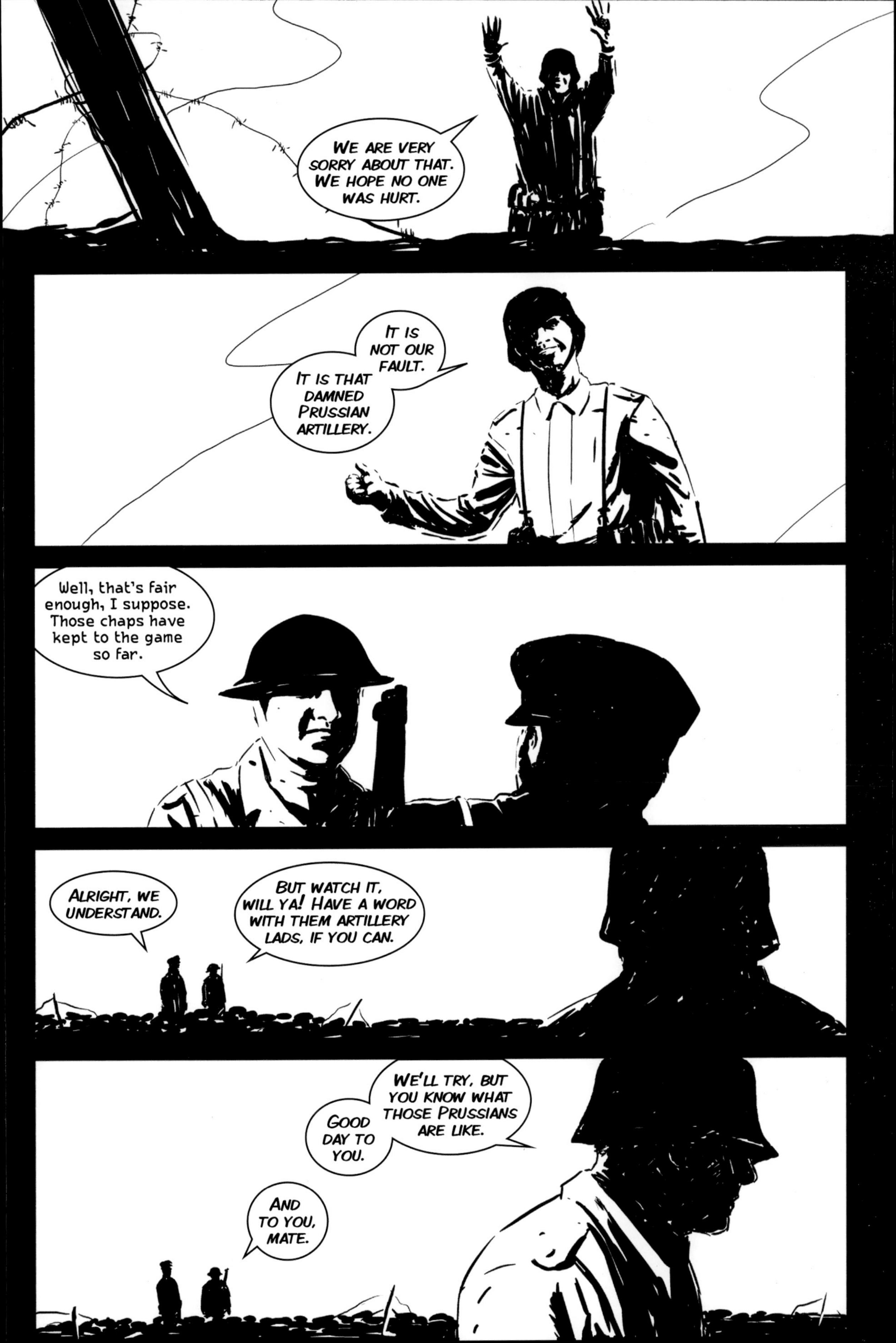
WE ARE VERY SORRY ABOUT THAT. WE HOPE NO ONE WAS HURT.
IT IS NOT OUR FAULT.
IT IS THAT DAMNED PRUSSIAN ARTILLERY.
Well, that's fair enough, I suppose. Those chaps have kept to the game so far.
ALRIGHT, WE UNDERSTAND.
BUT WATCH IT, WILL YA! HAVE A WORD WITH THEM ARTILLERY LADS, IF YOU CAN.
WE'LL TRY, BUT YOU KNOW WHAT THOSE PRUSSIANS ARE LIKE.
GOOD DAY TO YOU.
AND TO YOU, MATE.

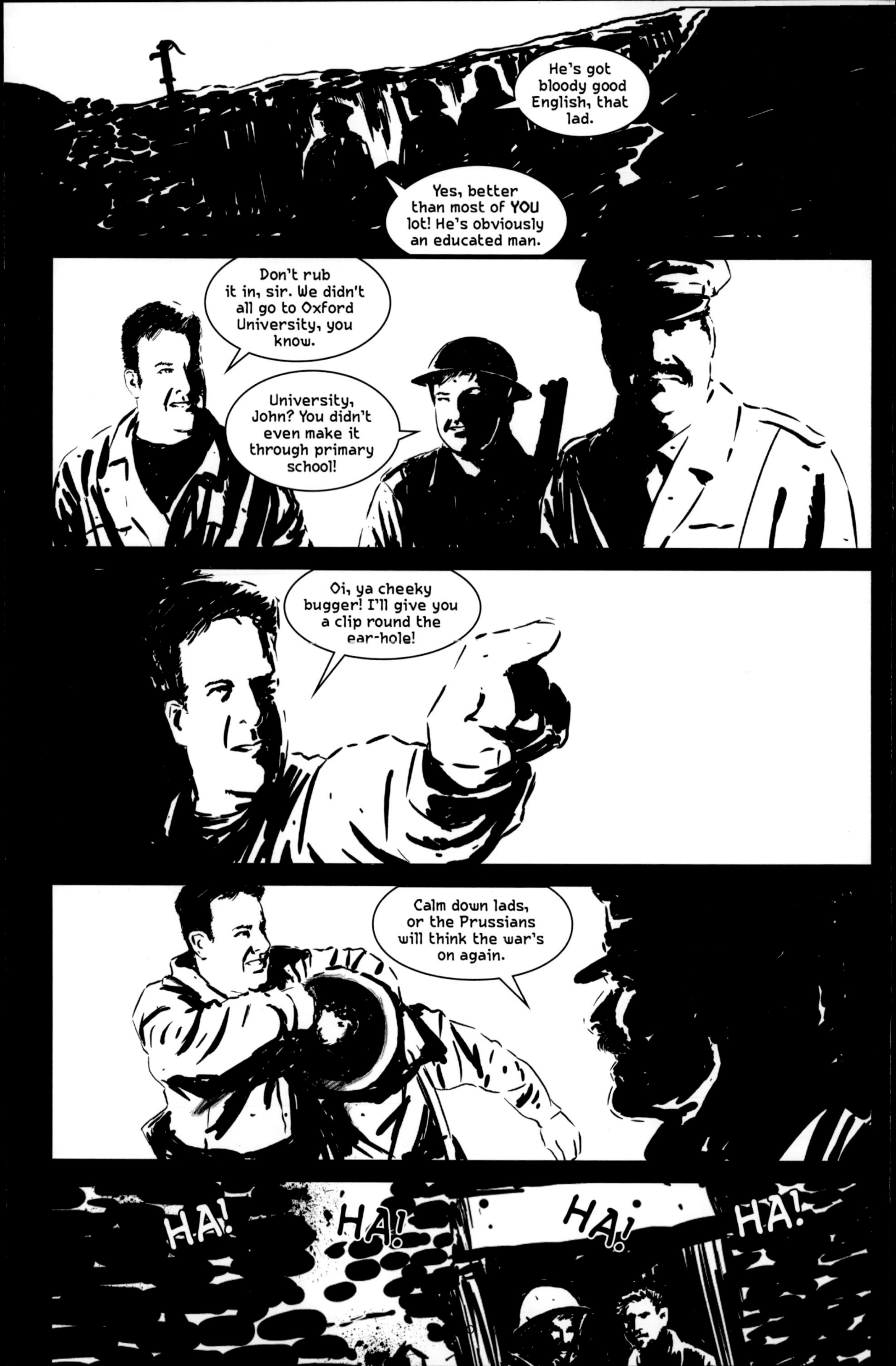
He's got bloody good English, that lad.
Yes, better than most of YOU lot! He's obviously an educated man.
Don't rub it in, sir. We didn't all go to Oxford University, you know.
University, John? You didn't even make it through primary school!
Oi, ya cheeky bugger! I'll give you a clip round the ear-hole!
Calm down lads, or the Prussians will think the war's on again.
HA! HA! HA! HA!

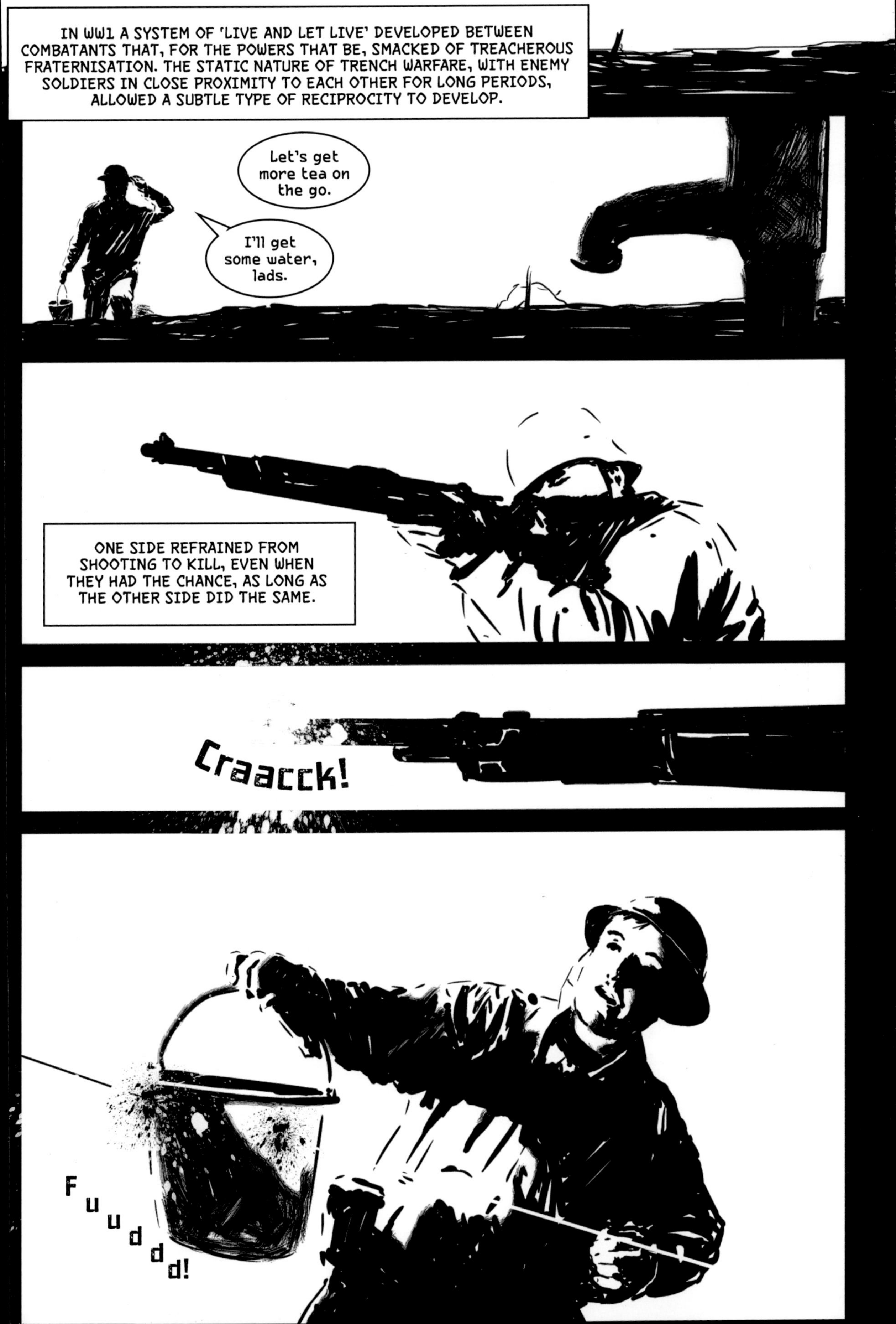
IN WW1 A SYSTEM OF 'LIVE AND LET LIVE' DEVELOPED BETWEEN COMBATANTS THAT, FOR THE POWERS THAT BE, SMACKED OF TREACHEROUS FRATERNISATION. THE STATIC NATURE OF TRENCH WARFARE, WITH ENEMY SOLDIERS IN CLOSE PROXIMITY TO EACH OTHER FOR LONG PERIODS, ALLOWED A SUBTLE TYPE OF RECIPROCITY TO DEVELOP.
Let's get more tea on the go.
I'll get some water, lads.
ONE SIDE REFRAINED FROM SHOOTING TO KILL, EVEN WHEN THEY HAD THE CHANCE, AS LONG AS THE OTHER SIDE DID THE SAME.
Craacck!
Fuuddd!

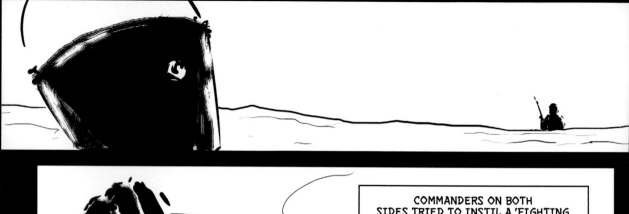

COMMANDERS ON BOTH SIDES TRIED TO INSTIL A 'FIGHTING SPIRIT'. THIS OFTEN RESULTED IN ONLY THE MOCK COMPLIANCE OF JUST PRETENDING TO ATTACK.

IN THE 1980S, RESEARCHERS STUDIED THIS BEHAVIOUR, LOOKING AT THE PERSONAL RECOLLECTIONS OF SOLDIERS IN WW1. THEY CONCLUDED IT WAS SIMILAR TO THE 'PRISONER'S DILEMMA GAME', IN WHICH A SITUATION OF MUTUAL RESTRAINT SEEMS PREFERABLE TO THE ALTERNATIVE OF BOTH SIDES SUFFERING PUNISHMENT.*

FOR SOME, THIS LIVE AND LET LIVE ATTITUDE INDICATES THAT CO-OPERATION MAY BE AS STRONG AS OR EVEN A STRONGER PART OF HUMAN NATURE THAN COMPETITION.

* TRENCH WARFARE 1914-1918: THE LIVE AND LET LIVE SYSTEM (1980) TONY ASHWORTH. EVOLUTION OF COOPERATION (2006) ROBERT AXELROD

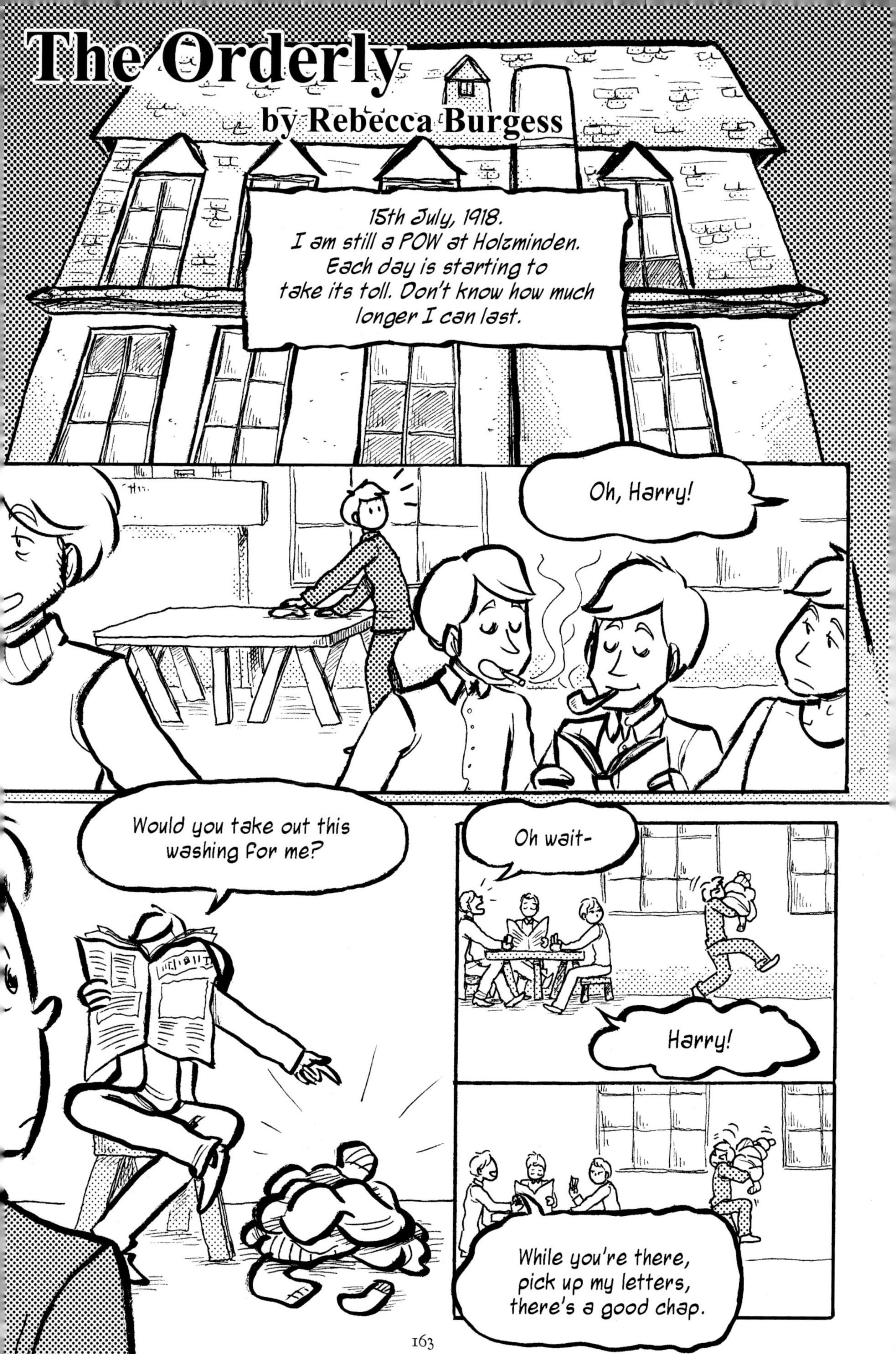
The Orderly
by Rebecca Burgess
15th July, 1918.
I am still a POW at Holzminden.
Each day is starting to
take its toll. Don't know how much
longer I can last.
Oh, Harry!
Would you take out this
washing for me?
Oh wait-
Harry!
While you're there,
pick up my letters,
there's a good chap.

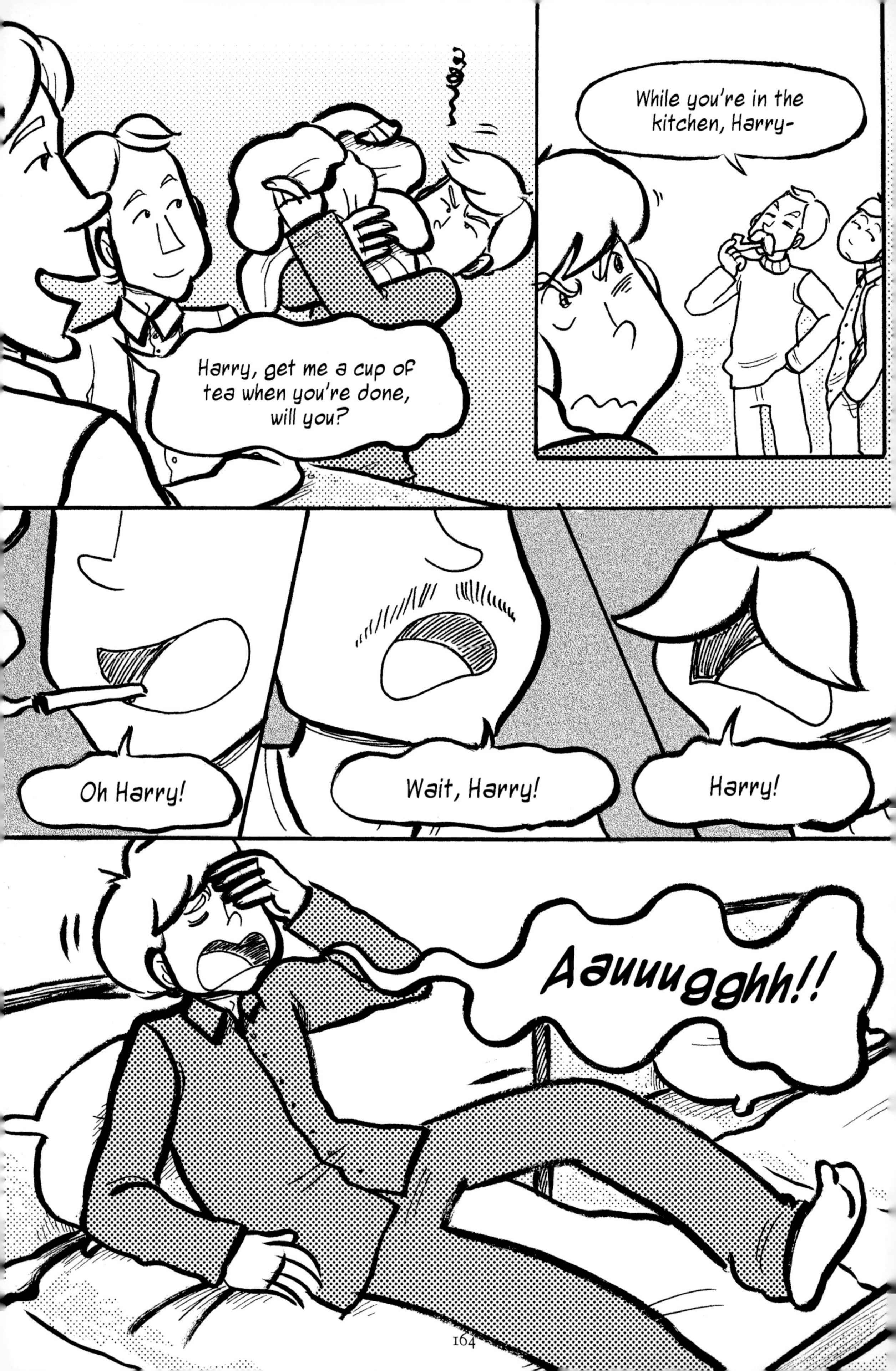
Harry, get me a cup of tea when you're done, will you?
While you're in the kitchen, Harry-
Oh Harry!
Wait, Harry!
Harry!
Aauuugghh!!

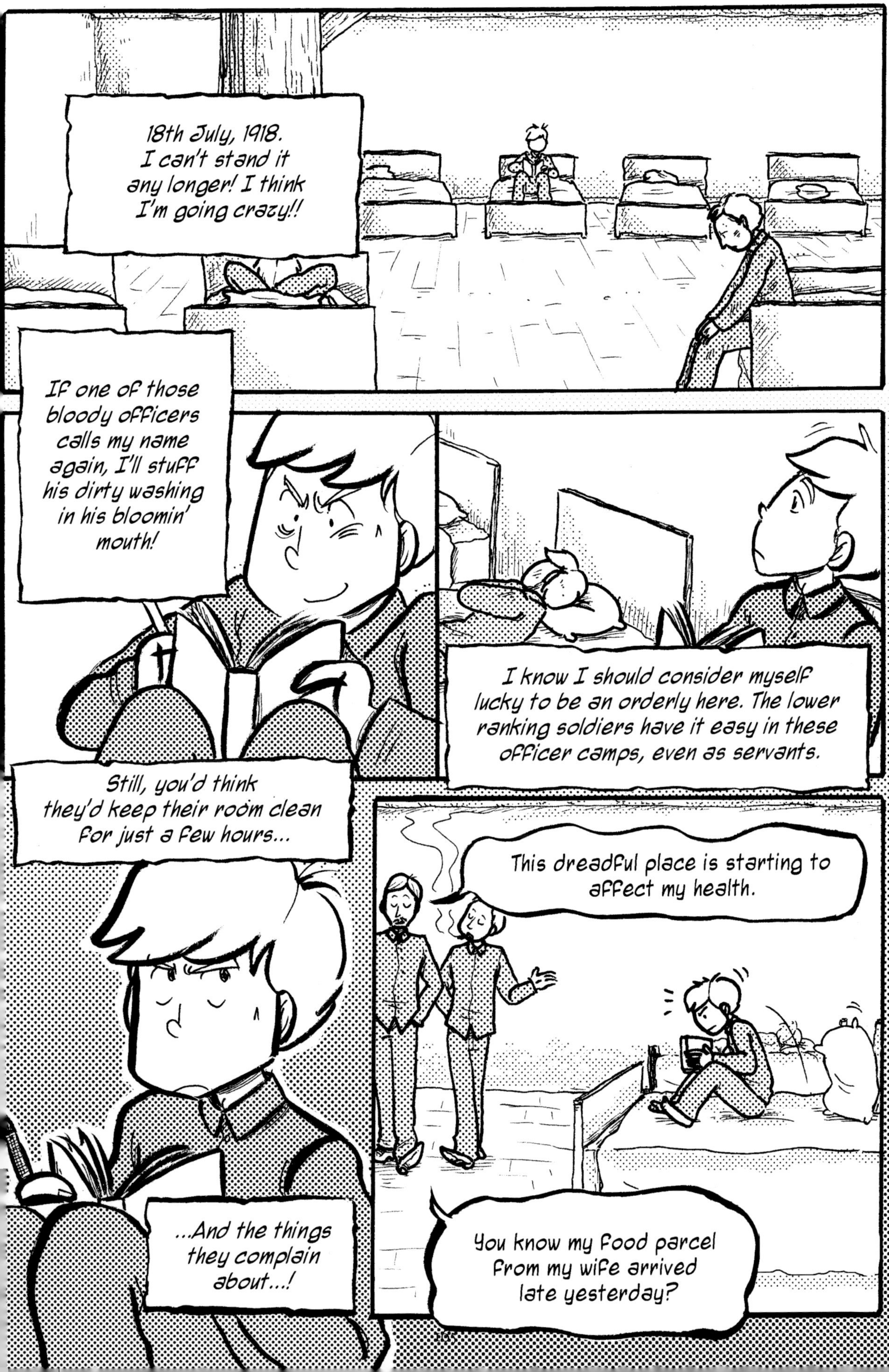

18th July, 1918. I can't stand it any longer! I think I'm going crazy!!
If one of those bloody officers calls my name again, I'll stuff his dirty washing in his bloomin' mouth!
I know I should consider myself lucky to be an orderly here. The lower ranking soldiers have it easy in these officer camps, even as servants.
Still, you'd think they'd keep their room clean for just a few hours...
This dreadful place is starting to affect my health.
...And the things they complain about...!
You know my food parcel from my wife arrived late yesterday?

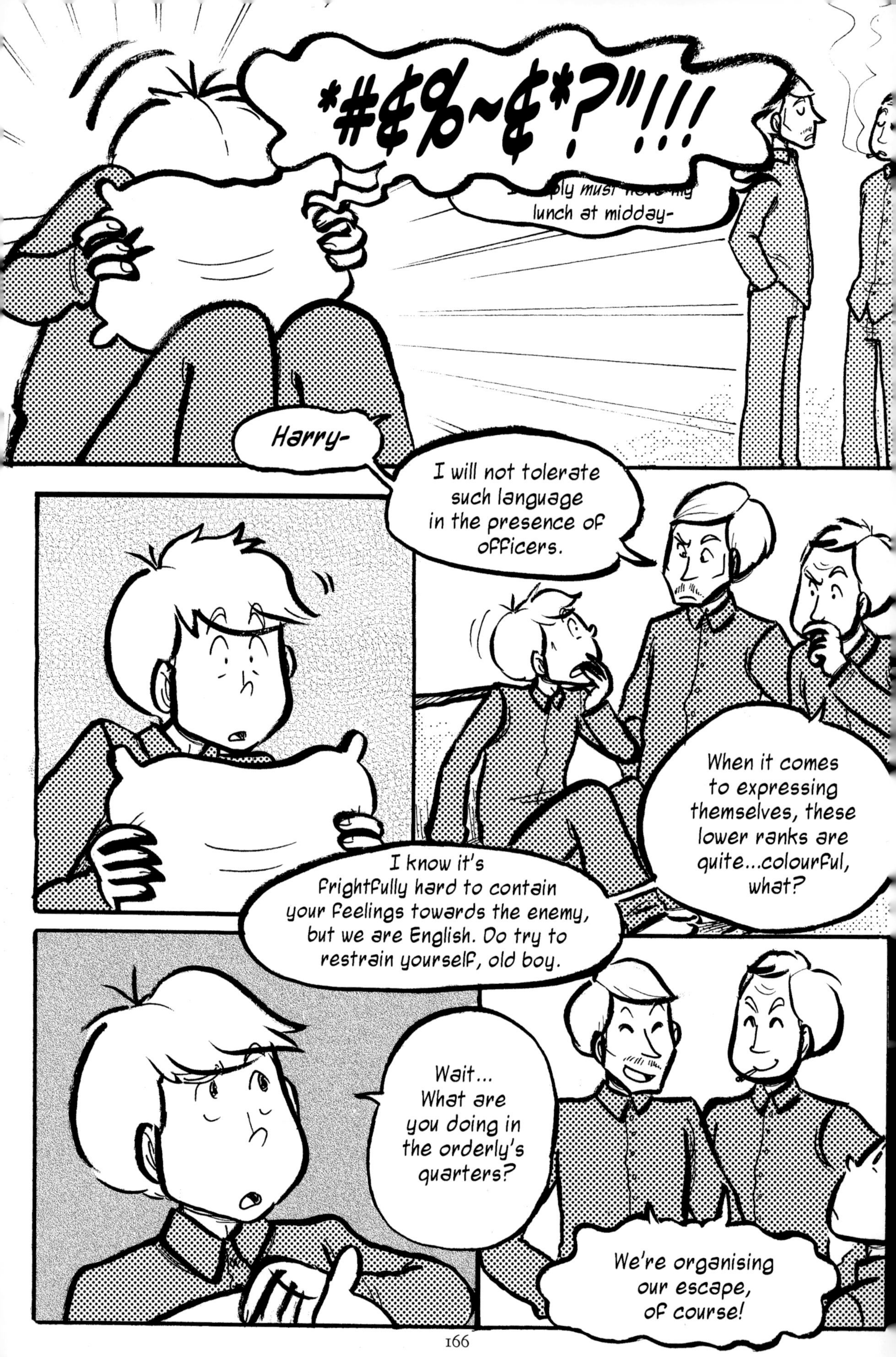

#$%~$?"!!!
...ply must ... lunch at midday-
Harry-
I will not tolerate such language in the presence of officers.
When it comes to expressing themselves, these lower ranks are quite...colourful, what?
I know it's frightfully hard to contain your feelings towards the enemy, but we are English. Do try to restrain yourself, old boy.
Wait... What are you doing in the orderly's quarters?
We're organising our escape, of course!

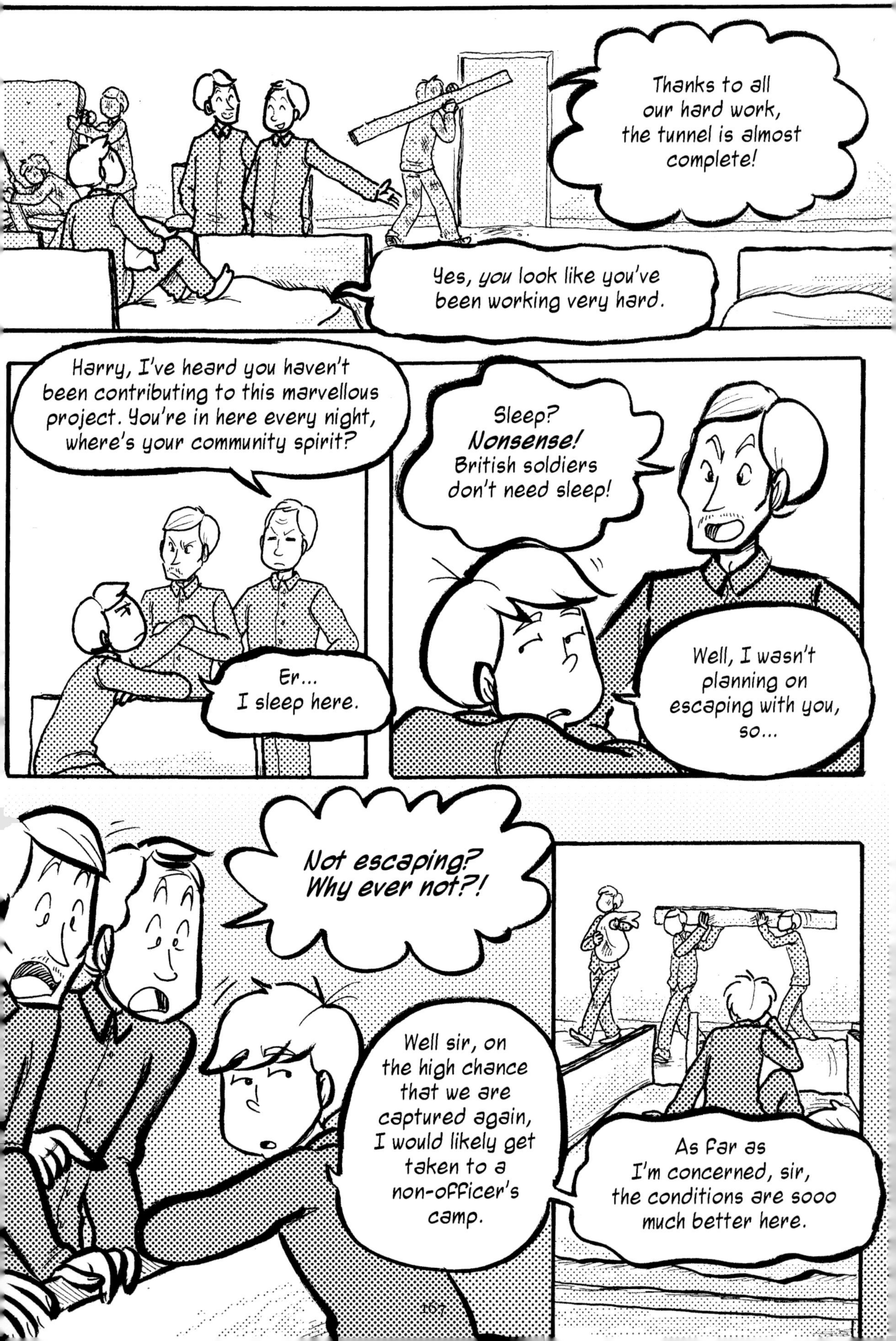
Thanks to all our hard work, the tunnel is almost complete!
Yes, *you* look like you've been working very hard.
Harry, I've heard you haven't been contributing to this marvellous project. You're in here every night, where's your community spirit?
Er... I sleep here.
Sleep? ***Nonsense!*** British soldiers don't need sleep!
Well, I wasn't planning on escaping with you, so...
Not escaping? Why ever not?!
Well sir, on the high chance that we are captured again, I would likely get taken to a non-officer's camp.
As far as I'm concerned, sir, the conditions are sooo much better here.

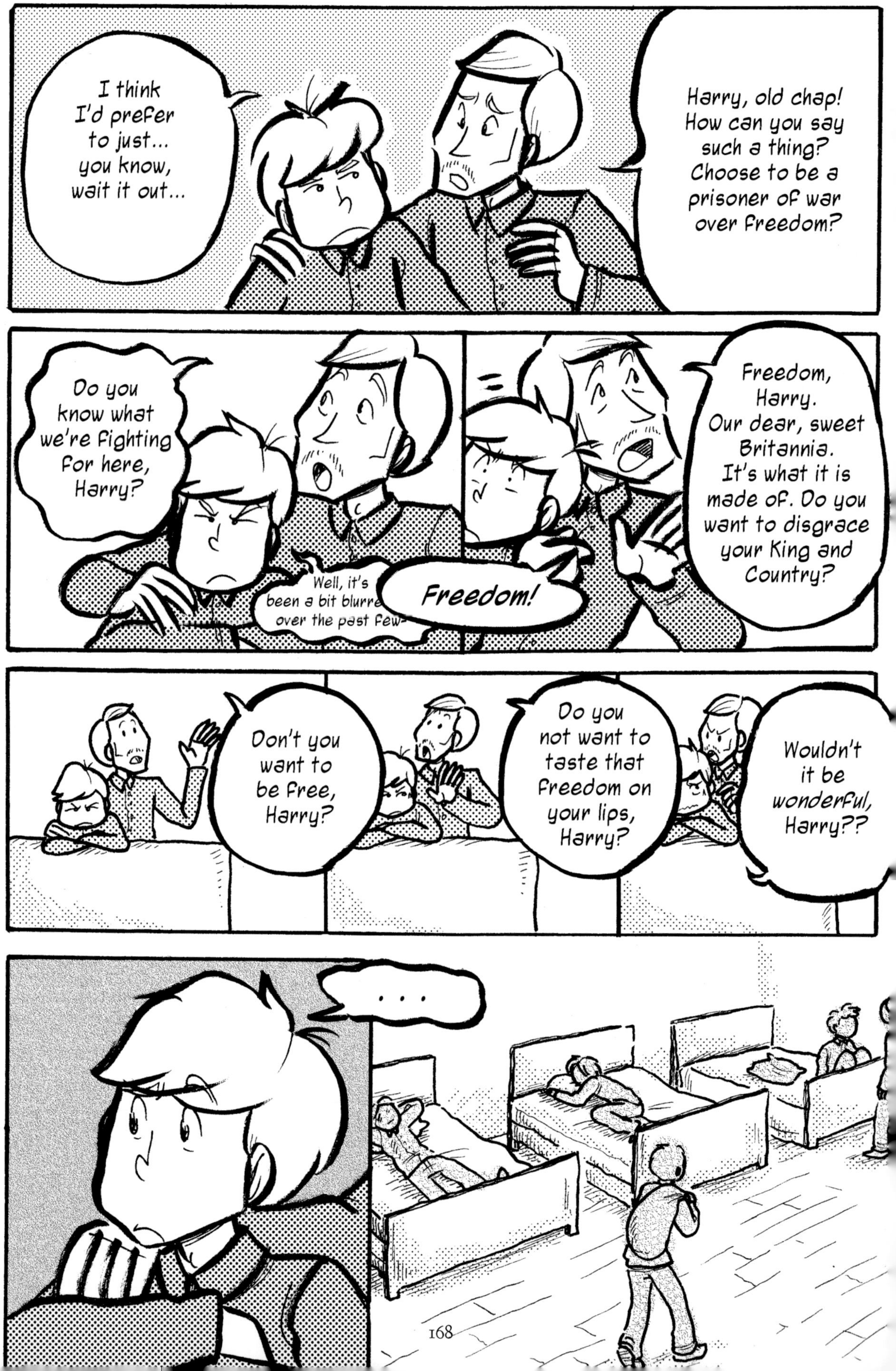
I think I'd prefer to just... you know, wait it out...
Harry, old chap! How can you say such a thing? Choose to be a prisoner of war over freedom?
Do you know what we're fighting for here, Harry?
Well, it's been a bit blurre over the past few-
Freedom!
Freedom, Harry. Our dear, sweet Britannia. It's what it is made of. Do you want to disgrace your King and Country?
Don't you want to be free, Harry?
Do you not want to taste that freedom on your lips, Harry?
Wouldn't it be wonderful, Harry??
. . .

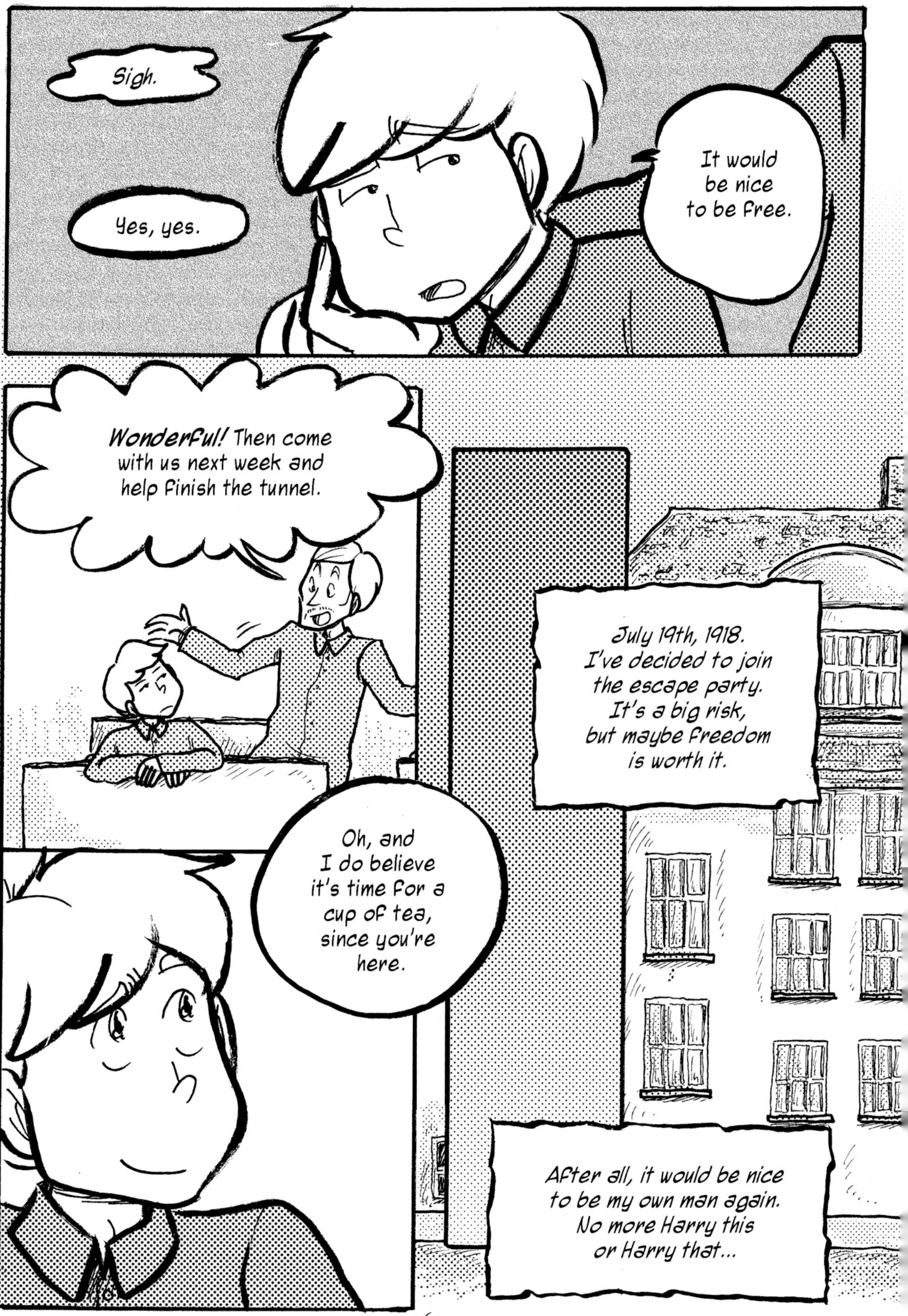
Sigh.
Yes, yes.
It would be nice to be free.
Wonderful! Then come with us next week and help finish the tunnel.
July 19th, 1918. I've decided to join the escape party. It's a big risk, but maybe freedom is worth it.
Oh, and I do believe it's time for a cup of tea, since you're here.
After all, it would be nice to be my own man again. No more Harry this or Harry that...

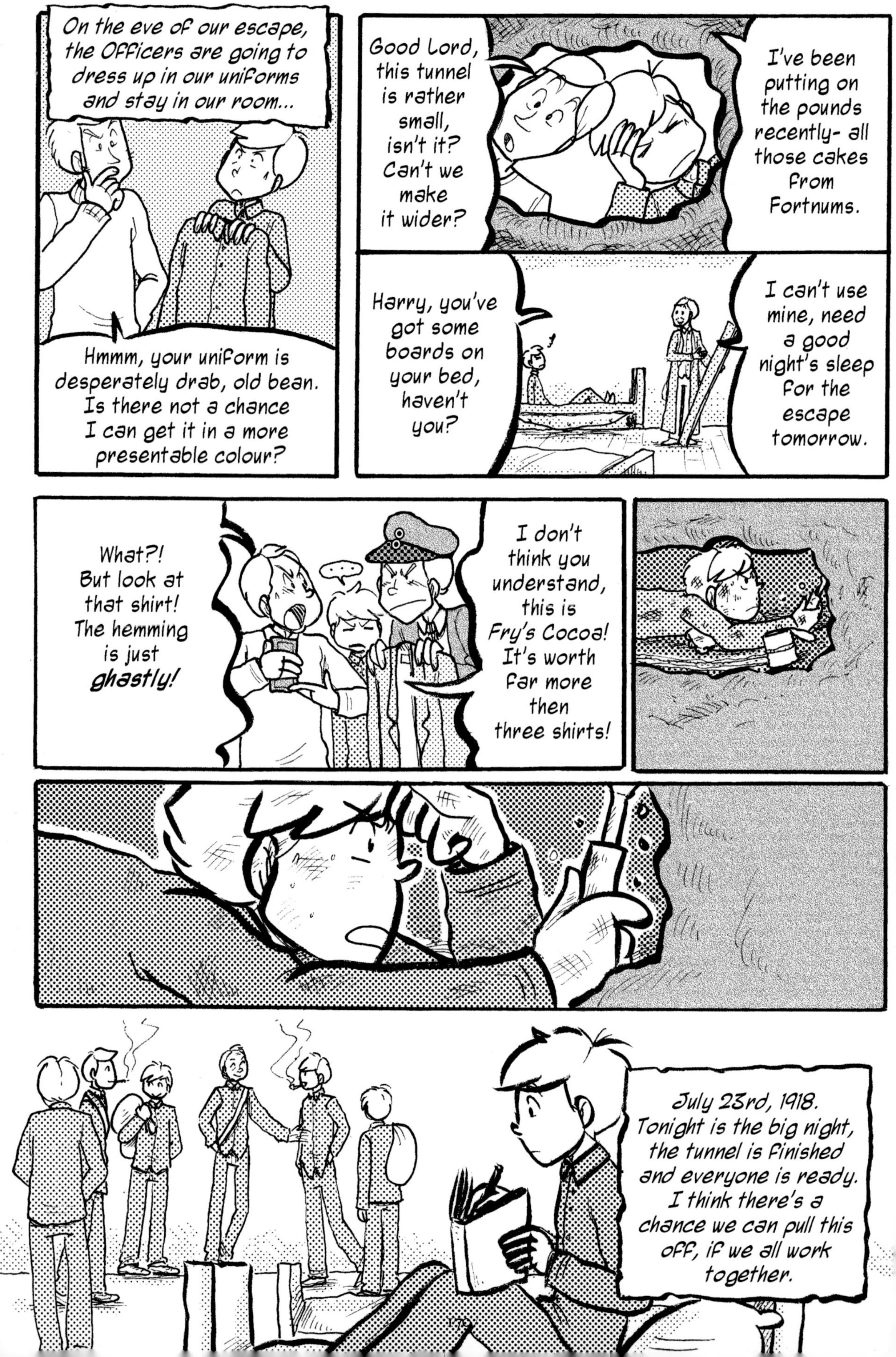
On the eve of our escape, the Officers are going to dress up in our uniforms and stay in our room...
Hmmm, your uniform is desperately drab, old bean. Is there not a chance I can get it in a more presentable colour?
Good Lord, this tunnel is rather small, isn't it? Can't we make it wider?
I've been putting on the pounds recently- all those cakes from Fortnums.
Harry, you've got some boards on your bed, haven't you?
I can't use mine, need a good night's sleep for the escape tomorrow.
What?! But look at that shirt! The hemming is just ***ghastly!***
I don't think you understand, this is *Fry's Cocoa!* It's worth far more then three shirts!
July 23rd, 1918. Tonight is the big night, the tunnel is finished and everyone is ready. I think there's a chance we can pull this off, if we all work together.

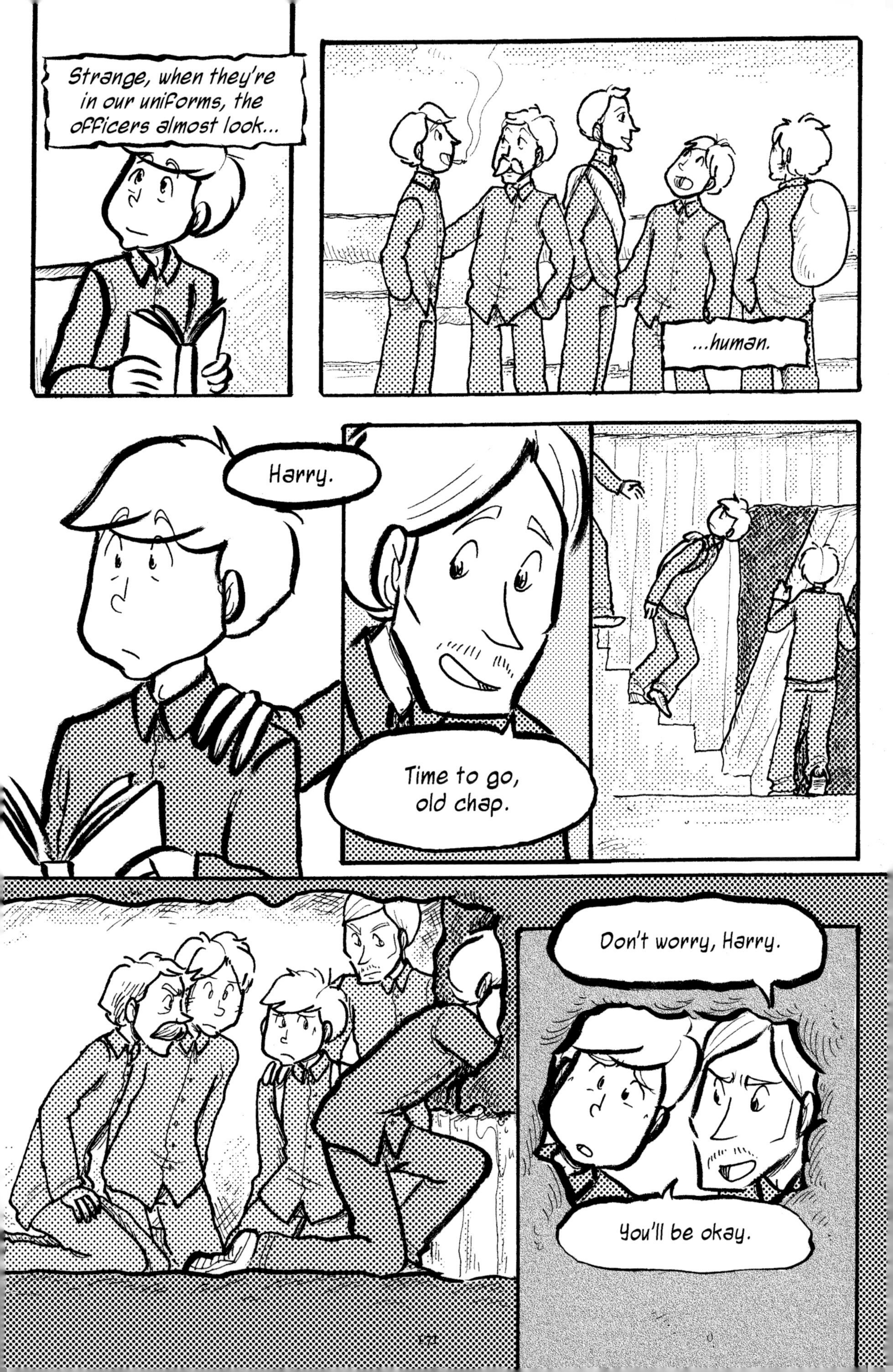
Strange, when they're in our uniforms, the officers almost look...
...human.
Harry.
Time to go, old chap.
Don't worry, Harry.
You'll be okay.

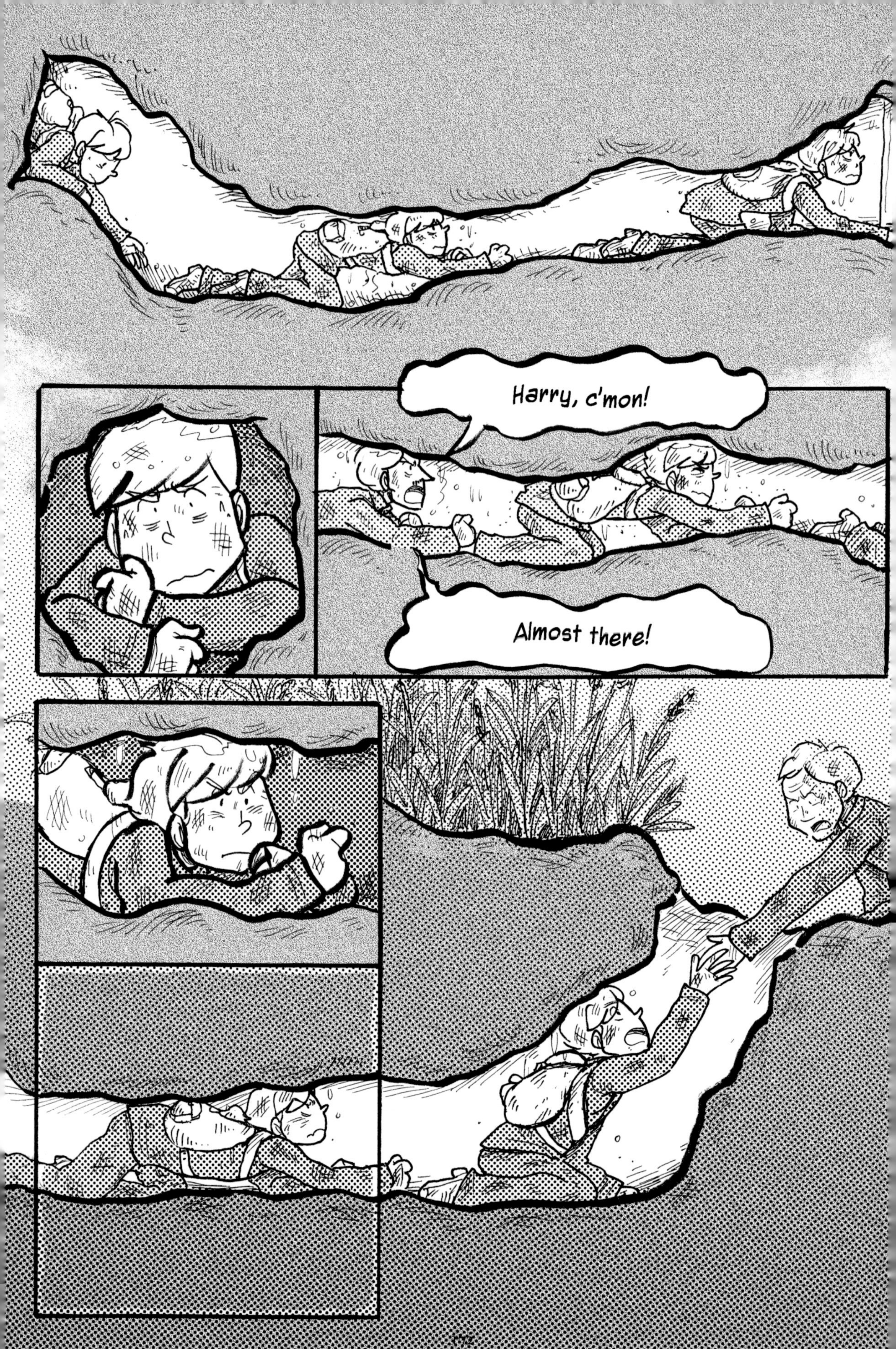
Harry, c'mon!
Almost there!

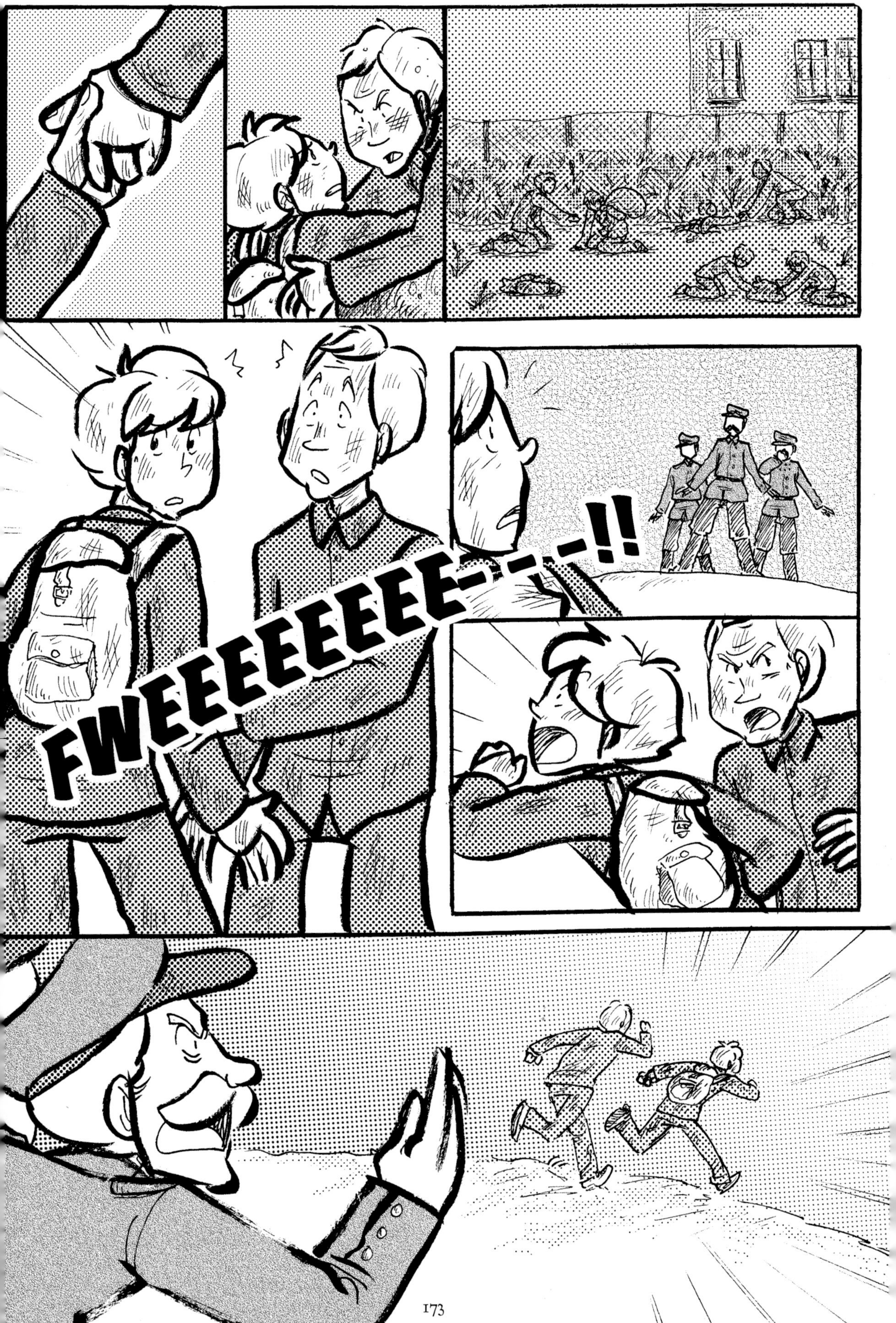
FWEEEEEEEEE---!!

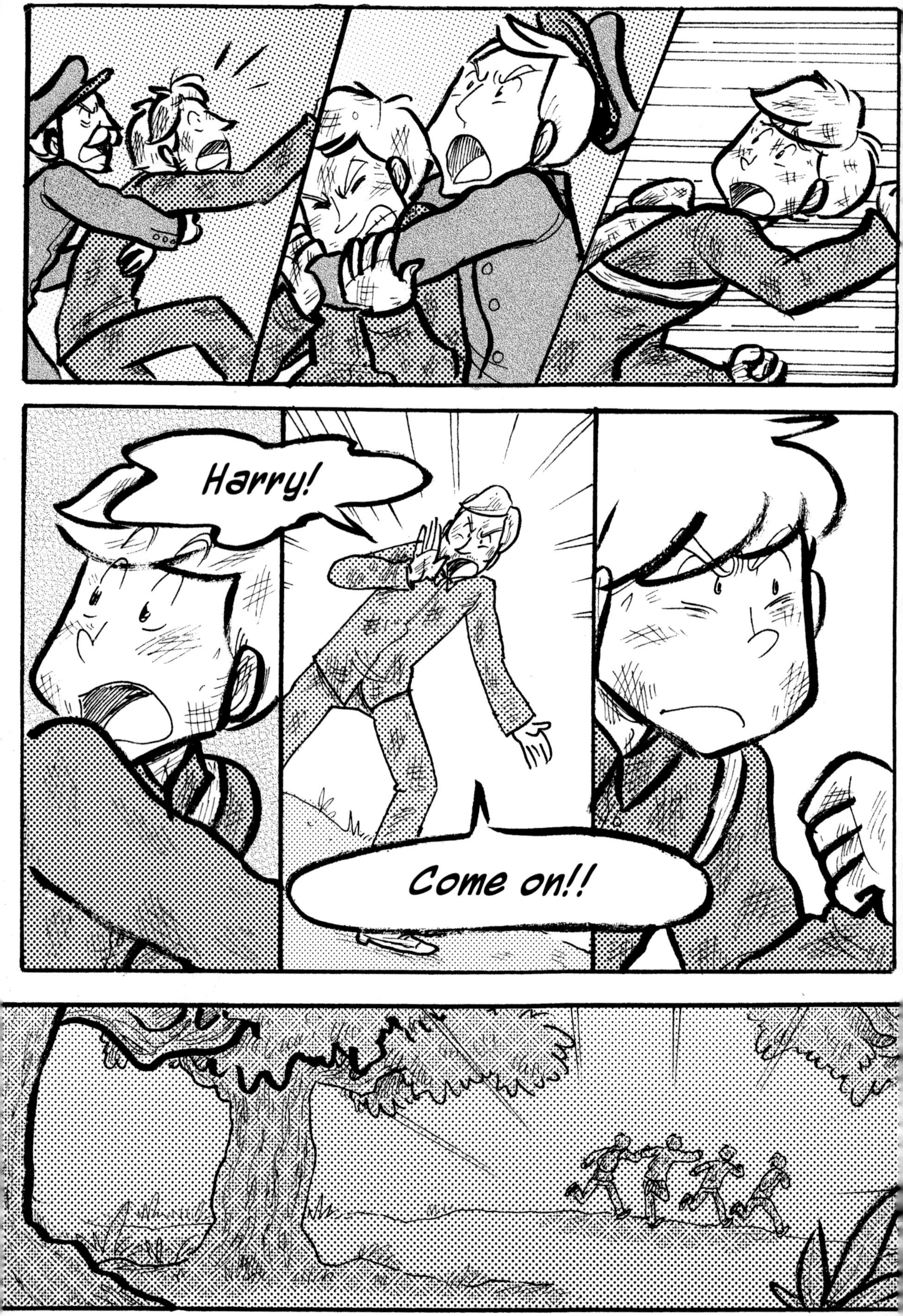
Harry!
Come on!!

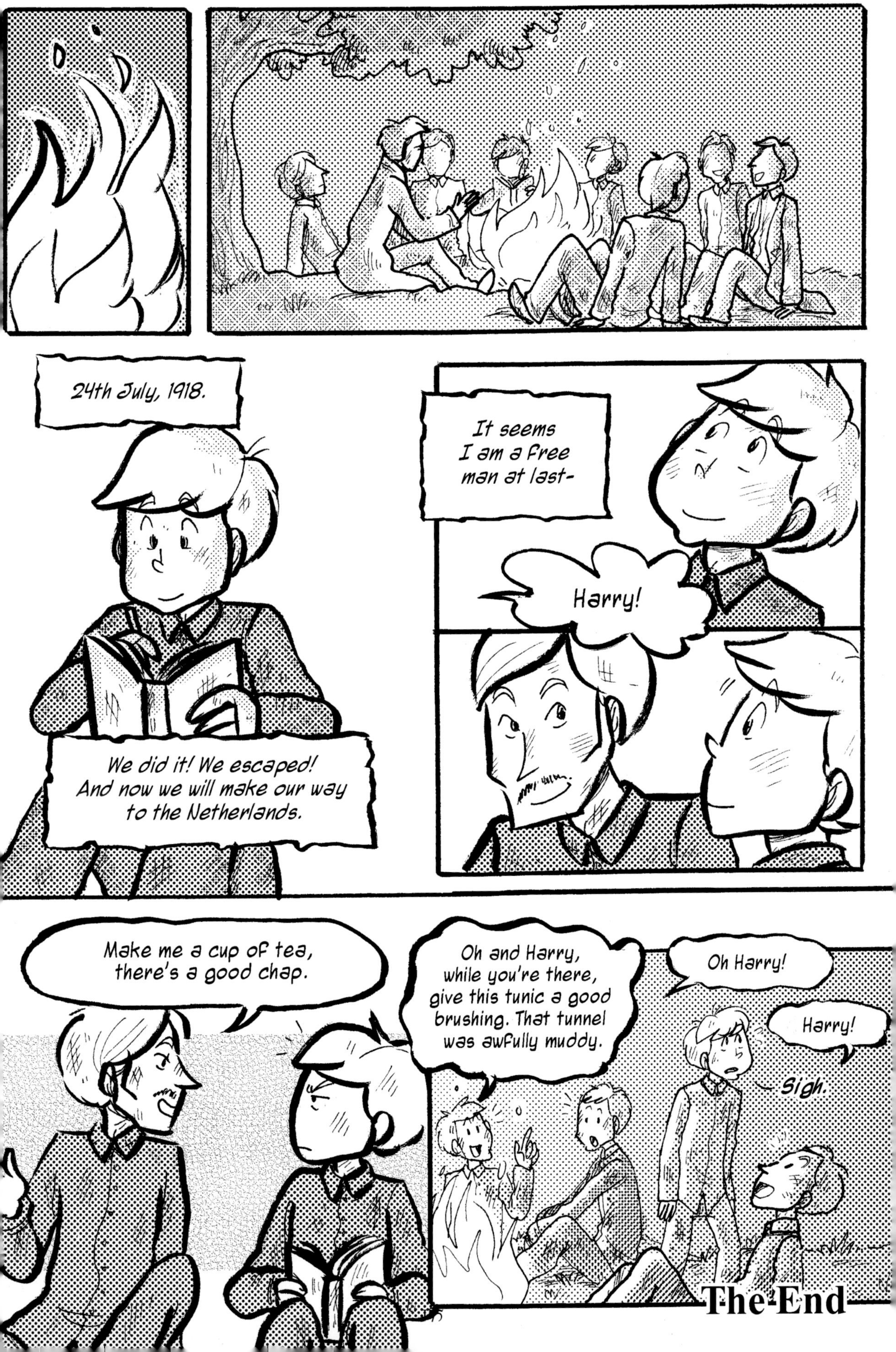

24th July, 1918.
We did it! We escaped!
And now we will make our way
to the Netherlands.
It seems
I am a free
man at last-
Harry!
Make me a cup of tea,
there's a good chap.
Oh and Harry,
while you're there,
give this tunic a good
brushing. That tunnel
was awfully muddy.
Oh Harry!
Harry!
Sigh.
The End

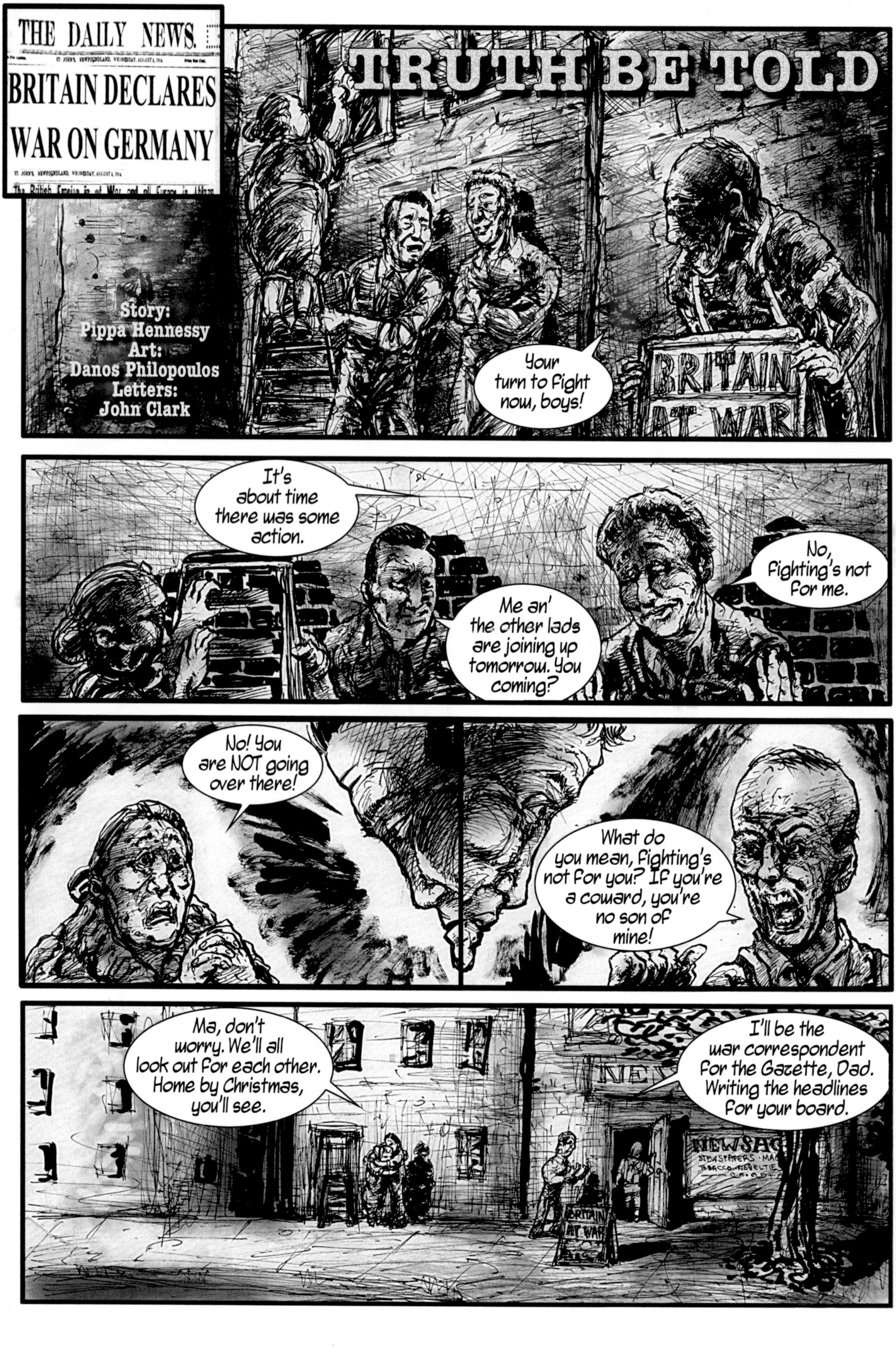
THE DAILY NEWS.
BRITAIN DECLARES WAR ON GERMANY
TRUTH BE TOLD
Story: Pippa Hennessy
Art: Danos Philopoulos
Letters: John Clark
Your turn to fight now, boys!
BRITAIN AT WAR
It's about time there was some action.
Me an' the other lads are joining up tomorrow. You coming?
No, fighting's not for me.
No! You are NOT going over there!
What do you mean, fighting's not for you? If you're a coward, you're no son of mine!
Ma, don't worry. We'll all look out for each other. Home by Christmas, you'll see.
I'll be the war correspondent for the Gazette, Dad. Writing the headlines for your board.
BRITAIN AT WAR

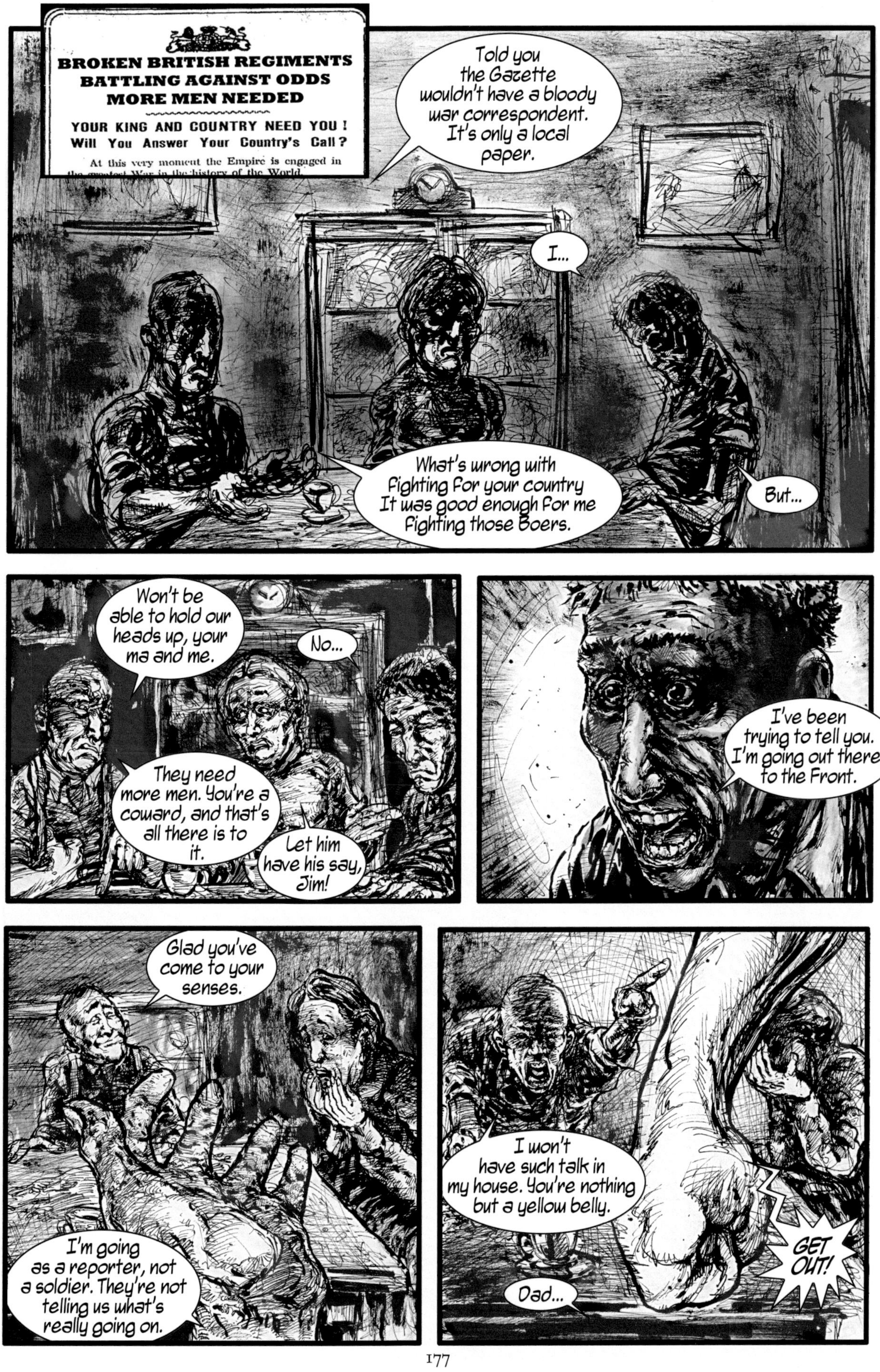
BROKEN BRITISH REGIMENTS
BATTLING AGAINST ODDS
MORE MEN NEEDED
YOUR KING AND COUNTRY NEED YOU !
Will You Answer Your Country's Call ?
At this very moment the Empire is engaged in
Told you the Gazette wouldn't have a bloody war correspondent. It's only a local paper.
I...
What's wrong with fighting for your country It was good enough for me fighting those Boers.
But...
Won't be able to hold our heads up, your ma and me.
No...
They need more men. You're a coward, and that's all there is to it.
Let him have his say, Jim!
I've been trying to tell you. I'm going out there, to the Front.
Glad you've come to your senses.
I'm going as a reporter, not a soldier. They're not telling us what's really going on.
I won't have such talk in my house. You're nothing but a yellow belly.
GET OUT!
Dad...

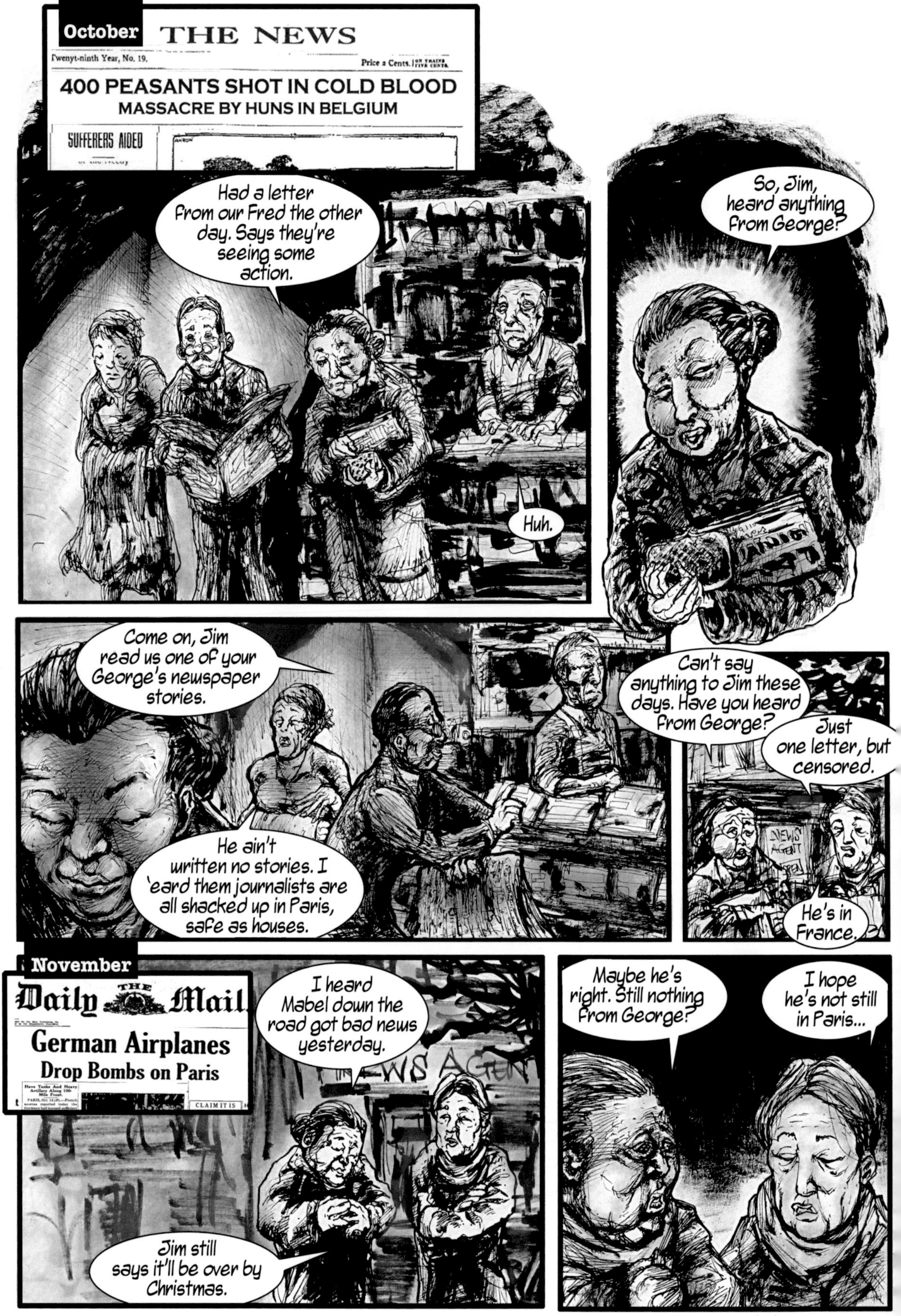

October
THE NEWS
Twenyt-ninth Year, No. 19.
Price 2 Cents.
400 PEASANTS SHOT IN COLD BLOOD
MASSACRE BY HUNS IN BELGIUM
SUFFERERS AIDED
Had a letter from our Fred the other day. Says they're seeing some action.
Huh.
So, Jim, heard anything from George?
Come on, Jim read us one of your George's newspaper stories.
He ain't written no stories. I 'eard them journalists are all shacked up in Paris, safe as houses.
Can't say anything to Jim these days. Have you heard from George?
Just one letter, but censored.
NEWS AGENT
He's in France.
November
Daily THE Mail
German Airplanes
Drop Bombs on Paris
CLAIM IT IS
I heard Mabel down the road got bad news yesterday.
Jim still says it'll be over by Christmas.
Maybe he's right. Still nothing from George?
I hope he's not still in Paris...

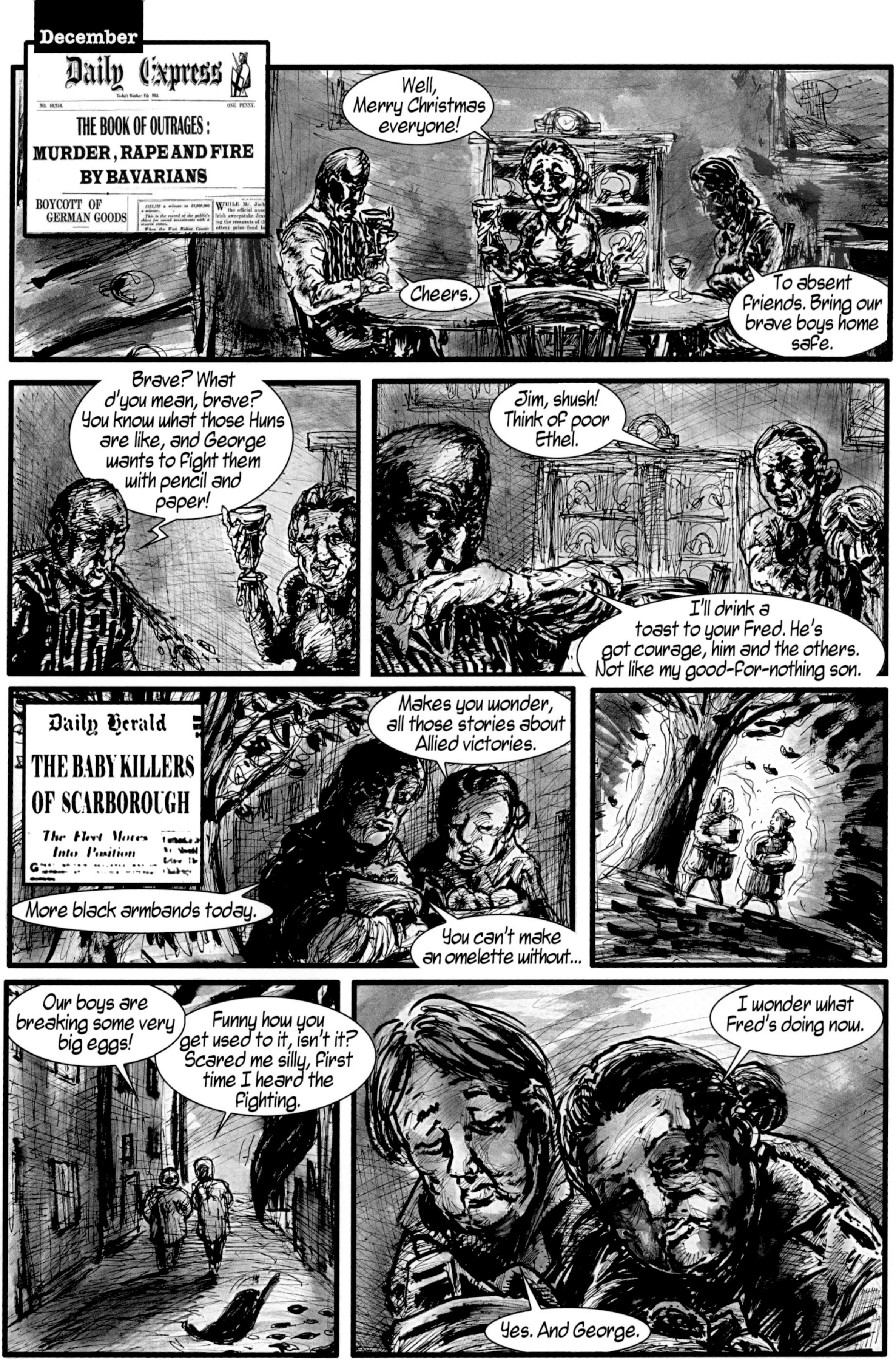
December
Daily Express
ONE PENNY.
THE BOOK OF OUTRAGES :
MURDER, RAPE AND FIRE
BY BAVARIANS
BOYCOTT OF
GERMAN GOODS
Well, Merry Christmas everyone!
Cheers.
To absent friends. Bring our brave boys home safe.
Brave? What d'you mean, brave? You know what those Huns are like, and George wants to fight them with pencil and paper!
Jim, shush! Think of poor Ethel.
I'll drink a toast to your Fred. He's got courage, him and the others. Not like my good-for-nothing son.
Daily Herald
THE BABY KILLERS
OF SCARBOROUGH
Makes you wonder, all those stories about Allied victories.
More black armbands today.
You can't make an omelette without...
Our boys are breaking some very big eggs!
Funny how you get used to it, isn't it? Scared me silly, first time I heard the fighting.
I wonder what Fred's doing now.
Yes. And George.

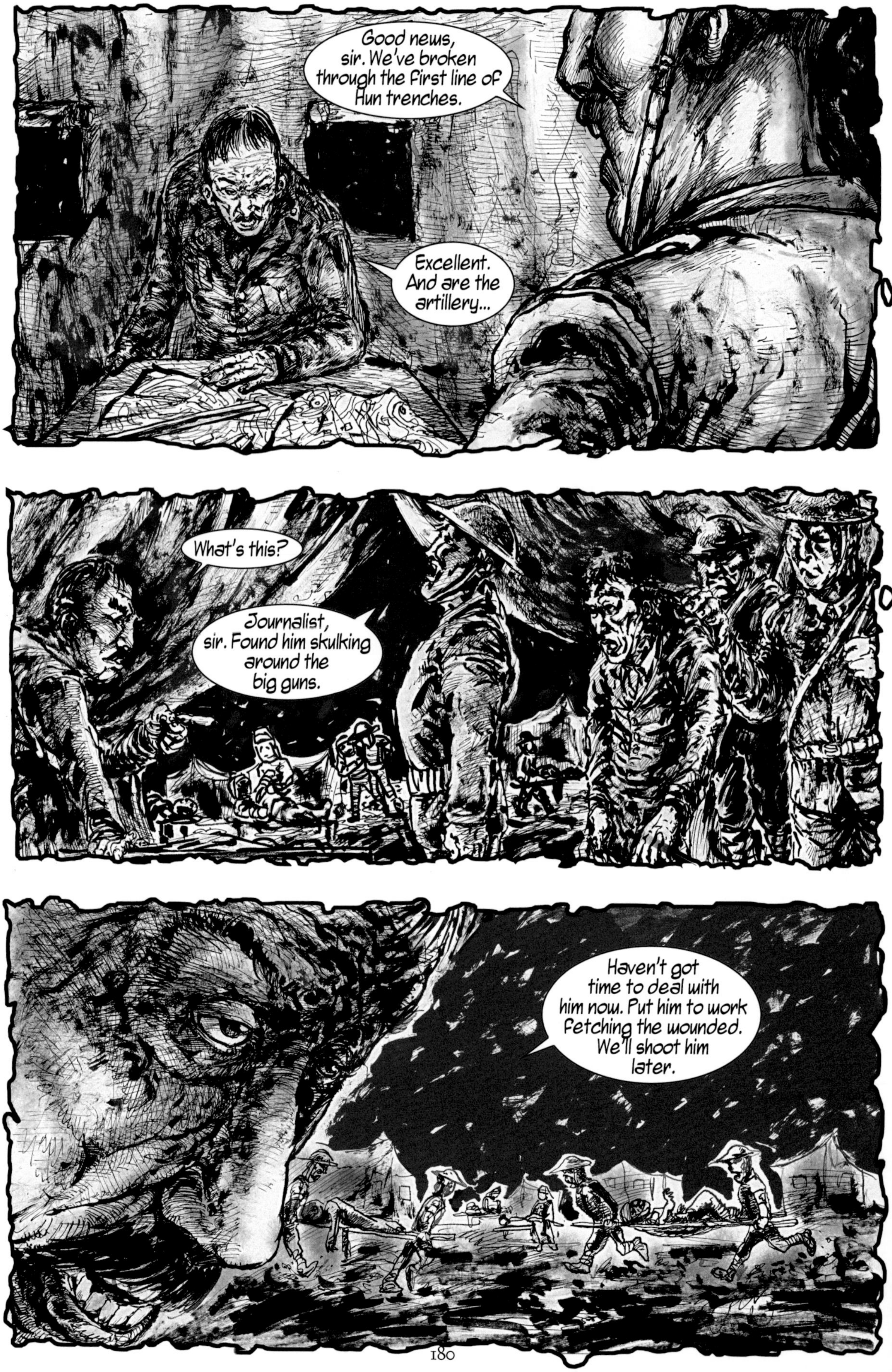
Good news, sir. We've broken through the first line of Hun trenches.
Excellent. And are the artillery...
What's this?
Journalist, sir. Found him skulking around the big guns.
Haven't got time to deal with him now. Put him to work fetching the wounded. We'll shoot him later.

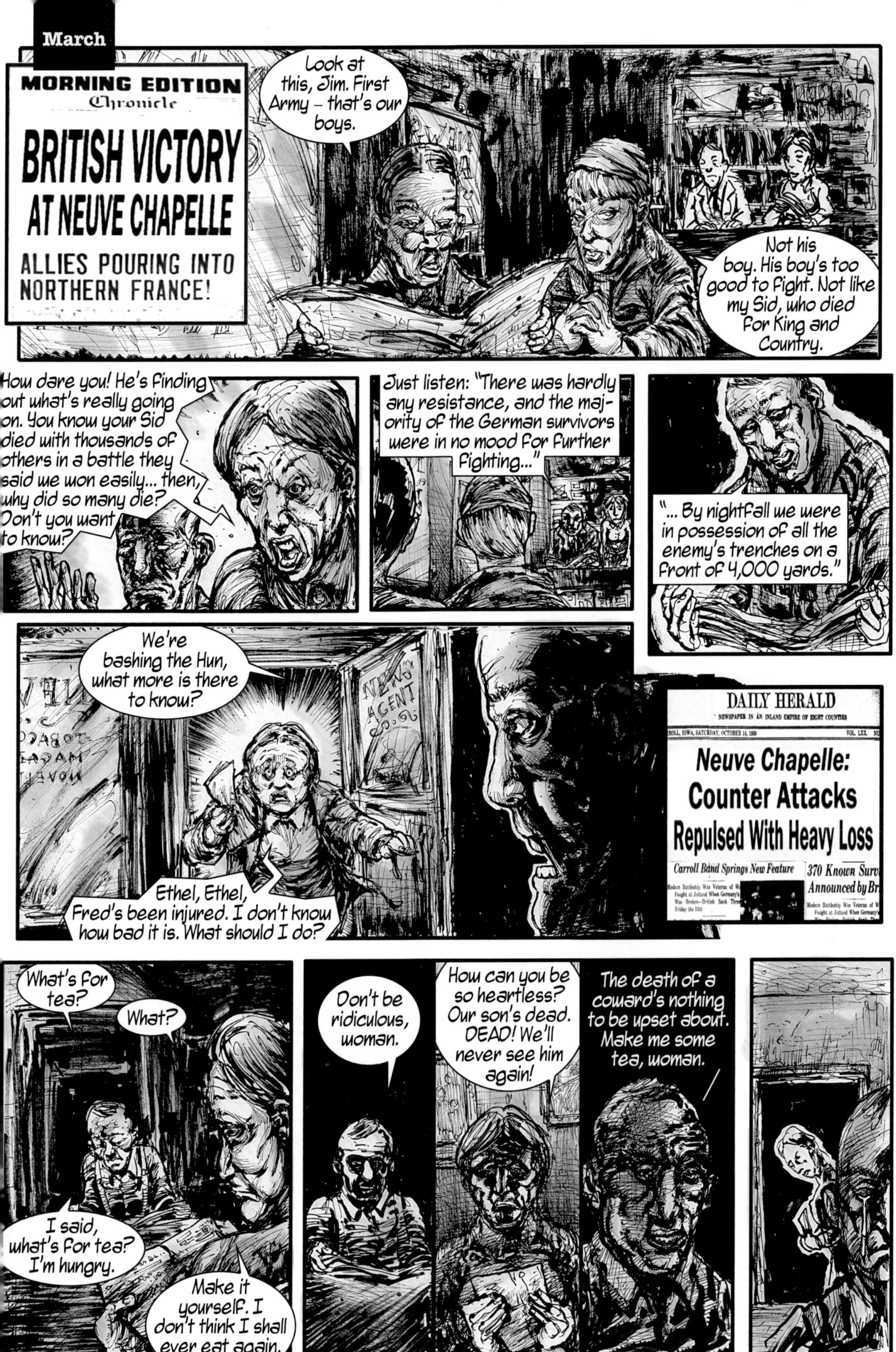
March
MORNING EDITION
Chronicle
BRITISH VICTORY AT NEUVE CHAPELLE
ALLIES POURING INTO NORTHERN FRANCE!
Look at this, Jim. First Army – that's our boys.
Not his boy. His boy's too good to fight. Not like my Sid, who died for King and Country.
How dare you! He's finding out what's really going on. You know your Sid died with thousands of others in a battle they said we won easily... then, why did so many die? Don't you want to know?
Just listen: "There was hardly any resistance, and the majority of the German survivors were in no mood for further fighting..."
"... By nightfall we were in possession of all the enemy's trenches on a front of 4,000 yards."
We're bashing the Hun, what more is there to know?
NEWS AGENT
DAILY HERALD
Neuve Chapelle: Counter Attacks Repulsed With Heavy Loss
Carroll Band Springs New Feature
Ethel, Ethel, Fred's been injured. I don't know how bad it is. What should I do?
What's for tea?
What?
I said, what's for tea? I'm hungry.
Make it yourself. I don't think I shall ever eat again.
Don't be ridiculous, woman.
How can you be so heartless? Our son's dead. DEAD! We'll never see him again!
The death of a coward's nothing to be upset about. Make me some tea, woman.

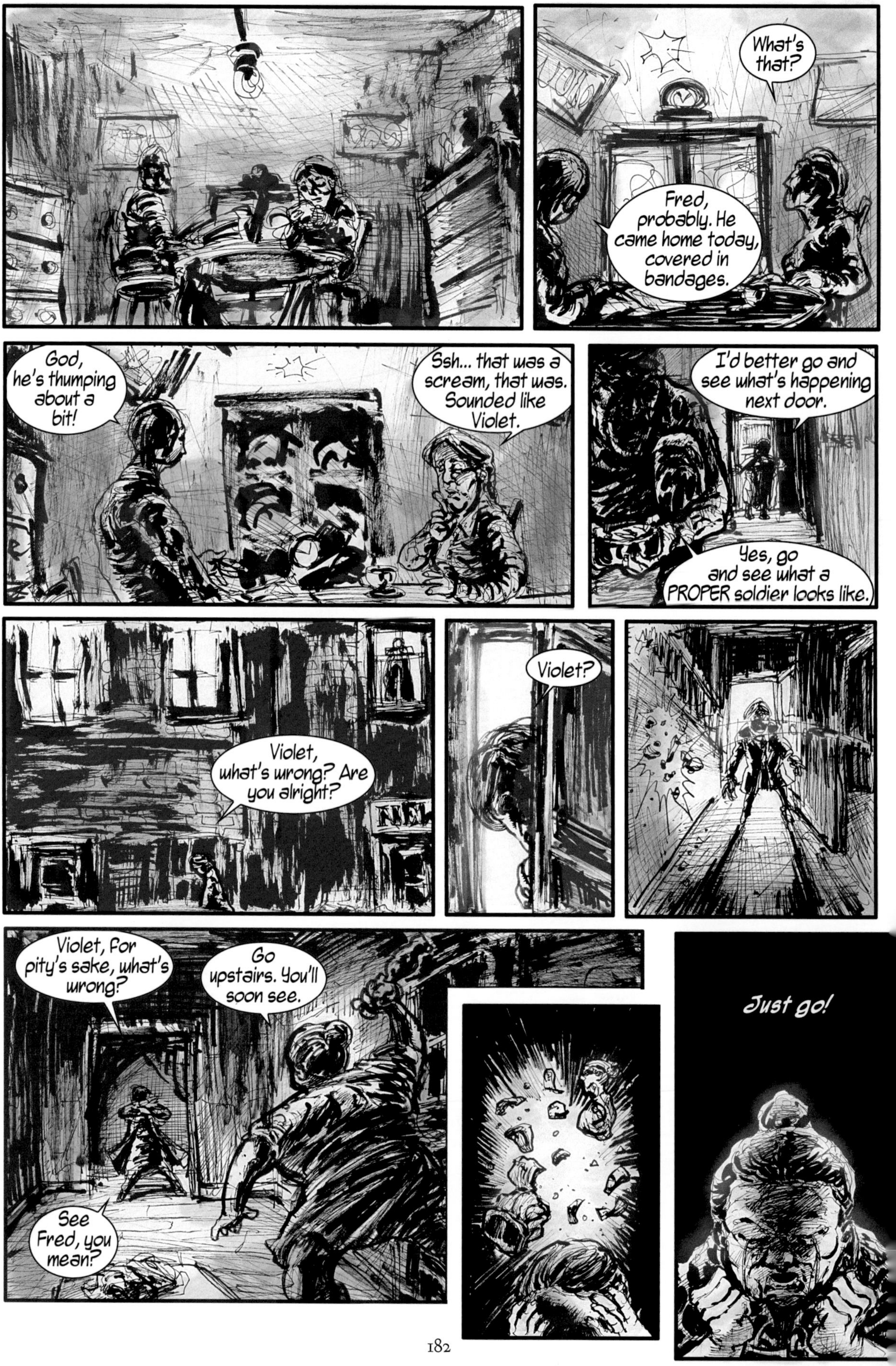
What's that?
Fred, probably. He came home today, covered in bandages.
God, he's thumping about a bit!
Ssh... that was a scream, that was. Sounded like Violet.
I'd better go and see what's happening next door.
Yes, go and see what a PROPER soldier looks like.
Violet, what's wrong? Are you alright?
Violet?
Violet, for pity's sake, what's wrong?
Go upstairs. You'll soon see.
See Fred, you mean?
Just go!

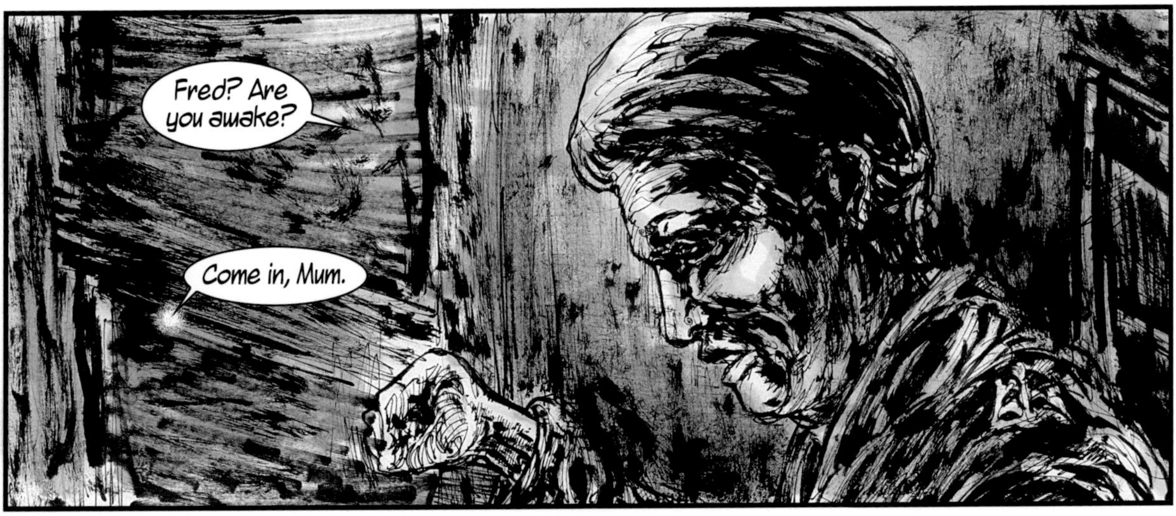
Fred? Are you awake?
Come in, Mum.

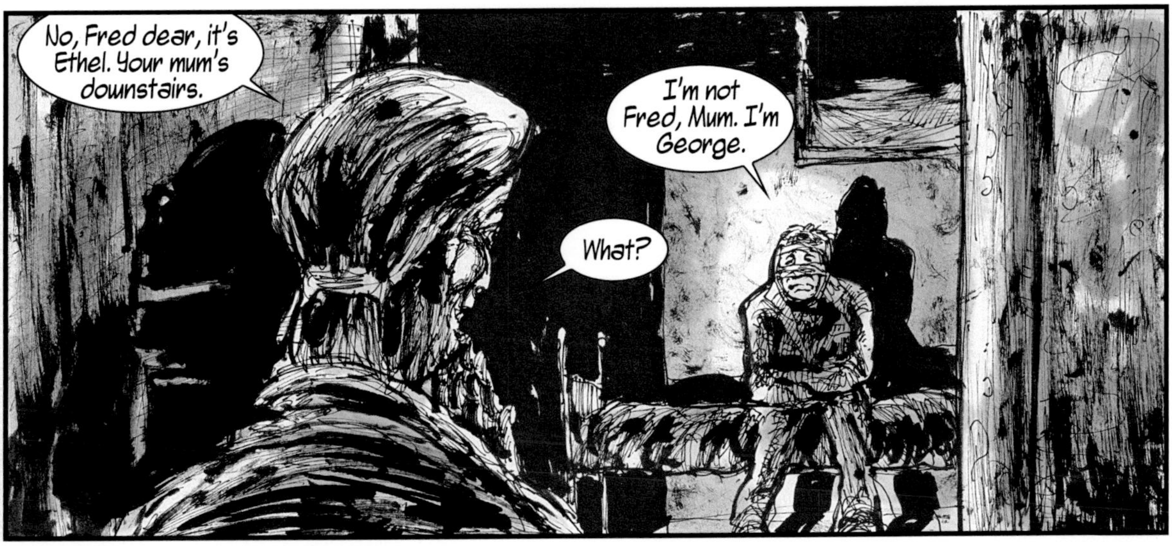
No, Fred dear, it's Ethel. Your mum's downstairs.
I'm not Fred, Mum. I'm George.
What?

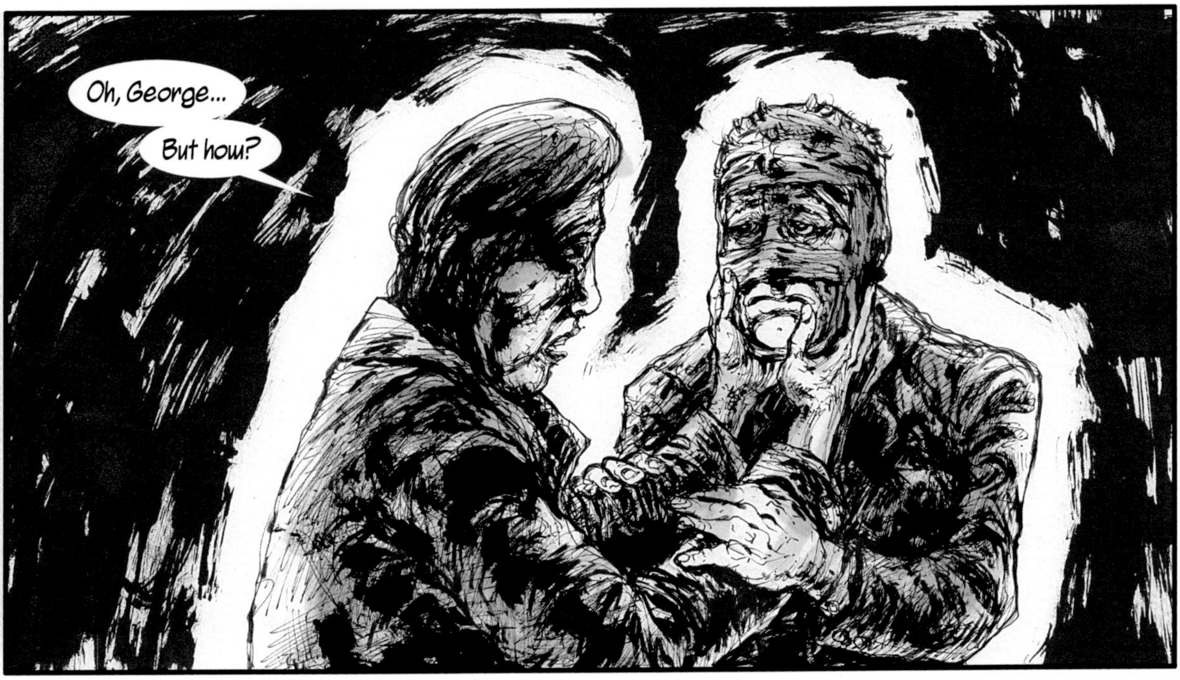
Oh, George...
But how?

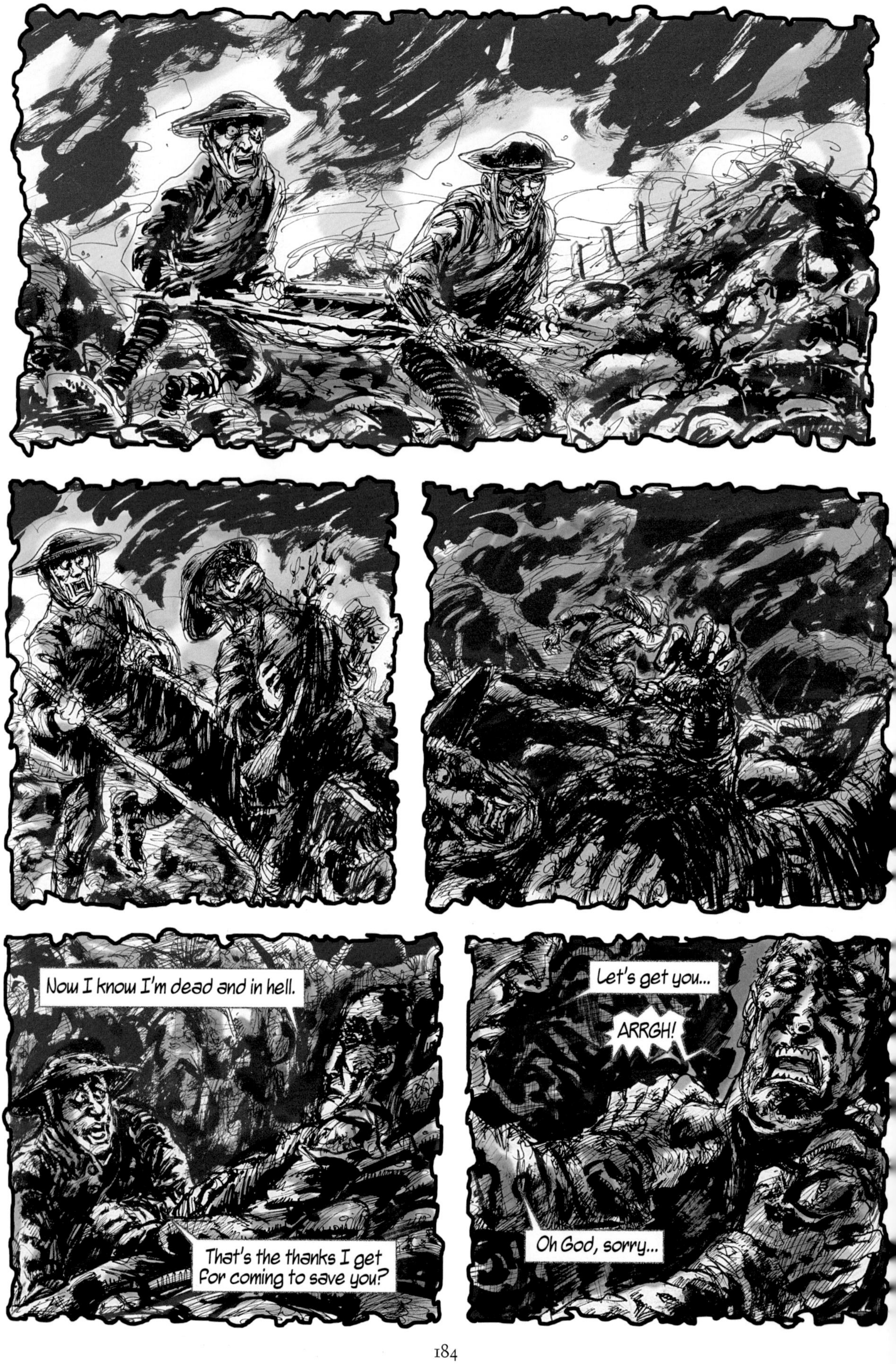
Now I know I'm dead and in hell.
That's the thanks I get for coming to save you?
Let's get you...
ARRGH!
Oh God, sorry...

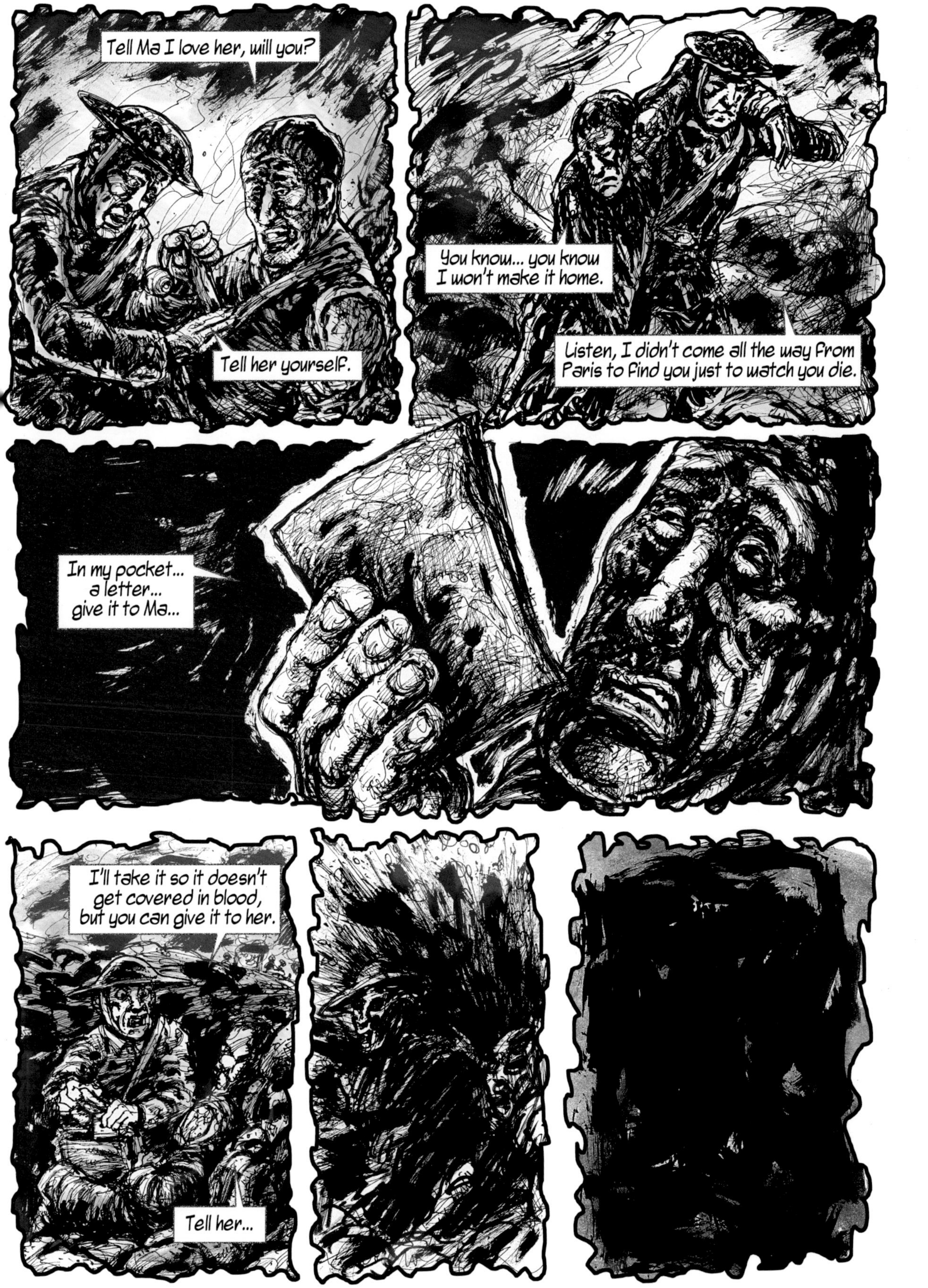
Tell Ma I love her, will you?
Tell her yourself.
You know... you know I won't make it home.
Listen, I didn't come all the way from Paris to find you just to watch you die.
In my pocket... a letter... give it to Ma...
I'll take it so it doesn't get covered in blood, but you can give it to her.
Tell her...

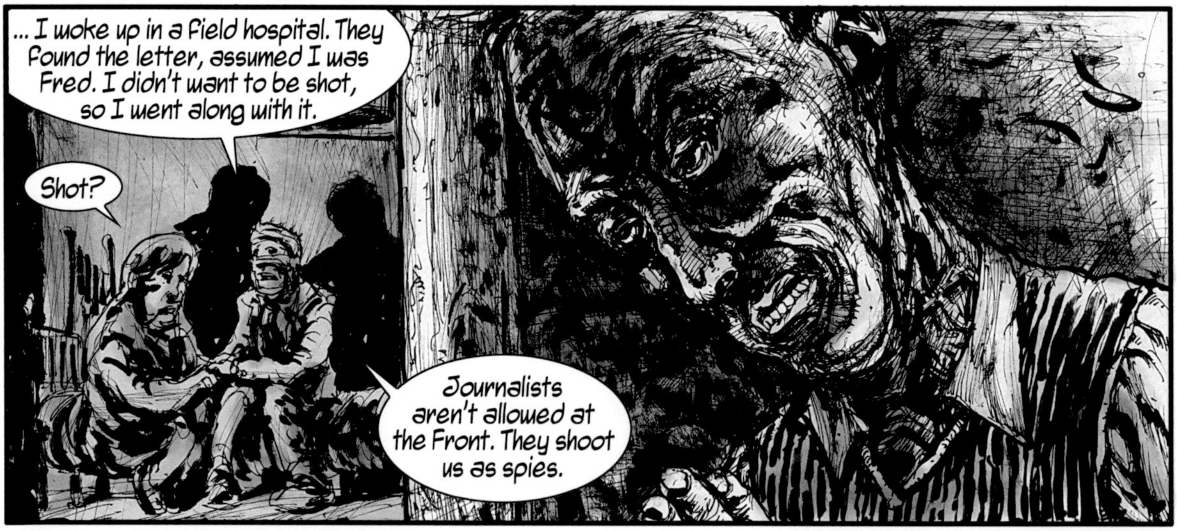
... I woke up in a field hospital. They found the letter, assumed I was Fred. I didn't want to be shot, so I went along with it.
Shot?
Journalists aren't allowed at the Front. They shoot us as spies.

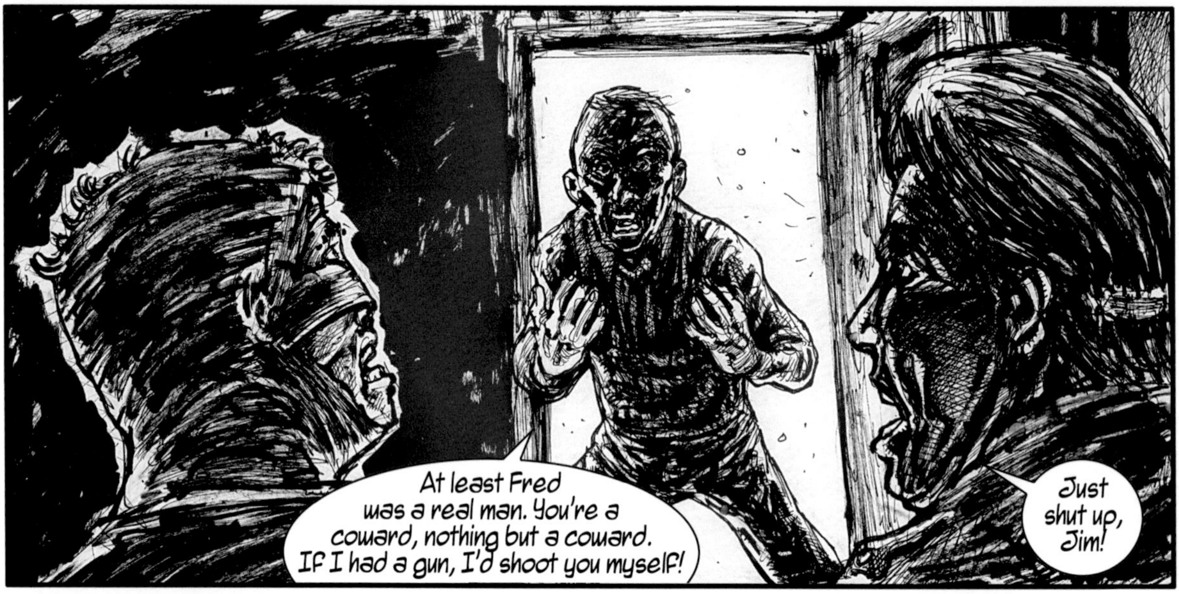
At least Fred was a real man. You're a coward, nothing but a coward. If I had a gun, I'd shoot you myself!
Just shut up, Jim!

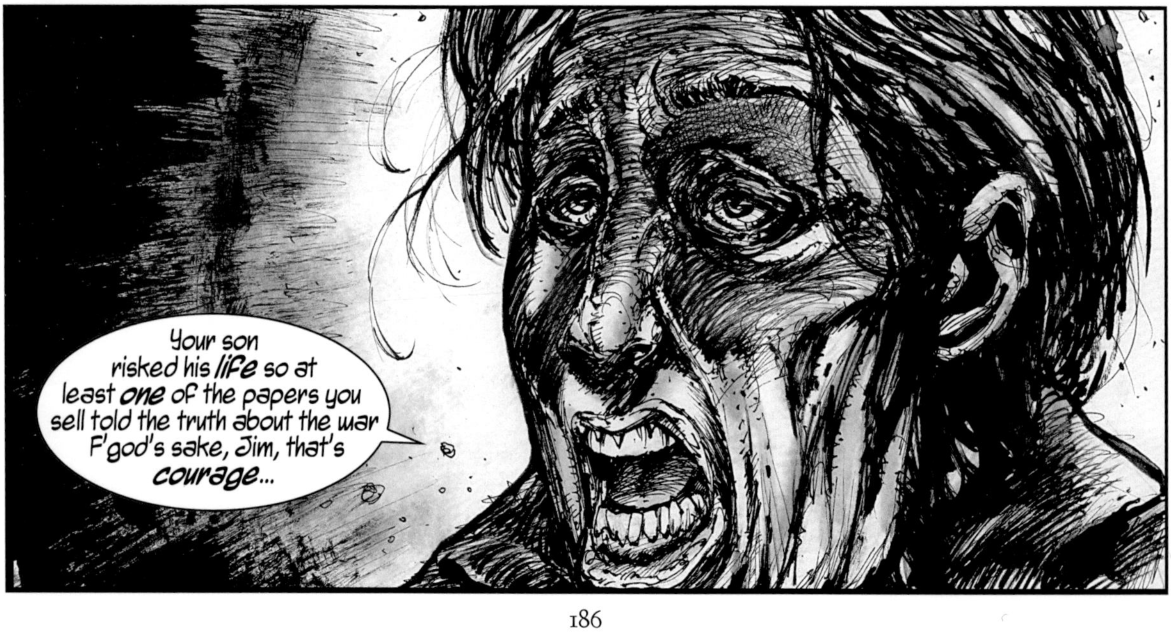
Your son risked his *life* so at least *one* of the papers you sell told the truth about the war F'god's sake, Jim, that's *courage*...

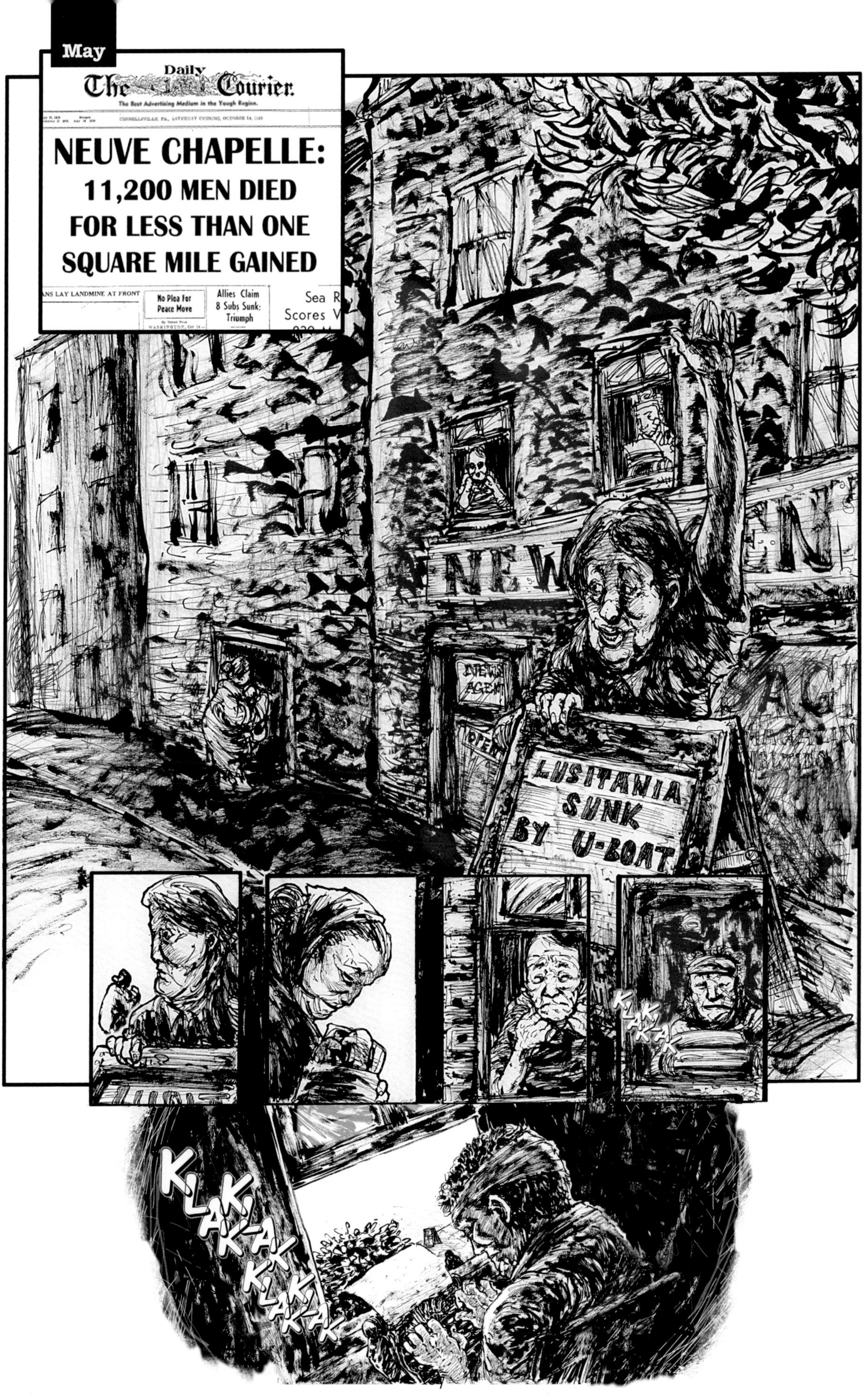

May
The Daily Courier
The Best Advertising Medium in the Yough Region.
NEUVE CHAPELLE:
11,200 MEN DIED
FOR LESS THAN ONE
SQUARE MILE GAINED
No Plea For Peace Move
Allies Claim 8 Subs Sunk: Triumph
NEWS
NEWS AGENT
LUSITANIA SUNK BY U-BOAT
KLAK-AK
KLAK-AK-AK-AK
KLAK-AK-AK

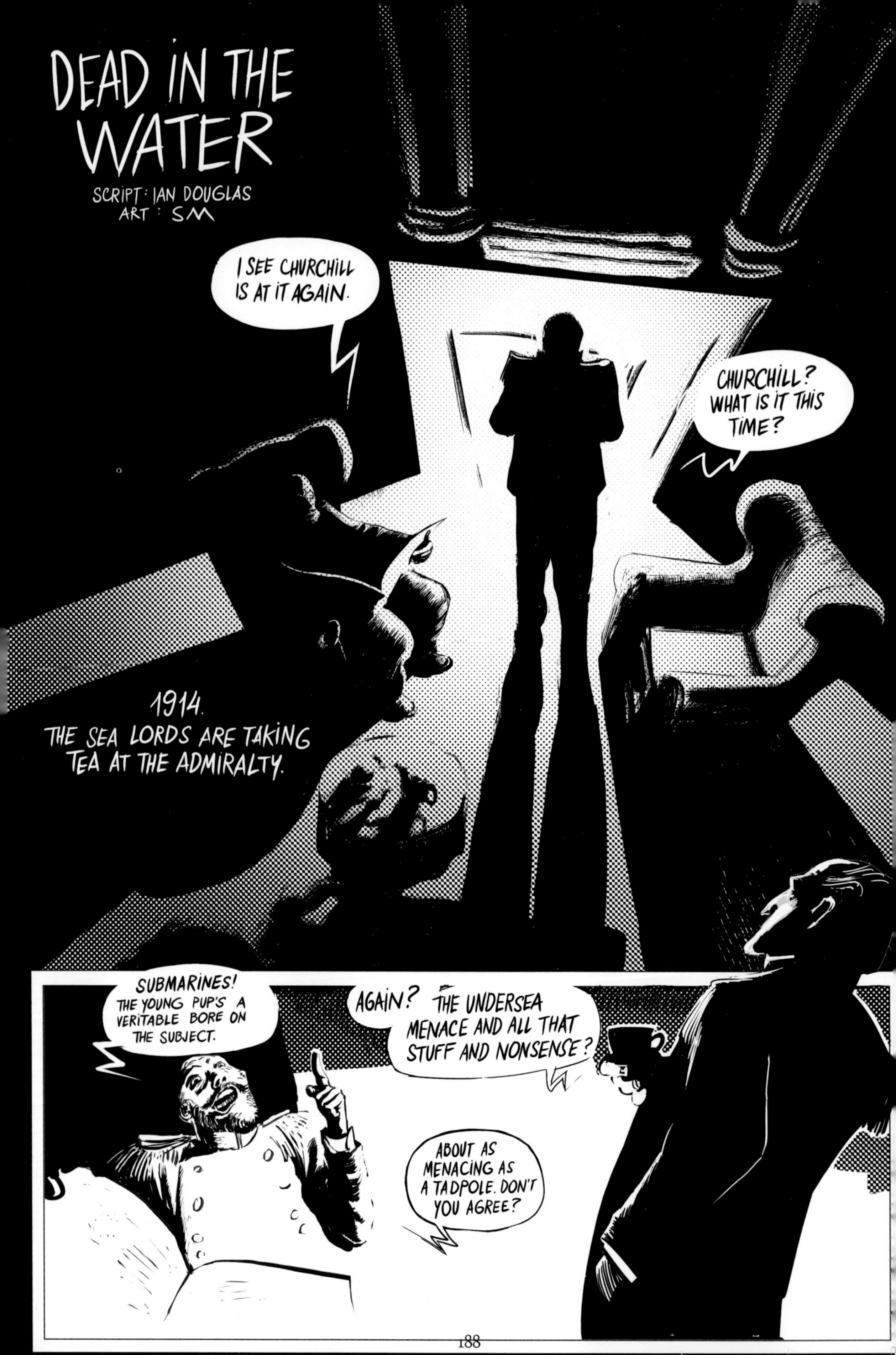
DEAD IN THE WATER
SCRIPT: IAN DOUGLAS
ART: SM
I SEE CHURCHILL IS AT IT AGAIN.
CHURCHILL? WHAT IS IT THIS TIME?
1914. THE SEA LORDS ARE TAKING TEA AT THE ADMIRALTY.
SUBMARINES! THE YOUNG PUP'S A VERITABLE BORE ON THE SUBJECT.
AGAIN? THE UNDERSEA MENACE AND ALL THAT STUFF AND NONSENSE?
ABOUT AS MENACING AS A TADPOLE. DON'T YOU AGREE?

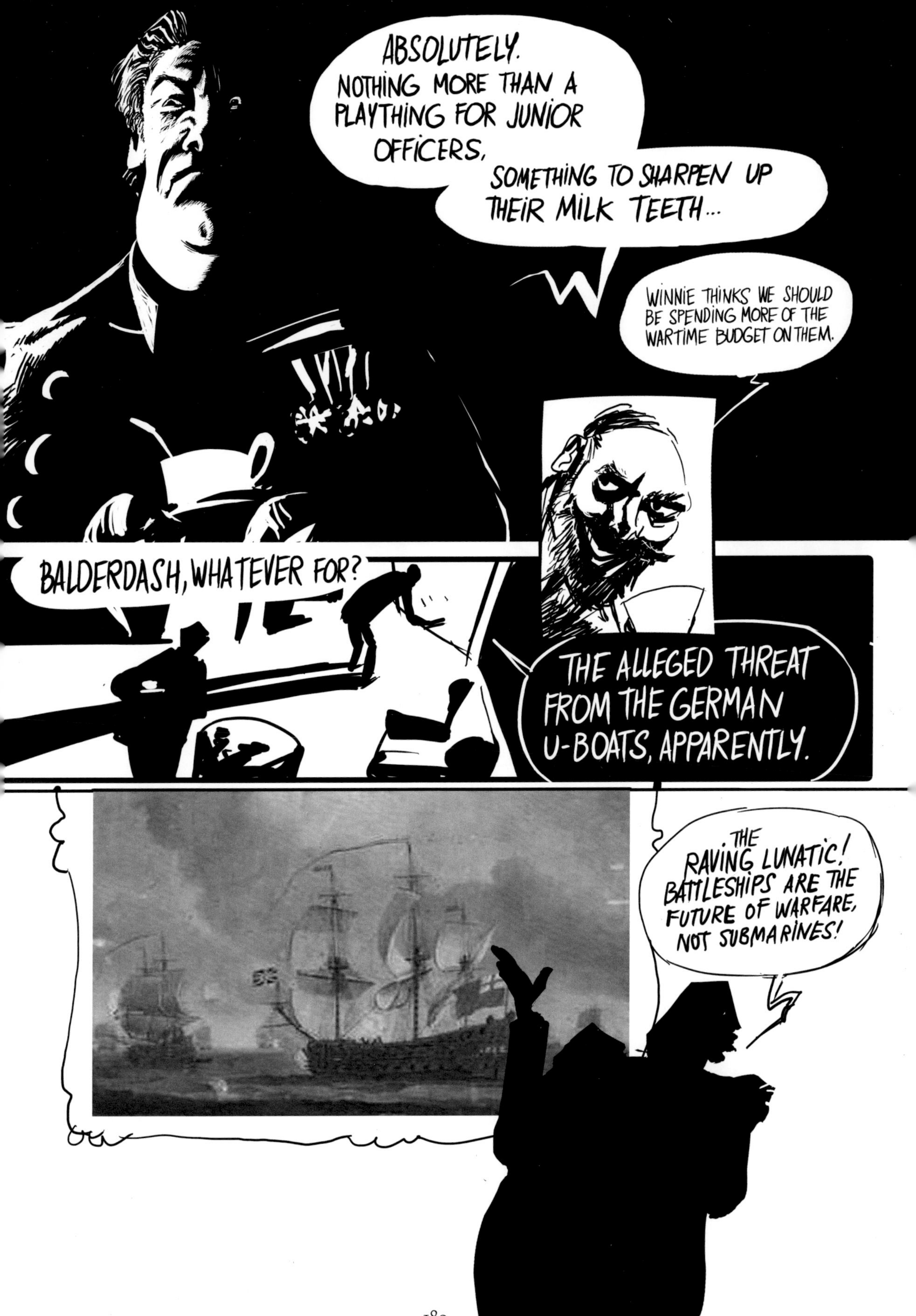
ABSOLUTELY. NOTHING MORE THAN A PLAYTHING FOR JUNIOR OFFICERS,
SOMETHING TO SHARPEN UP THEIR MILK TEETH...
WINNIE THINKS WE SHOULD BE SPENDING MORE OF THE WARTIME BUDGET ON THEM.
BALDERDASH, WHATEVER FOR?
THE ALLEGED THREAT FROM THE GERMAN U-BOATS, APPARENTLY.
THE RAVING LUNATIC! BATTLESHIPS ARE THE FUTURE OF WARFARE, NOT SUBMARINES!

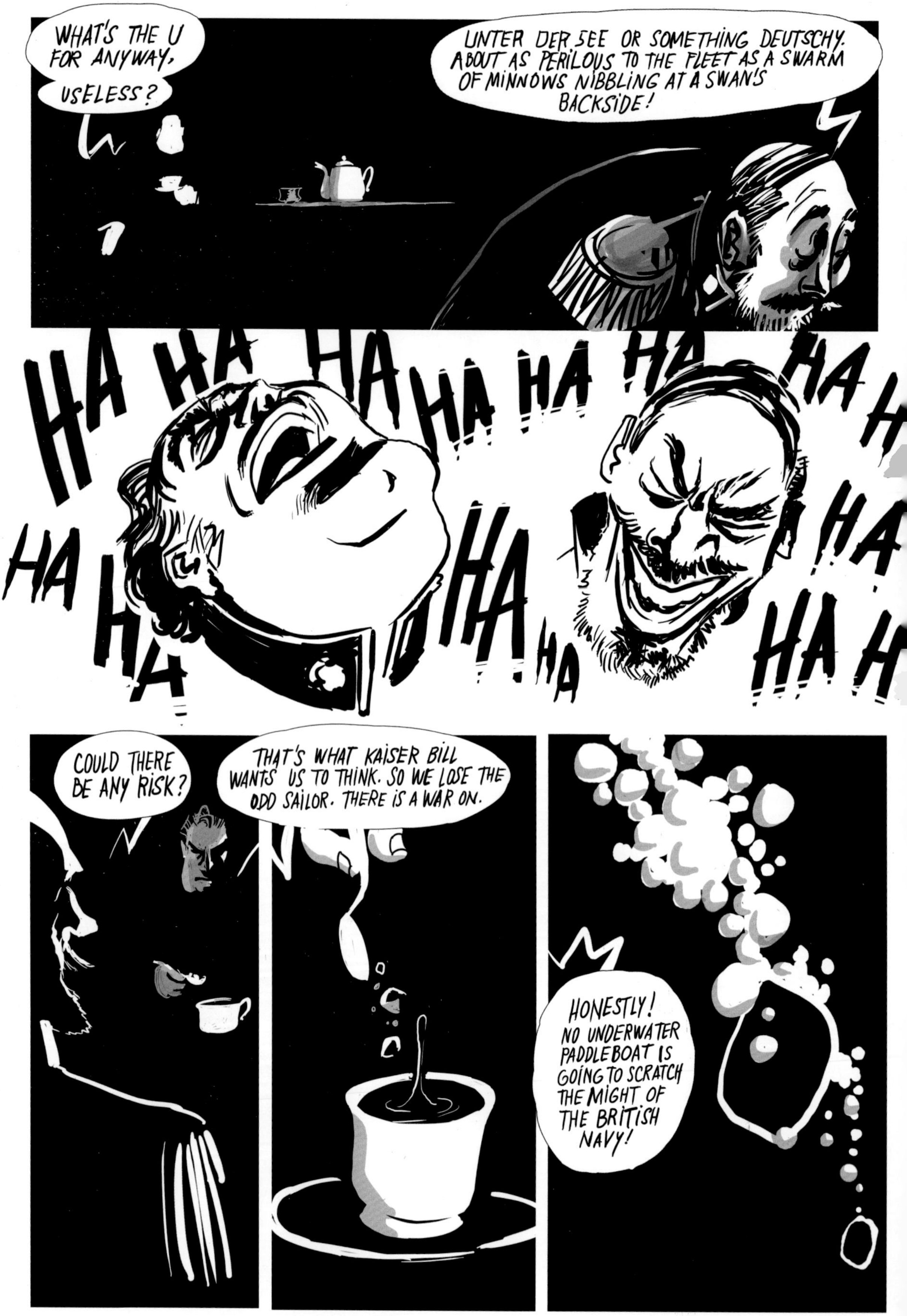
WHAT'S THE U FOR ANYWAY, USELESS?
UNTER DER SEE OR SOMETHING DEUTSCHY. ABOUT AS PERILOUS TO THE FLEET AS A SWARM OF MINNOWS NIBBLING AT A SWAN'S BACKSIDE!
HA HA HA HA HA HA HA HA HA HA HA HA HA HA HA HA HA HA
COULD THERE BE ANY RISK?
THAT'S WHAT KAISER BILL WANTS US TO THINK. SO WE LOSE THE ODD SAILOR. THERE IS A WAR ON.
HONESTLY! NO UNDERWATER PADDLEBOAT IS GOING TO SCRATCH THE MIGHT OF THE BRITISH NAVY!

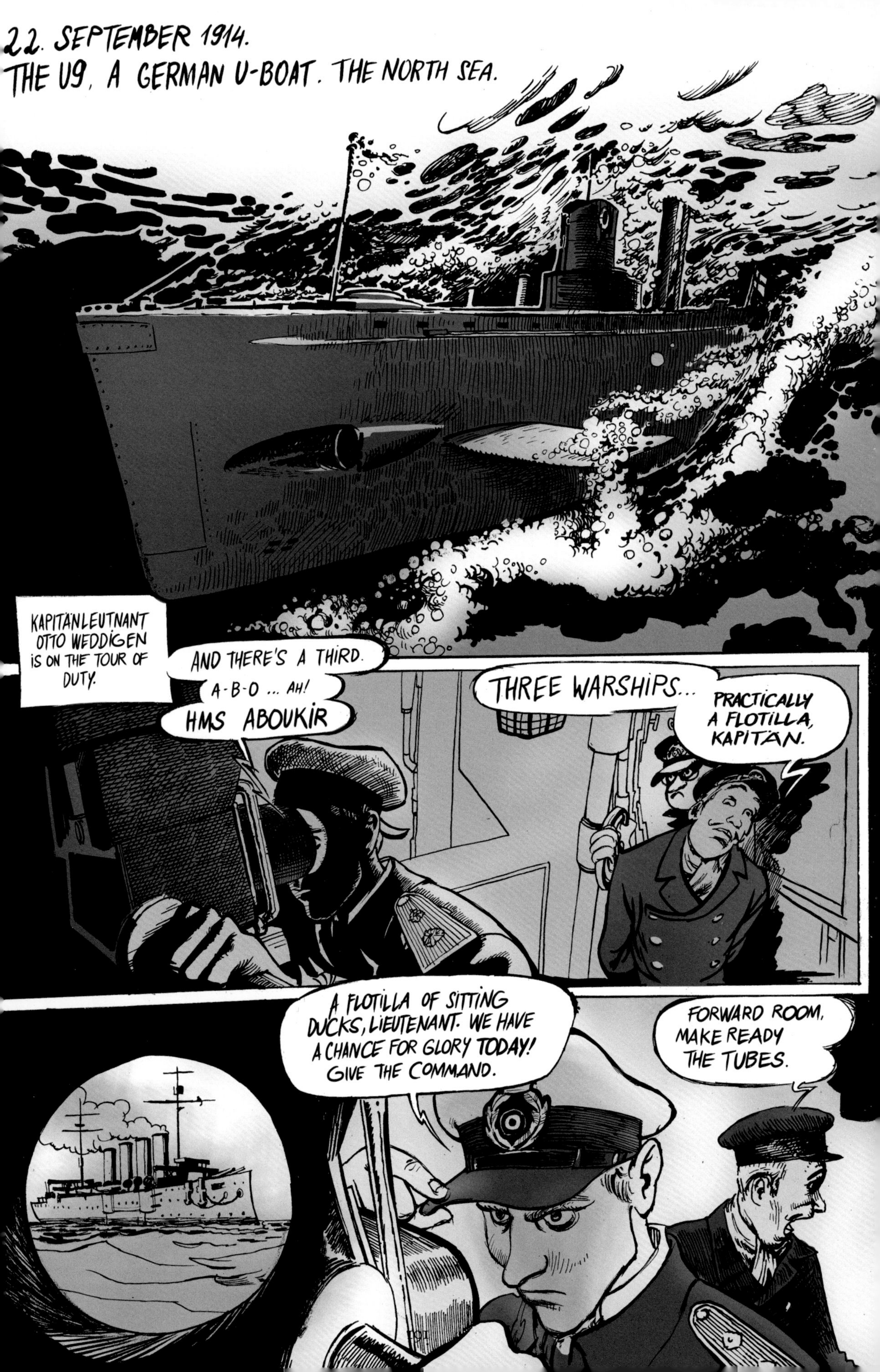
22. SEPTEMBER 1914.
THE U9, A GERMAN U-BOAT. THE NORTH SEA.
KAPITÄNLEUTNANT OTTO WEDDIGEN IS ON THE TOUR OF DUTY.
AND THERE'S A THIRD.
A-B-O ... AH!
HMS ABOUKIR
THREE WARSHIPS...
PRACTICALLY A FLOTILLA, KAPITÄN.
A FLOTILLA OF SITTING DUCKS, LIEUTENANT. WE HAVE A CHANCE FOR GLORY TODAY! GIVE THE COMMAND.
FORWARD ROOM, MAKE READY THE TUBES.

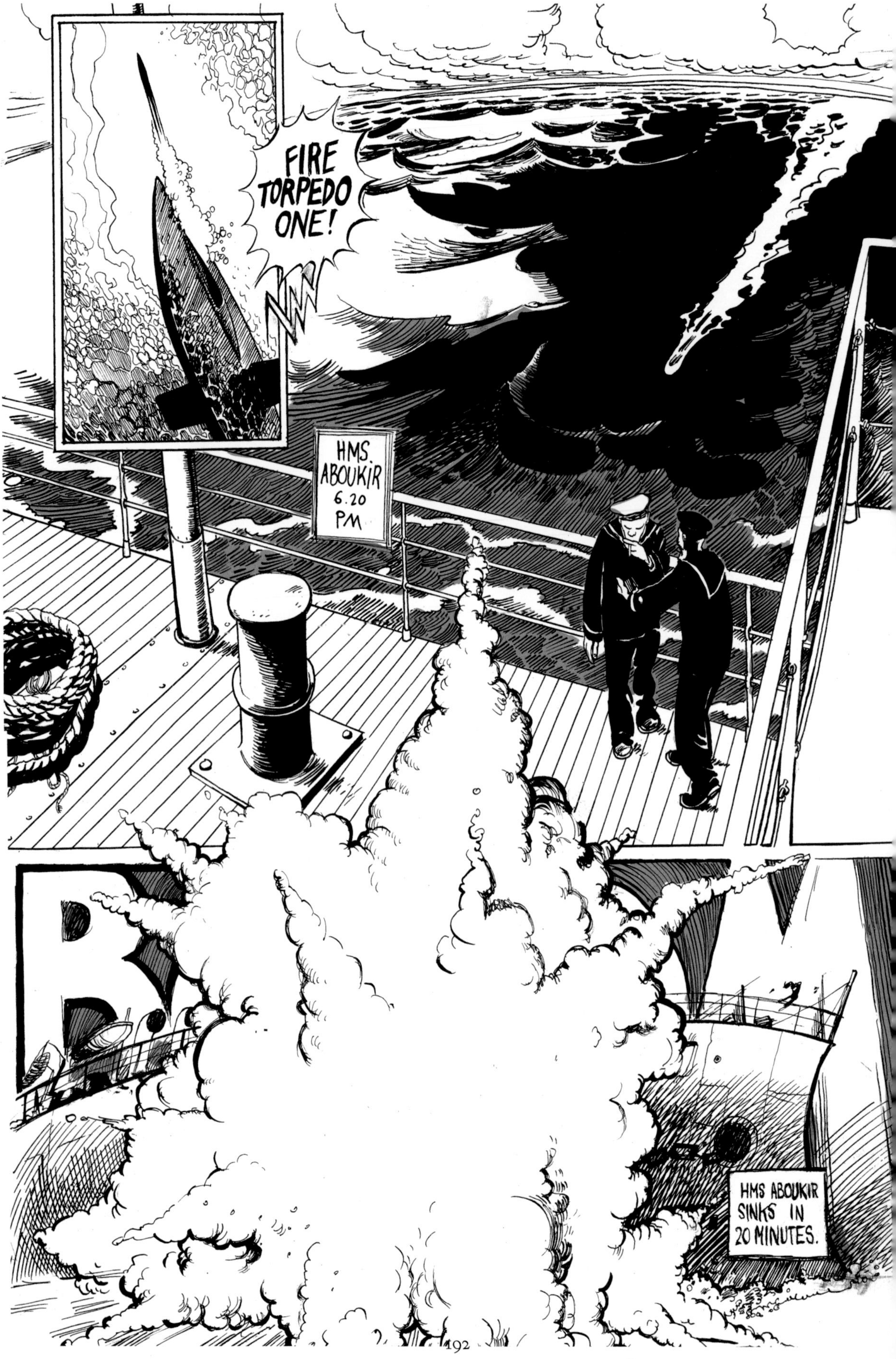
FIRE TORPEDO ONE!
HMS. ABOUKIR 6.20 PM
HMS ABOUKIR SINKS IN 20 MINUTES.

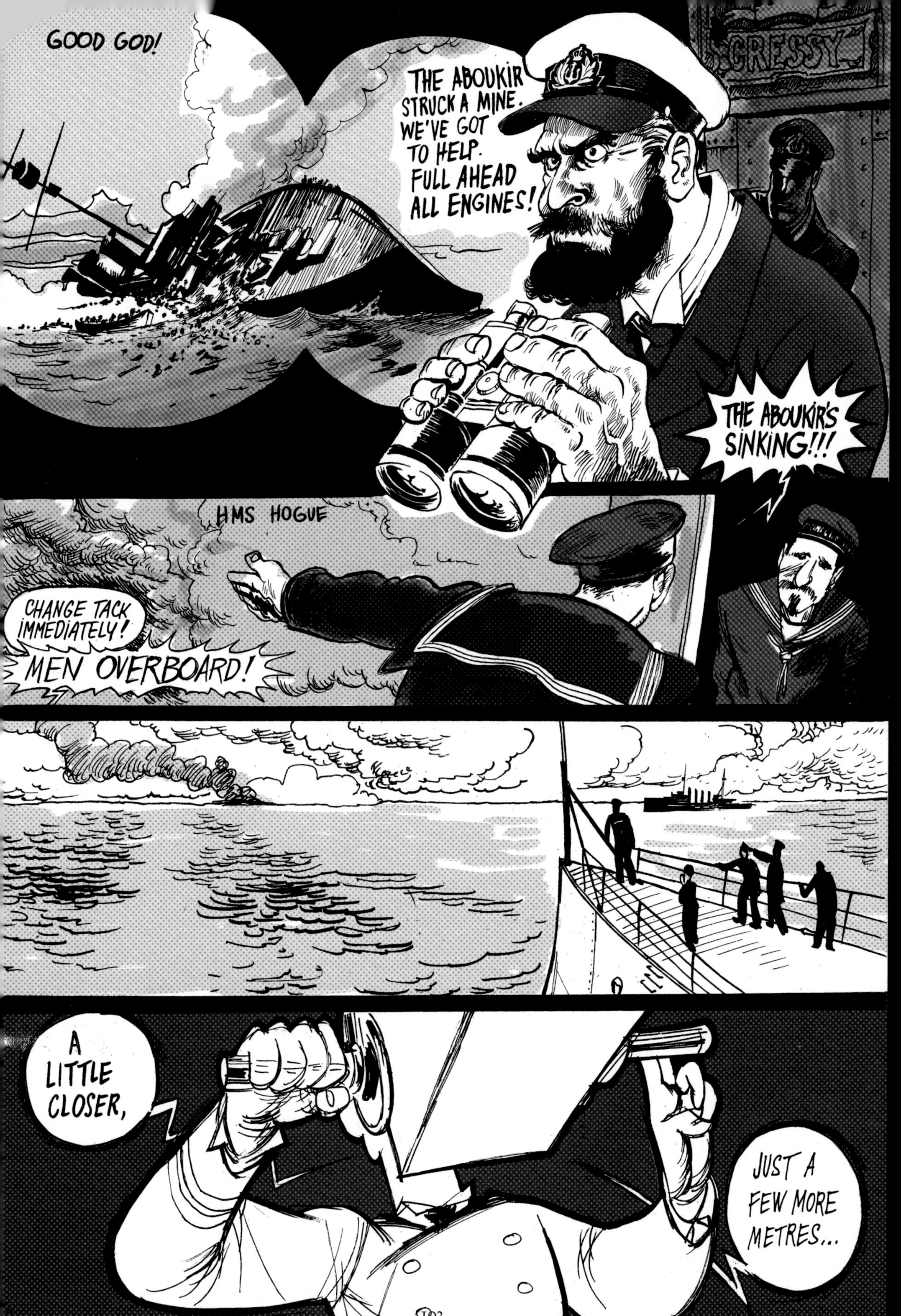
GOOD GOD!
CRESSY
THE ABOUKIR STRUCK A MINE. WE'VE GOT TO HELP. FULL AHEAD ALL ENGINES!
THE ABOUKIR'S SINKING!!!
HMS HOGUE
CHANGE TACK IMMEDIATELY!
MEN OVERBOARD!
A LITTLE CLOSER,
JUST A FEW MORE METRES...

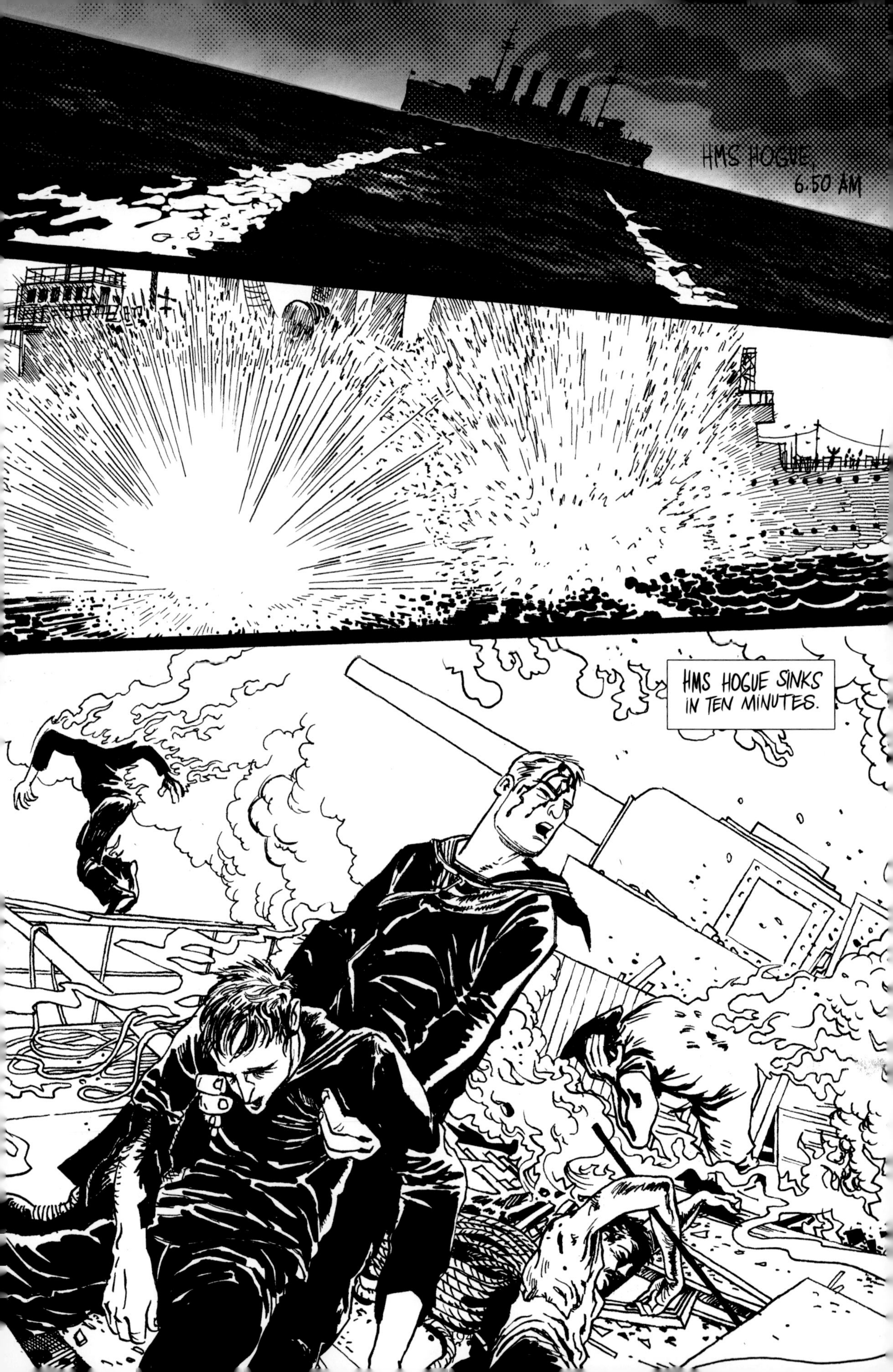
HMS HOGUE, 6:50 AM
HMS HOGUE SINKS IN TEN MINUTES.

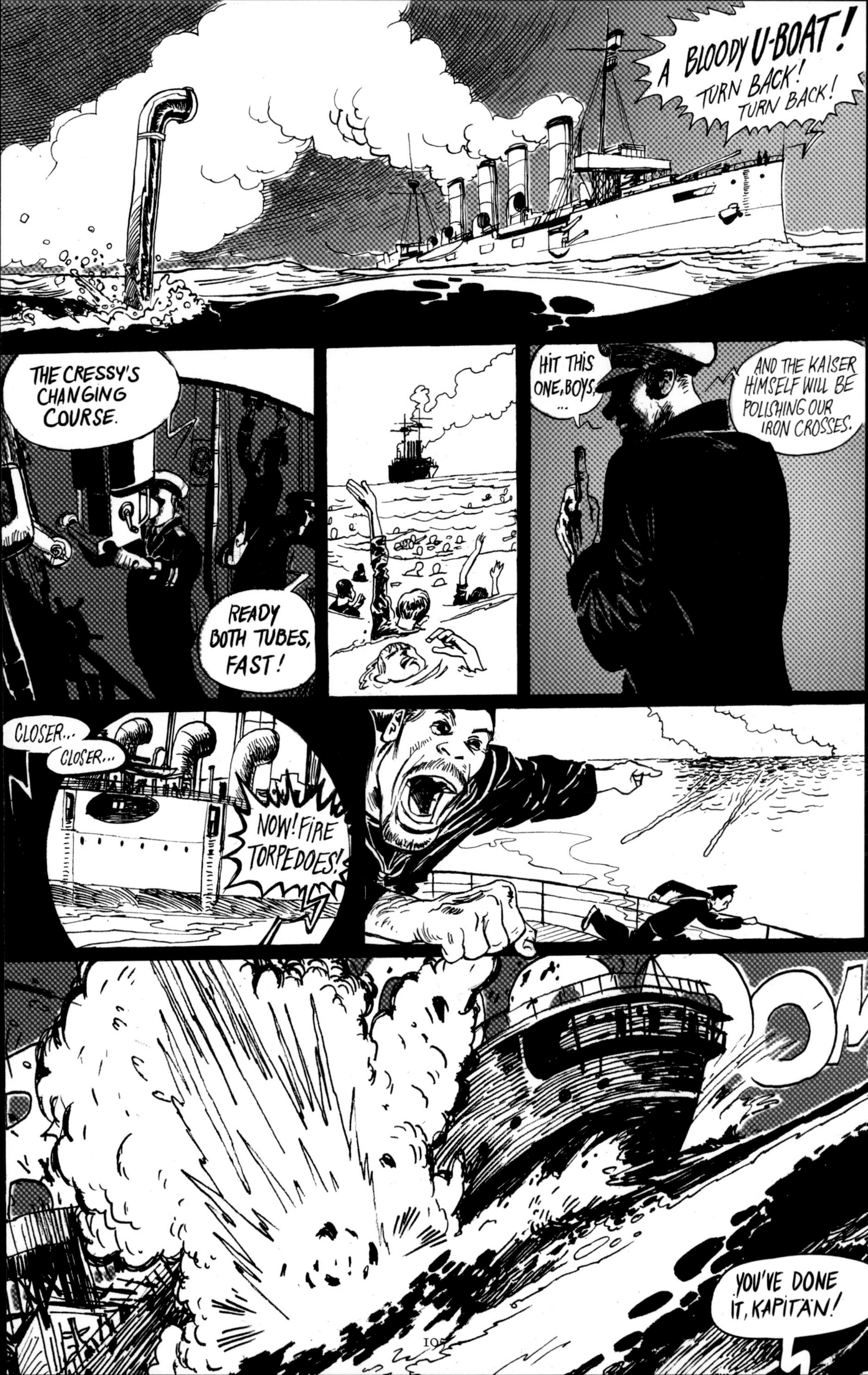
A BLOODY U-BOAT! TURN BACK! TURN BACK!
THE CRESSY'S CHANGING COURSE.
READY BOTH TUBES, FAST!
HIT THIS ONE, BOYS, ...
AND THE KAISER HIMSELF WILL BE POLISHING OUR IRON CROSSES.
CLOSER...
CLOSER...
NOW! FIRE TORPEDOES!
YOU'VE DONE IT, KAPITÄN!

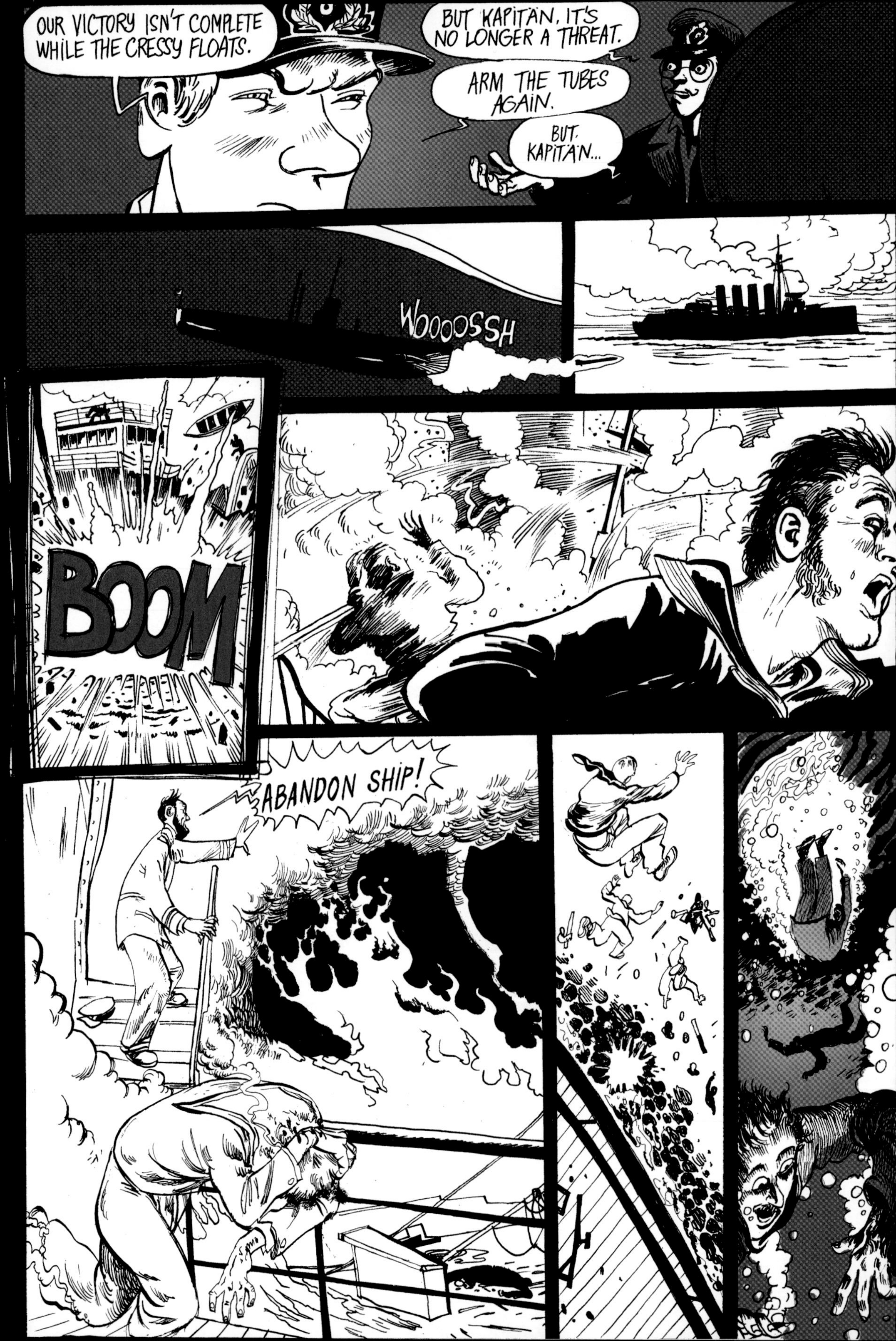
OUR VICTORY ISN'T COMPLETE WHILE THE CRESSY FLOATS.
BUT KAPITÄN, IT'S NO LONGER A THREAT.
ARM THE TUBES AGAIN.
BUT, KAPITÄN...
WOOOOSSH
BOOM
ABANDON SHIP!

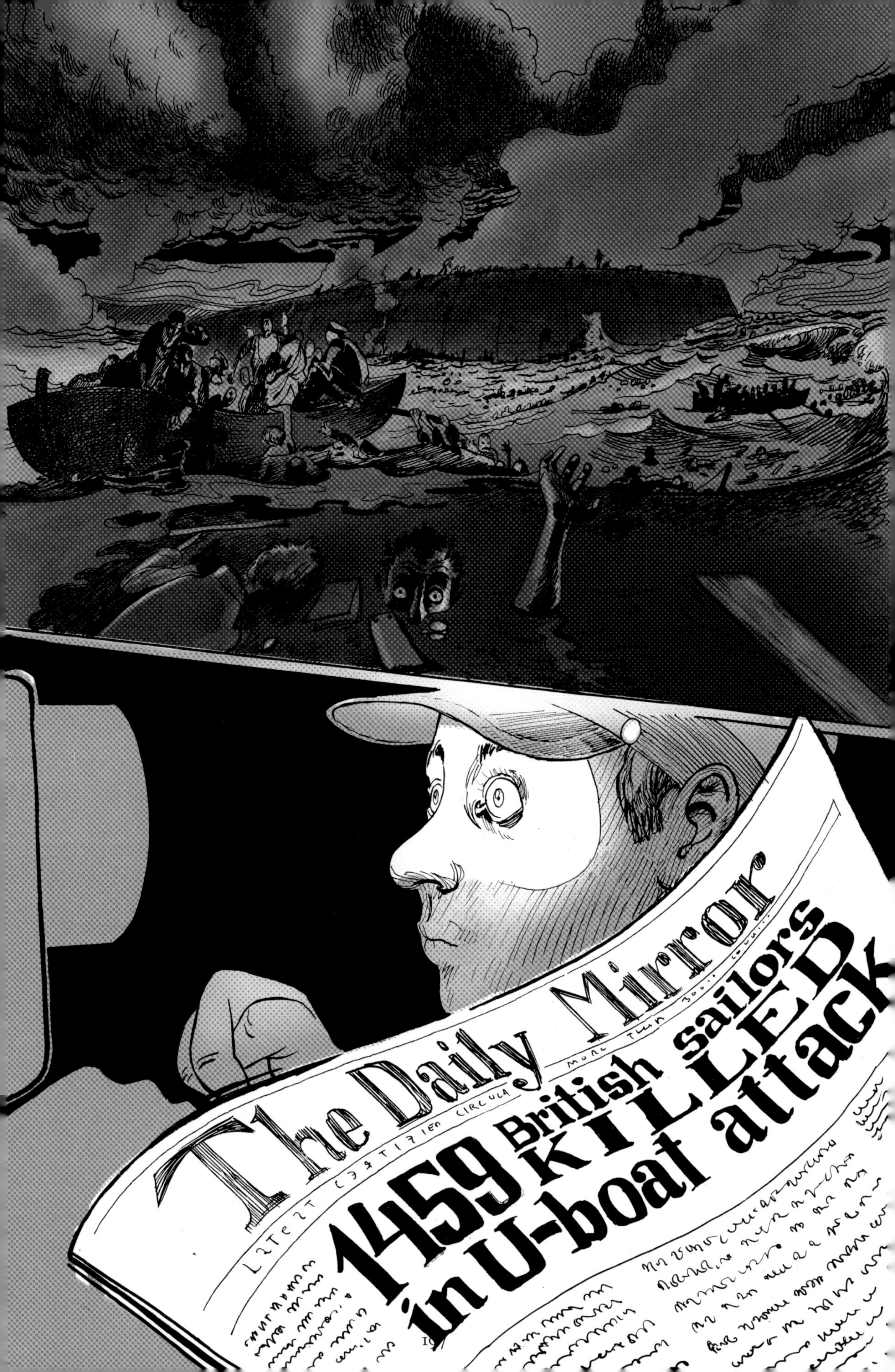
The Daily Mirror
1459 British sailors KILLED in U-boat attack

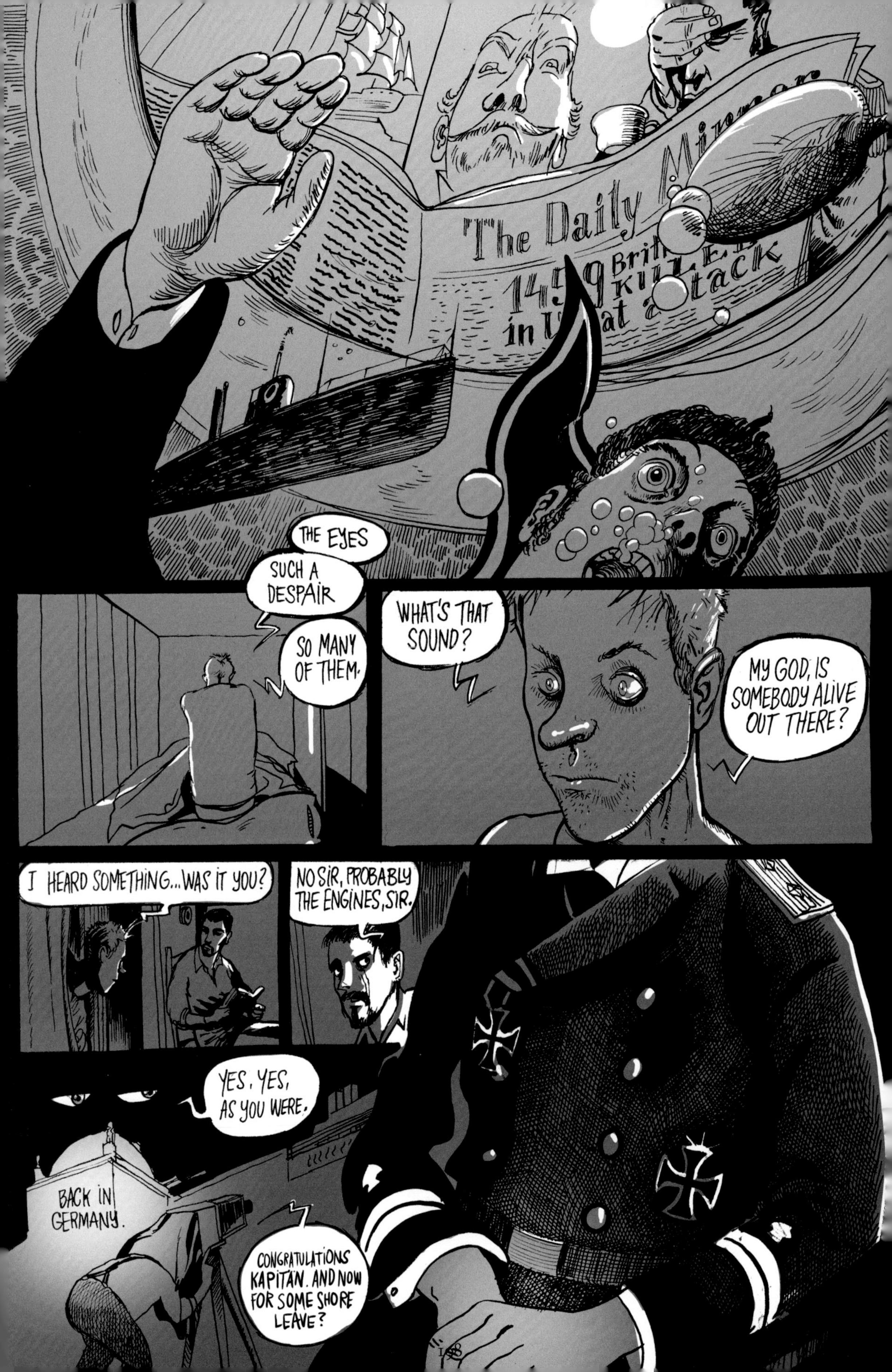

The Daily
THE EYES
SUCH A DESPAIR
SO MANY OF THEM.
WHAT'S THAT SOUND?
MY GOD, IS SOMEBODY ALIVE OUT THERE?
I HEARD SOMETHING... WAS IT YOU?
NO SIR, PROBABLY THE ENGINES, SIR.
YES, YES, AS YOU WERE.
BACK IN GERMANY.
CONGRATULATIONS KAPITÄN. AND NOW FOR SOME SHORE LEAVE?

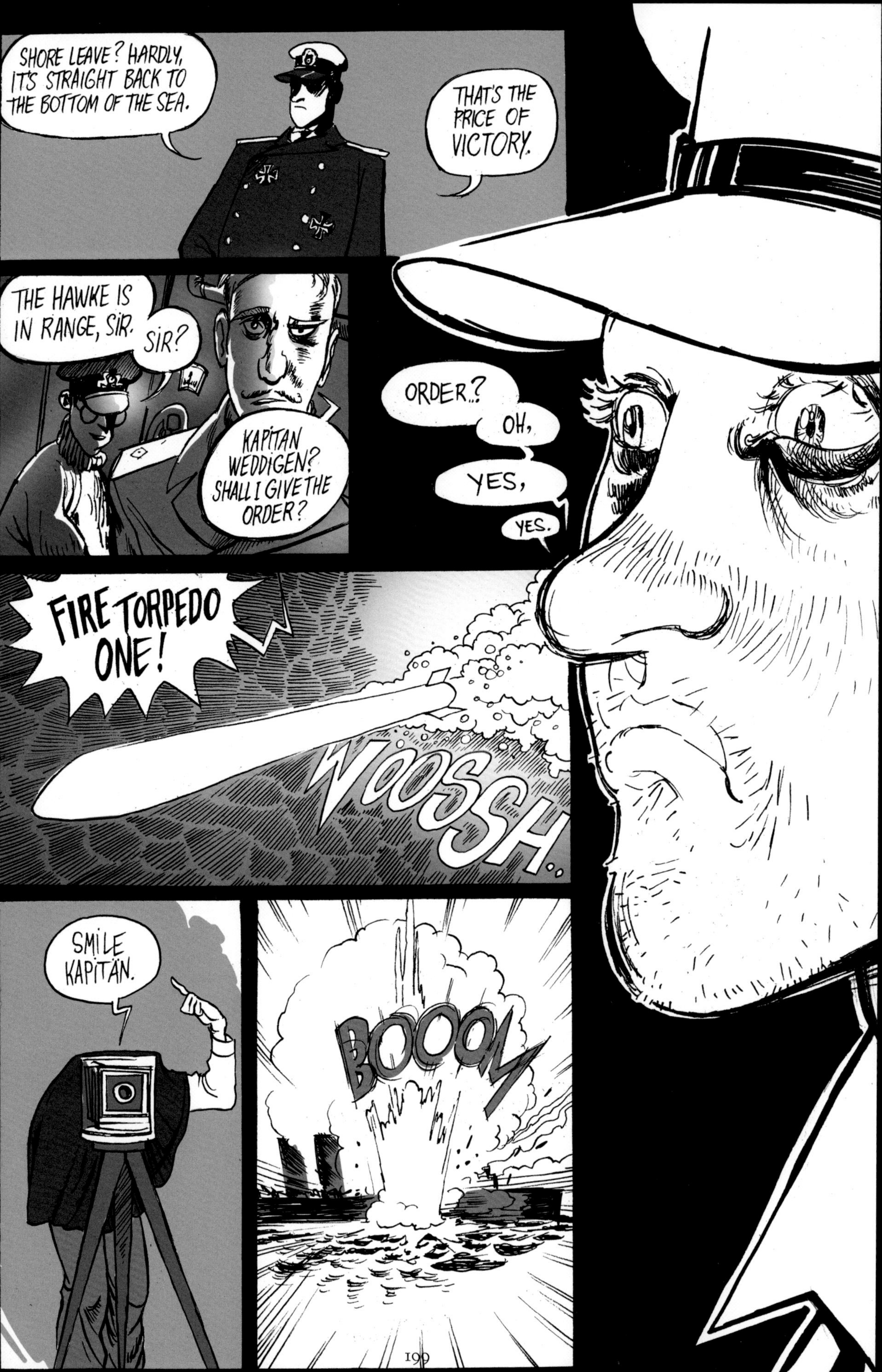
SHORE LEAVE? HARDLY, IT'S STRAIGHT BACK TO THE BOTTOM OF THE SEA.
THAT'S THE PRICE OF VICTORY.
THE HAWKE IS IN RANGE, SIR.
SIR?
KAPITAN WEDDIGEN? SHALL I GIVE THE ORDER?
ORDER..?
OH,
YES,
YES.
FIRE TORPEDO ONE!
WOOSSH..
SMILE KAPITÄN.
BOOOM

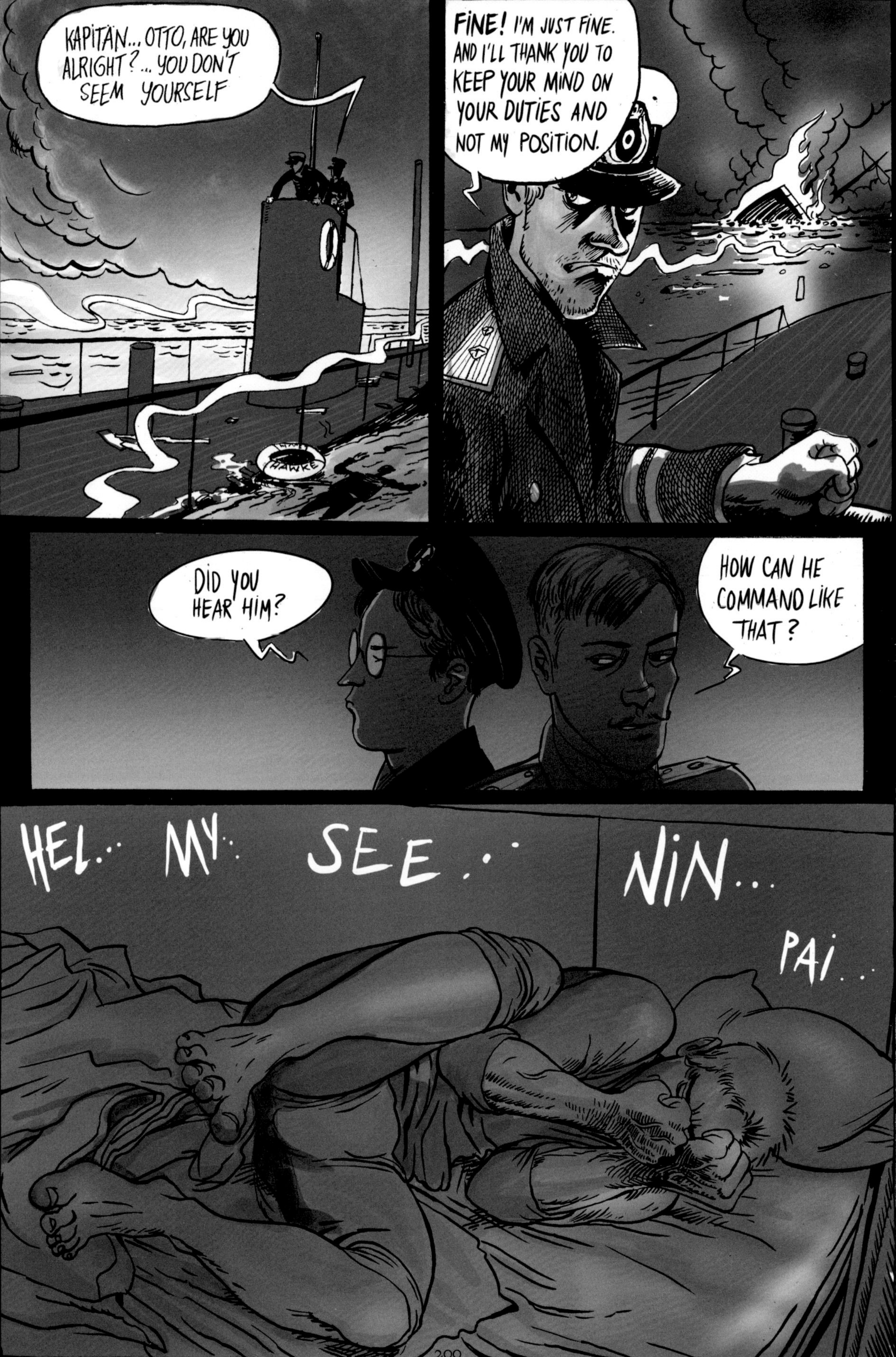

KAPITÄN..., OTTO, ARE YOU ALRIGHT?... YOU DON'T SEEM YOURSELF
FINE! I'M JUST FINE. AND I'LL THANK YOU TO KEEP YOUR MIND ON YOUR DUTIES AND NOT MY POSITION.
HAWKE
DID YOU HEAR HIM?
HOW CAN HE COMMAND LIKE THAT?
HEL... MY... SEE... NIN... PAI...

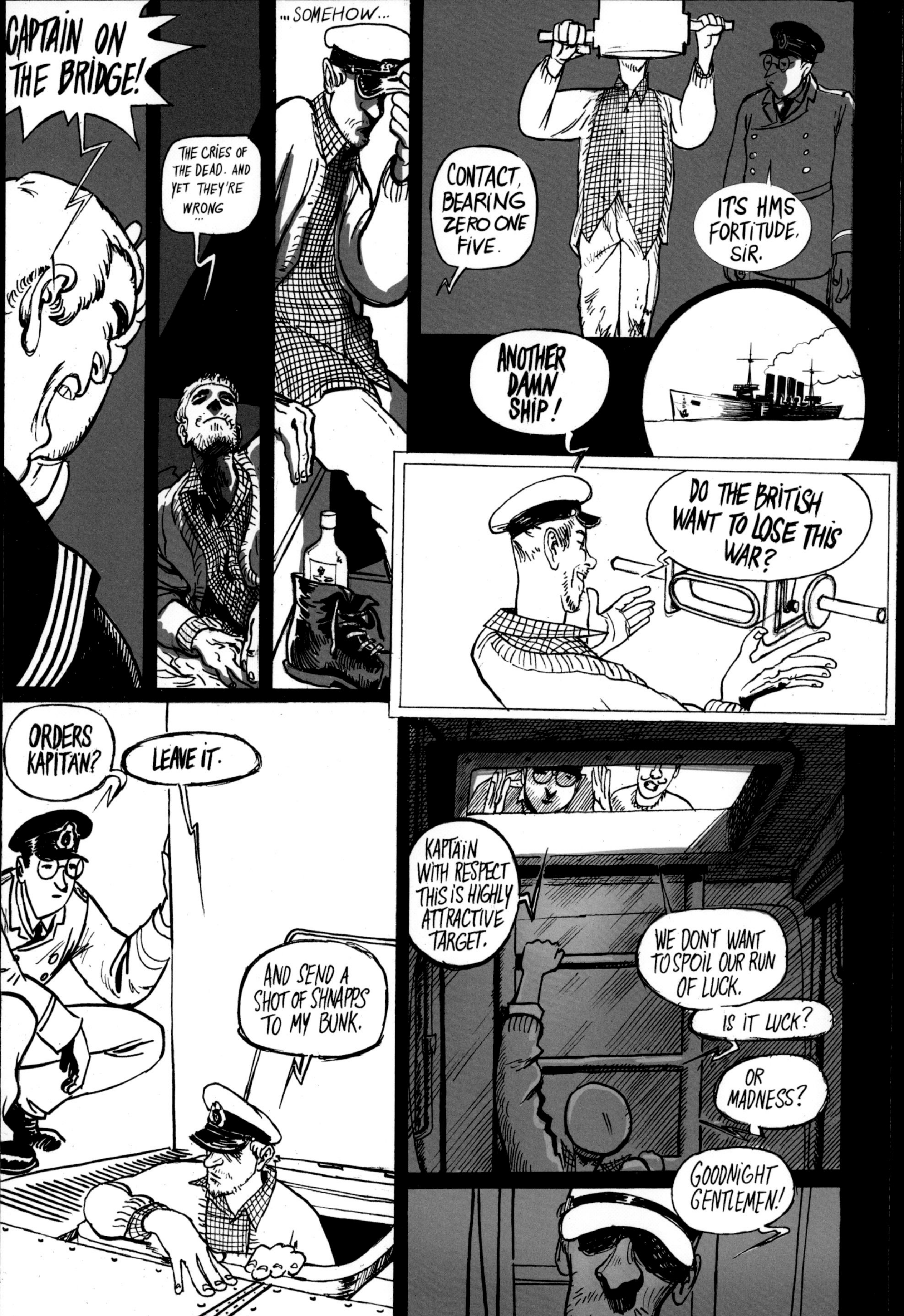
CAPTAIN ON THE BRIDGE!
THE CRIES OF THE DEAD. AND YET THEY'RE WRONG ...
...SOMEHOW...
CONTACT, BEARING ZERO ONE FIVE.
IT'S HMS FORTITUDE, SIR.
ANOTHER DAMN SHIP!
DO THE BRITISH WANT TO LOSE THIS WAR?
ORDERS KAPITÄN?
LEAVE IT.
AND SEND A SHOT OF SHNAPPS TO MY BUNK.
KAPTÄIN WITH RESPECT THIS IS HIGHLY ATTRACTIVE TARGET.
WE DON'T WANT TO SPOIL OUR RUN OF LUCK.
IS IT LUCK?
OR MADNESS?
GOODNIGHT GENTLEMEN!

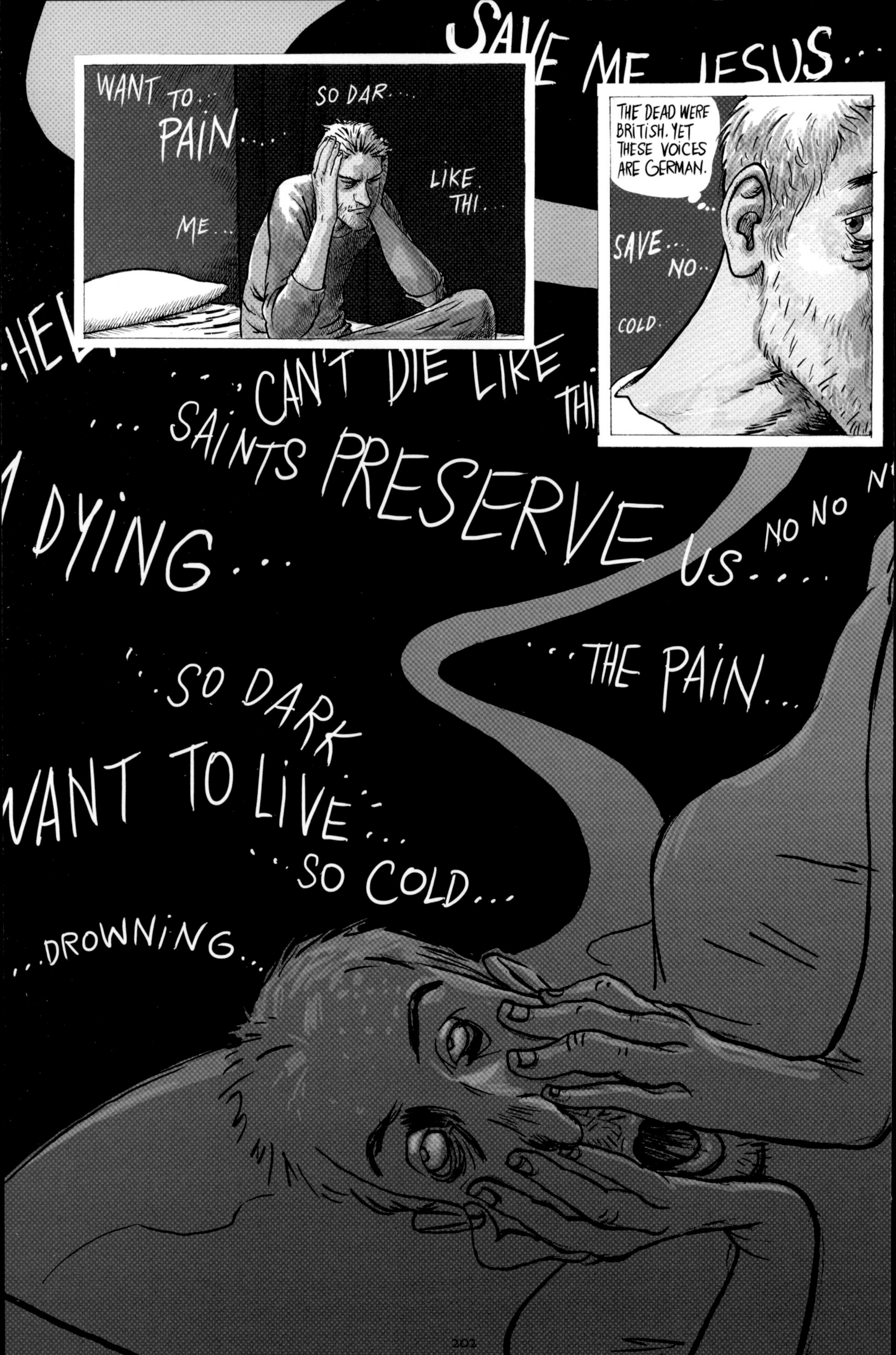
SAVE ME JESUS...
WANT TO...
SO DAR...
PAIN.....
LIKE. THI...
ME...
THE DEAD WERE BRITISH. YET THESE VOICES ARE GERMAN.
SAVE...
NO...
COLD...
...CAN'T DIE LIKE THI
...SAINTS PRESERVE US....
DYING...
NO NO
...THE PAIN...
...SO DARK
WANT TO LIVE...
...SO COLD...
...DROWNING...

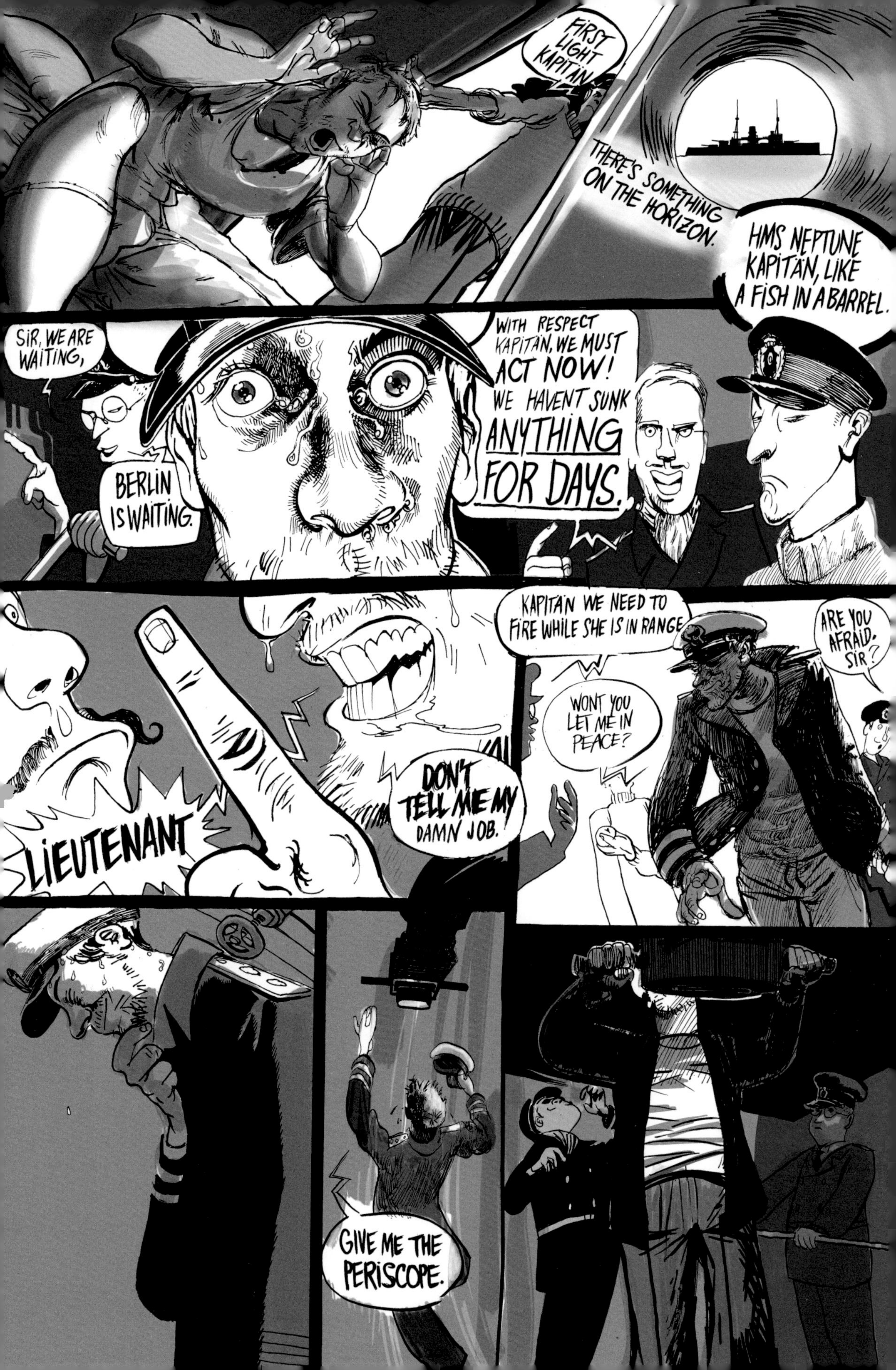
FIRST LIGHT KAPITÄN.
THERE'S SOMETHING ON THE HORIZON.
HMS NEPTUNE KAPITÄN, LIKE A FISH IN A BARREL.
SIR, WE ARE WAITING,
BERLIN IS WAITING.
WITH RESPECT KAPITÄN, WE MUST ACT NOW! WE HAVENT SUNK ANYTHING FOR DAYS.
LIEUTENANT
DON'T TELL ME MY DAMN JOB.
KAPITÄN WE NEED TO FIRE WHILE SHE IS IN RANGE
WONT YOU LET ME IN PEACE?
ARE YOU AFRAID, SIR?
GIVE ME THE PERISCOPE.

NEPTUNE'S PULLING OUT OF REACH...
KAPITÄN?
FIRE TORPEDO!!!
FIRE!
WOOSH
SO HOT!
MUST HAVE FRESH AIR...
SURFACE.
SURFACE!
- SPLASH.
NO.

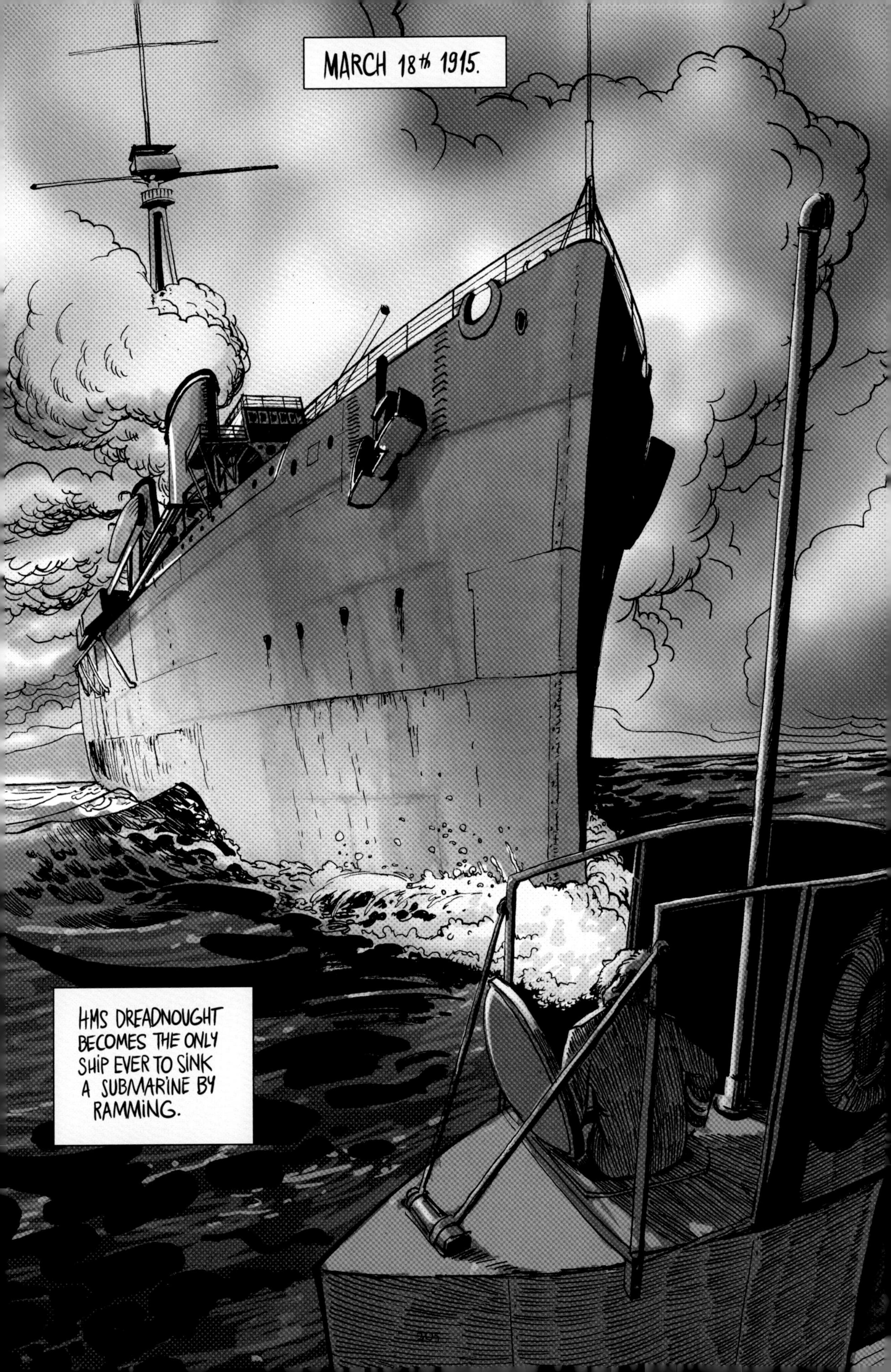
MARCH 18th 1915.
HMS DREADNOUGHT BECOMES THE ONLY SHIP EVER TO SINK A SUBMARINE BY RAMMING.

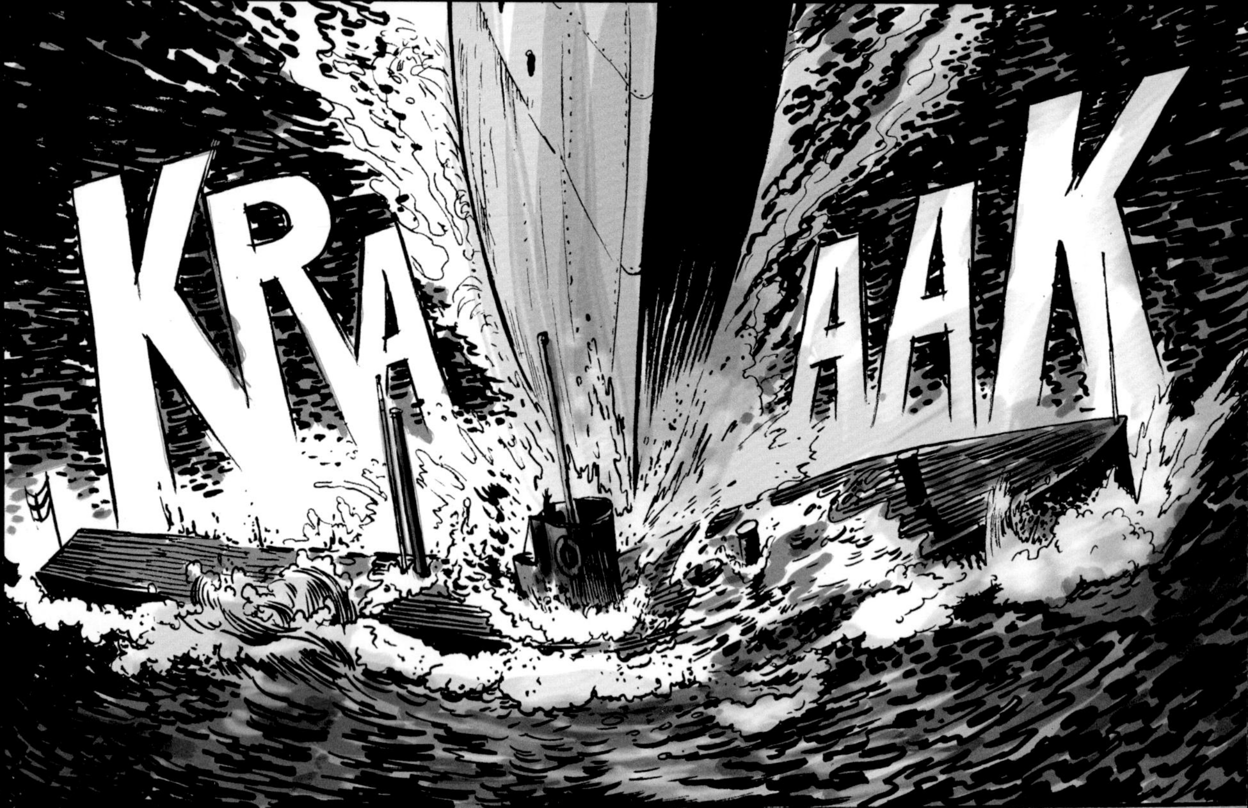
KRAAAK

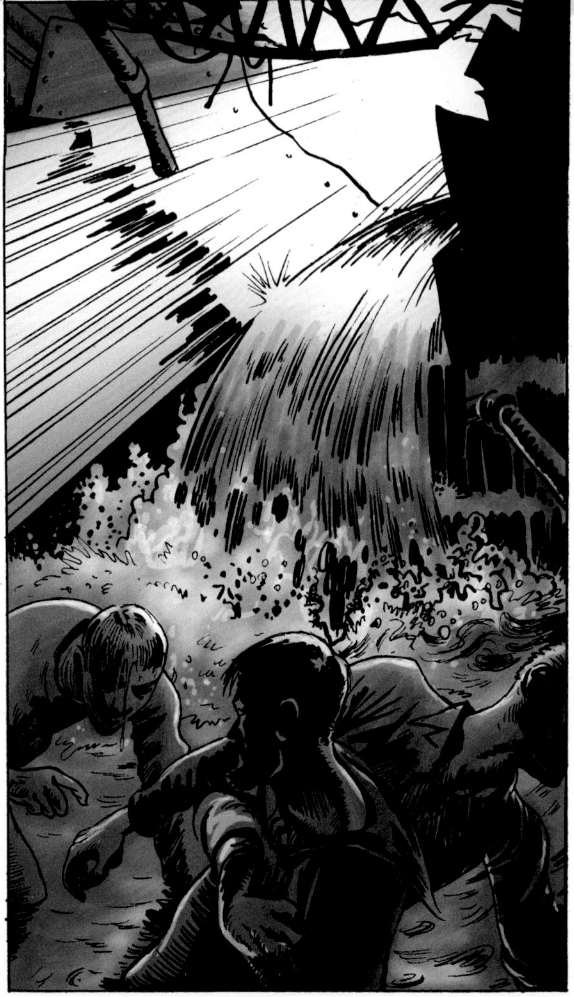

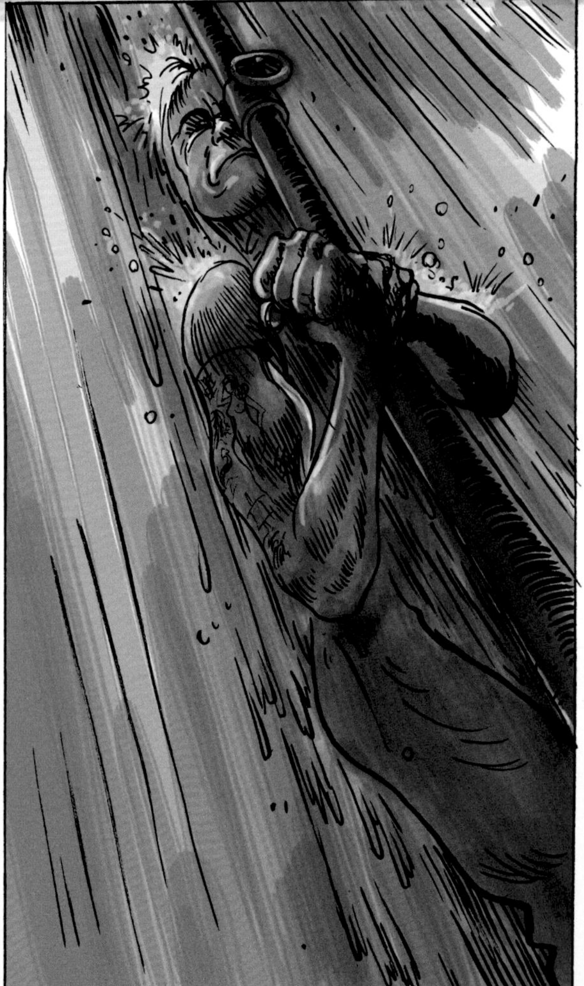

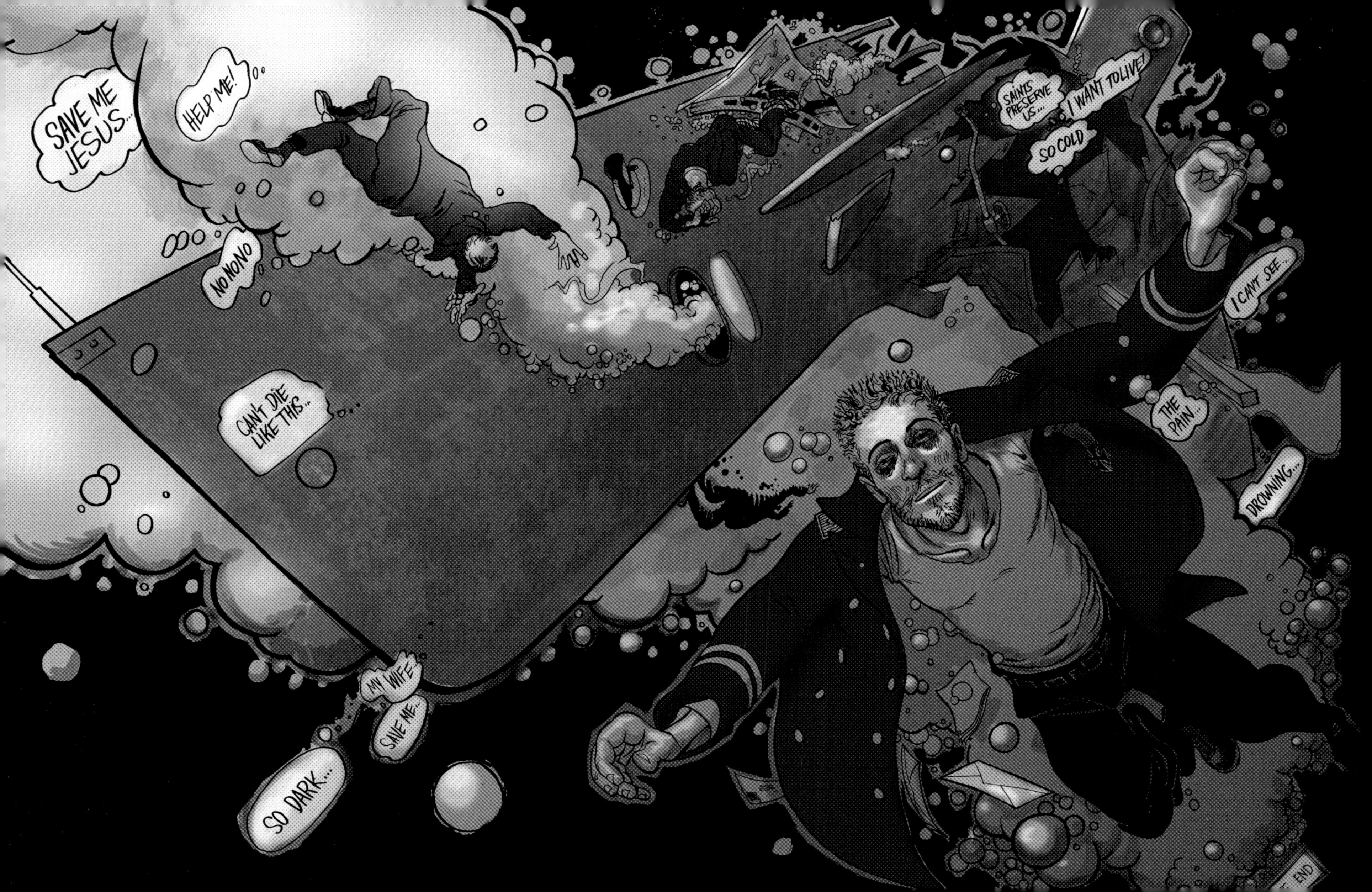
SAVE ME JESUS...
HELP ME!
NO NO NO
CAN'T DIE LIKE THIS..
SAINTS PRESERVE US...
I WANT TO LIVE!
SO COLD
I CAN'T SEE...
THE PAIN..
DROWNING...
MY WIFE
SAVE ME..
SO DARK...
END

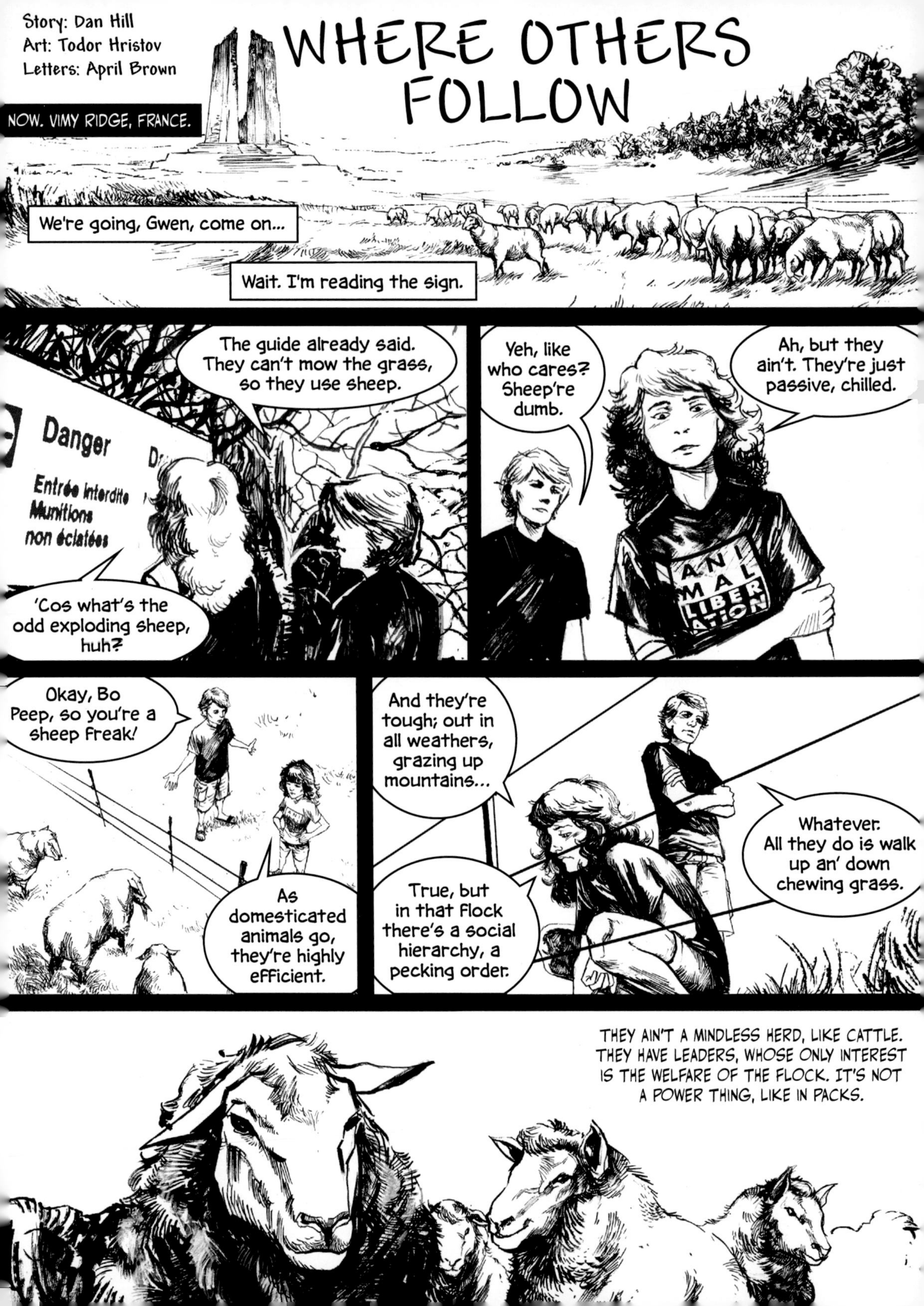
Story: Dan Hill
Art: Todor Hristov
Letters: April Brown
WHERE OTHERS FOLLOW
NOW. VIMY RIDGE, FRANCE.
We're going, Gwen, come on...
Wait. I'm reading the sign.
The guide already said. They can't mow the grass, so they use sheep.
Danger
Entrée interdite
Munitions
non éclatées
'Cos what's the odd exploding sheep, huh?
Yeh, like who cares? Sheep're dumb.
Ah, but they ain't. They're just passive, chilled.
ANIMAL LIBERATION
Okay, Bo Peep, so you're a sheep freak!
As domesticated animals go, they're highly efficient.
And they're tough; out in all weathers, grazing up mountains...
Whatever. All they do is walk up an' down chewing grass.
True, but in that flock there's a social hierarchy, a pecking order.
THEY AIN'T A MINDLESS HERD, LIKE CATTLE. THEY HAVE LEADERS, WHOSE ONLY INTEREST IS THE WELFARE OF THE FLOCK. IT'S NOT A POWER THING, LIKE IN PACKS.

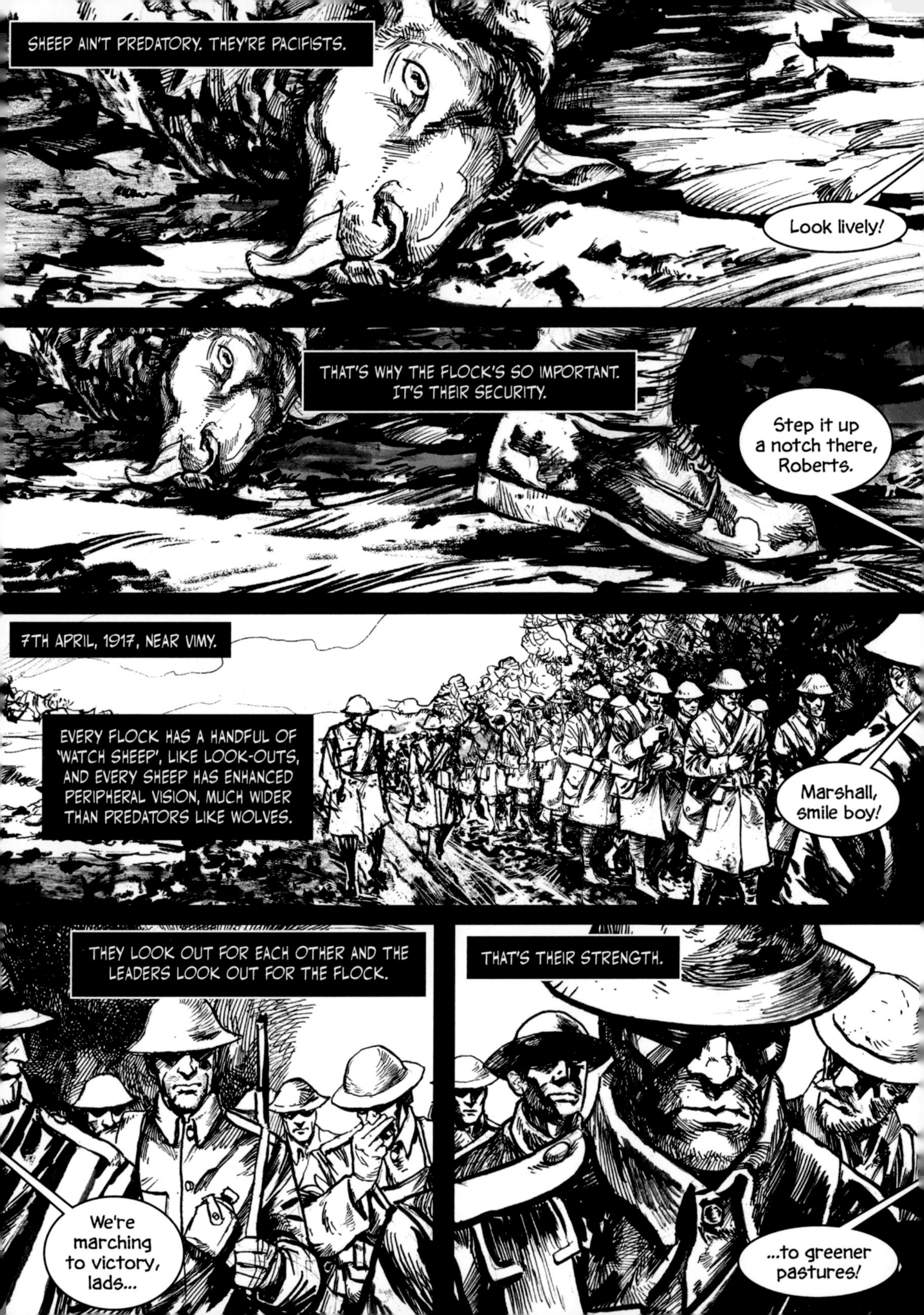
SHEEP AIN'T PREDATORY. THEY'RE PACIFISTS.
Look lively!
THAT'S WHY THE FLOCK'S SO IMPORTANT. IT'S THEIR SECURITY.
Step it up a notch there, Roberts.
7TH APRIL, 1917, NEAR VIMY.
EVERY FLOCK HAS A HANDFUL OF 'WATCH SHEEP', LIKE LOOK-OUTS, AND EVERY SHEEP HAS ENHANCED PERIPHERAL VISION, MUCH WIDER THAN PREDATORS LIKE WOLVES.
Marshall, smile boy!
THEY LOOK OUT FOR EACH OTHER AND THE LEADERS LOOK OUT FOR THE FLOCK.
We're marching to victory, lads...
THAT'S THEIR STRENGTH.
...to greener pastures!

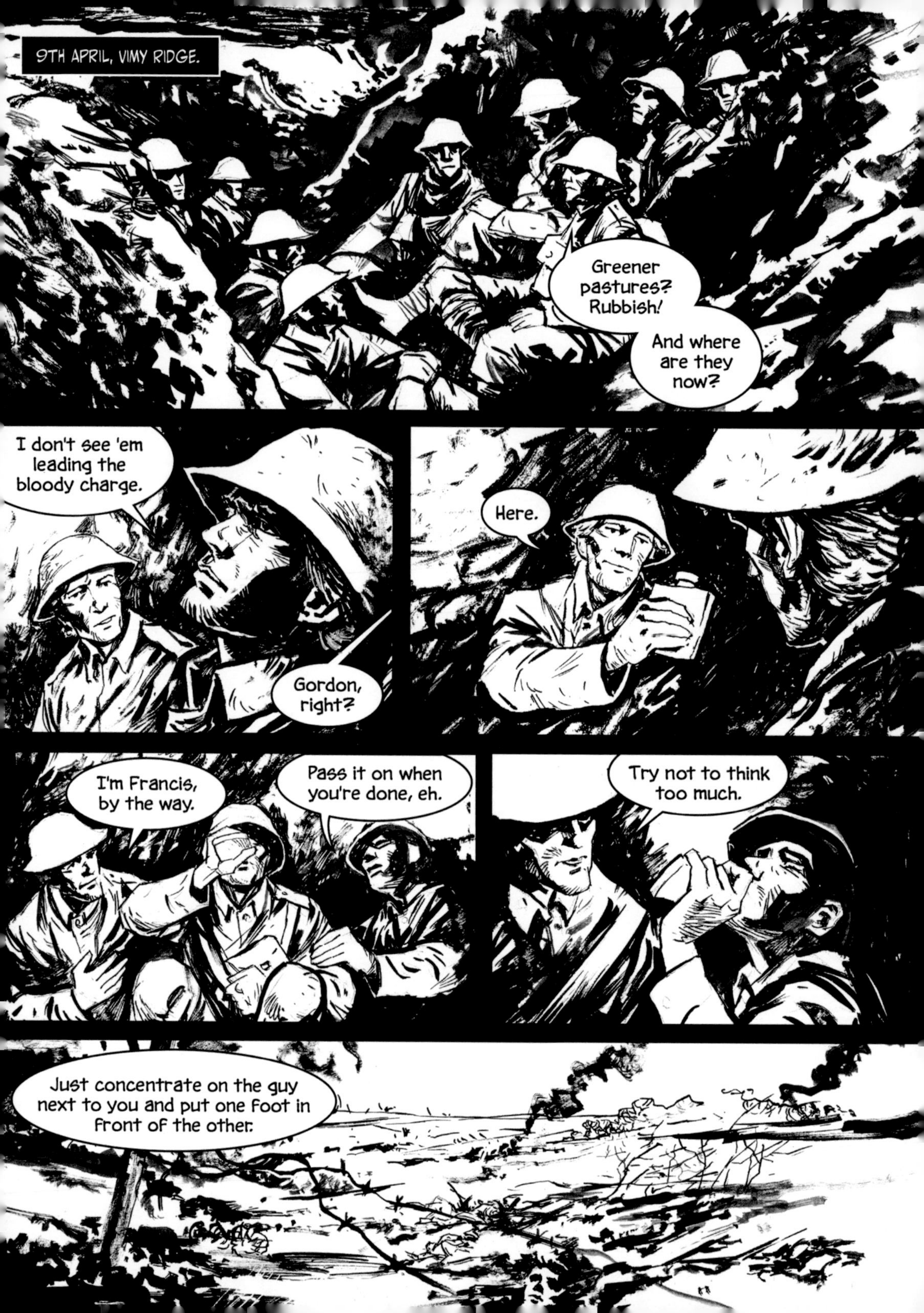

9TH APRIL, VIMY RIDGE.
Greener pastures? Rubbish!
And where are they now?
I don't see 'em leading the bloody charge.
Gordon, right?
Here.
I'm Francis, by the way.
Pass it on when you're done, eh.
Try not to think too much.
Just concentrate on the guy next to you and put one foot in front of the other.

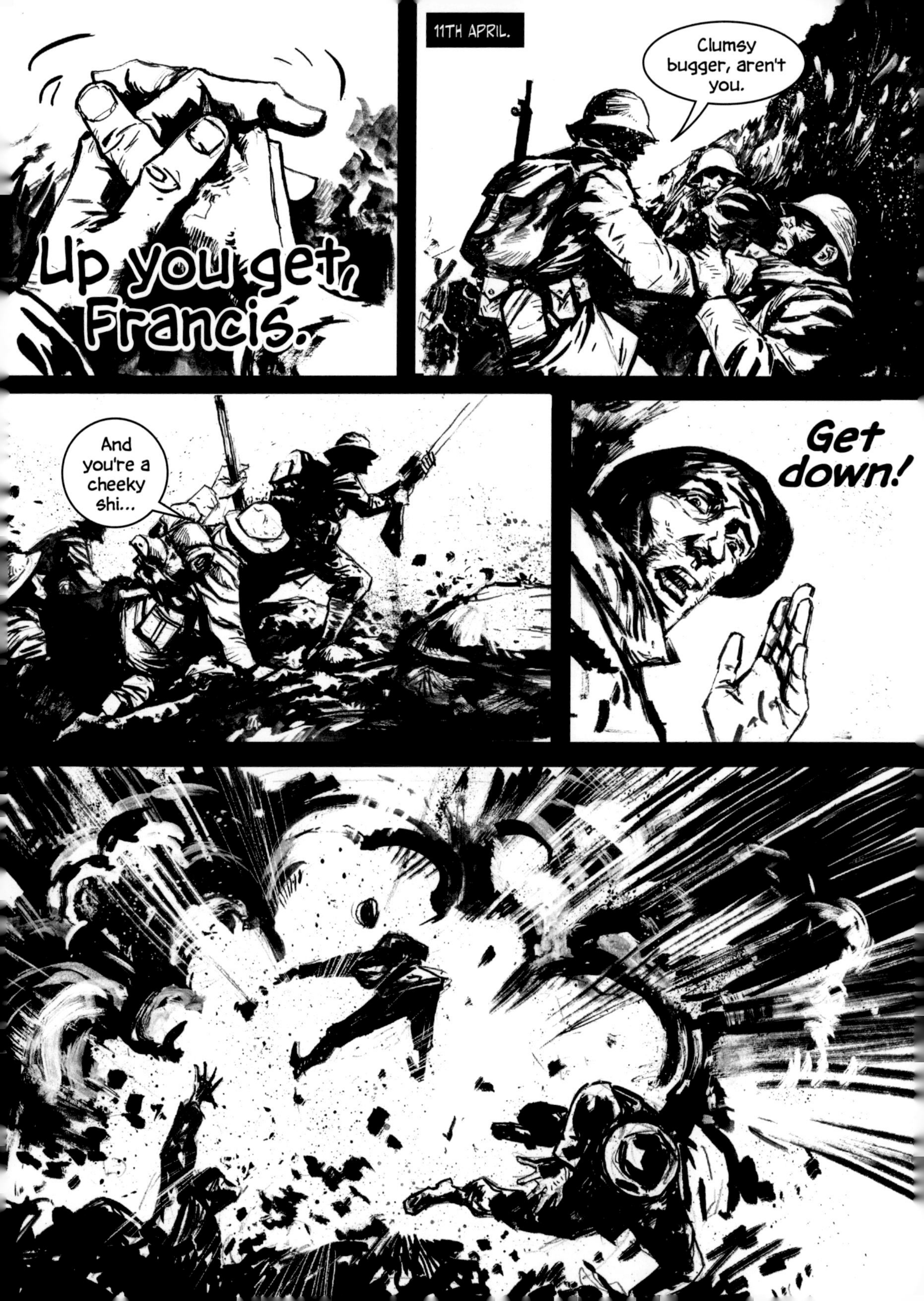
Up you get, Francis.
11TH APRIL.
Clumsy bugger, aren't you.
And you're a cheeky shi...
Get down!

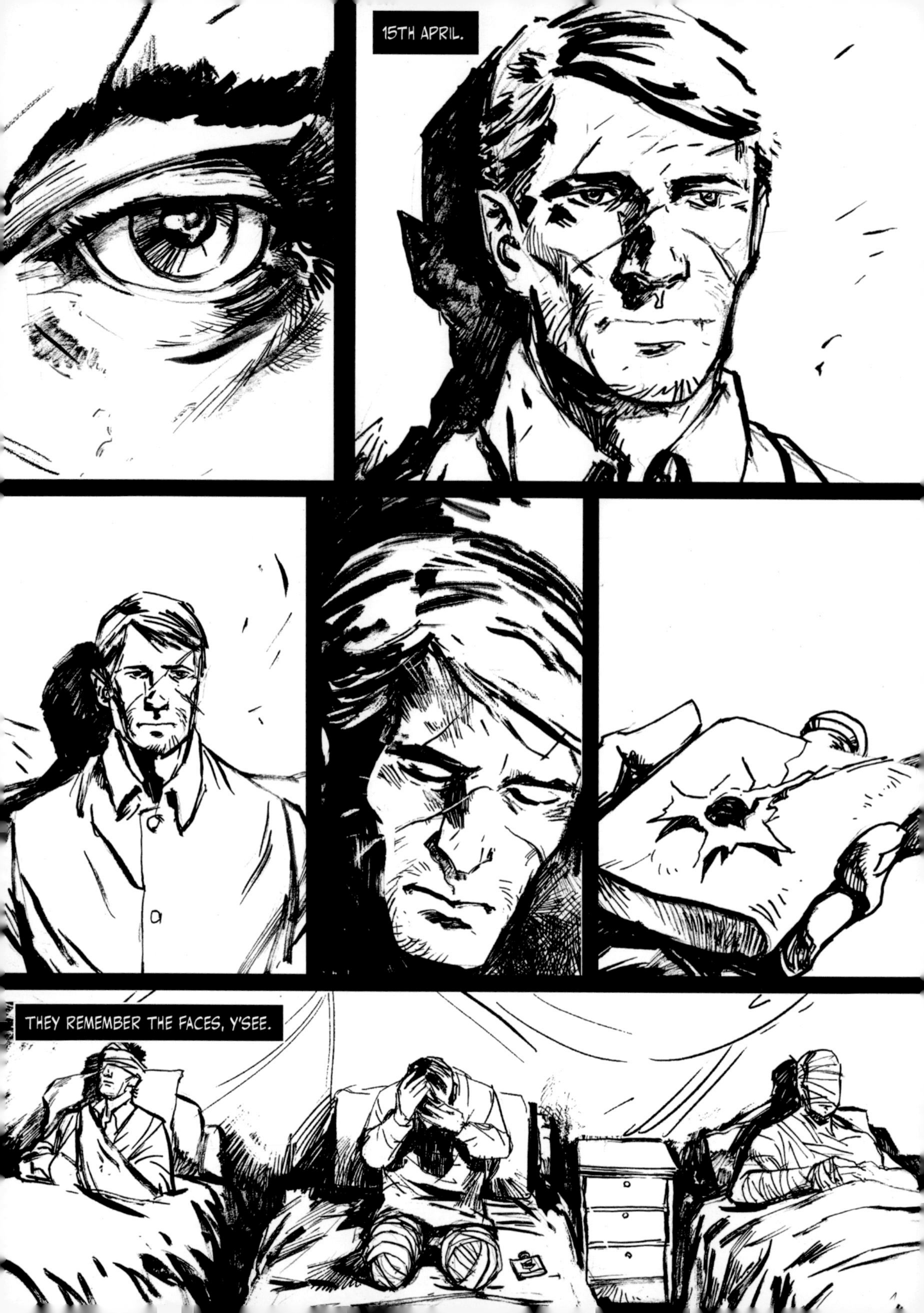
15TH APRIL.
THEY REMEMBER THE FACES, Y'SEE.

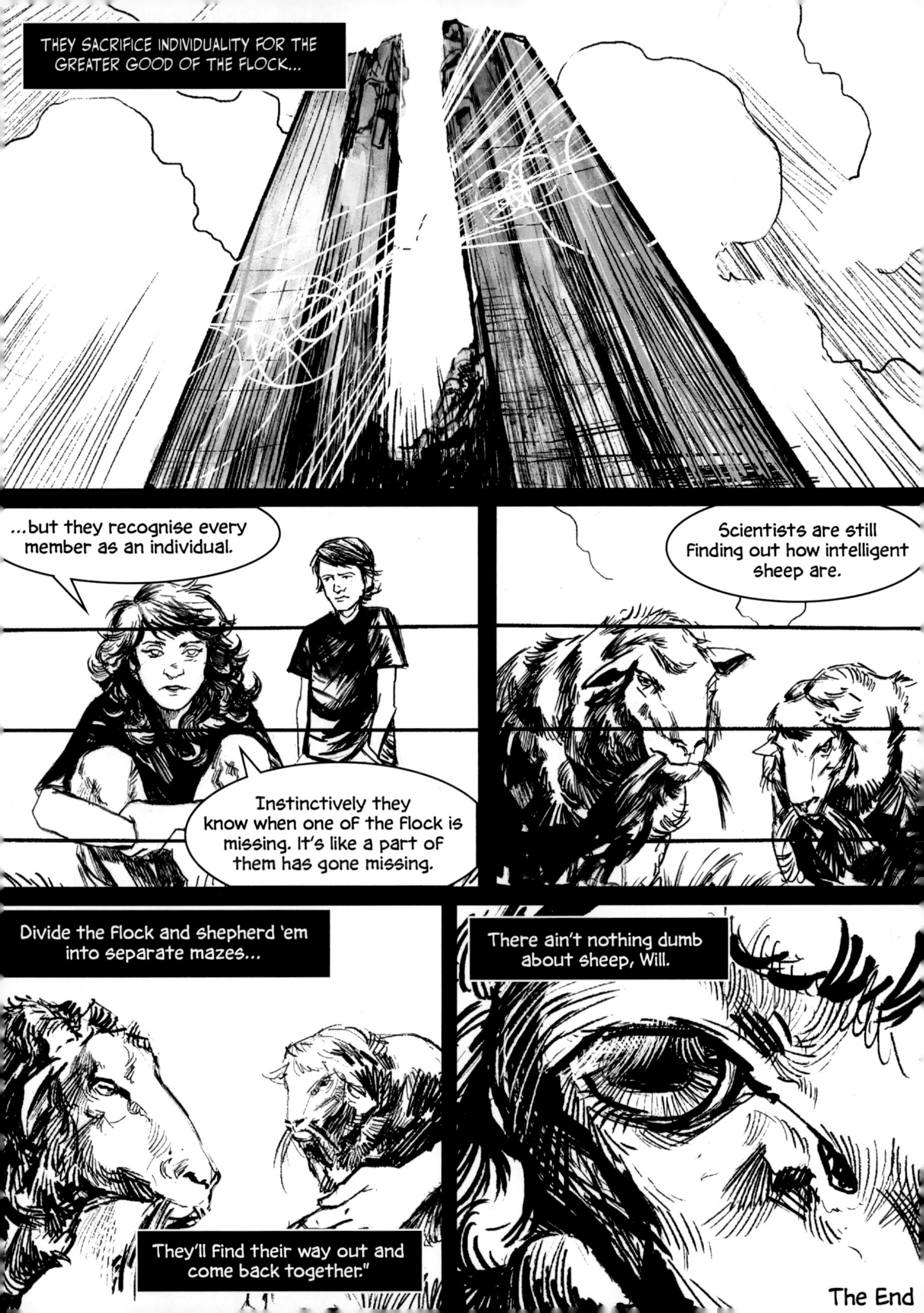
THEY SACRIFICE INDIVIDUALITY FOR THE GREATER GOOD OF THE FLOCK...
...but they recognise every member as an individual.
Instinctively they know when one of the flock is missing. It's like a part of them has gone missing.
Scientists are still finding out how intelligent sheep are.
Divide the flock and shepherd 'em into separate mazes...
They'll find their way out and come back together."
There ain't nothing dumb about sheep, Will.
The End

Go Home and Sit Still

Written by Selina Lock
Drawn by Arthur Goodman

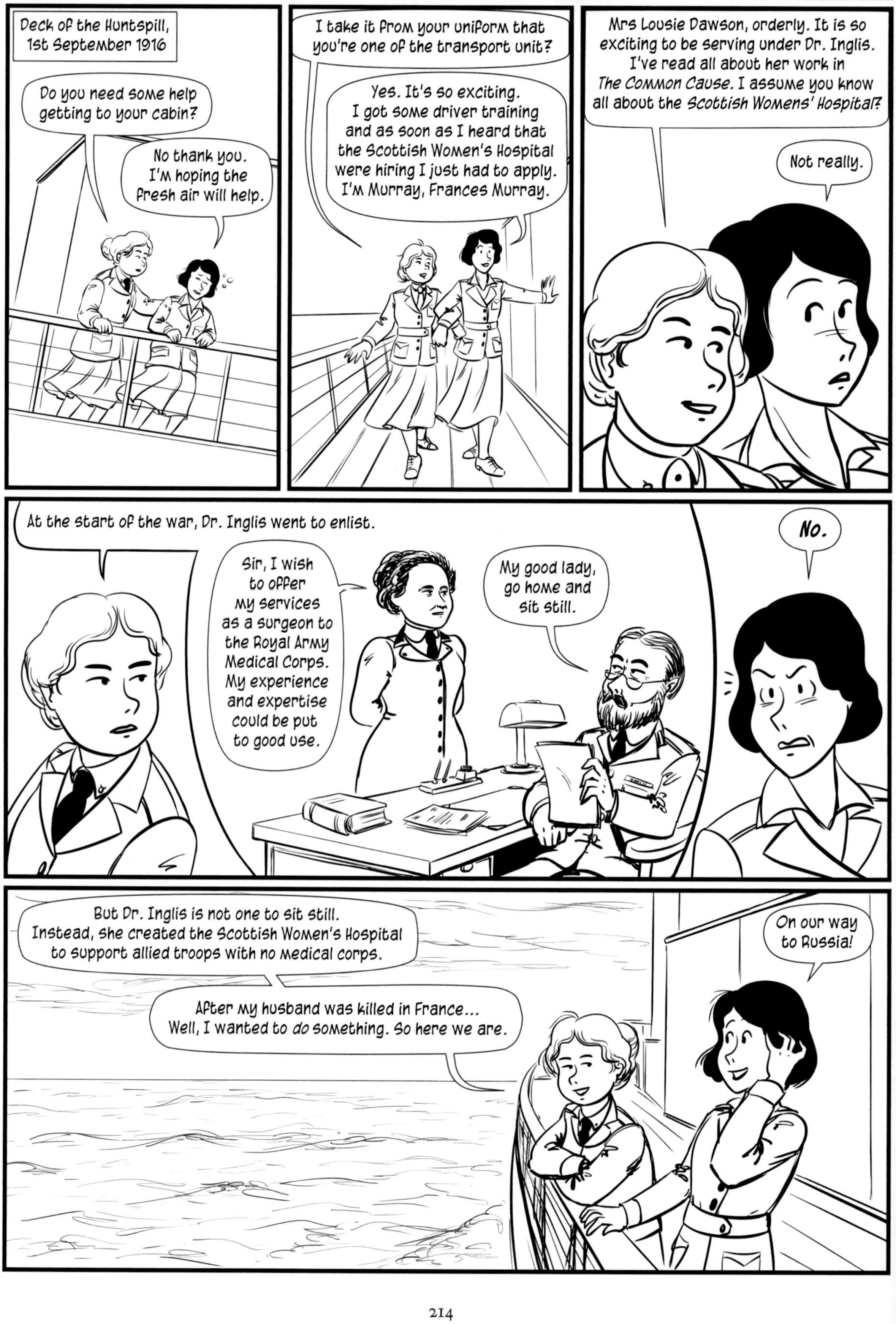
Deck of the Huntspill, 1st September 1916
Do you need some help getting to your cabin?
No thank you. I'm hoping the fresh air will help.
I take it from your uniform that you're one of the transport unit?
Yes. It's so exciting. I got some driver training and as soon as I heard that the Scottish Women's Hospital were hiring I just had to apply. I'm Murray, Frances Murray.
Mrs Lousie Dawson, orderly. It is so exciting to be serving under Dr. Inglis. I've read all about her work in *The Common Cause*. I assume you know all about the *Scottish Womens' Hospital*?
Not really.
At the start of the war, Dr. Inglis went to enlist.
Sir, I wish to offer my services as a surgeon to the Royal Army Medical Corps. My experience and expertise could be put to good use.
My good lady, go home and sit still.
No.
But Dr. Inglis is not one to sit still. Instead, she created the Scottish Women's Hospital to support allied troops with no medical corps.
After my husband was killed in France... Well, I wanted to *do* something. So here we are.
On our way to Russia!

Roll call on the Huntspill,
3rd September 1916.

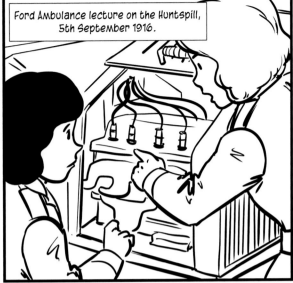

Ford Ambulance lecture on the Huntspill,
5th September 1916.

Disembarkation at Archangel,
12th September 1916.

Archangel, 12th September

Moscow, 17th September

Odessa, 22nd September

Reni, 30th September

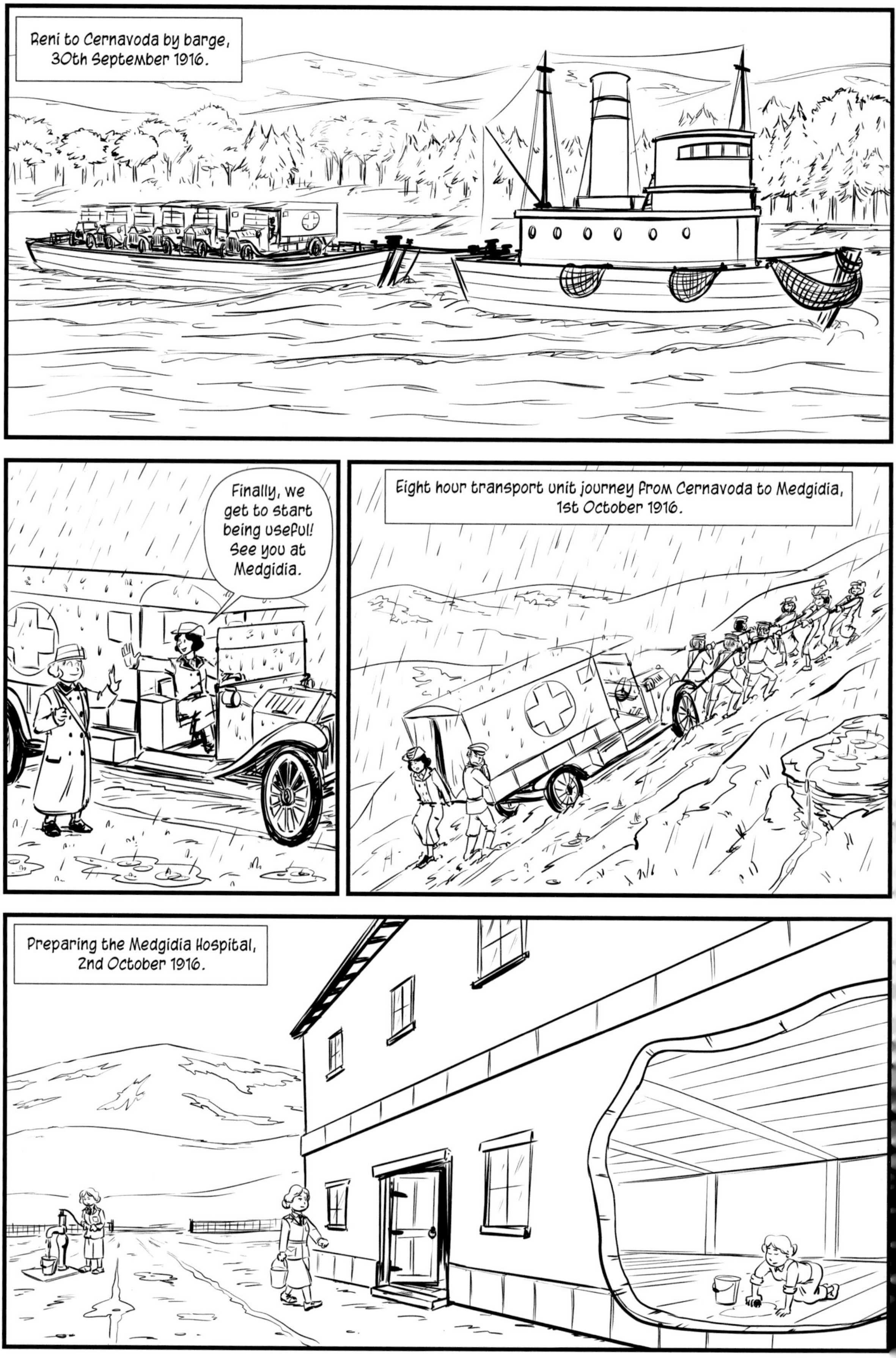
Reni to Cernavoda by barge, 30th September 1916.
Finally, we get to start being useful! See you at Medgidia.
Eight hour transport unit journey from Cernavoda to Medgidia, 1st October 1916.
Preparing the Medgidia Hospital, 2nd October 1916.

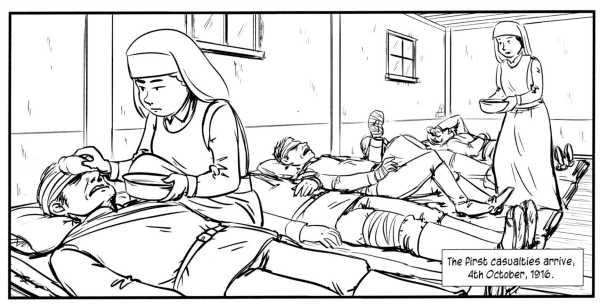

The first casualties arrive, 4th October, 1916.

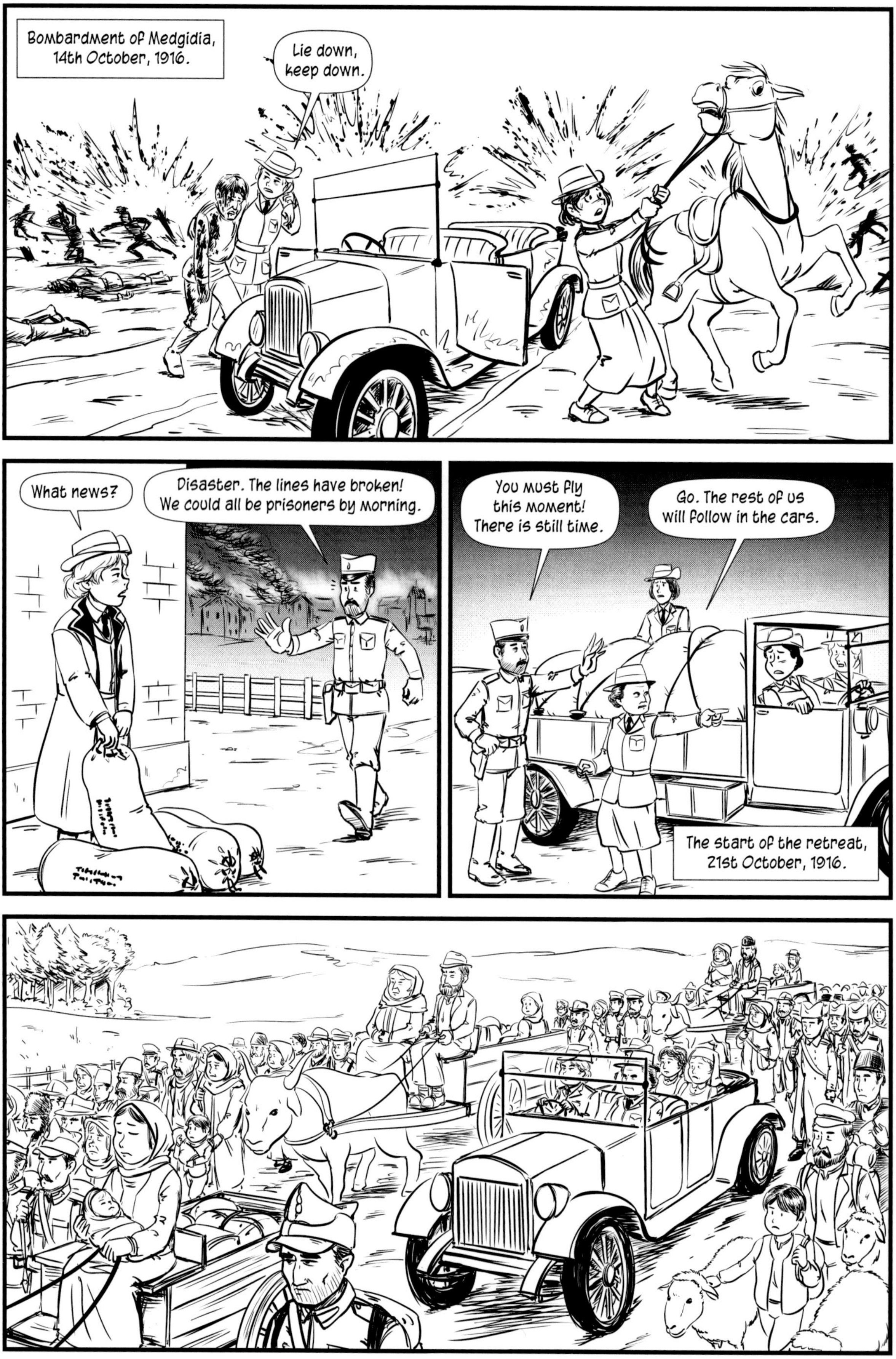
Bombardment of Medgidia,
14th October, 1916.
Lie down,
keep down.
What news?
Disaster. The lines have broken!
We could all be prisoners by morning.
You must fly
this moment!
There is still time.
Go. The rest of us
will follow in the cars.
The start of the retreat,
21st October, 1916.

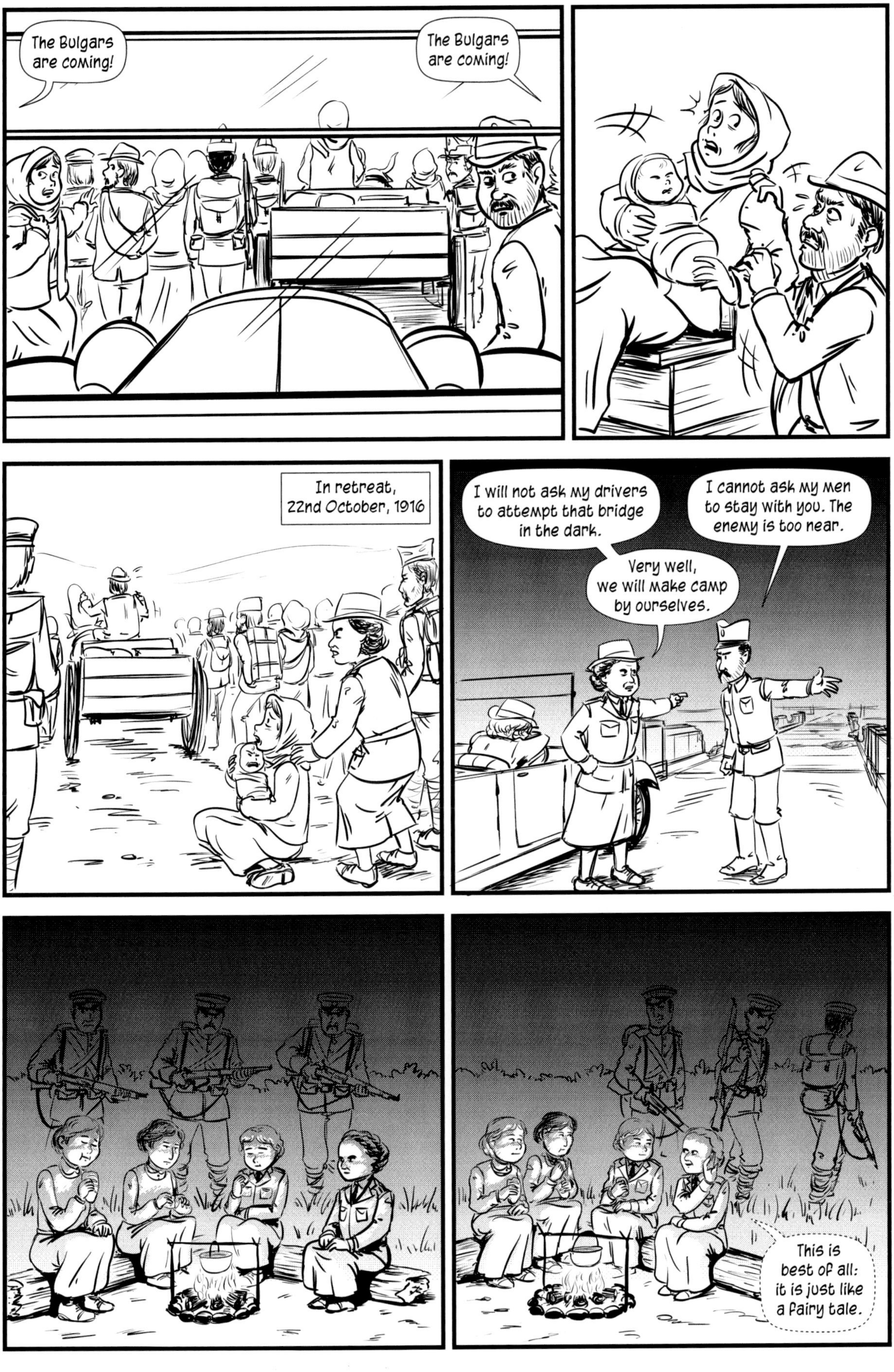

The Bulgars are coming!
The Bulgars are coming!
In retreat, 22nd October, 1916
I will not ask my drivers to attempt that bridge in the dark.
I cannot ask my men to stay with you. The enemy is too near.
Very well, we will make camp by ourselves.
This is best of all: it is just like a fairy tale.

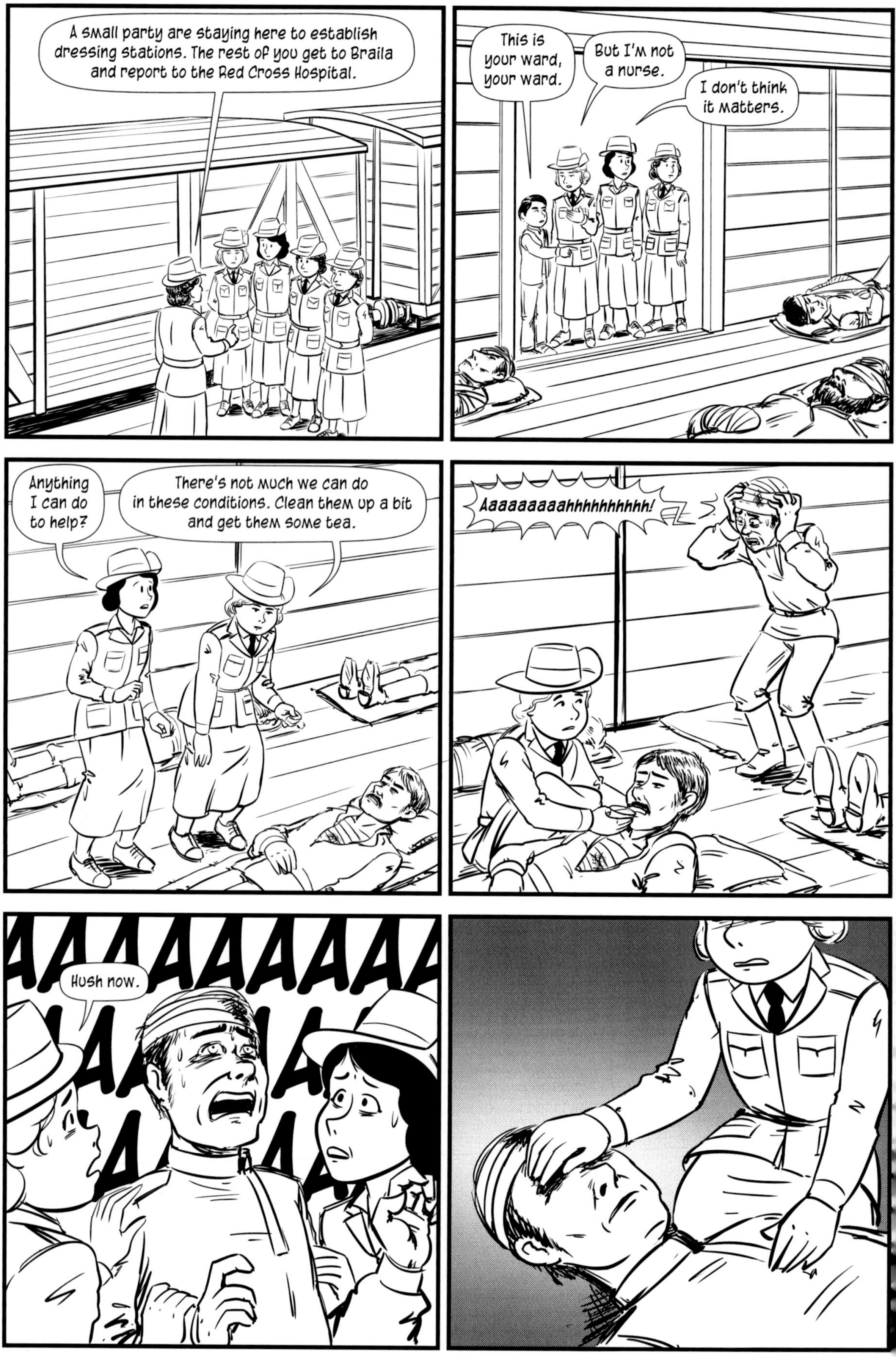
A small party are staying here to establish dressing stations. The rest of you get to Braila and report to the Red Cross Hospital.
This is your ward, your ward.
But I'm not a nurse.
I don't think it matters.
Anything I can do to help?
There's not much we can do in these conditions. Clean them up a bit and get them some tea.
Aaaaaaaaahhhhhhhhhh!
AAAAAAAAAAA
Hush now.

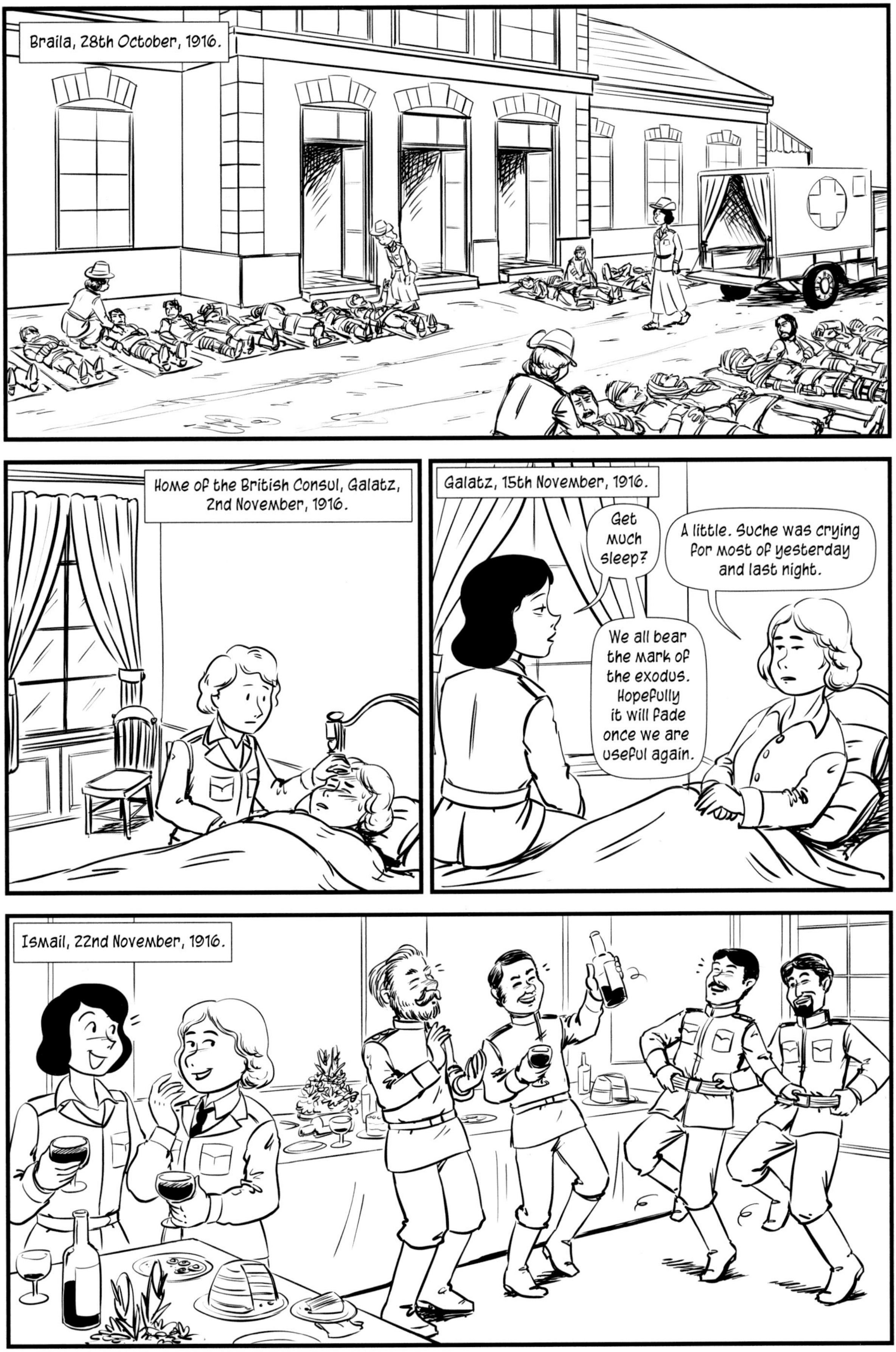
Braila, 28th October, 1916.
Home of the British Consul, Galatz, 2nd November, 1916.
Galatz, 15th November, 1916.
Get much sleep?
A little. Suche was crying for most of yesterday and last night.
We all bear the mark of the exodus. Hopefully it will fade once we are useful again.
Ismail, 22nd November, 1916.

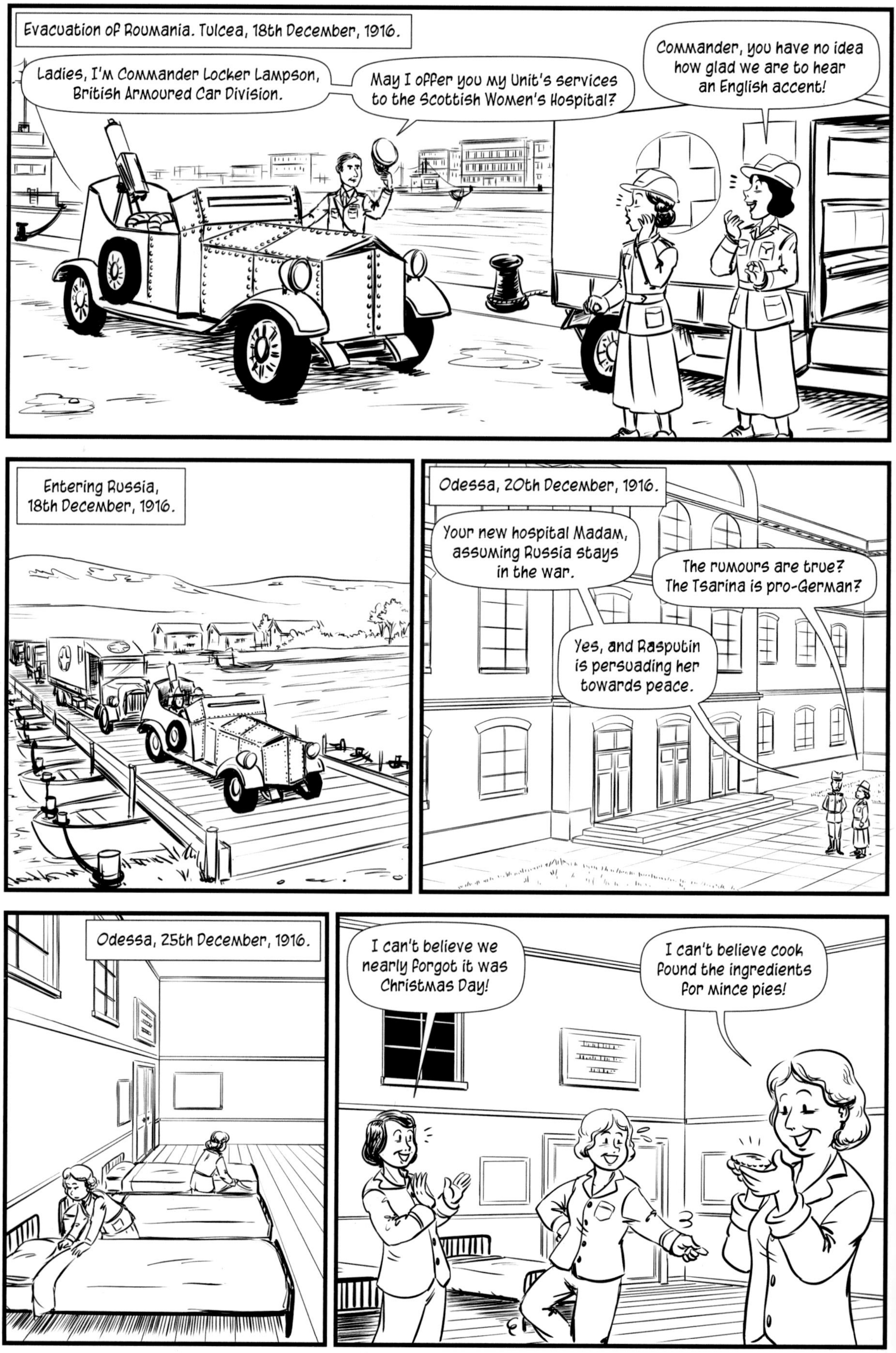
Evacuation of Roumania. Tulcea, 18th December, 1916.
Ladies, I'm Commander Locker Lampson, British Armoured Car Division.
May I offer you my Unit's services to the Scottish Women's Hospital?
Commander, you have no idea how glad we are to hear an English accent!
Entering Russia, 18th December, 1916.
Odessa, 20th December, 1916.
Your new hospital Madam, assuming Russia stays in the war.
The rumours are true? The Tsarina is pro-German?
Yes, and Rasputin is persuading her towards peace.
Odessa, 25th December, 1916.
I can't believe we nearly forgot it was Christmas Day!
I can't believe cook found the ingredients for mince pies!

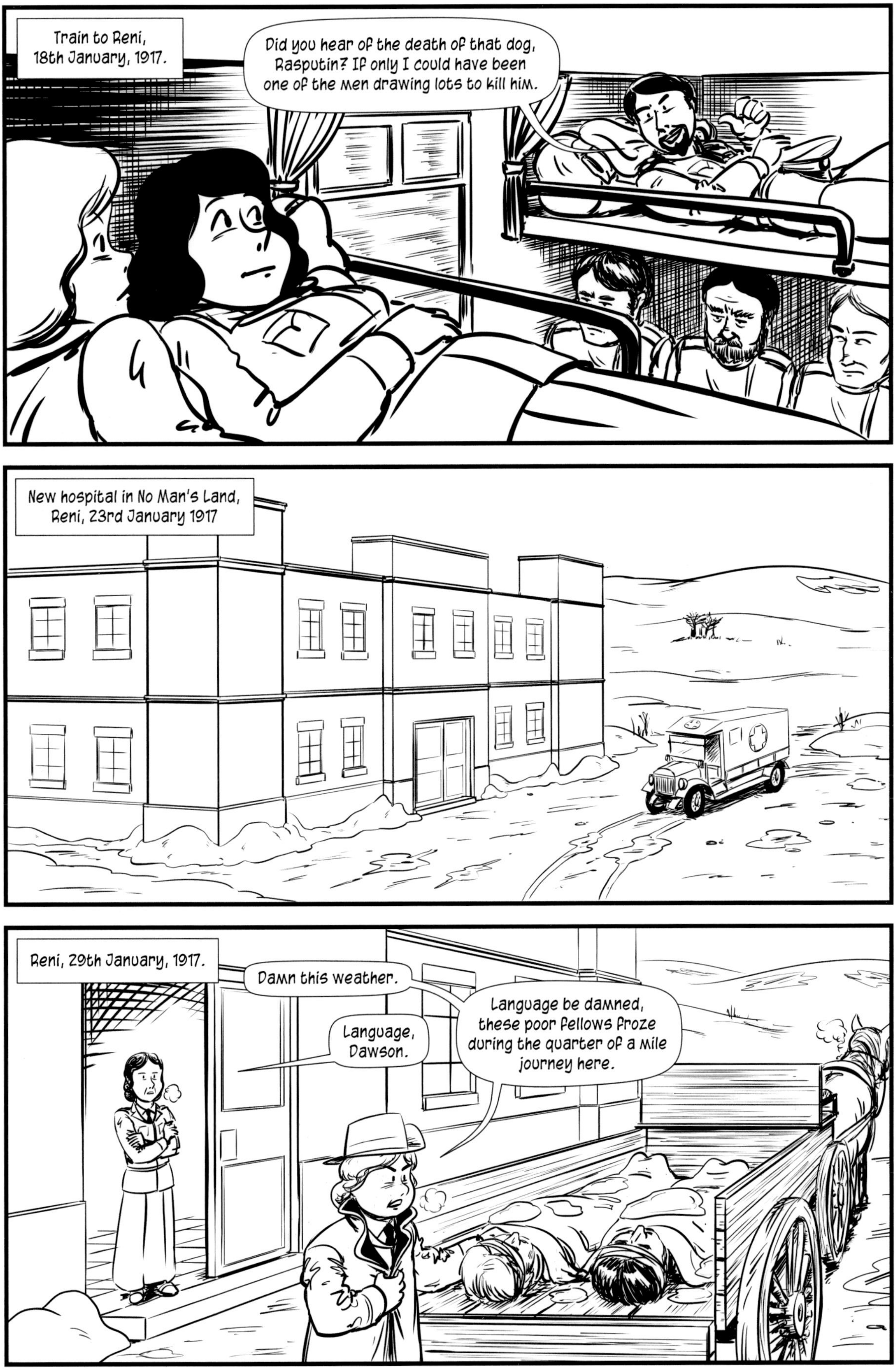
Train to Reni,
18th January, 1917.
Did you hear of the death of that dog, Rasputin? If only I could have been one of the men drawing lots to kill him.
New hospital in No Man's Land,
Reni, 23rd January 1917
Reni, 29th January, 1917.
Damn this weather.
Language, Dawson.
Language be damned, these poor fellows froze during the quarter of a mile journey here.

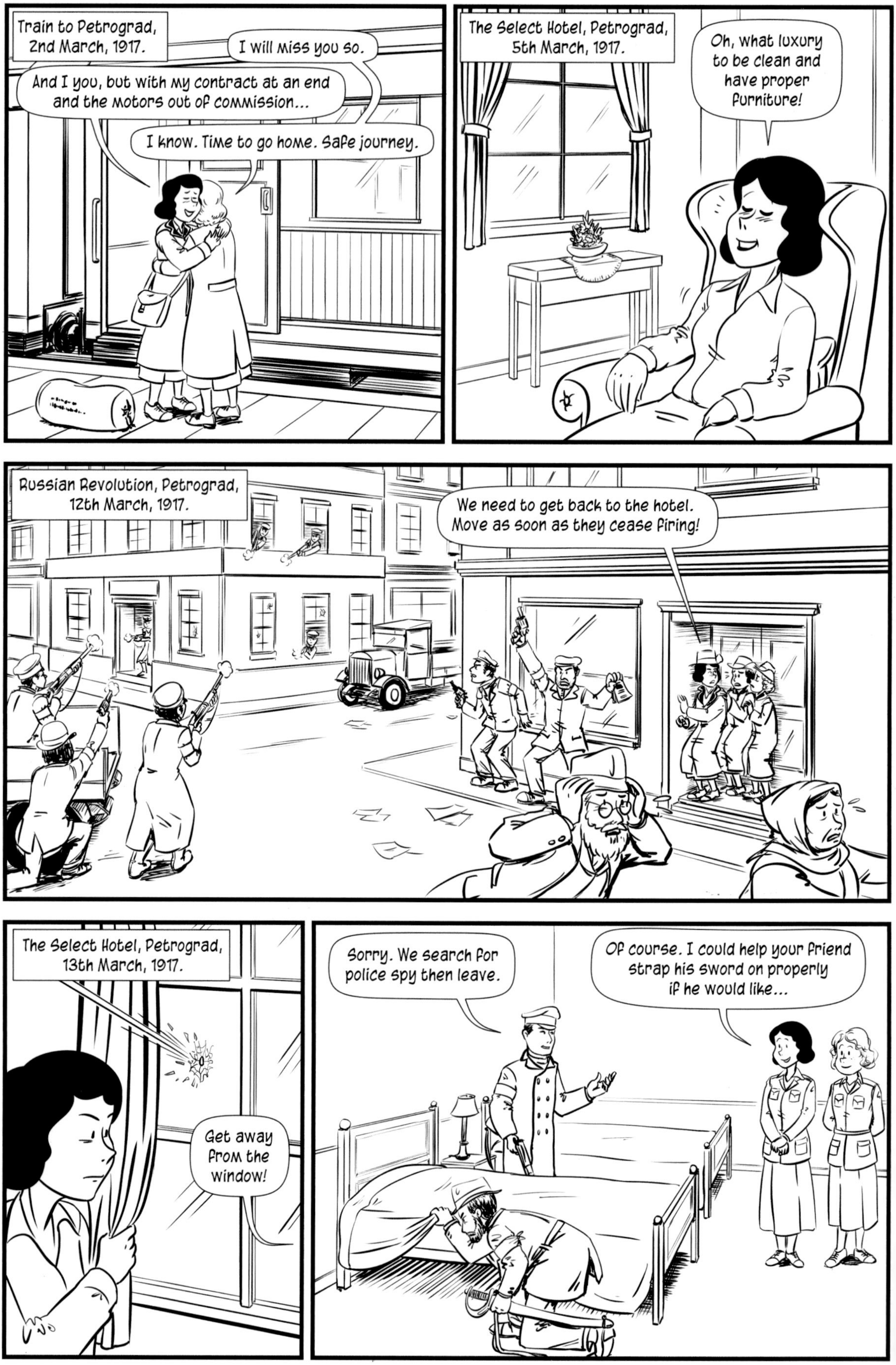

Train to Petrograd, 2nd March, 1917.
I will miss you so.
And I you, but with my contract at an end and the motors out of commission…
I know. Time to go home. Safe journey.
The Select Hotel, Petrograd, 5th March, 1917.
Oh, what luxury to be clean and have proper furniture!
Russian Revolution, Petrograd, 12th March, 1917.
We need to get back to the hotel. Move as soon as they cease firing!
The Select Hotel, Petrograd, 13th March, 1917.
Get away from the window!
Sorry. We search for police spy then leave.
Of course. I could help your friend strap his sword on properly if he would like…

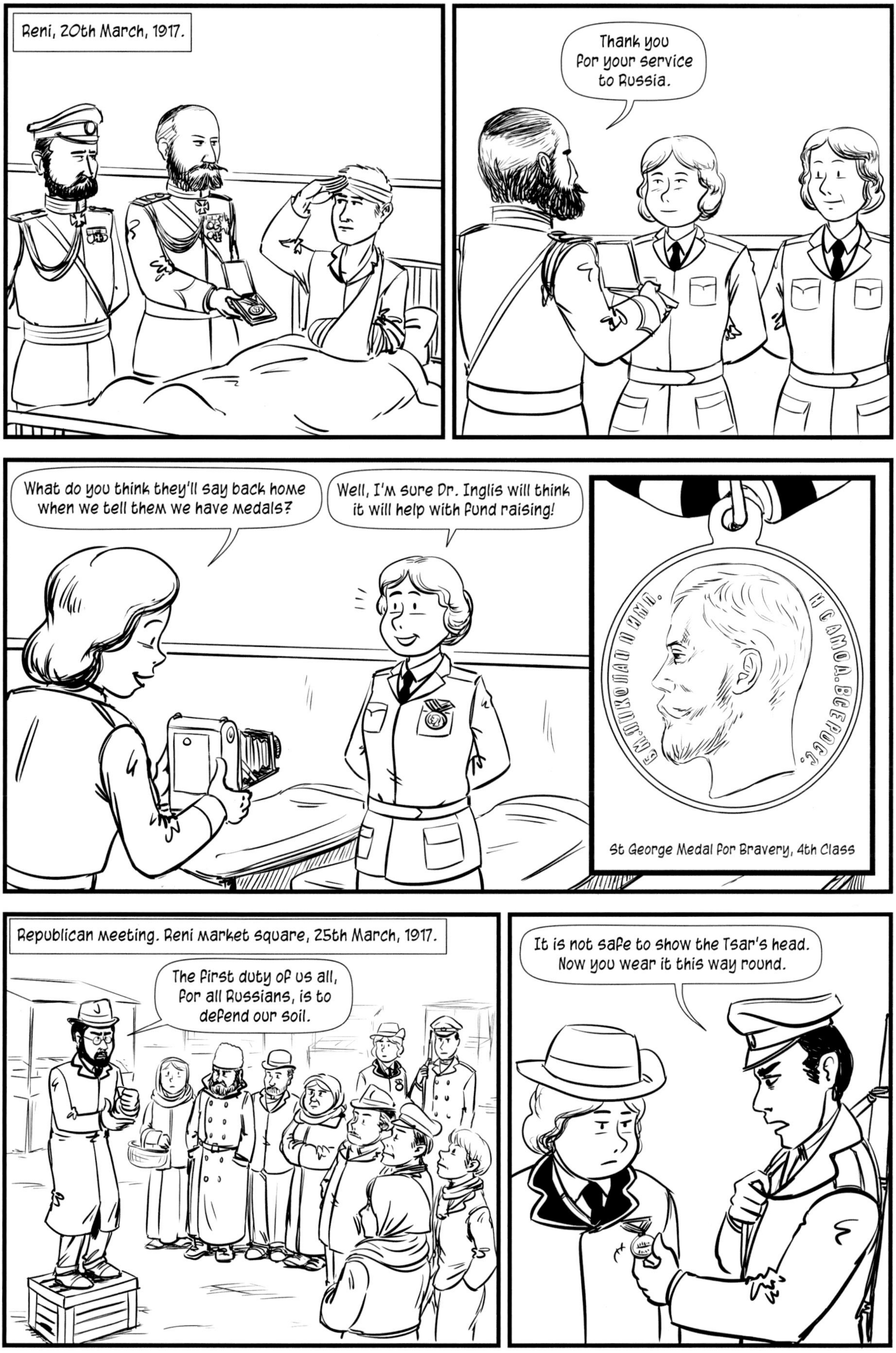
Reni, 20th March, 1917.
Thank you for your service to Russia.
What do you think they'll say back home when we tell them we have medals?
Well, I'm sure Dr. Inglis will think it will help with fund raising!
St George Medal for Bravery, 4th Class
Republican meeting. Reni market square, 25th March, 1917.
The first duty of us all, for all Russians, is to defend our soil.
It is not safe to show the Tsar's head. Now you wear it this way round.

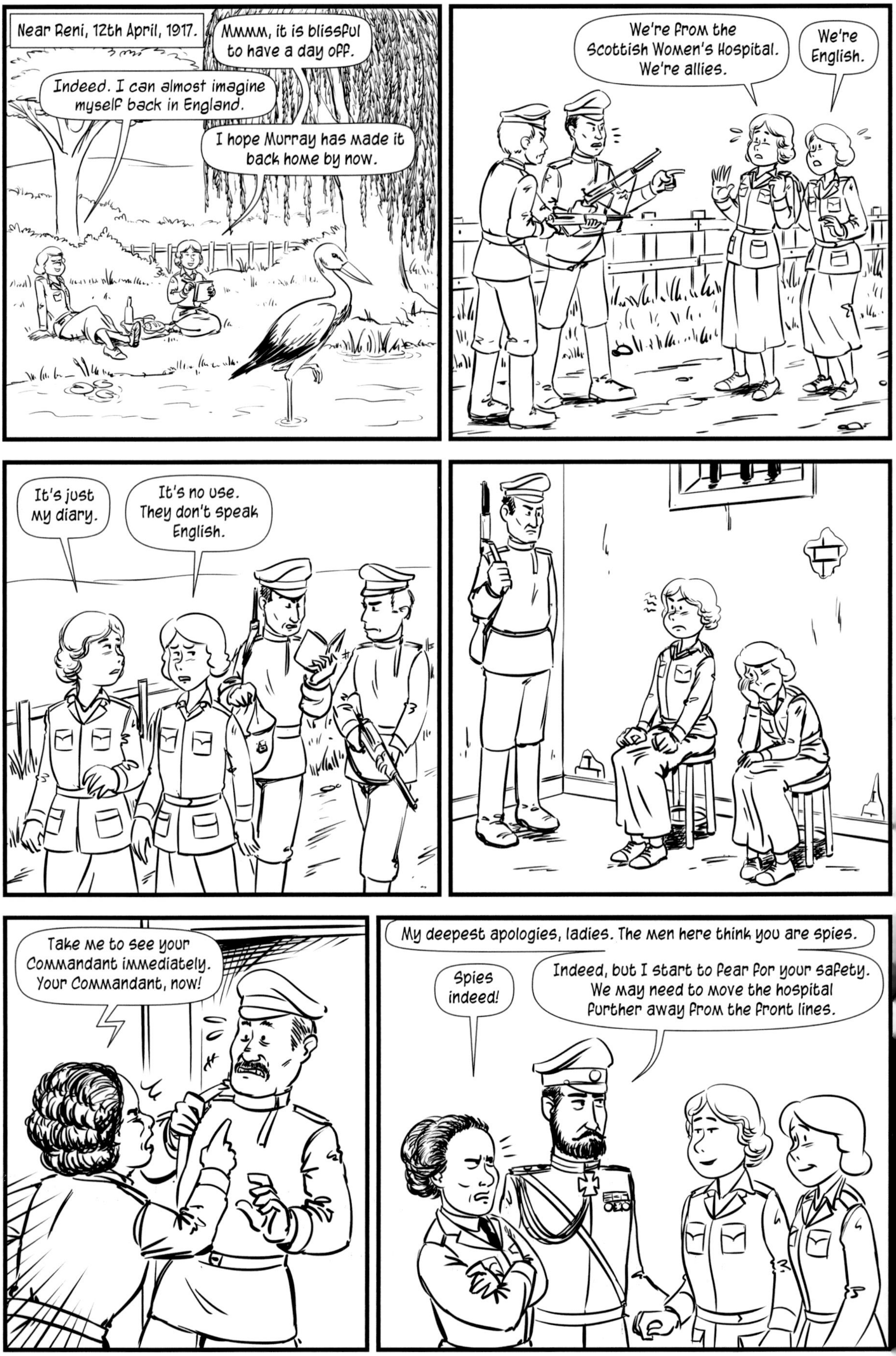
Near Reni, 12th April, 1917.
Mmmm, it is blissful to have a day off.
Indeed. I can almost imagine myself back in England.
I hope Murray has made it back home by now.
We're from the Scottish Women's Hospital. We're allies.
We're English.
It's just my diary.
It's no use. They don't speak English.
Take me to see your Commandant immediately. Your Commandant, now!
My deepest apologies, ladies. The men here think you are spies.
Spies indeed!
Indeed, but I start to fear for your safety. We may need to move the hospital further away from the front lines.

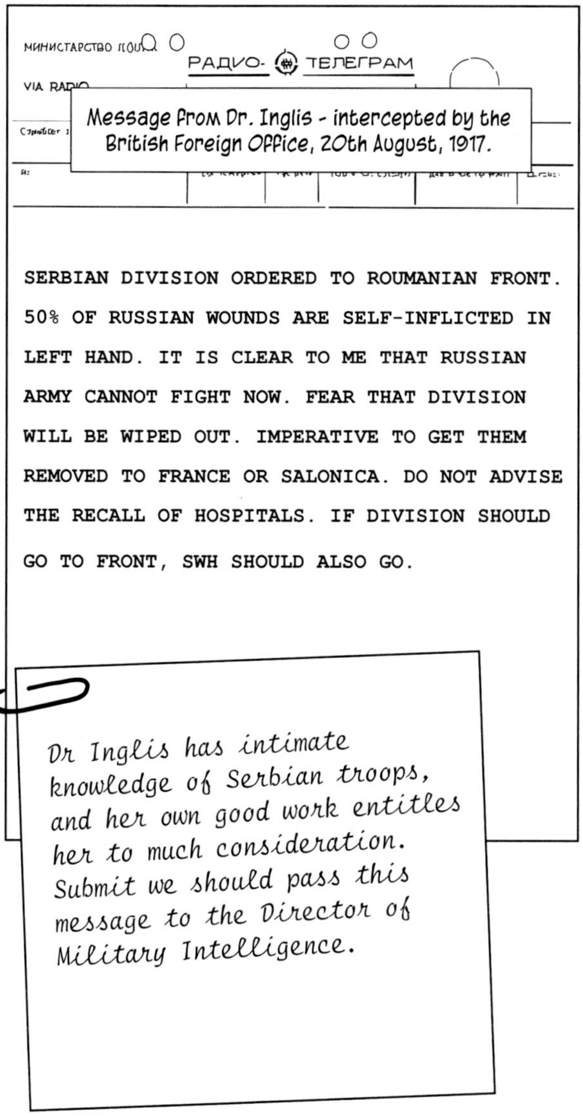
РАДИО- ТЕЛЕГРАМ
Message from Dr. Inglis - intercepted by the British Foreign Office, 20th August, 1917.
SERBIAN DIVISION ORDERED TO ROUMANIAN FRONT. 50% OF RUSSIAN WOUNDS ARE SELF-INFLICTED IN LEFT HAND. IT IS CLEAR TO ME THAT RUSSIAN ARMY CANNOT FIGHT NOW. FEAR THAT DIVISION WILL BE WIPED OUT. IMPERATIVE TO GET THEM REMOVED TO FRANCE OR SALONICA. DO NOT ADVISE THE RECALL OF HOSPITALS. IF DIVISION SHOULD GO TO FRONT, SWH SHOULD ALSO GO.
Dr Inglis has intimate knowledge of Serbian troops, and her own good work entitles her to much consideration. Submit we should pass this message to the Director of Military Intelligence.

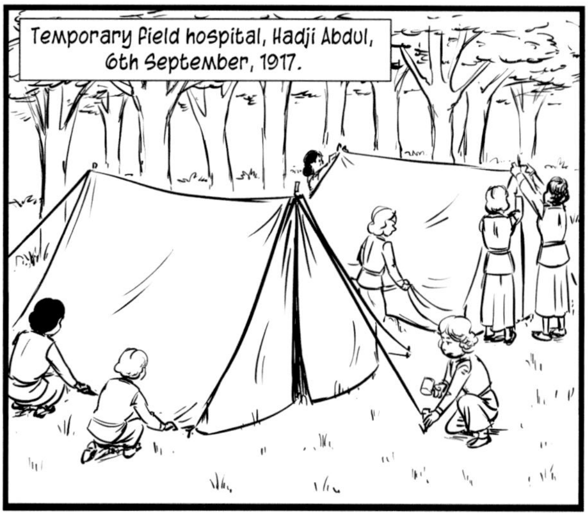
Temporary field hospital, Hadji Abdul, 6th September, 1917.

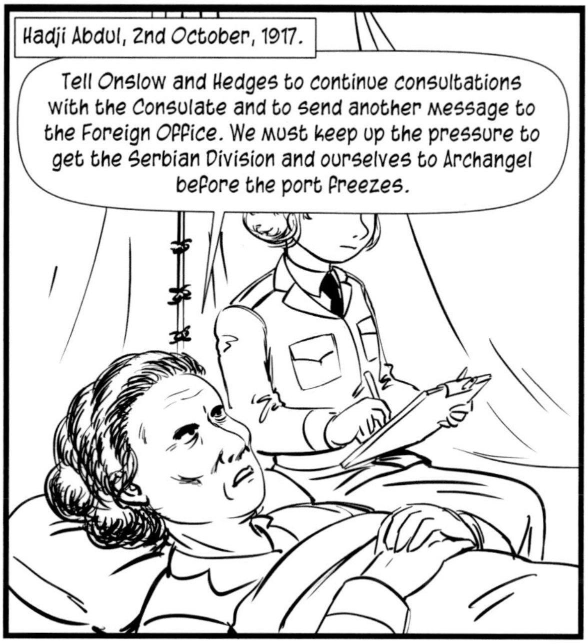
Hadji Abdul, 2nd October, 1917.
Tell Onslow and Hedges to continue consultations with the Consulate and to send another message to the Foreign Office. We must keep up the pressure to get the Serbian Division and ourselves to Archangel before the port freezes.

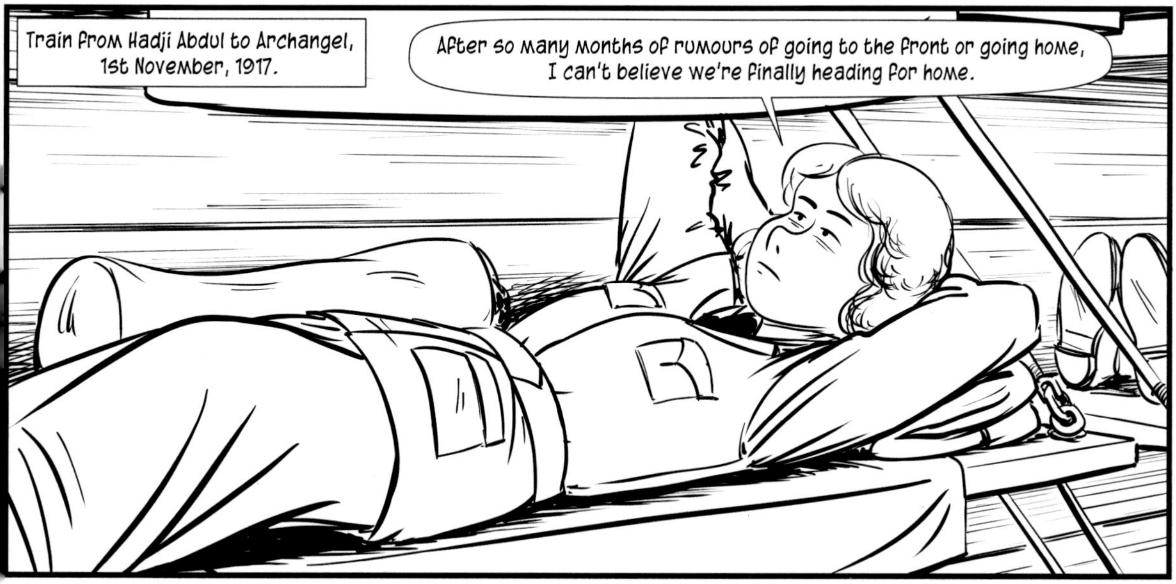
Train from Hadji Abdul to Archangel, 1st November, 1917.
After so many months of rumours of going to the front or going home, I can't believe we're finally heading for home.

River Ferry, Archangel, 10th November 1917.

We leave on the Porto Lisboa for England in the next few days. My heart grieves to leave Russia, but I long for home now.

Good luck to you Miss. The last convoy for England is believed lost. The Germans are torpedoing anything to leave port.

Porto Lisboa, Arctic Ocean, 17th November, 1917.

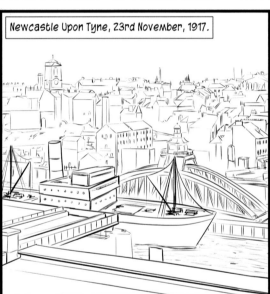

Newcastle Upon Tyne, 23rd November, 1917.

The Wilton Hotel, London, 26th November, 1917.

Welcome home. We were so worried that you hadn't got out of Russia, with the Bolshevik revolution and the strikes. Or that you'd be sunk in the Arctic!

The Wilton Hotel, London, 27th November, 1917.

Dr. Inglis died last night. We all knew she was ill, but I can't believe she's gone...

You've only been back a day! What a sad end to our Unit.

St Giles Cathedral, Edinburgh.

TO THE BELOVED AND HONOURED MEMORY OF ELSIE MAUD INGLIS SURGEON · PHILANTHROPIST FOUNDER · IN 1914 · OF THE SCOTTISH WOMEN'S HOSPITALS FOR SERVICE WITH THE ALLIES IN FRANCE · SERBIA AND RUSSIA BORN 1864 DIED · ON ACTIVE SERVICE · 1917

— MORS JANVA VITÆ —

Medical Faculty, Belgrade.

IN MEMORIAM
ELSIE INGLIS M.D.
AMICAE SERBORUM CERTISSIMAE
OBIIT ANNO MCMXVII
NOVEMBRIS DIE XV

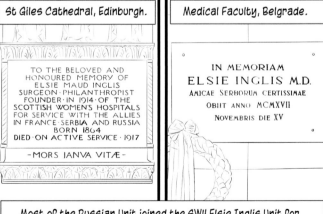

Most of the Russian Unit joined the SWH Elsie Inglis Unit for Macedonia or did war work for other women's organisations. After the war many of the women had careers as doctors, nurses, teachers, secretaries, academics and even the first woman barrister to appear at The Old Bailey.

The End

NO MORE THAN CATTLE...

SCRIPT: COLM REGAN
ART: MIKE-LITO

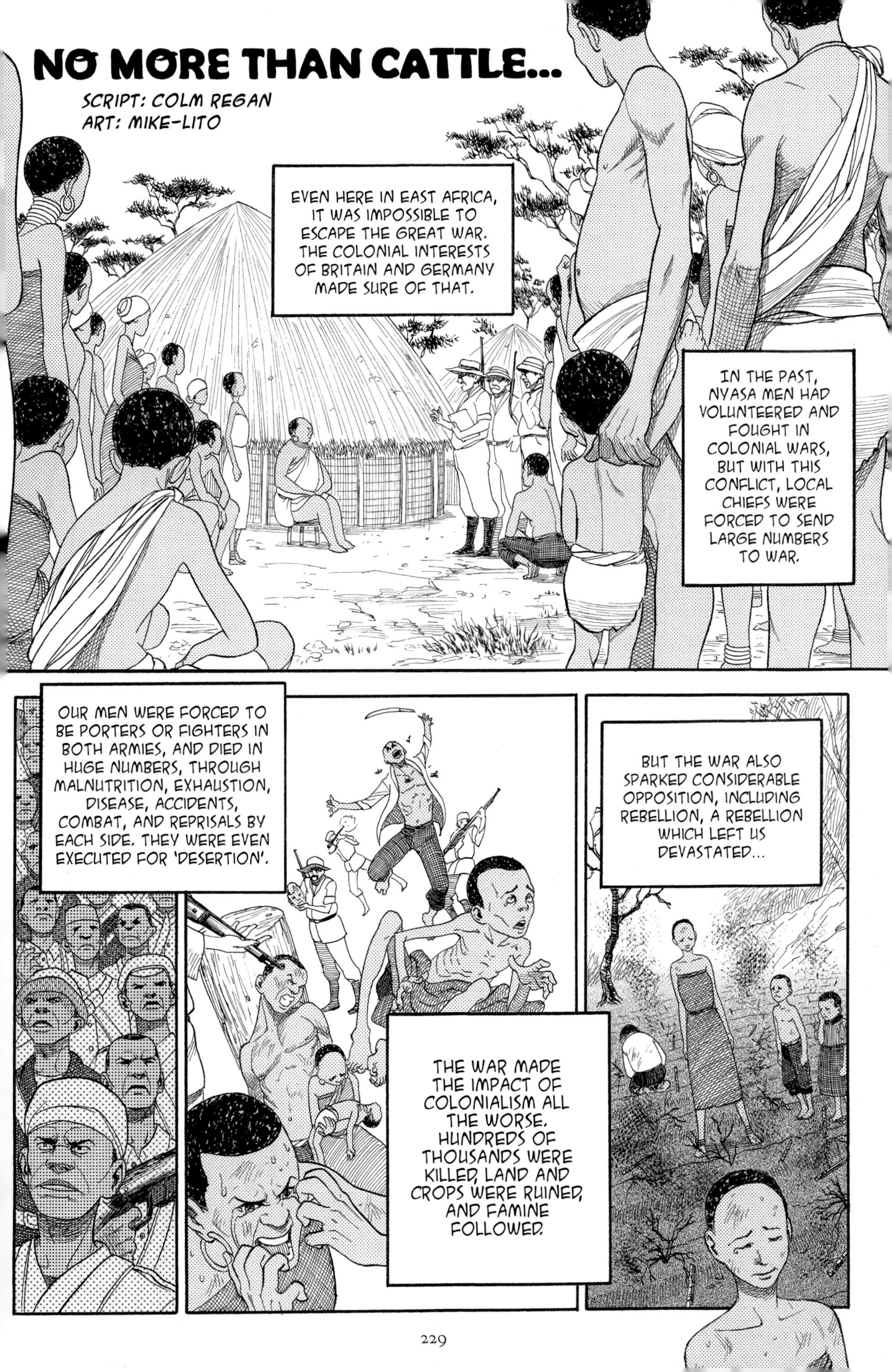
EVEN HERE IN EAST AFRICA, IT WAS IMPOSSIBLE TO ESCAPE THE GREAT WAR. THE COLONIAL INTERESTS OF BRITAIN AND GERMANY MADE SURE OF THAT.
IN THE PAST, NYASA MEN HAD VOLUNTEERED AND FOUGHT IN COLONIAL WARS, BUT WITH THIS CONFLICT, LOCAL CHIEFS WERE FORCED TO SEND LARGE NUMBERS TO WAR.
OUR MEN WERE FORCED TO BE PORTERS OR FIGHTERS IN BOTH ARMIES, AND DIED IN HUGE NUMBERS, THROUGH MALNUTRITION, EXHAUSTION, DISEASE, ACCIDENTS, COMBAT, AND REPRISALS BY EACH SIDE. THEY WERE EVEN EXECUTED FOR 'DESERTION'.
THE WAR MADE THE IMPACT OF COLONIALISM ALL THE WORSE. HUNDREDS OF THOUSANDS WERE KILLED, LAND AND CROPS WERE RUINED, AND FAMINE FOLLOWED.
BUT THE WAR ALSO SPARKED CONSIDERABLE OPPOSITION, INCLUDING REBELLION, A REBELLION WHICH LEFT US DEVASTATED...

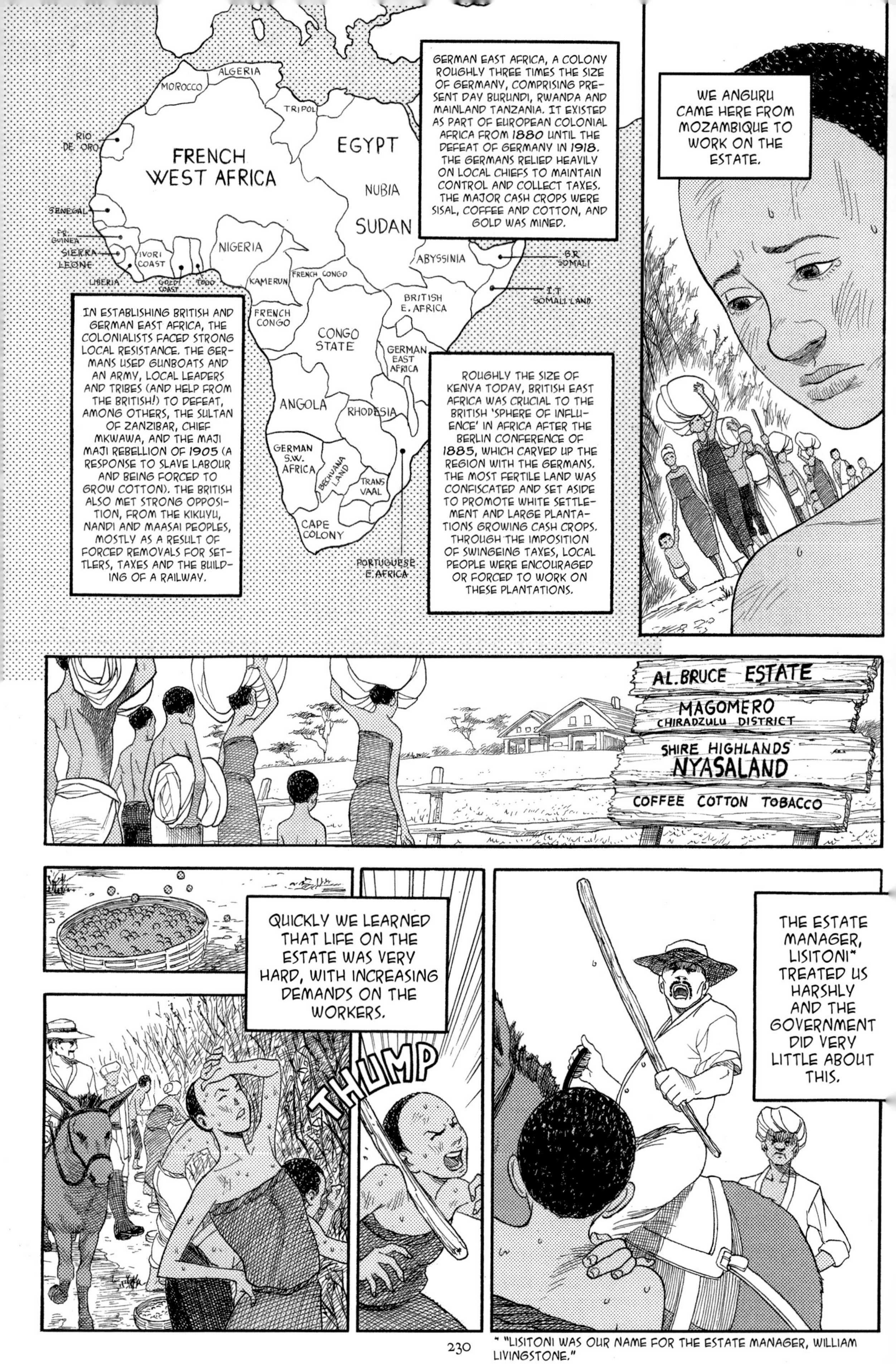

ALGERIA
MOROCCO
TRIPOLI
RIO DE ORO
FRENCH WEST AFRICA
EGYPT
NUBIA
SUDAN
SENEGAL
FR. GUINEA
SIERRA LEONE
LIBERIA
IVORI COAST
GOLD COAST
TOGO
NIGERIA
KAMERUN
FRENCH CONGO
ABYSSINIA
BR SOMALI
IT SOMALI LAND
BRITISH E. AFRICA
FRENCH CONGO
CONGO STATE
GERMAN EAST AFRICA
ANGOLA
RHODESIA
GERMAN S.W. AFRICA
BECHUANA LAND
TRANS VAAL
CAPE COLONY
PORTUGUESE E. AFRICA
GERMAN EAST AFRICA, A COLONY ROUGHLY THREE TIMES THE SIZE OF GERMANY, COMPRISING PRESENT DAY BURUNDI, RWANDA AND MAINLAND TANZANIA. IT EXISTED AS PART OF EUROPEAN COLONIAL AFRICA FROM 1880 UNTIL THE DEFEAT OF GERMANY IN 1918. THE GERMANS RELIED HEAVILY ON LOCAL CHIEFS TO MAINTAIN CONTROL AND COLLECT TAXES. THE MAJOR CASH CROPS WERE SISAL, COFFEE AND COTTON, AND GOLD WAS MINED.
IN ESTABLISHING BRITISH AND GERMAN EAST AFRICA, THE COLONIALISTS FACED STRONG LOCAL RESISTANCE. THE GERMANS USED GUNBOATS AND AN ARMY, LOCAL LEADERS AND TRIBES (AND HELP FROM THE BRITISH!) TO DEFEAT, AMONG OTHERS, THE SULTAN OF ZANZIBAR, CHIEF MKWAWA, AND THE MAJI MAJI REBELLION OF 1905 (A RESPONSE TO SLAVE LABOUR AND BEING FORCED TO GROW COTTON). THE BRITISH ALSO MET STRONG OPPOSITION, FROM THE KIKUYU, NANDI AND MAASAI PEOPLES, MOSTLY AS A RESULT OF FORCED REMOVALS FOR SETTLERS, TAXES AND THE BUILDING OF A RAILWAY.
ROUGHLY THE SIZE OF KENYA TODAY, BRITISH EAST AFRICA WAS CRUCIAL TO THE BRITISH 'SPHERE OF INFLUENCE' IN AFRICA AFTER THE BERLIN CONFERENCE OF 1885, WHICH CARVED UP THE REGION WITH THE GERMANS. THE MOST FERTILE LAND WAS CONFISCATED AND SET ASIDE TO PROMOTE WHITE SETTLEMENT AND LARGE PLANTATIONS GROWING CASH CROPS. THROUGH THE IMPOSITION OF SWINGEING TAXES, LOCAL PEOPLE WERE ENCOURAGED OR FORCED TO WORK ON THESE PLANTATIONS.
WE ANGURU CAME HERE FROM MOZAMBIQUE TO WORK ON THE ESTATE.
AL.BRUCE ESTATE
MAGOMERO
CHIRADZULU DISTRICT
SHIRE HIGHLANDS
NYASALAND
COFFEE COTTON TOBACCO
QUICKLY WE LEARNED THAT LIFE ON THE ESTATE WAS VERY HARD, WITH INCREASING DEMANDS ON THE WORKERS.
THUMP
THE ESTATE MANAGER, LISITONI* TREATED US HARSHLY AND THE GOVERNMENT DID VERY LITTLE ABOUT THIS.

* "LISITONI WAS OUR NAME FOR THE ESTATE MANAGER, WILLIAM LIVINGSTONE."

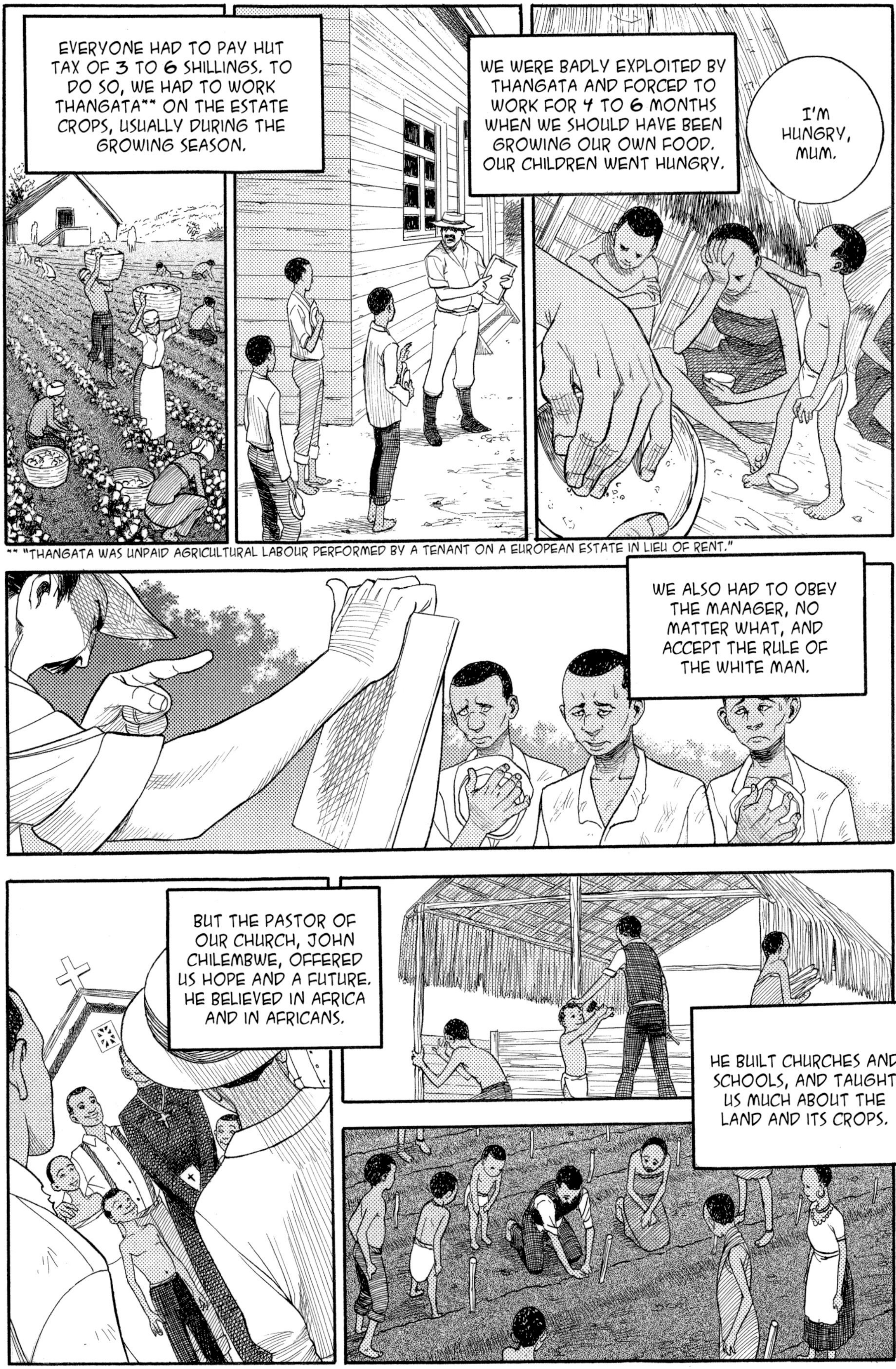
EVERYONE HAD TO PAY HUT TAX OF 3 TO 6 SHILLINGS. TO DO SO, WE HAD TO WORK THANGATA** ON THE ESTATE CROPS, USUALLY DURING THE GROWING SEASON.
WE WERE BADLY EXPLOITED BY THANGATA AND FORCED TO WORK FOR 4 TO 6 MONTHS WHEN WE SHOULD HAVE BEEN GROWING OUR OWN FOOD. OUR CHILDREN WENT HUNGRY.
I'M HUNGRY, MUM.
** "THANGATA WAS UNPAID AGRICULTURAL LABOUR PERFORMED BY A TENANT ON A EUROPEAN ESTATE IN LIEU OF RENT."
WE ALSO HAD TO OBEY THE MANAGER, NO MATTER WHAT, AND ACCEPT THE RULE OF THE WHITE MAN.
BUT THE PASTOR OF OUR CHURCH, JOHN CHILEMBWE, OFFERED US HOPE AND A FUTURE. HE BELIEVED IN AFRICA AND IN AFRICANS.
HE BUILT CHURCHES AND SCHOOLS, AND TAUGHT US MUCH ABOUT THE LAND AND ITS CROPS.

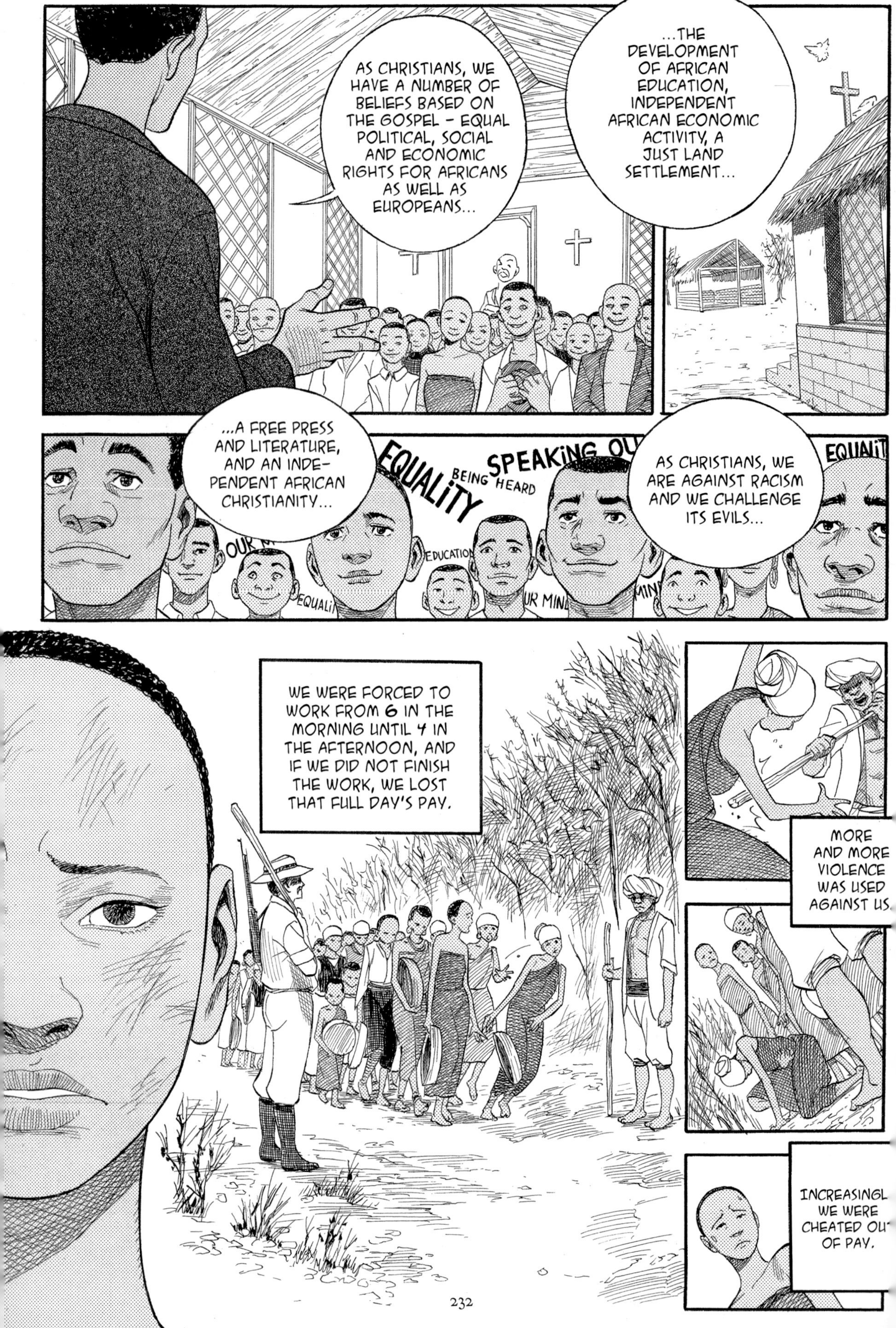

AS CHRISTIANS, WE HAVE A NUMBER OF BELIEFS BASED ON THE GOSPEL - EQUAL POLITICAL, SOCIAL AND ECONOMIC RIGHTS FOR AFRICANS AS WELL AS EUROPEANS...
...THE DEVELOPMENT OF AFRICAN EDUCATION, INDEPENDENT AFRICAN ECONOMIC ACTIVITY, A JUST LAND SETTLEMENT...
...A FREE PRESS AND LITERATURE, AND AN INDE-PENDENT AFRICAN CHRISTIANITY...
EQUALITY
BEING HEARD
SPEAKING OU
EDUCATION
AS CHRISTIANS, WE ARE AGAINST RACISM AND WE CHALLENGE ITS EVILS...
WE WERE FORCED TO WORK FROM 6 IN THE MORNING UNTIL 4 IN THE AFTERNOON, AND IF WE DID NOT FINISH THE WORK, WE LOST THAT FULL DAY'S PAY.
MORE AND MORE VIOLENCE WAS USED AGAINST US.
INCREASINGL WE WERE CHEATED OU OF PAY.

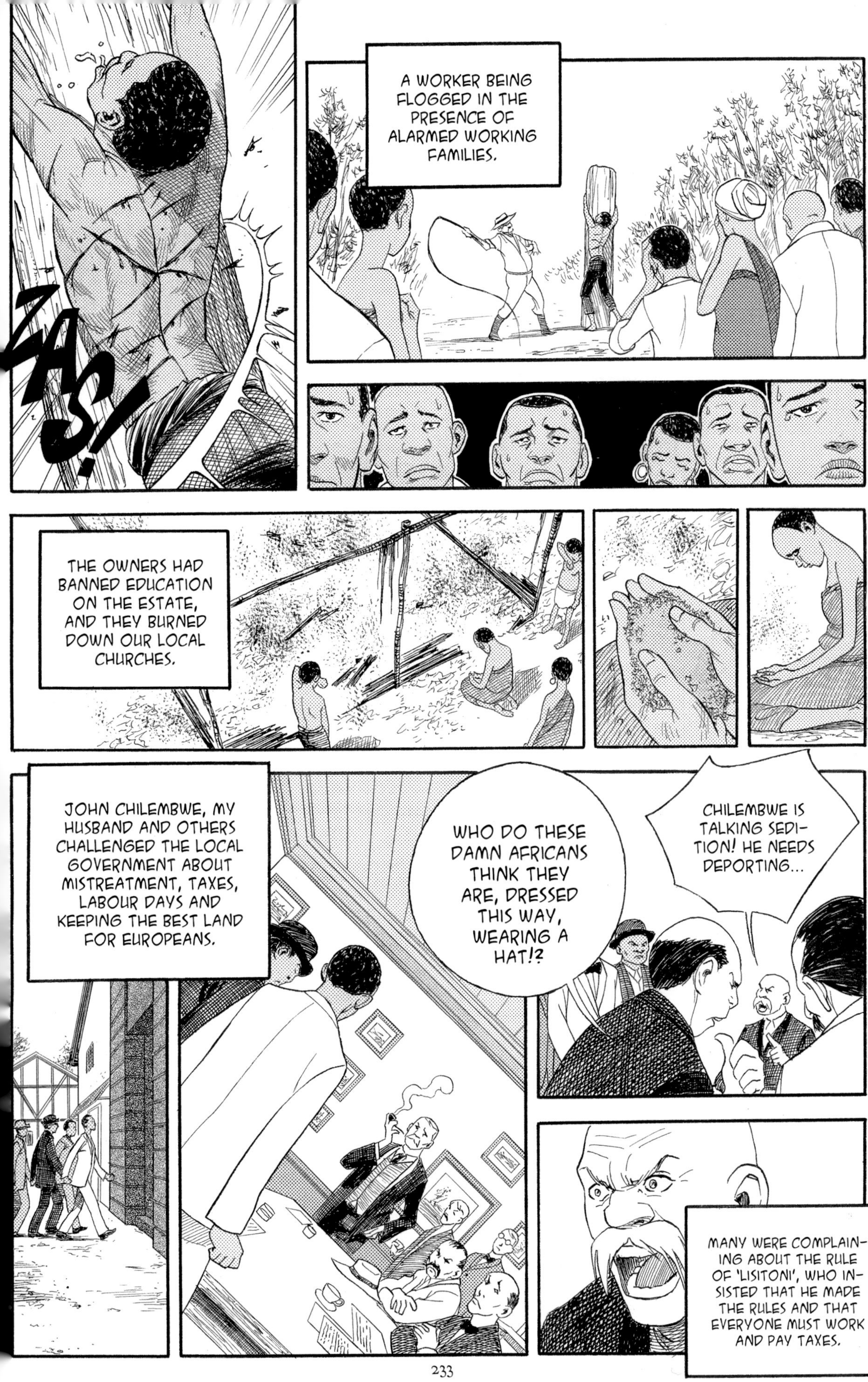
ZAS!
A WORKER BEING FLOGGED IN THE PRESENCE OF ALARMED WORKING FAMILIES.
THE OWNERS HAD BANNED EDUCATION ON THE ESTATE, AND THEY BURNED DOWN OUR LOCAL CHURCHES.
JOHN CHILEMBWE, MY HUSBAND AND OTHERS CHALLENGED THE LOCAL GOVERNMENT ABOUT MISTREATMENT, TAXES, LABOUR DAYS AND KEEPING THE BEST LAND FOR EUROPEANS.
WHO DO THESE DAMN AFRICANS THINK THEY ARE, DRESSED THIS WAY, WEARING A HAT!?
CHILEMBWE IS TALKING SEDI-TION! HE NEEDS DEPORTING...
MANY WERE COMPLAIN-ING ABOUT THE RULE OF 'LISITONI', WHO IN-SISTED THAT HE MADE THE RULES AND THAT EVERYONE MUST WORK AND PAY TAXES.

THINGS CHANGED COMPLETELY FOR US IN LATE 1914, WHEN THE EUROPEAN WAR CAME TO EAST AFRICA.

East Africa Standard

Mombasa, August 22nd, 1914

The duty of Europeans is not to fight each other but to keep control of the Africans.

THE WAR HERE WILL REQUIRE THOUSANDS OF PORTERS AND CARRIERS JUST TO SUPPLY TROOPS.

CERTAINLY. 'COURSE, THEY'LL HAVE TO BE AFRICANS.

THROUGH MY COUSIN, STORIES REACHED US OF THE MANY MEN KILLED AND INJURED IN THE WAR WITH THE GERMANS.

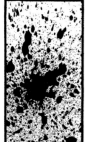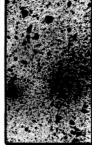

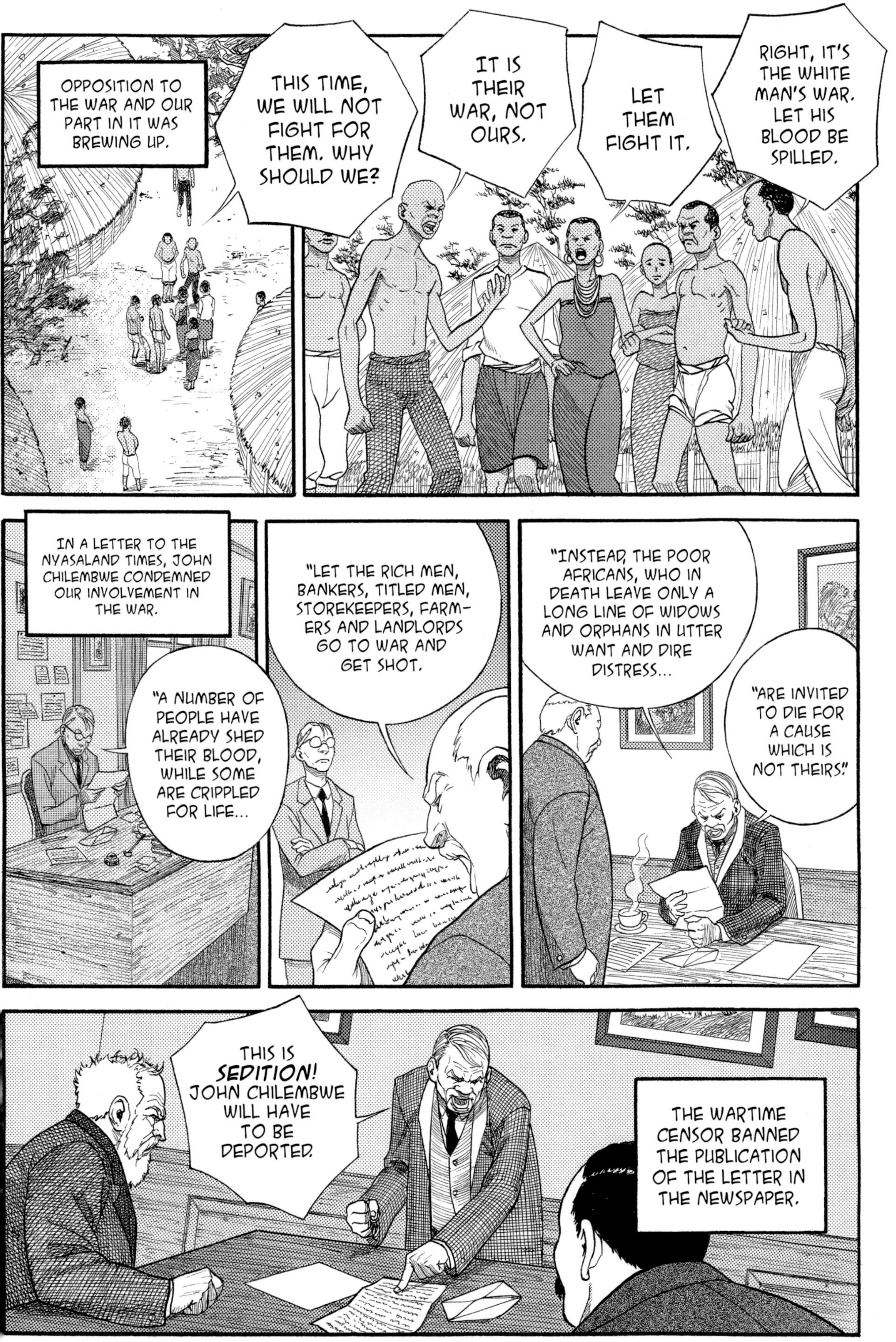
OPPOSITION TO THE WAR AND OUR PART IN IT WAS BREWING UP.
THIS TIME, WE WILL NOT FIGHT FOR THEM. WHY SHOULD WE?
IT IS THEIR WAR, NOT OURS.
LET THEM FIGHT IT.
RIGHT, IT'S THE WHITE MAN'S WAR. LET HIS BLOOD BE SPILLED.
IN A LETTER TO THE NYASALAND TIMES, JOHN CHILEMBWE CONDEMNED OUR INVOLVEMENT IN THE WAR.
"A NUMBER OF PEOPLE HAVE ALREADY SHED THEIR BLOOD, WHILE SOME ARE CRIPPLED FOR LIFE...
"LET THE RICH MEN, BANKERS, TITLED MEN, STOREKEEPERS, FARMERS AND LANDLORDS GO TO WAR AND GET SHOT.
"INSTEAD, THE POOR AFRICANS, WHO IN DEATH LEAVE ONLY A LONG LINE OF WIDOWS AND ORPHANS IN UTTER WANT AND DIRE DISTRESS...
"ARE INVITED TO DIE FOR A CAUSE WHICH IS NOT THEIRS!"
THIS IS *SEDITION!* JOHN CHILEMBWE WILL HAVE TO BE DEPORTED.
THE WARTIME CENSOR BANNED THE PUBLICATION OF THE LETTER IN THE NEWSPAPER.

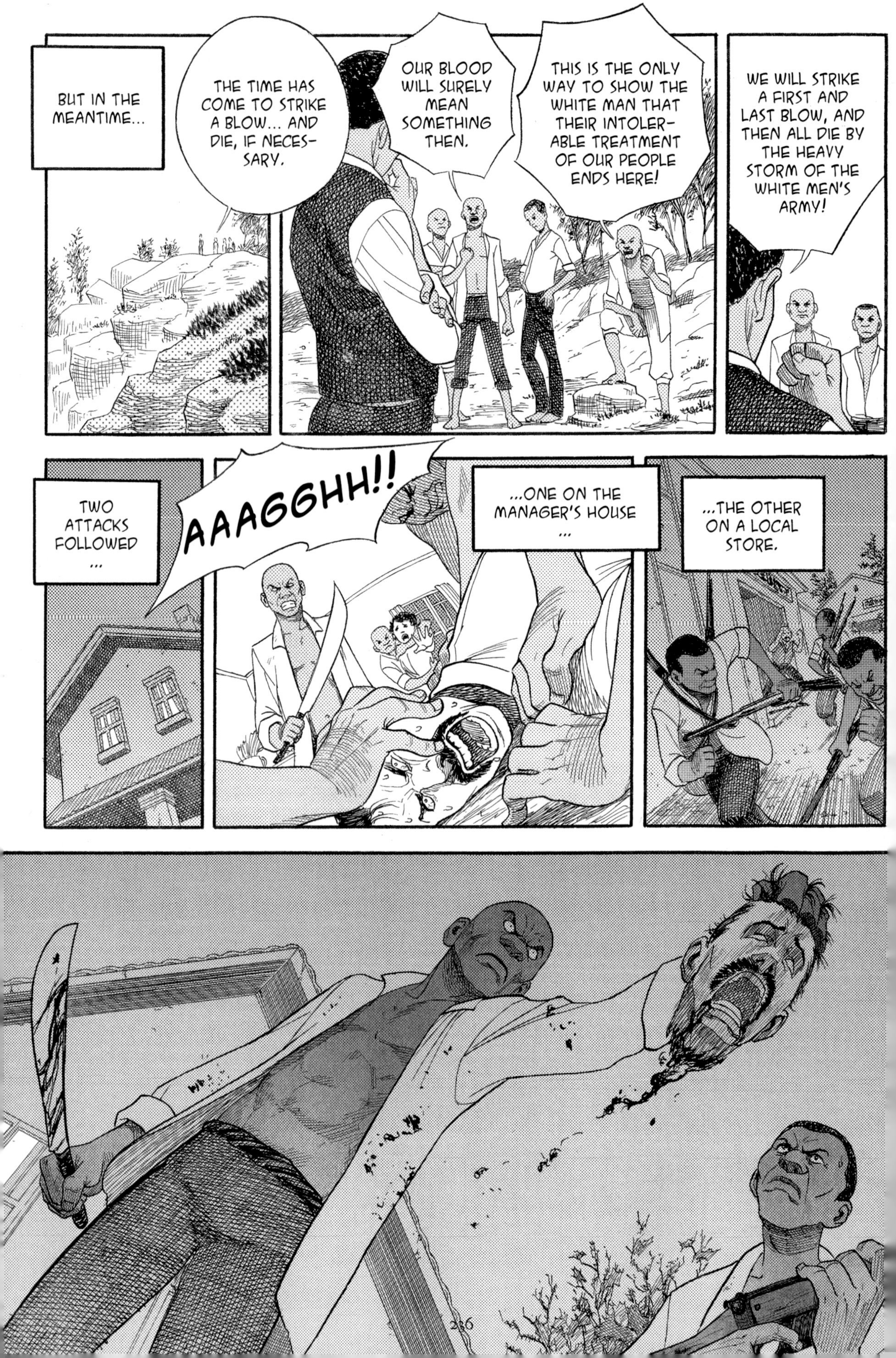

BUT IN THE MEANTIME...
THE TIME HAS COME TO STRIKE A BLOW... AND DIE, IF NECES-SARY.
OUR BLOOD WILL SURELY MEAN SOMETHING THEN.
THIS IS THE ONLY WAY TO SHOW THE WHITE MAN THAT THEIR INTOLER-ABLE TREATMENT OF OUR PEOPLE ENDS HERE!
WE WILL STRIKE A FIRST AND LAST BLOW, AND THEN ALL DIE BY THE HEAVY STORM OF THE WHITE MEN'S ARMY!
TWO ATTACKS FOLLOWED ...
AAAGGHH!!
...ONE ON THE MANAGER'S HOUSE ...
...THE OTHER ON A LOCAL STORE.

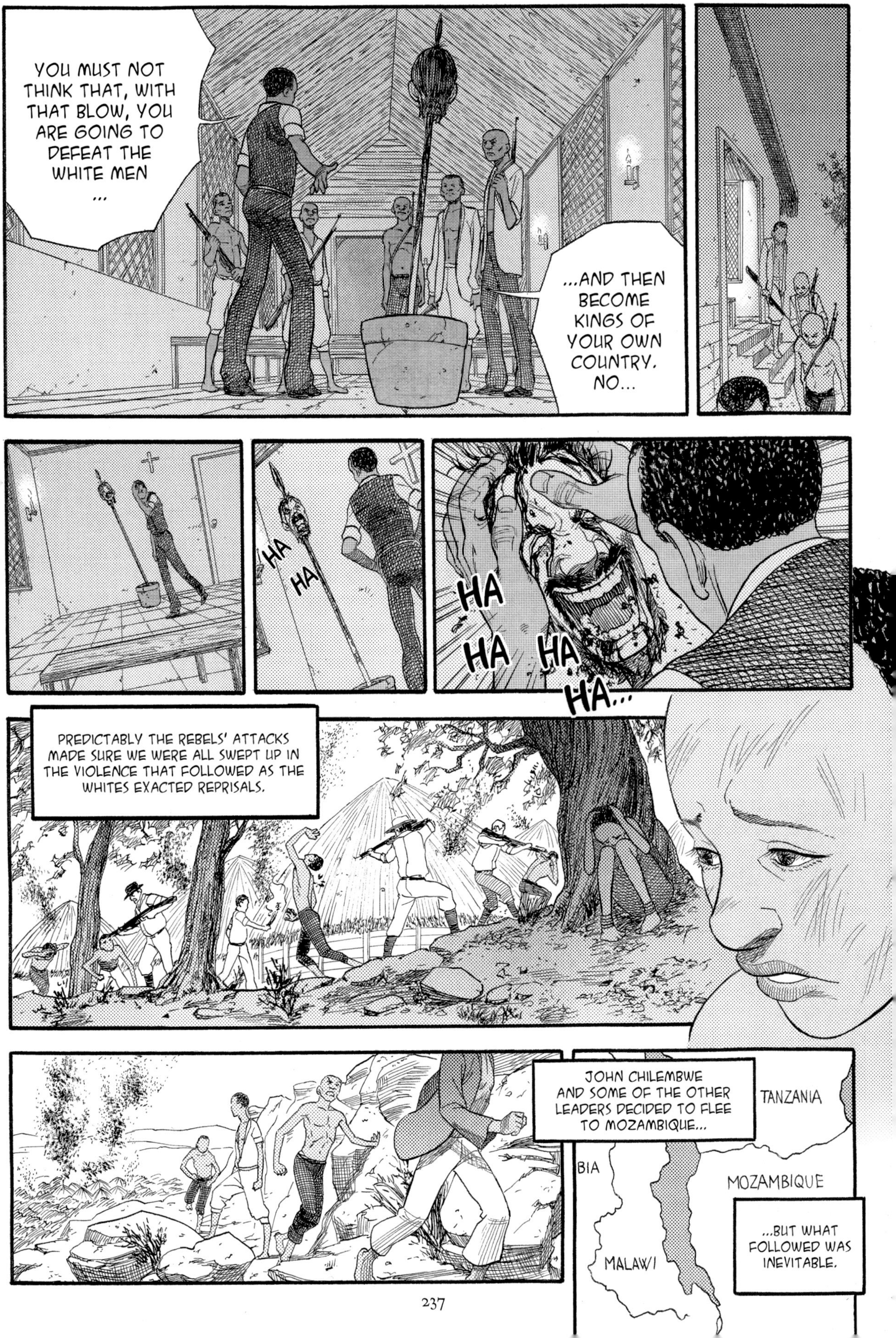
YOU MUST NOT THINK THAT, WITH THAT BLOW, YOU ARE GOING TO DEFEAT THE WHITE MEN ...
...AND THEN BECOME KINGS OF YOUR OWN COUNTRY. NO...
HA
HA
HA
HA HA
HA...
PREDICTABLY THE REBELS' ATTACKS MADE SURE WE WERE ALL SWEPT UP IN THE VIOLENCE THAT FOLLOWED AS THE WHITES EXACTED REPRISALS.
JOHN CHILEMBWE AND SOME OF THE OTHER LEADERS DECIDED TO FLEE TO MOZAMBIQUE...
TANZANIA
BIA
MOZAMBIQUE
MALAWI
...BUT WHAT FOLLOWED WAS INEVITABLE.

36 PEOPLE WERE EXECUTED AND HUNDREDS WERE KILLED.

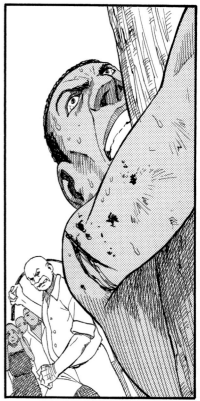

MANY OTHERS WERE SENTENCED TO LONG PRISON TERMS.

FOR THE CRIME OF SEDITION, THE COURT SENTENCES YOU, GEORGE MASANGANO...

...YOTAM LIFEYU AND JACKSON KOLIMBO, TO 10 YEARS...

CLACK

WE HOPE IN THE MERCY OF ALMIGHTY GOD THAT SOMEDAY THINGS WILL TURN OUT WELL...

...THAT THE GOVERNMENT WILL RECOGNISE OUR INDISPEN-SABILITY, AND THAT JUSTICE WILL PREVAIL.

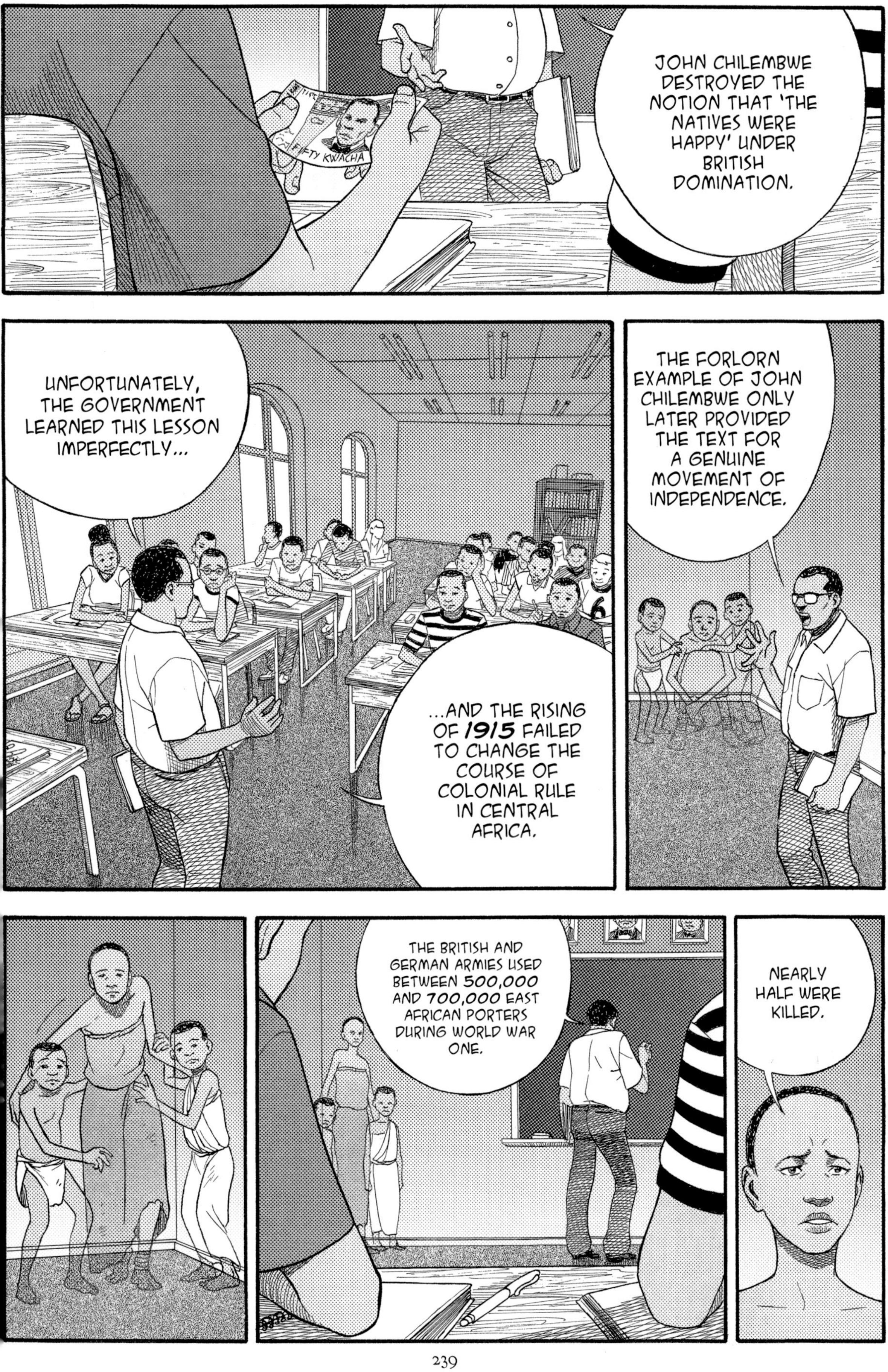
FIFTY KWACHA
JOHN CHILEMBWE DESTROYED THE NOTION THAT 'THE NATIVES WERE HAPPY' UNDER BRITISH DOMINATION.
UNFORTUNATELY, THE GOVERNMENT LEARNED THIS LESSON IMPERFECTLY...
...AND THE RISING OF 1915 FAILED TO CHANGE THE COURSE OF COLONIAL RULE IN CENTRAL AFRICA.
THE FORLORN EXAMPLE OF JOHN CHILEMBWE ONLY LATER PROVIDED THE TEXT FOR A GENUINE MOVEMENT OF INDEPENDENCE.
THE BRITISH AND GERMAN ARMIES USED BETWEEN 500,000 AND 700,000 EAST AFRICAN PORTERS DURING WORLD WAR ONE.
NEARLY HALF WERE KILLED.

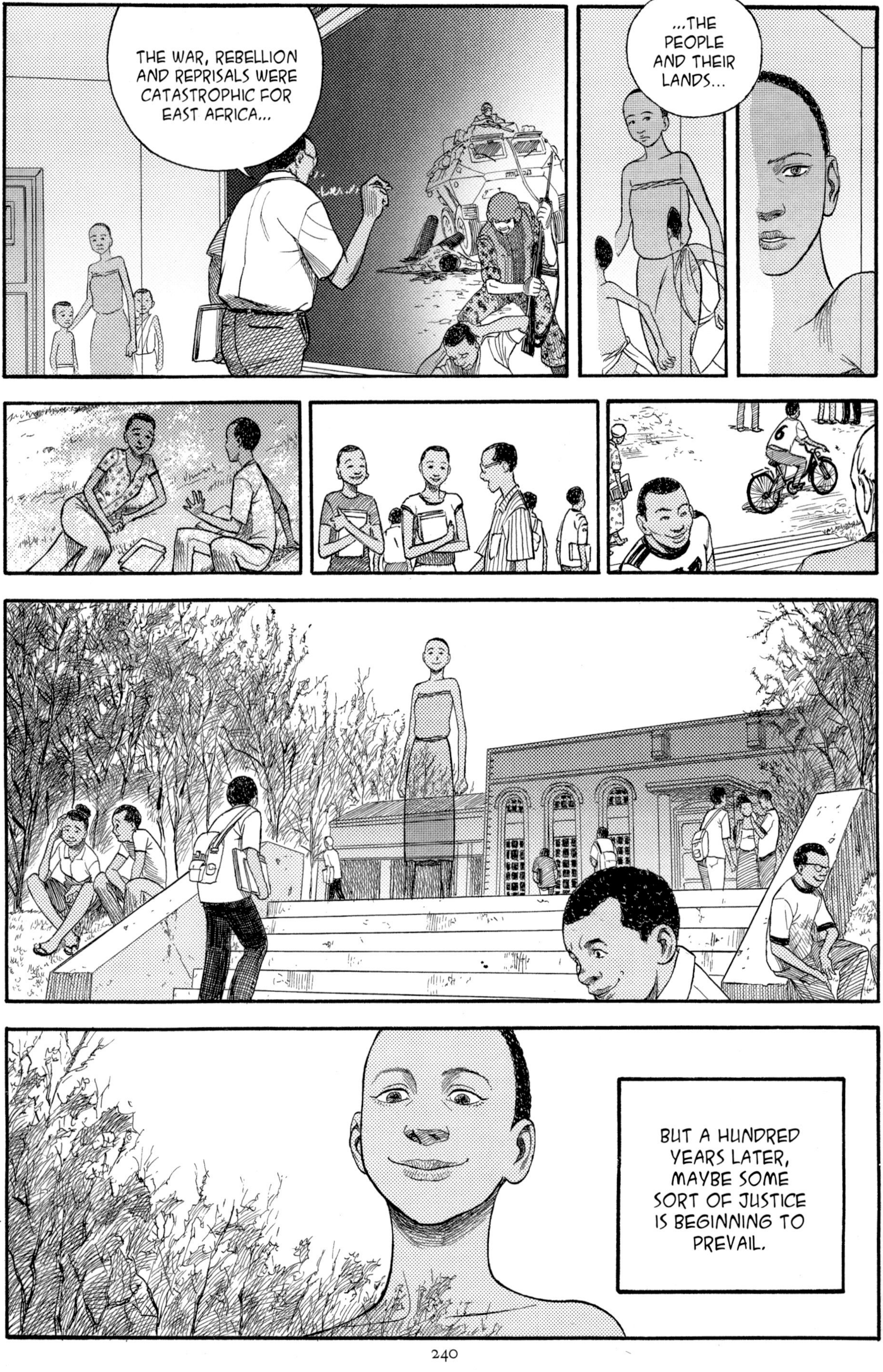
THE WAR, REBELLION AND REPRISALS WERE CATASTROPHIC FOR EAST AFRICA...
...THE PEOPLE AND THEIR LANDS...
BUT A HUNDRED YEARS LATER, MAYBE SOME SORT OF JUSTICE IS BEGINNING TO PREVAIL.

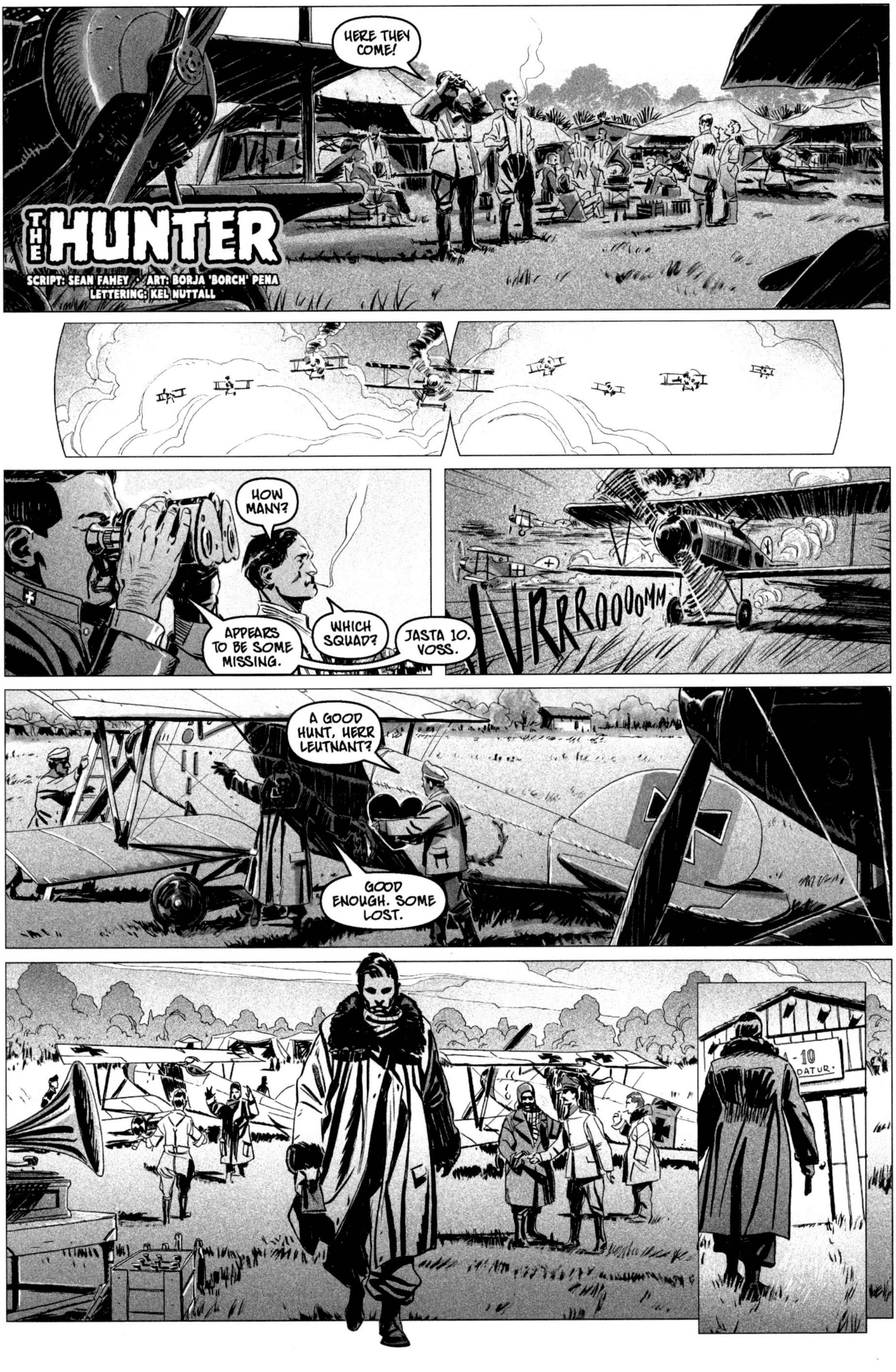

HERE THEY COME!
THE HUNTER
SCRIPT: SEAN FAHEY · ART: BORJA 'BORCH' PENA
LETTERING: KEL NUTTALL
HOW MANY?
APPEARS TO BE SOME MISSING.
WHICH SQUAD?
JASTA 10. VOSS.
VRRROOOOMM
A GOOD HUNT, HERR LEUTNANT?
GOOD ENOUGH. SOME LOST.

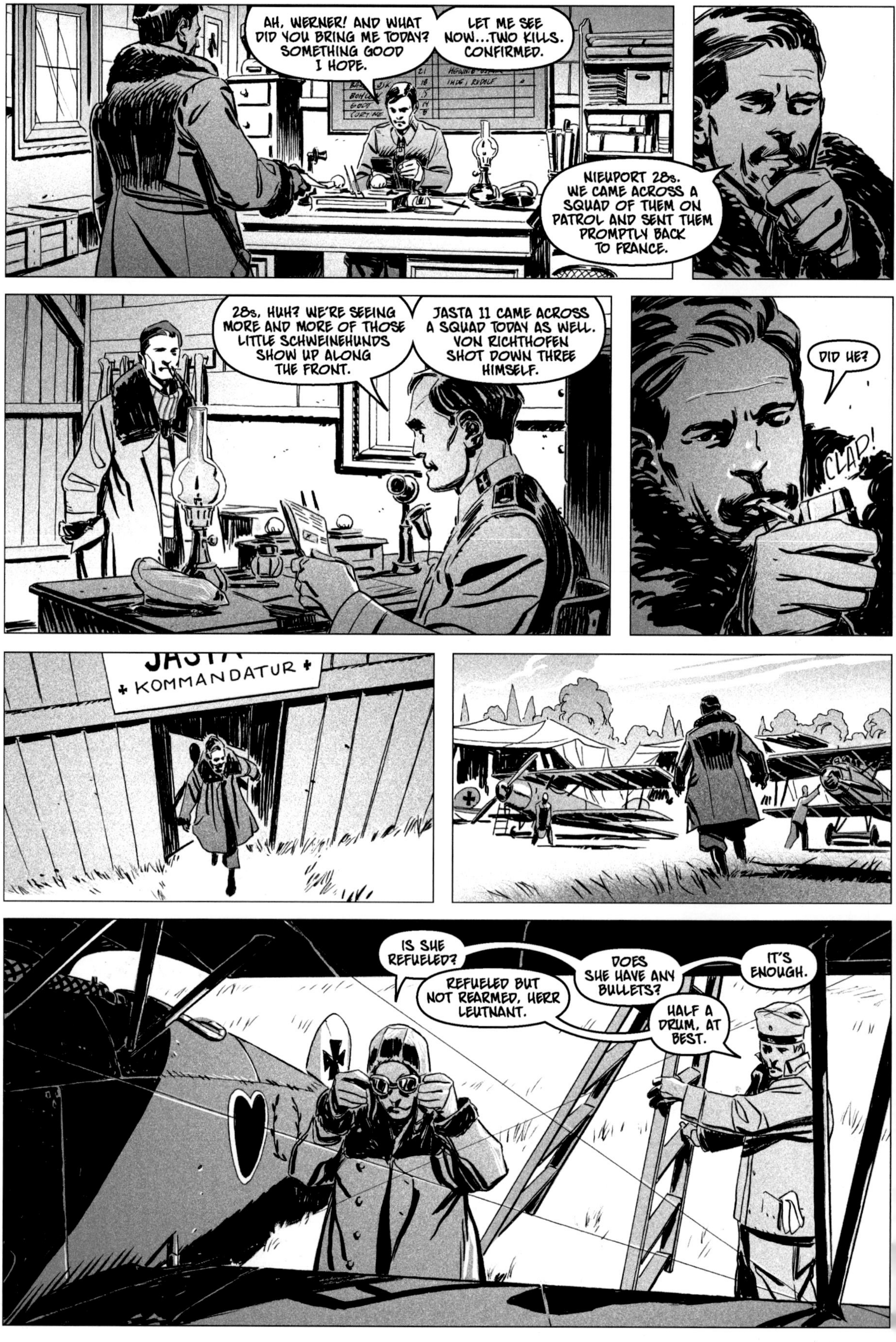
AH, WERNER! AND WHAT DID YOU BRING ME TODAY? SOMETHING GOOD I HOPE.
LET ME SEE NOW...TWO KILLS. CONFIRMED.
NIEUPORT 28s. WE CAME ACROSS A SQUAD OF THEM ON PATROL AND SENT THEM PROMPTLY BACK TO FRANCE.
28s, HUH? WE'RE SEEING MORE AND MORE OF THOSE LITTLE SCHWEINEHUNDS SHOW UP ALONG THE FRONT.
JASTA 11 CAME ACROSS A SQUAD TODAY AS WELL. VON RICHTHOFEN SHOT DOWN THREE HIMSELF.
DID HE?
CLAP!
KOMMANDATUR
IS SHE REFUELED?
REFUELED BUT NOT REARMED, HERR LEUTNANT.
DOES SHE HAVE ANY BULLETS?
HALF A DRUM, AT BEST.
IT'S ENOUGH.

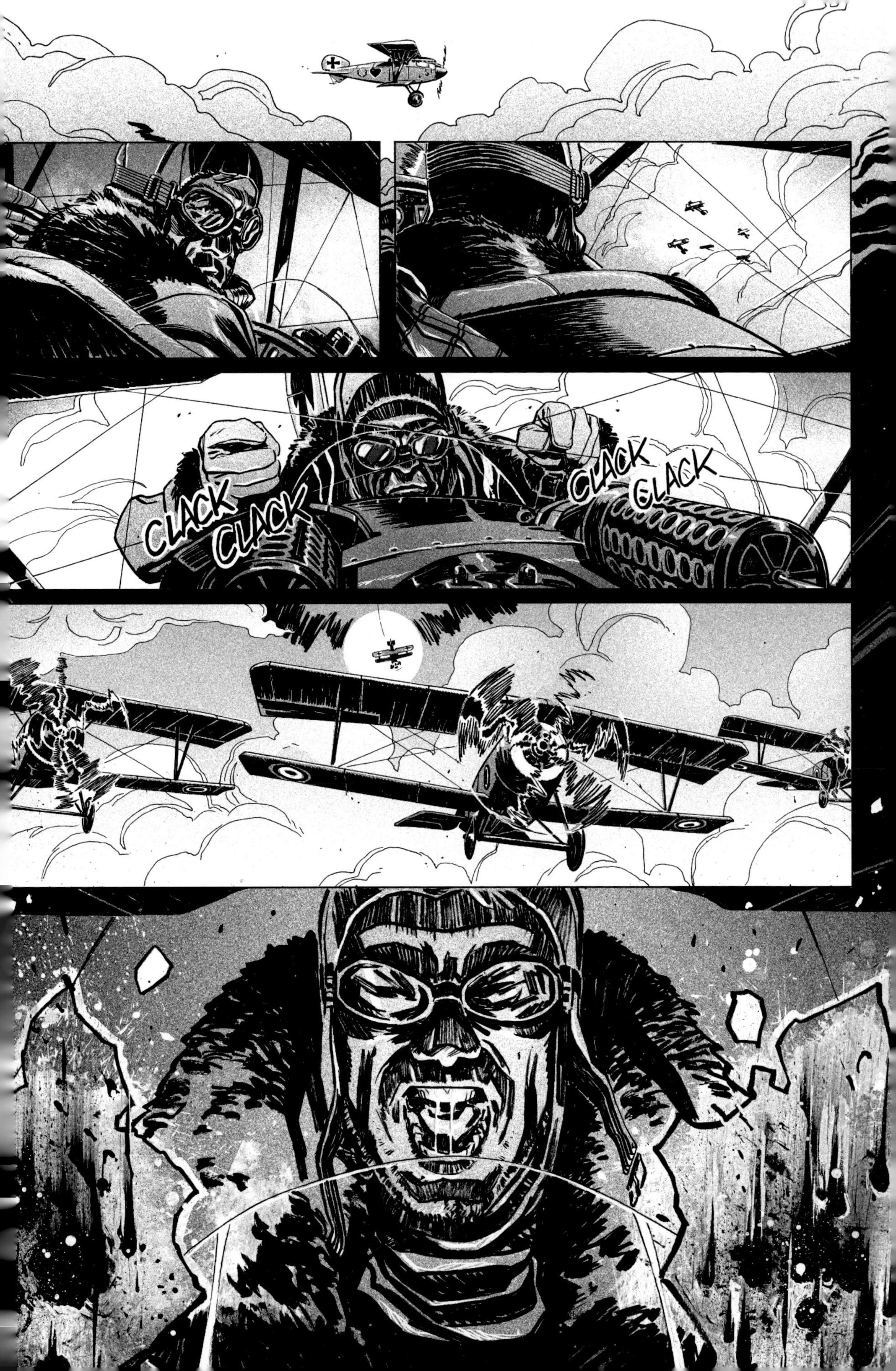
CLACK
CLACK
CLACK
CLACK

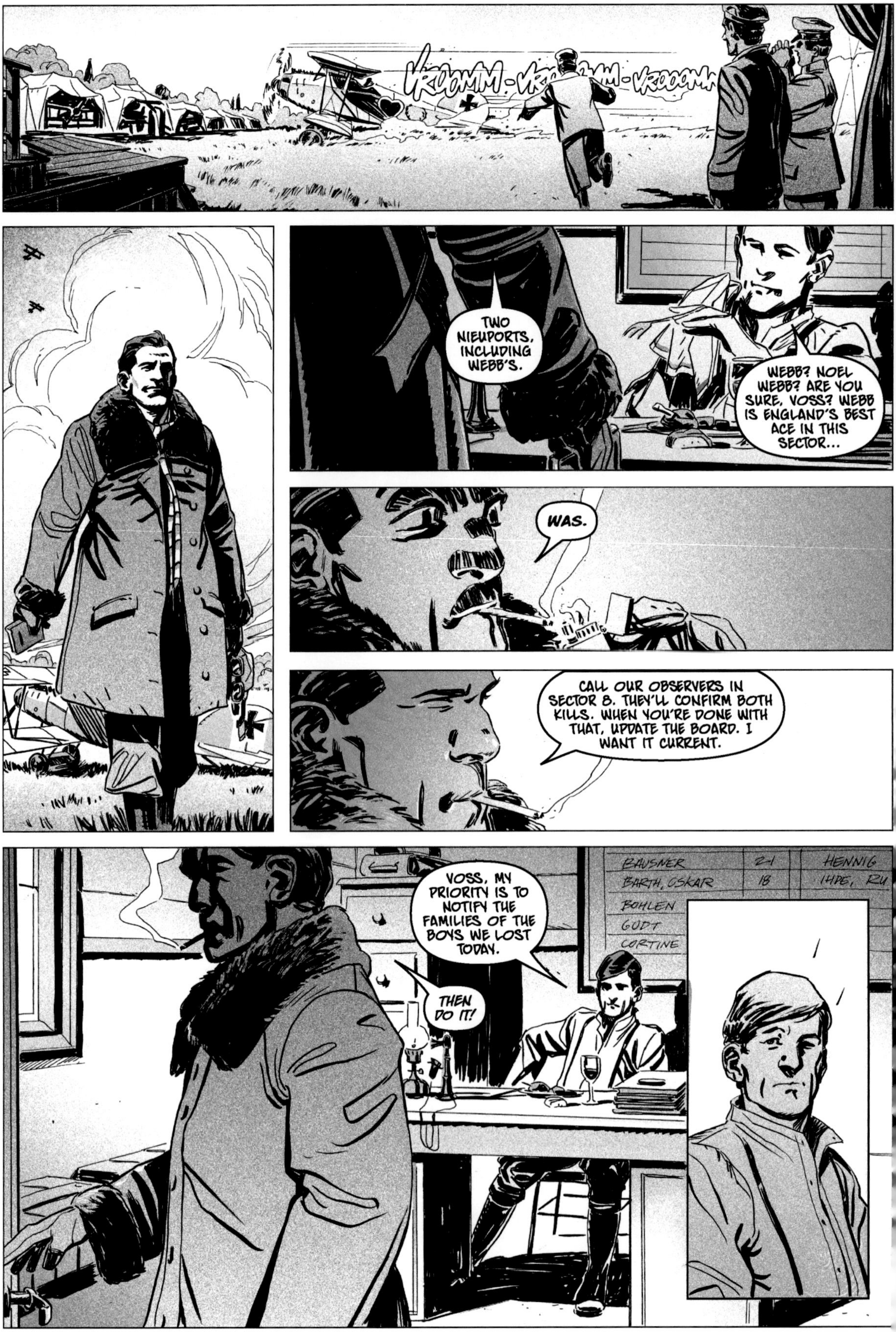
VROOMM -
TWO NIEUPORTS, INCLUDING WEBB'S.
WEBB? NOEL WEBB? ARE YOU SURE, VOSS? WEBB IS ENGLAND'S BEST ACE IN THIS SECTOR...
WAS.
CALL OUR OBSERVERS IN SECTOR 8. THEY'LL CONFIRM BOTH KILLS. WHEN YOU'RE DONE WITH THAT, UPDATE THE BOARD. I WANT IT CURRENT.
BAUSNER 21 HENNIG
BARTH, OSKAR 18 IHPE, RU
BOHLEN
GODT
CORTINE
VOSS, MY PRIORITY IS TO NOTIFY THE FAMILIES OF THE BOYS WE LOST TODAY.
THEN DO IT!

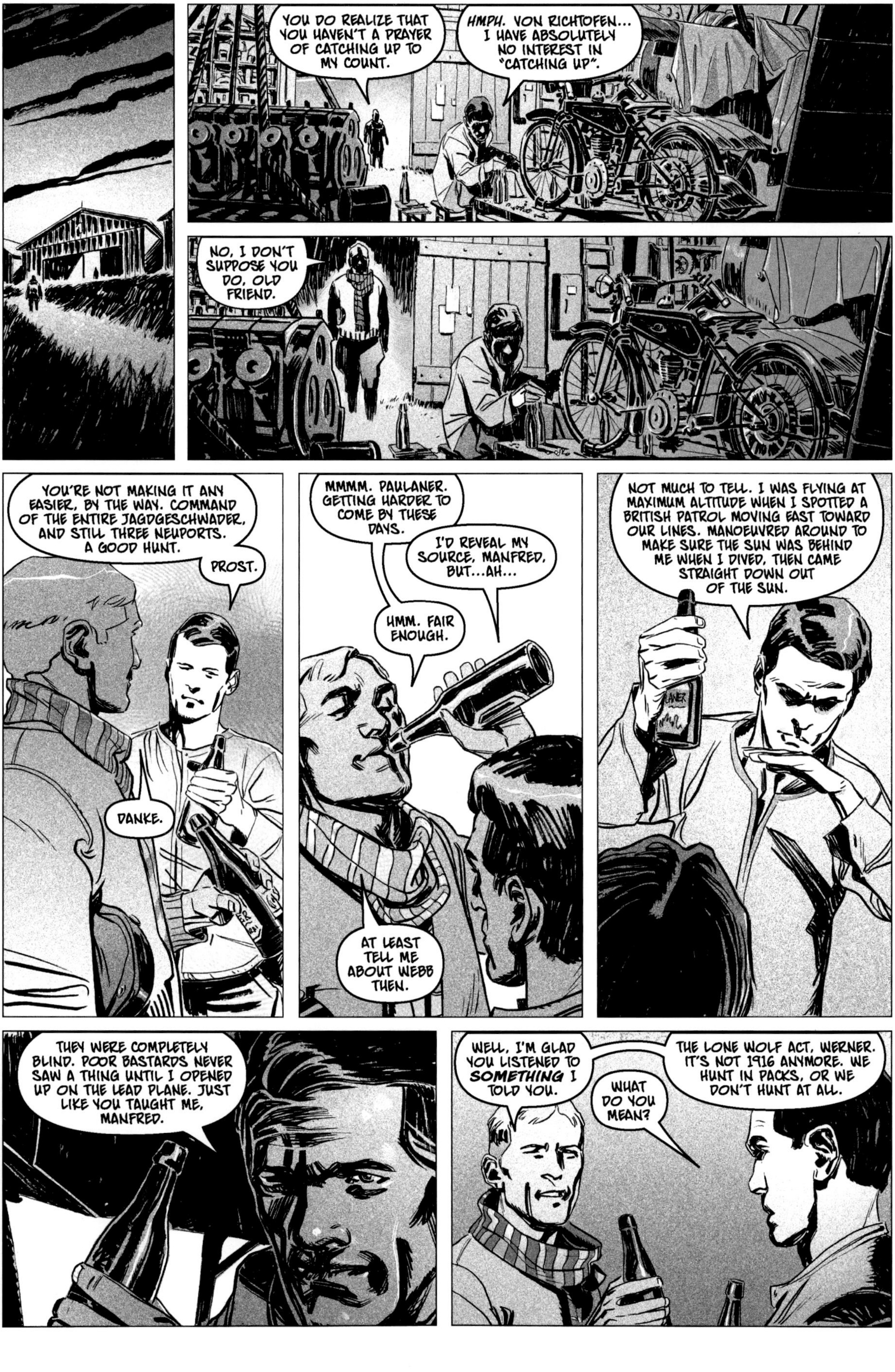

YOU DO REALIZE THAT YOU HAVEN'T A PRAYER OF CATCHING UP TO MY COUNT.
HMPH. VON RICHTOFEN... I HAVE ABSOLUTELY NO INTEREST IN "CATCHING UP".
NO, I DON'T SUPPOSE YOU DO, OLD FRIEND.
YOU'RE NOT MAKING IT ANY EASIER, BY THE WAY. COMMAND OF THE ENTIRE JAGDGESCHWADER, AND STILL THREE NEUPORTS. A GOOD HUNT.
PROST.
DANKE.
MMMM. PAULANER. GETTING HARDER TO COME BY THESE DAYS.
I'D REVEAL MY SOURCE, MANFRED, BUT...AH...
UMM. FAIR ENOUGH.
AT LEAST TELL ME ABOUT WEBB THEN.
NOT MUCH TO TELL. I WAS FLYING AT MAXIMUM ALTITUDE WHEN I SPOTTED A BRITISH PATROL MOVING EAST TOWARD OUR LINES. MANOEUVRED AROUND TO MAKE SURE THE SUN WAS BEHIND ME WHEN I DIVED, THEN CAME STRAIGHT DOWN OUT OF THE SUN.
THEY WERE COMPLETELY BLIND. POOR BASTARDS NEVER SAW A THING UNTIL I OPENED UP ON THE LEAD PLANE. JUST LIKE YOU TAUGHT ME, MANFRED.
WELL, I'M GLAD YOU LISTENED TO SOMETHING I TOLD YOU.
WHAT DO YOU MEAN?
THE LONE WOLF ACT, WERNER. IT'S NOT 1916 ANYMORE. WE HUNT IN PACKS, OR WE DON'T HUNT AT ALL.

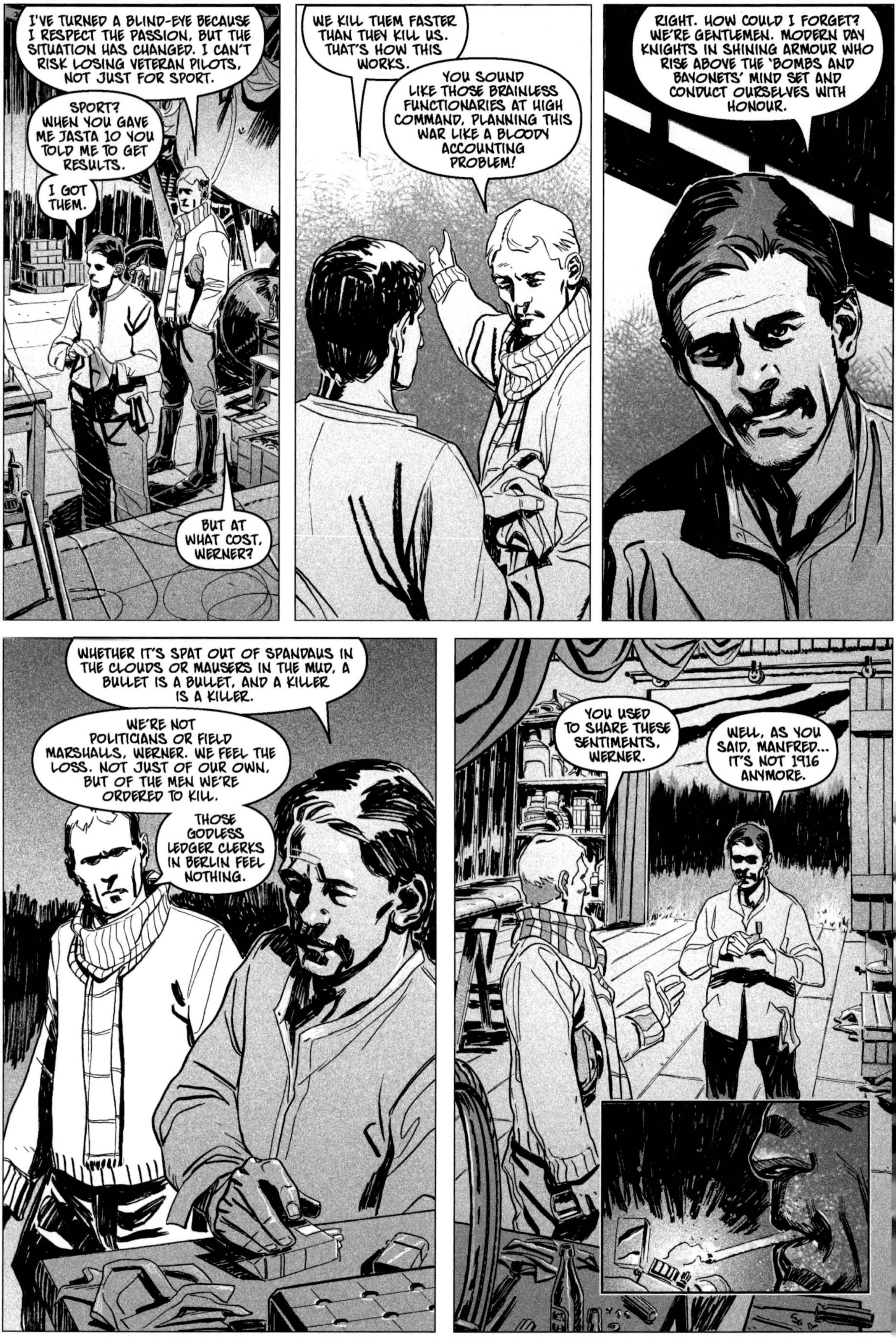
I'VE TURNED A BLIND-EYE BECAUSE I RESPECT THE PASSION, BUT THE SITUATION HAS CHANGED. I CAN'T RISK LOSING VETERAN PILOTS, NOT JUST FOR SPORT.
SPORT? WHEN YOU GAVE ME JASTA 10 YOU TOLD ME TO GET RESULTS.
I GOT THEM.
BUT AT WHAT COST, WERNER?
WE KILL THEM FASTER THAN THEY KILL US. THAT'S HOW THIS WORKS.
YOU SOUND LIKE THOSE BRAINLESS FUNCTIONARIES AT HIGH COMMAND, PLANNING THIS WAR LIKE A BLOODY ACCOUNTING PROBLEM!
RIGHT. HOW COULD I FORGET? WE'RE GENTLEMEN. MODERN DAY KNIGHTS IN SHINING ARMOUR WHO RISE ABOVE THE 'BOMBS AND BAYONETS' MIND SET AND CONDUCT OURSELVES WITH HONOUR.
WHETHER IT'S SPAT OUT OF SPANDAUS IN THE CLOUDS OR MAUSERS IN THE MUD, A BULLET IS A BULLET, AND A KILLER IS A KILLER.
WE'RE NOT POLITICIANS OR FIELD MARSHALLS, WERNER. WE FEEL THE LOSS. NOT JUST OF OUR OWN, BUT OF THE MEN WE'RE ORDERED TO KILL.
THOSE GODLESS LEDGER CLERKS IN BERLIN FEEL NOTHING.
YOU USED TO SHARE THESE SENTIMENTS, WERNER.
WELL, AS YOU SAID, MANFRED... IT'S NOT 1916 ANYMORE.

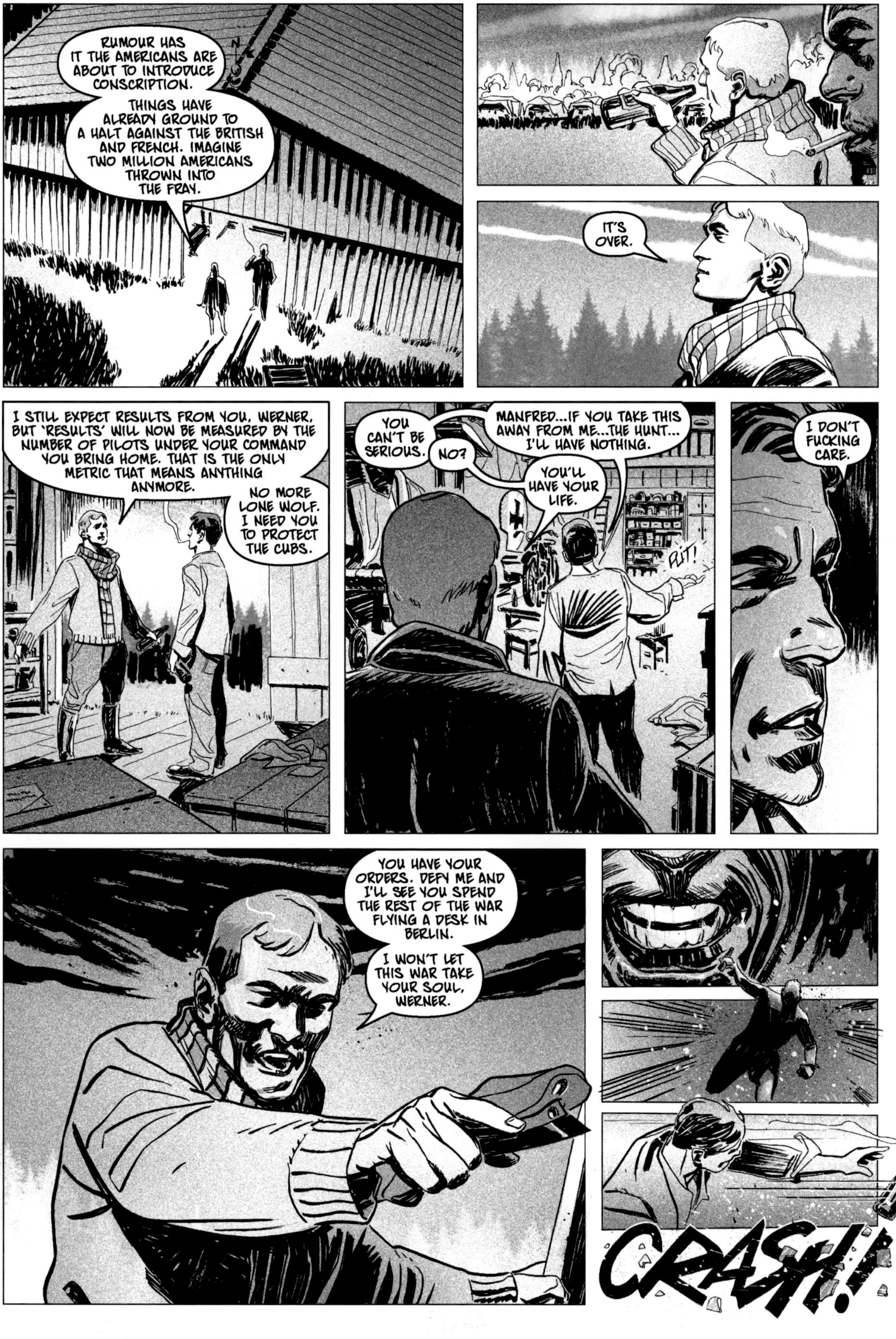
RUMOUR HAS IT THE AMERICANS ARE ABOUT TO INTRODUCE CONSCRIPTION.
THINGS HAVE ALREADY GROUND TO A HALT AGAINST THE BRITISH AND FRENCH. IMAGINE TWO MILLION AMERICANS THROWN INTO THE FRAY.
IT'S OVER.
I STILL EXPECT RESULTS FROM YOU, WERNER, BUT 'RESULTS' WILL NOW BE MEASURED BY THE NUMBER OF PILOTS UNDER YOUR COMMAND YOU BRING HOME. THAT IS THE ONLY METRIC THAT MEANS ANYTHING ANYMORE.
NO MORE LONE WOLF. I NEED YOU TO PROTECT THE CUBS.
YOU CAN'T BE SERIOUS.
NO?
MANFRED...IF YOU TAKE THIS AWAY FROM ME...THE HUNT... I'LL HAVE NOTHING.
YOU'LL HAVE YOUR LIFE.
PLIT!
I DON'T FUCKING CARE.
YOU HAVE YOUR ORDERS. DEFY ME AND I'LL SEE YOU SPEND THE REST OF THE WAR FLYING A DESK IN BERLIN.
I WON'T LET THIS WAR TAKE YOUR SOUL, WERNER.
CRASH!!

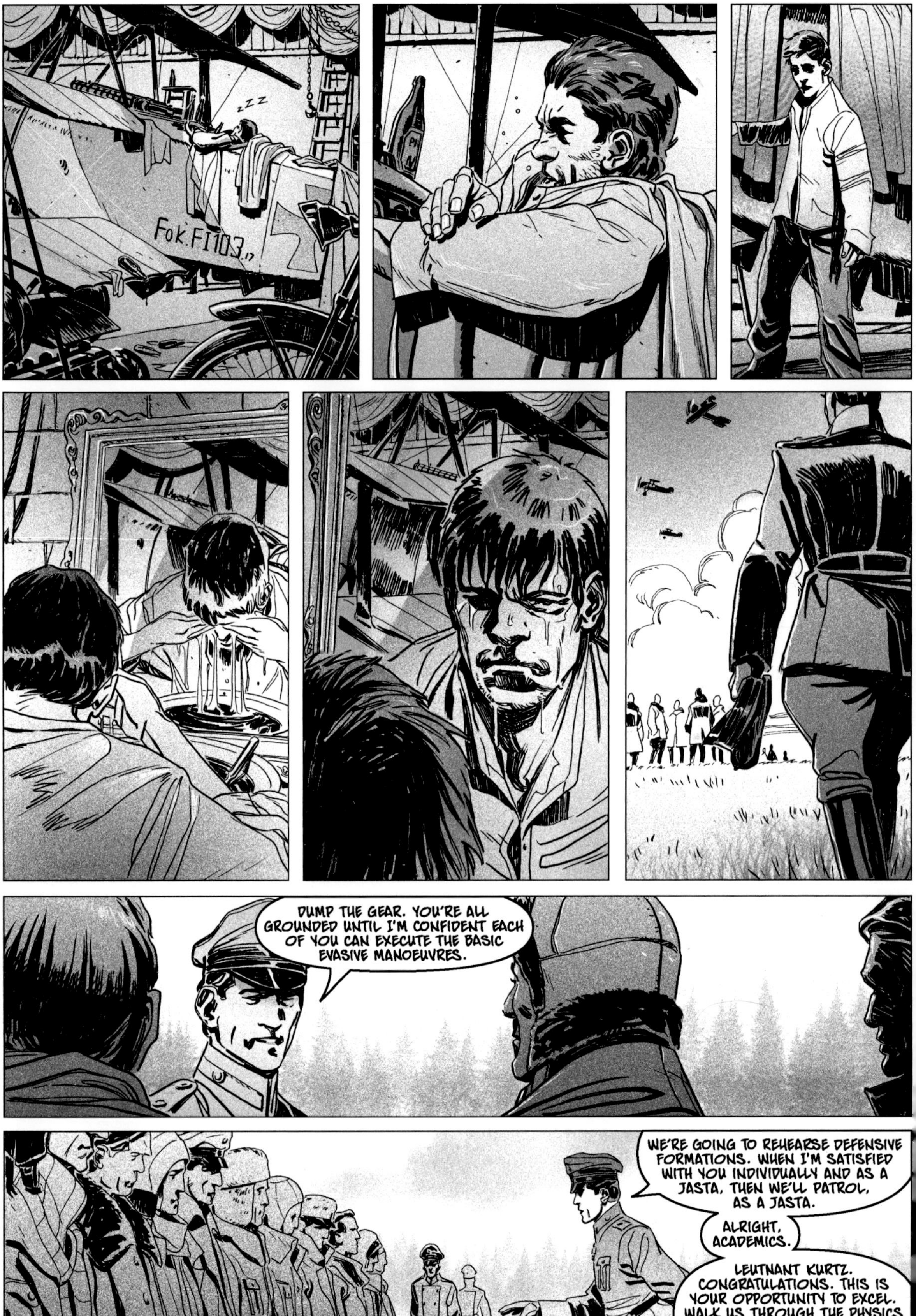
zZZ
Fok.FI103.17
DUMP THE GEAR. YOU'RE ALL GROUNDED UNTIL I'M CONFIDENT EACH OF YOU CAN EXECUTE THE BASIC EVASIVE MANOEUVRES.
WE'RE GOING TO REHEARSE DEFENSIVE FORMATIONS. WHEN I'M SATISFIED WITH YOU INDIVIDUALLY AND AS A JASTA, THEN WE'LL PATROL, AS A JASTA.
ALRIGHT, ACADEMICS.
LEUTNANT KURTZ. CONGRATULATIONS. THIS IS YOUR OPPORTUNITY TO EXCEL. WALK US THROUGH THE PHYSICS OF A BARREL ROLL FOLLOWED BY A DEFENSIVE SPIRAL.

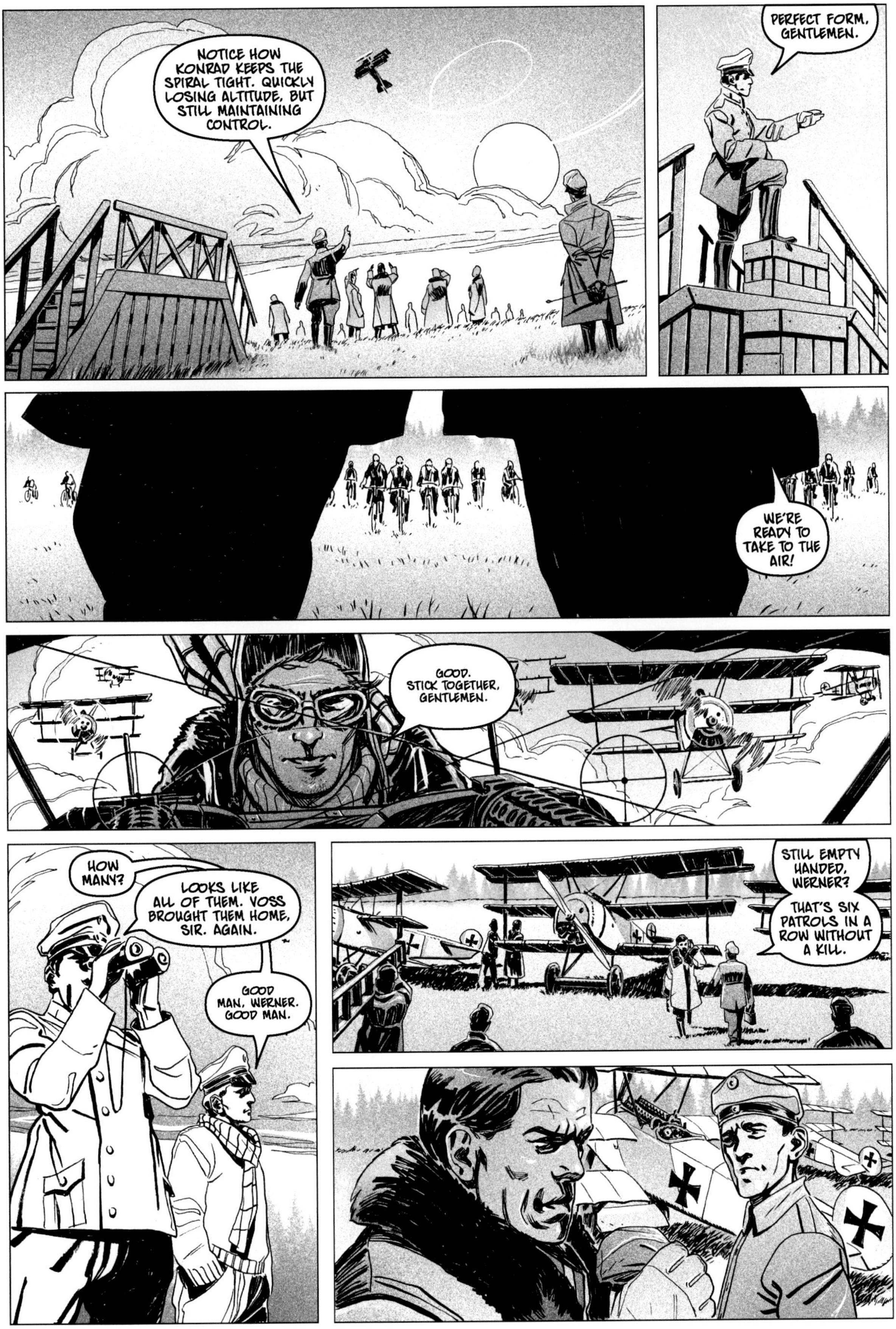
NOTICE HOW KONRAD KEEPS THE SPIRAL TIGHT. QUICKLY LOSING ALTITUDE, BUT STILL MAINTAINING CONTROL.
PERFECT FORM, GENTLEMEN.
WE'RE READY TO TAKE TO THE AIR!
GOOD. STICK TOGETHER, GENTLEMEN.
HOW MANY?
LOOKS LIKE ALL OF THEM. VOSS BROUGHT THEM HOME, SIR. AGAIN.
GOOD MAN, WERNER. GOOD MAN.
STILL EMPTY HANDED, WERNER?
THAT'S SIX PATROLS IN A ROW WITHOUT A KILL.

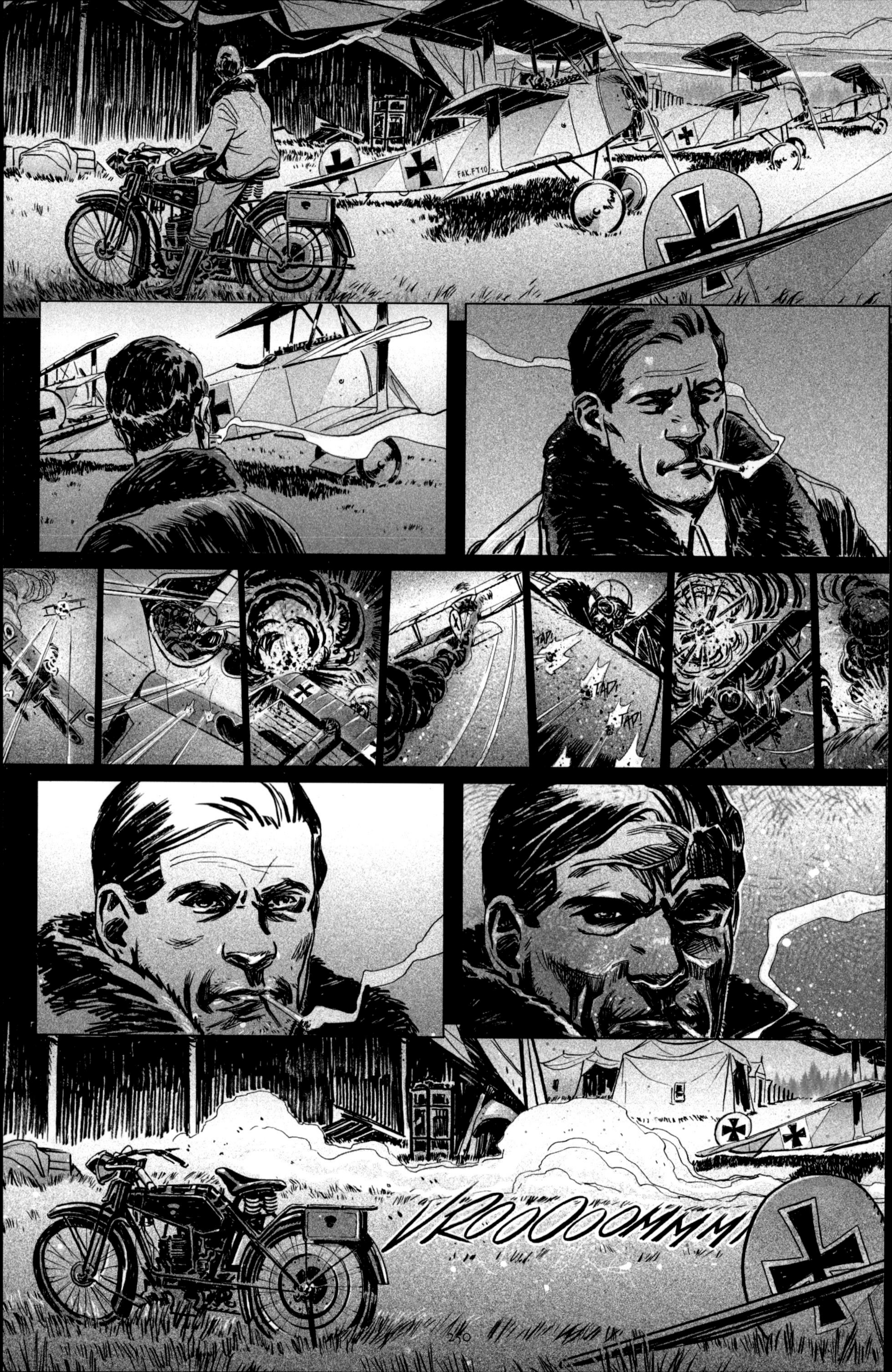
FAK.FT10
TAD!
TAD!
TAD!
VROOOOOMMMM

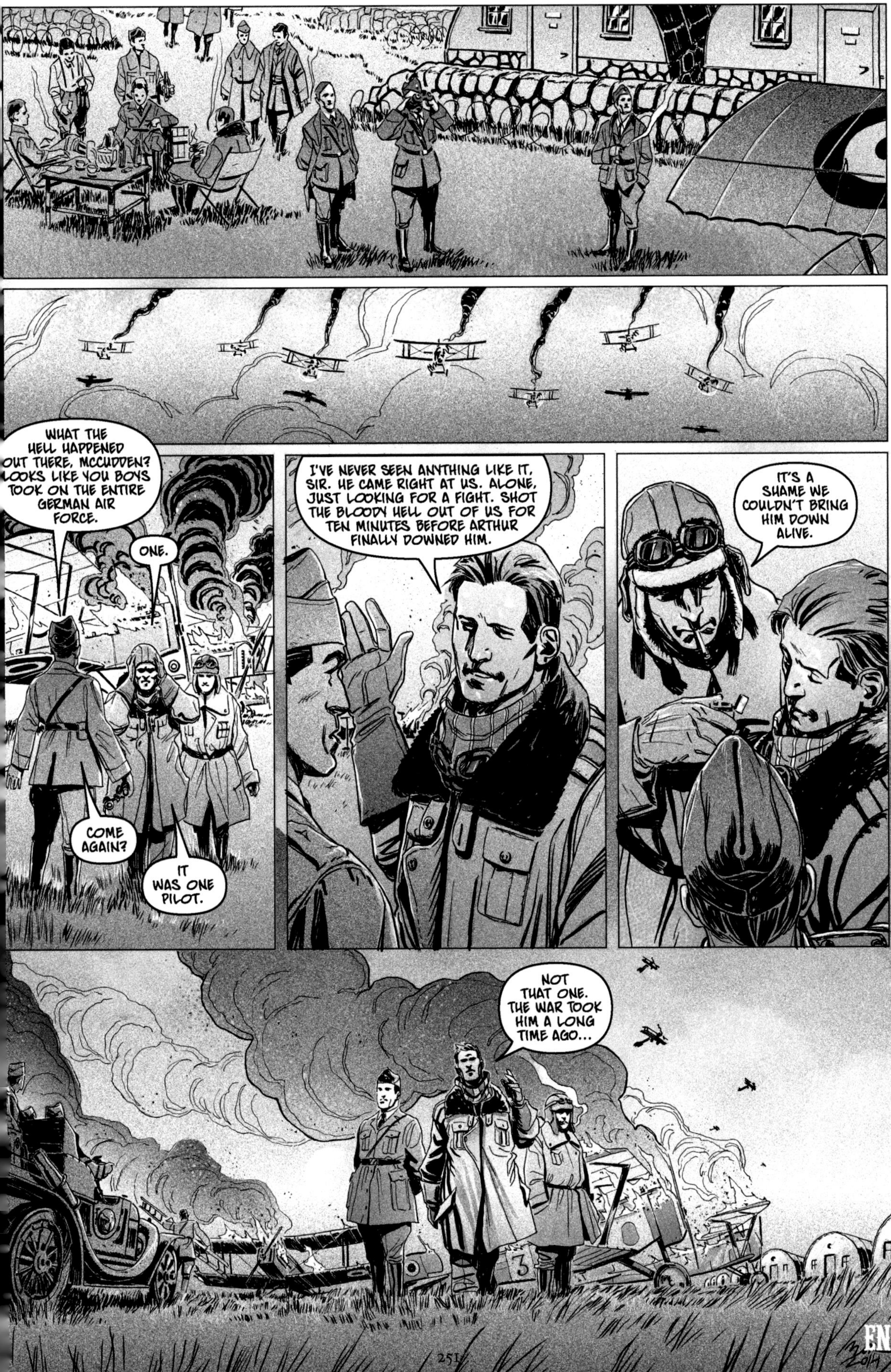
WHAT THE HELL HAPPENED OUT THERE, MCCUDDEN? LOOKS LIKE YOU BOYS TOOK ON THE ENTIRE GERMAN AIR FORCE.
ONE.
COME AGAIN?
IT WAS ONE PILOT.
I'VE NEVER SEEN ANYTHING LIKE IT, SIR. HE CAME RIGHT AT US. ALONE, JUST LOOKING FOR A FIGHT. SHOT THE BLOODY HELL OUT OF US FOR TEN MINUTES BEFORE ARTHUR FINALLY DOWNED HIM.
IT'S A SHAME WE COULDN'T BRING HIM DOWN ALIVE.
NOT THAT ONE. THE WAR TOOK HIM A LONG TIME AGO...
END

Mud, Lice and Vice

By Gary and Warren Pleece

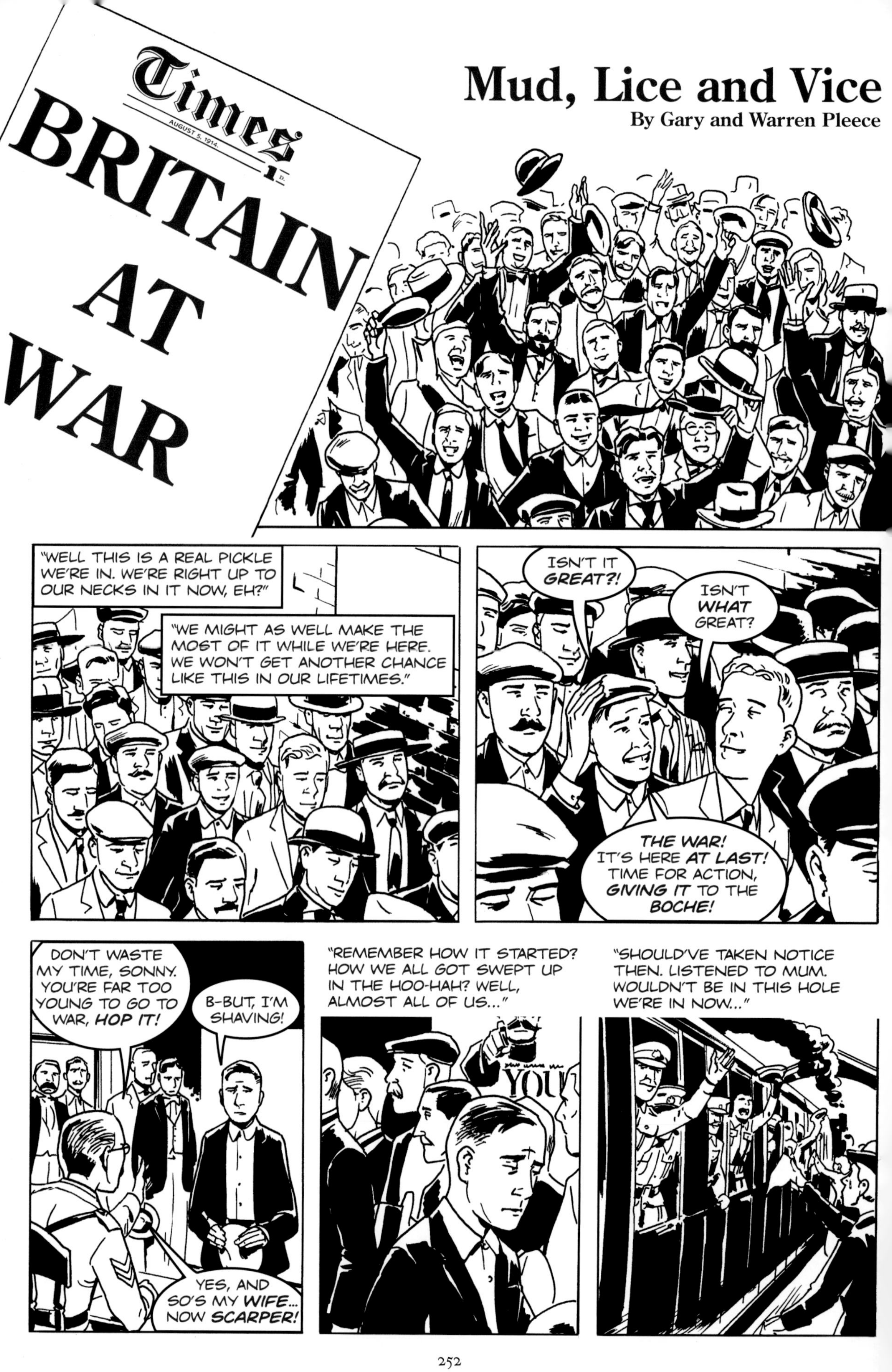
Times
AUGUST 5, 1914.
BRITAIN AT WAR
"WELL THIS IS A REAL PICKLE WE'RE IN. WE'RE RIGHT UP TO OUR NECKS IN IT NOW, EH?"
"WE MIGHT AS WELL MAKE THE MOST OF IT WHILE WE'RE HERE. WE WON'T GET ANOTHER CHANCE LIKE THIS IN OUR LIFETIMES."
ISN'T IT GREAT?!
ISN'T WHAT GREAT?
THE WAR! IT'S HERE AT LAST! TIME FOR ACTION, GIVING IT TO THE BOCHE!
DON'T WASTE MY TIME, SONNY. YOU'RE FAR TOO YOUNG TO GO TO WAR, HOP IT!
B-BUT, I'M SHAVING!
YES, AND SO'S MY WIFE... NOW SCARPER!
"REMEMBER HOW IT STARTED? HOW WE ALL GOT SWEPT UP IN THE HOO-HAH? WELL, ALMOST ALL OF US..."
YOU
"SHOULD'VE TAKEN NOTICE THEN. LISTENED TO MUM. WOULDN'T BE IN THIS HOLE WE'RE IN NOW..."

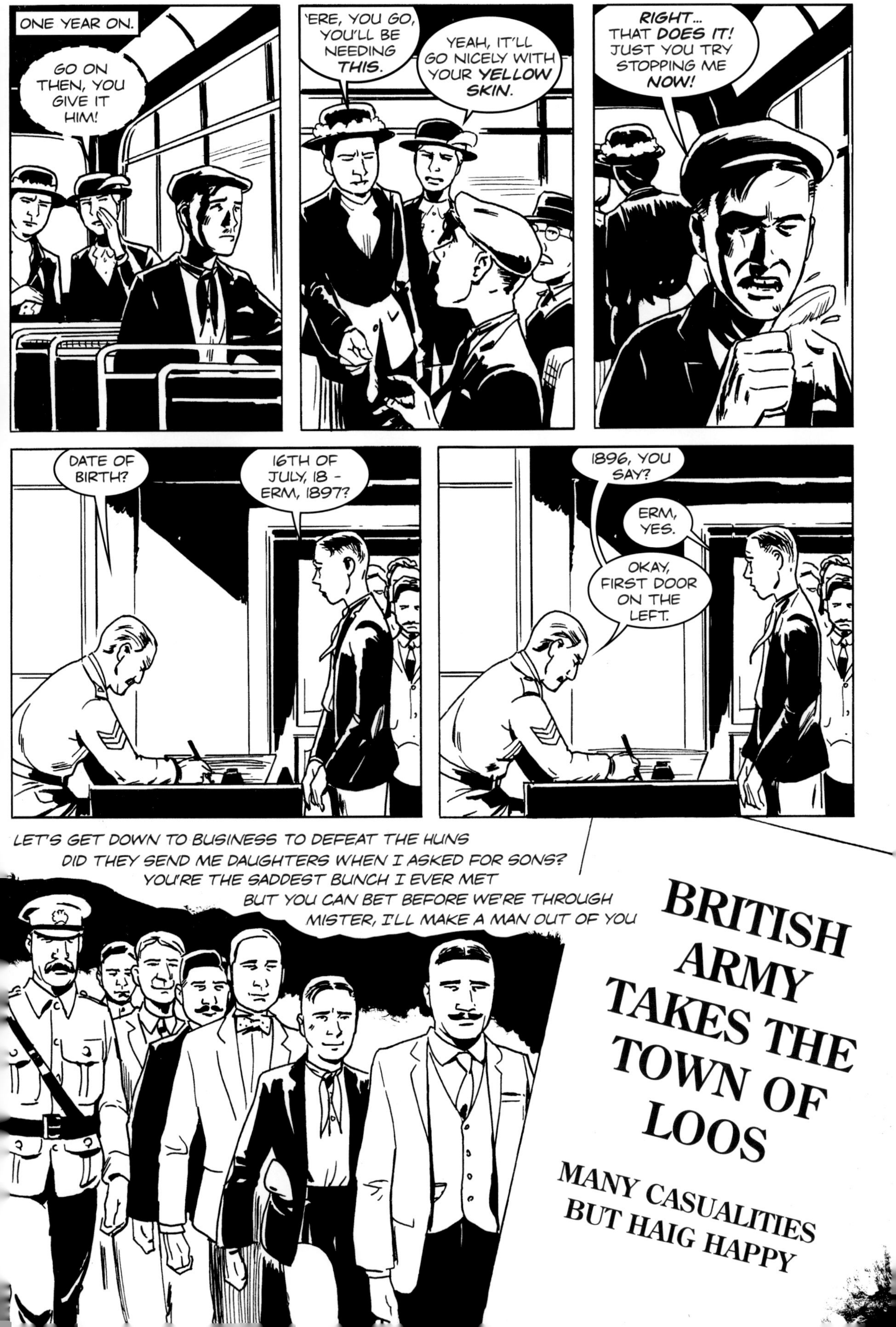
ONE YEAR ON.
GO ON THEN, YOU GIVE IT HIM!
'ERE, YOU GO, YOU'LL BE NEEDING THIS.
YEAH, IT'LL GO NICELY WITH YOUR YELLOW SKIN.
RIGHT... THAT DOES IT! JUST YOU TRY STOPPING ME NOW!
DATE OF BIRTH?
16TH OF JULY, 18 - ERM, 1897?
1896, YOU SAY?
ERM, YES.
OKAY, FIRST DOOR ON THE LEFT.
LET'S GET DOWN TO BUSINESS TO DEFEAT THE HUNS
DID THEY SEND ME DAUGHTERS WHEN I ASKED FOR SONS?
YOU'RE THE SADDEST BUNCH I EVER MET
BUT YOU CAN BET BEFORE WE'RE THROUGH
MISTER, I'LL MAKE A MAN OUT OF YOU
BRITISH ARMY TAKES THE TOWN OF LOOS
MANY CASUALITIES BUT HAIG HAPPY

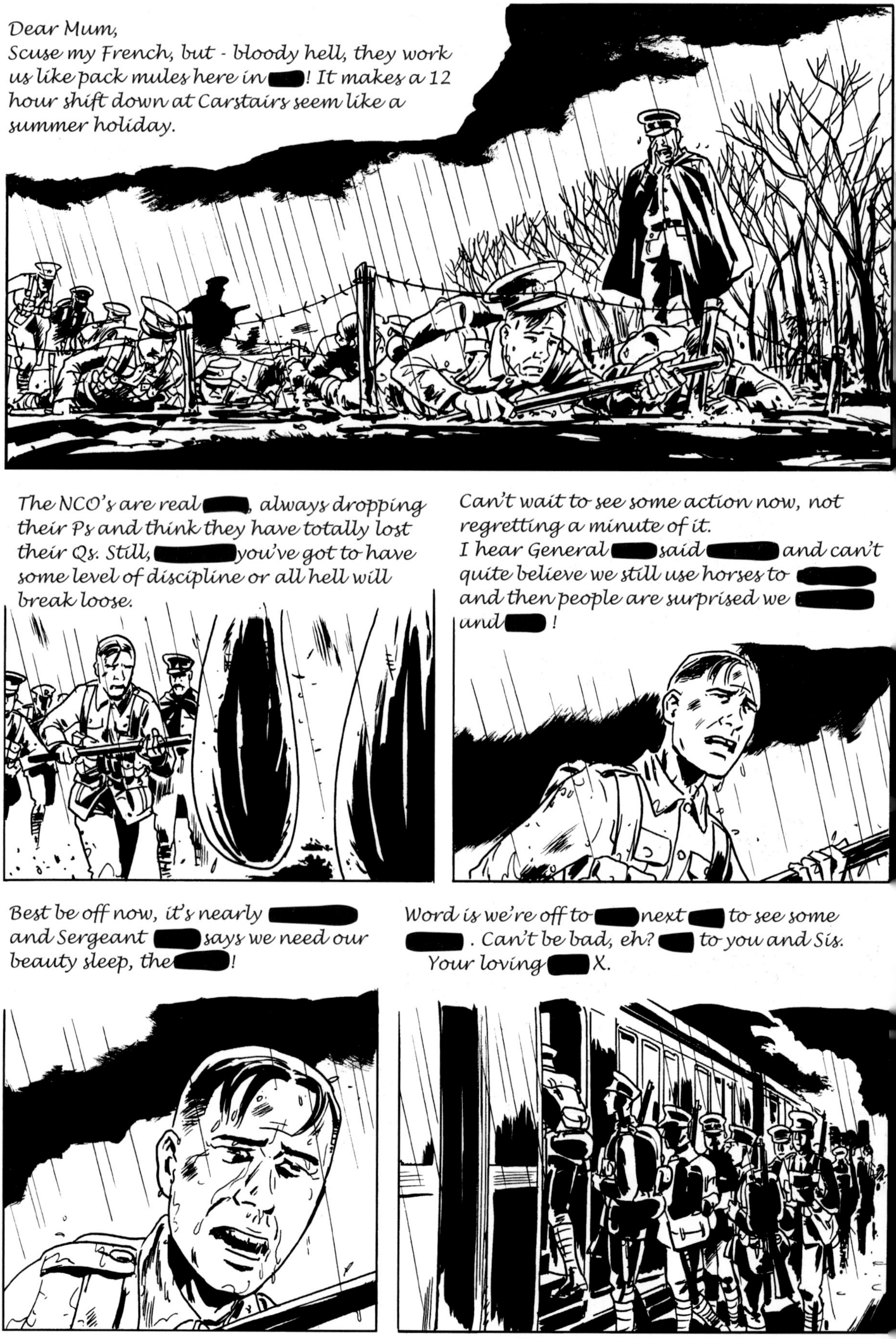
Dear Mum,
Scuse my French, but - bloody hell, they work us like pack mules here in [redacted]! It makes a 12 hour shift down at Carstairs seem like a summer holiday.
The NCO's are real [redacted], always dropping their Ps and think they have totally lost their Qs. Still, [redacted] you've got to have some level of discipline or all hell will break loose.
Can't wait to see some action now, not regretting a minute of it.
I hear General [redacted] said [redacted] and can't quite believe we still use horses to [redacted] and then people are surprised we [redacted] und [redacted] !
Best be off now, it's nearly [redacted] and Sergeant [redacted] says we need our beauty sleep, the [redacted]!
Word is we're off to [redacted] next [redacted] to see some [redacted]. Can't be bad, eh? [redacted] to you and Sis.
Your loving [redacted] X.

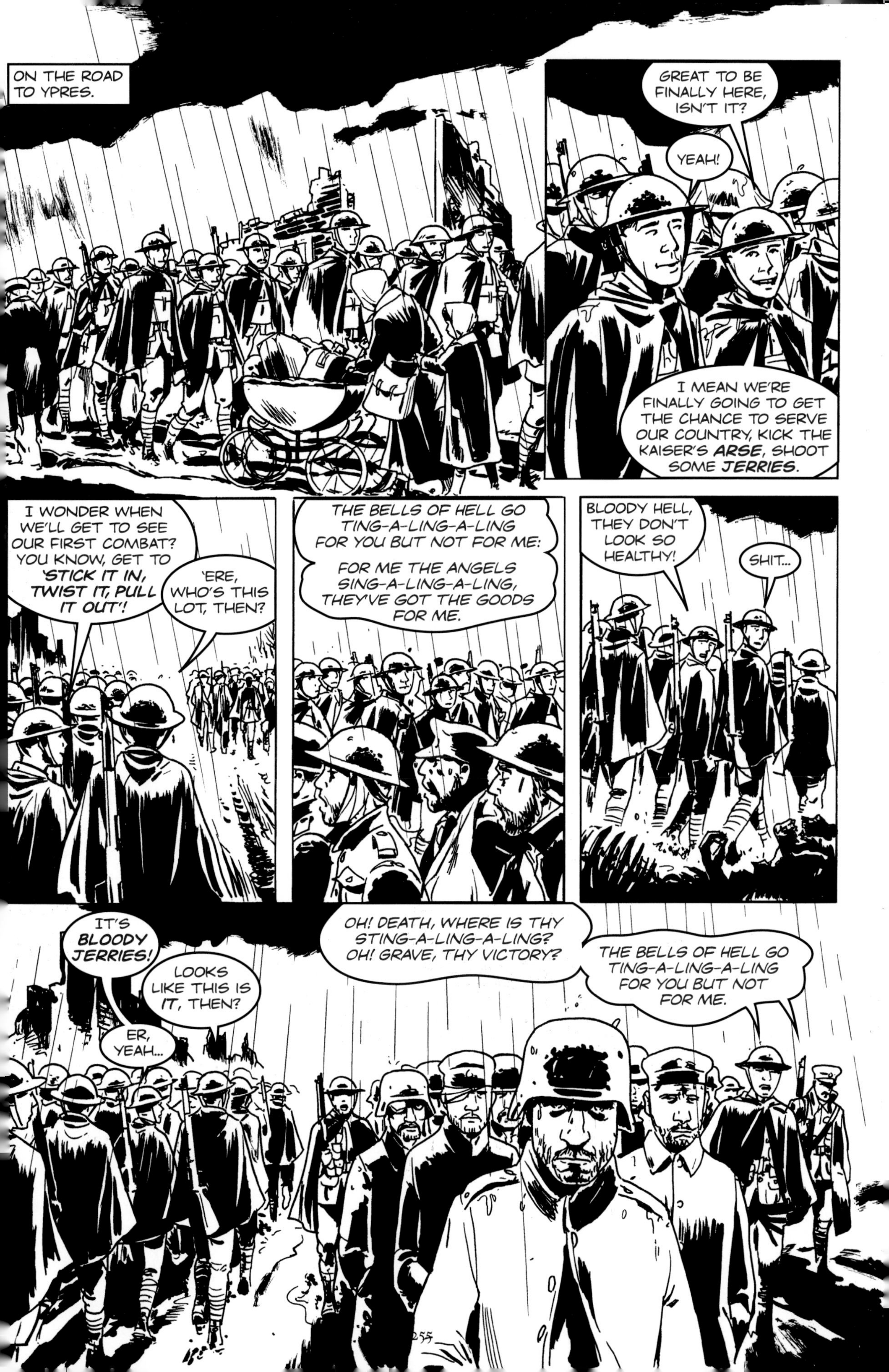

ON THE ROAD TO YPRES.
GREAT TO BE FINALLY HERE, ISN'T IT?
YEAH!
I MEAN WE'RE FINALLY GOING TO GET THE CHANCE TO SERVE OUR COUNTRY, KICK THE KAISER'S **ARSE**, SHOOT SOME **JERRIES**.
I WONDER WHEN WE'LL GET TO SEE OUR FIRST COMBAT? YOU KNOW, GET TO **'STICK IT IN, TWIST IT, PULL IT OUT'**!
'ERE, WHO'S THIS LOT, THEN?
THE BELLS OF HELL GO TING-A-LING-A-LING FOR YOU BUT NOT FOR ME:
FOR ME THE ANGELS SING-A-LING-A-LING, THEY'VE GOT THE GOODS FOR ME.
BLOODY HELL, THEY DON'T LOOK SO HEALTHY!
SHIT...
IT'S **BLOODY JERRIES!**
LOOKS LIKE THIS IS **IT**, THEN?
ER, YEAH...
OH! DEATH, WHERE IS THY STING-A-LING-A-LING? OH! GRAVE, THY VICTORY?
THE BELLS OF HELL GO TING-A-LING-A-LING FOR YOU BUT NOT FOR ME.

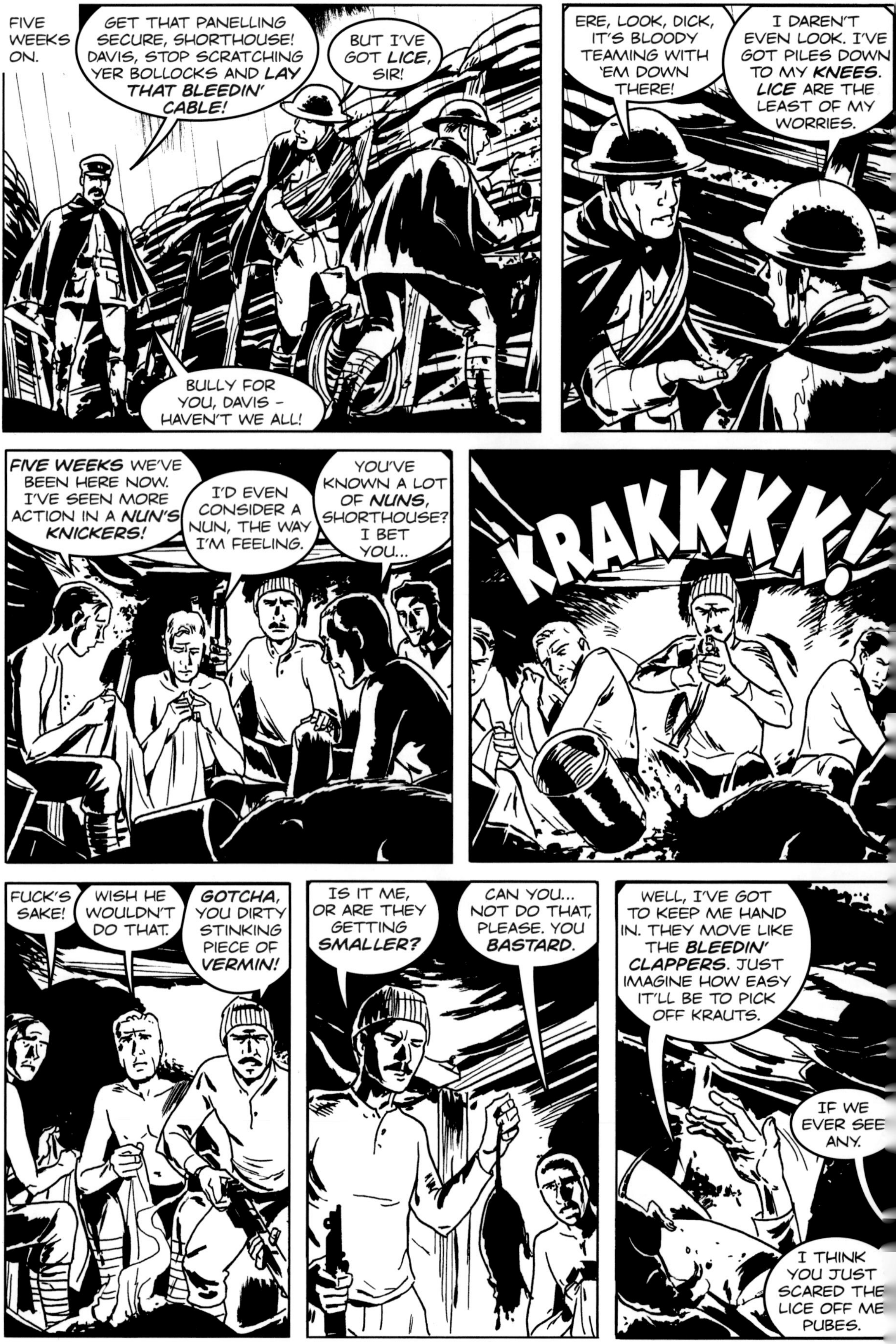
FIVE WEEKS ON.
GET THAT PANELLING SECURE, SHORTHOUSE! DAVIS, STOP SCRATCHING YER BOLLOCKS AND LAY THAT BLEEDIN' CABLE!
BUT I'VE GOT LICE, SIR!
BULLY FOR YOU, DAVIS – HAVEN'T WE ALL!
ERE, LOOK, DICK, IT'S BLOODY TEAMING WITH 'EM DOWN THERE!
I DAREN'T EVEN LOOK. I'VE GOT PILES DOWN TO MY KNEES. LICE ARE THE LEAST OF MY WORRIES.
FIVE WEEKS WE'VE BEEN HERE NOW. I'VE SEEN MORE ACTION IN A NUN'S KNICKERS!
I'D EVEN CONSIDER A NUN, THE WAY I'M FEELING.
YOU'VE KNOWN A LOT OF NUNS, SHORTHOUSE? I BET YOU...
KRAKKKK!
FUCK'S SAKE!
WISH HE WOULDN'T DO THAT.
GOTCHA, YOU DIRTY STINKING PIECE OF VERMIN!
IS IT ME, OR ARE THEY GETTING SMALLER?
CAN YOU... NOT DO THAT, PLEASE. YOU BASTARD.
WELL, I'VE GOT TO KEEP ME HAND IN. THEY MOVE LIKE THE BLEEDIN' CLAPPERS. JUST IMAGINE HOW EASY IT'LL BE TO PICK OFF KRAUTS.
IF WE EVER SEE ANY.
I THINK YOU JUST SCARED THE LICE OFF ME PUBES.

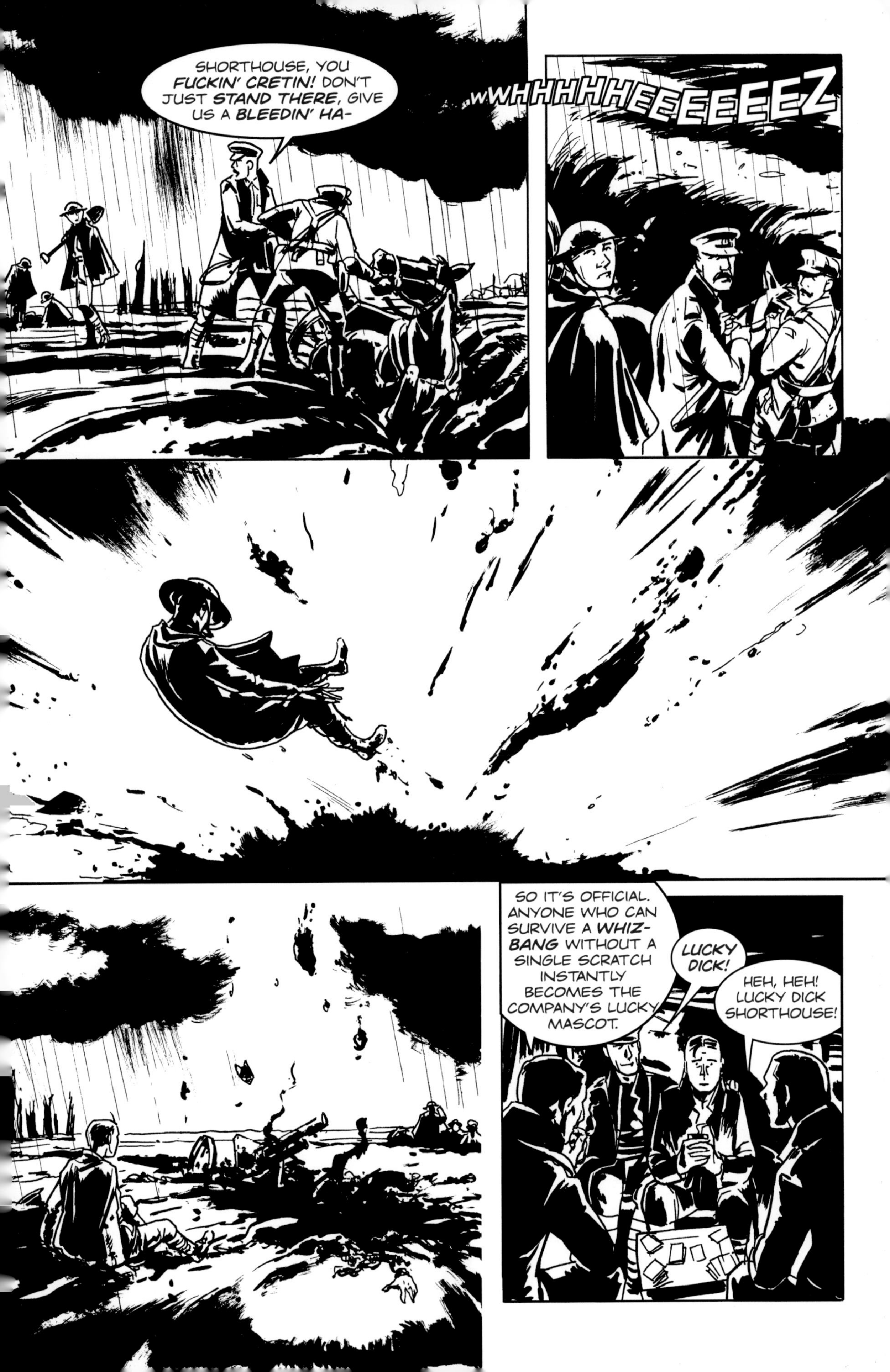

SHORTHOUSE, YOU FUCKIN' CRETIN! DON'T JUST STAND THERE, GIVE US A BLEEDIN' HA-
WWHHHHHEEEEEEEZ
SO IT'S OFFICIAL. ANYONE WHO CAN SURVIVE A WHIZ-BANG WITHOUT A SINGLE SCRATCH INSTANTLY BECOMES THE COMPANY'S LUCKY MASCOT.
LUCKY DICK!
HEH, HEH! LUCKY DICK SHORTHOUSE!

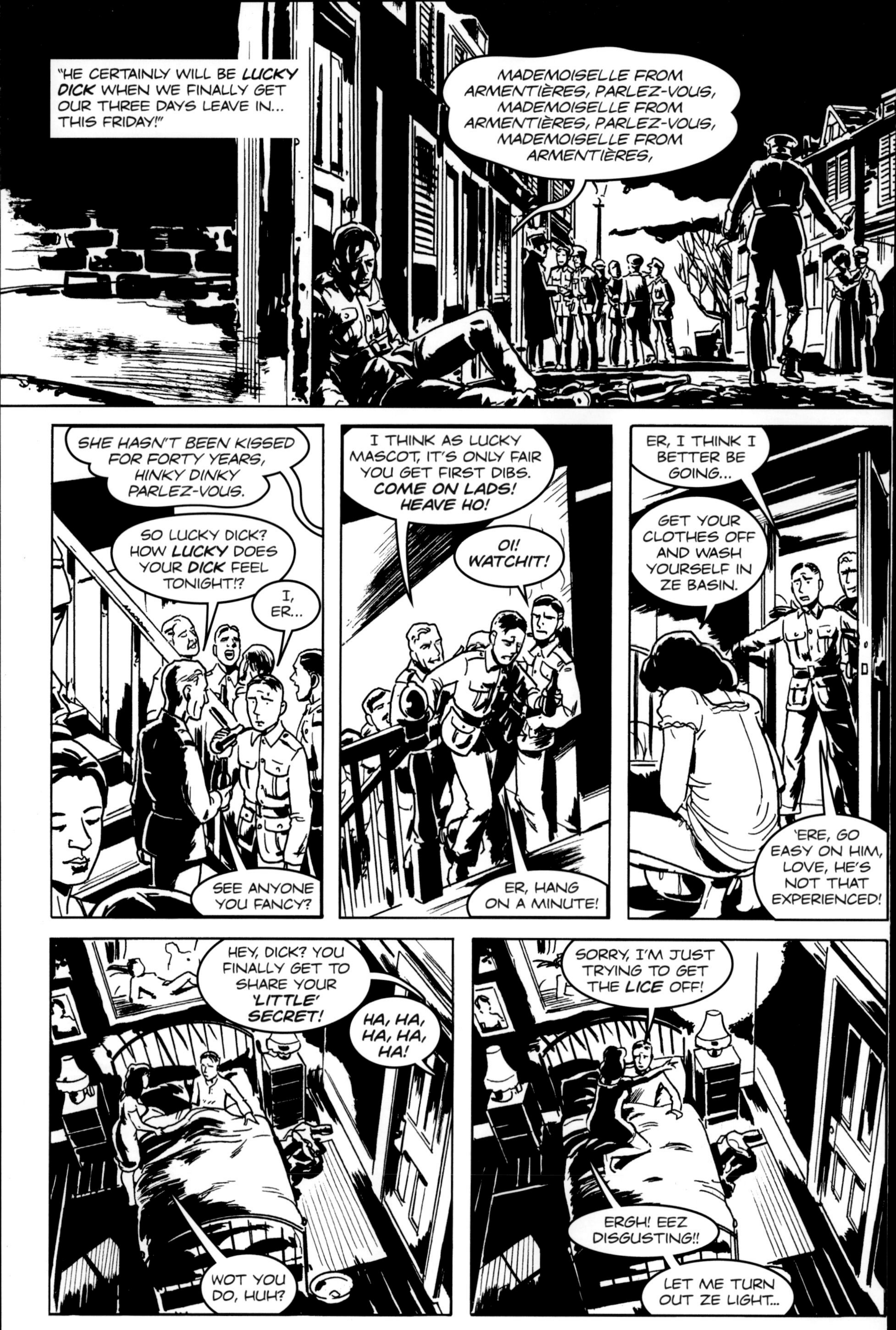
"HE CERTAINLY WILL BE **LUCKY DICK** WHEN WE FINALLY GET OUR THREE DAYS LEAVE IN... THIS FRIDAY!"
MADEMOISELLE FROM ARMENTIÈRES, PARLEZ-VOUS, MADEMOISELLE FROM ARMENTIÈRES, PARLEZ-VOUS, MADEMOISELLE FROM ARMENTIÈRES,
SHE HASN'T BEEN KISSED FOR FORTY YEARS, HINKY DINKY PARLEZ-VOUS.
SO LUCKY DICK? HOW **LUCKY** DOES YOUR **DICK** FEEL TONIGHT!?
I, ER...
SEE ANYONE YOU FANCY?
I THINK AS LUCKY MASCOT, IT'S ONLY FAIR YOU GET FIRST DIBS. ***COME ON LADS! HEAVE HO!***
OI! WATCHIT!
ER, HANG ON A MINUTE!
ER, I THINK I BETTER BE GOING...
GET YOUR CLOTHES OFF AND WASH YOURSELF IN ZE BASIN.
'ERE, GO EASY ON HIM, LOVE, HE'S NOT THAT EXPERIENCED!
HEY, DICK? YOU FINALLY GET TO SHARE YOUR ***'LITTLE' SECRET!***
HA, HA, HA, HA, HA!
WOT YOU DO, HUH?
SORRY, I'M JUST TRYING TO GET THE ***LICE*** OFF!
ERGH! EEZ DISGUSTING!!
LET ME TURN OUT ZE LIGHT...

Dear darling, Dicky. I hope the war is treating you well and that you are keeping out of harm's way and getting enough food down you. Me, Rosie and your Father all miss you terribly and we are always thinking of you.

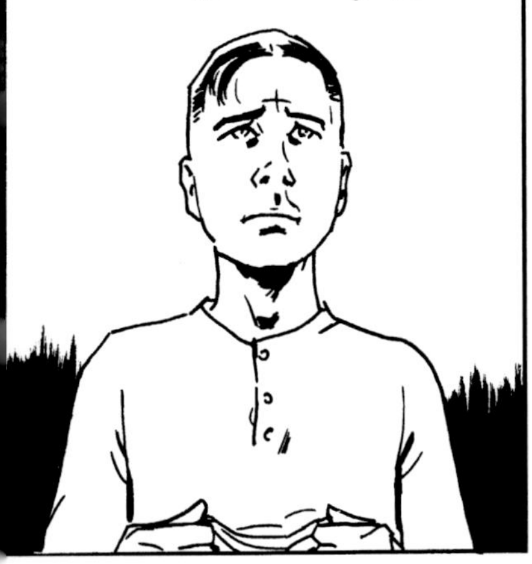

This year's crop of peaches and plums was a sorry affair, all blotchy and shrivelled.

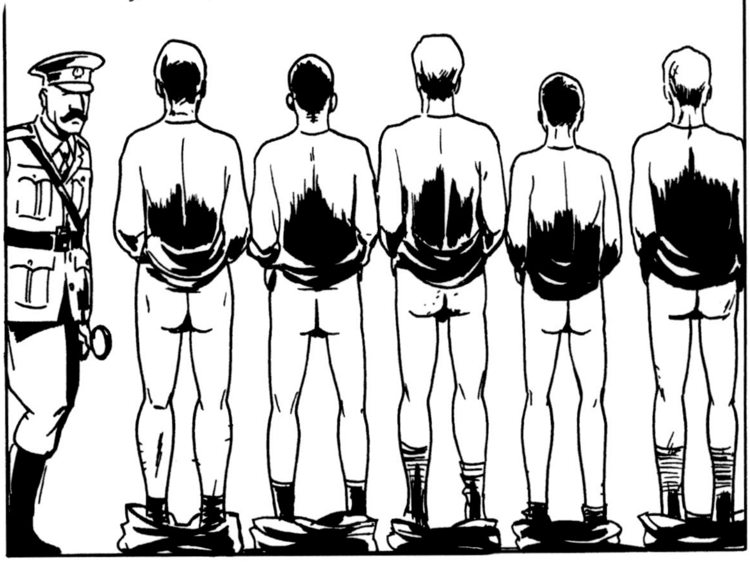

We tried making some of your favourite pies from this year's harvest. Wish I could have sent you some over, but I blame this blasted war.

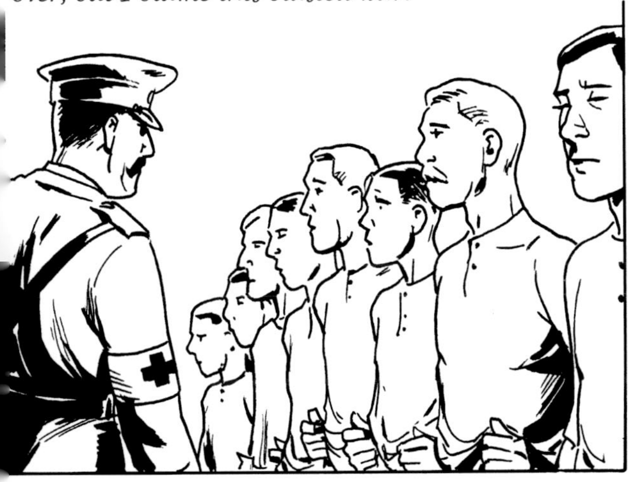

No amount of sugar coating could ever hope to cover up this year's sour and bitter plums...

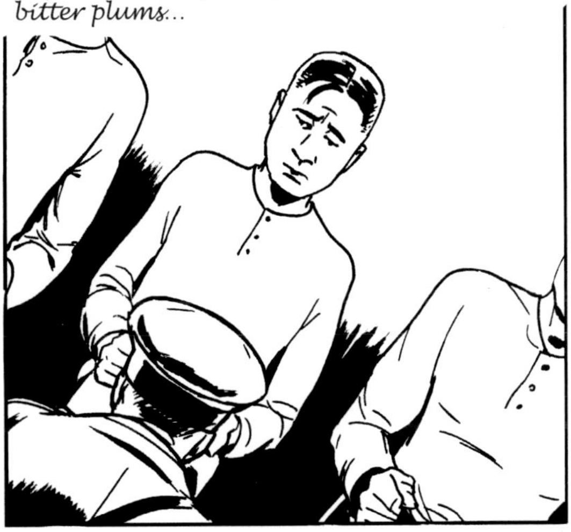

Hopefully Dad will have better luck with his carrots this winter.

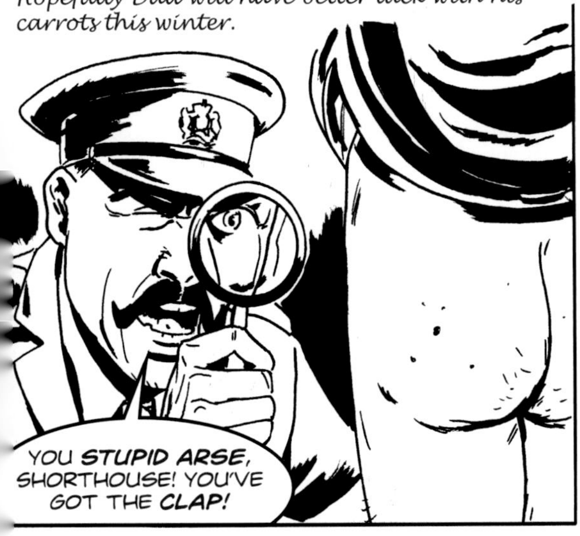
YOU STUPID ARSE, SHORTHOUSE! YOU'VE GOT THE CLAP!

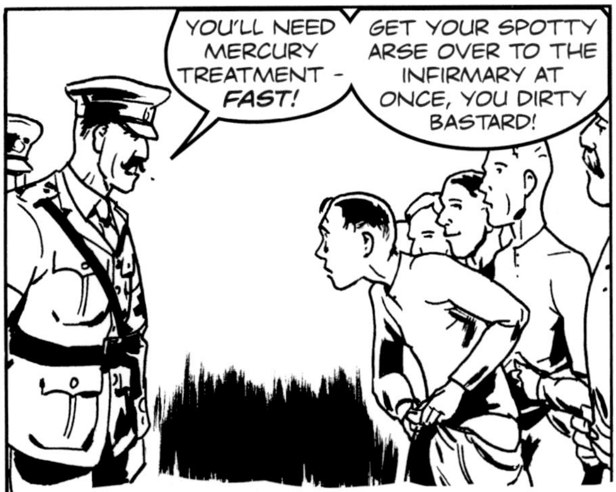
YOU'LL NEED MERCURY TREATMENT - FAST!
GET YOUR SPOTTY ARSE OVER TO THE INFIRMARY AT ONCE, YOU DIRTY BASTARD!

Best be off now, I've got a Spotted Dick in the oven.
Keep your pecker up, son.
Lot's of love,
Mother, Rosie and Father x

WE CAME WE SAW WE
CONQUERED,
WE SNIFFED, WE SCRATCHED,
WE BONKERED!

MUD, LICE AND VICE,
LITTLE OF IT IS VERY NICE,
BUT WE DON'T HOLD SWAY,
BY THE HUMDRUM DAY

WITH THE BULLETS
AND THE RATS
AND THE PLEASURE GAPS!

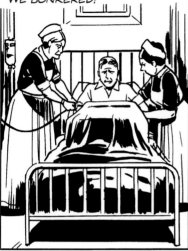  

*"Dear Chaps,
and Davis,"*

*"Thought I'd let you know that
I'm finally coming back to help
you sorry lot out..."*

*"Had quite enough of all this
lovely hot food, soft feathery
beds and sweetly perfumed
women..."*

*"I tell you, it's bloody
hard work over here on
civvy street. Seems only
fair that I take me
chances against the
Boche again. Tell Jacko
to save some lice pudding
for me.
Best regards, Dick."*

FOR
LUCK.

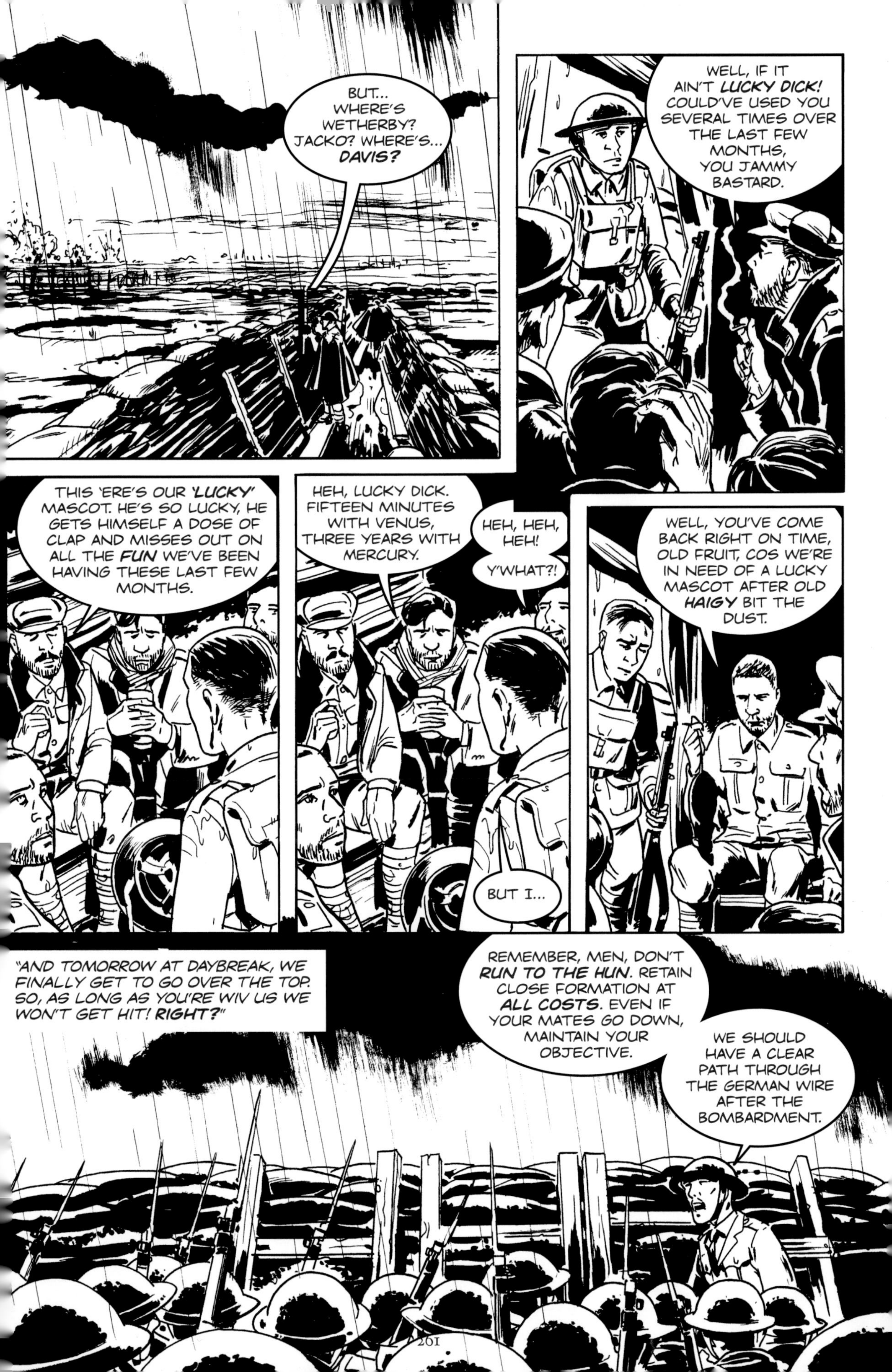
BUT... WHERE'S WETHERBY? JACKO? WHERE'S... **DAVIS?**
WELL, IF IT AIN'T **LUCKY DICK!** COULD'VE USED YOU SEVERAL TIMES OVER THE LAST FEW MONTHS, YOU JAMMY BASTARD.
THIS 'ERE'S OUR **'LUCKY'** MASCOT. HE'S SO LUCKY, HE GETS HIMSELF A DOSE OF CLAP AND MISSES OUT ON ALL THE **FUN** WE'VE BEEN HAVING THESE LAST FEW MONTHS.
HEH, LUCKY DICK. FIFTEEN MINUTES WITH VENUS, THREE YEARS WITH MERCURY.
HEH, HEH, HEH!
Y'WHAT?!
BUT I...
WELL, YOU'VE COME BACK RIGHT ON TIME, OLD FRUIT, COS WE'RE IN NEED OF A LUCKY MASCOT AFTER OLD **HAIGY** BIT THE DUST.
*"AND TOMORROW AT DAYBREAK, WE FINALLY GET TO GO OVER THE TOP. SO, AS LONG AS YOU'RE WIV US WE WON'T GET HIT! **RIGHT?**"*
REMEMBER, MEN, DON'T **RUN TO THE HUN**. RETAIN CLOSE FORMATION AT **ALL COSTS**. EVEN IF YOUR MATES GO DOWN, MAINTAIN YOUR OBJECTIVE.
WE SHOULD HAVE A CLEAR PATH THROUGH THE GERMAN WIRE AFTER THE BOMBARDMENT.

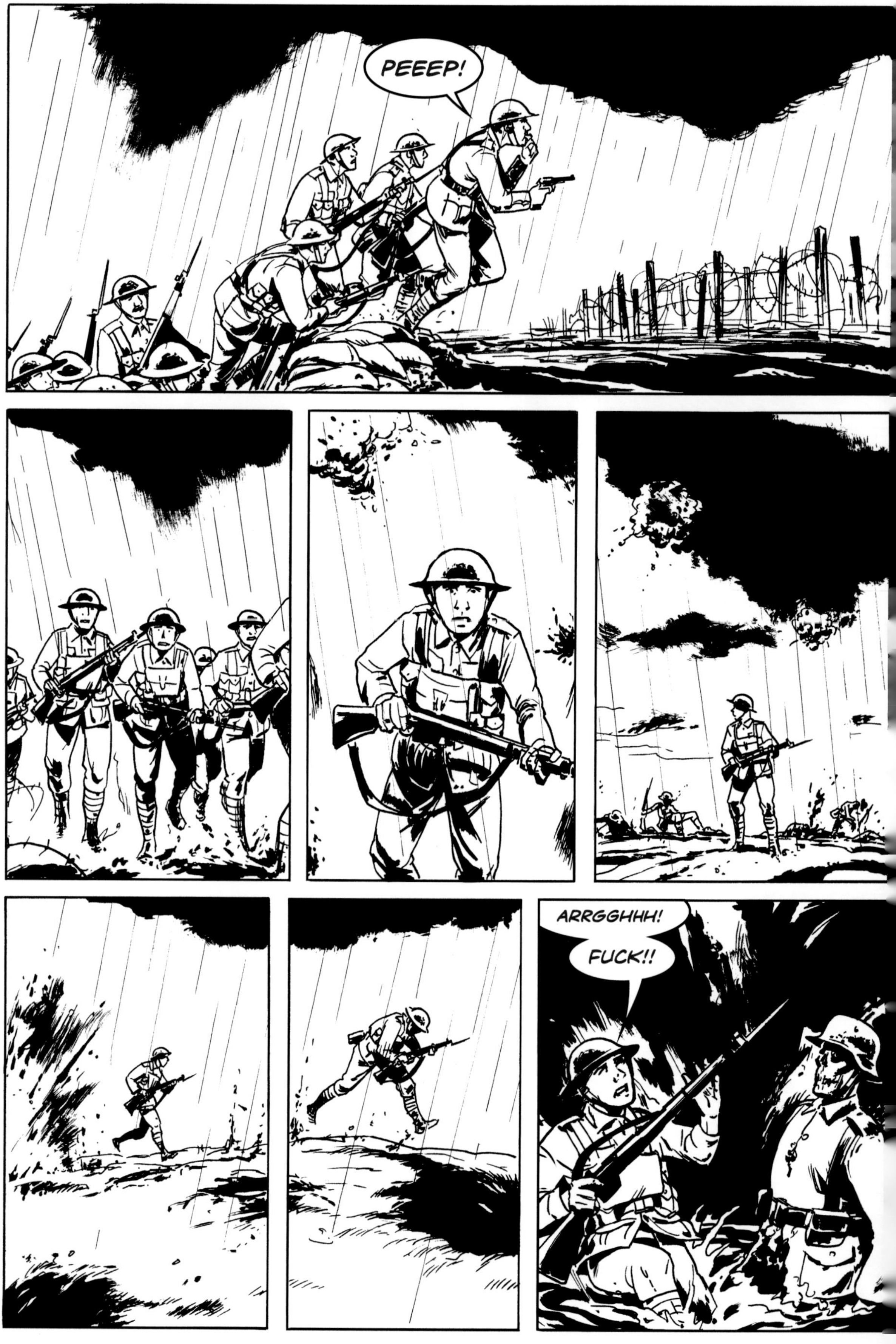
PEEEP!
ARRGGHHH!
FUCK!!

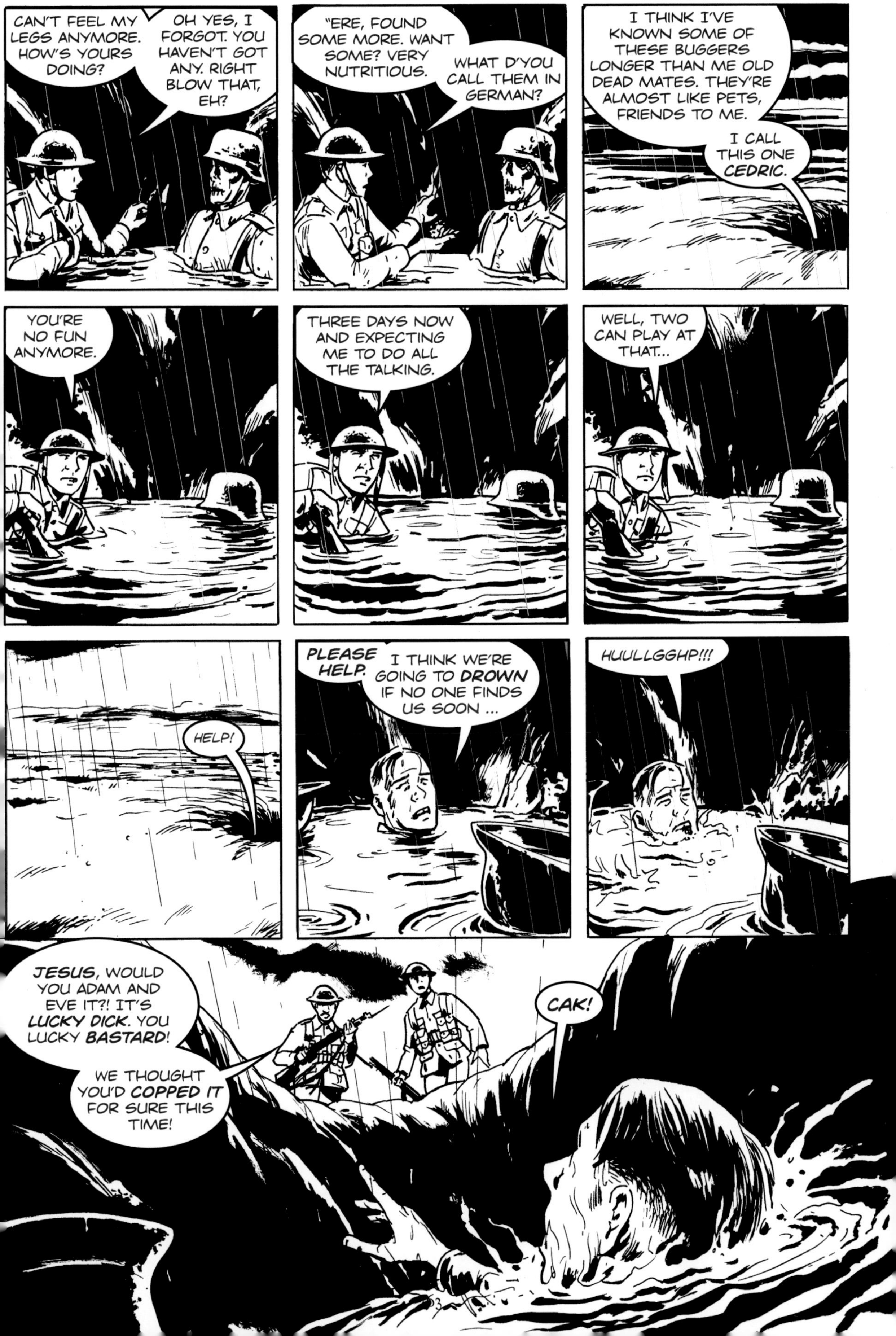
CAN'T FEEL MY LEGS ANYMORE. HOW'S YOURS DOING?
OH YES, I FORGOT. YOU HAVEN'T GOT ANY. RIGHT BLOW THAT, EH?
"ERE, FOUND SOME MORE. WANT SOME? VERY NUTRITIOUS.
WHAT D'YOU CALL THEM IN GERMAN?
I THINK I'VE KNOWN SOME OF THESE BUGGERS LONGER THAN ME OLD DEAD MATES. THEY'RE ALMOST LIKE PETS, FRIENDS TO ME.
I CALL THIS ONE **CEDRIC.**
YOU'RE NO FUN ANYMORE.
THREE DAYS NOW AND EXPECTING ME TO DO ALL THE TALKING.
WELL, TWO CAN PLAY AT THAT...
HELP!
PLEASE HELP.
I THINK WE'RE GOING TO **DROWN** IF NO ONE FINDS US SOON ...
HUULLGGHP!!!
JESUS, WOULD YOU ADAM AND EVE IT?! IT'S **LUCKY DICK**. YOU LUCKY **BASTARD**!
WE THOUGHT YOU'D **COPPED IT** FOR SURE THIS TIME!
CAK!

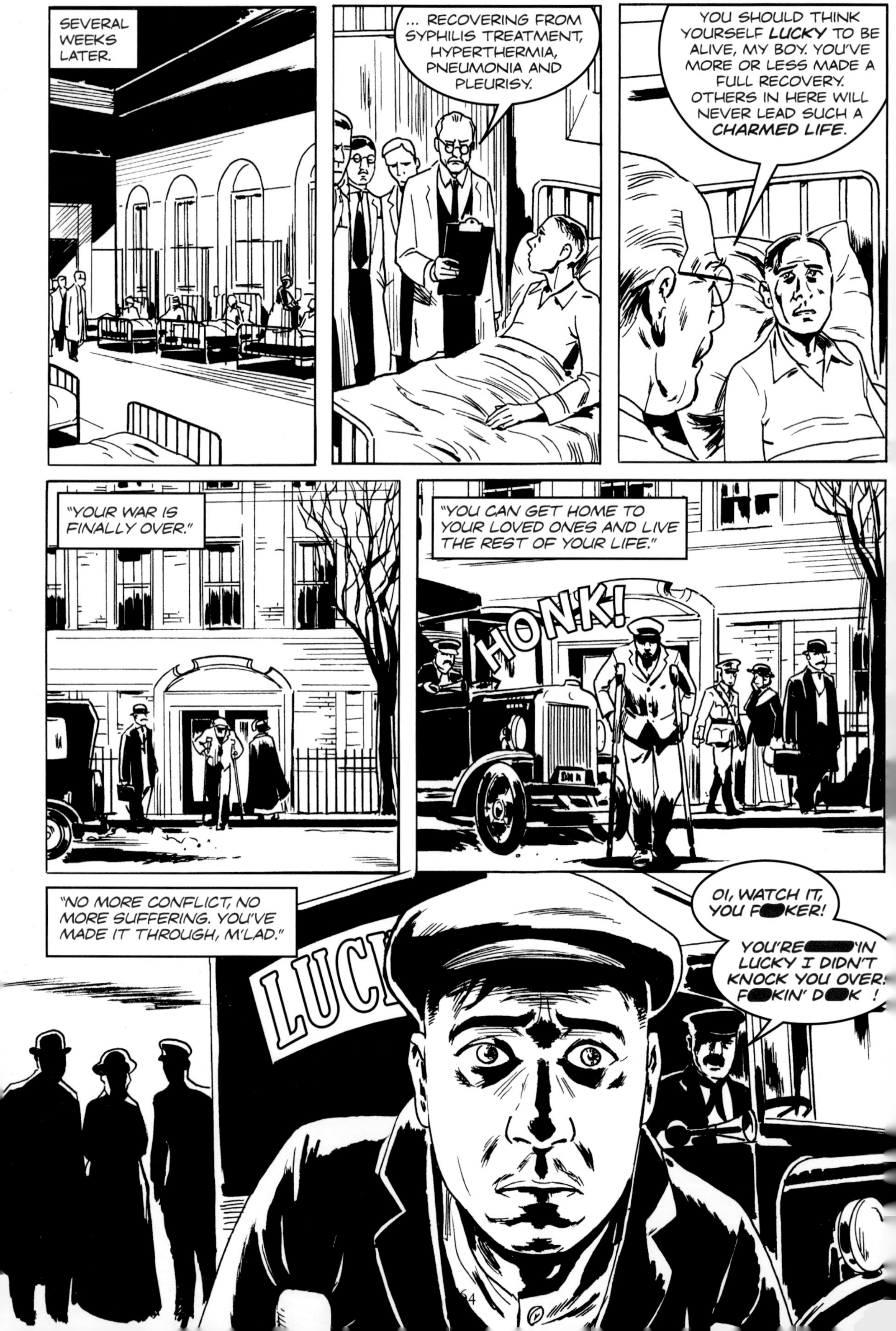
SEVERAL WEEKS LATER.
... RECOVERING FROM SYPHILIS TREATMENT, HYPERTHERMIA, PNEUMONIA AND PLEURISY.
YOU SHOULD THINK YOURSELF LUCKY TO BE ALIVE, MY BOY. YOU'VE MORE OR LESS MADE A FULL RECOVERY. OTHERS IN HERE WILL NEVER LEAD SUCH A CHARMED LIFE.
"YOUR WAR IS FINALLY OVER."
"YOU CAN GET HOME TO YOUR LOVED ONES AND LIVE THE REST OF YOUR LIFE."
HONK!
"NO MORE CONFLICT, NO MORE SUFFERING. YOU'VE MADE IT THROUGH, M'LAD."
OI, WATCH IT, YOU F[redacted]KER!
YOU'RE[redacted]'IN LUCKY I DIDN'T KNOCK YOU OVER! F[redacted]KIN' D[redacted]K !

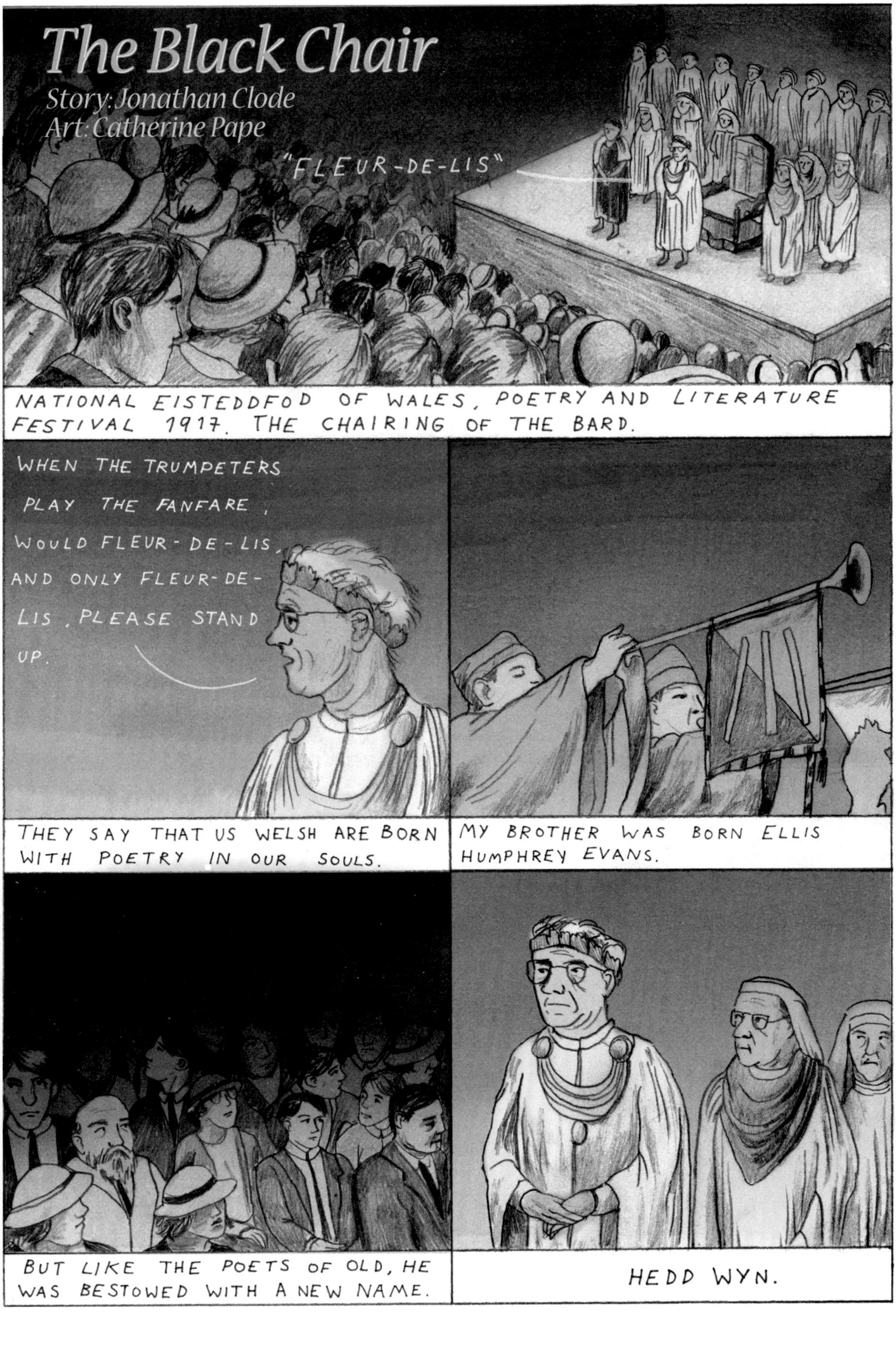
The Black Chair
Story: Jonathan Clode
Art: Catherine Pape
"FLEUR-DE-LIS"
NATIONAL EISTEDDFOD OF WALES, POETRY AND LITERATURE FESTIVAL 1917. THE CHAIRING OF THE BARD.
WHEN THE TRUMPETERS PLAY THE FANFARE, WOULD FLEUR-DE-LIS, AND ONLY FLEUR-DE-LIS, PLEASE STAND UP.
THEY SAY THAT US WELSH ARE BORN WITH POETRY IN OUR SOULS.
MY BROTHER WAS BORN ELLIS HUMPHREY EVANS.
BUT LIKE THE POETS OF OLD, HE WAS BESTOWED WITH A NEW NAME.
HEDD WYN.

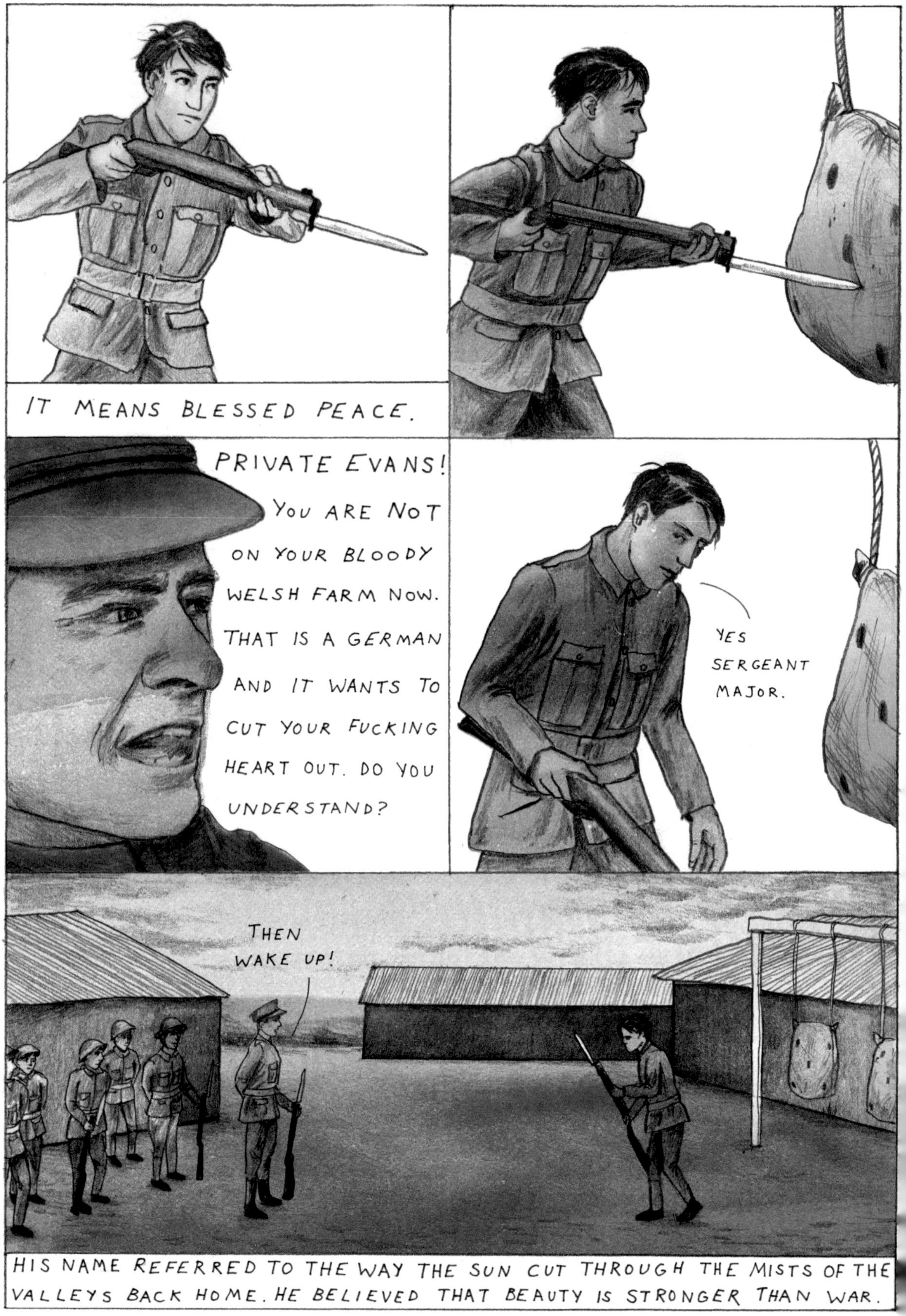
IT MEANS BLESSED PEACE.
PRIVATE EVANS! YOU ARE NOT ON YOUR BLOODY WELSH FARM NOW. THAT IS A GERMAN AND IT WANTS TO CUT YOUR FUCKING HEART OUT. DO YOU UNDERSTAND?
YES SERGEANT MAJOR.
THEN WAKE UP!
HIS NAME REFERRED TO THE WAY THE SUN CUT THROUGH THE MISTS OF THE VALLEYS BACK HOME. HE BELIEVED THAT BEAUTY IS STRONGER THAN WAR.

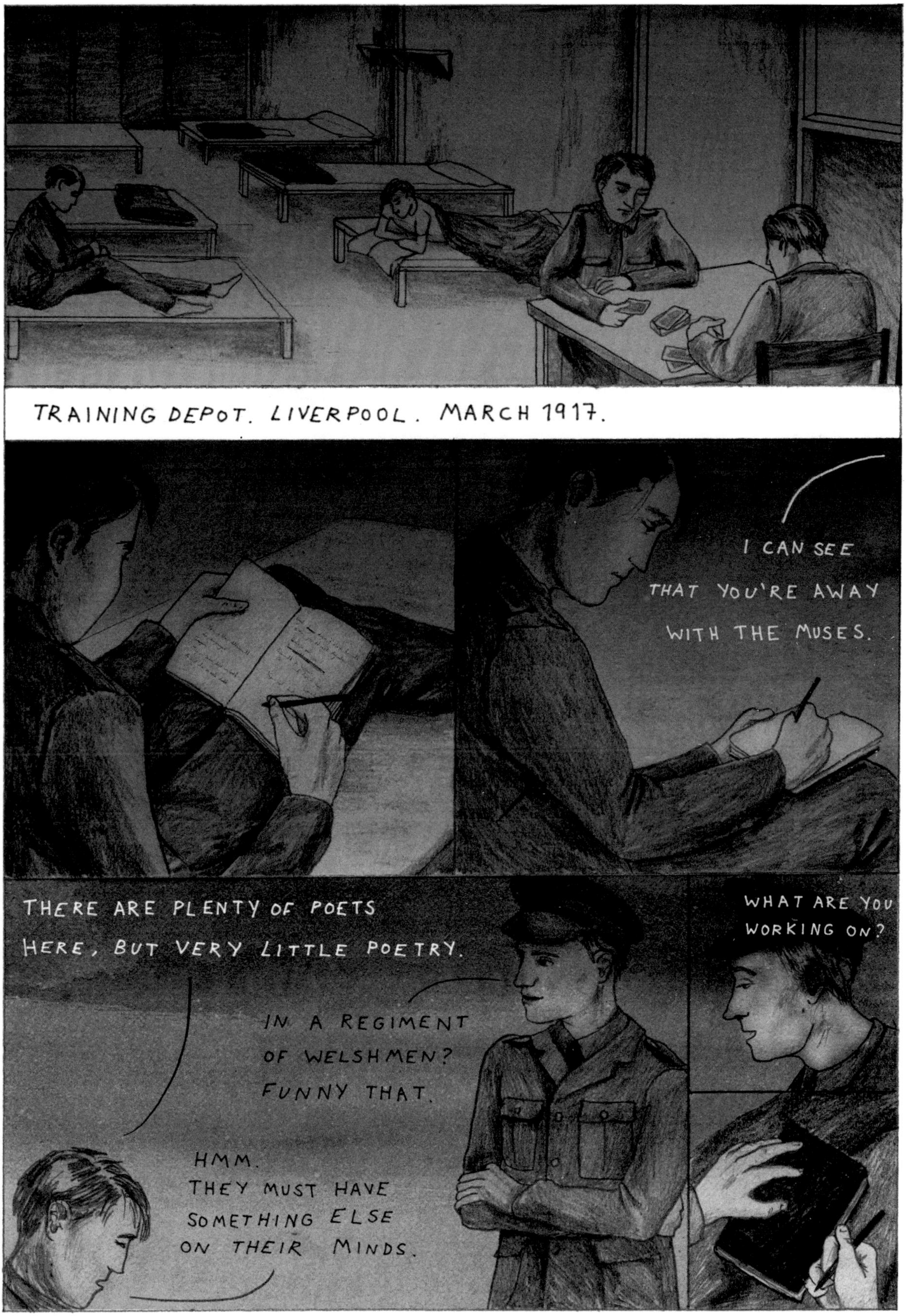
TRAINING DEPOT. LIVERPOOL. MARCH 1917.
I CAN SEE THAT YOU'RE AWAY WITH THE MUSES.
THERE ARE PLENTY OF POETS HERE, BUT VERY LITTLE POETRY.
IN A REGIMENT OF WELSHMEN? FUNNY THAT.
HMM. THEY MUST HAVE SOMETHING ELSE ON THEIR MINDS.
WHAT ARE YOU WORKING ON?

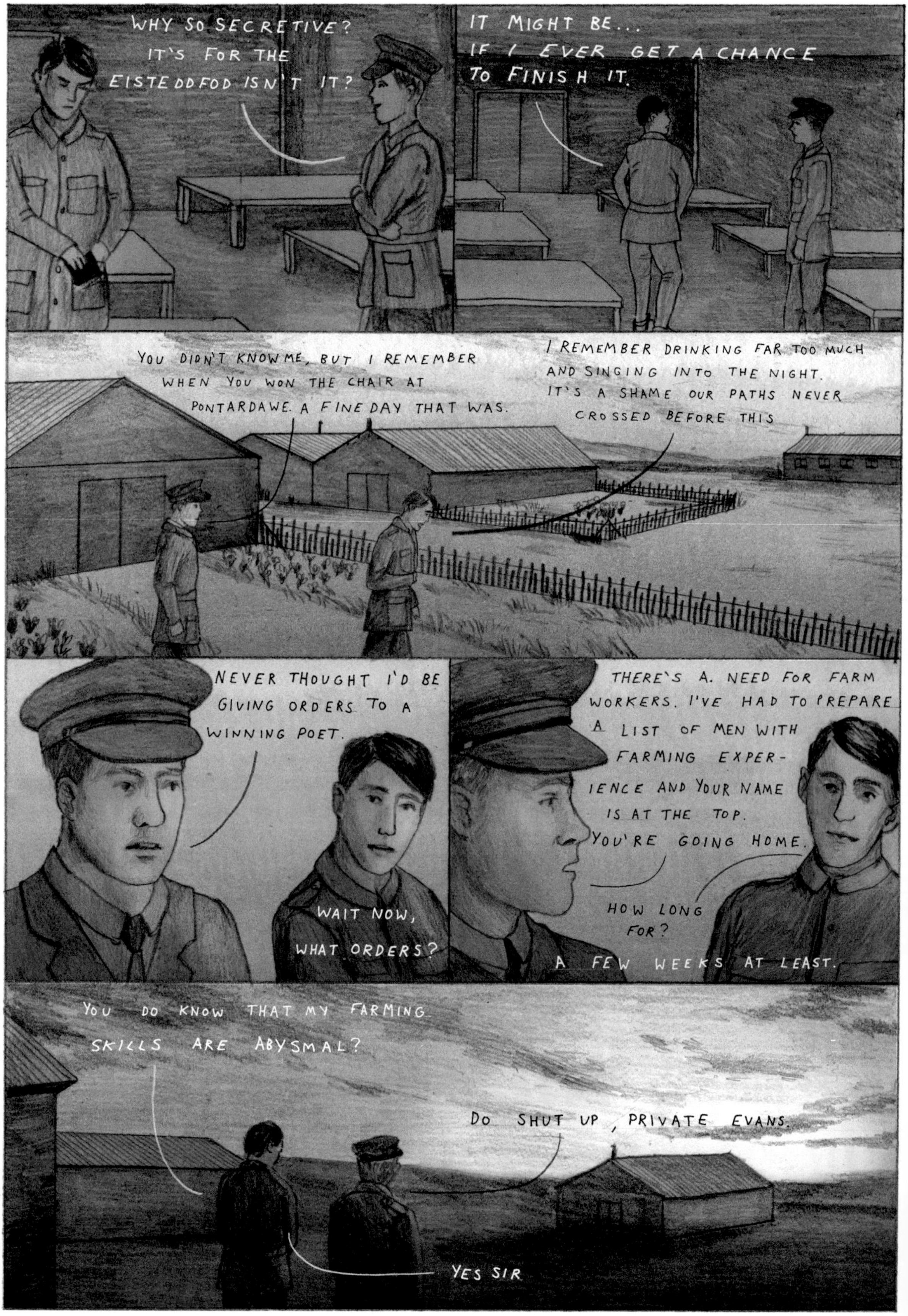
WHY SO SECRETIVE? IT'S FOR THE EISTEDDFOD ISN'T IT?
IT MIGHT BE... IF I EVER GET A CHANCE TO FINISH IT.
YOU DIDN'T KNOW ME, BUT I REMEMBER WHEN YOU WON THE CHAIR AT PONTARDAWE. A FINE DAY THAT WAS.
I REMEMBER DRINKING FAR TOO MUCH AND SINGING INTO THE NIGHT. IT'S A SHAME OUR PATHS NEVER CROSSED BEFORE THIS
NEVER THOUGHT I'D BE GIVING ORDERS TO A WINNING POET.
WAIT NOW, WHAT ORDERS?
THERE'S A NEED FOR FARM WORKERS. I'VE HAD TO PREPARE A LIST OF MEN WITH FARMING EXPERIENCE AND YOUR NAME IS AT THE TOP. YOU'RE GOING HOME.
HOW LONG FOR?
A FEW WEEKS AT LEAST.
YOU DO KNOW THAT MY FARMING SKILLS ARE ABYSMAL?
DO SHUT UP, PRIVATE EVANS.
YES SIR

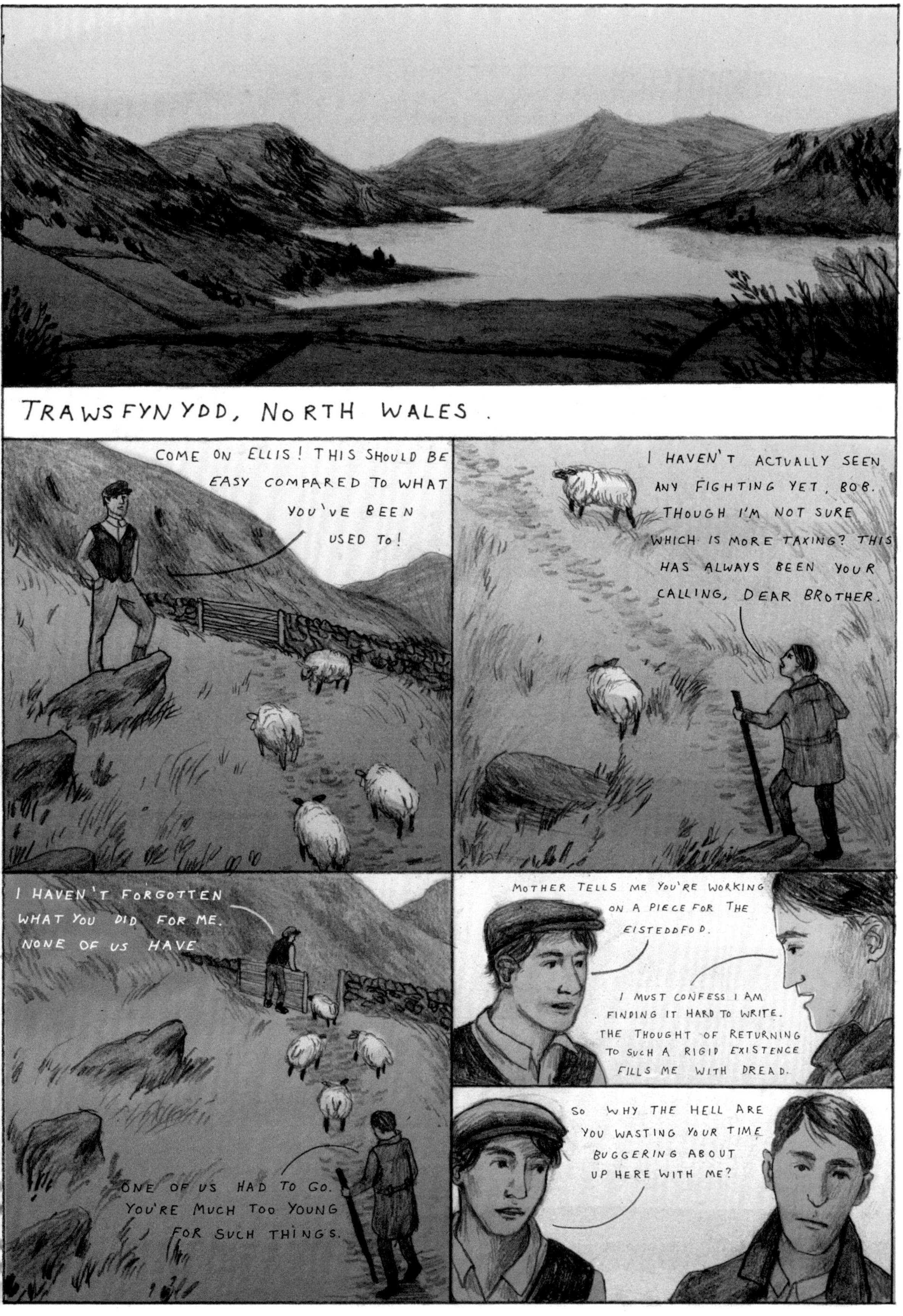
TRAWSFYNYDD, NORTH WALES.
COME ON ELLIS! THIS SHOULD BE EASY COMPARED TO WHAT YOU'VE BEEN USED TO!
I HAVEN'T ACTUALLY SEEN ANY FIGHTING YET, BOB. THOUGH I'M NOT SURE WHICH IS MORE TAXING? THIS HAS ALWAYS BEEN YOUR CALLING, DEAR BROTHER.
I HAVEN'T FORGOTTEN WHAT YOU DID FOR ME. NONE OF US HAVE
ONE OF US HAD TO GO. YOU'RE MUCH TOO YOUNG FOR SUCH THINGS.
MOTHER TELLS ME YOU'RE WORKING ON A PIECE FOR THE EISTEDDFOD.
I MUST CONFESS I AM FINDING IT HARD TO WRITE. THE THOUGHT OF RETURNING TO SUCH A RIGID EXISTENCE FILLS ME WITH DREAD.
SO WHY THE HELL ARE YOU WASTING YOUR TIME BUGGERING ABOUT UP HERE WITH ME?

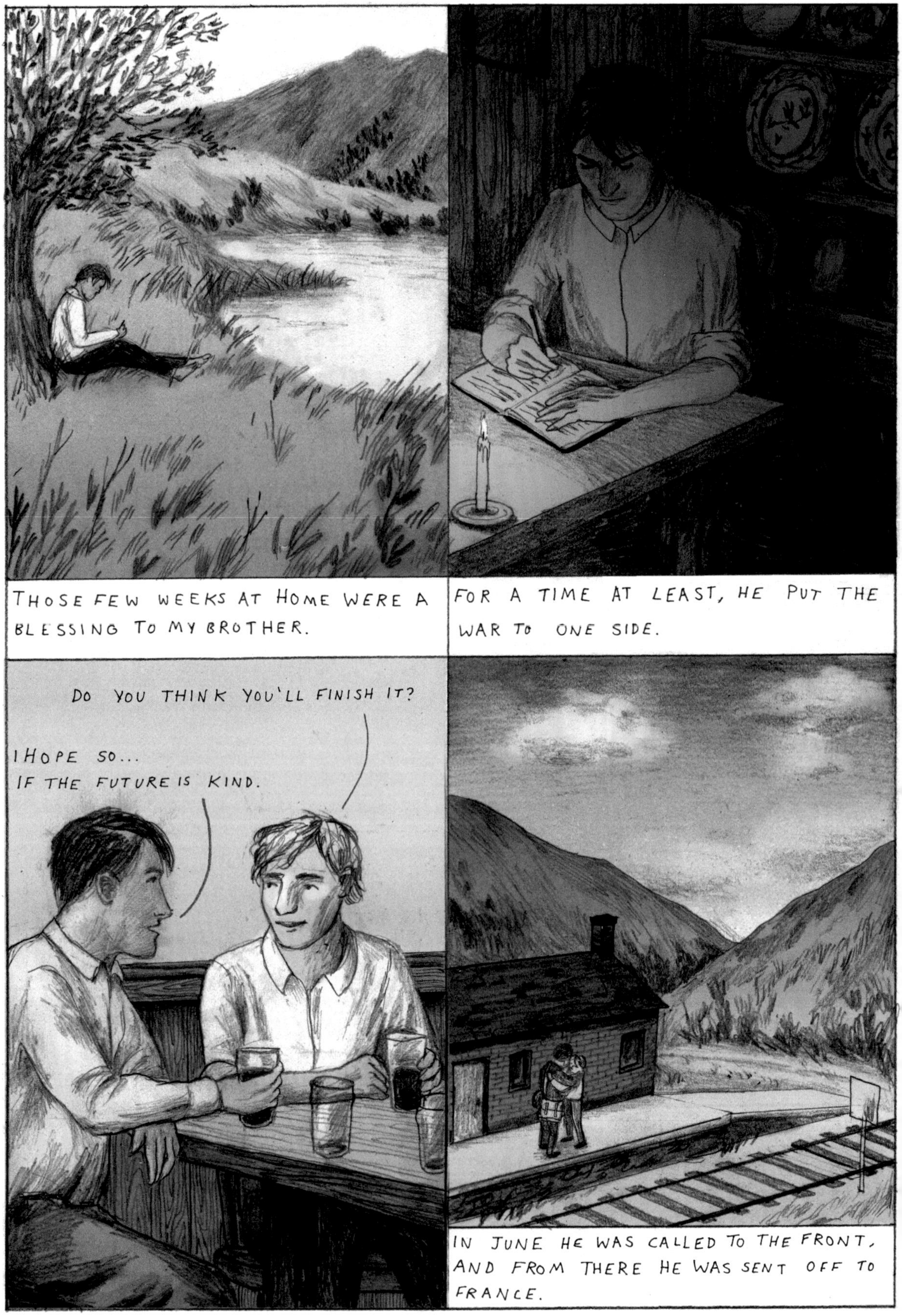
THOSE FEW WEEKS AT HOME WERE A BLESSING TO MY BROTHER.
FOR A TIME AT LEAST, HE PUT THE WAR TO ONE SIDE.
DO YOU THINK YOU'LL FINISH IT?
I HOPE SO... IF THE FUTURE IS KIND.
IN JUNE HE WAS CALLED TO THE FRONT, AND FROM THERE HE WAS SENT OFF TO FRANCE.

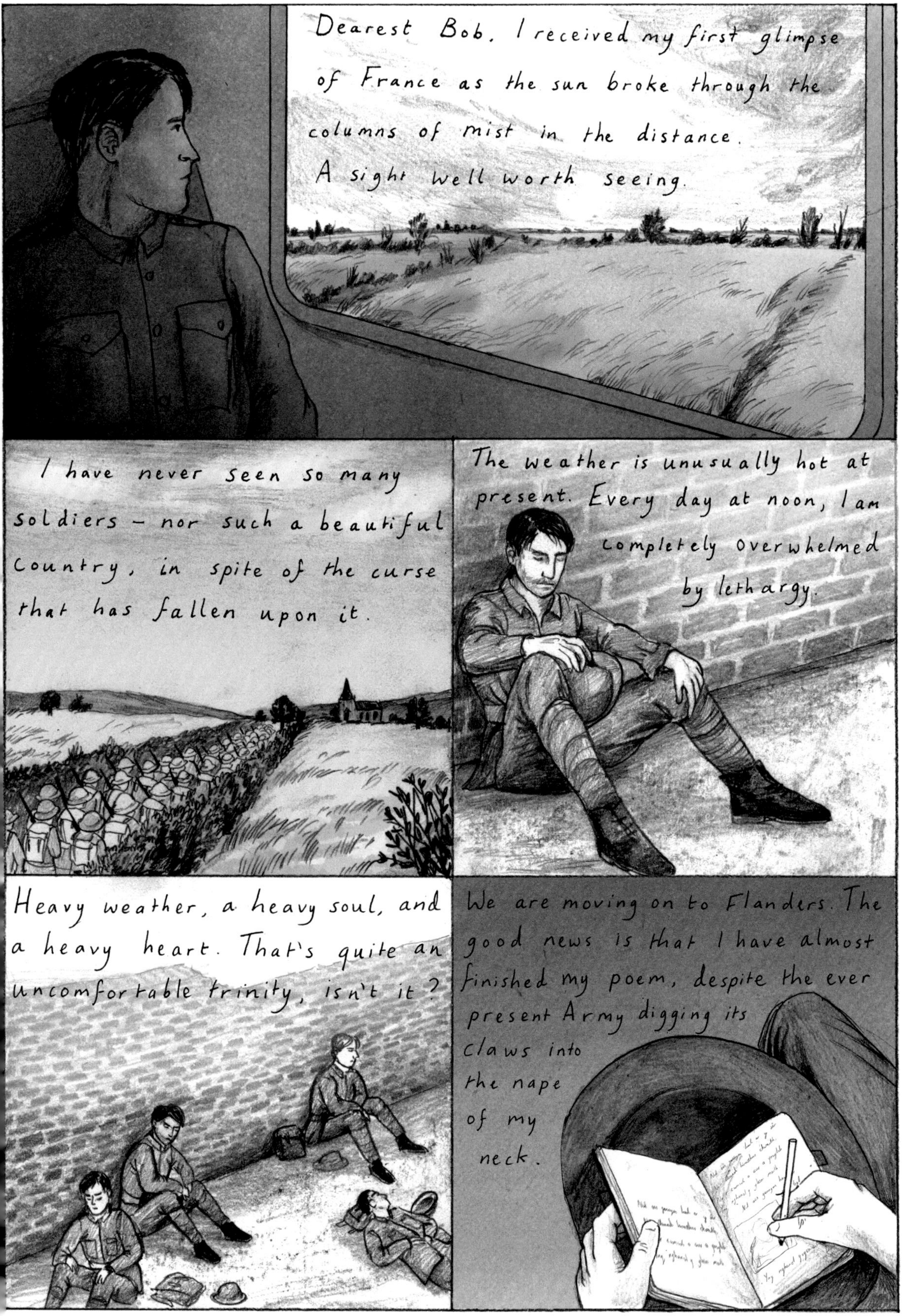
Dearest Bob. I received my first glimpse of France as the sun broke through the columns of mist in the distance. A sight well worth seeing.
I have never seen so many soldiers – nor such a beautiful country, in spite of the curse that has fallen upon it.
The weather is unusually hot at present. Every day at noon, I am completely overwhelmed by lethargy.
Heavy weather, a heavy soul, and a heavy heart. That's quite an uncomfortable trinity, isn't it?
We are moving on to Flanders. The good news is that I have almost finished my poem, despite the ever present Army digging its claws into the nape of my neck.

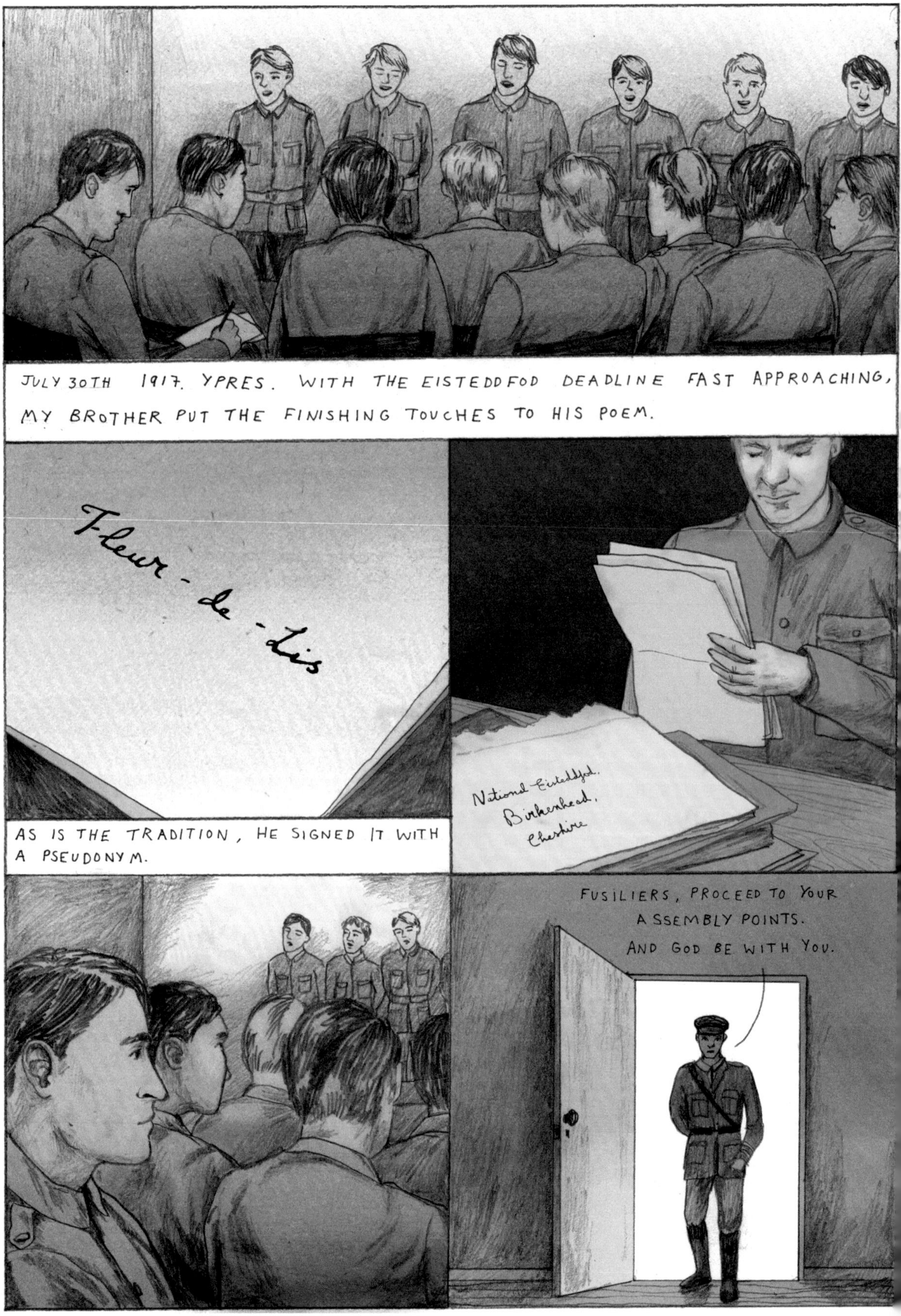
JULY 30TH 1917. YPRES. WITH THE EISTEDDFOD DEADLINE FAST APPROACHING, MY BROTHER PUT THE FINISHING TOUCHES TO HIS POEM.
Fleur-de-Lis
AS IS THE TRADITION, HE SIGNED IT WITH A PSEUDONYM.
National Eisteddfod. Birkenhead. Cheshire
FUSILIERS, PROCEED TO YOUR ASSEMBLY POINTS. AND GOD BE WITH YOU.

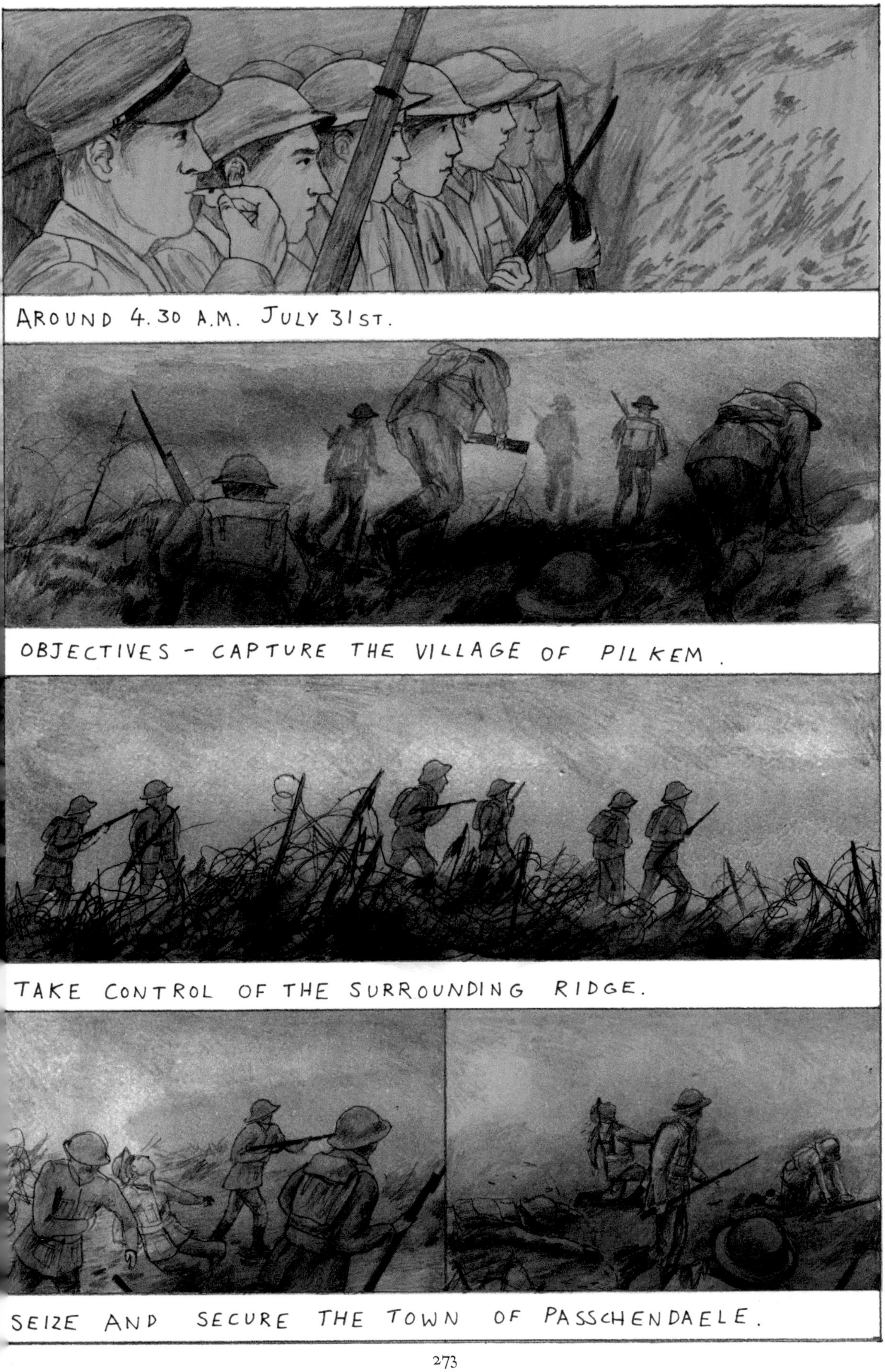
AROUND 4.30 A.M. JULY 31ST.
OBJECTIVES - CAPTURE THE VILLAGE OF PILKEM.
TAKE CONTROL OF THE SURROUNDING RIDGE.
SEIZE AND SECURE THE TOWN OF PASSCHENDAELE.

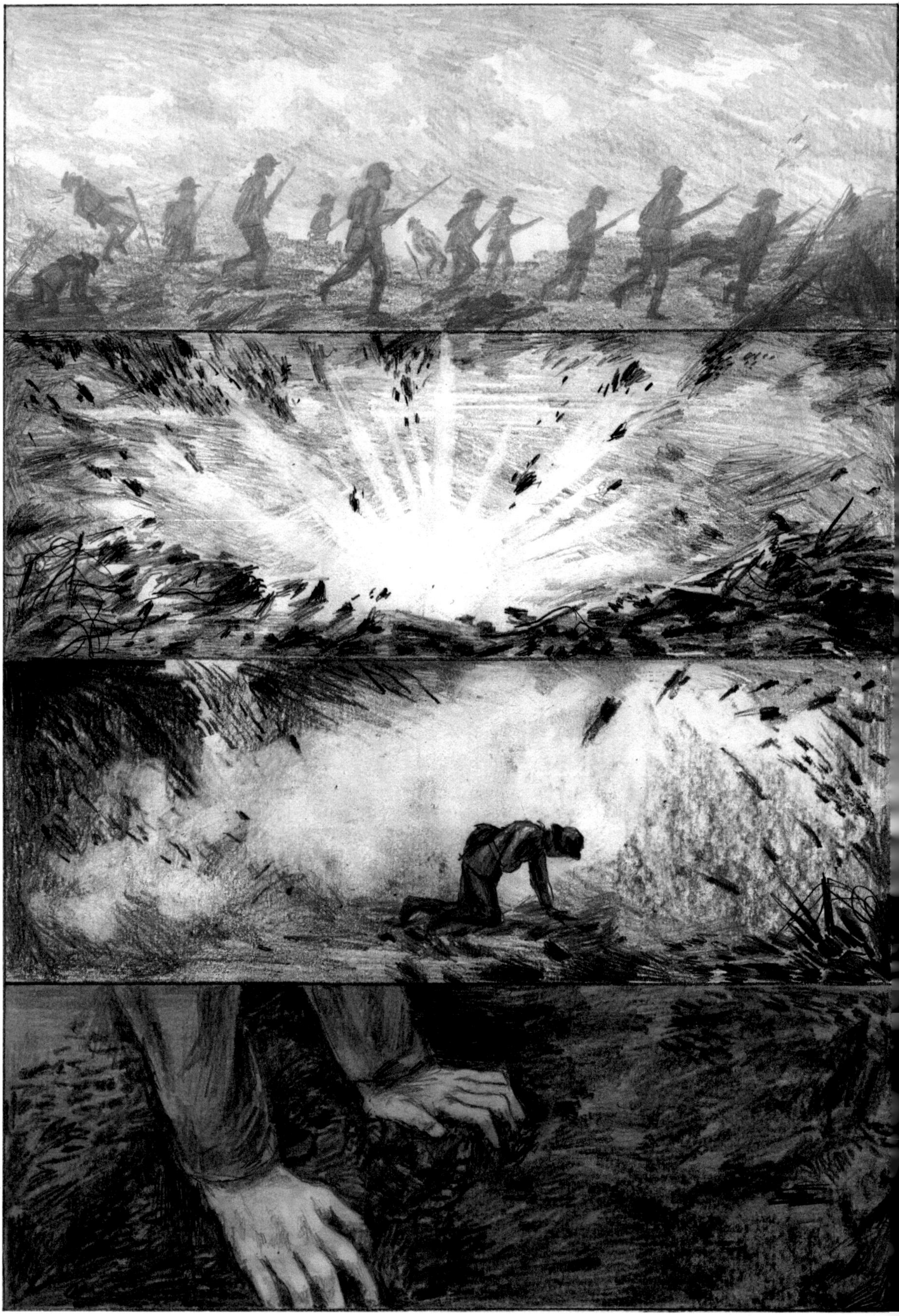

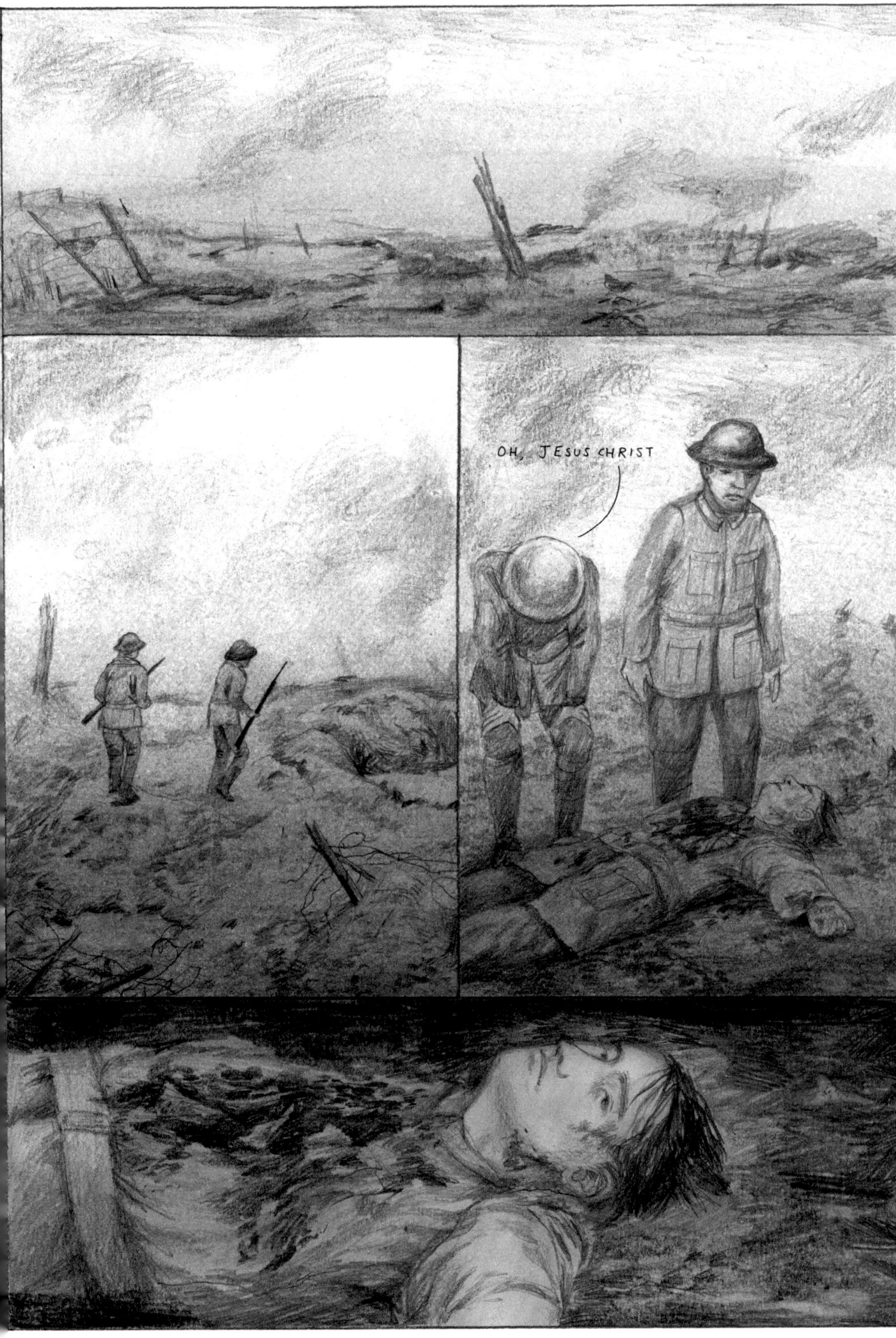
OH, JESUS CHRIST

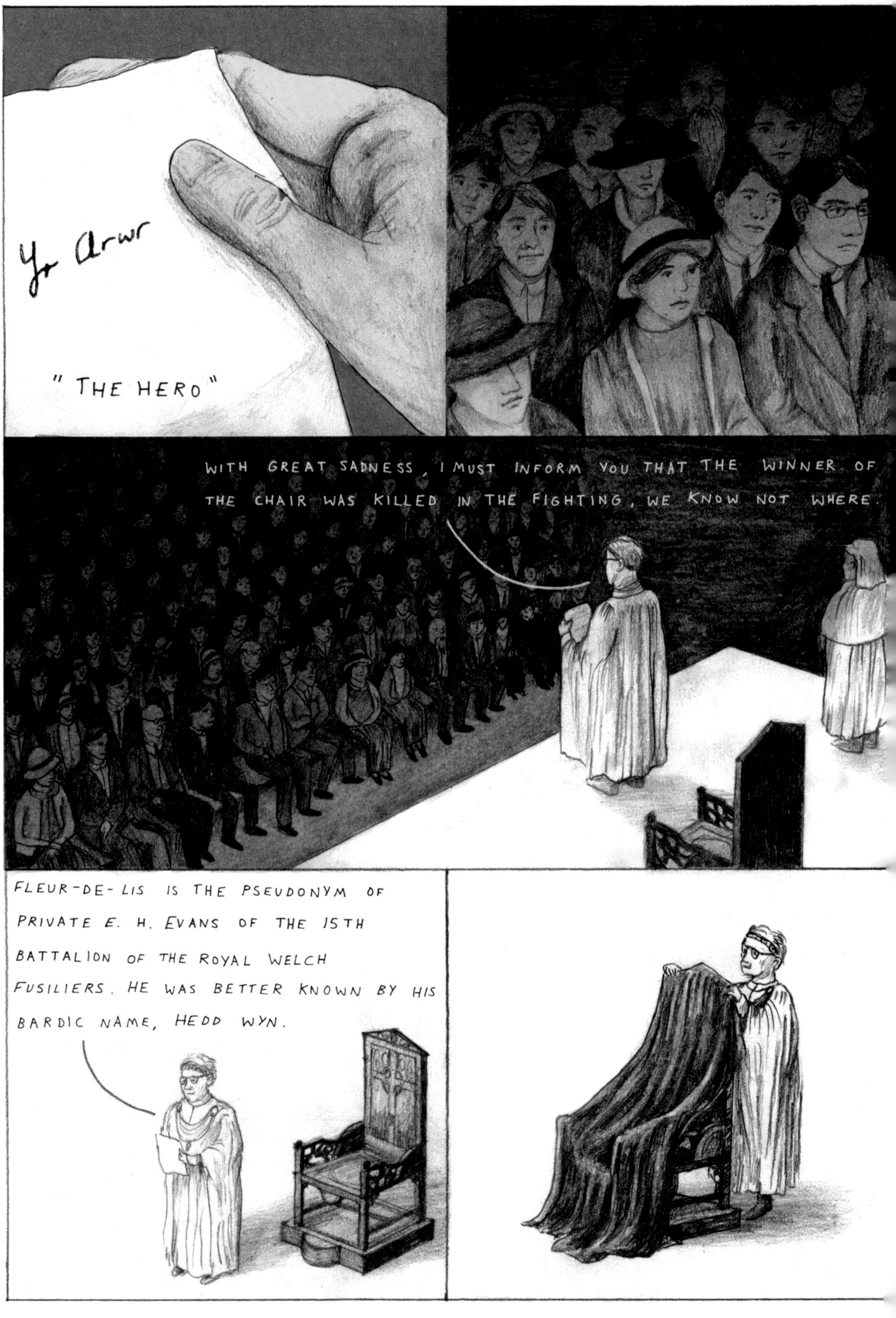
Yr Arwr
"THE HERO"
WITH GREAT SADNESS, I MUST INFORM YOU THAT THE WINNER OF THE CHAIR WAS KILLED IN THE FIGHTING, WE KNOW NOT WHERE.
FLEUR-DE-LIS IS THE PSEUDONYM OF PRIVATE E. H. EVANS OF THE 15TH BATTALION OF THE ROYAL WELCH FUSILIERS. HE WAS BETTER KNOWN BY HIS BARDIC NAME, HEDD WYN.

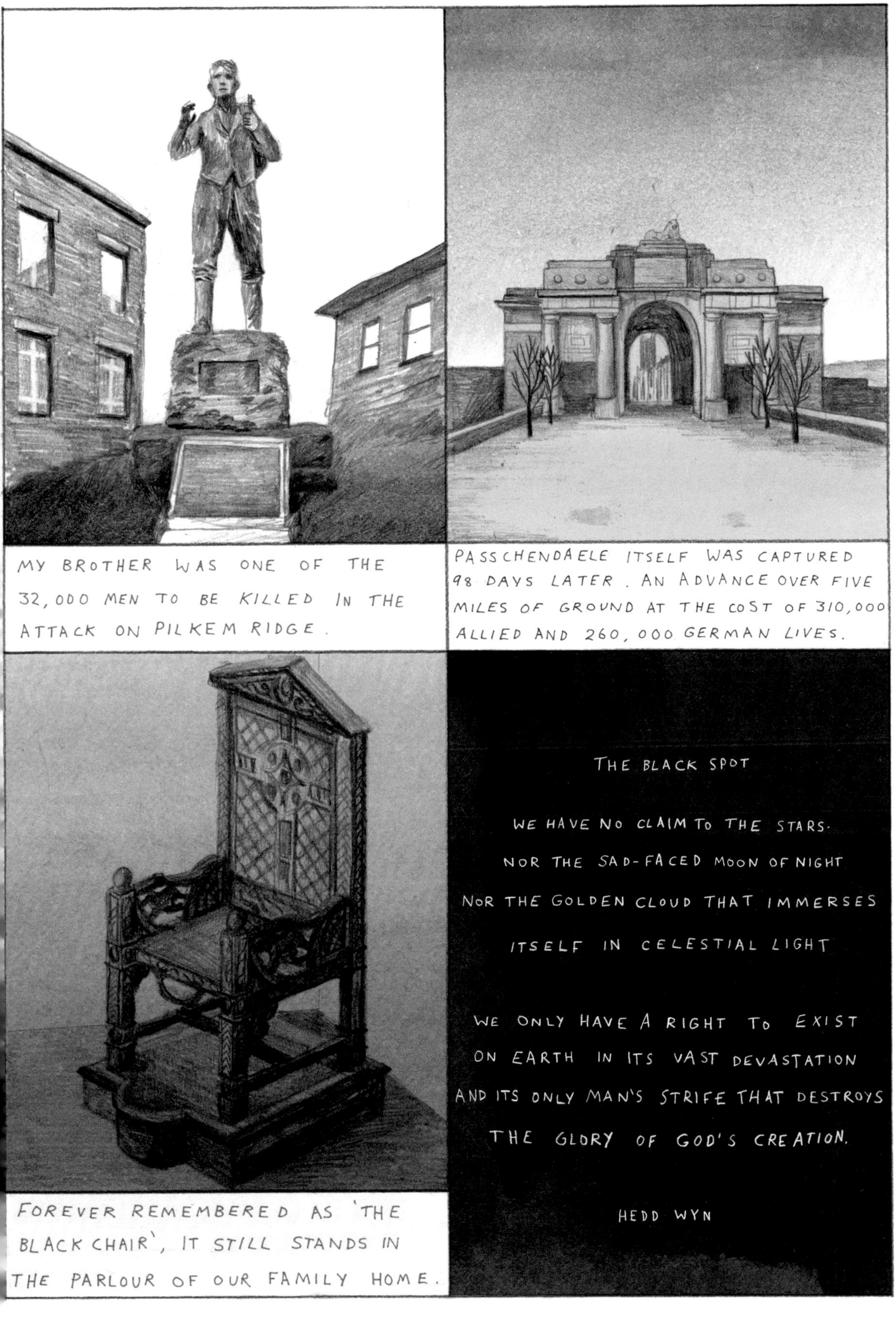
MY BROTHER WAS ONE OF THE 32,000 MEN TO BE KILLED IN THE ATTACK ON PILKEM RIDGE.
PASSCHENDAELE ITSELF WAS CAPTURED 98 DAYS LATER. AN ADVANCE OVER FIVE MILES OF GROUND AT THE COST OF 310,000 ALLIED AND 260,000 GERMAN LIVES.
FOREVER REMEMBERED AS 'THE BLACK CHAIR', IT STILL STANDS IN THE PARLOUR OF OUR FAMILY HOME.
THE BLACK SPOT
WE HAVE NO CLAIM TO THE STARS.
NOR THE SAD-FACED MOON OF NIGHT
NOR THE GOLDEN CLOUD THAT IMMERSES
ITSELF IN CELESTIAL LIGHT
WE ONLY HAVE A RIGHT TO EXIST
ON EARTH IN ITS VAST DEVASTATION
AND ITS ONLY MAN'S STRIFE THAT DESTROYS
THE GLORY OF GOD'S CREATION.
HEDD WYN

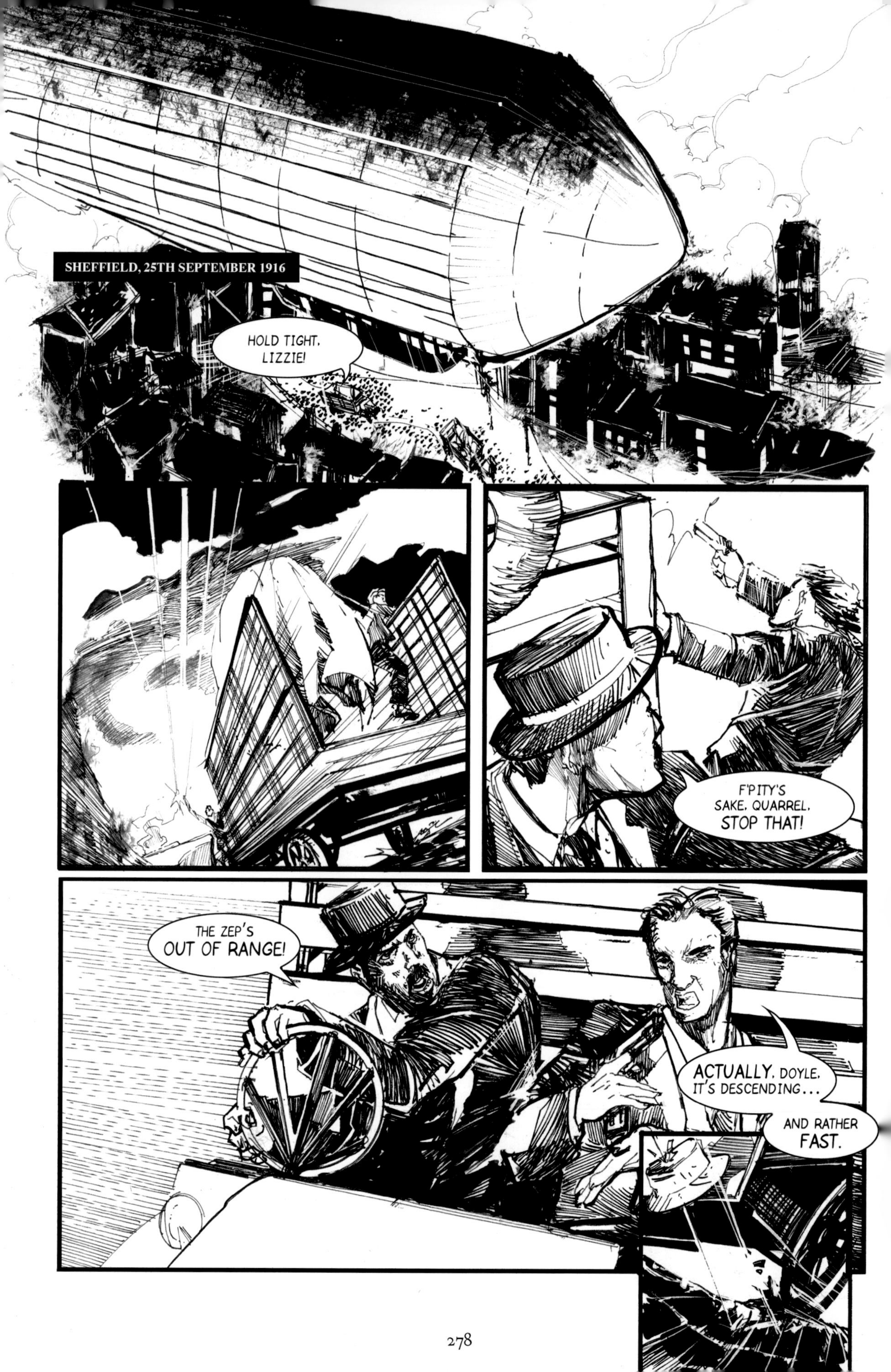
SHEFFIELD, 25TH SEPTEMBER 1916
HOLD TIGHT, LIZZIE!
F'PITY'S SAKE, QUARREL, STOP THAT!
THE ZEP'S OUT OF RANGE!
ACTUALLY, DOYLE, IT'S DESCENDING...
AND RATHER FAST.

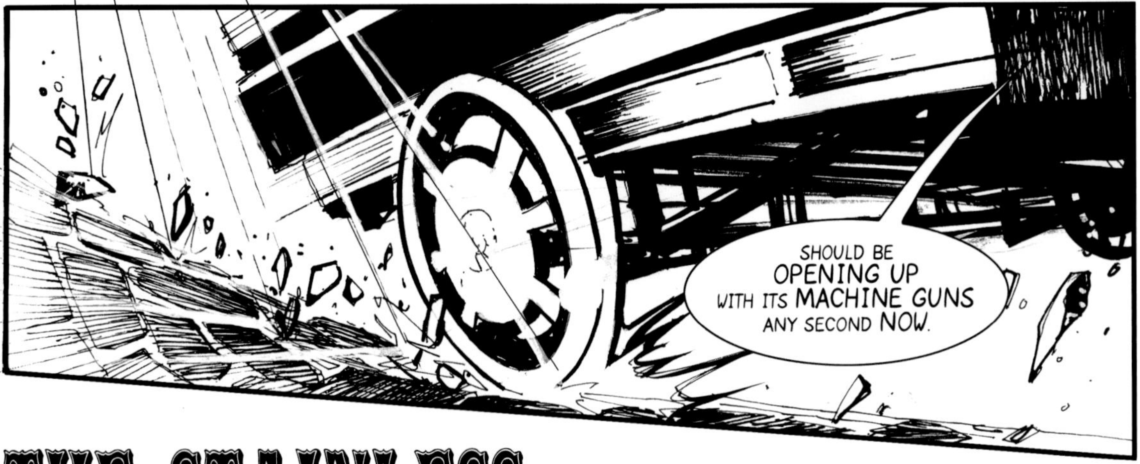
SHOULD BE OPENING UP WITH ITS MACHINE GUNS ANY SECOND NOW.

THE STAINLESS STEEL ELEPHANT

SCRIPT: Russell Wall & James Guy
ART: Ariela "Rie" Kristantina

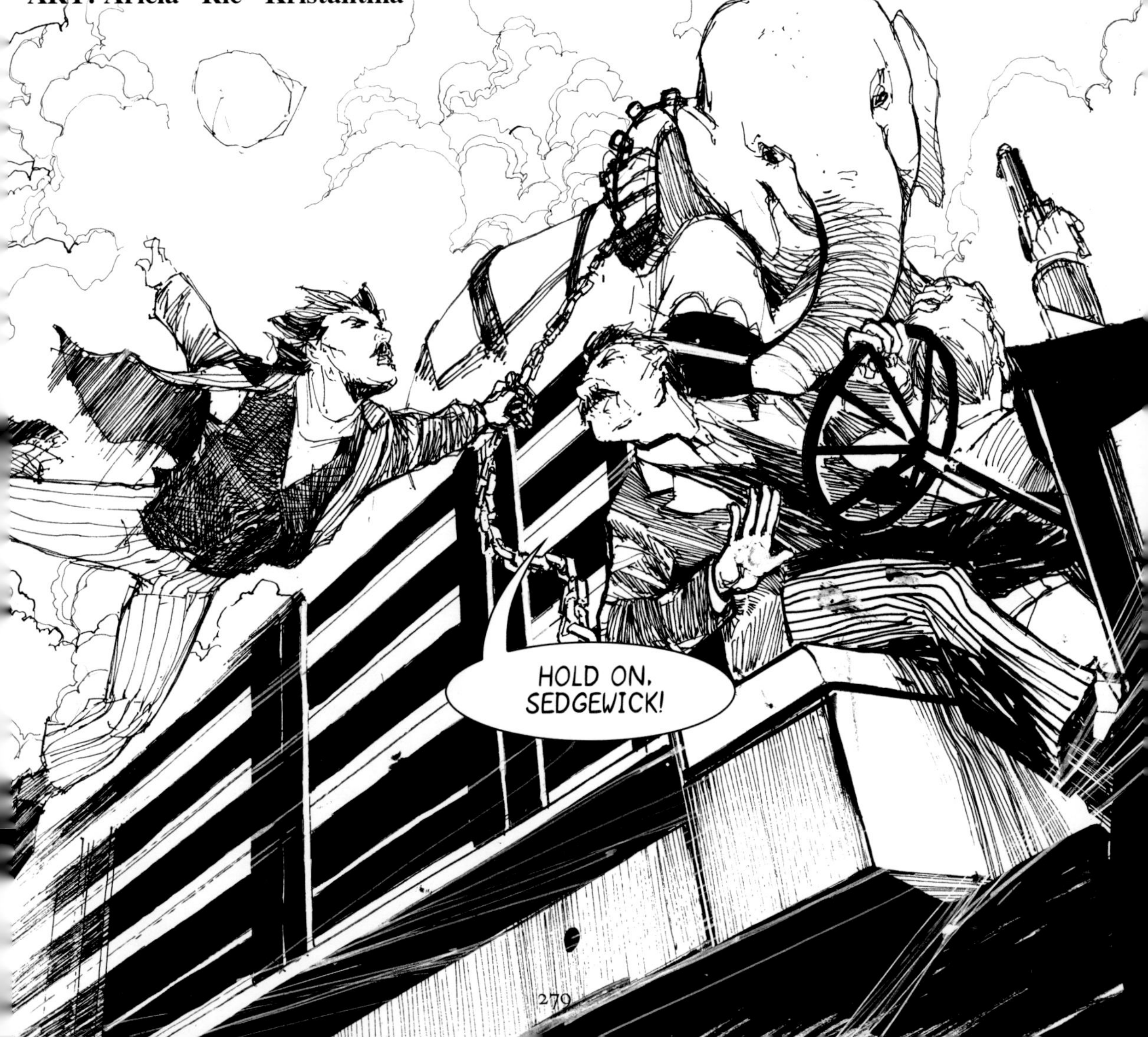
HOLD ON, SEDGEWICK!

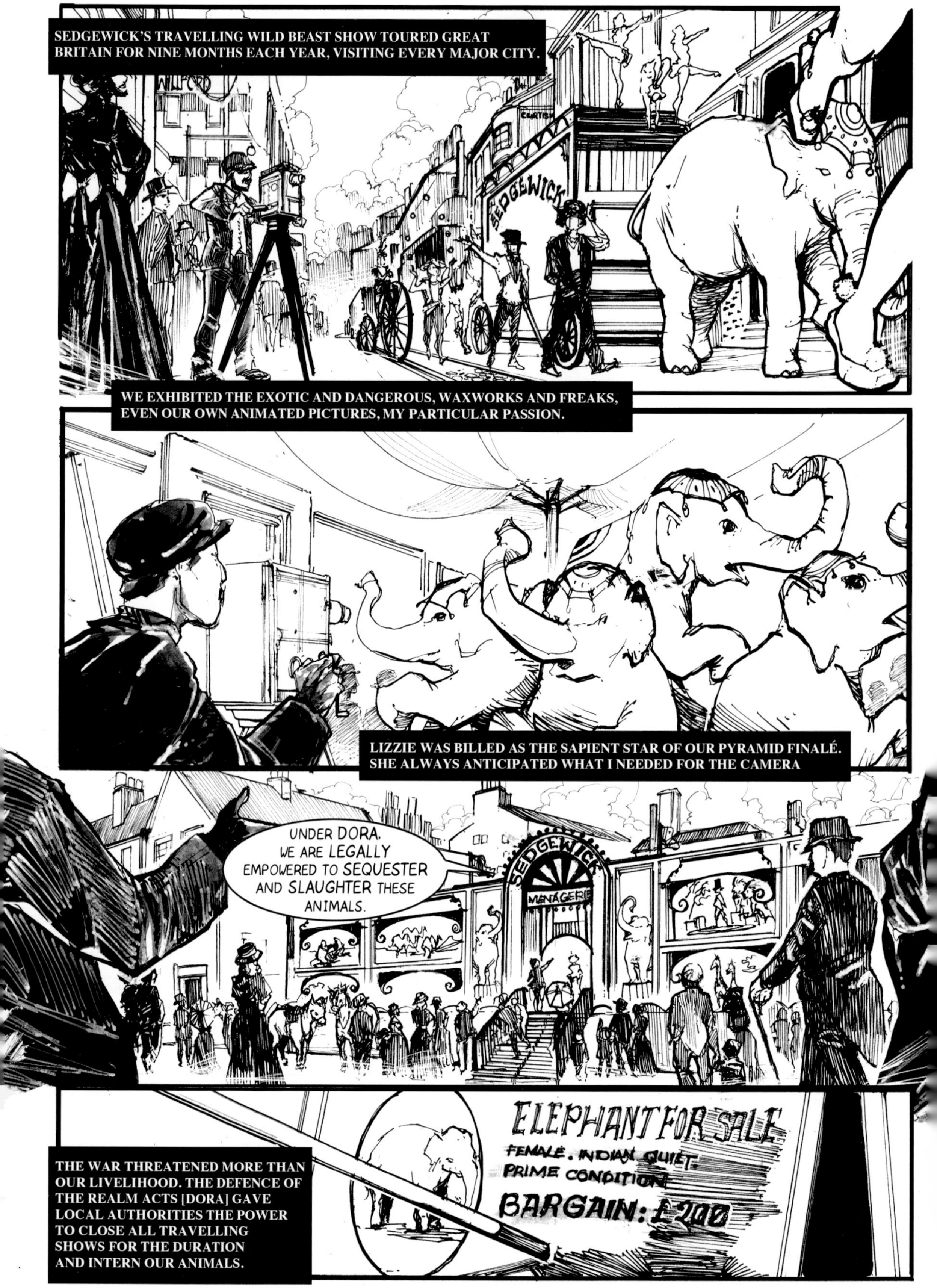
SEDGEWICK'S TRAVELLING WILD BEAST SHOW TOURED GREAT BRITAIN FOR NINE MONTHS EACH YEAR, VISITING EVERY MAJOR CITY.
SEDGEWICK
WE EXHIBITED THE EXOTIC AND DANGEROUS, WAXWORKS AND FREAKS, EVEN OUR OWN ANIMATED PICTURES, MY PARTICULAR PASSION.
LIZZIE WAS BILLED AS THE SAPIENT STAR OF OUR PYRAMID FINALÉ. SHE ALWAYS ANTICIPATED WHAT I NEEDED FOR THE CAMERA
UNDER DORA, WE ARE LEGALLY EMPOWERED TO SEQUESTER AND SLAUGHTER THESE ANIMALS.
SEDGEWICK
MENAGERIE
THE WAR THREATENED MORE THAN OUR LIVELIHOOD. THE DEFENCE OF THE REALM ACTS [DORA] GAVE LOCAL AUTHORITIES THE POWER TO CLOSE ALL TRAVELLING SHOWS FOR THE DURATION AND INTERN OUR ANIMALS.
ELEPHANT FOR SALE
FEMALE. INDIAN QUIET.
PRIME CONDITION
BARGAIN: £200

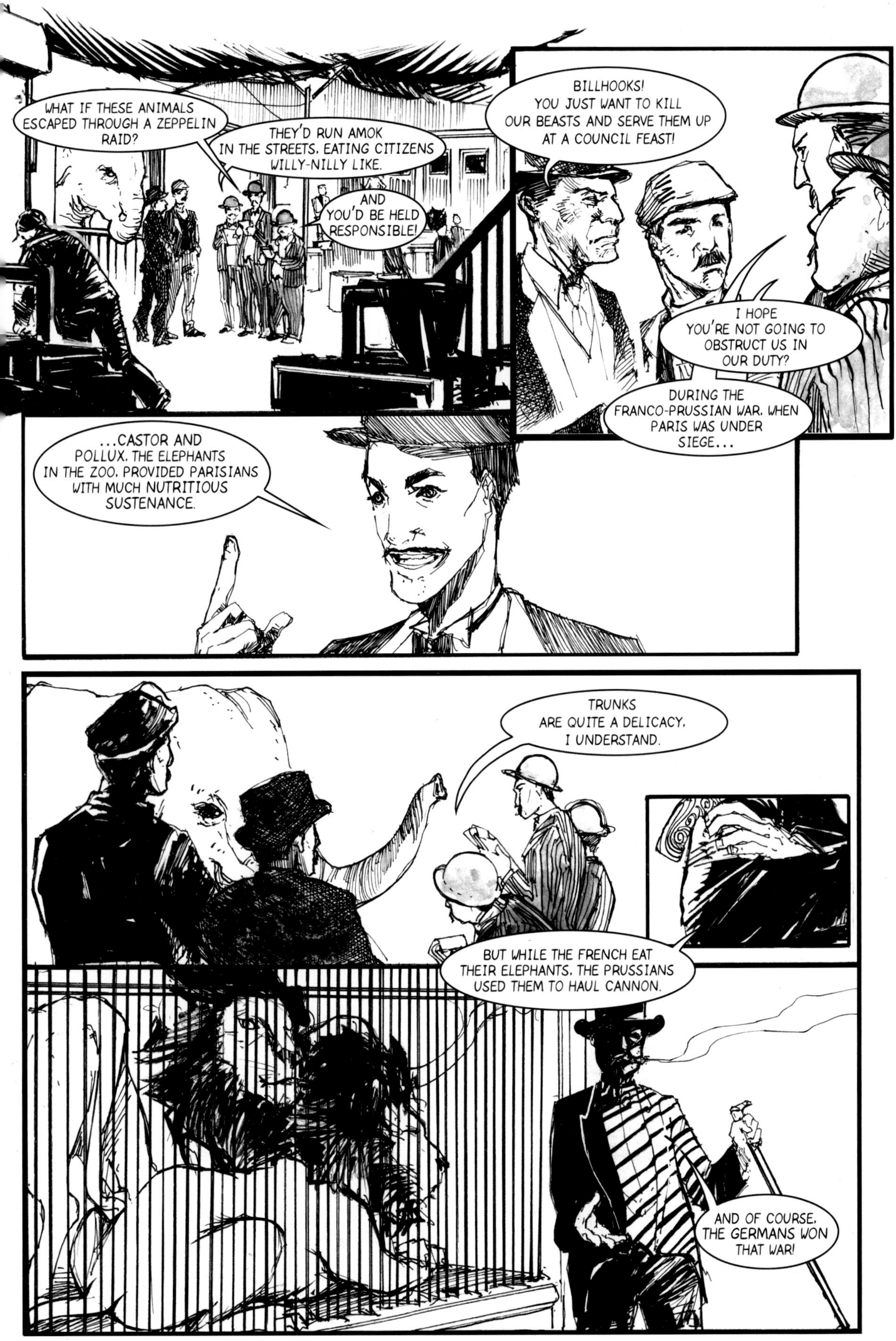
WHAT IF THESE ANIMALS ESCAPED THROUGH A ZEPPELIN RAID?
THEY'D RUN AMOK IN THE STREETS, EATING CITIZENS WILLY-NILLY LIKE.
AND YOU'D BE HELD RESPONSIBLE!
BILLHOOKS! YOU JUST WANT TO KILL OUR BEASTS AND SERVE THEM UP AT A COUNCIL FEAST!
I HOPE YOU'RE NOT GOING TO OBSTRUCT US IN OUR DUTY?
DURING THE FRANCO-PRUSSIAN WAR, WHEN PARIS WAS UNDER SIEGE...
...CASTOR AND POLLUX, THE ELEPHANTS IN THE ZOO, PROVIDED PARISIANS WITH MUCH NUTRITIOUS SUSTENANCE.
TRUNKS ARE QUITE A DELICACY, I UNDERSTAND.
BUT WHILE THE FRENCH EAT THEIR ELEPHANTS, THE PRUSSIANS USED THEM TO HAUL CANNON.
AND OF COURSE, THE GERMANS WON THAT WAR!

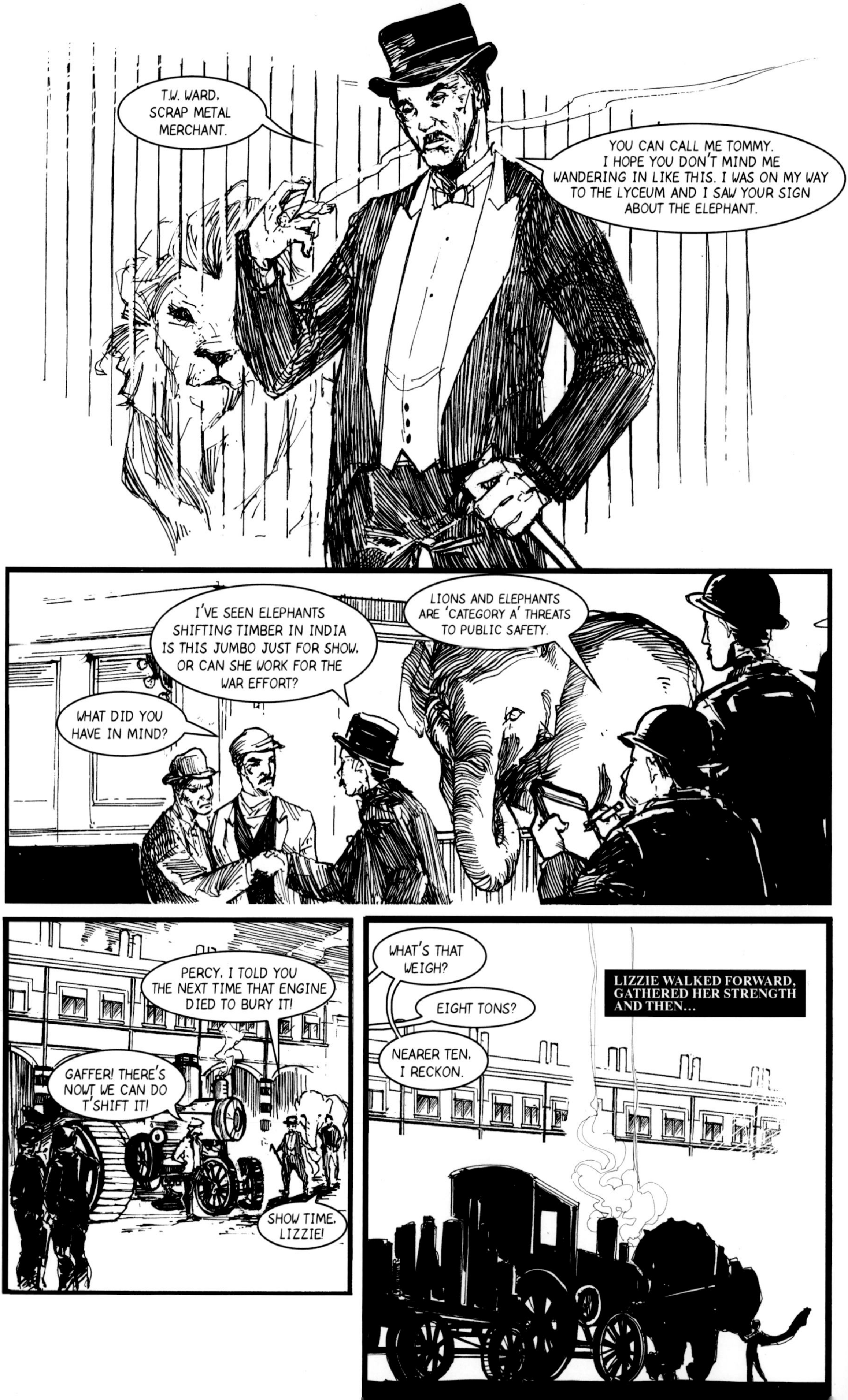
T.W. WARD, SCRAP METAL MERCHANT.
YOU CAN CALL ME TOMMY. I HOPE YOU DON'T MIND ME WANDERING IN LIKE THIS. I WAS ON MY WAY TO THE LYCEUM AND I SAW YOUR SIGN ABOUT THE ELEPHANT.
I'VE SEEN ELEPHANTS SHIFTING TIMBER IN INDIA IS THIS JUMBO JUST FOR SHOW, OR CAN SHE WORK FOR THE WAR EFFORT?
WHAT DID YOU HAVE IN MIND?
LIONS AND ELEPHANTS ARE 'CATEGORY A' THREATS TO PUBLIC SAFETY.
PERCY, I TOLD YOU THE NEXT TIME THAT ENGINE DIED TO BURY IT!
GAFFER! THERE'S NOWT WE CAN DO T'SHIFT IT!
SHOW TIME, LIZZIE!
WHAT'S THAT WEIGH?
EIGHT TONS?
NEARER TEN, I RECKON.
LIZZIE WALKED FORWARD, GATHERED HER STRENGTH AND THEN…

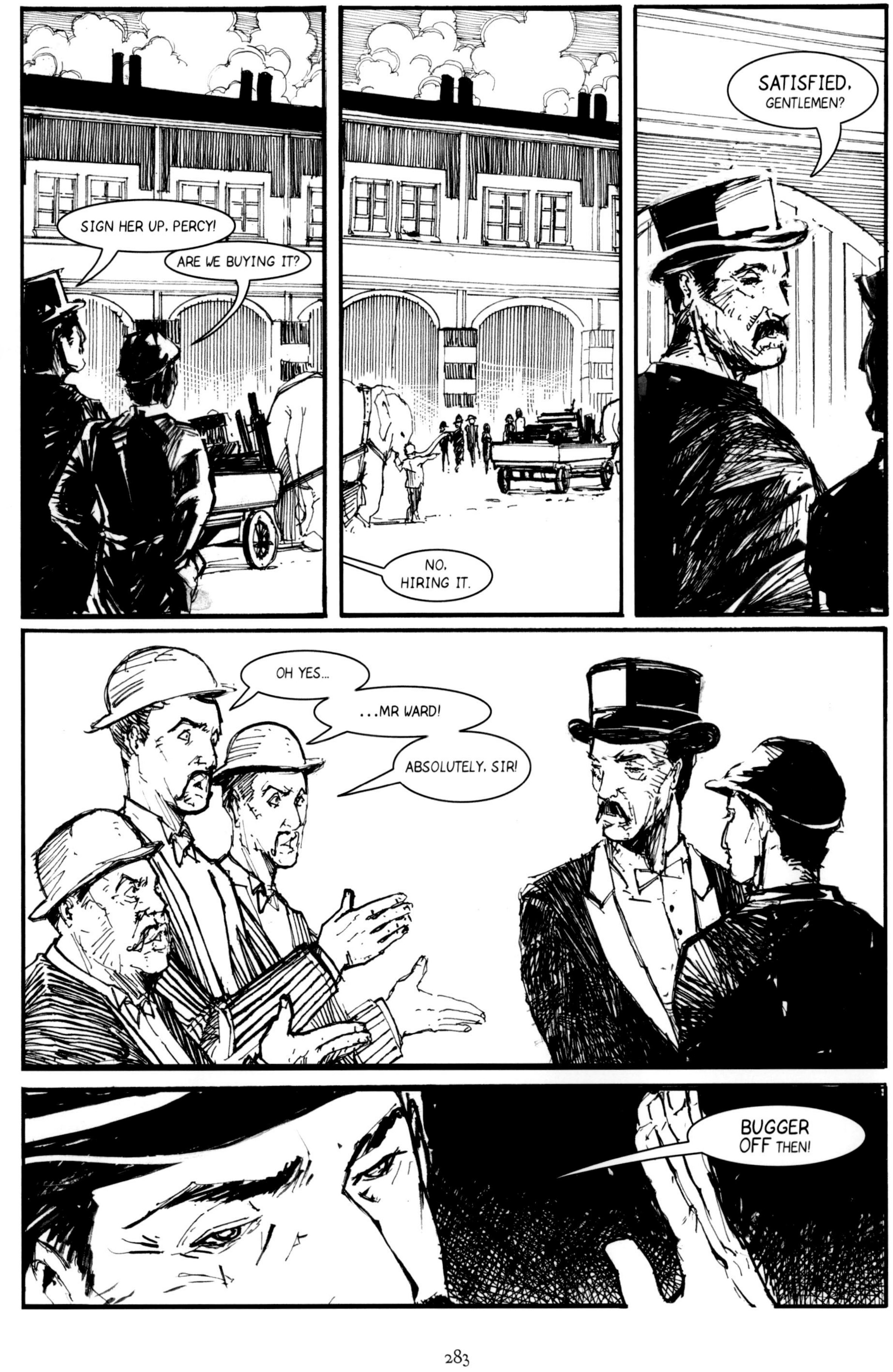
SIGN HER UP, PERCY!
ARE WE BUYING IT?
NO, HIRING IT.
SATISFIED, GENTLEMEN?
OH YES...
...MR WARD!
ABSOLUTELY, SIR!
BUGGER OFF THEN!

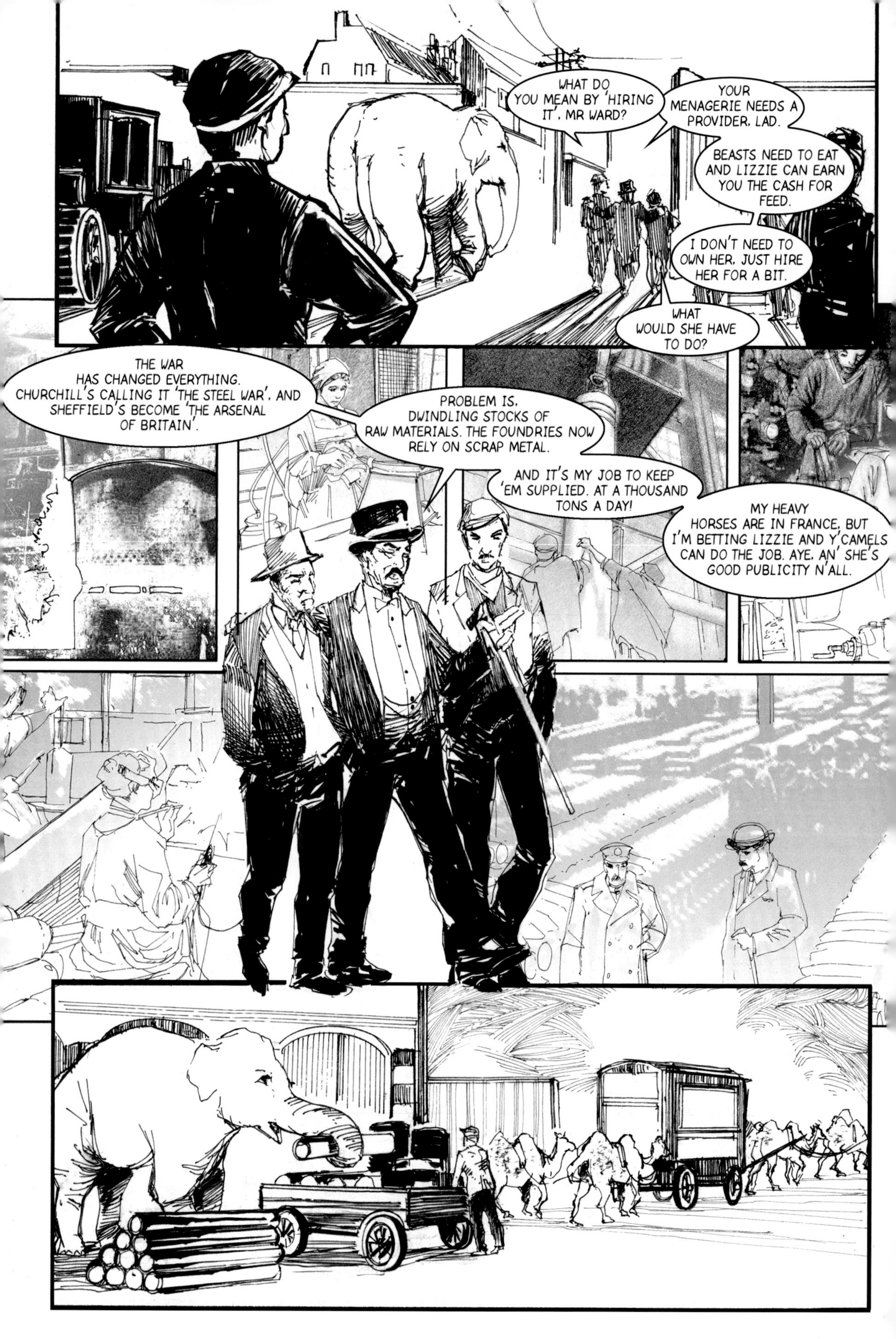
WHAT DO YOU MEAN BY 'HIRING IT', MR WARD?
YOUR MENAGERIE NEEDS A PROVIDER, LAD.
BEASTS NEED TO EAT AND LIZZIE CAN EARN YOU THE CASH FOR FEED.
I DON'T NEED TO OWN HER, JUST HIRE HER FOR A BIT.
WHAT WOULD SHE HAVE TO DO?
THE WAR HAS CHANGED EVERYTHING. CHURCHILL'S CALLING IT 'THE STEEL WAR', AND SHEFFIELD'S BECOME 'THE ARSENAL OF BRITAIN'.
PROBLEM IS, DWINDLING STOCKS OF RAW MATERIALS. THE FOUNDRIES NOW RELY ON SCRAP METAL.
AND IT'S MY JOB TO KEEP 'EM SUPPLIED. AT A THOUSAND TONS A DAY!
MY HEAVY HORSES ARE IN FRANCE, BUT I'M BETTING LIZZIE AND Y'CAMELS CAN DO THE JOB. AYE, AN' SHE'S GOOD PUBLICITY N'ALL.

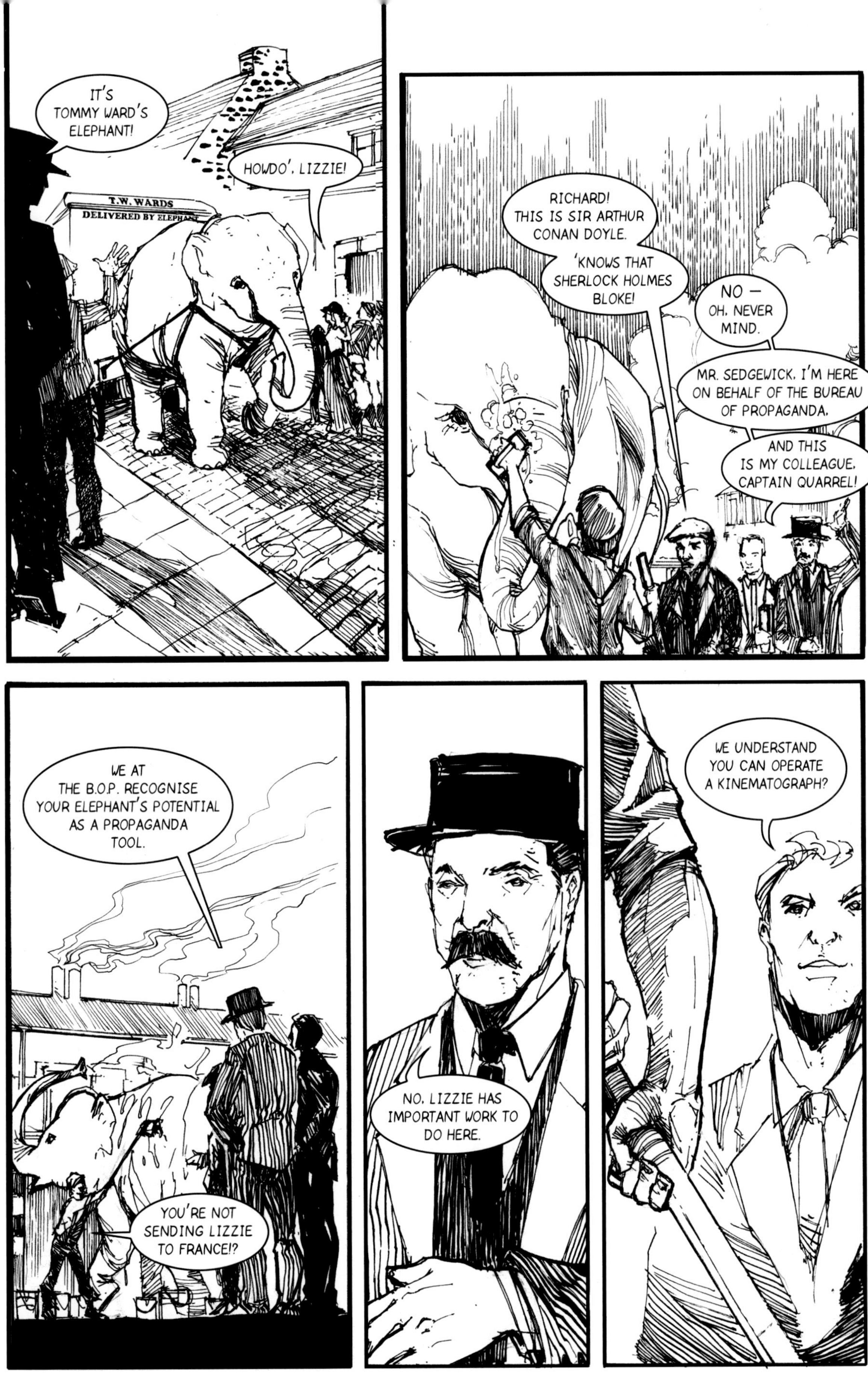

IT'S TOMMY WARD'S ELEPHANT!
HOWDO', LIZZIE!
T.W. WARDS
DELIVERED BY ELEPHANT
RICHARD! THIS IS SIR ARTHUR CONAN DOYLE.
'KNOWS THAT SHERLOCK HOLMES BLOKE!
NO — OH, NEVER MIND.
MR. SEDGEWICK, I'M HERE ON BEHALF OF THE BUREAU OF PROPAGANDA.
AND THIS IS MY COLLEAGUE, CAPTAIN QUARREL!
WE AT THE B.O.P. RECOGNISE YOUR ELEPHANT'S POTENTIAL AS A PROPAGANDA TOOL.
YOU'RE NOT SENDING LIZZIE TO FRANCE!?
NO, LIZZIE HAS IMPORTANT WORK TO DO HERE.
WE UNDERSTAND YOU CAN OPERATE A KINEMATOGRAPH?

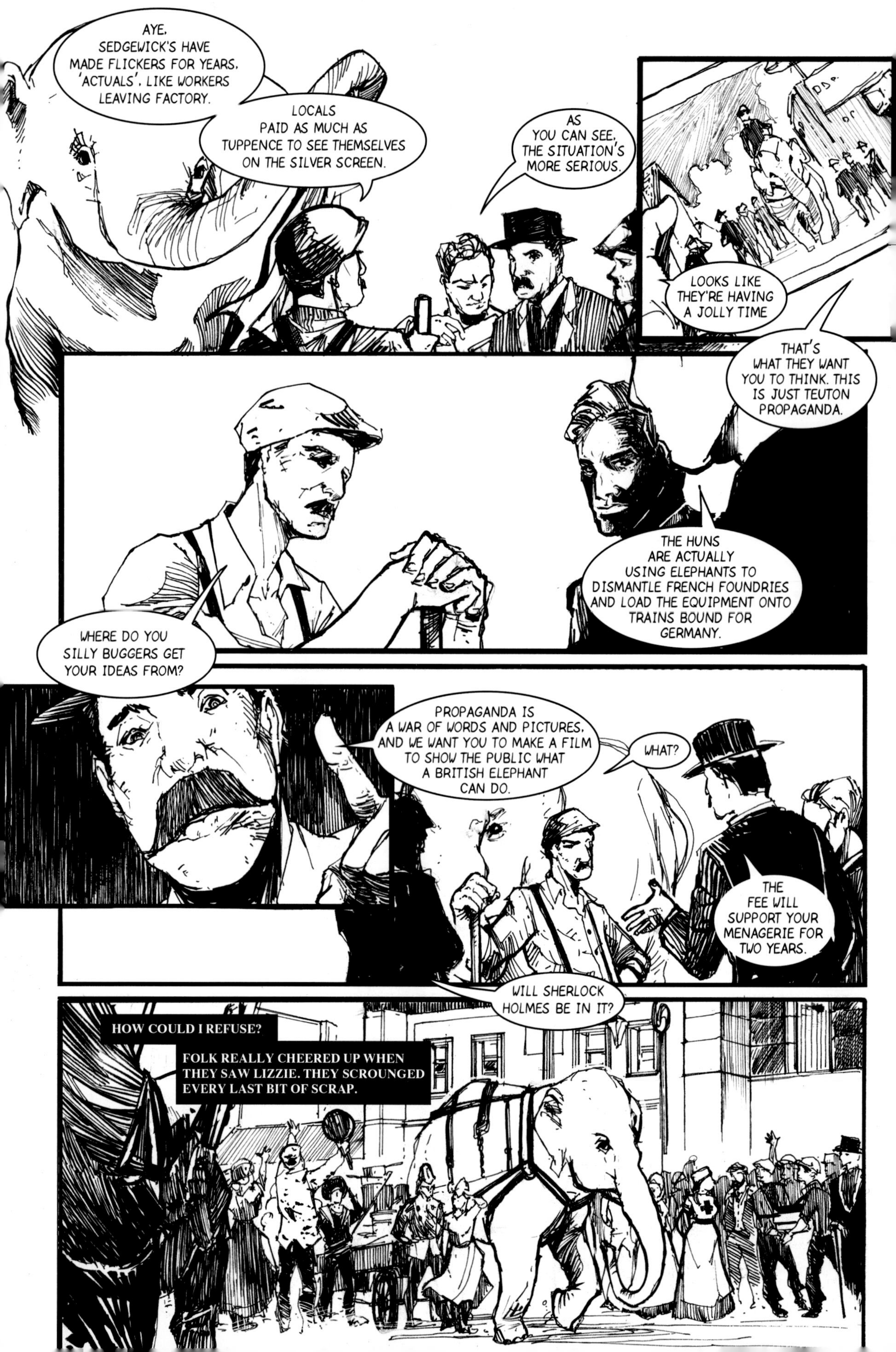
AYE, SEDGEWICK'S HAVE MADE FLICKERS FOR YEARS, 'ACTUALS', LIKE WORKERS LEAVING FACTORY.
LOCALS PAID AS MUCH AS TUPPENCE TO SEE THEMSELVES ON THE SILVER SCREEN.
AS YOU CAN SEE, THE SITUATION'S MORE SERIOUS.
LOOKS LIKE THEY'RE HAVING A JOLLY TIME
THAT'S WHAT THEY WANT YOU TO THINK. THIS IS JUST TEUTON PROPAGANDA.
THE HUNS ARE ACTUALLY USING ELEPHANTS TO DISMANTLE FRENCH FOUNDRIES AND LOAD THE EQUIPMENT ONTO TRAINS BOUND FOR GERMANY.
WHERE DO YOU SILLY BUGGERS GET YOUR IDEAS FROM?
PROPAGANDA IS A WAR OF WORDS AND PICTURES, AND WE WANT YOU TO MAKE A FILM TO SHOW THE PUBLIC WHAT A BRITISH ELEPHANT CAN DO.
WHAT?
THE FEE WILL SUPPORT YOUR MENAGERIE FOR TWO YEARS.
WILL SHERLOCK HOLMES BE IN IT?
HOW COULD I REFUSE?
FOLK REALLY CHEERED UP WHEN THEY SAW LIZZIE. THEY SCROUNGED EVERY LAST BIT OF SCRAP.

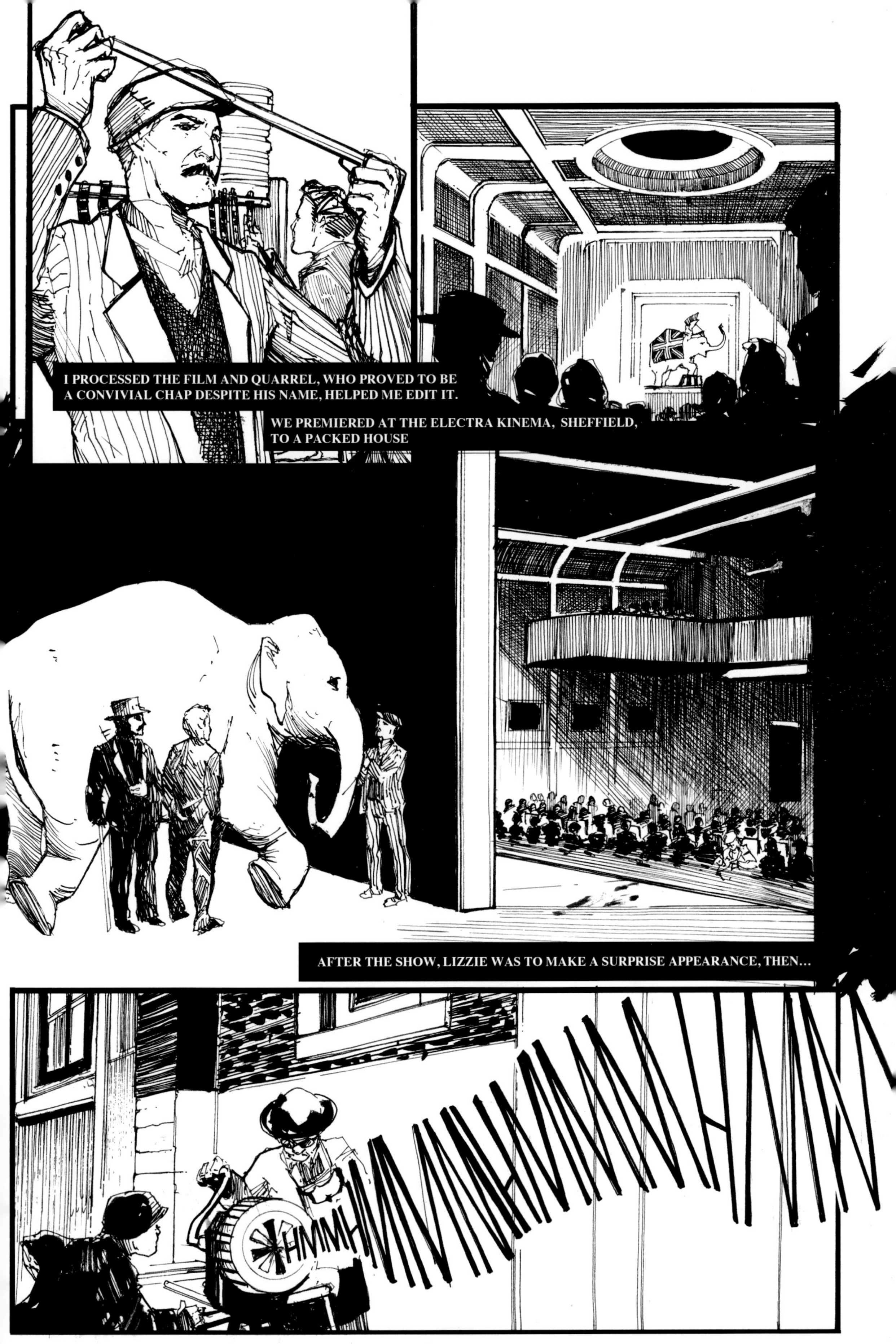
I PROCESSED THE FILM AND QUARREL, WHO PROVED TO BE A CONVIVIAL CHAP DESPITE HIS NAME, HELPED ME EDIT IT.
WE PREMIERED AT THE ELECTRA KINEMA, SHEFFIELD, TO A PACKED HOUSE
AFTER THE SHOW, LIZZIE WAS TO MAKE A SURPRISE APPEARANCE, THEN…
HMMHMMMMMMMMMMMMMMMMMMMM

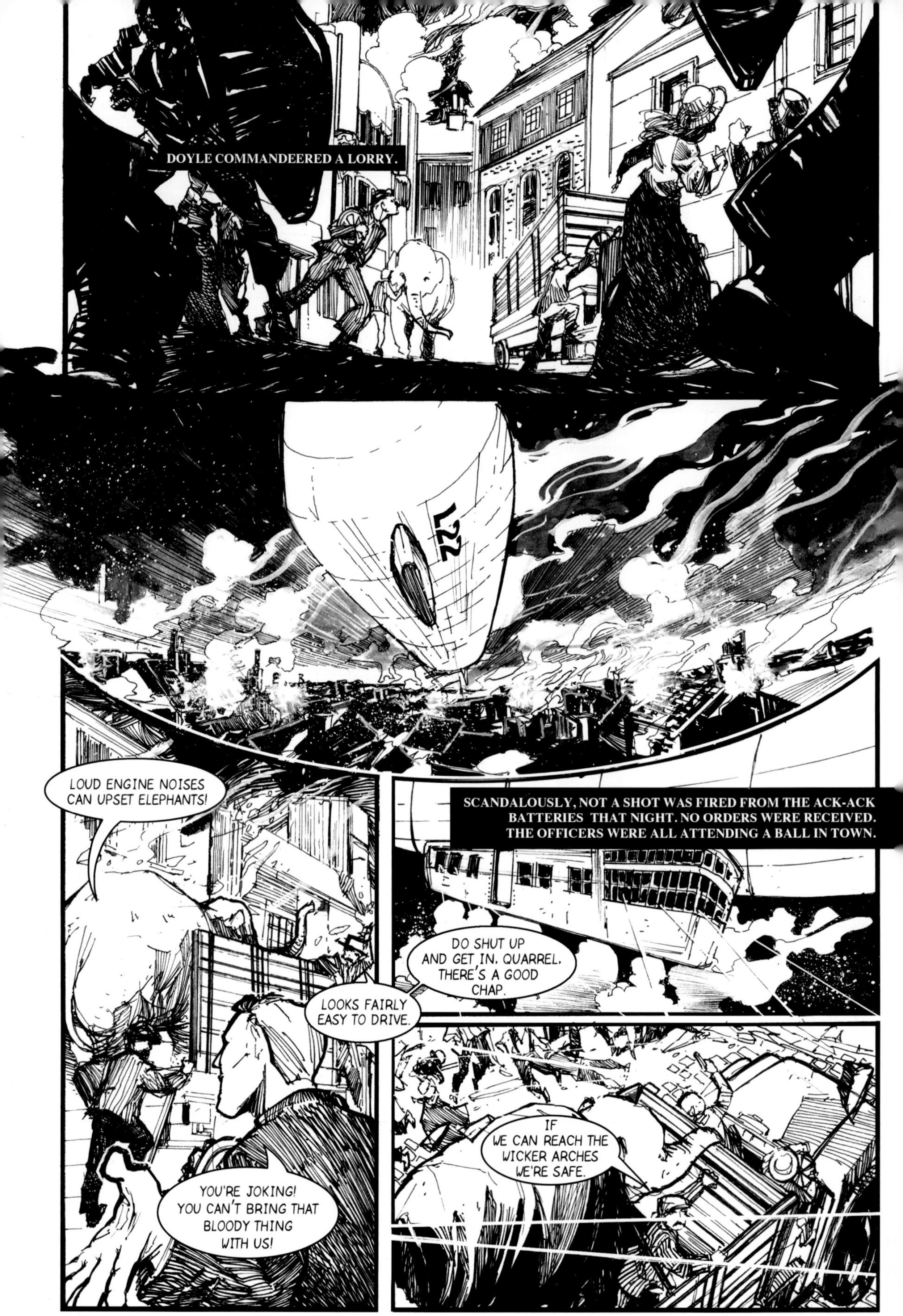
DOYLE COMMANDEERED A LORRY.
L22
LOUD ENGINE NOISES CAN UPSET ELEPHANTS!
SCANDALOUSLY, NOT A SHOT WAS FIRED FROM THE ACK-ACK BATTERIES THAT NIGHT. NO ORDERS WERE RECEIVED. THE OFFICERS WERE ALL ATTENDING A BALL IN TOWN.
DO SHUT UP AND GET IN, QUARREL, THERE'S A GOOD CHAP.
LOOKS FAIRLY EASY TO DRIVE.
YOU'RE JOKING! YOU CAN'T BRING THAT BLOODY THING WITH US!
IF WE CAN REACH THE WICKER ARCHES WE'RE SAFE.

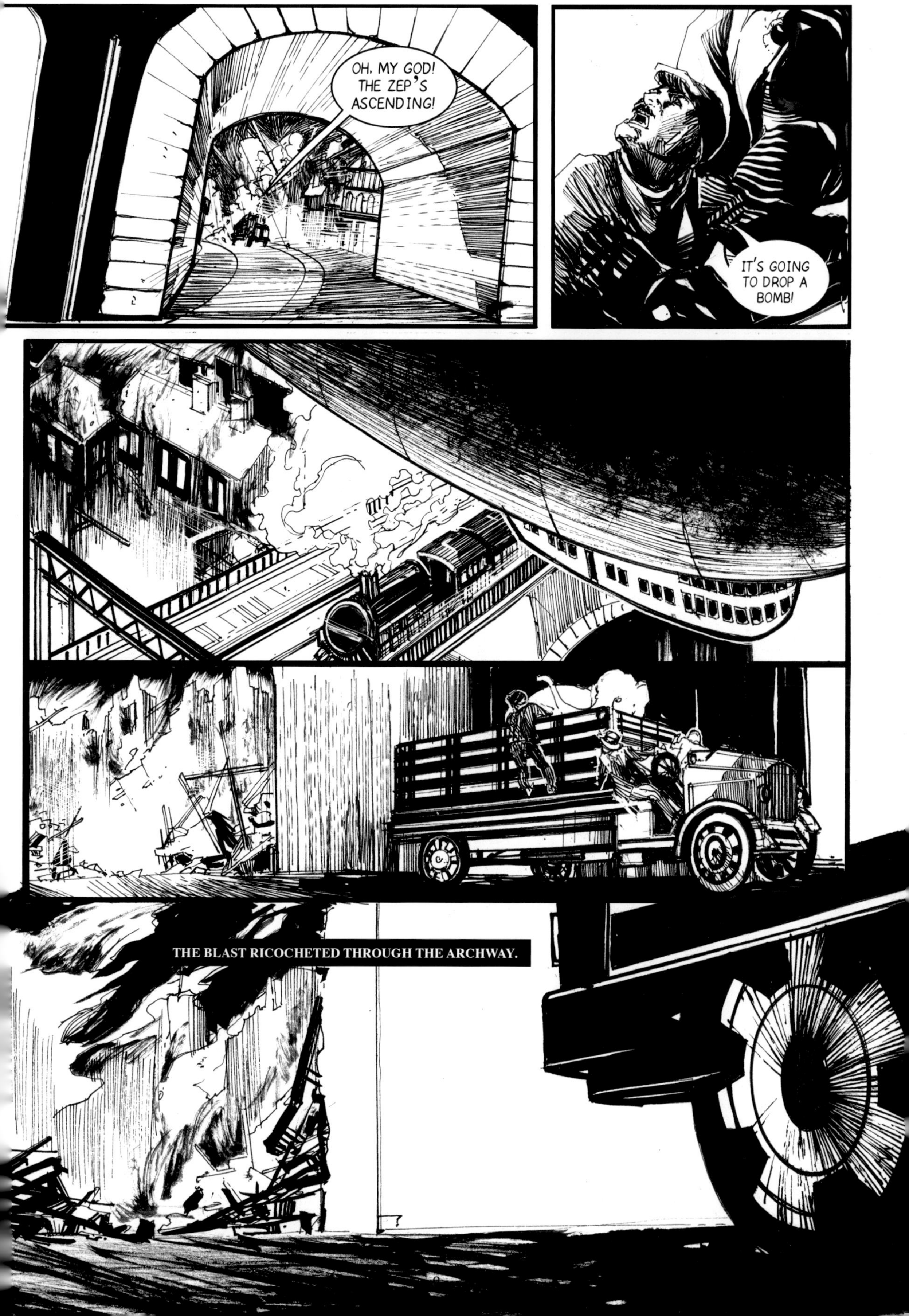
OH, MY GOD! THE ZEP'S ASCENDING!
IT'S GOING TO DROP A BOMB!
THE BLAST RICOCHETED THROUGH THE ARCHWAY.

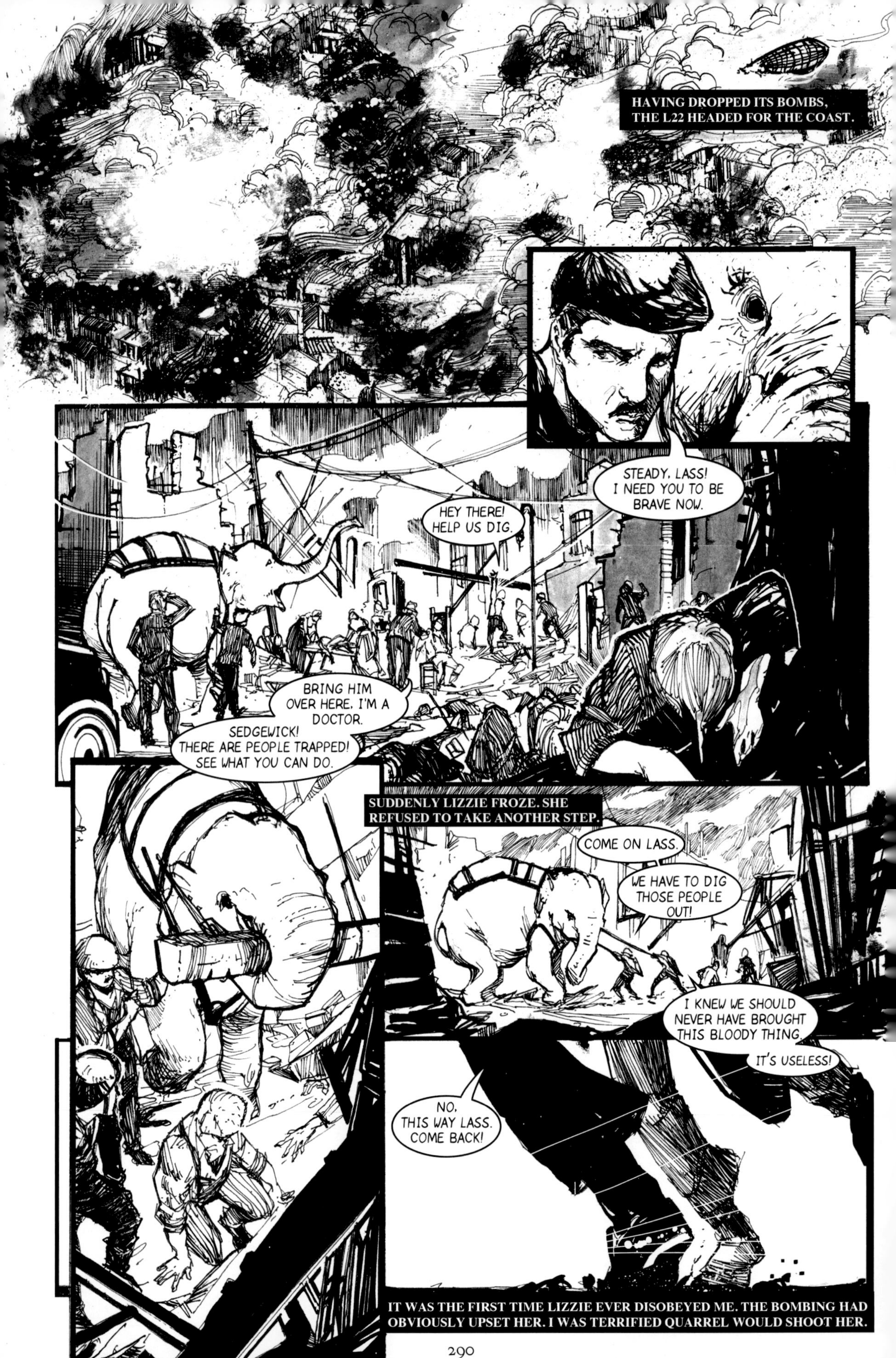
HAVING DROPPED ITS BOMBS, THE L22 HEADED FOR THE COAST.
STEADY, LASS! I NEED YOU TO BE BRAVE NOW.
HEY THERE! HELP US DIG.
BRING HIM OVER HERE, I'M A DOCTOR.
SEDGEWICK! THERE ARE PEOPLE TRAPPED! SEE WHAT YOU CAN DO.
SUDDENLY LIZZIE FROZE. SHE REFUSED TO TAKE ANOTHER STEP.
COME ON LASS.
WE HAVE TO DIG THOSE PEOPLE OUT!
I KNEW WE SHOULD NEVER HAVE BROUGHT THIS BLOODY THING.
IT'S USELESS!
NO, THIS WAY LASS. COME BACK!
IT WAS THE FIRST TIME LIZZIE EVER DISOBEYED ME. THE BOMBING HAD OBVIOUSLY UPSET HER. I WAS TERRIFIED QUARREL WOULD SHOOT HER.

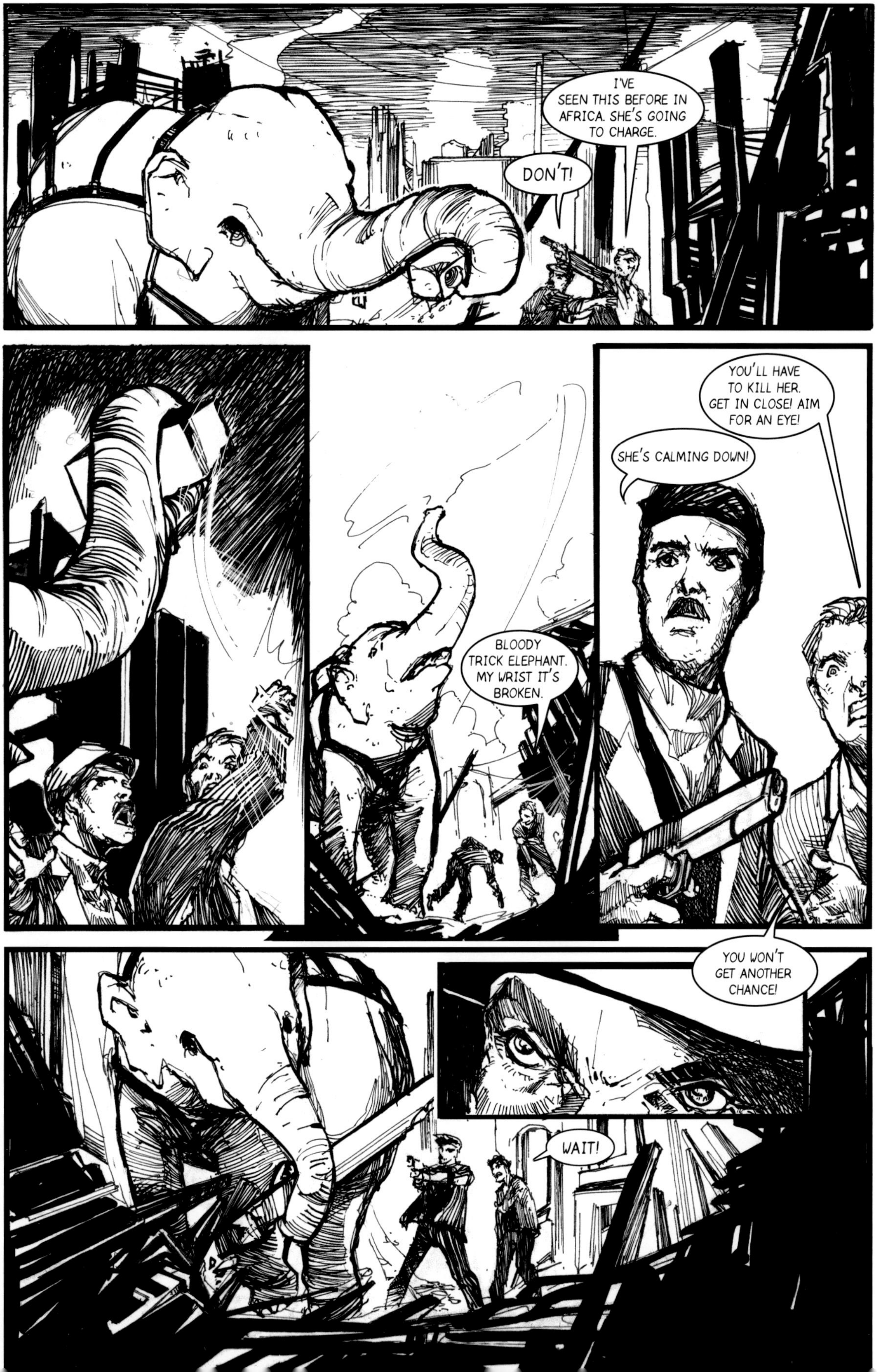
I'VE SEEN THIS BEFORE IN AFRICA. SHE'S GOING TO CHARGE.
DON'T!
BLOODY TRICK ELEPHANT. MY WRIST IT'S BROKEN.
YOU'LL HAVE TO KILL HER. GET IN CLOSE! AIM FOR AN EYE!
SHE'S CALMING DOWN!
YOU WON'T GET ANOTHER CHANCE!
WAIT!

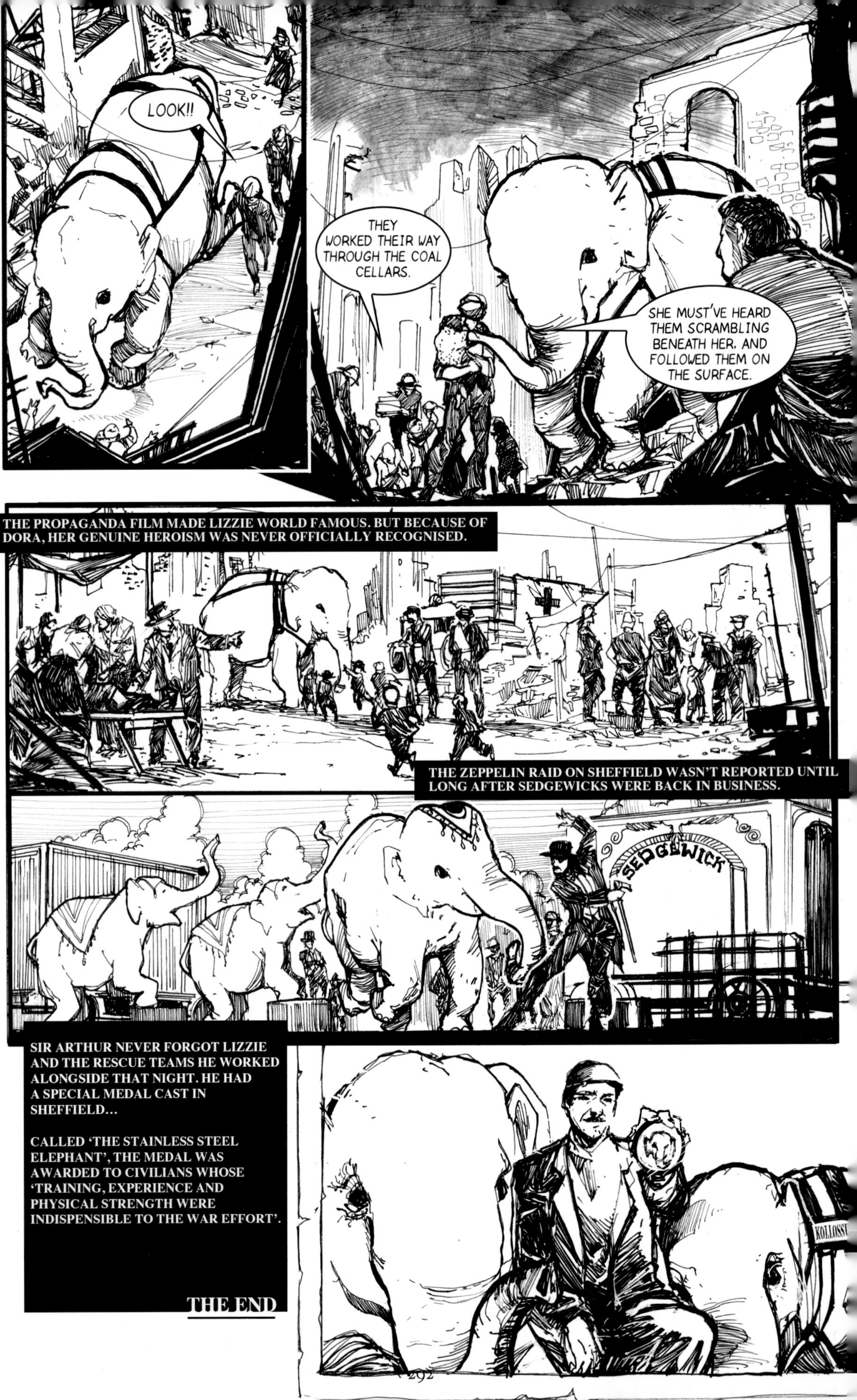
LOOK!!
THEY WORKED THEIR WAY THROUGH THE COAL CELLARS.
SHE MUST'VE HEARD THEM SCRAMBLING BENEATH HER, AND FOLLOWED THEM ON THE SURFACE.
THE PROPAGANDA FILM MADE LIZZIE WORLD FAMOUS. BUT BECAUSE OF DORA, HER GENUINE HEROISM WAS NEVER OFFICIALLY RECOGNISED.
THE ZEPPELIN RAID ON SHEFFIELD WASN'T REPORTED UNTIL LONG AFTER SEDGEWICKS WERE BACK IN BUSINESS.
SEDGEWICK
SIR ARTHUR NEVER FORGOT LIZZIE AND THE RESCUE TEAMS HE WORKED ALONGSIDE THAT NIGHT. HE HAD A SPECIAL MEDAL CAST IN SHEFFIELD…
CALLED 'THE STAINLESS STEEL ELEPHANT', THE MEDAL WAS AWARDED TO CIVILIANS WHOSE 'TRAINING, EXPERIENCE AND PHYSICAL STRENGTH WERE INDISPENSIBLE TO THE WAR EFFORT'.
THE END
KOLLOSSU

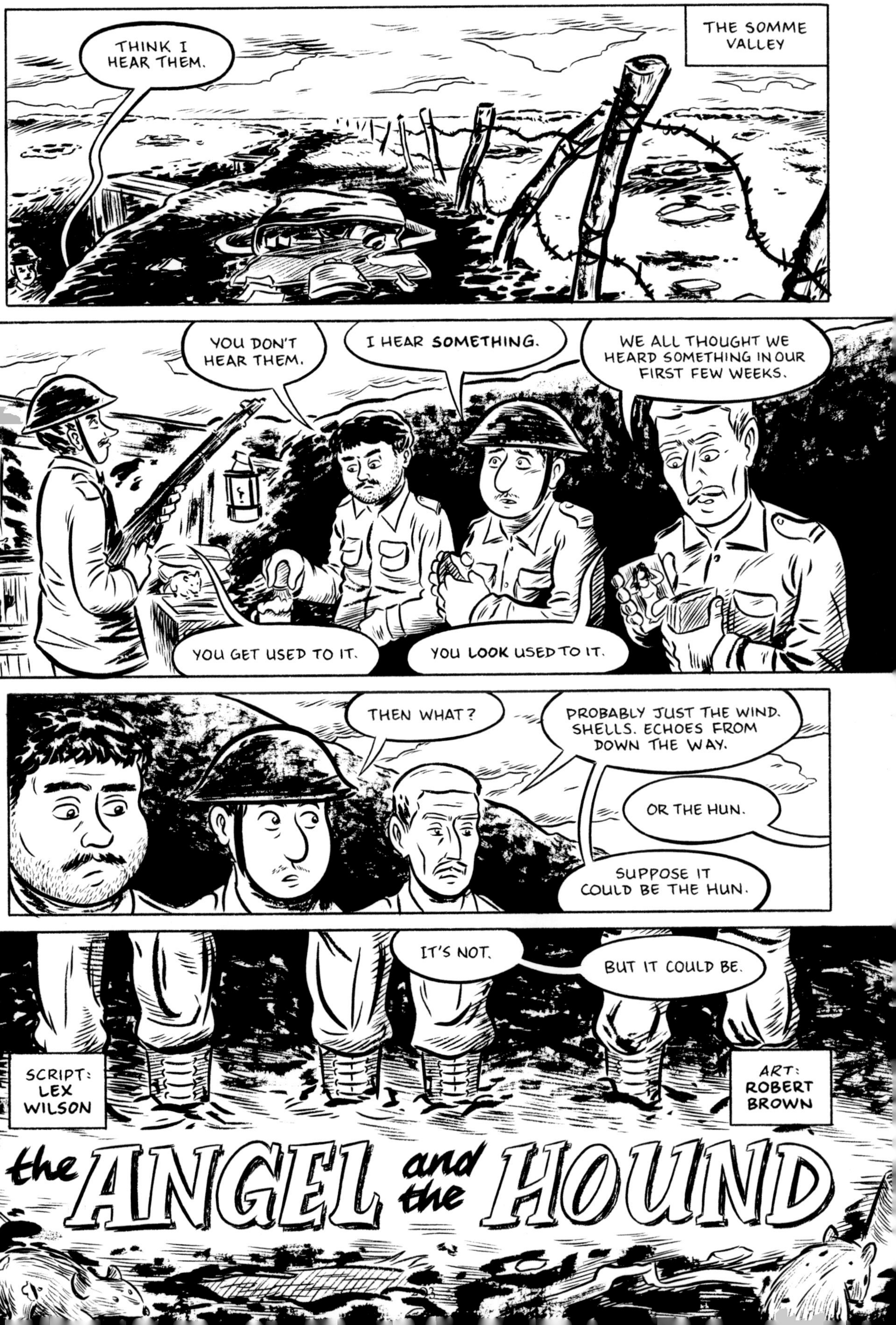
THE SOMME VALLEY
THINK I HEAR THEM.
YOU DON'T HEAR THEM.
I HEAR SOMETHING.
WE ALL THOUGHT WE HEARD SOMETHING IN OUR FIRST FEW WEEKS.
YOU GET USED TO IT.
YOU LOOK USED TO IT.
THEN WHAT?
PROBABLY JUST THE WIND. SHELLS. ECHOES FROM DOWN THE WAY.
OR THE HUN.
SUPPOSE IT COULD BE THE HUN.
IT'S NOT.
BUT IT COULD BE.
SCRIPT: LEX WILSON
ART: ROBERT BROWN
the ANGEL and the HOUND

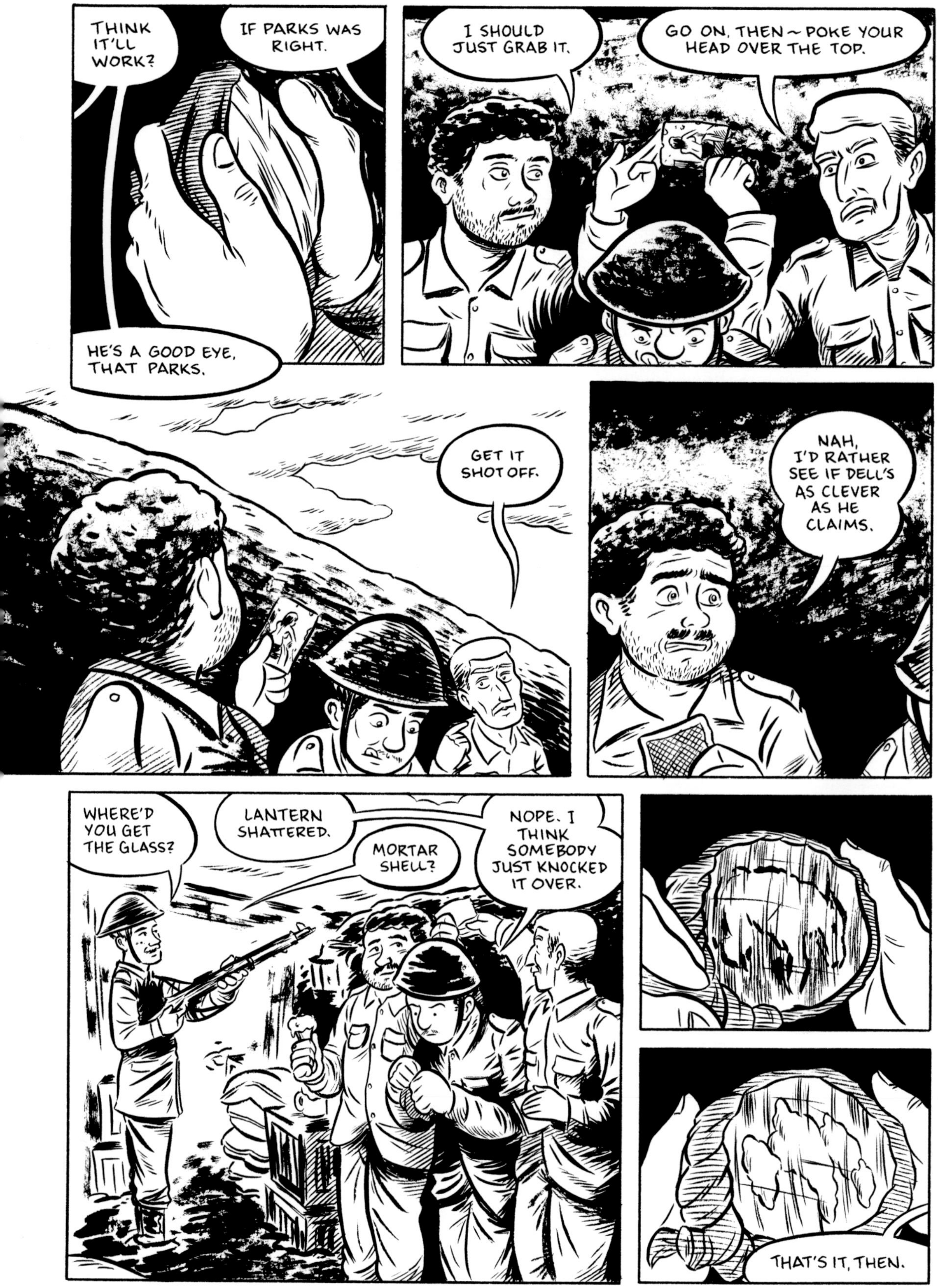
THINK IT'LL WORK?
IF PARKS WAS RIGHT.
HE'S A GOOD EYE, THAT PARKS.
I SHOULD JUST GRAB IT.
GO ON, THEN ~ POKE YOUR HEAD OVER THE TOP.
GET IT SHOT OFF.
NAH, I'D RATHER SEE IF DELL'S AS CLEVER AS HE CLAIMS.
WHERE'D YOU GET THE GLASS?
LANTERN SHATTERED.
MORTAR SHELL?
NOPE. I THINK SOMEBODY JUST KNOCKED IT OVER.
THAT'S IT, THEN.

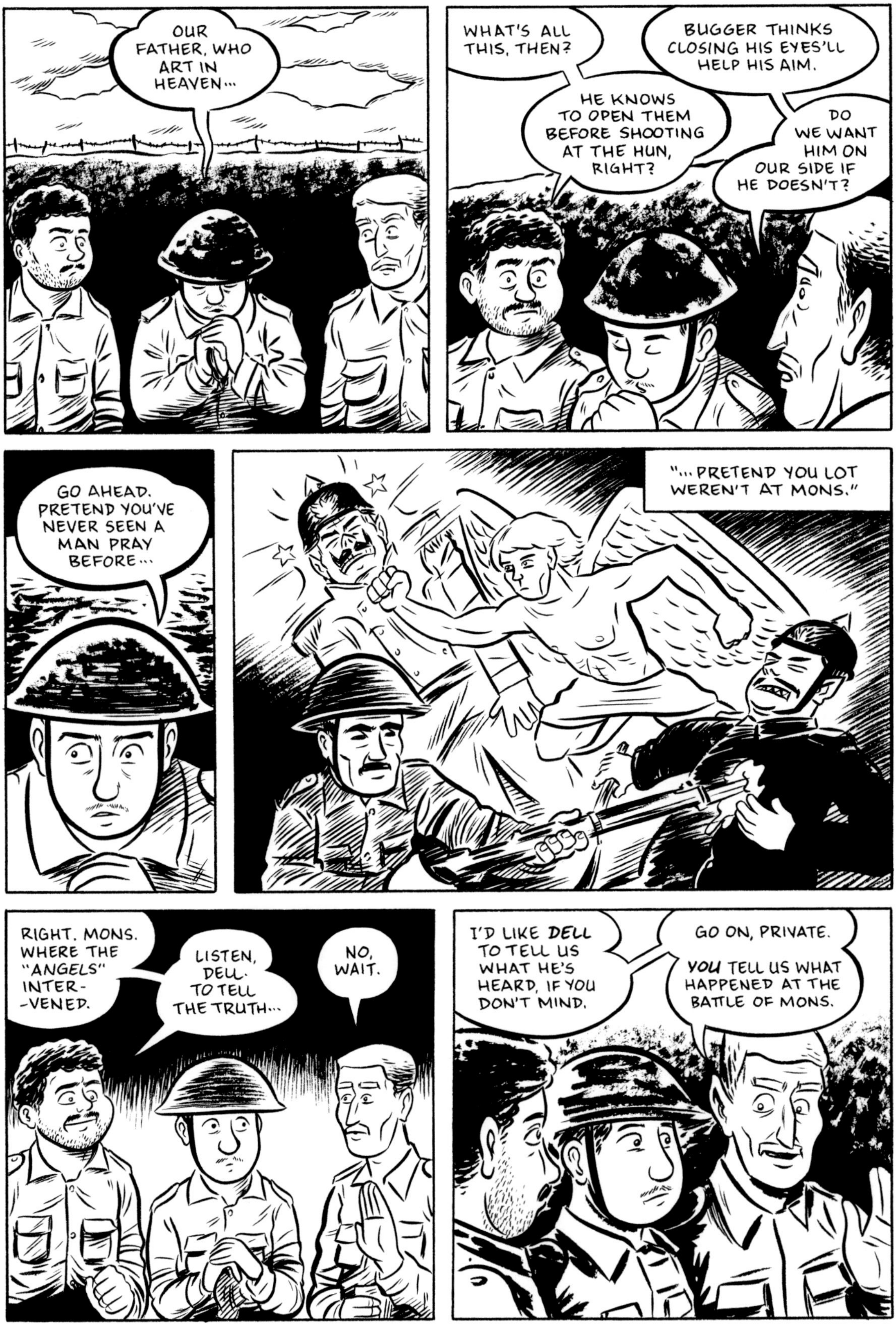
OUR FATHER, WHO ART IN HEAVEN...
WHAT'S ALL THIS, THEN?
BUGGER THINKS CLOSING HIS EYES'LL HELP HIS AIM.
HE KNOWS TO OPEN THEM BEFORE SHOOTING AT THE HUN, RIGHT?
DO WE WANT HIM ON OUR SIDE IF HE DOESN'T?
GO AHEAD. PRETEND YOU'VE NEVER SEEN A MAN PRAY BEFORE...
"...PRETEND YOU LOT WEREN'T AT MONS."
RIGHT. MONS. WHERE THE "ANGELS" INTER--VENED.
LISTEN, DELL. TO TELL THE TRUTH...
NO, WAIT.
I'D LIKE **DELL** TO TELL US WHAT HE'S HEARD, IF YOU DON'T MIND.
GO ON, PRIVATE.
YOU TELL US WHAT HAPPENED AT THE BATTLE OF MONS.

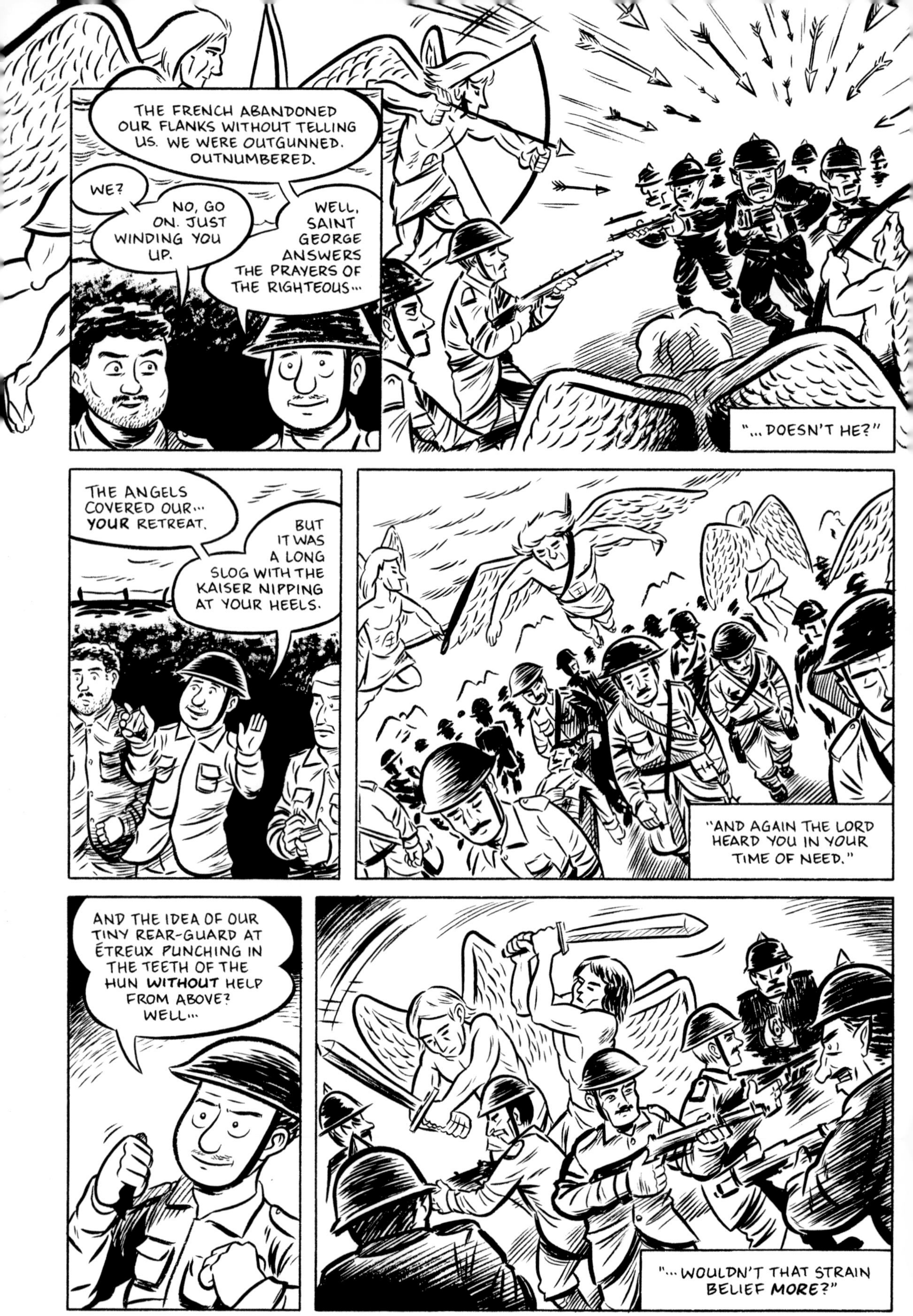
THE FRENCH ABANDONED OUR FLANKS WITHOUT TELLING US. WE WERE OUTGUNNED. OUTNUMBERED.
WE?
NO, GO ON. JUST WINDING YOU UP.
WELL, SAINT GEORGE ANSWERS THE PRAYERS OF THE RIGHTEOUS...
"...DOESN'T HE?"
THE ANGELS COVERED OUR... **YOUR** RETREAT.
BUT IT WAS A LONG SLOG WITH THE KAISER NIPPING AT YOUR HEELS.
"AND AGAIN THE LORD HEARD YOU IN YOUR TIME OF NEED."
AND THE IDEA OF OUR TINY REAR-GUARD AT ÉTREUX PUNCHING IN THE TEETH OF THE HUN **WITHOUT** HELP FROM ABOVE? WELL...
"...WOULDN'T THAT STRAIN BELIEF ***MORE***?"

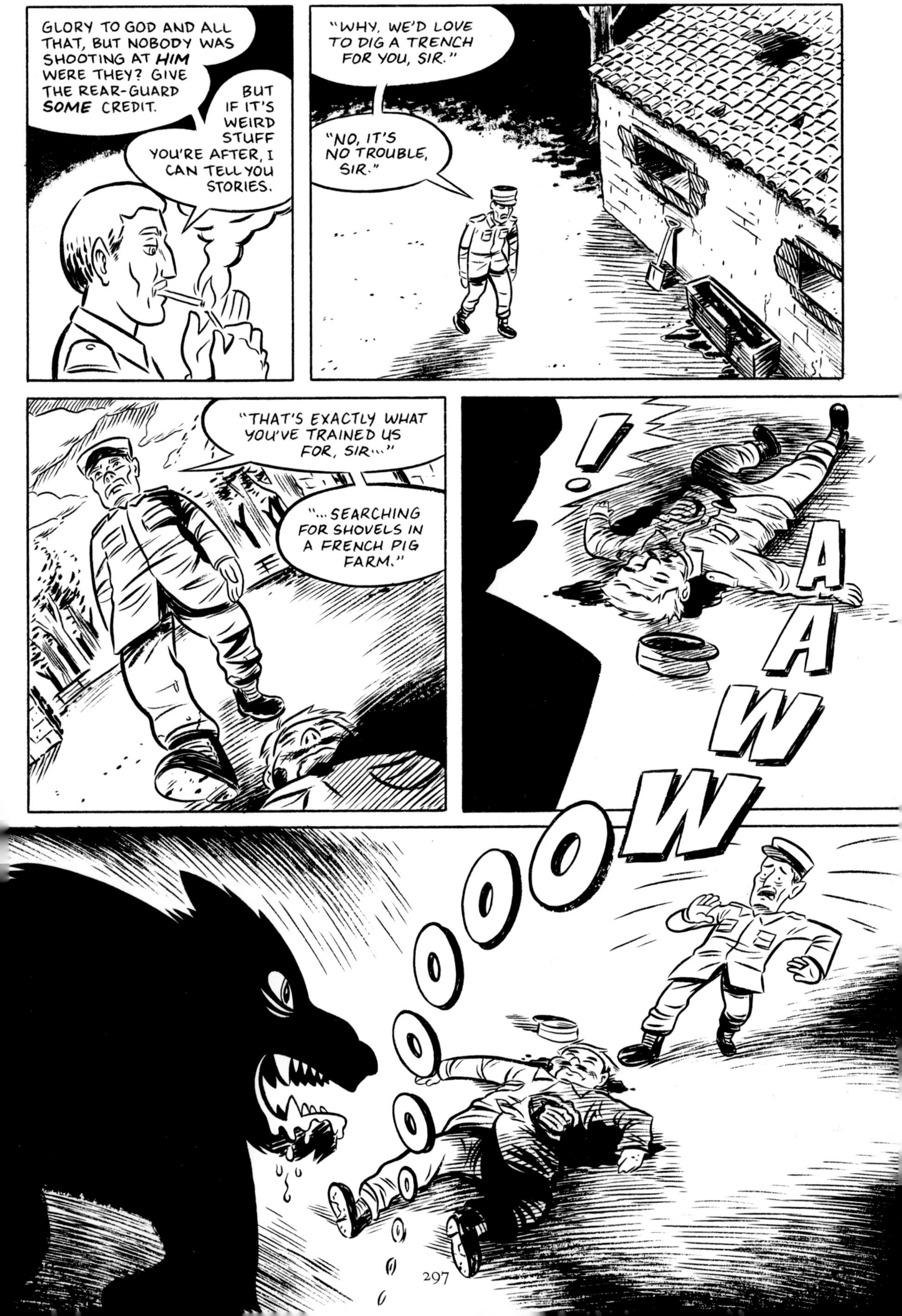
GLORY TO GOD AND ALL THAT, BUT NOBODY WAS SHOOTING AT HIM WERE THEY? GIVE THE REAR-GUARD SOME CREDIT.
BUT IF IT'S WEIRD STUFF YOU'RE AFTER, I CAN TELL YOU STORIES.
"WHY, WE'D LOVE TO DIG A TRENCH FOR YOU, SIR."
"NO, IT'S NO TROUBLE, SIR."
"THAT'S EXACTLY WHAT YOU'VE TRAINED US FOR, SIR..."
"...SEARCHING FOR SHOVELS IN A FRENCH PIG FARM."
!
AAWWOOOOOO

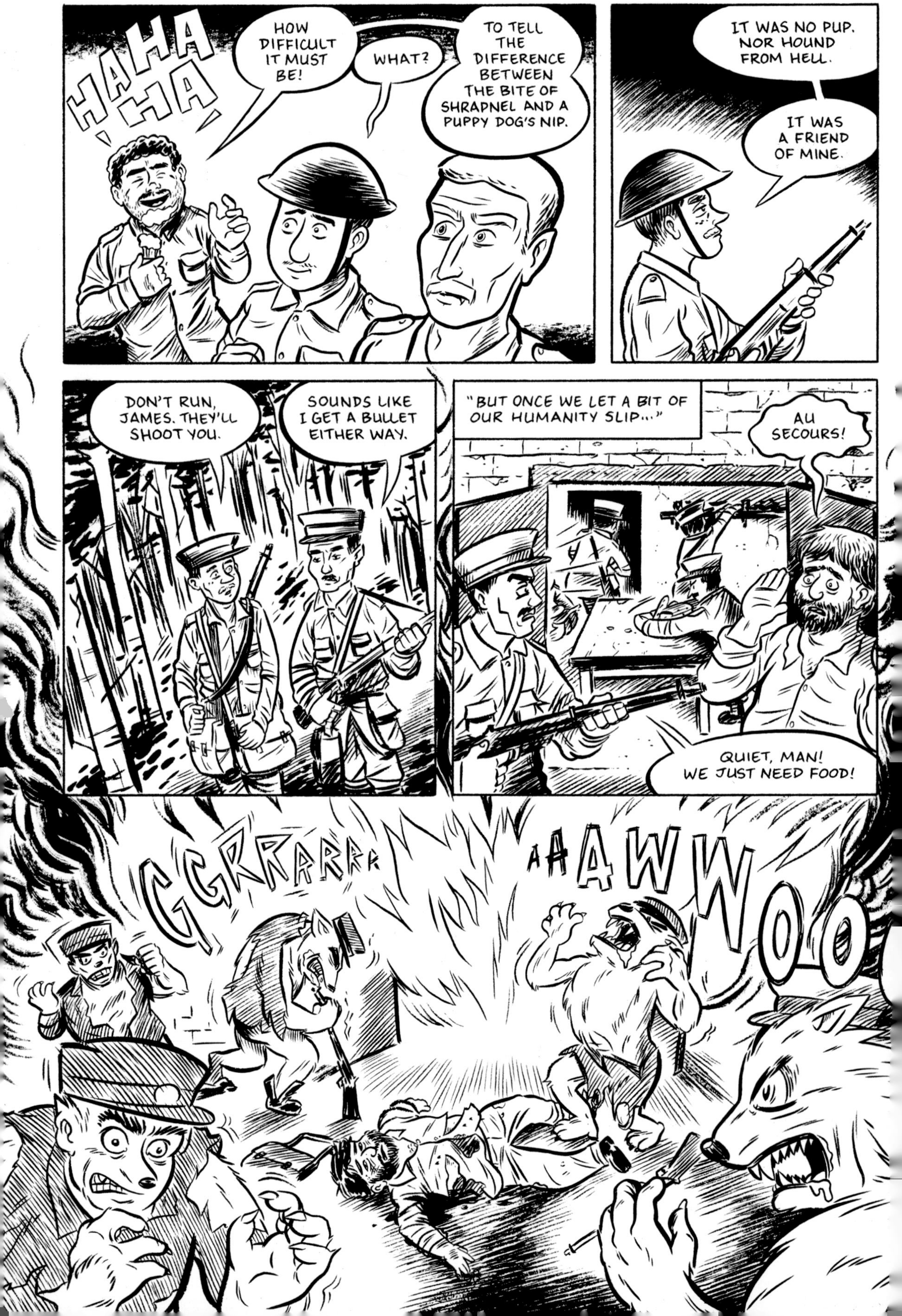
HAHA HA
HOW DIFFICULT IT MUST BE!
WHAT?
TO TELL THE DIFFERENCE BETWEEN THE BITE OF SHRAPNEL AND A PUPPY DOG'S NIP.
IT WAS NO PUP. NOR HOUND FROM HELL.
IT WAS A FRIEND OF MINE.
DON'T RUN, JAMES. THEY'LL SHOOT YOU.
SOUNDS LIKE I GET A BULLET EITHER WAY.
"BUT ONCE WE LET A BIT OF OUR HUMANITY SLIP..."
AU SECOURS!
QUIET, MAN! WE JUST NEED FOOD!
GGRRRRRR
AAAWWOOO

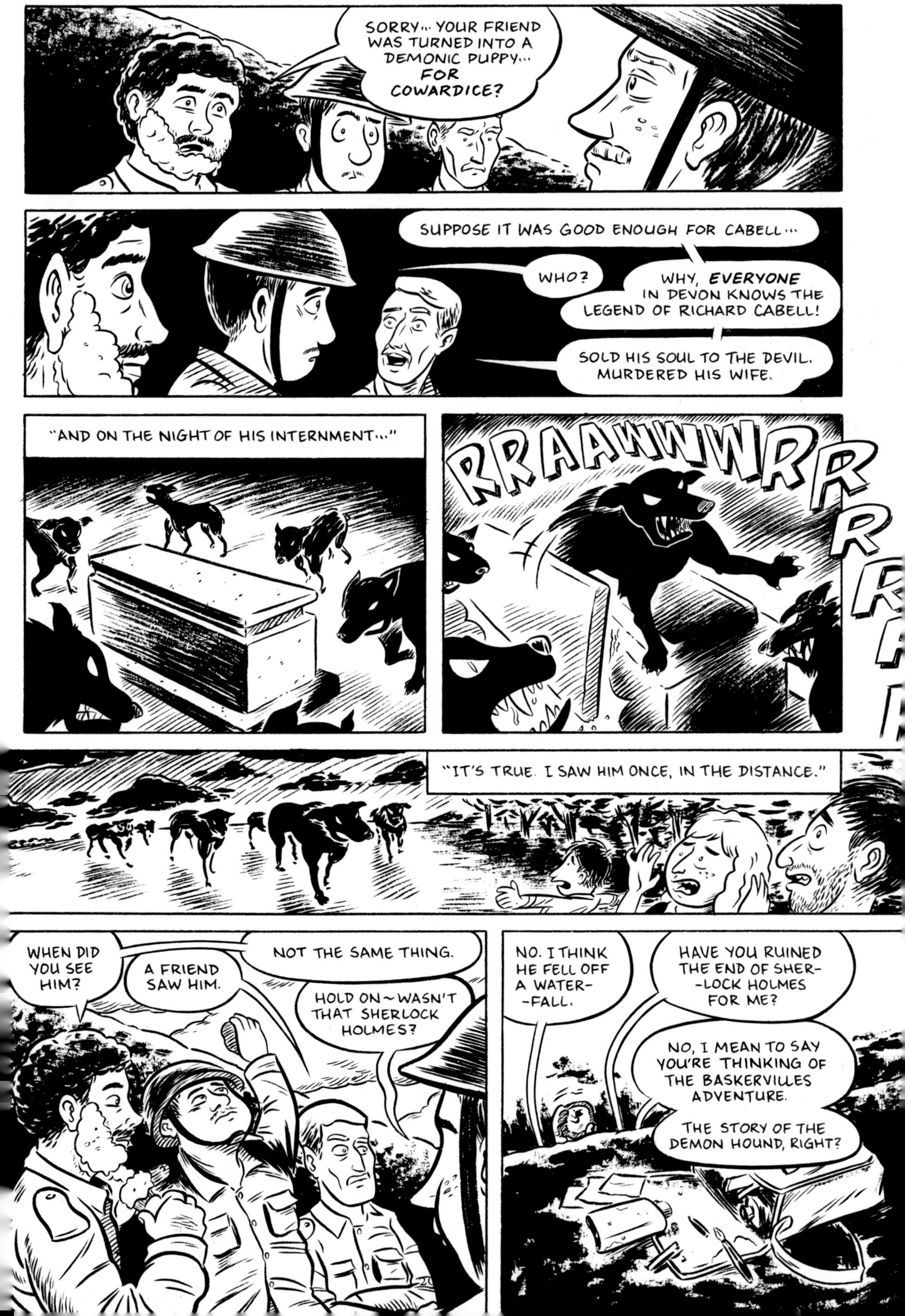
SORRY... YOUR FRIEND WAS TURNED INTO A DEMONIC PUPPY... FOR COWARDICE?
SUPPOSE IT WAS GOOD ENOUGH FOR CABELL...
WHO?
WHY, EVERYONE IN DEVON KNOWS THE LEGEND OF RICHARD CABELL!
SOLD HIS SOUL TO THE DEVIL. MURDERED HIS WIFE.
"AND ON THE NIGHT OF HIS INTERNMENT..."
RRAAWWWRRRRR
"IT'S TRUE. I SAW HIM ONCE, IN THE DISTANCE."
WHEN DID YOU SEE HIM?
A FRIEND SAW HIM.
NOT THE SAME THING.
HOLD ON~WASN'T THAT SHERLOCK HOLMES?
NO. I THINK HE FELL OFF A WATER-FALL.
HAVE YOU RUINED THE END OF SHER-LOCK HOLMES FOR ME?
NO, I MEAN TO SAY YOU'RE THINKING OF THE BASKERVILLES ADVENTURE.
THE STORY OF THE DEMON HOUND, RIGHT?

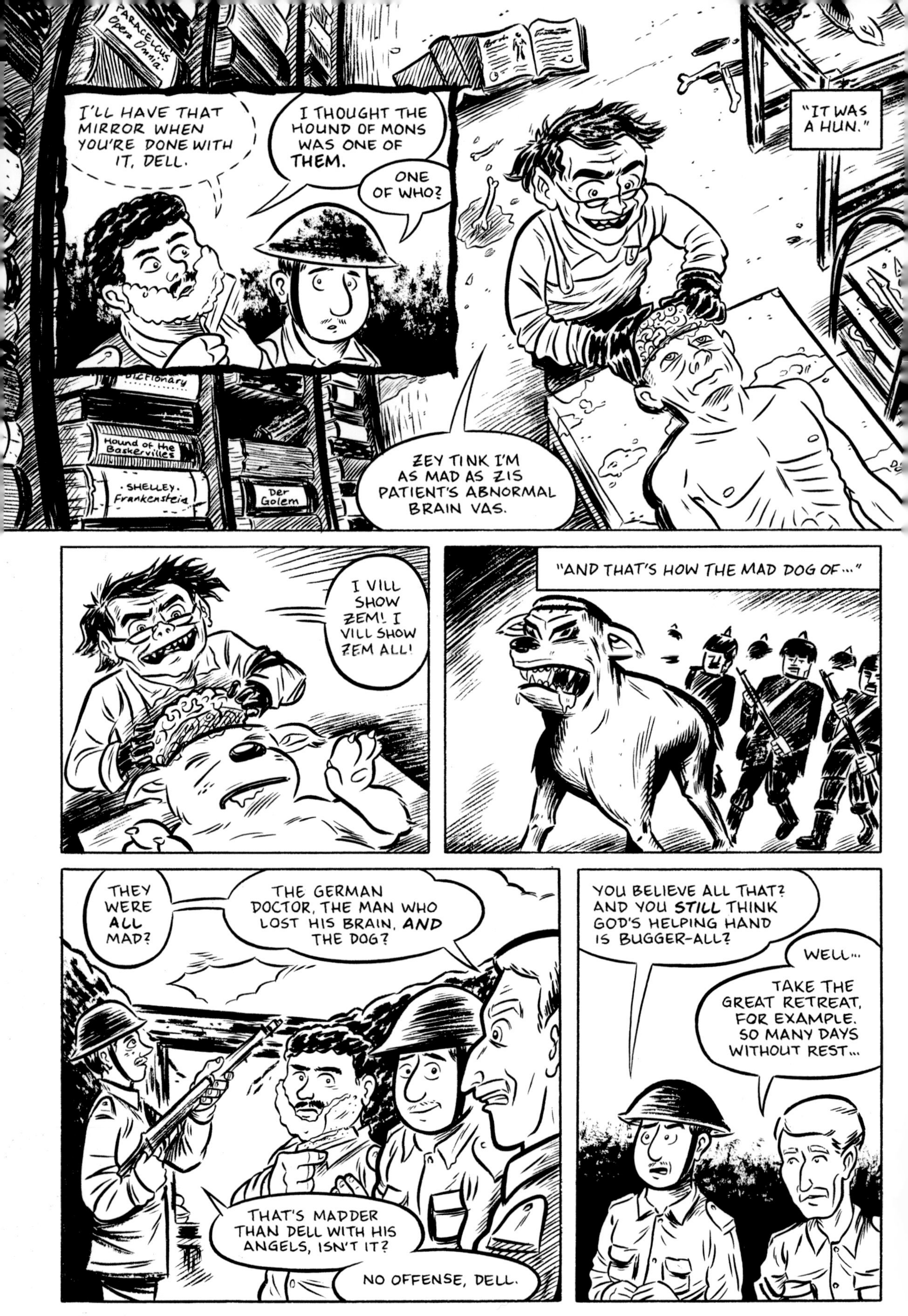

PARACELSUS Opera Omnia.
I'LL HAVE THAT MIRROR WHEN YOU'RE DONE WITH IT, DELL.
I THOUGHT THE HOUND OF MONS WAS ONE OF **THEM.**
ONE OF WHO?
Dictionary
Hound of the Baskervilles
SHELLEY. Frankenstein
Der Golem
"IT WAS A HUN."
ZEY TINK I'M AS MAD AS ZIS PATIENT'S ABNORMAL BRAIN VAS.
I VILL SHOW ZEM! I VILL SHOW ZEM ALL!
"AND THAT'S HOW THE MAD DOG OF..."
THEY WERE **ALL** MAD?
THE GERMAN DOCTOR, THE MAN WHO LOST HIS BRAIN, **AND** THE DOG?
THAT'S MADDER THAN DELL WITH HIS ANGELS, ISN'T IT?
NO OFFENSE, DELL.
YOU BELIEVE ALL THAT? AND YOU **STILL** THINK GOD'S HELPING HAND IS BUGGER-ALL?
WELL...
TAKE THE GREAT RETREAT, FOR EXAMPLE. SO MANY DAYS WITHOUT REST...

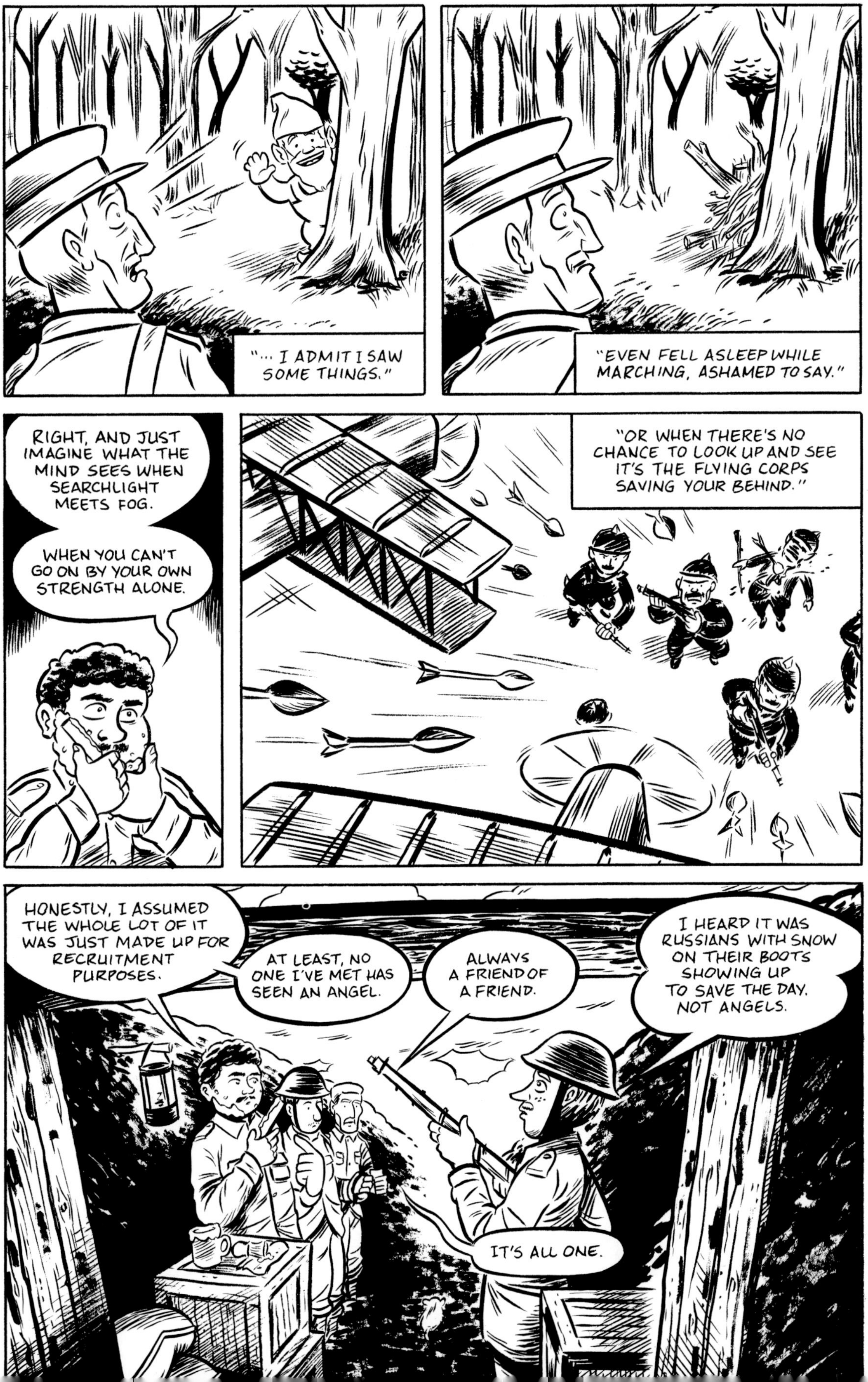
"... I ADMIT I SAW SOME THINGS."
"EVEN FELL ASLEEP WHILE MARCHING, ASHAMED TO SAY."
RIGHT, AND JUST IMAGINE WHAT THE MIND SEES WHEN SEARCHLIGHT MEETS FOG.
WHEN YOU CAN'T GO ON BY YOUR OWN STRENGTH ALONE.
"OR WHEN THERE'S NO CHANCE TO LOOK UP AND SEE IT'S THE FLYING CORPS SAVING YOUR BEHIND."
HONESTLY, I ASSUMED THE WHOLE LOT OF IT WAS JUST MADE UP FOR RECRUITMENT PURPOSES.
AT LEAST, NO ONE I'VE MET HAS SEEN AN ANGEL.
ALWAYS A FRIEND OF A FRIEND.
I HEARD IT WAS RUSSIANS WITH SNOW ON THEIR BOOTS SHOWING UP TO SAVE THE DAY. NOT ANGELS.
IT'S ALL ONE.

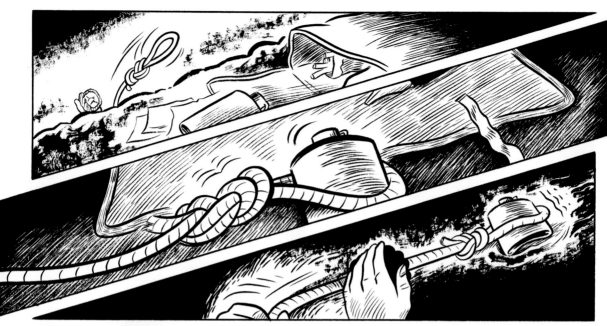

HEY! HE DID IT!

NEVER DOUBTED YOU FOR A SECOND!

IS IT FULL? HOW FULL IS IT?

FULL ENOUGH.

SO WHY ARE YOU SO INTERESTED IN THIS ANGEL NONSENSE ANYWAY?

SUPPOSE WE ALL HAVE OUR REASONS FOR SIGNING ON.

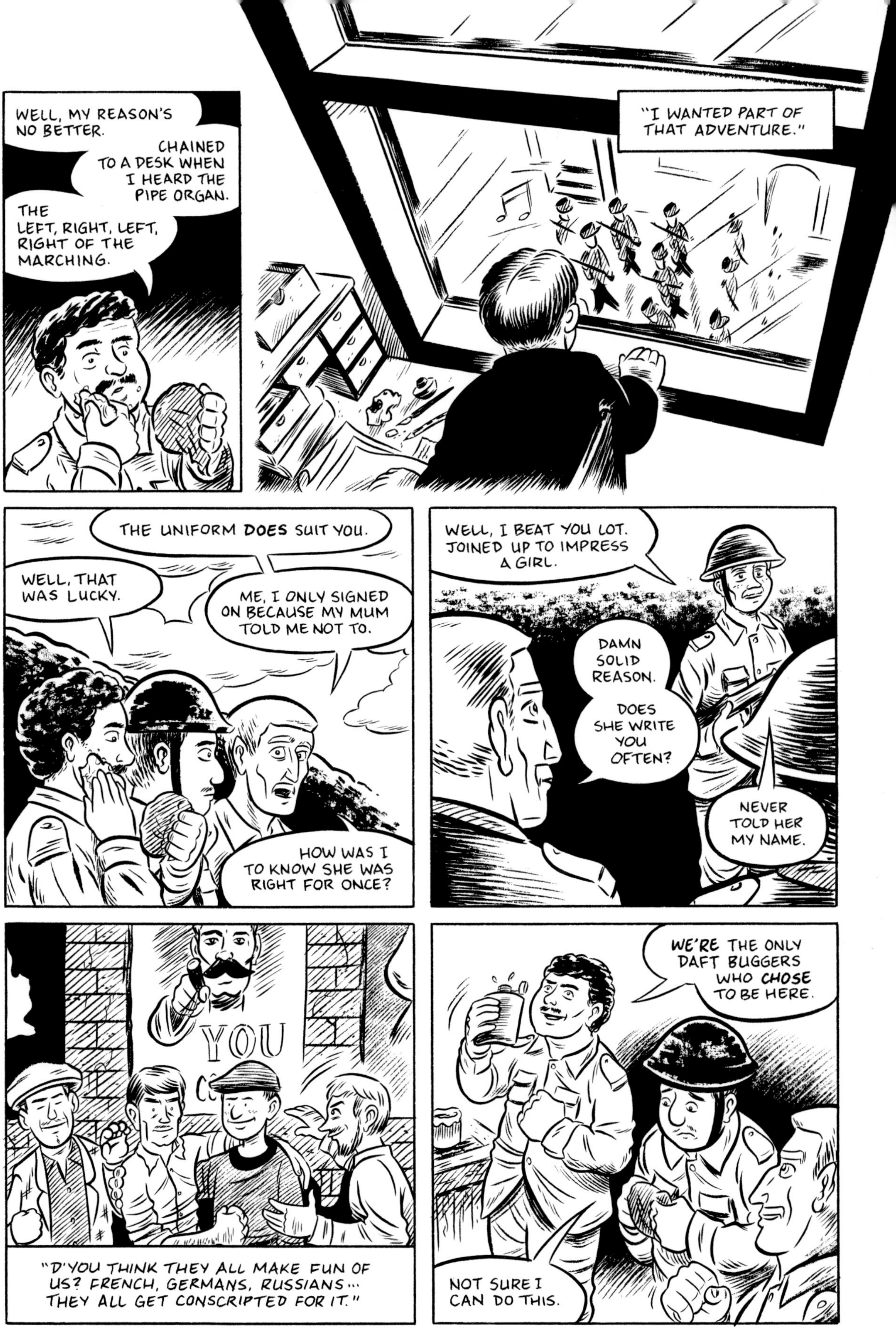
WELL, MY REASON'S NO BETTER.
CHAINED TO A DESK WHEN I HEARD THE PIPE ORGAN.
THE LEFT, RIGHT, LEFT, RIGHT OF THE MARCHING.
"I WANTED PART OF THAT ADVENTURE."
THE UNIFORM DOES SUIT YOU.
WELL, THAT WAS LUCKY.
ME, I ONLY SIGNED ON BECAUSE MY MUM TOLD ME NOT TO.
HOW WAS I TO KNOW SHE WAS RIGHT FOR ONCE?
WELL, I BEAT YOU LOT. JOINED UP TO IMPRESS A GIRL.
DAMN SOLID REASON.
DOES SHE WRITE YOU OFTEN?
NEVER TOLD HER MY NAME.
YOU
"D'YOU THINK THEY ALL MAKE FUN OF US? FRENCH, GERMANS, RUSSIANS... THEY ALL GET CONSCRIPTED FOR IT."
WE'RE THE ONLY DAFT BUGGERS WHO CHOSE TO BE HERE.
NOT SURE I CAN DO THIS.

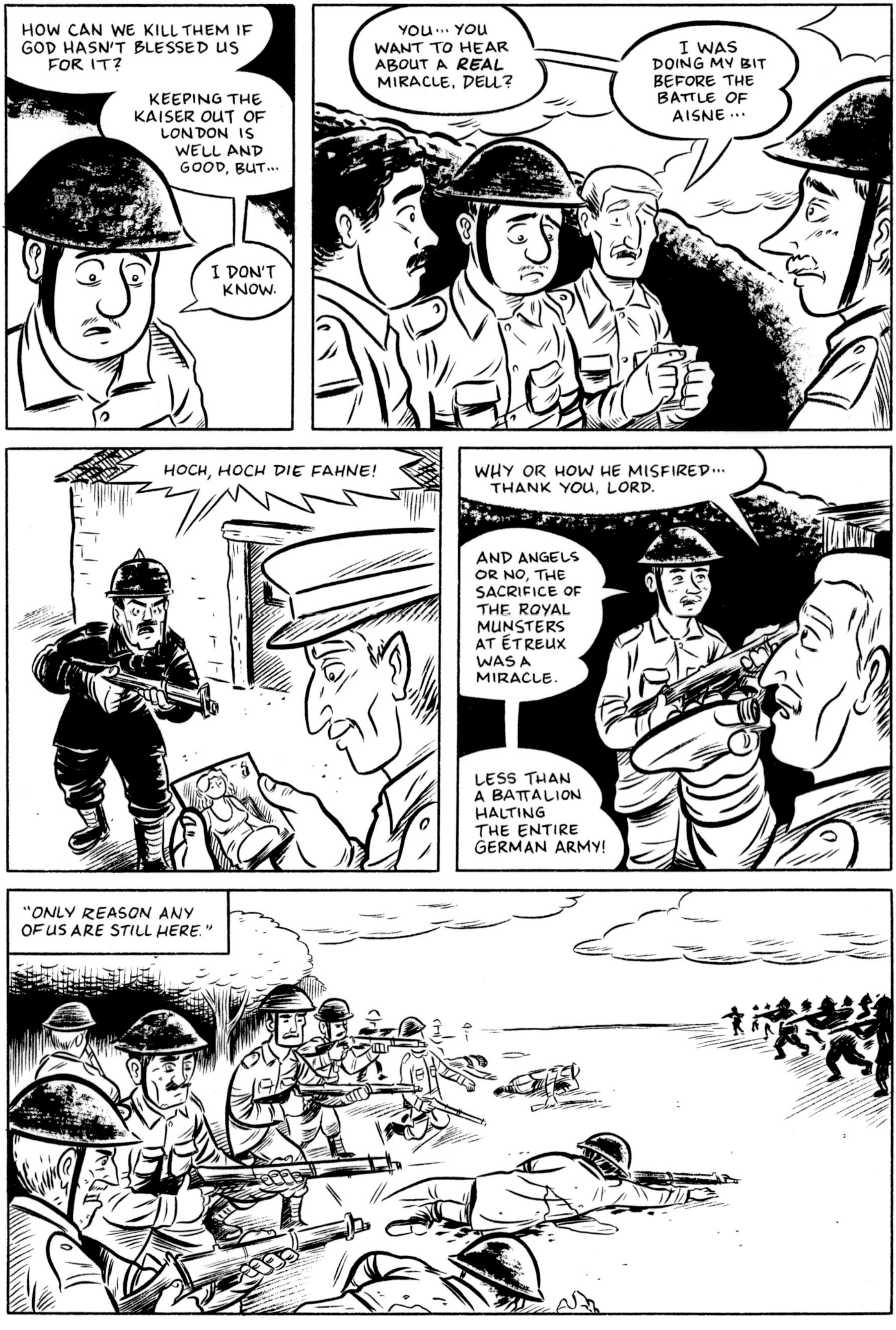
HOW CAN WE KILL THEM IF GOD HASN'T BLESSED US FOR IT?
KEEPING THE KAISER OUT OF LONDON IS WELL AND GOOD, BUT...
I DON'T KNOW.
YOU... YOU WANT TO HEAR ABOUT A **REAL** MIRACLE, DELL?
I WAS DOING MY BIT BEFORE THE BATTLE OF AISNE...
HOCH, HOCH DIE FAHNE!
WHY OR HOW HE MISFIRED... THANK YOU, LORD.
AND ANGELS OR NO, THE SACRIFICE OF THE ROYAL MUNSTERS AT ÉTREUX WAS A MIRACLE.
LESS THAN A BATTALION HALTING THE ENTIRE GERMAN ARMY!
"ONLY REASON ANY OF US ARE STILL HERE."

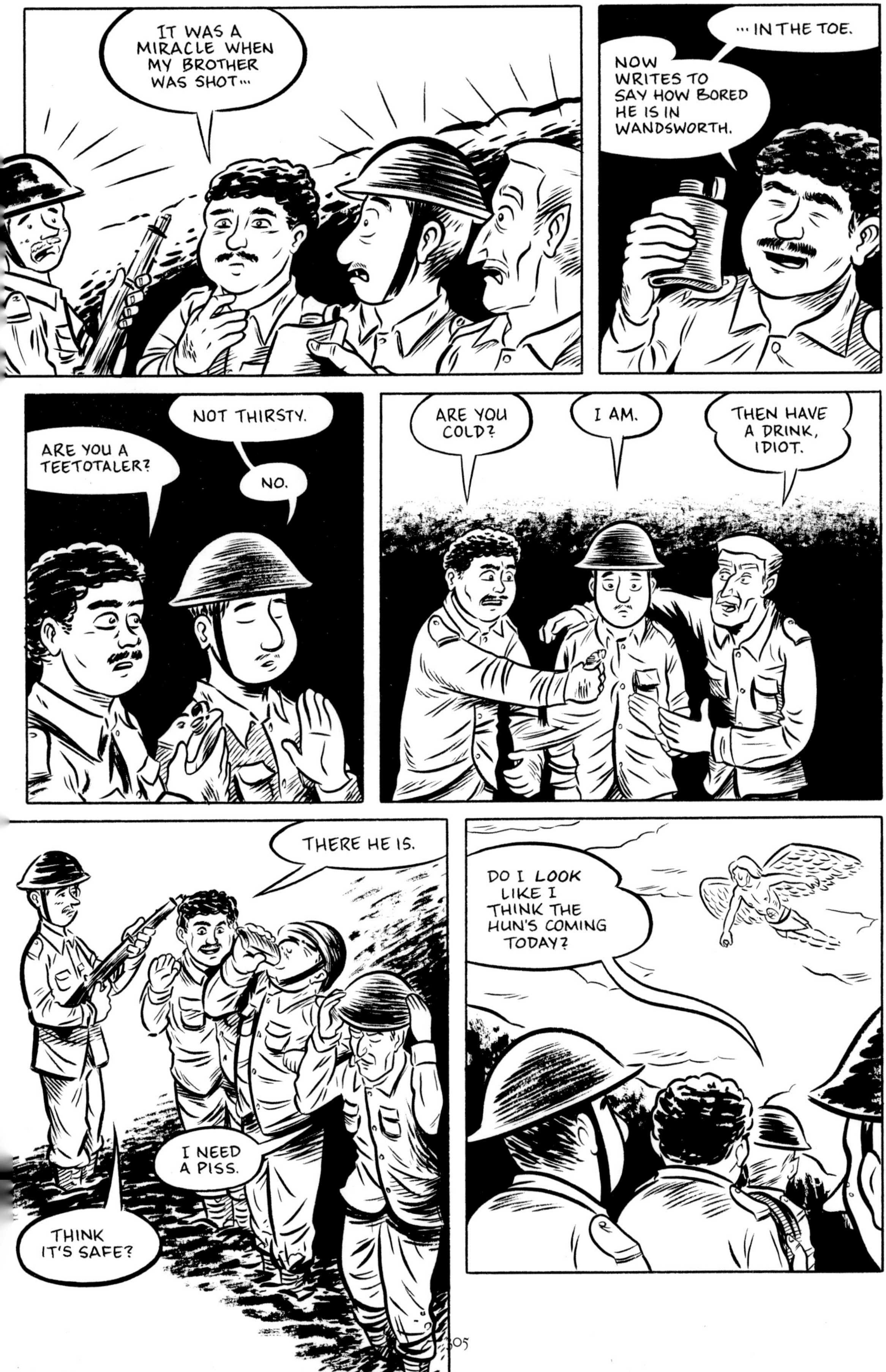

IT WAS A MIRACLE WHEN MY BROTHER WAS SHOT...
... IN THE TOE.
NOW WRITES TO SAY HOW BORED HE IS IN WANDSWORTH.
ARE YOU A TEETOTALER?
NOT THIRSTY.
NO.
ARE YOU COLD?
I AM.
THEN HAVE A DRINK, IDIOT.
THERE HE IS.
THINK IT'S SAFE?
I NEED A PISS.
DO I LOOK LIKE I THINK THE HUN'S COMING TODAY?

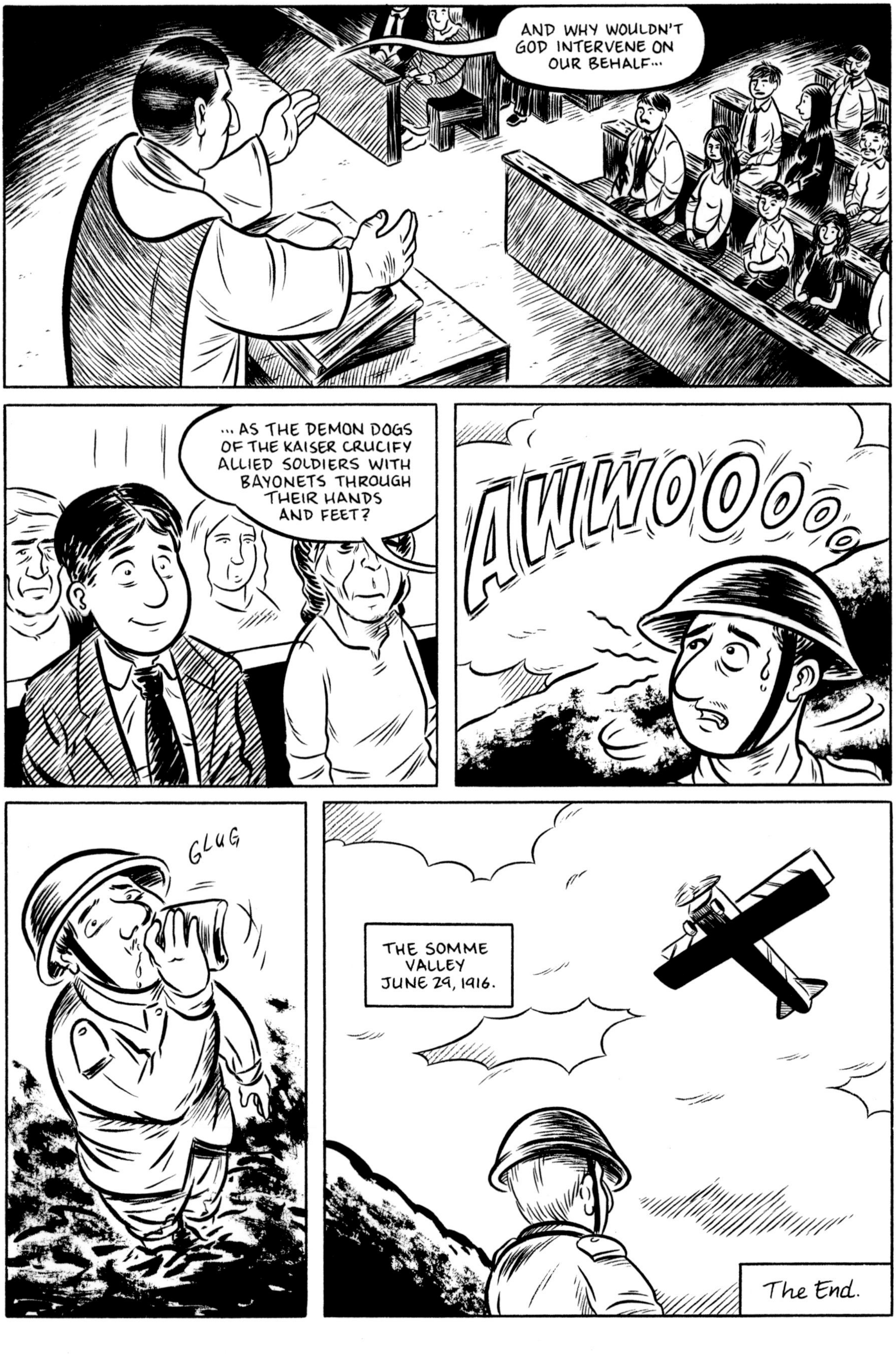
AND WHY WOULDN'T GOD INTERVENE ON OUR BEHALF...
...AS THE DEMON DOGS OF THE KAISER CRUCIFY ALLIED SOLDIERS WITH BAYONETS THROUGH THEIR HANDS AND FEET?
AWWOOOoo
GLUG
THE SOMME VALLEY JUNE 29, 1916.
The End.

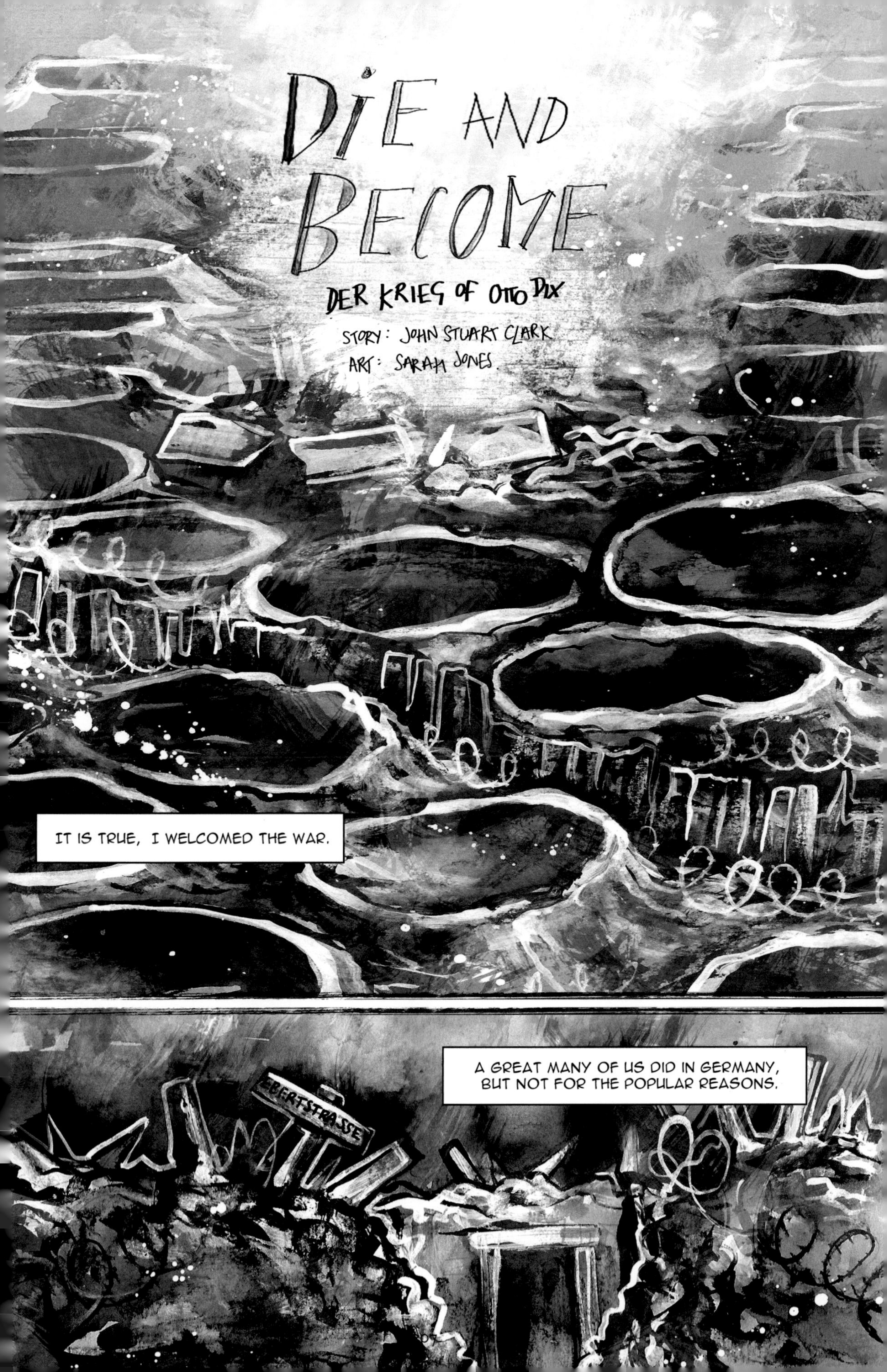
DIE AND BECOME
DER KRIEG OF OTTO DIX
STORY: JOHN STUART CLARK
ART: SARAH JONES.
IT IS TRUE, I WELCOMED THE WAR.
A GREAT MANY OF US DID IN GERMANY, BUT NOT FOR THE POPULAR REASONS.
EBERTSTRASSE

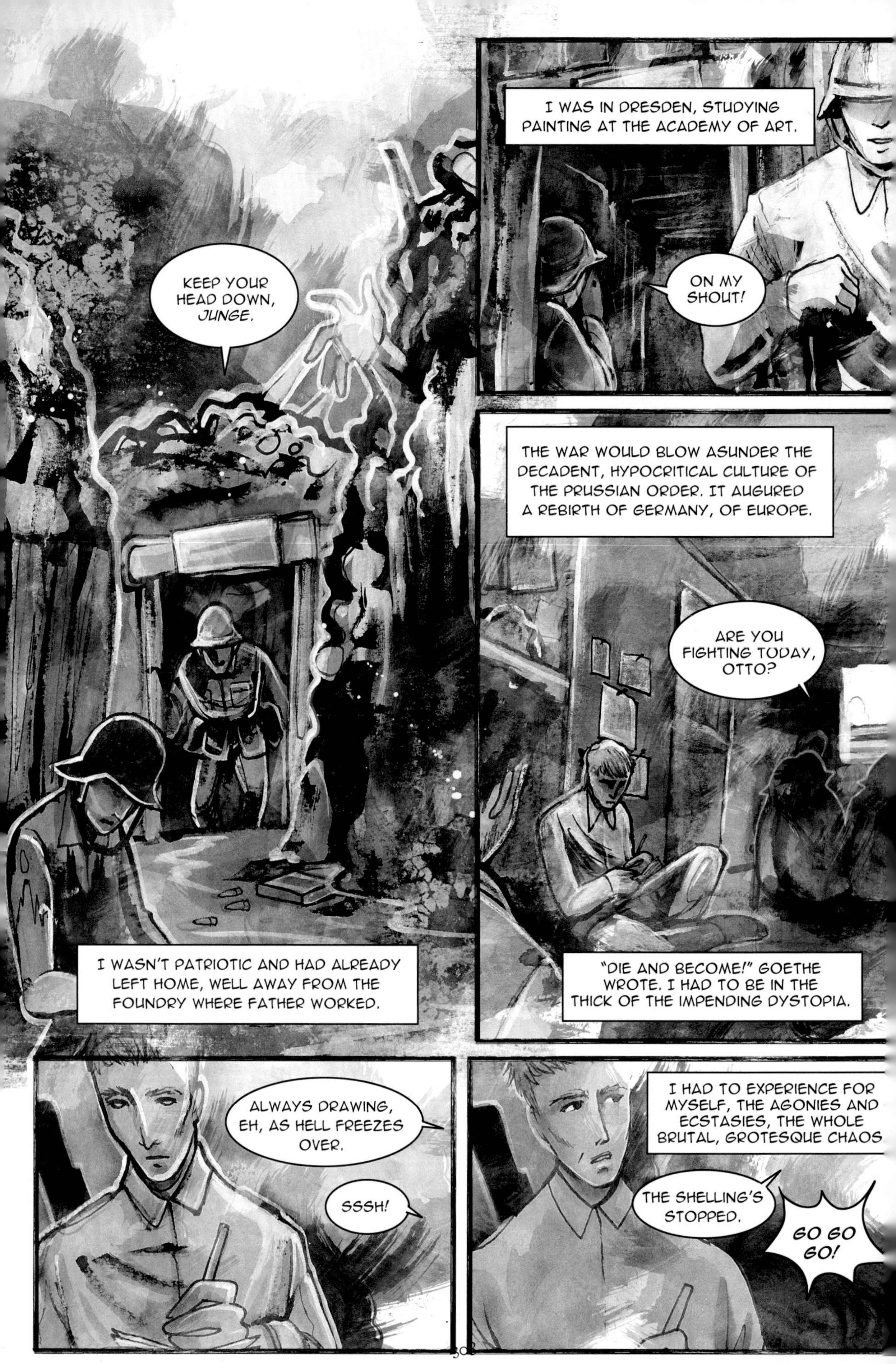
KEEP YOUR HEAD DOWN, JUNGE.
I WASN'T PATRIOTIC AND HAD ALREADY LEFT HOME, WELL AWAY FROM THE FOUNDRY WHERE FATHER WORKED.
I WAS IN DRESDEN, STUDYING PAINTING AT THE ACADEMY OF ART.
ON MY SHOUT!
THE WAR WOULD BLOW ASUNDER THE DECADENT, HYPOCRITICAL CULTURE OF THE PRUSSIAN ORDER. IT AUGURED A REBIRTH OF GERMANY, OF EUROPE.
ARE YOU FIGHTING TODAY, OTTO?
"DIE AND BECOME!" GOETHE WROTE. I HAD TO BE IN THE THICK OF THE IMPENDING DYSTOPIA.
ALWAYS DRAWING, EH, AS HELL FREEZES OVER.
SSSH!
I HAD TO EXPERIENCE FOR MYSELF, THE AGONIES AND ECSTASIES, THE WHOLE BRUTAL, GROTESQUE CHAOS
THE SHELLING'S STOPPED.
GO GO GO!

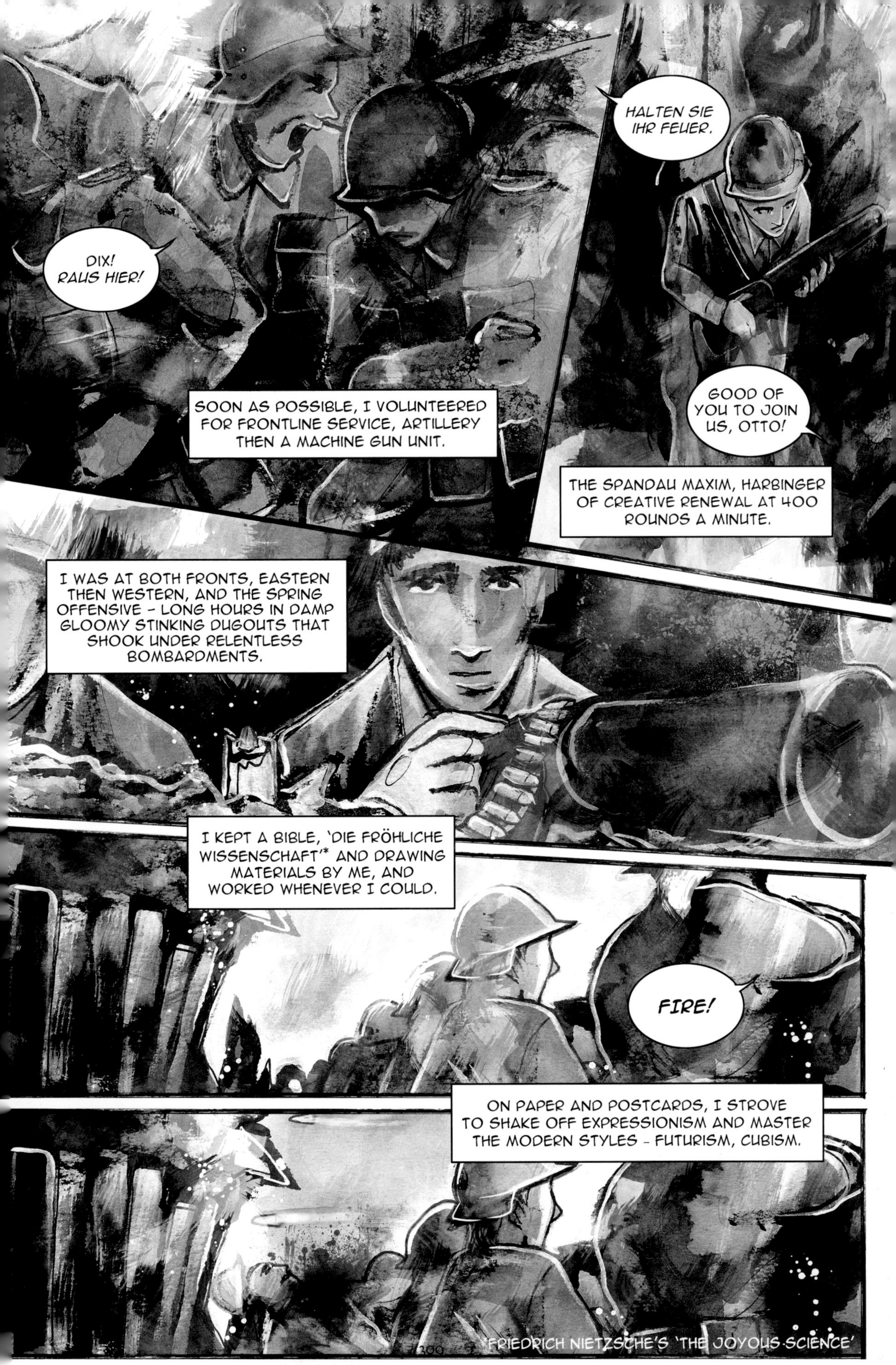
DIX! RAUS HIER!
SOON AS POSSIBLE, I VOLUNTEERED FOR FRONTLINE SERVICE, ARTILLERY THEN A MACHINE GUN UNIT.
HALTEN SIE IHR FEUER.
GOOD OF YOU TO JOIN US, OTTO!
THE SPANDAU MAXIM, HARBINGER OF CREATIVE RENEWAL AT 400 ROUNDS A MINUTE.
I WAS AT BOTH FRONTS, EASTERN THEN WESTERN, AND THE SPRING OFFENSIVE – LONG HOURS IN DAMP GLOOMY STINKING DUGOUTS THAT SHOOK UNDER RELENTLESS BOMBARDMENTS.
I KEPT A BIBLE, 'DIE FRÖHLICHE WISSENSCHAFT'* AND DRAWING MATERIALS BY ME, AND WORKED WHENEVER I COULD.
FIRE!
ON PAPER AND POSTCARDS, I STROVE TO SHAKE OFF EXPRESSIONISM AND MASTER THE MODERN STYLES – FUTURISM, CUBISM.
*FRIEDRICH NIETZSCHE'S 'THE JOYOUS SCIENCE'

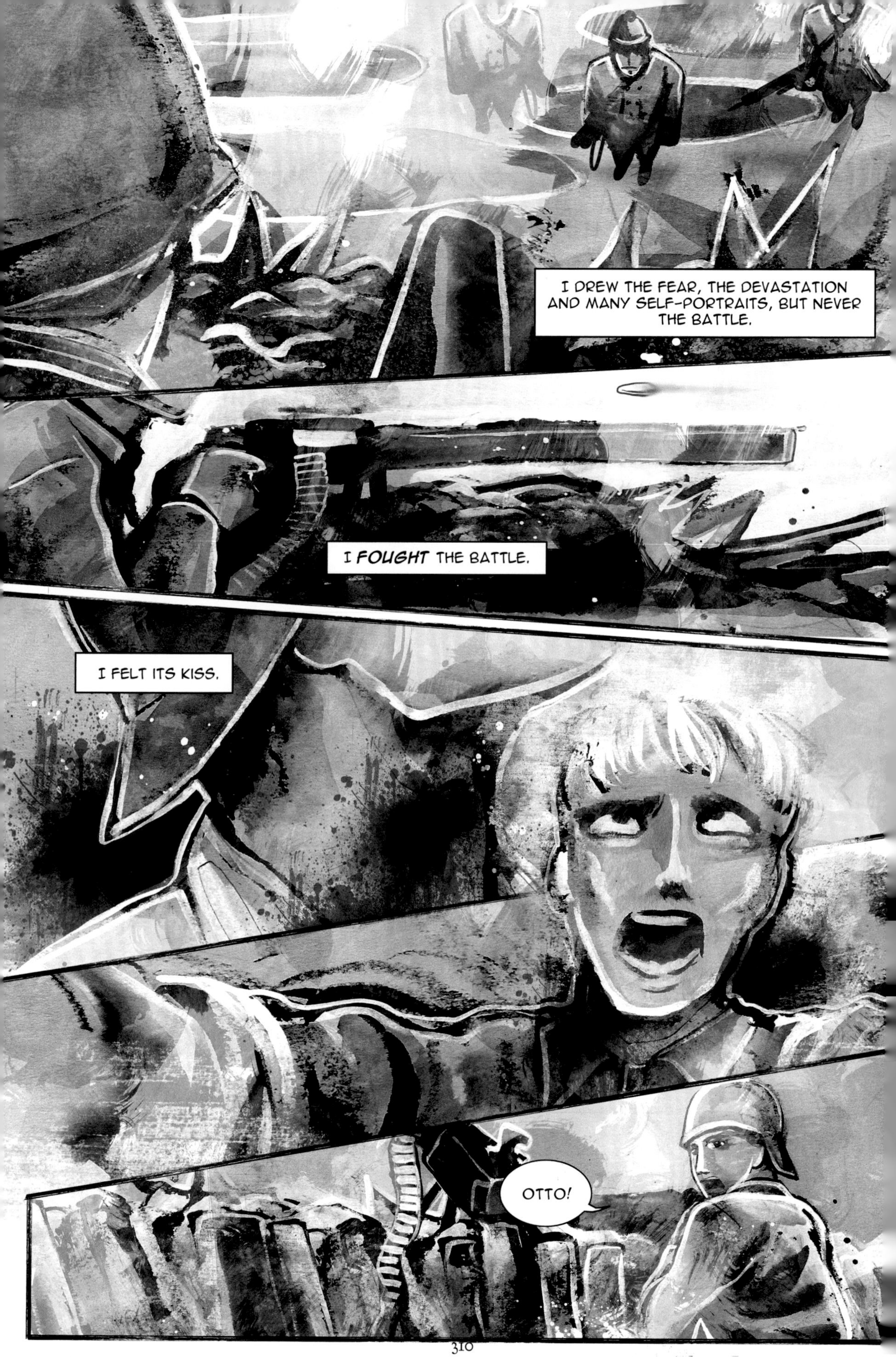
I DREW THE FEAR, THE DEVASTATION AND MANY SELF-PORTRAITS, BUT NEVER THE BATTLE.
I *FOUGHT* THE BATTLE.
I FELT ITS KISS.
OTTO!

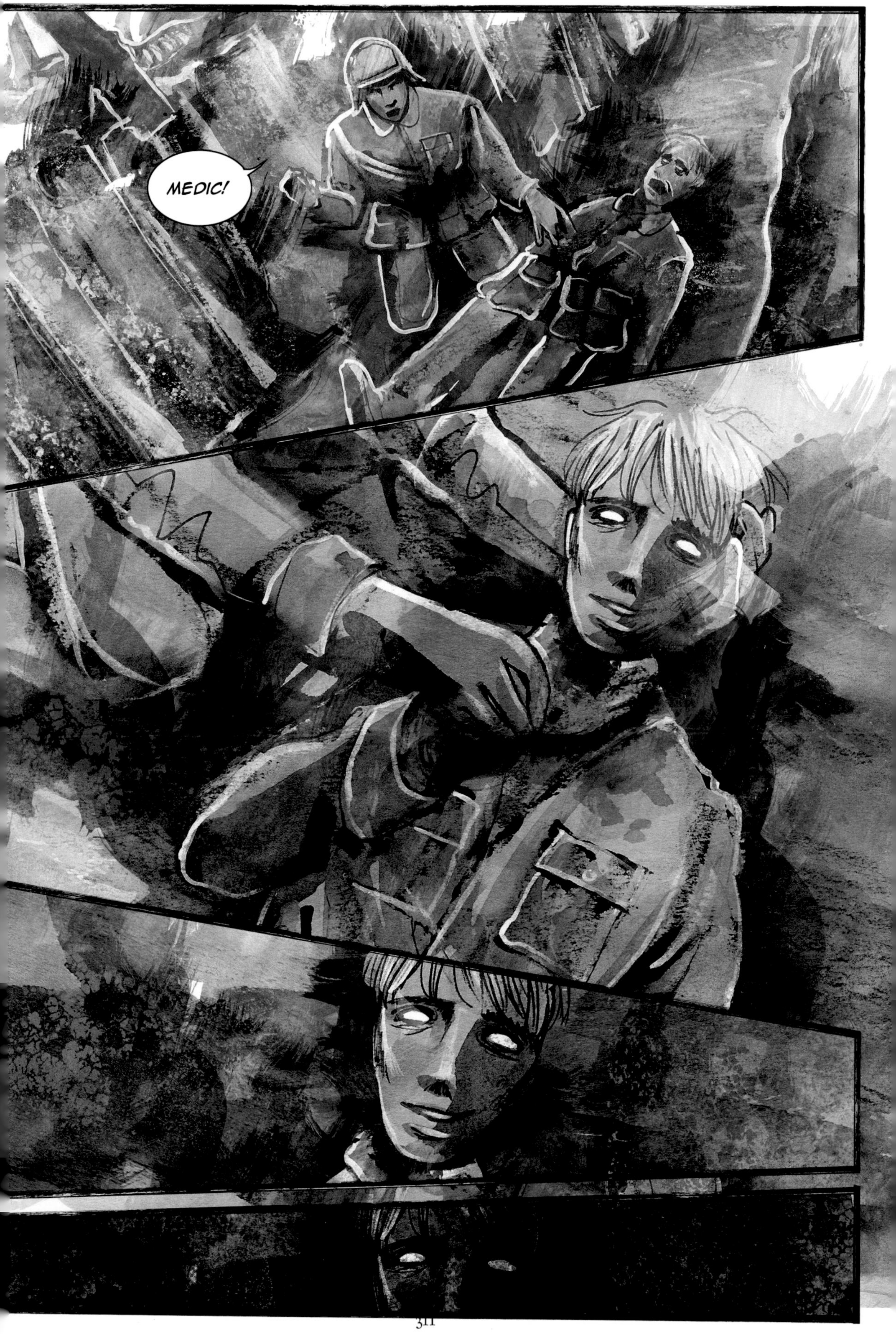
MEDIC!

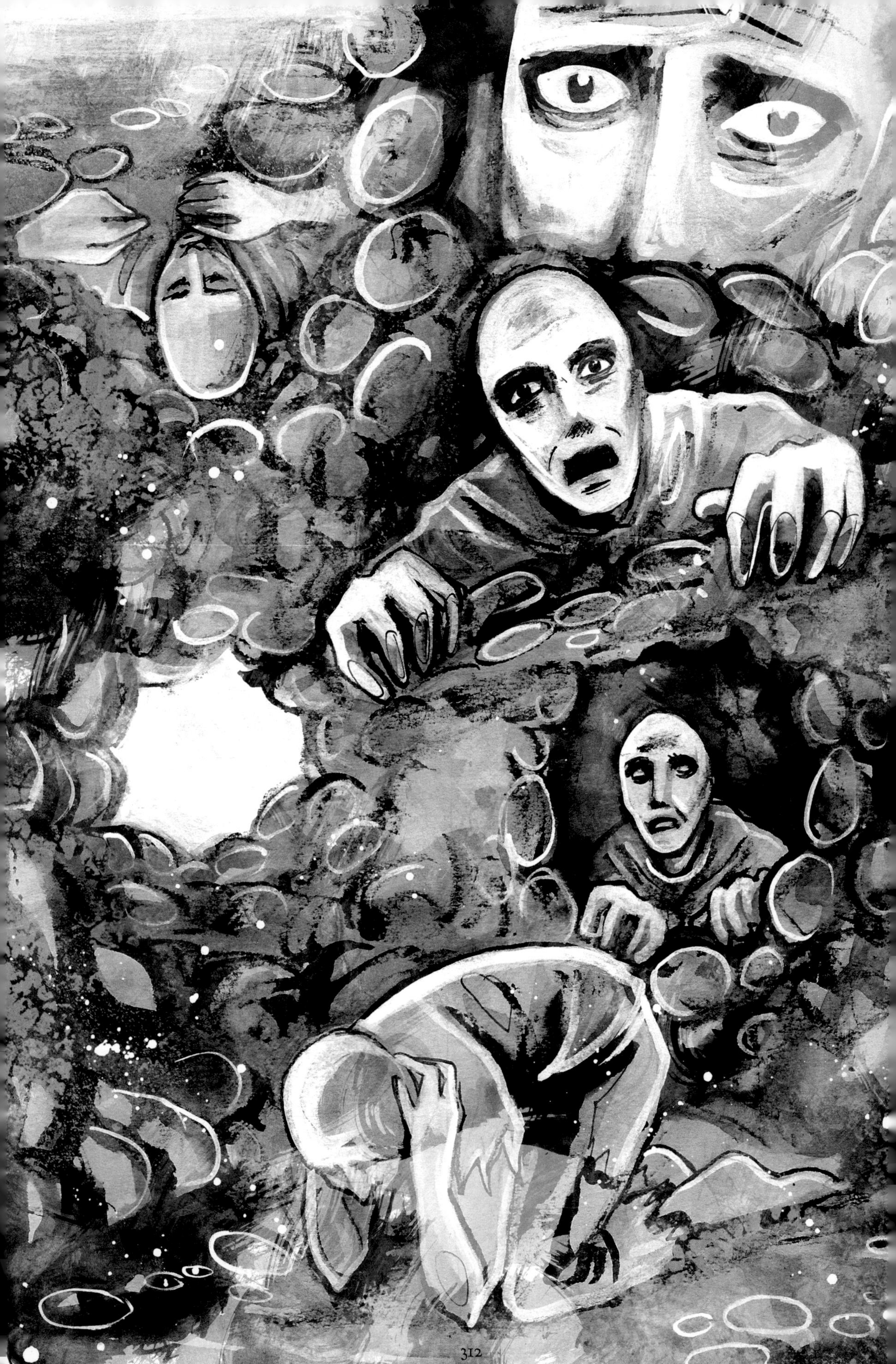

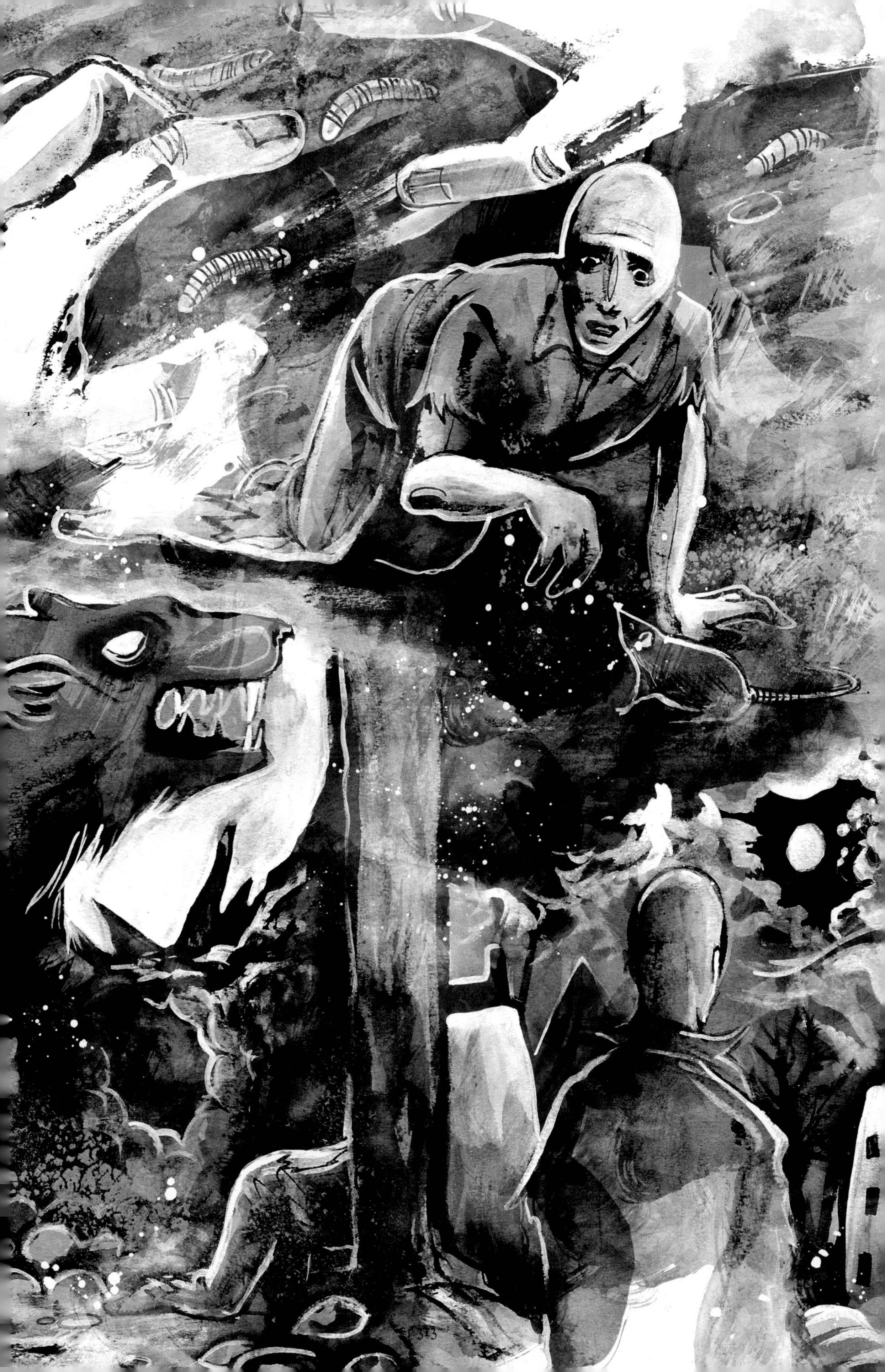

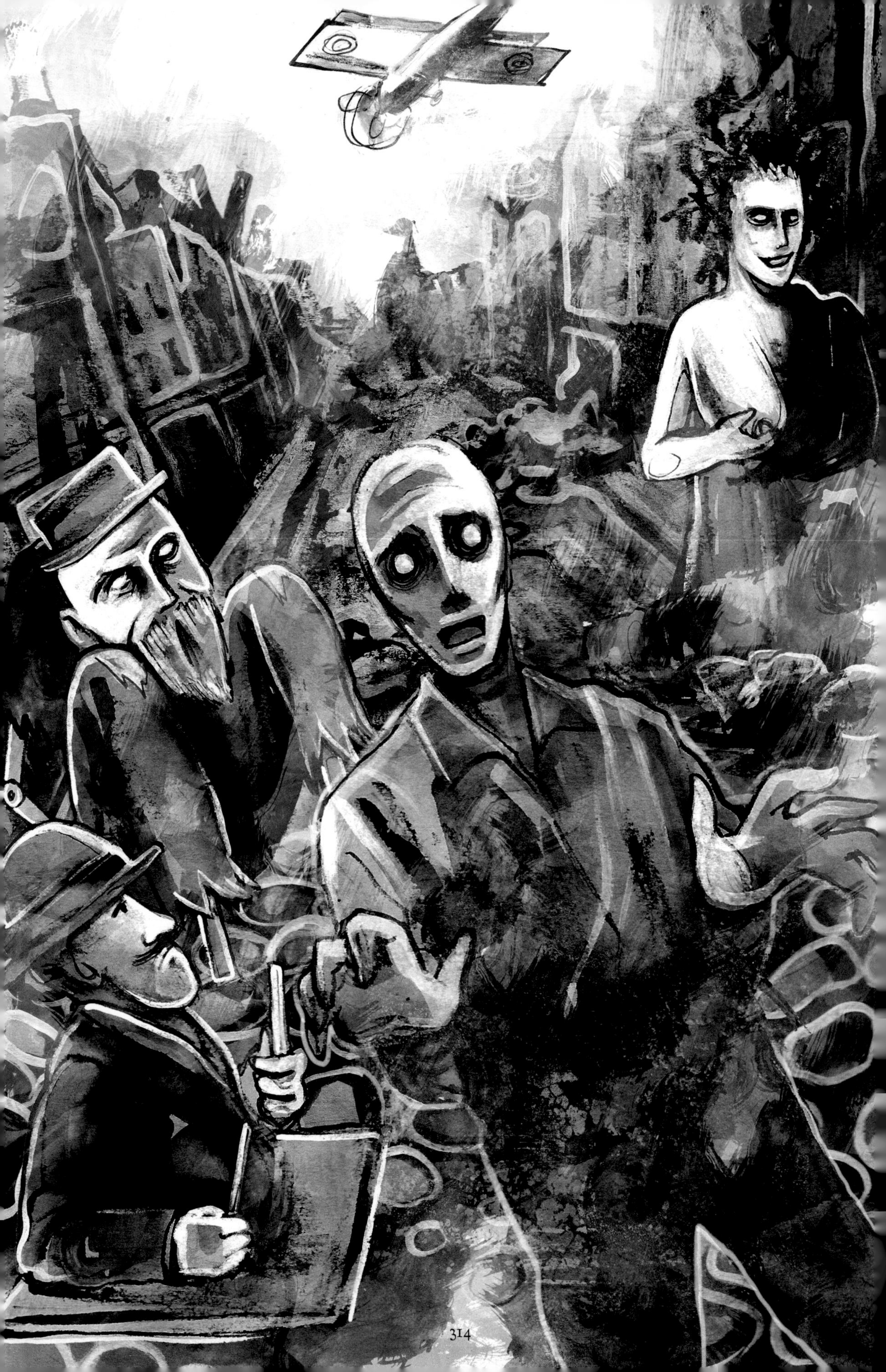

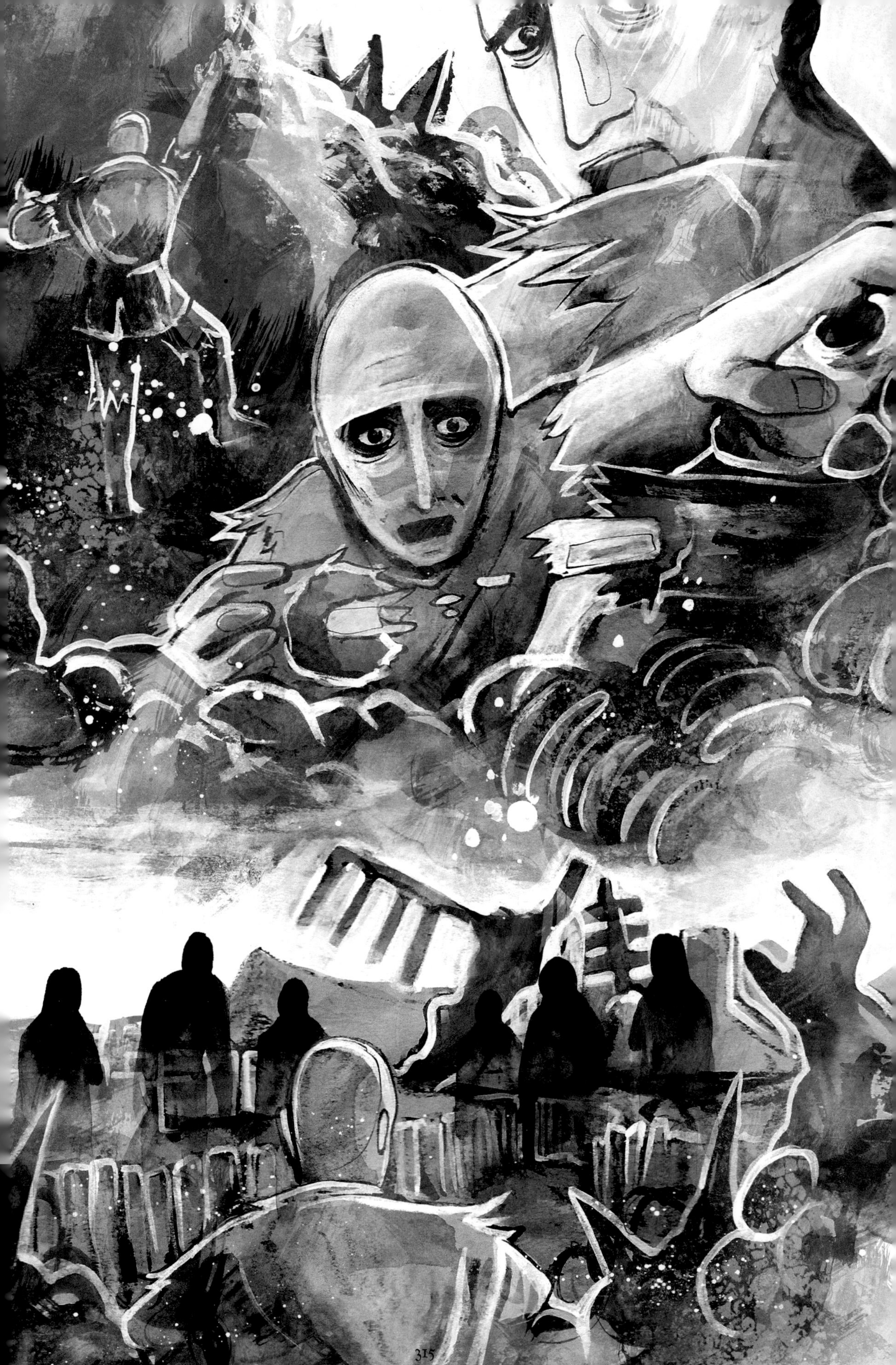

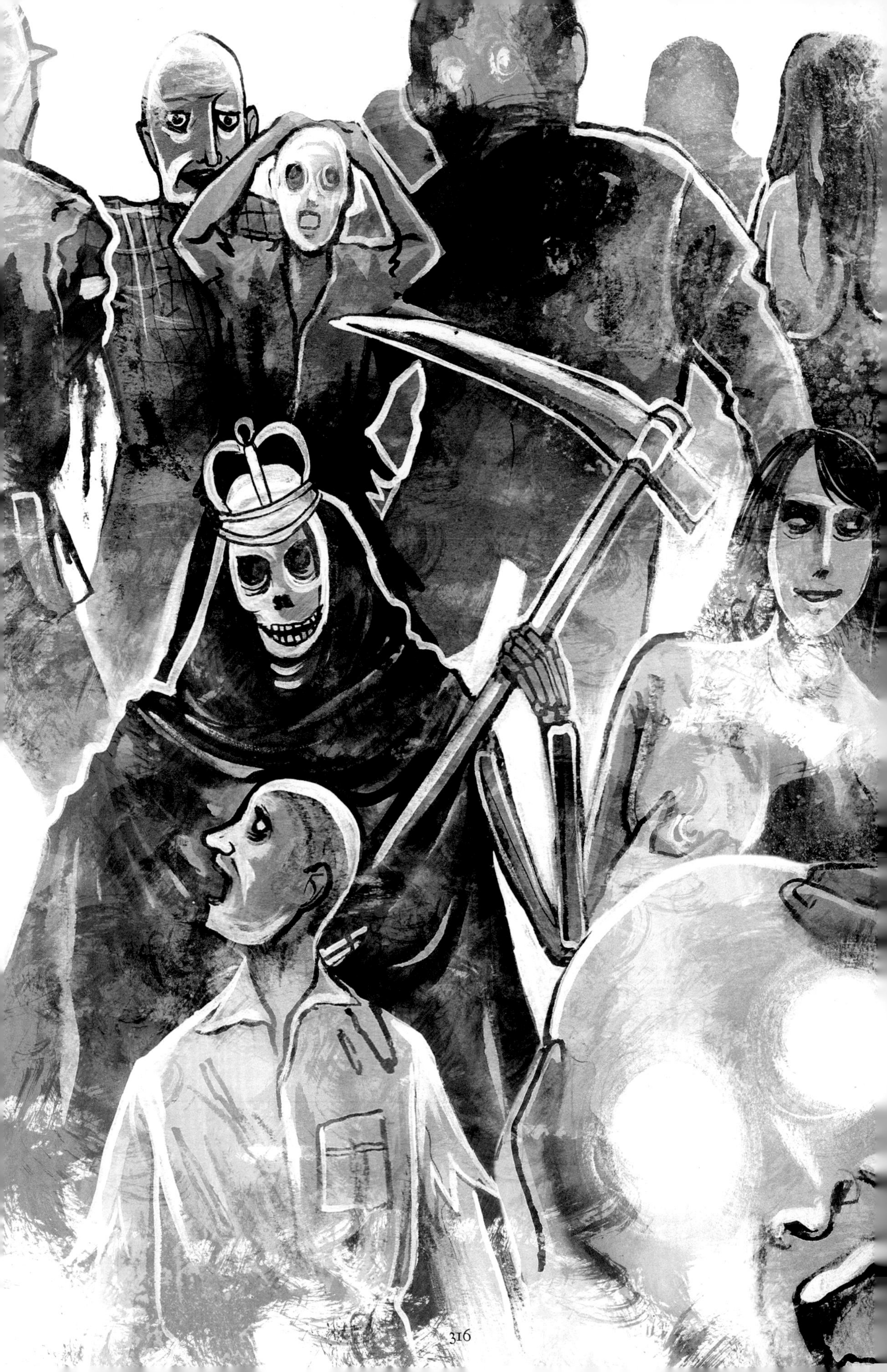

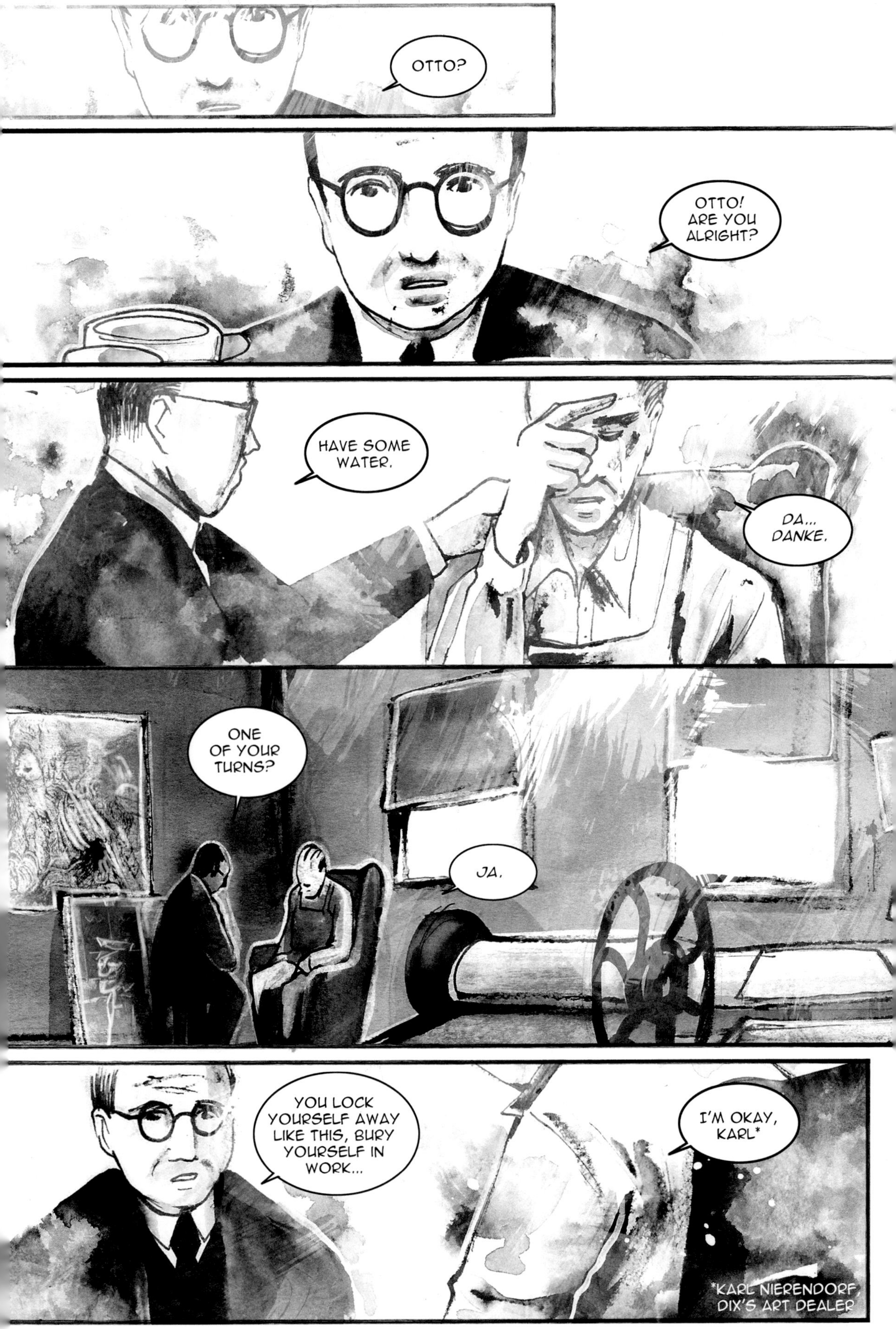
OTTO?
OTTO! ARE YOU ALRIGHT?
HAVE SOME WATER.
DA... DANKE.
ONE OF YOUR TURNS?
JA.
YOU LOCK YOURSELF AWAY LIKE THIS, BURY YOURSELF IN WORK...
I'M OKAY, KARL*
*KARL NIERENDORF, DIX'S ART DEALER

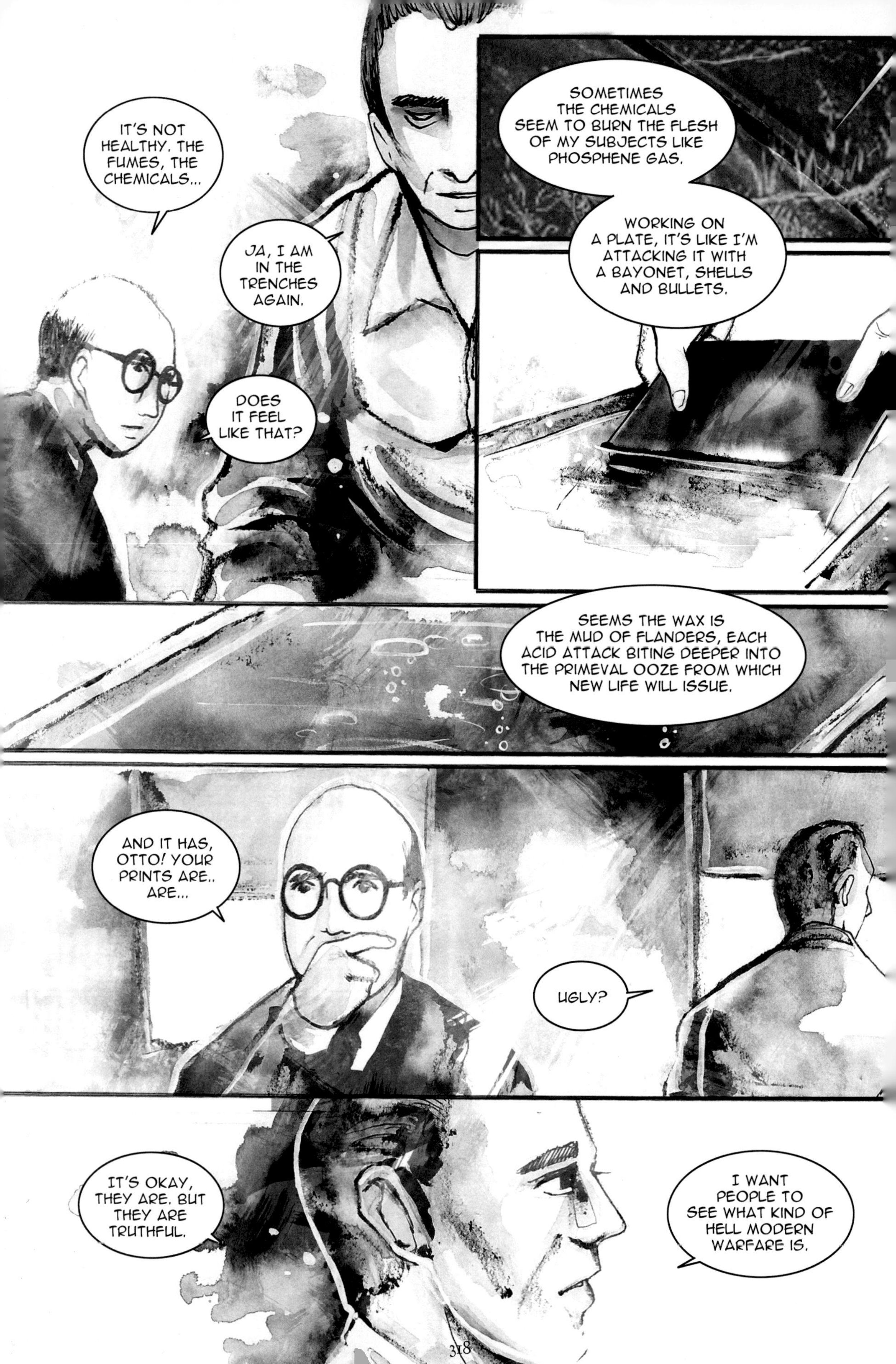
IT'S NOT HEALTHY. THE FUMES, THE CHEMICALS...
JA, I AM IN THE TRENCHES AGAIN.
DOES IT FEEL LIKE THAT?
SOMETIMES THE CHEMICALS SEEM TO BURN THE FLESH OF MY SUBJECTS LIKE PHOSPHENE GAS.
WORKING ON A PLATE, IT'S LIKE I'M ATTACKING IT WITH A BAYONET, SHELLS AND BULLETS.
SEEMS THE WAX IS THE MUD OF FLANDERS, EACH ACID ATTACK BITING DEEPER INTO THE PRIMEVAL OOZE FROM WHICH NEW LIFE WILL ISSUE.
AND IT HAS, OTTO! YOUR PRINTS ARE.. ARE...
UGLY?
IT'S OKAY, THEY ARE. BUT THEY ARE TRUTHFUL.
I WANT PEOPLE TO SEE WHAT KIND OF HELL MODERN WARFARE IS.

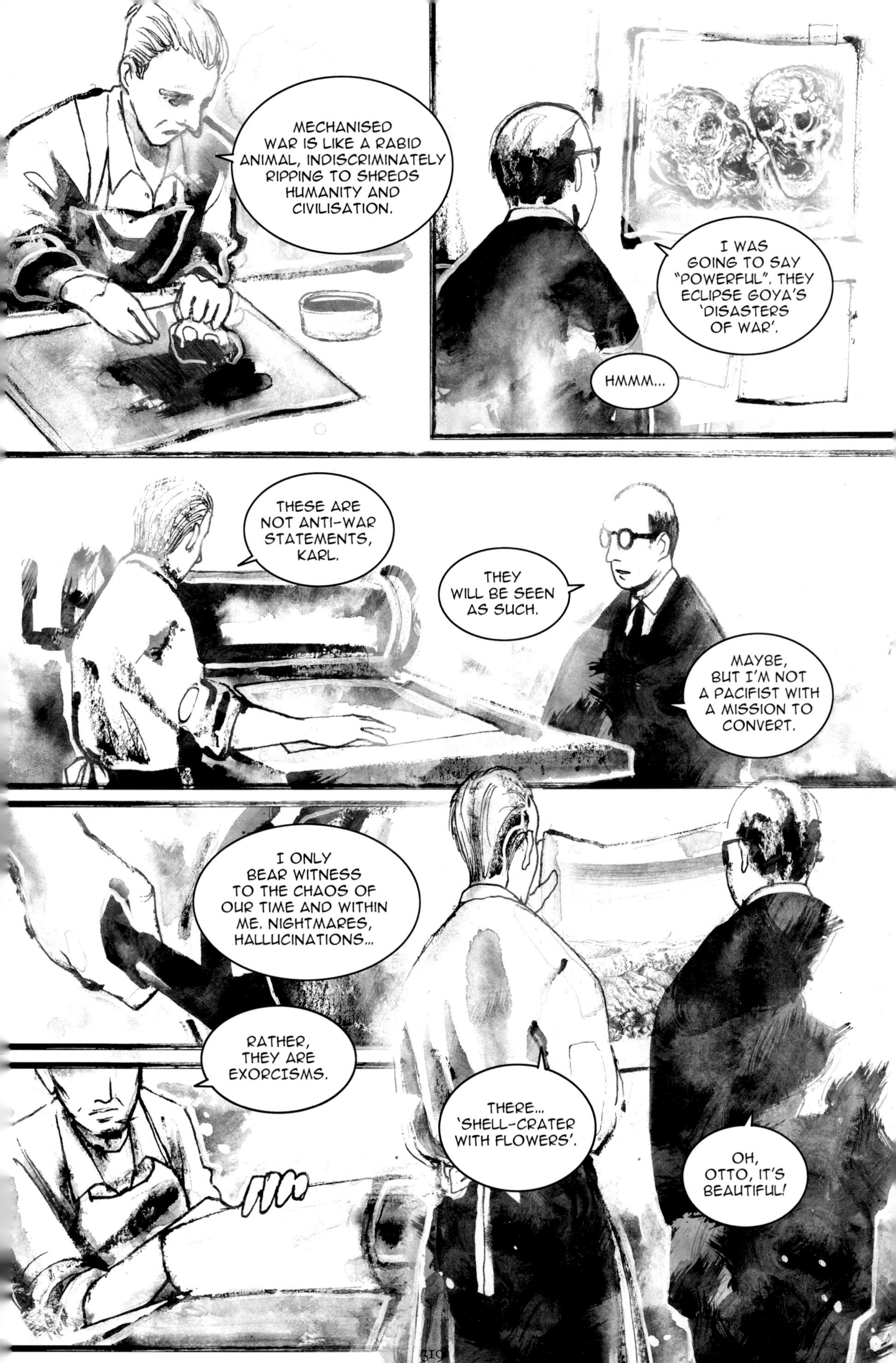
MECHANISED WAR IS LIKE A RABID ANIMAL, INDISCRIMINATELY RIPPING TO SHREDS HUMANITY AND CIVILISATION.
I WAS GOING TO SAY "POWERFUL". THEY ECLIPSE GOYA'S 'DISASTERS OF WAR'.
HMMM...
THESE ARE NOT ANTI-WAR STATEMENTS, KARL.
THEY WILL BE SEEN AS SUCH.
MAYBE, BUT I'M NOT A PACIFIST WITH A MISSION TO CONVERT.
I ONLY BEAR WITNESS TO THE CHAOS OF OUR TIME AND WITHIN ME. NIGHTMARES, HALLUCINATIONS...
RATHER, THEY ARE EXORCISMS.
THERE... 'SHELL-CRATER WITH FLOWERS'.
OH, OTTO, IT'S BEAUTIFUL!

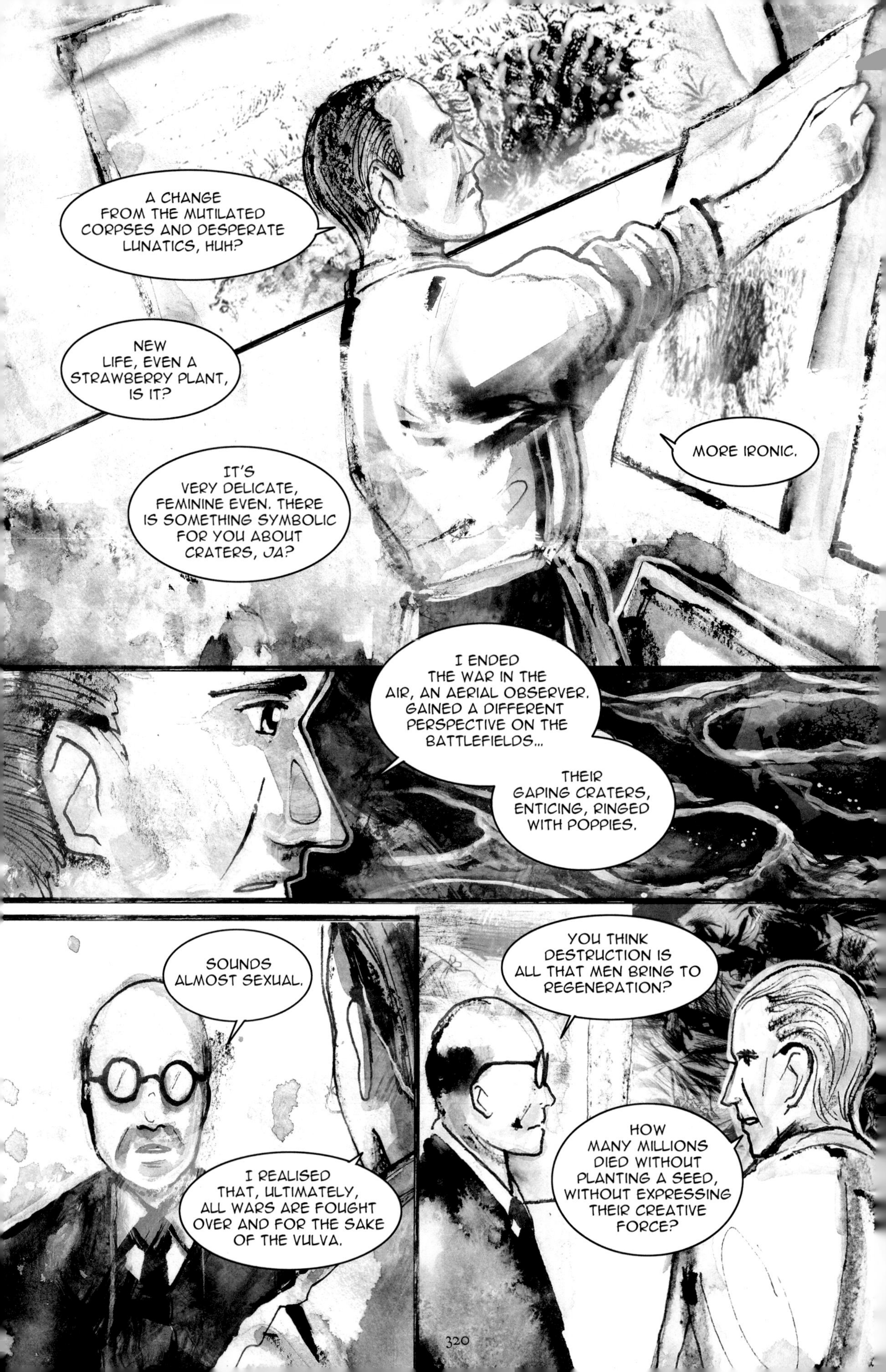
A CHANGE FROM THE MUTILATED CORPSES AND DESPERATE LUNATICS, HUH?
NEW LIFE, EVEN A STRAWBERRY PLANT, IS IT?
IT'S VERY DELICATE, FEMININE EVEN. THERE IS SOMETHING SYMBOLIC FOR YOU ABOUT CRATERS, JA?
MORE IRONIC.
I ENDED THE WAR IN THE AIR, AN AERIAL OBSERVER. GAINED A DIFFERENT PERSPECTIVE ON THE BATTLEFIELDS...
THEIR GAPING CRATERS, ENTICING, RINGED WITH POPPIES.
SOUNDS ALMOST SEXUAL.
I REALISED THAT, ULTIMATELY, ALL WARS ARE FOUGHT OVER AND FOR THE SAKE OF THE VULVA.
YOU THINK DESTRUCTION IS ALL THAT MEN BRING TO REGENERATION?
HOW MANY MILLIONS DIED WITHOUT PLANTING A SEED, WITHOUT EXPRESSING THEIR CREATIVE FORCE?

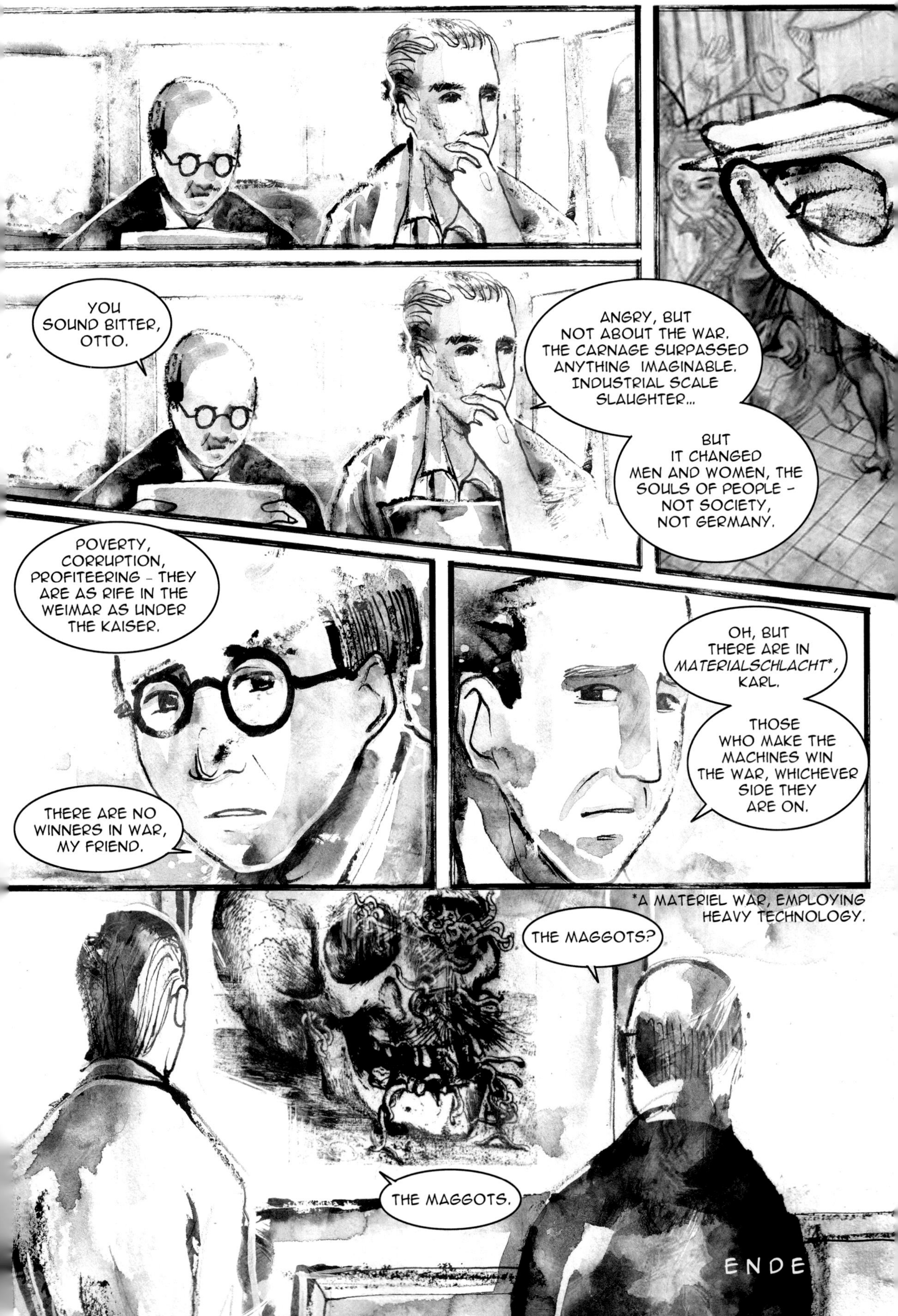
YOU SOUND BITTER, OTTO.
ANGRY, BUT NOT ABOUT THE WAR. THE CARNAGE SURPASSED ANYTHING IMAGINABLE. INDUSTRIAL SCALE SLAUGHTER...
BUT IT CHANGED MEN AND WOMEN, THE SOULS OF PEOPLE - NOT SOCIETY, NOT GERMANY.
POVERTY, CORRUPTION, PROFITEERING - THEY ARE AS RIFE IN THE WEIMAR AS UNDER THE KAISER.
THERE ARE NO WINNERS IN WAR, MY FRIEND.
OH, BUT THERE ARE IN *MATERIALSCHLACHT**, KARL.
THOSE WHO MAKE THE MACHINES WIN THE WAR, WHICHEVER SIDE THEY ARE ON.
*A MATERIEL WAR, EMPLOYING HEAVY TECHNOLOGY.
THE MAGGOTS?
THE MAGGOTS.
ENDE

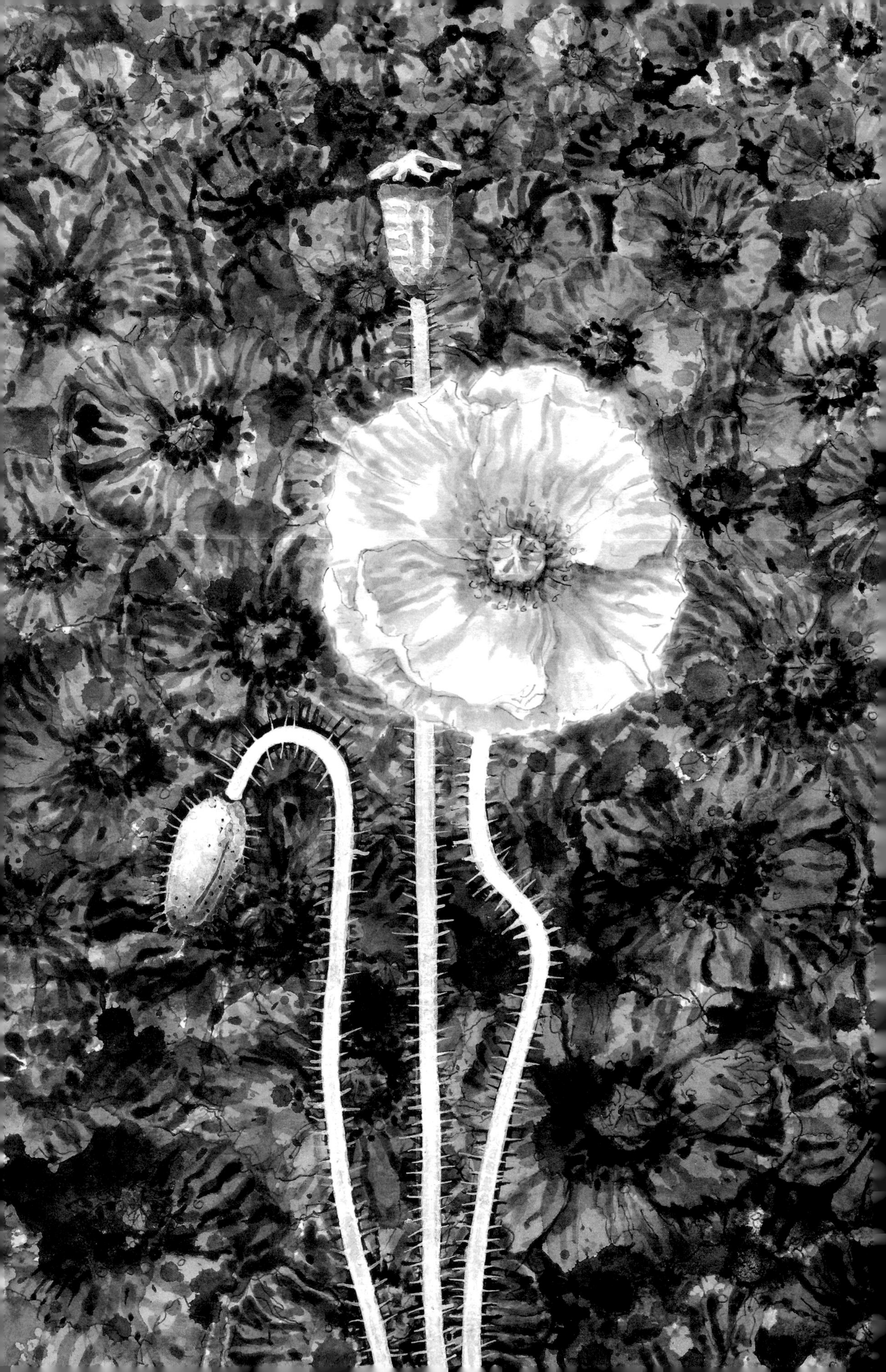

Memorial to the Mothers

Story: Joe Gordon

Art: Kate Charlesworth

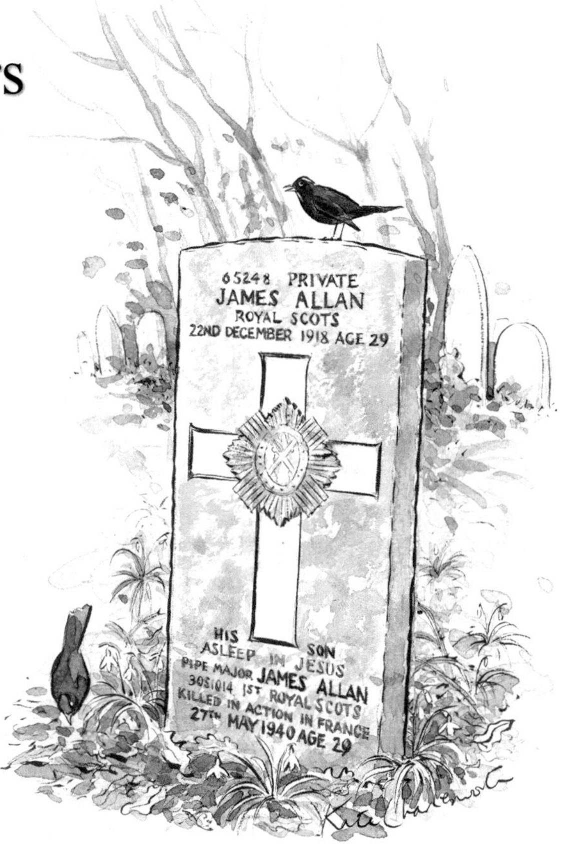

65248 PRIVATE
JAMES ALLAN
ROYAL SCOTS
22ND DECEMBER 1918 AGE 29
HIS SON
ASLEEP IN JESUS
PIPE MAJOR JAMES ALLAN
3051014 1ST ROYAL SCOTS
KILLED IN ACTION IN FRANCE
27TH MAY 1940 AGE 29

Close by my home lies an old cemetery, deliberately overgrown, the riot of foliage a small urban wildlife refuge enveloping the old headstones. Among the markers are a scattering of war graves; one has caught me eye many times on a walk. A simple stone with a cross engraved upon it and the insignia of the famous Royal Scots. "65248, Private James Allan", died 1918, aged 29.

There are so many like that across Britain and Europe, so many lives cut down like the harvest crop, allegiances and nationalities surrendered as they left this life and entered that grey realm of death where finally such distinctions matter no more.

What makes this memorial unusual is the second name, inscribed at the bottom of the stone: "Pipe Major James Allan, Killed in Action in France 1940". His son. The father fallen from The War To End All Wars, his lad taken in the one that soon followed. I've often considered this one grave summed up the bloody stupidity of nations solving differences through warfare, century after weary century, as if we are unable to evolve beyond this barbarous state.

But walking there recently, a different thought struck me – that there was another casualty of the wars whose name is not on that stone. Mrs. Allan, wife, mother, bereaved of husband by one war, of her darling boy by the next. And from that came the thought that each and every one of the many memorials that stand in honour of Remembrance also lacks entire regiments of casualties: the mothers of the fallen. The mothers who received a wound as devastating as any soldier upon

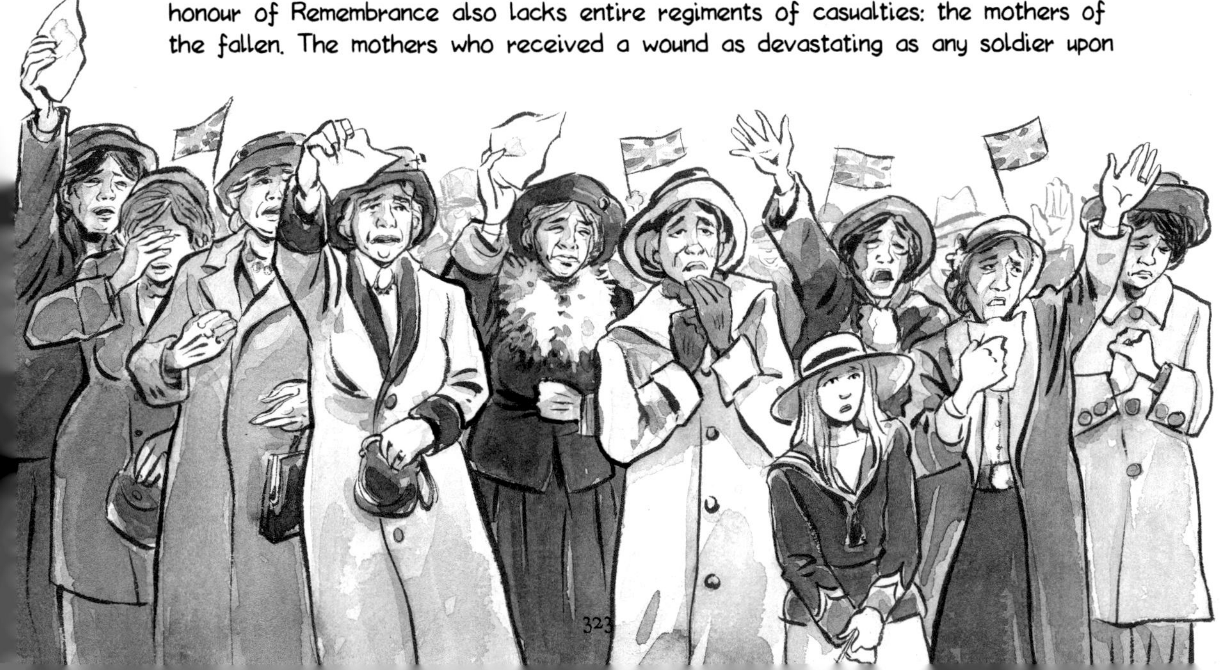

a battlefield. A bayonet wound to the heart that beat for her loved ones in the way only a mother's can. A bullet wound that penetrated to the soul. A deep, all-pervading sorrow and loss which seeped into her as surely as the dreadful poison gas of the Western Front, breathed in with the news of her loss, permeating every aspect of her body and spirit.

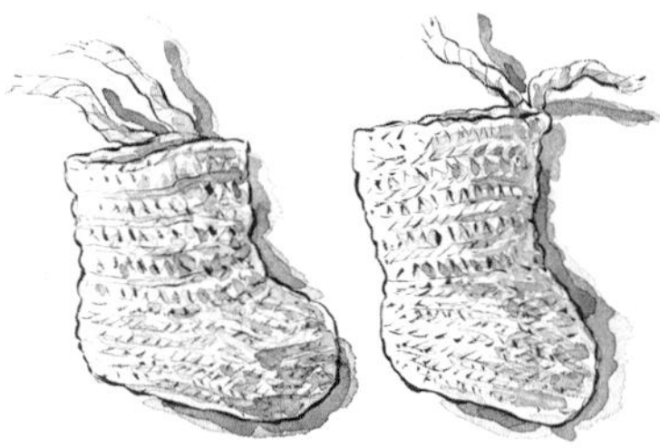

The mothers of the fallen are the walking wounded of our wars. In public they walk upright, blinking tears but trying to be what is expected, the brave, proud mother, sorrowful for her loss yet proud of her boys for doing their duty for King, Kaiser, Czar, or for God, for their country. Proud of their honourable and courageous service, of bravery in the face of monstrous suffering, she tries to carry her self respectfully for their memory and sacrifice, given at the behest of political leaders who have never, in any age, grasped the real meanings of those concepts of honour and courage that the rank and file soldier knows.

But inside she is as dreadfully wounded as any of those maimed in body or mind in the trenches. In public she is steady and stolid. In her mind she is screaming why my boy, why my man? Did he die quickly, did he linger in pain? Did he lie in agony screaming for her? She's heard the stories, how many a brave man, in mortal pain screams for she who gave him life, whose body bore him, whose blood and love nurtured him. Make the pain stop, mum, please save me, make it stop, make it go away, kiss it and make it all better. Oh please, mum, please make it stop. I tried to be good, why is this happening, why does it hurt so much... She'll never know.

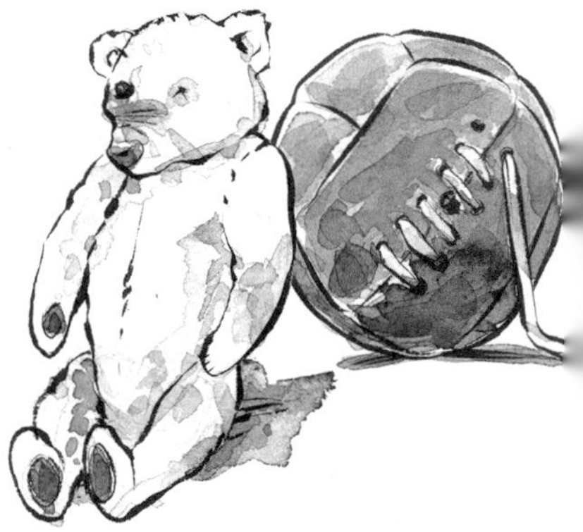

His old comrades may visit to pay their respects, but they'll never tell her anything save that he was brave and it was over quickly, that he never knew a thing. Never would they burden her with what they really saw; mates choking in clouds of vile vapours, or ripped apart by shells, or dying slowly caught in wire or mud, screaming for hours. Or the ones they simply never found again, whatever remained of them unrecognizable, or else swallowed by the violated Earth, vanished, erased from the Book of Life.

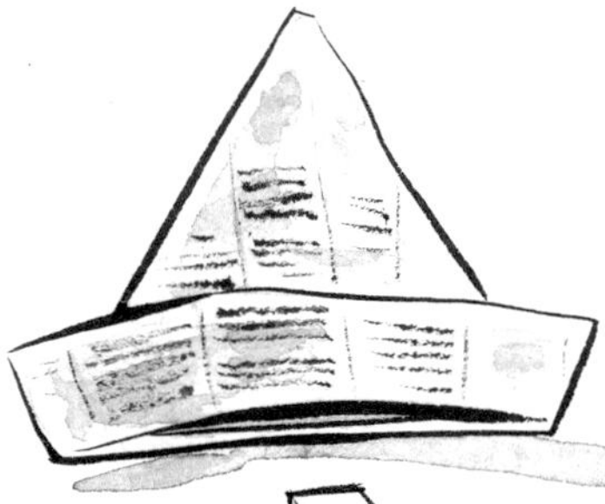

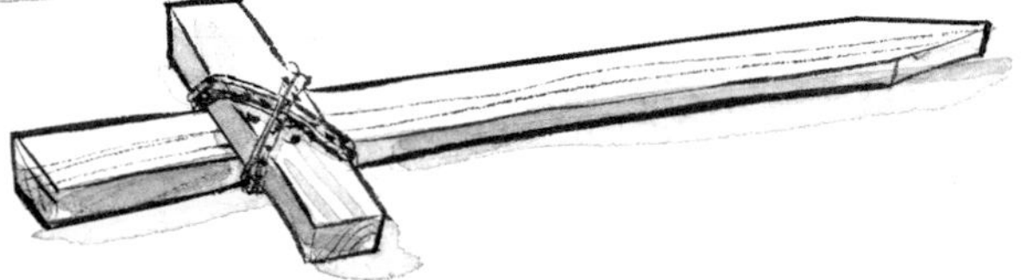

Hiding the truth of the charnel house of battlefield is the only mercy they can give her, for the sake of their lost brother in arms. But for the rest of her days she'll dream of him and his end, and blame herself for not being able to protect him, her blood, her life.

Behind each and every name on those memorials, from grand obelisk in fine stone to the humble wooden board with painted lettering in an old church or society house, are the ranks of the casualties never mentioned on those markers, regiment after regiment of mothers. They fell as surely as their boys and each time they see a new war and new young lads cut down, new recruits to their black-veiled regiment, their heart bleeds a little more and they wonder was it not enough? That you took my boys, was it not enough? How could it not be enough? How could anyone decide to send yet more young lads off to another war again. And again. And again.

And what really did they fight for? For lofty ideals of freedom or the malicious manœuvrings of politicians who saw warfare as another method for gaining new lands, resources and prestige, while they themselves risked little. How easily 'the old lie' was spoken by those who issued the orders but who never risked death in cold waters as their ship was ripped apart, suffered in trenches or, in a new twist on ancient warfare, fell in flames from the skies as the magical new science of flying, only just born, was malformed and reshaped to industrial scale killing. So easy for those who never risk their lives or their loved ones to cry noble sentiments, "Dulce et Decorum est, Pro patria mori."

Did that bereft mother's love turn to burning anger? Did she blame those who lead us with excuses into such butchery then lacked the vision or courage to end it? Or did the place where once love for her child lived turn into a dark place filled with hate? Did the mother in a British village burn with hatred for all Germans for what they did to her boy? Did the mother in Hamburg rage against all Britons for mangling her young — oh so damned young — blue eyed boy. Or did their weeping hearts overflow with sympathy and

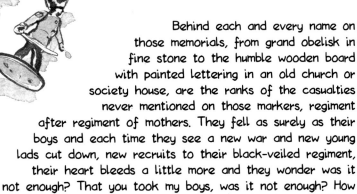

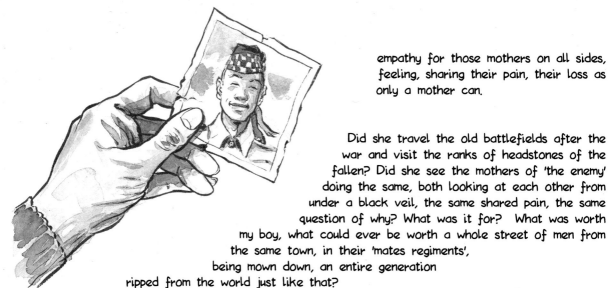

empathy for those mothers on all sides, feeling, sharing their pain, their loss as only a mother can.

Did she travel the old battlefields after the war and visit the ranks of headstones of the fallen? Did she see the mothers of 'the enemy' doing the same, both looking at each other from under a black veil, the same shared pain, the same question of why? What was it for? What was worth my boy, what could ever be worth a whole street of men from the same town, in their 'mates regiments', being mown down, an entire generation ripped from the world just like that?

Each war that followed that War to End All Wars has been a betrayal of those so sacrificed, a betrayal to each generation of mothers who loved and lost and mourned, limping through the rest of their lives with a hole in their soul, a phantom pain of loss no less real than the phantom pain in the lost limb of a maimed veteran.

Perhaps the decision to go to war should never be decided by men in wood panelled offices of state, but by a committee of mothers on both sides, advised by those who have seen war and what it does to soft human bodies, to the fragile mind and very soul.

And then perhaps we might finally learn to stop, for what mother really, truly believes anything was worth her bonnie boy?

END

Acknowledgements

The editors are immensely grateful to all those contributors credited for the scripts, art and lettering who shared our commitment and vision, and worked so hard for no financial reward. We would also like to thank Pat Mills, Charis Campbell, Gareth Kitchen, Paul Gravett, Bill Badham, Charlie Adlard, Tommy Clark, David Tattersfield, Tony Bennett, Ian Brookes, Sandy Bywater, John Freeman, Zoe Sussmeyer, publicist Jonathan Purves and the Arch Druid, Jim Nest, for their invaluable help and support.

Finally, we are indebted to John Anderson from Soaring Penguin Press, who believed in what we were doing and encouraged us to carry on doing it.

JC & JSC
http://toendallwarscomic.wordpress.com/

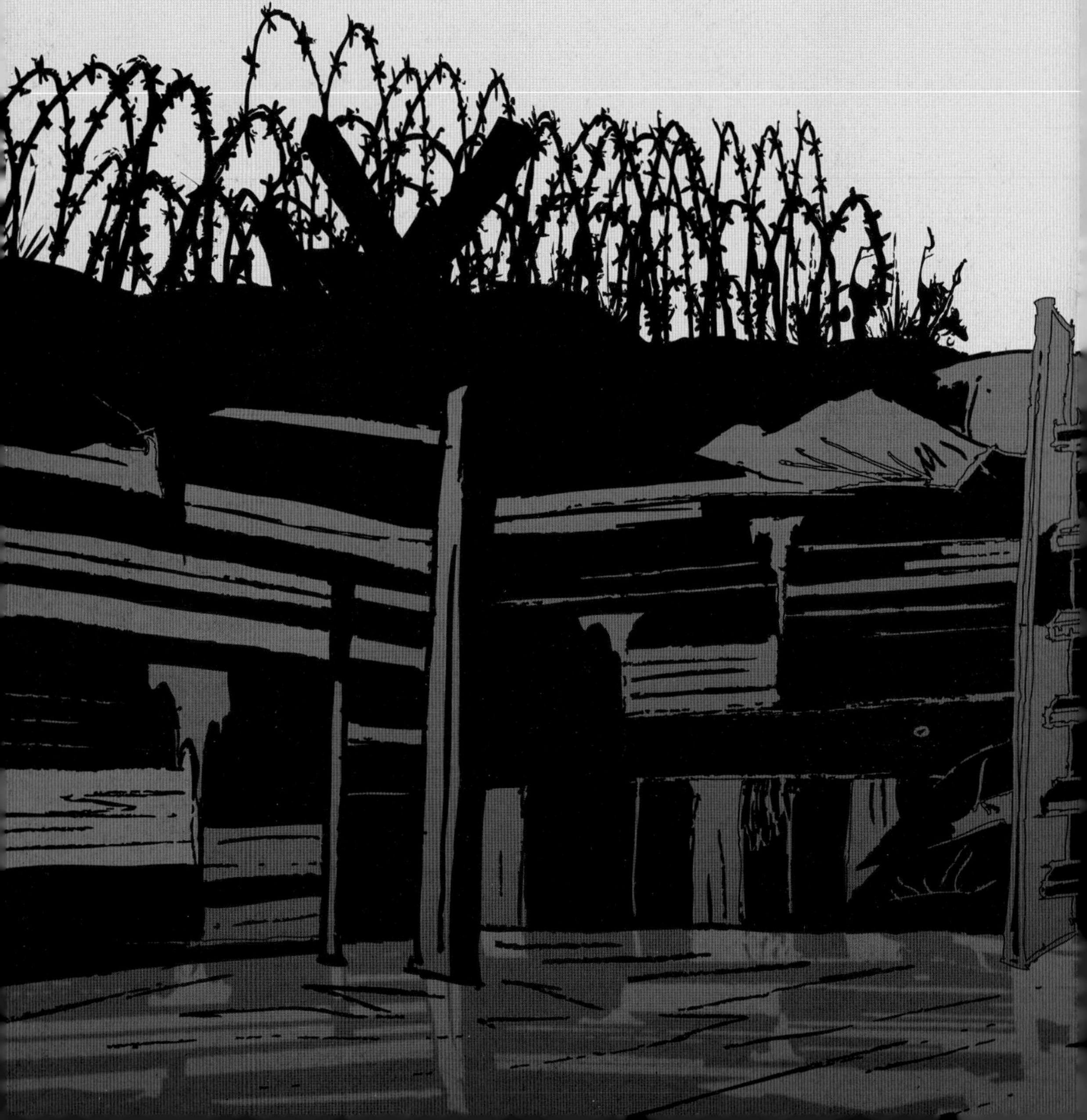

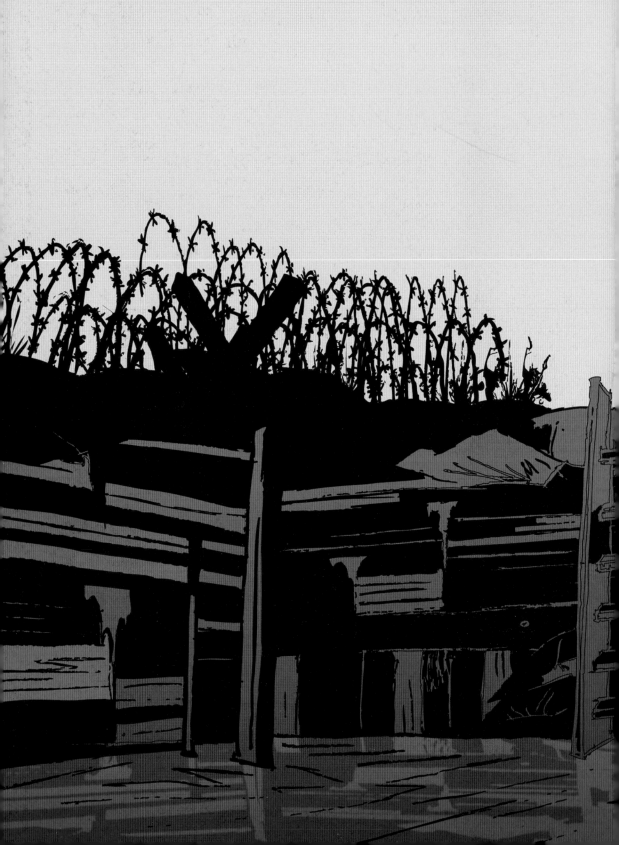